What a Time I Am Having

I Am Having

SELECTED LETTERS OF MAX PERUTZ

This photograph always hung on Max's office wall. He also included it in an album made two or three years before his death. His caption for the photo reads: "My skis. Niedere Tauern. Winter 1930." It was with these skis in 1930 that Max first tasted success; he and his team of three brought victory for their school. In June 2000, on the weekly radio programme Desert Island Discs, Max chose skis as his luxury: "you never know, it might snow."

What a Time I Am Having

SELECTED LETTERS OF MAX PERUTZ

Edited by

Vivien Perutz

COLD SPRING HARBOR LABORATORY PRESS
Cold Spring Harbor, New York • www.cshlpress.com

What a Time I Am Having
SELECTED LETTERS OF MAX PERUTZ

Publisher	John Inglis
Acquisition Editor	John Inglis
Director of Development, Marketing, and Sales	Jan Argentine
Developmental Editor	Judy Cuddihy
Project Coordinators	Inez Sialiano and Mary Cozza
Permissions Coordinator	Carol Brown
Production Manager	Denise Weiss
Production Editor	Mala Mazzullo
Desktop Editor	Lauren Heller
Book Marketing Manager	Ingrid Benirschke
Sales Account Managers	Jane Carter and Elizabeth Powers

Front cover: Cover portrait and design by Tina Wendon, © 2009 Tina Wendon
www.tinawendon.com

Back cover photograph: In the Engadine, June 1946

Library of Congress Cataloging-in-Publication Data

Perutz, Max F.
  What a time I am having : selected letters of Max Perutz / edited by
Vivien Perutz.
     p. cm.
  Includes bibliographical references and index.
  ISBN 978-0-87969-864-5 (hardcover : alk. paper)
  1. Perutz, Max F. 2. Molecular biologists–Austria–Vienna–Biography. 3.
Molecular biologists–Great Britain–Biography. 4. Perutz, Max
F.–Correspondence. I. Perutz, Vivien. II. Title.
  QH31.P248A3 2008
  572.8092–dc22

                    2008035808

10 9 8 7 6 5 4 3 2 1

All World Wide Web addresses are accurate to the best of our knowledge at the time of printing.

All Cold Spring Harbor Laboratory Press publications may be ordered directly from Cold Spring Harbor Laboratory Press, 500 Sunnyside Blvd., Woodbury, New York 11797-2924. Phone: 1-800-843-4388 in Continental U.S. and Canada. All other locations: (516) 422-4100. FAX: (516) 422-4097. E-mail: cshpress@cshl.edu. For a complete catalog of all Cold Spring Harbor Laboratory Press publications, visit our website at http://www.cshlpress.com/.

*For Robin and Liesel, my two greatest supporters
during the long gestation of this project*

ALSO FROM COLD SPRING HARBOR LABORATORY PRESS

Related Titles

I Wish I'd Made You Angry Earlier: Essays on Science, Scientists, and Humanity by Max F. Perutz

Max Perutz and the Secret of Life by Georgina Ferry

The Eighth Day of Creation: The Makers of the Revolution in Biology (25th Anniversary Edition) by Horace Freeland Judson

Other History of Science Titles

A Passion for DNA: Genes, Genomes, and Society by James D. Watson

Dorothy Hodgkin: A Life by Georgina Ferry

George Beadle, An Uncommon Farmer: The Emergence of Genetics in the 20th Century by Paul Berg and Maxine Singer

We Can Sleep Later: Alfred D. Hershey and the Origins of Molecular Biology edited by Franklin W. Stahl

Contents

Preface

My father, Max Perutz, was a prolific letter writer. He nurtured his skills as a writer from his teenage years, first in letters he wrote to an English girl friend and later to his family, honing his ability to tell a good story and to breathe life into his observations of people and places. Unwittingly he was also writing a much better autobiography than the one he had barely begun when he died. No recollection could have matched the brilliance and directness with which these letters reflect salient features of his personality. We see in turn the chemistry student of wealthy parents in pre-war Vienna; the research student in Cambridge, who became a refugee 18 months after his arrival; the interned "enemy alien" and the naturalised British officer employed to travel to the United States on a hare-brained project to build an airstrip of ice in the mid Atlantic; the ever-optimistic scientist working on an intractable problem, the structure of haemoglobin; and finally the highly regarded member of the scientific community still battling with science.

Most excitingly, at the centre of this volume, in the 1950s, we witness the laying of the foundation stones of a new and spectacularly successful science, molecular biology, and the infrastructure needed to support it. By the end of this decade the small unit in a physics laboratory, which Max directed, had grown exponentially. It was shortly to become the Medical Research Council Laboratory of Molecular Biology (LMB), a laboratory that he chaired until 1979 and that has won more Nobel prizes than any other worldwide. In addition Max's letters provide vignettes of his struggles and eureka moments as a scientist; of life in Britain in the lean years of the 1940s and early 1950s; impressions of the United States in 1943 and on many later visits; and work on the Jungfraujoch in Switzerland studying the glacier, his second line of research in the early years. The letters convey his excited delight in the latest scientific advances made by his friends and colleagues; his interest in politics and history figures prominently; and just occasionally he recounts gossip that is still fascinating today. Max's private thoughts were expressed in many letters, but they also served as a medium to practise for his public writing, especially for *The New York Review of Books* and the *London Review of Books*. In 1996, to his great delight, he won the Lewis Thomas Prize, awarded by the Rockefeller University in New York, "honoring the scientist as poet." His final collection of essays can be found in *I Wish I'd Made You Angry Earlier* published by Cold Spring Harbor Laboratory Press in 1998 and 2003.

The English girl friend to whom Max wrote for many years was Evelyn Machin (née Baxter). She had spent several months in Vienna with her aunt and uncle, the closest friends of Max's parents, before going up to Oxford. She remained a good friend and kindly returned his letters shortly before her death. The family letters fall into four large groups: those my father wrote more or less fortnightly to his sister, Lotte, who emigrated to the United States after Hitler's invasion of Austria; those addressed primarily to my mother, to whom he wrote almost daily whenever he or she was away; those to my maternal grandparents, to whom my father wrote informatively until my grandfather's death in 1952; and those to my brother Robin and his family. Lotte preserved a fair number of my father's letters from the 1940s, 1980s, and 1990s; my mother, who was a hoarder by nature, threw nothing away and her collection is at its richest in the intervening years. Robin, who was as assiduous as my mother in preserving all the letters he and his family received, spent two long periods abroad as a student and moved away from Cambridge in 1972.

Luckily one of my mother's absences coincided with one of the most exciting and tense moments of Max's scientific career: the discovery that attaching heavy atom derivatives to a haemoglobin molecule would solve the phase problem that had stood in the way of unravelling the structure of proteins. But mostly it was he who was absent, travelling to conferences, giving lectures, or doing an experiment that could not be done in Cambridge. What was most important, he always told us in explaining these absences, was to see the work going on elsewhere, particularly in the United States. My father wrote to Robin as a fellow chemist about science and especially about his developing ideas regarding the mechanics of haemoglobin as it binds the oxygen we breathe in and then releases it to the muscles. He would also amuse himself by recounting his adventures for Robin and his family, once cheap telephone calls to my mother had deprived him of the pleasure of writing home.

In addition to family letters, I have drawn on the copies of letters still in my father's office when he died, which will be deposited in the archive of Churchill College, Cambridge; on the letters preserved in a number of archives; and on those which friends have given me. I have also included my father's diaries from London and then North America in 1943, parts of those from trips to the Middle East and to Moscow in 1961, and the one from Stockholm on the occasion of the receipt of the Nobel Prize in 1962. The only years from which few private letters survive are the later 1930s. A bomb destroyed my father's letters home to Vienna along with the contents of his parents' flat, so that his first impressions of England, Cambridge and the Cavendish laboratory are lost. He himself threw out almost all of his files on moving into a smaller office in 1979. I was unable to access letters in The British National Archives of the 1960s and 1970s.

My chief problem has not been survival but the selection of excerpts from my father's voluminous correspondence. I have tried to ensure that my parents' privacy remains intact and have omitted almost all of my father's frequent references to his health, which was a continual source of anxiety. I have cut virtually all the passages that would have revealed his care and concern for the lives and well-being of family and friends. If this volume portrays Max as excessively self-centred, my excisions are the cause. I have left them invisible. I have preserved eccentricities of English in the early letters where they do not make comprehension difficult, but have corrected the odd error or spelling mistake as Max would have wished me to do.

I have been fortunate in having the assistance of two friends of my father, the historian Brendan Simms, like my father a Fellow of Peterhouse, and Alan Weeds, first a research student at LMB and from 1969 a member of the staff. Their additions to my introductions to each decade appear in italics. Brendan has explained the context of my father's political comments in the letters my father wrote during his undergraduate years. Alan has been meticulous in going through the parts of the scientific correspondence which as an art historian by profession I am incompetent to judge. He advised me which scientific passages should be included and has added scientific notes which are signed AW. Kiyoshi Nagai and my brother Robin Perutz have provided further expert guidance. Alan also helped me to decide on the exclusion of the correspondence on the controversy that broke out over Jim Watson's revelation in *The Double Helix* that my father had shown Francis Crick a Medical Research Council report on the work of Rosalind Franklin. This report contained a vital clue, which Jim Watson had failed to relay to Crick after hearing Franklin lecture, and which enabled

Crick and Watson to build the double-helical model of DNA. The grounds for exclusion are that the entire lengthy and repetitive correspondence will now be published on the web and that it has had a considerable airing in a number of books. The best discussion of this issue is probably that of Horace Judson in *The Eighth Day of Creation*, but see also Georgina Ferry's *Max Perutz and the Secret of Life* and Soraya de Chadarevian's *Designs for Life: Molecular Biology after World War II*.

The Royal Society and Mavis Blow have kindly allowed me to reproduce an excellent memoir written for *The Biographical Memoirs of the Royal Society* by Mavis's late husband, David Blow. David was my father's research student in the mid 1950s and continued to work in the same laboratory for many years. There readers will find a more technical account of my father's scientific research than is provided in the notes. A few paragraphs that duplicate material to be found elsewhere in the volume have been omitted.

My brother Robin has answered countless questions, read the proofs meticulously, and helped me in innumerable other ways. I am also grateful to my father's cousin, Alice (Liesel) Frank Stock, my sister-in-law, Sue Perutz, and Georgina Ferry for their advice and support. Ferry's biography, *Max Perutz and the Secret of Life,* and some of the material she assembled have lightened my task.

Unless otherwise stated, all the letters were written from home, that is, before May 1936 from Vienna or the family's house in the village of Reichenau, and later from Cambridge, England. The originals of the letters from October 1932 to May 1936 are in German, as is the occasional letter thereafter. My translations draw on those made for Georgina Ferry by Barbara Hott and Linde Davidson. Roy and Alice (Liesel) Frank Stock, Ron Gray, Daria von Esterházy, and my brother Robin have all assisted me. Later letters often contain the odd German word or phrase; because many of these are not precisely translatable, I have kept the German and given an approximate translation.

I am grateful to Georgina Ferry and my publisher, John Inglis, for encouraging me to undertake this enterprise and to archivists and others for assistance in locating and often copying many of my father's letters: Shannon Bohle and Ludmila Pollock at Cold Spring Harbor Laboratory; Donald Borton at the Venter Institute; Becky Cape at the Lilly Library, Indiana University, Bloomington; Tim Driscoll at Harvard University; Elizabeth Ennion at King's College, Cambridge; Annette Faux at the Medical Research Council Laboratory of Molecular Biology; Colin Harris at the Bodleian Library in Oxford; Adam Perkins at Cambridge University Library; Char-lotte Sturm at the Rockefeller Foundation; and Blair Worden. I am also grateful to the recipients or their representatives for permission to copy them: Her Majesty the Queen, Don and Nancy Abraham, Bruce Alberts, Lucy Annan, Martin Bernal, Ann Corden (née Hartridge), Claudio Cuello, The Literary Estate of Lord Dacre of Glanton, David Edsall, Jean Floud, Horst Fuhrmann, Clare Goodman, Ron Gray, Martin Harwit, Richard Himsworth, Luke Hodgkin, Blaise Machin, Sir John Major, Hans Mark, Bob May, Rita Levi Montalcini, Marion, Robin, Sue and Tim Perutz, the Rocke- feller Archive Foundation, Alice Sievert, Monsignor Sorondo, Lady Thatcher, Patience Thomson, Lord Waldegrave, Duscha Weisskopf, Jim Wat- son, and the Zuckerman Archive University of East Anglia. Photographs have generously been given to me for reproduction by Gerhard Bodo, Robin Carrell, Anne Corden, David Edsall, John Gurdon, Richard Himsworth, Hugh Huxley, Beth Ingram, Blaise Machin, Kiyoshi Nagai, Hilary Wallace, and Shuguang Zhang. At the MRC Laboratory of Molecular Biology Annette Faux has also supplied photos, and she and Michael Fuller have answered a number of my questions.

My editor, Judy Cuddihy, could not have been more supportive. She has guided this project with intelligence and sensitivity. All the staff at Cold Spring Harbor Laboratory Press have been a pleasure to work with. Last but not least I am grateful to my cousin, Tina Wendon, for the fine cover and especially for the painting reproduced there. Her imaginative intuition and skill have transformed a mediocre photograph into an image that brings my father to life.

VIVIEN PERUTZ
Cambridge, July 2008

Timeline: A Life in Dates

1905   Brother (Franz) born

1909   Sister (Lotte) born

1914   Max born

1932   Student of chemistry, University of Vienna

1933   Trip to Lapland, northern Norway and Jan Mayen

1936   Cambridge, research student at Peterhouse and Cavendish Labora-
       tory with J.D. Bernal

1937   Started work on haemoglobin

1938   Austria invaded, now a refugee; member of Gerald Seligman's Swiss
       glacier research team

1940   Ph.D. completed under W.L. Bragg; interned as an enemy alien

1941   Returned to Cambridge

1942   Married Gisela Peiser

1943   Worked on Habbakuk project; British citizenship

1944   Daughter Vivien born

1947   Foundation of MRC Unit for the study of Molecular Structure of Bio-
       logical Systems

1948   First glacier expedition organised by Max to study mechanism of glacier
       flow

1949   First post-war trip to Austria; son Robin born

1950   Completion of glacier study

1951   Experimental proof of Linus Pauling's α-helical structure of poly-
       peptide chains

1953   Method for solving protein structures by attaching heavy atom derivatives
       (the solution of the phase problem)

1954   Fellow of The Royal Society

1959   First three-dimensional structure of haemoglobin at 5.5Å

1961   Weizmann lectures in Israel preceded by trip to Cyprus, Lebanon, and
       Jordan; conference in Moscow

1962   MRC Laboratory of Molecular Biology opened; Nobel Prize in Chemistry
       with John Kendrew

1963   Structure of human deoxy-haemoglobin; Dunham lectures at Harvard;
       founding chairman of the European Organisation for Molecular Biology;
       Commander of the British Empire (CBE)

1968   Structure of horse oxy-haemoglobin at 2.8Å; molecular basis of haemoglo-
       bin diseases

1970s Structures of abnormal haemoglobins and spectroscopic studies of
       haem–haem interaction

1970   Proposed mechanism of action of haemoglobin

1971   Royal Medal of The Royal Society; marriage of Robin to Sue Gray

1975   Companion of Honour (CH)

1978   Grandson Timothy born

1979   "Retirement"; Copley Medal of The Royal Society

1981   Member of the Pontifical Academy of Sciences; granddaughter Marion
       born

1983   Adaptation of haemoglobin in different species

1985   Publication of "Enemy Alien" essay in *The New Yorker*

1986   How haemoglobin acts as a drug receptor

1987   Asked to chair the MRC's committee for research into therapies for AIDS;
       Ordre pour le Mérite (Germany)

1988   Order of Merit (OM)

1994   Huntington's disease and molecular zippers

1996   Lewis Thomas Prize, "honoring the scientist as poet"

2002   Death; last scientific papers on amyloid published

List of Correspondents and People Referred to by First Name or Nickname

Her Majesty, The Queen

Abraham, Don, collaborated with Max for many years on attaching drugs to haemoglobin; medicinal chemist

Alberts, Bruce, President of the National Academy of Sciences

Annan, Noel, married to a distant cousin of Gisela; historian; Provost of King's College, Cambridge 1956–66; Provost of University College 1966–78; Vice-Chancellor of London University 1978–81

Anne, see Hartridge

Annemarie, see Wendrina

Baxter, Evelyn, see Machin

Bernal, John Desmond, Max's first Ph.D. supervisor as head of the Crystallographic Laboratory at the Cavendish in Cambridge; from 1938 Professor of Physics at Birkbeck College, London; scientific advisor to Lord Louis Mountbatten during World War II. With Dorothy Hodgkin (Crowfoot) in 1934, he took the first X-ray diffraction picture of a protein crystal.

Bragg, W. Lawrence, Max's second Ph.D. supervisor and later collaborator; Nobel Prize in Physics, 1915, with his father for the solution by X-ray diffraction of the structure of salt; Cavendish Professor 1938–53; Director of the Royal Institution 1953–66

Crick, Francis, joined Max in 1949; Nobel Prize in Physiology or Medicine with James Watson and Maurice Wilkins in 1962. He worked at LMB until 1975, when he moved to the Salk Institute in California.

Cuello, Claudio, was Chair of the McGill University Department of Pharmacology and Therapeutics.

Dardozzi, Renato, Director of the Chancery of the Pontifical Academy of Sciences

Daria, see Weissel

Davis, Bernard, microbiologist at Harvard University

Dorothy, see Hodgkin

Edsall, John T., biochemist who ended his career as Emeritus Professor at Harvard University; colleague and friend from 1943

Eirich, Fritz, 9 years older than Max, keen mountaineer, amateur botanist, and professional polymer chemist; took on the role of an elder brother from at least 1928; lifelong friend. Met Max because his closest school friend was Willy Teller, Evelyn Machin's cousin, and the son of Max's parents' closest friends. Emigrated from Vienna to Cambridge and then to the United States where he became a professor at Brooklyn Polytechnic

Eirich (née Dehne), Maria, nicknamed Wopp, wife of Fritz, Vivien's godmother

Fan, see Fankuchen

Fankuchen, Isidore, American crystallographer, who was working in the Cavendish in Cambridge when Max became a research student there

Floud, Jean, sociologist, Principal of Newnham College 1972–83. Met Max at Edward Shils' memorial where she gave the address. She subsequently became a family friend

Francis, see Crick

Franz (Frank), see Perutz

Fritz, see Eirich

Fuhrmann, Horst, historian and fellow member of Pour le Mérite

Gowans, James (Jim), Secretary, i.e. chief executive, of the Medical Research Council 1977–87

Granichstaedten, Heini, fellow chemistry student in Vienna; companion on expedition to Scandinavia; interned with Max; one of his two closest friends; committed suicide in 1954 when he mistakenly thought his business had gone bankrupt

Gray, Ron, father of Sue Perutz

Hartridge, Anne (Corden), girlfriend and lifelong friend; physiotherapist

Haurowitz, Felix, husband of Max's cousin, Gina; professor of biochemistry at the Charles University in Prague, then in Istanbul, and finally at Indiana University, Bloomington

Heini, see Granichstaedten

Himsworth, Harold, Secretary, i.e. chief executive, of the Medical Research Council 1949–68

Hodgkin, Dorothy Crowfoot, friend from the late 1930s until her death in 1994; she solved the molecular structures in three dimensions of insulin, penicillin, and vitamin B12; Nobel Prize in Chemistry 1964

Hughes, Tom, physical chemist; co-worker on the Jungfraujoch in 1938 and lifelong friend

Jaeger, René, friend from 1930 when he attended the same school as Max; keen mountaineer

Falkner, Dr., unknown

Jimmy, see Perutz

John, see Kendrew

Kendrew, John, joined Max as a research student in 1945; shared Nobel Prize in Chemistry in 1962 with Max for discovery of structure of myoglobin

Kiyoshi, see Nagai

Levi-Montalcini, Rita, neurologist; Nobel Prize in Physiology or Medicine 1986

Lotte, see Perutz

Luke, see Wendon

Machin, Evelyn, the niece of Max's parents' closest friends, girl friend and lifelong friend, Robin's godmother; taught German; became an archaeologist in retirement; poet and amateur painter

Major, John, Prime Minister 1990–97

Mark, Hans, son of Hermann Mark, one of Max's professors in Vienna, who in the U.S. worked on the Habbakuk project.

May, Robert (Bob), President of the Royal Society

Miller, H.M., worked for The Rockefeller Foundation

Mott, Nevill, Cavendish Professor of Physics 1954–7, Nobel Prize in Physics 1977

Nagai, Kiyoshi, Max's post-doc and later colleague working on haemoglobin at LMB

Pauling, Linus, author of *The Nature of the Chemical Bond and the Structure of Molecules and Crystals,* 1939, which set many purely empirical aspects of chemistry on a theoretical basis; proposer of the α-helical structure of polypeptides 1950 and author of many further key papers; Nobel Prize in Chemistry 1954; Nobel Peace Prize 1962 for his campaign against nuclear weapons and their testing

Peiser, Herbert and Nelly, parents-in-law

Peiser, Steffen, brother-in-law

Perutz, Franz (Frank), brother

Perutz, Hugo and Dely, parents

Perutz, Gisela, wife

Perutz, Jimmy, nephew; son of Franz and Senta

Perutz, Lotte, sister

Perutz, Marion, granddaughter

Perutz, Robin, son

Perutz, Senta, wife of Franz

Perutz, Sue, daughter-in-law

Perutz, Timothy, grandson

Perutz, Vivien, daughter

Pomerat, Gerard, worked for The Rockefeller Foundation

Popper, Karl, philosopher of science and of politics; professor at the London School of Economics

René, see Jaeger

Roch, André, engineer, mountaineer and photographer; Director of the Swiss Avalanche Research Centre, Davos

Silvers, Robert, editor of *The New York Review of Books* for which Max wrote many articles

Sorondo, Marcelo Sánchez, prelate and philosopher; Chancellor of the Pontifical Academy of Sciences

Steffen, see Peiser

Thatcher, Margaret, Prime Minister 1979–1990

Thomson, Patience, friend, daughter of Lawrence Bragg; expert on dyslexia; teacher, writer and publisher

Tom, see Hughes

Trevor-Roper, Hugh, (Lord Dacre), historian, Master of Peterhouse (Max's college) 1980–87

Udvarhelyi, Híradó, unknown

Waldegrave, William, Chancellor of the Duchy of Lancaster in John Major's Cabinet with special responsibility for science

Watson, James (Jim), came to work in Max's unit in 1951; Nobel Prize in Physiology or Medicine with Francis Crick and Maurice Wilkins, 1962, for the solution of the structure of DNA; Chancellor Emeritus of Cold Spring Harbor Laboratory

Weaver, Warren, Director of Natural Sciences at the Rockefeller Foundation, New York, which funded Max and his unit

Weissel, Daria, wife of Werner

Weissel, Werner, attended Max's secondary school from 1930; cardiologist; closest lifelong friend

Weisskopf, Victor (Viki), friend; physicist; director of CERN, who in that capacity helped Max when he chaired the European Molecular Biology Organisation; member of the Pontifical Academy of Sciences

Wendon, Luke, son of Hans and Annemarie

Wendrina (anglicised to Wendon) Hans and Annemarie, Gisela's uncle and aunt.

Werner, see Weissel

Wopp, see Eirich, Maria

Wyman, Jeffries, biophysicist at Harvard, later joined the haemoglobin group at the University of Rome; council member of the European Molecular Biology Organisation

Zuckerman, Solly, zoologist; chief scientific adviser first at the Ministry of Defence and later to the British Government

List of Illustrations

All photographs are © Vivien and Robin Perutz unless otherwise specified.

Memoir

1930s

1960s

1970s

Archival Repositories of the Letters

Bodleian Library Manuscripts at the University of Oxford

To Hugo and Dely Perutz, November 24, 1940 (SPSL 336/2, fol. 150)
To the Aliens War Service Department, March 17, 1941 (SPSL 336/2, fol. 151)
To Esther Simpson, September 14, 1941 (SPSL 336/2, fol. 164)
To Dorothy Hodgkin, September 12, 1943 (Eng. c. 5707 [H 180])
To Dr Falkner, March 15, 1965 (Eng. c.2419 [F23])
To Jeffries Wyman, February 23, 1966 (Eng. c.2440 [G4])
To Jeffries Wyman, February 2, 1967 (Eng. c.2440 [G11])
To Dorothy Hodgkin, March 2, 1992 (Eng. c. 5707 [H 182])

Cambridge University Library Manuscript Collection Add. 8287 J178

To John Desmond Bernal, March 21, 1938
To John Desmond Bernal, July 12, 1938
To John Desmond Bernal December 6, 1939

Harvard University Archives

To John T. Edsall, December 12, 1947 (HUG4352.5–box 13)
To John T. Edsall at Harvard, January 15, 1964 (HUG 4352.5.4–box 14)
To John T. Edsall, December 12, 1965 (HUG 4352.5.4–box 14)
To John T. Edsall, September 7, 1969 (HUG 4352.5.4–box 24)
To John T. Edsall. May 6, 1970 (HUG 4352.5.4–box 24)
To John T. Edsall, August 22, 1978 (Accession 10257–box 2)
To John T. Edsall, October 29, 1978 (Accession 10257–box 3)
To John T. Edsall. May 19, 1981 (Accession 12020–box 5)
To John T. Edsall, September 27, 1983 (Accession 12057–box 5)
To John T. Edsall, November 26, 1983 (Accession 12057–box 5)
To John T. Edsall, November 12, 1984 (Accession 12057–box 5)
To John T. Edsall, January 18, 1986 (12020–box 5)
To John T. Edsall, February 17, 1986 (Accession 12020–box 5)

To John T. Edsall, November 30, 1986 (Accession 12020–box 5)
To John T. Edsall, August 2, 1994 (Accession 13606–box 3)

Lilly Library, Indiana University, Bloomington Coll LMC1538 Correspondence: Max Perutz file

To Felix Haurowitz, August 1, 1937
To Felix Haurowitz, July 28, 1953
To Felix Haurowitz, September 21, 1953
To Felix Haurowitz, September 20, 1956
To Felix Haurowitz, April 19, 1957
To Felix Haurowitz, December 13, 1959
To Felix Haurowitz, December 8, 1973
To Felix Haurowitz, December 26, 1973
To Felix and Gina Haurowitz, December 6, 1980

King's College, Cambridge

To Noel Annan, May 3, 1989 (NGA/5/1/787)

Medical Research Council Laboratory of Molecular Biology, Cambridge

To Harold Himsworth, September 20, 1955
To Harold Himsworth, August 24, 1956
To Harold Himsworth, October 24, 1958
To Harold Himsworth, May 3, 1959
To Harold Himsworth, January 25, 1961
To Harold Himsworth, February 9, 1961
To Harold Himsworth, December 12, 1962

Courtesy Ava Helen and Linus Pauling Papers, Oregon State University Pauling Archives, Box 304.1

To Linus Pauling, August 5, 1946
To Linus Pauling, April 21, 1958
To Linus Pauling, December 14, 1950

The National Archives of the United Kingdom

To Harold Himsworth, April 6, 1953 (FD1 426)

The Rockefeller Foundation Archive New York

To Warren Weaver, January 26, 1941 Record Group 1.1; Series 200D; Box 43; Folder 563

To HM Miller, August 8, 1942 Record group 1.1; Series 401D, Box 43, Folder 564

To Gerard Pomerat, August 8, 1955 Record group 1.1; Series 401D, Box 44, Folder 365

To Gerard Pomerat, August 15, 1955 Record group 1.1; Series 401D, Box 44, Folder 365

To Gerard Pomerat, August 30, 1955 Record group 1.1; Series 401D, Box 44, Folder 562

To Gerard Pomerat, October 12, 1955 Record group 1.1; Series 401D, Box 44, Folder 568

To Gerard Pomerat September 16, 1957 Record group 1.1; Series 401D, Box 44, Folder 569

To Gerard Pomerat October 1, 1959 Record group 1.1; Series 401D, Box 44, Folder 570

To Gerard Pomerat, July 21, 1961 Record group 1.1; Series 401D, Box 44, Folder 572

Venter Institute Archive Perutz Papers

To John Edsall. July 18, 1948 (B3F17)

To Solly Zuckerman, February3, 1989 (B3F5)

To Bernard Davis, January 7, 1992, (Box 3 F2)

To Rita Levi-Montalcini, May 18, 1992 (B3F6)

To Hans Mark, May 20, 1992 (B3F17)

To Claudio Cuello, October 5, 1992 (B3F5)

To Hírado Udvarhelyi, August 17, 1995 (B3F10)

To Rita Levi-Montalcini, February 16, 1996 (B3F6)

Private Collections

Letters to Don Abraham, Jean Floud, and Patience Thomson are in the recipients' collections. Letters to Steffen Peiser are in Clare Goodman's collection.

All the other letters are now in the Perutz family archive. As mentioned in the Preface, the copies of letters from Max's office files, but not the private correspondence, will be deposited in the archive of Churchill College, Cambridge.

Memoir of Max Perutz

by David Blow

Max Ferdinand Perutz OM CH CBE
19 May 1914 – 6 February 2002

David Blow (1931–2004). Blow became Max's research student in 1954; he remained on the scientific staff of the MRC Unit and then the MRC Laboratory of Molecular Biology until 1977, when he became Professor of Biophysics at Imperial College.

Max Ferdinand Perutz OM CH CBE
19 May 1914 – 6 February 2002
Elected FRS 1954

By D.M. Blow FRS

Biophysics Section, Blackett Laboratory, Imperial College, London SW7 2AZ, UK

SCIENTISTS WILL REMEMBER MAX PERUTZ for his outstanding analysis of the molecular structure, properties and allosteric mechanism of haemoglobin, but his wonderful clarity and simplicity in writing on the widest range of topics has made him famous far beyond the haemoglobin fraternity. He left many autobiographical essays on different events in his life, and his writings are quoted frequently in this memoir. Indeed, to a large extent, it is written by Max Perutz himself!

Introduction

The pioneers of X-ray crystallography in Britain have included an impressive series of characters. Several of them, outstandingly Sir Lawrence Bragg, Dame Kathleen Lonsdale, and Dorothy Crowfoot Hodgkin, have had a lasting influence on the ethos of research. They have demonstrated honesty in competition, straightforwardness in collaboration, and respect for colleagues.

Max Perutz must unquestionably be included in this elite group. He possessed a wonderful humanity, a deep respect for individual points of view, and an utter honesty in resolving scientific and personal issues. This attitude is encapsulated in the quotation on a plaque in the vestibule of the Max Perutz lecture theatre at the Laboratory of Molecular Biology, "In science, truth always wins."

As his own status developed, the young man who had chosen a research problem deemed impossible by many of his peers began to demonstrate a

Adapted from the memoir published by The Royal Society. (*Biogr. Mem. Fellows R. Soc. Lond.* **50:** 227–256, 2004). Biographical information that is covered in the section introductions and letters of this book has been deleted from this memoir.

deep and imaginative insight, which led him forward through the technical, administrative, and intellectual difficulties. His skill at apparently effortless organization was matched by an uncanny insight into people's abilities, and his qualities of respect and persuasiveness gained him their support and loyalty. His creative command of written English, and his way of organizing a complex set of ideas into a simple logical progression, made his influence wider and more immediate.

Of all these qualities, the humanity projected most strongly, putting strangers at ease and smoothing his relations with colleagues. At the same time, his honesty could make him appear harsh. If he decided not to continue an appointment he would tell its holder directly, face to face, in terms that allowed no further negotiation.

Prewar Cambridge

After 3 years as an undergraduate at the University of Vienna studying Chemistry, Max left to begin studying for a Ph.D. in Cambridge which he gained in January 1940.

There the physiologist Gilbert Adair (FRS 1939) gave Perutz beautiful haemoglobin crystals. From these, Max recalls, "I obtained rich X-ray diffraction patterns. I was hooked! I proudly showed my X-ray photographs to all my friends, but when asked what they meant I changed the subject, because I had no idea" (40).* Adair had determined the molecular mass of haemoglobin by osmotic pressure measurements to be close to 67000 daltons, and had shown by oxygen binding measurements that the molecule contained four haem groups. The unit cell of horse methaemoglobin revealed that such a molecule must lie on a twofold symmetry axis, and must therefore consist of two identical halves (1). Perutz also measured the polarization dichroism, which showed that the four haems lie roughly normal to the crystallographic a axis (2). These were the first specific insights into protein structure ever gained through the study of crystals.

Postwar Cambridge

In 1938 a new Cavendish Professor had arrived in Cambridge, a Nobel laureate honoured for his solution of the first crystal structures, W.L. (later Sir) Lawrence Bragg FRS. With his help, Perutz obtained a three-year ICI

---

*Numbers in this form refer to the Perutz bibliography at the end of the text.

Fellowship, which supported his work until 1947. In the autumn of 1945 a Wing Commander in the Royal Air Force, John (later Sir John) Kendrew (FRS 1960), just returned to the UK from India for demobilization, came to call on Max. In Delhi he had been with A.V. Hill, and in 1944 he was sent to Mountbatten's headquarters in Ceylon (Sri Lanka), where he renewed his acquaintance with Bernal. His journey home had taken him through Los Angeles, where he made a pilgrimage to Pasadena to meet Linus Pauling (ForMemRS 1948). These contacts had made Kendrew enthusiastic for structural work on proteins, and Max welcomed him warmly. Kendrew became a research student working under Bragg, to study crystals of normal and foetal sheep haemoglobin in collaboration with Perutz (Holmes 2001).

In the later war years, Perutz made few publications, but 'The composition and swelling properties of haemoglobin crystals' (4), published in 1946, was of far-reaching importance. A crisis was, however, looming. In the following year both Perutz and Kendrew would reach the end of their funding. "Going backwards and forwards on my bicycle between the Cavendish Laboratory and the Molteno Institute, I was the living link between Biology and Physics, but I was a chemist incapable of teaching either subject, and neither the university nor any of the colleges had a place for me." Keilin suggested to Bragg that an approach might be made to the Medical Research Council (MRC) for support. This approach, following a presentation to the Secretary of the MRC, Sir Edward Mellanby FRS, was brilliantly successful, and an MRC Unit for the Study of the Molecular Structure of Biological Systems was established in October 1947, with Perutz as Director and Kendrew as part-time member.

During the war years, Perutz had recorded three-dimensional X-ray diffraction data on horse methaemoglobin, and measured the intensities of some 7000 Bragg reflections visually. The conventional approach to crystal structure analysis would have been to calculate a Fourier synthesis of the intensities, a Patterson function. "One or two weeks" hard work on a hand calculator allowed me to do a two-dimensional Fourier summation with a hundred terms, but three-dimensional Fourier summations of a protein seemed out of the question at first. Later, after the work by Dorothy Hodgkin (FRS 1947) on penicillin, the three-dimensional Patterson function was calculated tediously, using many thousands of Hollerith cards. Its most prominent feature suggested parallel rods of density packed hexagonally 10.5 Å apart, showing strong features at intervals of 5 Å (6). Noting that the spacings corresponded to the equatorial and meridional arcs observed on diffraction patterns of α-keratin, Perutz 'concluded, rashly, that haemoglobin consisted of close-packed, α-keratin-like polypeptide chains' (40). This insight was gloriously near to the truth, but attempts at more detailed interpretation led into deep trouble.

Francis Crick (FRS 1959) had nearly completed a doctorate in physics at University College when his laboratory was destroyed by a bomb in 1940. After war service with the Admiralty, he turned to biology with an MRC studentship to work at the Strangeways Laboratory, Cambridge, from 1947, but by 1949 he knew of Perutz's work and sought to transfer to the Cavendish. "He hadn't got a reputation. He just came and we talked together and John and I liked him." He registered anew as research student under Max. "The first thing Francis did was to read everything we had done. Then he started criticising" (quoted by Judson 1979). "He calculated what I ought to have done, namely the theoretical density in the rods" of the Patterson function. This calculation suggested "that only about one-third of the molecule consisted of parallel polypeptide chains of the [keratin] type. When the real structure emerged, it became clear that the vector rod was due to α-helices which make up just 7% of the molecule!" (40).

"Bragg made Kendrew and me build atomic models to explore the helical structures that the stereochemistry of polypeptides allowed with a 5.1 Å repeat, representing what he suspected was the repeat of amino acid residues along the fibre axis of α-keratin. We built models with two-, three-, and four-fold screw symmetry without being aware of the planarity due to the partial double-bond character of the peptide bond. We published these in the autumn of 1950" (7,40).

In June 1951 Pauling published a hypothetical structure for a polypeptide chain, the α-helix (Pauling et al. 1951). Max read it on a Saturday morning. "I was thunderstruck." Their helix had a pitch of 5.4 Å, rather than 5.1 Å. It "was strain-free; all the amide groups were planar and every carbonyl group formed a perfect hydrogen bond." But "how could Pauling and Corey's helix be right, however good it looked, if it had the wrong repeat? I had an idea." In the proposed α-helix successive peptide bonds advance 1.5 Å along the axis, so "this regular repeat should give rise to a strong X-ray reflection of 1.5 Å spacing from planes perpendicular to the fibre axis." Perutz's clear insight, before any detailed theory of helical diffraction had been formulated, is notable. He realized that this short spacing would not be observed using conventional fibre diffraction technique, because the fibre needs to be tilted to bring these planes into a diffracting position. The same afternoon, he mounted a horse hair at 31° to the incident X-ray beam, and "found a strong reflection at 1.5 Å spacing, exactly as demanded by Pauling and Corey's α-helix" (8,41). It was discovered later that the 5.1 Å spacing observed in diffraction from keratin is due to the helical repeat of two α-helices twisting round each other.

When Max recounted this to Bragg on the Monday morning, "I told him the idea was sparked off by my fury over having missed building that beautiful structure myself." Bragg's memorable response "I wish I'd made you angry earlier" (26) was used by Perutz almost 50 years later as the title of a book of essays (41).

Bernal had suggested that study of crystals in different states of hydration might make possible the direct analysis of the molecular structure (1). Bragg showed how this idea could be used to study the signs of the *h0l* reflections (whose phase is limited to 0° or 180° by symmetry). If the Fourier transform of X-ray scattering from this plane of the haemoglobin structure can be explored at close intervals, the signs can change only where the molecular transform passes through a point of zero scattering power. In this way sign relations could be established between *h0l* reflections (Bragg 1953). Using his expertise in shrinking and swelling protein crystals (4), Perutz was able to make this idea work (9). It provided the first indications about the *h0l* signs, but did not seem able to be extended into three dimensions.

The vision of protein structure determination seemed as far away as ever. "I pursued both the Patterson and the Bernal approach to exhaustion, with meagre results which I largely misinterpreted, but in a circuitous way they did finally lead me to the solution of the phase problem and of protein structures" (40).

The Golden Decade, 1952–62

In October 1951 Jim Watson (ForMemRS 1981) arrived unannounced at Max's laboratory. At 22, he was 12 years younger than Crick. "They shared the sublime arrogance of men who have rarely met their intellectual equals." This irritated Bragg, but their approach to DNA, a problem "that could only be solved by a tremendous leap of imagination," was recognized and tolerated by Perutz, who saw that "like Leonardo [they] often achieved most when they seemed to be working least" (29). The resulting publication describing the structure of DNA (Watson and Crick 1953) brought the MRC Unit into the limelight for the first time.

One feature of Perutz's role in the discovery of the double helix was controversial. Although Watson had seen X-ray photographs of DNA taken by Rosalind Franklin at King's College, London, he had not noted the precise details she had given in a lecture. These data were also given in the working papers of a MRC committee (Medical Research Council 1952), which Perutz showed to Watson and Crick. This information, especially the statement of the symmetry of crystals of the A form of DNA, was crucial to solving the structure. Perutz later described Watson's account in *The Double Helix* (Watson 1968) as picturing "Wilkins and Miss Franklin jealously trying to keep their data secret, and Watson and Crick getting hold of them in an underhand way, through a confidential report passed on by me." This "does an injustice to one of the greatest discoveries of the century. The report was not confidential and contained no data that Watson had not already heard about from Miss Franklin and Wilkins. Crick might have had this more than a year earlier if Watson had taken notes at a seminar given by Miss Franklin. I realized later that, as a matter of courtesy, I should have asked Randall for permission to show it to Watson and Crick, but I saw no reason for withholding it" (17). This letter drew an unqualified apology from Watson (1969).[1]

While the DNA structure was coming out, protein crystallography seemed stuck. To calculate the structure from the X-ray scattering, it is necessary to know the phases of the scattered orders of diffraction. Perutz had only an uncertain method, based on the shrinkage stages of haemoglobin crystals, applicable only to the *h0l* orders, which had phases either zero or π (11). Another method, known as isomorphous replacement, had been shown by Bijvoet to be applicable to non-centrosymmetric structures (Bokhoven et al. 1951), but depended on changes of diffracted intensity considered too small to be used for proteins. Crick's quantitative work on haemoglobin had shown that the scattering from protein crystals was weaker than had been imagined, and indicated that Bijvoet's method might be feasible. In 1953 Max himself made a breakthrough that allowed the "phase problem" to be solved.

"One day the mail brought me reprints from a stranger at Harvard, Austin Riggs." They showed that the sulphydryl groups of the haemoglobin molecule can be ligated with silver or mercury ions. "Had Riggs' papers arrived a few years earlier I might have doubted that the presence of two mercury atoms would produce significant intensity changes but in fact I had recently measured the absolute intensity from a haemoglobin crystal" (24). Perutz realized that "the electrons of a heavy atom, being concentrated in a small sphere, would scatter in phase, and that their contribution should produce measurable intensity changes," despite being only a tiny fraction of the electrons in the crystal (33). His biochemist colleague Vernon Ingram (FRS 1970) prepared crystals containing the heavy atoms. "These [intensity] changes would provide the correct phases only if the attachment of the heavy atom left the structure of the protein molecules unaltered. When I first tried the method, I was not at all sure that these stringent demands would be fulfilled. . . . I developed my first X-ray photograph of mercury haemoglobin [and] I was jubilant when the diffraction spots appeared in exactly the same positions as in the mercury-free protein, but with slightly altered intensity, just as I had hoped" (33). He fetched Bragg to the dark-room. "We realized that the phase problem which had baffled us for 16 years was at last solved, and Bragg went around telling everyone generously that I had discovered a goldmine" (40).

Measurements were speedily made of the *h0l* intensity changes when a heavy atom was substituted. These changes confirmed that the heavy atoms were attached to a unique site in the molecule. From this knowledge, the signs of the *h0l* reflections could be established, and showed themselves beautifully consistent with the sign relations obtained from the shrinkage stages of the crystals (12). For the other reflections, because of the chirality of protein molecules, the phase may take any value between 0 and 2π. It took a few years more to develop the method for these reflections. It required attachment of mercurials to the other 'buried' sulphydryl site, to create other significantly different derivatives. This did not prove easy.

In 1954, immediately after the first publication using isomorphous replacement to determine protein phases, Perutz was elected a Fellow of The Royal Society. Among his distinguished proposers were Bernal, Bragg, Kathleen Lonsdale, Dorothy Hodgkin, William Astbury, and A.V. Hill.

Some years before, Kendrew had transferred his attention to the crystal structure of myoglobin, a molecule only a quarter the size of haemoglobin. Myoglobin has no sulphydryl groups, and Kendrew's team worked hard to find how to attach heavy atoms to a protein molecule without such groups. In time, they found four derivatives with heavy atoms at identifiable sites. The smaller size of the myoglobin molecule, which gave more robust and better-ordered crystals with simpler diffraction patterns, gave Kendrew's group a substantial advantage. In 1958 a three-dimensional model of myoglobin using diffraction to 6.0 Å resolution showed a curiously looped sausage of density, interpreted as α-helix, winding around the density of the haem group (Kendrew et al. 1958).

Figure 1. The 5.5 Å resolution structure of haemoglobin, represented in Perutz's famous model. (From the frontispiece of I Wish I'd Made You Angry Earlier *[42].)*

In September 1959 Perutz and colleagues, using 40,000 measurements from crystals of haemoglobin and six heavy-atom derivatives, calculated the three-dimensional structure at 5.5 Å resolution. It "proved itself at first sight. The conformation of the two pairs of chains in horse haemoglobin closely resembled that found by Kendrew. No conceivable combination of errors could have produced that striking similarity" (40). This structure was published in 1960 (15), alongside a preliminary description of an electron density map of myoglobin at 2.0 Å resolution that had required 200,000 measurements (Kendrew et al. 1960). It was illustrated by a famous representation of the molecule as white and black slabs of thermosetting plastic, which has become the symbol of Perutz's work on haemoglobin (see Figure 1 above).

Many other factors were crucial to that success. Max had recruited an excellent high-vacuum engineer, Tony Broad, who designed a high-intensity fine-focus rotating-anode X-ray generator. At first these machines were hugely unreliable, but they provided a far brighter X-ray source, of appropriate size, than was available anywhere else. Max made himself ill with the effort of visual estimation of thousands of X-ray diffraction spots on small films, but Kendrew identified an automatic scanning densitometer (designed by Peter Walker in Edinburgh), which could tirelessly scan the intensities of lines of spots. David Blow (FRS 1972) developed methods of analysis to determine phase angles reliably. The calculation of Fourier transforms would have been unthinkable without the power of the first general stored-program computer, EDSAC1, developed by Maurice Wilkes and his colleagues in the nearby Mathematical Laboratory. Kendrew wrote the world's first two-dimensional Fourier transform computer programs for EDSAC1. Later, Michael Rossmann (ForMemRS 1996) wrote a three-dimensional program for its more powerful successor, EDSAC2. Fiendish ingenuity (and many miles of paper tape) were required to make these calculations with the tiny amount of memory available. All of these innovations were brought together in a timely way to achieve the result.

The Unit had other amazing successes during these years. Hugh Huxley (FRS 1960), building on his Ph.D. work under Max, established with Jean Hanson (FRS 1967) the sliding-filament model for muscle contraction. Vernon Ingram, using techniques invented by Fred Sanger (FRS 1954), made a detailed study of peptide fragments of human haemoglobin and of sickle-cell haemoglobin. Long before the amino acid sequence of haemoglobin, or even of myoglobin, was known, Ingram determined the exact single amino acid substitution responsible for sickle-cell disease. Francis Crick and Sydney Brenner (FRS 1965) demonstrated that the DNA code was a three-letter code, and Crick formulated his "central dogma."

Also in 1954 Bragg had retired and moved to the Royal Institution, and the Cavendish Professorship was taken by Sir Nevill Mott FRS. Mott, although encouraging to Perutz, felt that his work should not be accommodated in the Physics Department and sought to transfer the Unit to a different department, but none was willing to offer adequate resources. A desperate compromise was reached, in which the Unit moved out of the Physics buildings in 1957 and took over a hut in the car park, erected for temporary wartime use (see Figure 2). Happily the X-ray generators remained in the basement of the Cavendish Laboratory's Austin Wing. In the following years, the group of scientists attracted to work with Perutz, Kendrew, Crick, and Brenner became far too large to do experimental work in the hut. Every unused room in the vicinity was adopted for use. Kendrew built his model of myoglobin in the recently vacated cyclotron room at the Cavendish, while Brenner and his colleagues used Lord Rutherford's former stable for experiments in molecular genetics.

The situation was obviously unsustainable. In summer 1957, even before moving into the hut, Perutz had joined Sanger in proposing to the MRC, led since 1949 by Sir Harold Himsworth FRS as Secretary, that new

Figure 2. Perutz with his team outside the "hut" in 1958. Standing from the left: Larry Steinrauf, Dick Dickerson, Hilary Muirhead, Michael Rossmann, Ann Cullis, Bror Strandberg, two unknown people and Max. Seated are Leslie Barnett and Mary Pinkerton. (Reproduced by courtesy of the Laboratory of Molecular Biology.)

accommodation was needed for their research. This proposal was taken seriously by Himsworth, who promptly initiated discussions with the university and with the heads of the relevant scientific departments. In early 1958, Crick and Perutz made a major submission to the MRC (14) with an extensive supporting document (13) emphasizing that molecular biology "had changed from a subject of speculation and uncertainty to an exact science" within six years. Perutz made the case to the Council personally (Medical Research Council 1958). "I spent a sleepless night worrying about it, but as soon as I entered the Council room one of the members told me it was the most interesting report he had ever read and the Council approved our plans that same day" (37). Much greater difficulties were encountered with the university, on such questions as the relation of the university to the proposed Laboratory of Molecular Biology (LMB), its control over its size and conditions of employment, and above all, its site. Himsworth's strong and active support kept the embattled proposal alive, and in 1959 the enthusiastic plan by Professor J.S. Mitchell FRS to place the Laboratory adjacent to his Radiotherapeutics Department on the site of the new hospital began to appear the most favourable solution. The distance of two miles from the centre of Cambridge was a major disappointment, but the plan to set up a Postgraduate Medical School at the hospital in the future was some compensation. The 1958 award of the Nobel Prize for Medicine to Sanger concentrated minds on the proposal. At this late stage some Heads of Department complained that the group should not be moved so far away, but none was able to offer significant space closer to the centre.

Himsworth allowed a legacy to the MRC from Cusrow Wadia of Bombay to be used towards the cost of the buildings, and both the MRC and the Wellcome Trust made generous contributions towards capital equipment. The building was designed and constructed rapidly, and began to be occupied in February 1962. It was opened by The Queen on 28 May 1962. In October 1962 the award of the Nobel Prize for Medicine to F.H.C. Crick, J.D. Watson and M.H.F. Wilkins FRS was announced, followed by a further announcement on 1 November that the Nobel Prize for Chemistry was awarded to J.C. Kendrew and M.F. Perutz.

Max recalled that after the Nobel award ceremony in Stockholm, "it was for me to lead The Queen to dinner. She [was] a woman in her 70's, a sister of Mountbatten under whom I worked during the war. My brief acquaintance with her brother provided plenty of topics for talk."[2] In his Nobel Banquet Speech Max quoted a prayer of Sir Francis Drake to emphasize the long passage that still remained before structural analysis might give deep insight into biology: "Despite the 25 years for which I have been at it, the task which I have set myself has only just begun."

European Molecular Biology

Perutz had forged strong links with American scientists in the 1950s. Many visitors came to his laboratory for extended periods, including Jim Watson, Donald Caspar, Howard Dintzis, Alex Rich, Bob Parrish, Hal Wyckoff, Dick Dickerson, and Lyle Jensen. Linus Pauling's son Peter was Kendrew's graduate student. The influential Harvard scientists John Edsall, Jefferies Wyman, and Paul Doty visited several times. Max's former students Francis Crick, Hugh Huxley, and David Blow went to US laboratories for postdoctoral study.

With few exceptions, the most notable being the laboratories of Jacques Monod (ForMemRS 1968) and Vittorio Luzzatti in Paris and Walter Hoppe's in Munich, there was much less contact with European workers, despite the fact that Perutz and Kendrew were both fluent linguists, widely acquainted with European scientists. "Young Americans who recognised the promise of the new subject could easily get fellowships. . . but young Europeans had no such possibilities. In America there were summer schools where the pioneers could teach, but there were no funds for such activities in Europe."[3] It was partly a different economic regime, but, perhaps more importantly, many European universities were rigidly departmentalized, giving even less encouragement to interdisciplinary work than Cambridge.

The same issues worried European physicists, and Viktor Weisskopf, Director-General of CERN, was particularly keen to strengthen the growing influence of physical science on biology. In March 1962, with EURATOM sponsorship and support behind the scenes from Weisskopf, the Laboratorio Internazionale di Genetica e Biofisica was set up in Naples, with Adriano Buzzati-Traverso as Director.

A new impetus came from a bizarre event, which Max describes in his dramatic style.

> At the height of the Cuban missile crisis in [October][4] 1962, Leo Szilard, an eccentric Hungarian-born physicist, packed up his wife and belongings and fled Washington for Geneva. There he walked into the office of Victor Weisskopf, the director of CERN, with the words "I am the first refugee from the Third World War.". . . [Szilard] had been one of the initiators and early pioneers of the American atomic bomb project, but his qualms after Hiroshima made him turn from physics to molecular biology. Szilard suggested to Weisskopf the formation of an international laboratory of molecular biology on the model of CERN.[3]

True to form, Szilard wasted no time. He telephoned Crick to invite him to form the laboratory, but Crick refused, saying "not my glass of champagne." He spoke to Sydney Brenner (whom he knew well as a phage geneticist), who identified John Kendrew as the man he needed. Brenner says "Szilard had not heard of Kendrew, and I had to explain to him that he was a Nobel prizewinner"—this dates the conversation to after the prize was announced on 1 November. As a result, Kendrew accompanied by Jim Watson went to Geneva on the way back from Stockholm in December 1962, and discussed with Weisskopf and Szilard the possibility of setting up a CERN-like centre for molecular biology (Tooze 1981).[5] The project was ambitious because molecular biology was not yet widely recognized, and because anything emulating CERN, even remotely, would require strong inter-governmental support.

Weisskopf set up a meeting in Ravello in September 1963, ostensibly to organize an Italian Physical Society course to be given by biologists, but designed to bring together interested senior figures from a number of European countries, including Perutz, Kendrew, Brenner, and Conrad Waddington FRS from the UK. Before this meeting, a great deal of consultation took place, and two views began to emerge. One, promoted by Kendrew, was for a well-endowed international laboratory, a centre that could be used to train and coordinate research in fundamental biology for scientists throughout Europe; another view, formulated particularly by Waddington, sought to establish a widely based federal European organization that would sponsor training courses and fund postdoctoral fellowships and international exchanges at existing laboratories. These two proposals were not incompatible, and a draft proposal agreed between Kendrew and Waddington included both aspects. Perutz later noted, "I was convinced that the laboratory project was premature and . . . we must first build up molecular biology in Europe."[3] At the Ravello meeting, the European Molecular Biology Organization (EMBO) was established, its Executive Committee supported by two subcommittees, a Laboratory Subcommittee chaired by Kendrew, and a Federal Organization Subcommittee chaired by Buzzati-Traverso, with Waddington as a member.

It was unusual for Perutz to attend a meeting of this kind, because he preferred to spend time in the laboratory or in scientific discussion with colleagues (or, otherwise, in high mountains, which are not convenient from Ravello). Even more unusually, he agreed to be listed as a proposed member of the Executive Committee. Brenner says that during the meeting, when he was nominated by Jefferies Wyman to be the chairman, he was a bit cornered but accepted it with good grace. This acceptance reflects the great importance that Perutz attached to developing biology in continental Europe. "I helped to found the European Molecular Biology Organization of which I was the first chairman for six years. Apart from that I have always avoided committees" (Hargittai 1999).

To initiate the proposed organization and laboratory was a huge task. The first problem was to find financial resources. Max's wonderful persuasive and confidence-building skills were exactly what EMBO needed. "I went to see Butenandt (a member of the original EMBO Council), who was chairman of the Max Planck Gesellschaft, but crucially chairman of the Volkswagen Foundation, a large fund to support research and teaching in science, and had no difficulty in persuading him to lend us his support. He asked me to draft an application."[3] CERN generously provided accommodation for meetings. By July 1964 a draft constitution had been finalized (subsequently approved under Swiss law, giving EMBO a legal existence); the

Swiss Government undertook a diplomatic initiative to persuade other European governments to participate; Perutz's draft application to the Volkswagen Foundation was approved for submission; and R.K. Appleyard of EURATOM was invited to be the first executive secretary (Tooze 1981).

EMBO had everything except money. Israeli scientists were anxious to have a part in the embryonic organization and Aharon Katchalski of the Weizmann Institute (whose brother Ephraim, later to be President of Israel, was on the EMBO Council) rapidly organized a contribution from the Israeli government, enough to get going. Another helpful contribution was made by the Swiss Interpharma. Before the end of 1965 the Volkswagen Foundation awarded a grant of $687,000 for three years, renewed for a further three years in 1968, and EMBO's future began to look secure.

Max continued as EMBO's chairman until January 1969, with Raymond Appleyard as secretary, and with the active participation of John Kendrew as Secretary General of the European Molecular Biology Council. By this time intergovernmental support had been agreed. Kendrew "became the moving spirit in the founding of EMBL, which would never have come into being but for his drive and shrewd diplomacy."[3]

Structural Analysis of Oxy- and Deoxy-Haemoglobin

Meanwhile, with characteristic aplomb, Perutz had set up a simple structure for running his new laboratory in Cambridge (see Figure 3). "I persuaded the Medical Research Council to appoint me Chairman of the Governing Board rather than Director, a Board to be made up of Kendrew, Crick, Sanger, and me. This arrangement reserved major decisions of scientific policy to the Board and left their execution to me. The Board met only rarely. The Board never directed the laboratory's research but tried to attract, or to keep, talented young people and give them a free hand. My job was to take an interest in their research and to make sure that they had the means to carry it out" (37).

That was a severe enough task, even when the laboratory started with 25 scientific staff and a similar number of visitors and students. But Max appeared to do it effortlessly, and to have ample time to push forward his own research. "Seeing the Chairman standing at the laboratory bench or the X-ray tube, rather than sitting at his desk, set a good example and raised morale" (37).

The path from the model of haemoglobin at 5.5 Å resolution to the map at 2.8 Å, which would show the orientation of nearly every amino acid, was long and frustrating. Aware of the inconvenience and labour-intensive character of recording X-ray diffraction photographically at that time, Max decided

Figure 3. Max Perutz drawn by Sir Lawrence Bragg in 1964.

to use a diffractometer for the task (see Figure 4). The diffractometer, originally designed by Uli Arndt (FRS 1982), worked excellently, but advance calculation of the settings for every reflection, after the crystal orientation had been accurately determined, created a logistical problem, and a postdoctoral assistant made errors in aligning the diffractometer. Max decided to collect the data himself. Blow and Tim Gossling rallied round to set up a system in which the laboratory's new in-house computer could control data collection online. "[Uli] Arndt and [Frank] Mallett helped me to keep it running day and night for 15 months while I measured the intensities of some 100,000 reflections between 5.5 and 2.8 Å spacing from crystals of the native protein and three heavy atom derivatives. The final electron density map was so beautiful that I soon forgot the tedium of data collection" (40). This final model, fully consistent with the interpretation of the 5.5 Å map, gave crucial details of the interactions between the α and β subunits, showing how the α subunit makes extensive (but very different) interactions with the β_1 and β_2 subunits (16).

It had long been known that the binding of oxygen to haemoglobin was cooperative. That is to say, the binding of the first oxygen molecule increases its affinity for oxygen. Max set his student Hilary Muirhead onto the struc-

Figure 4. Max Perutz at the diffractometer. (Photograph taken in 1980, reproduced by courtesy of Cambridge Newspapers Ltd.*)*

ture determination of a deoxygenated form of haemoglobin, and crystals of the human form were found to be favourable. Muirhead obtained a structure at 5.5 Å resolution in October 1962, and, "interrupted by the announcement of the Nobel Prize," Max observed a structure composed of α and β subunits identical to those in horse oxyhaemoglobin, but the β-chains were moved further apart. This gave "a first glimpse of the transition for which Monod [Monod et al. 1963] was to coin the name 'allosteric'."

"The theory says that cooperative substrate binding may arise in proteins with two or more structures in equilibrium. In one structure [T] the subunits would be constrained by strong bonds that would oppose substrate binding. In the other structure [R] these constraints would be relaxed. In the transition between them, the symmetry would be conserved, so that the activity of all the subunits would be either equally low or equally high" (40). This model made strong, testable predictions, which led to discovery that 2,3-diphospho-glycerate, present in blood, acts as an allosteric effector of haemoglobin—its binding modifies the oxygen equilibrium by stabilizing the deoxy structure.

By 1970 Perutz and colleagues had obtained electron density for horse deoxyhaemoglobin at the same resolution, 2.8 Å, as the map of oxyhaemo-globin, and similar data for human deoxyhaemoglobin. These results not only confirmed the rearrangement of subunits but also revealed changes in subunit structure when oxygen is bound. In his insightful 1970 paper (18) Perutz noted especially a movement of the iron atoms relative to the plane of the haem group. In oxyhaemoglobin the haem iron is close to the haem plane, but in deoxyhaemoglobin it is displaced from the plane by at least 0.5 Å. A study of metal-ion field theory enabled him to correlate this displacement with the change of magnetic spin state of the iron atom depending on its 5-fold or 6-fold coordination. J.L. Hoard had observed a change in the Fe–N$_{porphyrin}$ distance according

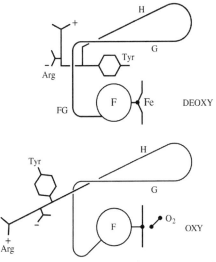

Figure 5. Perutz's 1970 sketch of the "trigger" that transforms a small movement of the haem iron into a reorganization of helix H. (Reprinted with permission from Nature **228**: 726–739. Copyright 1970 Macmillan Magazines Limited.)

to the spin state of ferric porphyrins (Hoard 1968). In 1970 the corresponding ferrous porphyrin structures had not been determined, but Pauling (1960, p. 518) had predicted a similar change in Fe–N distance. It was also uncertain whether the haem iron's distance from the proximal histidine would depend on the spin state. Perutz observed that in the β-chain of deoxy-haemoglobin, valine E11 is so close to the porphyrin ring that it must move to allow an oxygen molecule to be accommodated. He also noted that salt bridges formed by the carboxyterminal residues of the α- and β-chains make constraints that stabilize the deoxy form of haemoglobin.

By a brilliant series of insights, Perutz related the tiny displacements at the haem to the major reorganization of the interactions between the α$_1$- and β$_2$-chains on oxygenation, "like the flea that makes the elephant jump" (see Figure 5). He supported his interpretation by studies of the effects on oxygen binding and iron oxidation of a ligand (bis-maleimidomethyl ether) that blocks some of the subunit interactions, and the role of 2,3-diphosphoglycerate in the structural change. Perutz concludes his paper with a critique of the detail of the allosteric hypothesis (Monod et al. 1963). Of the suggestion that only two stable states are accessible to allosteric oligomers, he comments, "These words ring prophetically." The authors' assumption, which they discuss explicitly, that all subunits in one state are unreactive and all in the other are reactive, whether or not they are liganded, he finds too simple: "The haemoglobin subunits change their structure in response, not to the change in quaternary structure, but to the binding of ligand." He ends, "It is remarkable that there should be such an exceedingly complex, subtle and elegant instrument of respiratory transport, exploiting a difference in atomic radius of 13 per cent between the covalent and ionic forms of iron" (18). It is also remarkable that such a detailed, thorough, and rigorous analysis of this hugely complex mechanism should have been possible so soon after the first sight of a map at atomic resolution, remembering that it took two people three months just to build the model. This paper perhaps represents the pinnacle of Perutz's achievements on haemoglobin.

But it is far from the end of the story. "The evidence for the stereochemistry of the cooperative mechanism seemed so obvious and convincing that I expected everyone to accept it, but it failed to convince even my closest colleagues" [with the exception of Bragg, Crick, and Monod] (40). Controversy raged about the iron atom positions (whether in or out of the haem plane) until resolved in 1984 by structural results on deoxyhaemoglobin at a resolution of 1.74 Å (21). Conflicting measurements on the magnetic susceptibilities of various haemoglobins cast doubt on the role of the spin state of iron in triggering the structural change. Other controversies centred on the properties of dimeric haemoglobin, and the amino acids responsible for the Bohr effect (a change of oxygen affinity with pH). Max vindicated himself against these criticisms, but did not enjoy the controversy.

Mutant Haemoglobins And Species Adaptations

Vernon Ingram's demonstration in Perutz's laboratory in 1957 that sickle-cell disease follows from a single change to the amino acid sequence of haemoglobin, glutamate to valine at residue β6, started a new branch of medicine that Max named "molecular pathology." Many pathological variants of human haemoglobin could be detected by electrophoresis, and Perutz began a long and productive collaboration with Hermann Lehmann (FRS 1972), who collected samples worldwide. As detailed structural data emerged, the exact symptoms of each mutant gave new information about the function of different features of the haemoglobin molecule. "Fine modulations of physiological properties [could] be understood on the basis of atomic models" and related to clinical problems (19). "It was the first time that the causes of human disease could be seen at the atomic level. Abnormalities that defied simple explanations often revealed new properties of haemoglobin or new features of the allosteric mechanism" (40). A stream of papers, many reporting new X-ray structures for mutant haemoglobins, appeared from 1971 onwards. Later, site-directed mutagenesis became possible and the first synthetic mutant haemo-globins were reported in 1985 (22). These papers allowed the function of indi-vidual amino acids to be determined with increasing sophistication.

Although many of these examples represent rare, if not unique, muta-tions, sickle-cell disease is a major killer, especially in countries where malaria is prevalent. Perutz made little progress against sickle-cell disease. He recognized that the sickle-cell mutation, which gives some protection against malaria in alleles, must have happened several times (Pagnier et al. 1984). He tried to build on evidence that the sickle-cell mutant molecules aggregate into fibres by the association of valine β6 with phenylalanine β85 and leucine β86 of another molecule (Schechter et al. 1987), without success.

Other important diseases are linked to the need of mammals for foetal haemoglobin with higher oxygen affinity than the mother's. In humans, there is an embryonic haemoglobin E whose haemoglobin chains both dif-fer from the adult, which is replaced during development by foetal haemo-globin F with one variant chain. The absence or defectiveness of a gene for any of the chains leads to the widespread disease thalassaemia, which, like the sickle-cell trait, offers protection against malaria. "The high incidence of thalassaemia in malarial islands of Melanesia and its rarity in malaria-free islands inhabited for only 3000 years [shows that] Darwinian selection must have operated in historical times" (30).

Another active study concerned the needs of different animals for oxy-gen transport, and the consequent evolution of their haemoglobin. The requirements for haemoglobin in deep-sea fish, high-flying geese, ele-phants, and mice are very different. Camel and llama haemoglobins differ by a single amino acid change that alters oxygen affinity. Haemoglobin led the way in a neo-Darwinian analysis of natural selection and the evolution-ary tree at the molecular level. Perutz used some of these examples in his critique of Karl Popper's view of evolution (25).

As his world-famous laboratory expanded and diversified, Perutz remained personally committed to the study of haemoglobin in all its aspects. He continually sought depth and thoroughness in his studies, and embraced new techniques whenever he found they could throw light on a problem. The prayer of Sir Francis Drake, which he had quoted in his Nobel acceptance speech to suggest that the Prize acknowledged only the first step in the task he had undertaken, was used again as the motto of *Science is Not a Quiet Life* in 1997 (40), to indicate a sense of achievement: "When Thou givest Thy Servants to endeavour in any great matter, grant us also to know that it is not the beginning, but the continuing of the same, until it is thoroughly finished which yieldeth the true glory."

Structural Biology and Molecular Medicine

In this way research on a single protein, haemoglobin, led Perutz into a direct involvement in clinical problems. It was always his ambition to repay the tremendous investment made by the MRC into molecular biology with advances in medical knowledge. He encouraged many new approaches to disease at the LMB, but all too often the result was excellent diagnosis, deep insight into the nature of a disease, but no effective therapy.

The 1974 Wilson government challenged the MRC to demonstrate nationally that they were giving value for money in medical research. After reports by Lord Rothschild FRS and Sir Frederick (later Lord) Dainton FRS in 1971, more direct and intrusive administrative mechanisms had begun to appear. With Max's retirement looming, the MRC set up a committee under David Phillips FRS (later Lord Phillips of Ellesmere) to formulate future policy for the support of molecular biology. It has been suggested that the criticism in Phillips's report on the LMB was a consequence of professional rivalry between a laboratory securely supported by the MRC, and their opposite numbers in Oxford working in an insecure university environment (Chadarevian 2002, footnote 15, p. 342). The conflict between the LMB and the Phillips report is more reasonably represented as a difference of dogma. Phillips was an organization man, seeking efficient deployment of research resources, and recognizing that government holds the key to funding from the top downwards. Perutz was the antithesis of this, believing that research succeeds by the recognition of excellent workers and by the encouragement of creativity in the laboratory, with controls from above that are almost invisible. He admired the MRC's record as an autonomous body free from political pressures, with a tradition of excellence and far-sighted policy, "matched by an understanding of the human relations needed to motivate scientists to do creative work" (28). The ethos of the time was with Phillips, but Perutz had already proved his case by the wonderful achievements of the LMB. The report (Medical Research Council 1976) caused some anxiety at Cambridge, but its long-term effects were not serious.

Meanwhile, the LMB's first big breakthrough with obvious clinical application followed from the growing understanding of the immune system, and marked one of the first successes of cloning technology. Köhler &

Milstein (1975) found a means of maintaining growth of lymphocytes while secreting monoclonal antibodies, which led to their Nobel Prize.

When Max reached retirement age in 1979 he passed on the chairmanship of the Laboratory, but his personal research and his involvement in the scientific problems and aspirations of those around him continued with little apparent change. Progress on medical applications remained sparse for several years.

From about 1986 human immunodeficiency virus (HIV) was recognized as a major threat to world health. Unusually for him, Max accepted from the MRC a coordinating role to identify anti-viral compounds, vaccines, and new specific drugs, as part of a national Directed Programme to tackle the disease by all available methods. Assisted by Raymond Dwek (FRS 1998), he travelled extensively, and did not hesitate to enlist aid from American drug companies where he thought they could act more rapidly than the MRC. Progress again appeared agonizingly slow.

One of the significant achievements of molecular biological approaches to HIV therapy has been the design of drugs on the basis of the crystal structures of target enzymes. The worldwide adoption of Perutz's methods meant that the LMB was no longer the key player in structure determination.

Meanwhile, there were other important developments. "For me [Max wrote], the turning point came with Hermann Waldmann's and Greg Winter's humanized rat anti-T-cell antibody that produced long remissions in two terminally-ill leukemia patients (Riechmann et al. 1988). Waldmann and Winter could never have engineered that antibody if others before them had not solved the structures of several antibodies by X-ray analysis" (33). Wider application has followed and several reshaped antibodies have been approved for the therapy of infectious viral disease and cancers, and for use in transplant surgery. In 1992 Max Perutz published a textbook *Protein Structure: New Approaches to Disease and Therapy* (33), which emphasizes successful applications of structural analysis to medicine. Even at this recent date, the book mostly presents hopeful lines of research, and there are no completed success stories.

But within a year or so, a series of almost chance observations diverted the focus of Max's scientific work away from haemoglobin for the first time, and led him at 80 years of age to a series of highly original studies concentrated on neurodegenerative diseases, especially Huntington's disease. In 1991 he had reviewed a book (31) presenting the discovery of restriction enzymes, and their role in detection of inherited diseases, which chose recent developments in diagnosis of Huntington's disease as the main theme.

In 1992, the amino acid sequence of the octameric haemoglobin of *Ascaris*, known for its very high oxygen affinity, revealed a repetitive amino acid sequence at the carboxy terminus of the monomer. Perutz and others proposed that repetitive sequences of the octamer associate as an eight-stranded antiparallel β-barrel, stabilized by charged interactions, which was named a "polar zipper" (32). This led to the recognition of other types of repetitive sequences that might be similarly stabilized.

In Huntington's disease, a protein (huntingtin) shows a polyglutamine tract of variable length at its carboxy terminus. Similar polyglutamine sequences are observed in proteins associated with other neurodegenerative diseases. The suggestion that huntingtin might oligomerize through a polyglutamine antiparallel cross-β structure was supported by X-ray diagrams of fibres drawn from a synthetic glutamine polypeptide (34). The molecular aggregation is believed to lead to the formation of amyloid aggregates (35). Sequences of up to 37 glutamine residues are harmless, but proteins with 40 or more precipitate as insoluble fibres (42). The delay in onset of the disease depends on the length of this repetitive sequence. With Alan Windle FRS, Perutz demonstrated a convincing relationship to the kinetics observed for the nucleation of crystals (44).

Outside the Laboratory

Perutz was appointed CBE in 1963, at the same time that John Kendrew became KBE. His colleagues knew Max did not want an honour that would confer an honorary title, which he felt would erect an artificial barrier when talking to junior workers. He received The Royal Society's Royal Medal in 1971, and the Copley Medal in 1979. In 1975 he became a Companion of Honour, and in 1988 he was appointed to the Order of Merit.

Perutz always took a lively interest in general issues, including science, religion, history, and politics. This was one of the factors that made the tearoom at the LMB such a success. Although much of the talk would be about the latest paper from a competitor, or a new idea for an experiment, more general subjects were discussed, not only at the table where Max happened to be sitting.

Max read widely and had an exceptionally retentive memory. His writing is full of apparently effortless literary allusions. He was an outstanding communicator, and seemed never to repeat the same lecture. Although he often spoke on haemoglobin to specialized audiences, he regularly addressed other scientific gatherings, and in later life, many other audiences from school sixth forms to local meetings of the University of the Third Age. He spoke fluent French and Italian, as well as his native languages of German and English, and travelled widely as a speaker.

After his retirement, Max began to write many book reviews and was a frequent contributor to the *London Review of Books* and the *New York Review of Books*. Reviews of biographies of famous scientists were a favourite. One of their subjects is Fritz Haber, the chemist whose obsession with poison gases brought German triumphs in World War I but who was dismissed from his later secret work manufacturing poison gases by the Nazis in 1933 because he was a Jew (36). Another subject was his Austrian heroine Lise Meitner (ForMemRS 1955), whose collaboration in 1938–39 with her nephew Otto Frisch (FRS 1948) first demonstrated the possibility of a uranium fission chain reaction (39).

He frequently spoke out publicly on political and moral issues. One of his campaigns related to the increasing burden on scientists of detailed committee decisions in deciding what research should be supported. In an essay entitled "The new Marxism" (28) he contrasts the haphazard organization of British science in 1930–45 with the Soviet Union where science was organized on Bernal's Marxist principles. Despite the much larger numbers of scientists employed there, few significant advances were made. He then attacks a 1989 report from the Advisory Board for the Research Councils (ABRC) proposing a monolithic structure headed by the Chief Science Advisor to the Department of Education and Science "responsible for developing, promulgating and implementing a coordinated policy for science and engineering" with senior positions allocated to "scientists or engineers who have had training and experience in management, so as to equip them with the necessary knowledge to carry out their accounting, marketing, and policy roles. Experience in research is not mentioned. The new council would present to the Secretary of State a Five-Year Plan. I thought I was reading a document by Brezhnev's Politburo." He cites the MRC's long history of supporting outstanding scientists without detailed intervention in their work, by an autonomous Council free from political pressures, among which not less than three-quarters of the members are appointed on account of their qualifications in science. He appeals that the ABRC "will not suppress the MRC which is one of the world's most successful and internationally acknowledged research organisations" (28). William Waldegrave's reorganization of research funding, which closed the Science and Engineering Research Council, the Agricultural Research Council and several others, left the MRC virtually untouched.

Among his other campaigns were the need for the Catholic world to adopt contraception (he was a Foreign Member of the Pontifical Academy of Sciences), the prospects offered by genetically manipulated crops for the Third World, the advantages of storage of human genetic data, and of gene therapy. He published a closely reasoned history of the concept of human rights from Aeschylus to the present day (38). "I find it tragic that just when the gradually evolving concept of human rights has at last been given the force of international law, the concept of human duties should have fallen into unprecedented disrepute, threatening the disintegration of our society." He maintained his long interest in the protection of religious minorities, and for worldwide freedom of intellectual activity, supporting the modern-day successors of the wartime SPSL.

In October 2001, just before his terminal illness was identified, he was seeking support from senior Cambridge academics for a brief letter to *The Times*. This concerned the response to the terrorist attack of 11 September on New York and Washington, and included the following:

"1. Avoid war—do not go to war or start a war! (This is exactly what the terrorists want to achieve.)"

"2. Avoid military actions against innocent people. Military retaliation does not solve the problem of fanaticism, but instead fuels the anger by demanding 'counter'-revenge."

To quote his own words, already cited above (18)—"these words ring prophetically."

Notes

1 Perutz's statement is not disputed by any of the surviving central players. Fuller (2003), however, says that views differ over the degree of confidentiality of the committee papers.

2 Perutz, M.F. (1962) *Stockholm 1962*. Unpublished note for family circulation, appending the Banquet speech, in the hands of the Perutz family.

3 Manuscript notes made by Perutz for a speech at the opening of the new EMBO building in 1998, in his files at his death.

4 Perutz's note reads "December" but Lanouette and Silard (1992) give the date precisely as Saturday, 27 October.

5 Krige (2002) questions whether this meeting actually occurred, because it is not mentioned in CERN files. The Kendrew papers [Bodleian Library, Oxford, Folder F1] confirm it in at least two places, one being his speech at the inauguration of the EMBL in May 1978. There can be no doubt that it took place.

Acknowledgments

I thank the many people who have given me advice and information in preparing this memoir. Gisela Perutz, Robin Perutz, and Vivien Perutz have been unfailingly helpful to me. John Finch FRS and Annette Lenton of the LMB have given considerable assistance. Amongst others I should mention particularly Raymond Appleyard, Uli Arndt FRS, Sydney Brenner FRS, the late Francis Crick FRS, Raymond Dwek FRS, Michael Fuller, Frank Gannon, István Hargittai, Geoffrey Hattersley-Smith, Richard Henderson FRS, Mary Holmes, Vernon Ingram FRS, Eduard Kellenberger, John Kilmartin FRS, Aaron Klug FRS, Hilary Muirhead, Fred Sanger FRS, Bruno Strasser, Sir John Meurig Thomas FRS, Jim Watson ForMemRS, and Maurice Wilkins FRS. I thank Annette Faux and Annette Lenton of the LMB, Pam Lane of the Medical Research Council, and Karen Peters and Martin Carr of The Royal Society for their help.

References to other Authors

Bokhoven, C., Schoone, J.C., and Bijvoet, J.M. 1951. The Fourier synthesis of the crystal structure of strychnine sulphate pentahydrate. *Acta Crystallogr.* **4:** 275–280.

Bragg, Sir Lawrence 1953. X-ray analysis of the haemoglobin molecule. *Proc. R. Soc. Lond.* B **141:** 67–69.

Chadarevian, S. de 2002. *Designs for Life. Molecular Biology after World War II.* Cambridge University Press.

Fuller, W. 2003. Who said 'helix'? *Nature* **424:** 876–878.

Hargittai, I. 1999. Max Perutz (recorded conversation). *Chem. Intelligencer*, January, 17–21.

Hoard, J.L. 1968. Some aspects of heme stereochemistry. In *Structural Chemistry and Molecular Biology* (ed. A. Rich & N. Davidson), pp. 573–594. San Francisco: Freeman.

Holmes K.C. 2001. John Cowdery Kendrew. *Biogr. Mems Fell. R. Soc. Lond.* **47:** 311–332.

Judson, H.F. 1979. *The Eighth Day of Creation.* London: Jonathan Cape.

Kendrew, J.C., Bodo, G., Dintzis, H.M., Parrish, R.G., Wyckoff, H., and Phillips, D.C. 1958. A 3-dimensional model of the myoglobin molecule obtained by X-ray analysis. *Nature* **181:** 662–666.

Kendrew, J.C., Dickerson, R.E., Strandberg, B.E., Hart, R.G., Davies, D.R., Phillips, D.C., and Shore, V.C. 1960. Structure of myoglobin: 3-Dimensional Fourier synthesis at 2 Å resolution. *Nature* **185:** 422–427.

Köhler, G. and Milstein, C. 1975. Continuous cultures of fused cells secreting antibody of predefined specificity. *Nature* **256:** 495–497.

Krige, J. 2002. The birth of EMBO and the difficult road to EMBL. *Stud. Hist. Phil. Biol. Biomed. Sci.* **33:** 547–564.

Lanouette, W. with Silard, B. 1992. *Genius in the Sshadows: A Biography of Leo Szilard, the Man Behind the Bomb.* New York: Charles Scribner's Sons/Maxwell MacMillan.

Medical Research Council 1952. Report to Biophysics Committee, circulated 15 December.

Medical Research Council 1958. Paper 58/408. Minute 95, Council Minutes, 18 April 1958.

Medical Research Council 1976. Subcommittee to Review Molecular Biology. Report to MRC Cell Board. MRC 76/610, file S1202/1, vol. 2.

Monod, J., Changeux, J.-P., and Jacob, F. 1963. Allosteric proteins and molecular control systems. *J. Mol. Biol.* **6**: 306–329.

Pauling, L. 1960 *The Nature of the Chemical Bond*, 3rd edn. Ithaca: Cornell University Press.

Pauling, L., Corey, R.B., and Branson, H.R. 1951. The structure of proteins: Two hydrogen-bonded configurations of the polypeptide chain. *Proc. Natl Acad. Sci. USA* **37**: 205–211.

Pagnier J., Mears, J.G., Dunda-Belkhodia, O., Schaefer-Rego, K.E., Beldjord, C., Nagel, R.L., and Labie, D. 1984. Evidence for the multicentric origin of the sickle cell hemoglobin gene in Africa. *Proc. Natl Acad. Sci. USA* **81**: 1771–1773.

Riechmann, L., Clark, M., Waldmann, H., and Winter G. 1988. Reshaping human antibodies for therapy. *Nature* **332**: 323–327.

Schechter A.N., Noguchi, C.T., and Rodgers G.P. 1987. Sickle cell disease. In *The Molecular Basis of Blood Diseases* (ed. G. Stammatopoyannopoulos, A. W. Nienhuis, P. Leder & P. W. Majerus). Philadelphia: W. B. Saunders.

Seymour, C.A. 1993. Citation for Max Ferdinand Perutz for an Honorary Fellowship of the Royal College of Physicians, London. Copy held by The Royal Society's Archivist.

Tooze, J. 1981. A brief history of the European Molecular Biology Organisation. *EMBO J.*, sample copy, 1–6.

Watson, J.D. 1968. *The Double Helix*. New York: Athaeneum.

Watson, J.D. 1969. [untitled] *Science* **164**: 1539.

Watson, J.D. and Crick, F.H.C. 1953. A structure for deoxyribose nucleic acid. *Nature* **171**: 737–738.

Bibliography

The following Perutz publications are those referred to directly in the original text.

(1) 1938 (With J.D. Bernal and I. Fankuchen) An X-ray study of chymotrypsin and haemoglobin. *Nature* **141**: 523–524.

(2) 1939 Absorption spectra of single crystals of haemoglobin in polarized light. *Nature* **143**: 731–733.

(3) (With G. Seligman) A crystallographic investigation of glacier structure and the mechanism of glacier flow. *Proc. R. Soc. Lond.* A **172**: 335–360.

(4) 1946 The composition and swelling properties of haemoglobin crystals. *Trans. Faraday Soc.* B **42**: 187–195.

(5) 1947 A description of the iceberg aircraft carrier and the bearing of the mechanical properties of wood pulp on some problems of glacier flow. *J. Glaciol.* **1**: 95–104.

(6) 1949 An X-ray study of horse methaemoglobin. II. *Proc. R. Soc. Lond.* A **195**: 474–499.

(7) 1950 (With W.L. Bragg and J.C. Kendrew) Polypeptide chain configurations in crystalline proteins. *Proc. R. Soc. Lond.* A **203**: 321–357.

(8) 1951 The 1.5 Å reflexion from proteins and polypeptides. *Nature* **168**: 653–656.

(9) 1952 (With W.L. Bragg) The structure of haemoglobin. *Proc. R. Soc. Lond.* A **213**: 425–435.

(10)   (With J.A.F. Gerrard and A. Roch) Measurement of the velocity distribution along a vertical line a glacier. *Proc. R. Soc. Lond.* A **213**: 546–558.

(11) 1954 The structure of haemoglobin. III. Direct determination of the molecular transform. *Proc. R. Soc. Lond.* A **225**: 264–286.

(12)   (With D.W. Green & V.M. Ingram) The structure of haemoglobin. IV. Sign determination by the isomorphous replacement method. *Proc. R. Soc. Lond.* A **225**: 287–307.

(13) 1958 *Recent advances in molecular biology.* MRC Paper 58/303. Published almost unchanged as 'Some recent advances in molecular biology,' *Endeavour* **17**: 190–203 (1958).

(14)   (With F.H.C. Crick) *The case for a laboratory of molecular biology.* MRC Paper 58/307.

(15) 1960 (With M.G. Rossmann, A.F. Cullis, H. Muirhead, G. Will, and A.C.T. North) Structure of haemoglobin. A three-dimensional Fourier synthesis at 5.5 Å resolution obtained by X-ray analysis. *Nature* **185**: 416–422.

(16) 1968 (With H. Muirhead, J.M. Cox and L.C.G. Goaman) Three-dimensional Fourier synthesis of oxyhaemoglobin at 2.8 Å resolution. II. The atomic model. *Nature* **219**: 131–139.

(17) 1969 DNA helix. *Science* **164**: 1537–1539.

(18) 1970 Stereochemistry of cooperative effects in haemoglobin. *Nature* **228**: 726–739.

(19) 1971 (With H. Morimoto and H. Lehmann) Molecular pathology of human haemoglobin: stereochemical interpretation of abnormal oxygen affinities. *Nature* **232**: 408–413.

(20) 1978 Hemoglobin structure and respiratory transport. *Scient. Am.* **239**: 92–125. Republished as 'The secret of life' in (41), pp. 255–277.

(21) 1984 (With G. Fermi, B. Shaanan, and R. Fourme) The crystal structure of human deoxyhaemoglobin 1.74 Å resolution. *J. Mol. Biol.* **175**: 159–174.

(22) 1985 (With K. Nagai and C. Poyart) Oxygen binding properties of human mutant haemoglobins synthesized in *Escherichia coli*. *Proc. Natl Acad. Sci. USA* **82**: 7252–7255.

(23) That was the war: enemy alien. *New Yorker*, August. Republished in (29), pp. 101–136, and in (41), pp. 73–106.

(24) Early days of protein crystallography. *Methods Enzymol.* **114A**: 3–18.

(25) 1986 A new view of Darwinism. *New Scientist*, 2 October, 36–38. Republished as 'Darwin, Popper and evolution' in (29), pp. 217–223, and as 'Darwin was right' in (41), pp. 201–208.

(26) 1987 I wish I'd made you angry earlier. *The Scientist*, February 23. Republished in (42), pp. 173–175.

(27) Keilin and the Molteno. *Cambridge Review*, October, 152–157. Republished in *The Biochemist*, Apr/May, 17–20 (1992), and in G. Semenza & R. Jaenicke (eds) Selected topics in the history of biochemistry, personal recollections, V. *Comprehensive Biochem.* **40**: 57–66 (1997).

(28) 1989 The new Marxism. *New Scientist* 15 July, 72–73.

(29) *Is Science Necessary? Essays on Science and Scientists.* London: Barrie & Jenkins.

(30) 1991 Hemoglobin. In *Encyclopaedia of Human Biology* (ed. R. Dulbecco), vol. 4, pp. 135–144. New York: Academic Press.

(31) Dangerous misprints. (Review of *Genome* by J. Bishop & M. Waldhoz.) *London Review of Books*, 26 September. An updated version appears in (41), pp. 191–195.

(32) 1992 (With I. De Baere, L. Liu, L. Moens, J. Van Beeumen, C. Gielens, J. Richelle, C. Trotman, J. Finch, and M. Gerstein) Polar zipper sequence in the high-affinity hemoglobin of *Ascaris suum*: Amino acid sequence and structural interpretation. *Proc. Natl Acad. Sci. USA* **89**: 4638–4642.

(33) *Protein Structure. New Approaches to Disease and Therapy.* New York: Freeman.

(34) 1994 (With T. Johnson, M. Suzuki, and J.T. Finch) Glutamine repeats as polar zippers: Their possible role in inherited neurodegenerative diseases. *Proc. Natl Acad. Sci. USA* **91**: 5355–5358.

(35) 1995 (With K. Stott, J.M. Blackburn, and P.J. Butler) Incorporation of glutamine repeats makes proteins oligomerize: Implications for inherited neurodegenerative diseases. *Proc. Natl Acad. Sci. USA* **92**: 6509–6513.

(36) The Cabinet of Dr Haber. (Review of *Fritz Haber, Chemiker, Nobelpreisträger, Deutscher, Jude: eine Biographie* by D. Stolzenberg.) *New York Review of Books*, 20 June. Also published in *Recherche* **297**: 78–84 (1997) and as 'Friend or foe of mankind?' in (41), pp. 3–16.

(37) 1996   The Medical Research Council Laboratory of Molecular Biology. *Mol. Med.* **2**: 659–662.

(38)   By what right do we invoke human rights? *Proc. Am. Phil. Soc.* **140**: 135–147. Republished in *Eur. Rev.* **5**: 123–133 (1997) and in (41), pp. 215–226.

(39) 1997   A Passion for Science. (Review of *Lise Meitner: A Life in Physics* by R.L. Sime.) *New York Review of Books*, 20 February. Republished as 'Splitting the atom' in (41), pp. 17–30.

(40)   *Science Is Not a Quiet Life. Unravelling the Atomic Mechanism of Haemoglobin*. London: Imperial College Press.

(41) 1998   *I Wish I'd Made You Angry Earlier. Essays on Sscience, Scientists and Humanity*. New York: Cold Spring Harbor Laboratory Press; and Oxford University Press (1999).

(42) 1999   Glutamine repeats and neurodegenerative diseases: molecular aspects. *Trends Biochem. Sci.* **24**: 58–63.

(43) 2000   Diary. *London Review of Books*, 6 July, 35.

(44) 2001   (With A.H. Windle) Cause of neural death in neurodegenerative disease attributed to expansion of glutamine repeats. *Nature* **412**: 143–144.

1930s

"One of the aims of my English stay is to search for a different path to the future."

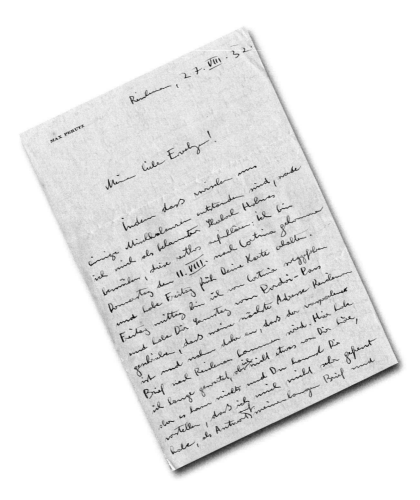

Translation of letter on page 33

My dear Evelyn!

As a well-known Sherlock Holmes, because we've exchanged several messages with corny puns, I'll make an effort at complete clarification. I arrived in Cortina on Thursday, 2 August and got your card on Friday. I left on Friday morning and wrote to you on Saturday from the Pordoi Pass that my next address would be Reichenau and therefore believed that the next, promised letter would arrive there. I waited here for ages, to see whether I'd hear anything from you, but nothing came, and you can imagine that I was not best pleased to have only a card in reply to my long letter and many cards.

WHEN EVELYN MACHIN RETURNED HIS EARLY LETTERS, Max, then in his eighties, was amazed at his own good fortune during his student years: no domestic duties, several circles of friends to go out with, visits to the theatre and cinema, trips to the mountains in the three annual university vacations and on many weekends, not to speak of plenty of time to read, a great contrast to the years of relative hardship that were to follow. Skiing and rock climbing were his great loves: "Skiing early in this century was quite a different sport from that it has become today. There were no more than half a dozen lifts in the whole of Austria. You strapped seal skins to the bottom of your skis, the grain of which kept you from slipping back, and pushed up the mountain by your own efforts, often laying your own track in virgin snow. Finding the best route, both uphill and down, was part of the challenge. The thrill of laying a virgin track through silent, snow-covered woods or up vast sunlit slopes on a frosty morning gave you a high much greater than any drug could have done, and the descent, after 3 or 4 hours' climb, was a wonderful climax to the day. There was none of today's cult of equipment. A pair of hickory skis, a windproof suit and leather boots were all that were needed. A reduced excursion ticket on the train was the only expense."[1] The family's house in the village of Reichenau, to which Max escaped the moment term was over, was just over 40 miles from Vienna and at the threshold of the Alps. From there it was only a short cycle ride to the Rax, an ideal playground for a budding rock climber.

In translating these letters, I have attempted to make the English idiomatic while preserving the character of the German text and Max's punctuation. I have chosen a few typical passages from the letters to portray the character of his life and feelings and, in addition, descriptions of three trips including a remarkable adventure across Lapland on foot and with the small boat that travelled annually to the island of Jan Mayen, 590 miles from the Norwegian coast. I have also included all of his infrequent comments on his scientific

---

[1] Unpublished biographical note.

studies at the University of Vienna, contemporary politics, and anti-Semitism, but only one of his many responses to Evelyn's letters and poems.

In the paragraphs that follow, Brendan Simms explains the rationale of Max's views in the light of contemporary politics:

The young Max Perutz was pitched into what was essentially a three-way struggle between the ruling Conservative (Christian-Social) Catholic Clerical Fascists, the mainly Social Democratic left, and the Austrian Nazis. Only the former unambiguously supported an independent Austria, with both the left and the extreme right favouring some form of unity with Germany proper (while bitterly disputing everything else). It is clear that faced with this choice, Max favoured the Catholic Conservatives, even if he was unhappy with some of their repressive policies. He had been brought up as a Catholic, and did not lose his faith until the mid-1930s; he speaks approvingly in early May 1933 of the "government ... keeping a firm grip ... and ... really trying to preserve Austria"; and in late February 1934, he breathes a sigh of relief that a left-wing rising in support of "a red revolution and soviet republic" had been "prevented in time." Indeed, as Engelbert Broda, a scientist who knew Max during the war, notes Max "continued to consider himself an Austrian"[2] long after he had to leave Vienna.

After the Nazi takeover of power on 30 January 1933, Austria's position became more precarious. Hitler was an implacable advocate of Anschluss, the incorporation of Austria into the German Reich. Max obviously followed developments across the border closely. Thus his reference on 7 February 1933 to disarmament and the quality of newspapers in America and Great Britain, is surely an allusion to Hitler's interview in the Daily Mail *the previous day in which disarmament and his demand for a rapid dismantling of the Versailles peace treaty figured prominently. Some six weeks later, Max was ruminating about the mysterious fire that burned down the Reichstag. Because this gave Hitler a pretext to push through the Enabling Act, and thus dictatorial powers for himself, it was long assumed that the Nazis were behind the deed themselves, using the communists as a scapegoat. Interestingly, Max did not jump to that conclusion himself: "Who set fire to the Reichstag? The communists, the Nazis, a lone fanatic or madman ... The fire of course was very opportune for Hitler; but whether he really had it started, that's very much the question." In fact, recent scholarship now agrees that the Reichtsag was*

---

[2]Cited in Dokumentationsarchiv des öesterreichischen Widerstandes (DÖW) (ed.) 1992. *Öesterriecher im Exil Grossbritannien 1938–1945*, p. 277. DÖW, Vienna.

burned down by an insane Dutch communist Marinus van der Lubbe, act-
ing on his own initiative.

Shortly after (27 April 1933 and 5 May 1933), Max notes the escalating
terror in Germany. He refers to concentration camps, which by mid-1933
held nearly 30,000 people. He also mentions the experience of his uncle,
August Frank, a judge in Munich, who is hounded out of his job, as a direct
result of the Orwellian "Law for the re-establishment of the Professional Ser-
vice," enacted on 8 April 1933 and designed to purge Jews from government
employment.

All of this explains Max's ambivalence towards the steady erosion of
political rights within Austria itself. For on 4 March 1933, after a long period
of instability, the Christian Social Chancellor Engelbert Dollfuss invoked
emergency powers dating back to the First World War to set aside parlia-
mentary government. Protests from the left and right were broken up by the
police. In time, most political parties were banned, and freedom of expres-
sion was severely curtailed. As Max remarked critically on 17 March 1933,
"our government thinks that what Hitler can do, they can also do and there
are clear signs of a passion for dictatorship." On the other hand, Dollfuss had
banned the Nazi party and paramilitary displays in general ("there is a gen-
eral ban on uniforms" 5 May 1933). Dollfuss was thus the best hope Austria
had of holding out against Hitler, while simultaneously containing the threat
of social revolution from below. Here Max is not afraid to defend the cleri-
cal fascist state against the charge of disproportionate force against the
armed workers holed up in the Karl Marx Hof in late February 1934. Any-
body who knows the topography of that complex can only agree with him
that there was no other way of reducing it than by the use of artillery. Max
makes no mention of the assassination of Dollfuss by Austrian Nazis on 25
July during a failed coup attempt, probably because he was then incommu-
nicado on a trip to Scandinavia.

To Evelyn Baxter, August 5, 1932

One evening Dr. Strauss came to see my father; he is a very clever man and
I therefore talked to him about what I am going to study; he said that there's
no point today in doing a programme for 4 or 5 years and that I should study
whatever I find most interesting; I think he is right and I will therefore study
chemistry because it's really pointless in today's world to rack my brain over

Evelyn Baxter   *Max as a teenager*

what I'm going to do with it when I finish. Mind you, I only decided while writing this letter and must still talk it over with my parents.[3]

To Evelyn Baxter, August 27, 1932

Our rendez-vous worked brilliantly, that is, Hoefft, the Weissel brothers and me, and altogether from the point of view of its programme our trip [rock-climbing in the Dolomites] worked perfectly. It only rained for 5 minutes during the entire 2 weeks. In the first week we had 2 rest days and even so I found that week more strenuous as I wasn't in training and the climbs were really incredibly long. Monte Cristallo especially, it took us 8 hours as we climbed up the wrong way for two hours and had to go back down and climb up the right route for a further two and a half hours [to get to the same altitude]. Altogether on that day I climbed for 8 hours and walked for 4. In Cor-

---

[3] In 1995, on the occasion of his friend Fritz Eirich's 90th birthday, Max quoted this letter and went on to write: "They were not at all pleased when I did, because they wanted me to read law in preparation for running the family textile firm, but Fritz persuaded them to let me have my way. I don't know what he said to them because I was not there, but they must have found the combination of his charm and lucidity of mind irresistible. For this single act I owe Fritz a debt which I can never repay."

tina a great clean up followed and civilisation; mind you, during the rest of the trip I was the one who washed most. In the second week the Weissel brothers stank like pigs and you could hardly go near them when they took off their shoes. Did you know that my parents and Lotte [Max's sister] were also in the Dolomites? We met them in the most expensive hotel in which sadly we had to eat and spend a night and they paid all my and Hoefft's bills which as you can imagine didn't displease us. The Weissel brothers who are great fanatics left in the meantime and did two extra climbs. At the end of the first week I was really tired and had to make an effort to get over it; the second week I enjoyed more and more as time went on. The weariness wasn't from walking and nothing to do with my body, but the ceaseless studying [of the guidebook]. What would we do tomorrow? Could we do it? Could we get up it? Would I be able to find the route? Would it work well? And so on. It got a bit much; when the others rested, it was always me who had to look in the guidebook to see how the climb continued. Apart from that we irritated one another: Hoefft was dreadfully nervous, the elder Weissel slurped, all the others put together had studied the climbs less thoroughly than me and always interfered in an idiotic way which got on my nerves dreadfully and then there were other trivial things. In the second week the many worries ceased, as we found our rucksacks lighter and especially because it was so incredibly beautiful on the Rosengarten we were less bothered by other things. We had no more rest days, and so we ran out of food and didn't pass any village where we could get fresh supplies[4]; at the huts the rations weren't very ample, but the prices were, and so we were never quite full up. On the peaks our rations consisted of a few sugar lumps, a small piece of chocolate and dry bread, but for all that we had wonderful views, which ought to fill up a climber who's enchanted by nature. So with all this I was 5 to 6 kilos lighter when I got back to Reichenau than when I left.... Hoefft suffered from his walking boots, the Weissels from their climbing shoes, I from my rucksack and trousers and all of us from our hands because of the sharp rocks.

Our best trips were on the Rosengarten right at the end, first because the landscape is so wonderful and secondly because they were shorter, finer climbs which appealed most to us. [After the others left] I stayed at the hut one more day and did my only climb with a guide: the ascent of the 3 Vajolet towers. I told [the guide] that I had only 200 lire but he didn't mind and took me all the same although the climb normally costs 500. I think it was

---

[4]The paths in the Dolomites that go from hut to hut lie well above the valleys in which the villages lie.

(Left to right) Werner Weissel, his brother Walter, Titi Hoefft, and Max on the summit of Grosse Zinne (Cima Grande in Italian).

thanks to Willy's introduction and my youthful enthusiasm. The guide was a particularly nice chap and climbed incredibly well in a way I've never seen. The climb included two moves that were the hardest that I've ever done and the rest wasn't easy so I learned a lot.

The whole trip was as beautiful as one could wish; I learned a lot and gained a lot of experience; apart from that I saw an incredible amount in 14 days; I was on 15 peaks some over, some a little under 3000 meters.[5]

To Evelyn Baxter, October 25, 1932

Thank you very much for your letter which pleased me very much as I'd given up hope of ever hearing from you again. Of course I don't excuse anything and as usual I am furious and had already determined not to write to you any more, but as you see I did not act on this decision.

I have again got endless things to report. A few weeks ago there was a glider day with Robert Kronfeld which was particularly beautiful and interesting. He demonstrated the various ways of starting your flight with a glider. Kronfeld had himself towed 800 meters up and then performed the wildest artistic stunts which to date had only been done with motor-driven

---

[5]On a postcard of the Marmolata from this trip, Max pointed to the apex of the rocky peak of 3346 meters and proudly wrote: "got here today."

Max's photo of the Vajolet towers

Max's photo of a friend (possibly René Jaeger) rock climbing that he labeled "between heaven and earth."

aeroplanes. All kinds of loops, flying on his back and sides, dives which he himself had tried out for the first time the previous day. I believe that the Prater had never been as crowded. Everyone was very enthusiastic.

The following week on Tuesday Rudolf [the family's chauffeur] had his day off and went with his wife to the Wienerwald; on the way home he heard a cyclist ringing his bell behind him, he turned round and the same moment the cyclist rode into him and he hit the footpath with his head and was knocked unconscious. The first aid people took him to hospital immediately and he was told that he had a slight head injury and concussion, and he died the next day of a fractured skull. You can imagine how upset we were because he was the most decent and best person you could imagine. Everybody liked him, I don't think he had a single enemy, and he was a wonderful chauffeur. He was part of the family, had been with us for nine years. His death is hard to believe. The man who had been a chauffeur for 25 years and had driven on the most dangerous roads, spent four years at the front in the war, then gets run down by a cyclist in the Wienerwald and dies from this. From then on I had a lot to do because I was the locum chauffeur and drove from dawn to dusk for ten days.

I haven't been to the theatre but I have read a lot, *The Diary of a Young Lady of Fashion 1764–65* [by Cleone Knox], *The Story of San Michele* by Axel Munthe, *The Picture of Dorian Gray* [by Oscar Wilde], *Kim* by Kipling, *The Devil's Disciple, Caesar and Cleopatra, Widowers' Houses* by GBS [George Bernard Shaw], *Those Charming People* by Michael Arlen and now I am starting *Elizabeth and Essex* by [Lytton] Strachey. I can't say which I like best but they are excellent books and I enjoyed each in its own way. I forgot to mention one other *The Women of Andros* by [Thornton]Wilder.[6]

To Evelyn Baxter, December 7, 1932

Don't imagine that you alone have feasted on exams and work[7]; recently I too have largely devoted myself to these tremendous delights. It began on 3 November when I went to the Institute of Chemistry for the first time. Then came the great miracle, my entire family, my friends and acquaintances were all dumbfounded: I who had never worked in my life began to work like a

---

[6]Max spent the months between school and university perfecting his English, even taking an exam as an interpreter in the autumn of 1932.

[7]Evelyn was in her first term at Oxford and would have sat prelims.

madman. Already on day two I had a 14-hour day. Now I go to the lab at 8, work without a lunch break, come home at 6 and work again until 10. And when you've worked through a practical and theoretical introduction to chemistry, you have to take an exam. The material that you have to master is enormous and everyone tries to get it over and done with as quickly as possible.[8]

This is what happened on Monday in the English seminar which Lotte attends. Someone looked out of the window from the seminar to see what the noise was about. At that moment a Jewish doctor who'd been beaten up staggered in followed by 15 youths. Behind Lotte sat a very hardworking boy who looks very Jewish with an artificial arm and a leather hand, a boy who had never harmed anyone; he was quite helpless, but these 15 boys pounced on him and hit him so hard in the face with leather belts that he collapsed. Two benches away Lotte's notes were quite splashed with blood. I don't think any commentary is necessary. At the University there are similar incidents and punch-ups every day.

As to work in the Institute of Chemistry I am very agreeably surprised. I imagined that the atmosphere would be terribly aggressive and tense. The atmosphere is smelly, but otherwise very friendly. I have never seen anybody fight; Jews, people with swastikas, Christian Socialists and Socialists cooperate as good friends (so far); they wear the same uniform, which is a white lab coat, under which political identity and convictions seem hidden. If you ever hear a mad rumpus it is at most a waterfight in the lab which happens when the technician is absent. The whole environment is most agreeable and informal [*gemütlich*]; of course you have work to do which you are interested in; moreover we have good conversations and sometimes we laugh all day long. So far I prefer it to school, particularly because you can come and go as you wish from eight in the morning to six in the evening. Two people always work at one bench. I work with a former schoolmate who was in the same class as me throughout at the Theresianum; he always got As. He is the only one in the whole room who openly wears a swastika!! Of course we get on brilliantly.[9] There are all kinds of girls there from small and dark and fat to tall and blonde and slim and pretty. The lectures I go to are quite good and you are hardly ever bored. So far I like it very much there.

Now after the exam I have as much to do as ever, as there are a thousand things you have to follow up, go through and absorb, but sadly you can't learn the whole of chemistry in one go.

---

[8]In Austria courses were not of a set duration; you took exams when you were ready.

[9]The irony in this comment becomes apparent from the later letters.

My lab work over the next months (years) consists of conducting 37 analyses; how long it takes is a matter of luck. One analysis can take three weeks and then it turns out to be wrong and you have to repeat it. Enough of chemistry!

To Evelyn Baxter, January 21, 1933

In case you are interested I can tell you what my work consists of. I am doing qualitative analysis which means I get mixtures of chemical compounds which I have to analyse. When I've finished an analysis, it's checked and if it's correct I get a stamp to say it's accepted; if not you have to repeat it. Of course it's always very nerve-racking to see whether it will be accepted as each is a lengthy process. All this is very interesting. Then on average I have two lectures a day, some of which are very good.

To Evelyn Baxter, February 7, 1933

For once I feel compelled to compliment you on your home country; England is really the only decent country in Europe; English politicians are the only ones who want disarmament; [Ramsay] Macdonald's [British Prime Minister] speech at the disarmament conference was marvellous, he finally called a spade a spade and made specific recommendations. Then England behaved impressively regarding the ban on arms export to the Far East and it is really incredible that not even this one measure could be agreed on in the League of Nations. Thirdly, England is the only country that defends her subjects; other countries would not bother with the people under arrest in Russia, and England threatens to break off diplomatic relations. You are right if you are proud of it. I can't tell you much about the conditions here because I noticed that English and American newspapers have a better grasp of Austrian politics in a few paragraphs than our papers with their pages of drivel.

In the last few weeks I have taken a real interest in politics, understandably, which is why I need to read 3 to 4 newspapers a day, which of course takes a lot of time; but it is worth the effort to follow what's going on in the world.

To Evelyn Baxter, March 17, 1933

I say nothing of friend Hitler as things here are taking such an amazing course, everything goes so completely against expectation that what you say one day, can be quite ridiculous the next. Who set fire to the Reichstag? The Communists, the Nazis, a lone fanatic or madman like the railway assassin [Sylvestre] Matuschka? The fire of course was very opportune for Hitler; but whether he really had it started, that's very much the question. The effect on Austria is that our government thinks that what Hitler can do, they can also do and there are clear signs of a passion for dictatorship. There's great agitation here about the American banks, my father was stunned.[10]

To Evelyn Baxter, April 4, 1933

Recently I read several books, among them *Marie Antoinette* by Stefan Zweig and *Die Feindlichen Brüder*: [*Inventur der europäischen Probleme*] by [Carlo] Sforza, 1933. The first is wonderful and the second also very interesting. You can imagine that I definitely don't agree with [George Bernard] Shaw's *Black Girl* [*in her Search for God*] (have you read it?). What he says might perhaps be valid for England but for the way in which religion is taught here, it does not apply since the Catholic Church has adapted its interpretation of the Bible to modern science to a greater extent, and that contradiction which Shaw criticised between religion and science doesn't apply. His criticism of the New Testament and Christian belief is absurd, just as in general his attacks are no longer valid. He's getting old. Please excuse my criticism of a book which you gave me; I know that it's very tactless of me and not at all nice. On the other hand it would have shown lack of character and be against my convictions had I not done so. I hope you will understand me aright as always and don't take it amiss.

I've also got a large request to make. In *The Times* I saw the first pictures of the flight over Everest. Please send me all the pictures of it that you can find. This flight interests me particularly as it's really a wonderful achievement. I'd also be very pleased to have any news about the current Everest expedition wherever you can find it. I'm very curious to see whether the ascent succeeds.[11]

---

[10]There had been a run on the gold reserves and currency holdings of the American banks bankrupting some of them; newly inaugurated as president on 6 March, Roosevelt had halted the run by temporarily closing the banks and rushing the Emergency Banking Act through Congress, which succeeded in reviving the fortunes of those banks that had remained solvent.

[11]Max writes in another letter that he had agreed to go to the Himalayas in the summer of 1937 with his sister's Norwegian boy friend Arne Naess, future professor of philosophy in Oslo. In fact he went home to Austria from Cambridge and visited the Jungfraujoch in preparation for his first glacier expedition as a crystallographer under Gerald Seligman in 1938.

To Evelyn Baxter, April 27, 1933

My parents are terribly upset about the events in Germany, especially my father. He grew up in a world of material values, while today financial agreements, laws, property and so-called secure positions and possessions have lost any kind of permanence; he's disturbed that the law and rules no longer exist; in England of course and western Europe this is still different. I never believed in it, I'm not surprised.

You can't imagine how the Hitler psychosis has also hit all young people here; there are only a few exceptions who can still see clearly and can see how insane and absurd this movement is. Wiltschko, my old friend, has regrettably become a member of the SS[12]; only Weissel and Hoefft are still with me. The lab is still very apolitical, but not because of a lack of Nazis but because of a lack of Jews.[13] Today work started again. I heard that the atmosphere in England is very anti-German and that people are outraged about the anti-Semitic measures. I'd be very pleased if you sent me a little report about what people think about things in England. Are German goods boycotted? Here and in Czechoslovakia, in Jewish circles all German goods are boycotted; it's especially true of Czech industry because the German owners are almost all Jewish, and the Czech owners boycott them all the more. In Switzerland there is a quiet boycott of all German products; even when I was there, I heard from all Christians how outraged they were by the measures. Enough of politics!

To Evelyn Baxter, May 5, 1933

We hear from everybody who comes from Germany that the vehemently denied "horror stories" from Germany are not exaggerated at all but in fact understated. The terror which is going on there is apparently indescribable, especially in Munich, because a lot of people whom they dislike apparently don't go to concentration camps but are simply shot. Nobody dares to say a word, people are arrested in the middle of the night and disappear. My uncle [August Frank], who has worked as a judge in Munich since before 1914, which means that according to civil service law he is entitled to

---

[12]I found to my surprise that eight months later he turned up unexpectedly to spend a day with Max in the country.

[13]Max's ancestors were Jews but he was brought up as a Catholic and at school had presumably not been regarded as Jewish since he went to the Catholic rather than the Jewish classes in religious instruction.

remain in his position, is not being made redundant but is to be given a lowly position in the countryside instead of his high-profile position in Munich. Since he is quite old and would not get used to it, he is planning to move to Prague. Obviously my aunt writes all this between the lines under a false name, so that outsiders would get a different meaning, because apparently there are spies everywhere who open letters. Supposedly this also happens with transit mail, which is why I'm trying to send this letter via Switzerland. Our government is keeping a firm grip, there is a general ban on uniforms and it is really trying to preserve Austria; well-informed circles think that they will hold out. We would leave the city, if it came to it, before we got arrested, and would go to Czechoslovakia, since we have nothing here except Reichenau. But the danger is not that great because of the dangerous diplomatic complications which a union with Austria would entail for Germany. It has also emerged in a number of local elections that the Nazis are not able to achieve an absolute majority, but only 30 to 33 per cent of the votes and this percentage could be even lower if the voting age were lowered from 24 to 21 as planned.

To Evelyn Baxter, May 25, 1933

There are great expectations that Nazism won't reach Austria. The Government has started to make great propaganda for a free Austria, new Austrian patriotism is budding, [Engelbert] Dollfuss [the Austrian Chancellor] is very busy, appears to be getting a loan at long last, his actions are being supported with money and I think if he lasts one more year, the battle is won. The best measure is if lots of foreigners come here because then it seems the Germans wouldn't come in such numbers. Make propaganda for us in England because the English are a thousand times preferable to the Huns.

The situation here is much better now. People no longer passively watch Nazi expansion but actively fight it. The mood has changed considerably.

To Evelyn Baxter, June 6, 1933

A week ago on Saturday the Catholic students held a commemoration for war veterans at the University, where Dollfuss was supposed to speak. The Nazis promised the Rector [President/Vice-Chancellor] not to disturb the ceremony.

Continuation (a), seen from the Left: Shortly before the start, Nazi students hurled themselves from a ramp into the auditorium, shouted "Heil Hitler" etc., assaulted the Catholic students and brutally hit them with steel batons and knuckledusters. When the Austrian Chancellor arrived and a few people stumbled towards him covered in blood, he instructed the police to take action, who then for the first time entered free academic ground.

Continuation (b), seen from the Right: Finally the Jewish press has achieved its goal: academic ground has been violated. When at 12.30 there happened to be a few National Socialist students left in the auditorium, they were assaulted by the Catholic students who outnumbered them and abused them in the most brutal way with the weapons they had brought. The NS students, however, withstood manfully, which made the officials order the police to chase these brave champions of the national cause off University ground.

The result of it all: The University has been closed for 14 days because of the big disturbance among the students. The time lost for work will be made up in the summer.

To Evelyn Baxter, July 8, 1933

My father's business is going very badly like industry in general in Czechoslovakia. I turn over and over in my mind feeble plans of ways to avoid becoming a textile industrialist in a Czech village, forgetting chemistry and, when the factory goes bankrupt, finding myself without anything. On the other hand, as a chemist I can hardly earn enough to live on before I am thirty. Luckily there is time—one has to consider what will be lost to the research community if I do not concentrate on science and instead devote myself to a business career. It will be very sad if the Nobel Prize has to be handed to somebody unworthy of it.

To Evelyn Baxter. Karasjok, July 23, 1933

If you travel alone, you feel lonely, if you travel with others, they get on your nerves. Never mind: let's be generous explorers, overcome the trivial irritations of the day and with unerring gaze penetrate the innermost soul of the wonders of the world.[14] I don't want to talk now about the bus ride which took us on the only road in the world (built like a scenic railway) which leads to the Arctic Ocean and which brought us to Ivalo in Inner Lapland, nor about the car journey to Inari where a reindeer galloped at 50 km an hour in front of us, nor about etc. Yes, I think this is the right point to start a description of our journey.

---

[14]Unidentified quotation?

Car on a ferry

So, the day after my last letter I met my companions: Heini Granich-staedten [a fellow chemistry student] and Dr. [Werner] Weissel [Max's school friend, who had just completed his first year as a medical student]; since we had organised everything that was complicated, we travelled next day first by train and then, as said, by bus. The road goes through vast forests and over many rivers, over which there are no bridges but very fine ferries: rafts, which are suspended from cables stretched over the river, with which you can pull them over by hand. For passengers there are generally boats for public use on these rivers. Ivalo is an up and coming place, because it lies at the centre of the tourist route in Lapland; there's a new tourist inn there, its fittings quite up to date; on the whole the land along the road is sparsely populated: there are only two kinds of civilisation, pretty primitive (Lapps) and quite up to date (Finnish and Swedish immigrants). Frequently you see both very close to one another.

In Ivalo we enquired again about our route; but we failed because no one had ever done it; in Ivalo Dr. Weissel, who in Vienna had been full of pluck, suddenly declared that he would much rather take the standard route. When we told him that he should have thought this through in Vienna, in the end he came along. It seems I'm not a very good judge of people. In Vienna I liked him a lot and now I discover daily that he's a terrible swine. From Ivalo we proceeded by car and boat to the most unknown shore of a pretty unknown and enchantingly beautiful lake. Where we landed, there was a Lapp hut and there we saw the first real Lapps. They were sitting on the bank and were repairing fishing nets. They hardly looked up when we came, although strangers can hardly land there more than twice a year. They were completely indifferent. We stayed there a short while, I even photographed them but they refused to be disturbed. From there we proceeded on a small track, then without any path using map and compass to a large river called the Tana Elv that runs from Lapland into the Arctic Ocean. The bonus of hiking here is that time does not constrain you, as the sun shines day and night. On the first day we went on till midnight, when we had a wonderful view of the midnight sun from a peak. There we pitched our first camp; in fact at 69 degrees of latitude it was so warm that we could sleep without a tent. The next day we reached a large lake—to our great satisfaction it was even the place we'd intended to reach—so big that you can hardly see the other end of it. No one lives there or in its vicinity. We went swimming and it wasn't even that cold. In the afternoon we went on, only a thunderstorm halted us, quite a nasty experience in these barren wastes. Then we tramped on till late into the night over mountains, through swamps and rivers, and only pitched our tent very late. On the way among other things we saw a few wild reindeer. In the night it began to rain and we had the unpleasant surprise that the tent, guaranteed

One of Max's companions shrouded in a mosquito net fording the Peldojoki.

waterproof, wasn't just wet on the outside. Then came a tough day; we walked from 11.30 to 4 o'clock the following morning with short breaks; even I got large blisters. So much for the programme. The area is quite different from what we'd expected. Hills up to 500 m. In the valley, lakes, marshes, and lush vegetation—often we had to work hard to cut our way through the primeval forest. The forest consisted mainly of birches, which for us was an unusual sight. Sometimes the landscape even looked like a cultivated park: the ground covered in white flowering moss, with scattered birches. But, as experience demonstrates, descriptions of landscapes are tedious for everyone except the writer. The only dangerous parts were the marshes, because you can sink into them if you don't cross in the right place. The midges are unpleasant; you can't imagine the swarms of them. They bite through gloves, socks, shirt, they creep into the tent, hundreds of them buzz around you; they bite day and night, when it's sunny and when it rains; if you've no midge oil or net, they eat you alive, that is, you get ill from the loss of blood.

The night before last we came to the first Lapp hut on the Tana Elv. There were two relatively new huts. We knocked on one—nothing. We looked in: inside a fire was burning in the hearth and on a bed on the floor lay an unidentifiable something, all wrapped in reindeer hides. We knocked, we called, we shouted, all that we got was a deep grunt. Finally we gave up and looked into the neighbouring house. In that there was a woman and a small child. The woman hardly looked up and didn't answer our greeting, and showed not the slightest surprise at our visit; besides on our arrival we made quite some noise outside the huts, and she never even looked out. The whole area is a region where other mad people come at most occasionally.

Skoganvarre, July 24, 1933 In the meantime we have seen a lot. A road to Karasjok is being built; it only goes to within 8 km of the place; to get there you have to go on foot. We missed the bus of course and had to go as tramps along the road, were picked up by a car and brought here. Here in the guest house they asked us whether we could pay because generally Germans pay nothing. Only when we said we were Austrian did we get anything to eat.

To describe our Lapp experiences further: after we realised that no boat was available, with which we could have travelled further, we gave up the idea. In the next house two hours further on, our arrival was similarly played out; we pitched our tent, slept 8 hours and in the morning the people were friendlier. It seems they were afraid of the wild strange men. However, there was no boat there either. Later we heard that at this time of year

Heini Granichstaedten seated at the front crossing the Tenojoki on the way to Karasjok.

The captain of the boat

the men are with the reindeer by the sea. Apparently they had also taken the boats along. The only people at home were very old men, women and children. After we had even got something to eat and conducted a lively conversation in Finnish—the young Lapp woman had been to school and was quite intelligent—we found there was a boat after all an hour later to Karasjok, the centre of Norwegian Lapland. Now we are off to Nordkapp. I'm very much hoping for a letter from you in Hammerfest.

To Evelyn Baxter. The Steamship of the Vesteraalens Shipping Line, Norway, August 20, 1933

I have not written to you for a long time and have seen so much since that I hardly know where I should begin. Should I write amusingly, adventurously, romantically or sentimentally or tell you of my journey or bring out a few salient points. All difficult problems!

The conscientious traveller up the Norwegian coast must go to Nordkapp. So in Hammerfest we hired a small motor boat and set off. The boat shook terribly, the fog became ever thicker, the wind ever fiercer, for 8 hours the current drove us on, then we gave up and stopped.

The Susan

The captain of the Susan

Since our principle was not to see what every conscientious northern tourist sees but what nobody else looks at, we weren't put out by this mishap.

We travelled in fog all the way from Hammerfest to Tromsø. In Tromsø our great adventure began. It's called Jan Mayen, a small island in the Arctic Ocean that lies north of Iceland between Spitzbergen and Greenland. On the island there's a Norwegian meteorological station with a three-man team that stays on the island for a year. Once a year a ship travels to Jan Mayen which brings the team, fresh food, coal, etc. This year in addition an Austrian polar expedition that carried out magnetic measurements of the earth over-wintered there. We travelled with the annual ship. It was a giant 60 tonner and answered to the name Susan. Inside there was a hole in which I slept.[15] It travelled through the fjords for the first few hours, then came the open sea and the lurching began. Three of the Norwegians and my two friends got seasick that same evening; amazingly I developed into a sailor impervious to the weather and felt well.

Another five Norwegians also accompanied us. One was the head of the northern observatory in Tromsø and erected observation instruments in Jan Mayen; another was a meteorologist who checked the instruments in Jan Mayen; in addition the team for the next year consisted of two telegraphers and a cook. One of the telegraphers had been on one of Amundsen's North Pole expeditions and had spent 7 years on the pack ice. He'd formerly spent two winters on Jan Mayen.

The weather improved and we got a favourable wind; after 4 days Jan Mayen appeared. At first a grey stripe on the horizon, then the glaciers of the Beerenberg emerged above the clouds. After another half day we arrived and gave three gun salutes, the ship dropped anchor 200 meters from the island and we landed with a rowing boat. Arriving by rocket on the moon could hardly be more sensational than this volcanic island. The earth is coal-black sand out of which small black or red pointed stone slopes rise; the wind draws wild shapes in the sand. Further off there are small mountains which in part have bright red rock walls, in part are overgrown with bright green moss. This green is quite fascinating and stabs your eyes and is attractive all the same. Above it all, an extinct volcano[16] of 2300 m rises that is completely covered with glaciers; the glaciers reach right down to the sea. You can't compare the landscape with anything, as it's quite unique in the world.

The station stands on a small slope c. 200 m from the shore. The island has no harbour. All the cargo, almost 30,000 kilos, had to be brought in in small boats then hoisted up with a primitive contraption and then brought to the station. Unloading is possible only when the sea is calm. We left almost immediately and wanted to tour the south side of the island. At first we came to the hut where 50 years ago the Austrian polar expedition had over-wintered. Then we wanted to go further south; but such thick fog developed that we had to return to the station. There we helped energetically with unloading but had to stop because of the high seas. Sadly the account will become far too long; if I go on writing in such detail, it'll take me till the day after tomorrow. A tremendous hurricane blew up and the

---

[15]The German is "Loch" not "Laderaum", i.e., hole, not hold.

[16]The Beerenberg is not extinct but unusual in that it emits lava from apparently distant vents which form scoria cones.

Dropping anchor at Jan Mayen

ship had to put out to sea so as not to be smashed on the coast. We were invited by the Norwegians as we had brought no food with us and so lived as guests of the Norwegian state. There was talk of four weeks. Jan Mayen is a storm centre, no one knew how long it might last. After two days the wind turned and we were able to go on unloading. On the last day brilliant weather; went on a volcano dating from only 1814.[17]

Departure from Jan Mayen. After 12 hours a strong east wind which the ship struggled against in vain. We made no headway. The next day the motor failed; the whole day they kept saying it would only take two hours to repair. Finally it worked; an hour later it died again. It's only a small 80 HP; it worked a few more times then it packed up altogether and we were stationary in heavy seas far from anywhere for a whole day. In the storm the engine had dropped down on one side. There was nothing to be done. The sails were hoisted but the wind was so bad that we hardly advanced.

---

[17]This "volcano" must be one of the Beerenberg's scoria cones.

Eventually it was decided to proceed on half an engine. The wind improved slightly and we advanced a little. It rocked terribly; every meal was a drama; despite every precaution the plates slid over the whole table; in the middle of the night the coffee pot landed on the cabin floor.

Because of the sails the ship heeled over steeply. Besides it was packed to capacity so I had to sleep on the floor. All the Austrian polar expedition staff badly sea sick. Every morning the captain got out his medieval sextant and tried to establish our position. The results were dubious. So it continued in this way for days. Sometimes the wind was better, sometimes worse, never good. Eventually after seven days two shadows on the horizon—land! Soon there was more and as the hours went by the fantastic chain of the Lofoten islands rose before us.[18] After an 8 day journey we had landed in Stamsund instead of Tromsø, blown 250 km off course. The attraction of the journey to Jan Mayen was not only its adventurous nature, we learned the most interesting things about the polar and seal hunting expeditions, and about Norway; we got to know a completely different kind of person; it was a very interesting and stimulating experience.

Dolomite-like forms, glaciers, wild rock towers, rising out of the sea cleft by fjords and lakes; on the coast small fishing villages—these are the Lofoten and here we set off on the next hikes. The interior of the island is relatively unknown, the peaks rarely climbed. We completed two hikes, one difficult, erected our tent by an enchanting lake, lovely weather—it was ideal. After three days we decided to share in the ordinary activities of the locals and to join in the deep sea fishing. We went out into the Raftsund [Fjord] in a fishing boat. You let the line down to 2 meters above the seabed, you are very busy especially watching to see if a fish bites. After 4 hours I had caught 4 fish; we had 2 for supper; they were very good. So for 2 days we lived in a fishing village. Yesterday we went with the local ship to Svolvaer, the capital of the Lofoten and in the evening with this fast ship to Trondheim.

The departure from the Lofoten was moving. The ship slipped slowly though the water which was glittering in the soft evening light. Just as we were happy to see the jagged outline of the wild towers emerge from the sea, 10 days ago from the Susan, so they sank again like a beautiful dream, a black silhouette against a dark red evening sky, so we distanced ourselves from the land for which we had yearned and sped back to the daily routine of civilisation.

---

[18]The islands are just off the Norwegian coast south of Tromsø.

The companion who got on my nerves left us long ago, the second left today so I'm on my own now.[19]

To Evelyn Baxter. Dünaburg (Daugavpils), Latvia, September 6, 1933

The final adventure, mind you, a rather shabby one. While I went for a walk at the station, the train left with my luggage inside it; it's now 8.00 pm, the next train to Warsaw departs at 4.30 in the morning. If I still had plenty of money left, it wouldn't matter, but I've none left and am quite hungry. Never mind! The pleasure of writing you a letter, Evelyn, will help me get through this night.

Your letter gave me enormous pleasure. I was especially pleased about the interest you took in my travels. You'd even like me to send my diary; I wrote it on loose sheets, mostly on swaying ships and every two or three weeks I sent it home instead of a letter with my news. It runs to over 60 pages! If I have time I want to rework it somewhat, that is, organise it. You can have whichever version you prefer but the original will be hard to read.

As far as I'm aware, I last wrote to you on the journey to Trondheim— it feels ages ago but I think in reality it wasn't. Altogether I feel as if I'd been away from home a year, I've seen and experienced so many different things.

From Trondheim I went into a fjord, went over the high mountains by car and then out through another fjord and south to Bergen. I spent two days there, it's a charming town. Then with the Bergen railway to Oslo where I spent 2 days. There's lots to see there—the Viking ships are tremendously impressive—then I've never seen so many attractive people as in this town. It's quite an extensive town but everything happens on one long street; you walk up and down here, go shopping, go to the pictures, to the theatre and, above all, all the young people have a good time here. It's amazing how much beauty you see. You go up and down 20 times and are riveted. Altogether I think that that life in Norway is closer to the classical ideal of beauty than was the case in the classical period and countries. The people are attractive, clever, brave, honest, friendly, they have a really classical calmness; you never see someone shouting without reason, getting worked up, fidgeting in a nervous and restless way. I forgot to say that the people

---

[19]In fact Werner Weissel remained Max's closest friend until his death in 1994. Max was as close to Heini but their friendship ended in 1954 with Heini's tragic suicide.

have a lot of taste and a sense of beauty; the women in the small towns rarely lack taste; the women in Oslo are charmingly dressed; the Norwegians have at least as much appreciation of the beauty of the landscape as any enthusiastic foreigner.

I have improved my English on this journey; first the people here are used to German German [as opposed to Austrian German] and find my German hard to understand. And I also spent a lot of time talking to English people.

6 hours to go—luckily Latvia is full of Jews. They speak German and hence I could at least make myself understood because I didn't take a Latvian dictionary along. I got on quite well in Norwegian. I could say all the easy things, but I couldn't understand the replies; I could read the newspaper quite well.

From Oslo I went to Stockholm, without doubt the most beautiful city with lots to see—I've not seen nearly everything—and yet I almost prefer Oslo. In Oslo, altogether in Norway, everything is quite different from other countries, while Stockholm is a normal large city. Yesterday morning I left on the ship to Riga and arrived here at lunchtime; I hope only part of my luggage has been stolen in the meantime.

I read 2 good books on the journey, *Angel Pavement* by [J.B.] Priestley and *First Person Singular* by [W. Somerset] Maugham, very good short stories. Now I'm reading *Point Counter Point* by [Aldous] Huxley and hope I'll find it at the next station because I left it on the seat not in my case.

Travelling alone has advantages; I'd never have spoken to so many people if I'd not been alone. You hear all kinds of interesting things and get to know the country better.

To Evelyn Baxter, November 1, 1933

It may be lack of taste to underline this but it has to be said; so far as I'm aware, I was always very nice to you; so that you should have no bad memories of me, I will do you a last favour: you don't need to write me a farewell letter.

Half an hour ago I was told that you have got engaged; I can't say I'm delighted about it—apparently it is the custom to write to say so in letters of congratulation—but I hope you will believe me that I wish you all the happiness imaginable.

You would have spared me a lot of thought if you had told me that you were engaged to Tom and later that you were engaged to . . . (I don't know his name). You were a riddle to me—have made me reflect sadly on my lack of understanding of human nature. It was depressing to know you so well and not to have guessed what you are really like. Now all is clear to me—you and your poems—the riddle is solved. Don't think that I never imagined that you didn't love someone else; but I did think you'd write to me if you got engaged. You didn't want to hurt my feelings; that was nice of you.

People said all sorts of nasty things about you—your aunt is an old gossip. I defended you as best I could. The image I have of you nobody could spoil. And now even less. For it hasn't assumed any ugly traits but on the contrary is clearer, purer and more beautiful.

You take yourself too seriously and that often disturbs other people, because you are too young. But believe me, in the long run nobody is happy who looks upon himself as a caricature. It seems I am so fond of you because you belong to the other extreme. Of course I won't go in for tragic gestures as I'm not the sort to; I can't write to you that I can't live without you, because I've seen I can. I've realised that it's better to be unhappy in love than not to love at all. . . .

To Evelyn Baxter, December 8, 1933

Although you really know that it's out of the question that I quite forgot about you over the last few weeks, you may well be thinking I did. I got your touching letter of the 4 November and I was very pleased that as always you understood me correctly. It's a wonderful feeling to write to somebody who never misunderstands you.

A mountain of hard work rests on my tired head. Only rarely have I been as busy. First I stand every day from morning to evening in the laboratory. Then secondly in the small hours I try to squeeze some intellectual products out of my tired empty brain and as you can imagine this is a very laborious and fruitless task. The result is an article about Jan Mayen which some people like but my mother finds too boring and dry for anyone to accept it. Thirdly in the autumn I decided that I ought to entertain myself and therefore I interested myself a little more in my friends (male and female) and I've found a few new ones. We drink, dance, go to the theatre and all the things you have to do in company. Among my new friends Heini Granichstaedten who came to Lapland and Jan Mayen is the most important; he is a good sport. There are people in whom you discover their bad qualities only after a lengthy time and there are some in whom you discover their good qualities only later. He belongs to the latter. Gretl [Schloegl], tall, blond, beautiful, intelligent, not such a splendid character[20] but because she is charming and has this blinding beauty it compensates for her character. She is a colleague and works in the laboratory next to me. Originally I wasn't in love with her but when my friends Wildstrehel and Weissel got passionate about her, jealousy caught me and I fell in love with her. Now I stand here poor idiot and am a function of her moods.[21] And depending on whether I am seeing her today, whether she's been with me or with my friends, I'm either very happy or sad to death.[22] Anyway it crystallised itself and she fell in love with Weissel though she likes me very much but what can I do with that—my usual fate.

My profound deliberations about human beings have come to the conclusion that you have to presume from the beginning that they are swines or that they are stupid. If you presume both, you won't be disappointed, particularly if you consider yourself one of them. For this purpose you take forceps, seize your intelligence and place it on a high tower, the rest of the self should be left down below to make sure that none of your emotions remain attached to it. From the tower you consider this creature which runs around down below, and you will immediately realise what a miserable drip he is.

To Evelyn Baxter, January 14, 1934

My current occupation is quantitative analysis, that is, thanks to very accurate methods one determines the exact content of a solution of a mineral, or a compound of several elements to within one ten thousandth of a gram. It's the least interesting part of my course. Speaking of that, I went to a lecture on physical chemistry which was extraordinarily interesting; it was on the latest theories of atomic research. The boldness with which these men construct their hypotheses which are usually not wholly right but which are partly so is often astounding. Compared with their intellectual athletics, their surprising conclusions, Sherlock Holmes is a duffer who's slow on the uptake. In the play by Kurt Goetz[23] which I wrote to you about before, Sherlock Holmes also appears. Goetz shows in masterly fashion that Sherlock Holmes is only a SH because he always starts by looking for the obvious and by doing that astounds

---

[20]Later he confessed he had misjudged her.

[21]This is a quotation from Goethe's *Faust*.

[22]This is a quotation from Goethe's *Egmont*. I am indebted to Ron Gray for pointing out this quotation and that above.

[23]This is a reference to Goetz's play *Dr. Job Praetorius* (1932), in which Holmes and Watson must solve the puzzling death of Dr. Praetorius, a professor killed in a car crash. The play has political undertones, as Ron Gray pointed out.

his audience. Modern atomic theories, however, astonish by the remoteness of the thought processes. Sometimes only the results appear plausible.

To Evelyn Baxter, January 25, 1934

Is what you have to learn in Oxford really interesting? What are the professors like? Here they are quite mixed as of course it's rare that the outstanding ones get the chairs rather than those who enjoy the most patronage. As it happens, mine are really good.

Last week I went to a ball, tedious as usual and very elegant; though I did meet two pretty and nice girls, which has never happened to me before at such a party.

Have you seen the film *Torero*? I've rarely laughed so much.

Two nice Nazi tricks: at the reception of the Italian secretary of state 400 of the Home Guard in civvies were sent to the railway station to shout hurrah and long live [Italy]. Some Nazis mingled with them in an informal way and screamed "Heil Hitler" before he arrived. The police then viciously beat up the entire home guard which is a government agency and chased them off, while in fact it was a Nazi demonstration.

Unknown perpetrators stuffed the exhaust of the Minister of Commerce, [Friedrich] Stockinger, full of paper swastikas; when the minister drove through the city strewing swastikas, the first policeman of course arrested him.

In addition, it now means that the Nazi danger changes every month; it's either serious or definitely overcome. No one knows what will happen next.

To Evelyn Baxter, February 23, 1934

You are or were unhappy as you didn't have a proper home and yearned for real parents full of understanding for you. What you dreamed of is an illusion as it doesn't exist even when parents have an ideal marriage.[24] It is almost absurd how little the parents of most of my friends and my own understand us and can penetrate into what occupies our minds. It is absurd that you think you have lost all your ambitions and will never in your life be anything because you aren't now. You have so much willpower and energy in you that they can't be broken; it's just when you can't make up your mind that you think they've vanished; you only have to be cheerful for a week and then they'll suddenly reappear.

---

[24]Evelyn's parents were divorced; in contrast, Max's parents were devoted to one another.

If you think that a narrow horizon especially in political matters is a speciality of Oxford students you are wrong. It is the expression of a healthy people; our free-thinking minds, which are too critical to join a political party and be happy with the ideas of the masses, are a manifestation of Jewish degeneration.

You moan that your ambition has vanished and that you have no prospects. You have little to go on about. In the course of the last year I've given up thinking things through as otherwise you get too depressed without being able to do anything. What will happen if the Nazis come? I'll have to leave Austria, friends, mountains, studies, everything that makes life a pleasure will be gone! What shall I do when my degree is finished? Put my mortarboard on my head and sit in Bělohrad?[25] What will happen to my father's firm when he no longer goes to the office, his partner totally incompetent and my brother too stupid to run it alone? I won't get any nearer answering these questions. In addition the firm is already going very badly because of the foreign exchange embargo in the Balkans and the crisis.

On Thursday in Kitzbühel I had one of the most beautiful experiences of my life. There's now a small aeroplane there with which you can make round trips. I made a plan to take one as soon as I heard about it, as it was quite cheap. The weather was wonderful on Thursday, so I decided to fly to the Grossglockner, Austria's highest mountain. In the afternoon the pilot, the owner of the plane, also a young pilot and I soared upwards. The well-known mountains of Kitzbühel looked very nice, the skiers, who were drawing ridiculously slow curves through the slopes, the village with its colourful old houses and the lively crowds (it is full of English, French, Italian, Czech and Hungarian people). As we neared the Hohe Tauern [a mountain range in Carinthia], over the peaks we saw snow whirled up by the wind into giant pennants, soon we noticed that a fierce south-west gale had blown up and we felt the first gusts, once the plane fell 50 meters, then it immediately climbed back; we had to fly over two mountain ranges and gained the necessary height with difficulty as the wind always blew us down, but in the narrow valleys by circling madly it gained height again. We soon succeeded in crossing a narrow pass to reach the Glockner. You can't imagine the fantastic landscape made by the bizarre forms and wild, vertical mountain faces over which we flew. The storm became increasingly fierce, and the aircraft was hurled about wildly. At the Glockner the pilot turned round at 3000 m and flew back to the narrow pass of 2500 m, the storm forced the weak craft

---

[25]The Czech village with the textile factory owned by his mother and aunts.

down 600 meters. The pilot flew back again, tried to gain height but in vain, we could again not get across the pass, the storm got fiercer, another shot again in vain and also the third go failed; every time the pilot had to make a sharp turn away from the pass. It was unbelievably nerve-racking and exciting: Would it work? What would we do if we could not get across? Now he began to search for an upwind and flew close to the mountain face; the gusts repeatedly forced us down. Finally he found a tremendous upwind on a mountain face, flew right into it, and spiralled upwards on full throttle in steep curves of a kind I've only seen in air shows. We rose high and he flew to the pass and we got over it. The craft is so small and light that it kept fluttering in the storm. We still had to cross two mountain ranges; the second pilot suddenly got sick, he threw up uninhibitedly; as it approached the ranges the plane fell a little in a far from comfortable manner, but it got over both, and we were able to land in the quiet valley of Kitzbühel, the adventure at an end. It was really exciting and I'm absolutely delighted with the beautiful and dramatic course this trip took.

As I'd only enough money left for my journey, I returned to Vienna that evening. Here work in the lab has begun again; thanks to the flight over the Glockner I've no money and so am leading a restricted life.

Today I finished reading *The Fountain* [by Charles Morgan], a wonderful book with so much in it that it would be absurd to say anything about

The aeroplane on the snow after its safe landing in Kitzbühel.

it. There was a lot in it from which I could learn because as you know my ideal is also stillness, the contemplative life, to be invulnerable. But as he himself says, everyone has to find his own way there. In fact not even Norwitz stays invulnerable, when he discovers that his beloved wife loves another. If you are loved it is easy to construct a philosophy and live according to it, to achieve contemplation stillness, invulnerability as Lewis does. The ideas in the book are excellent.

To Evelyn Baxter, February 24, 1934

The events in Vienna have been completely misinterpreted abroad and also in the English newspapers I've read. I'm very well informed both through our local papers and my wide-ranging connections.

It started with the police wanting to search a working-class block of flats for arms and the workers shooting the police. Many people say this was an accidental cause and that in any case the Social Democrats wanted to stir up trouble that day. The unrest spread over Vienna, a general strike was proclaimed (only a small proportion of the workers responded, because people here are not so keen on socialist ideas), the Republican Guard [Republikanische Schutzbund] occupied power and railway stations. The bobbies on the beat were taken prisoner; when the police tried to liberate the buildings and forcibly enter the houses, they were shot with automatic weapons. Subsequent events you'll know from the newspapers. But the following has been misunderstood. Everyone abroad is horrified that the workers' flats were bombarded by artillery. The council blocks, especially the giant Karl Marx Hof in Heiligenstadt, which you'll doubtless remember, were turned into fortresses with large armament stores as it now transpires (for instance, the lavatory windows, which all looked out onto the street, were built as places for snipers and had concrete supports for machine guns); people were shooting from the apartment blocks into the streets and onto the tram lines; the apartment blocks were made of thick reinforced concrete and could only be taken with artillery. That they had to be attacked and occupied is clear as the situation was untenable and the affair had to be settled as quickly as possible, because you can't take a fortress in a big city by cutting off its food supply.

The death toll has been greatly exaggerated; it is at most 200–300 and not about 2000–3000 as the papers write. Admittedly that's more than enough.

Certainly people now say that it's good that it went off quickly and relatively lightly; meanwhile in the council blocks they found several hundred machine-guns, many thousands of weapons and huge munitions depots in the cellars; the Czech Social Democrat party sent them the weapons, as I learned yesterday as a Czech Social Democrat told an acquaintance in Prague, that on the Sunday preceding the events in Vienna he packed weapons for the social democrats here, which they immediately passed on to the Austrian embassy. In Josefstadt [a district of Vienna] they found a huge depot of explosives under a gasometer so carelessly stored that the whole district could have blown up.

Civilians suffered little in this civil war. It was played out only in the council blocks, that is, in the large apartment blocks built by the local authority for workers after the war (but also positioned at strategic points!) and only between armed groups, that is, the Republican Guard on one side and the Home Guard, army and police on the other; the government troops were more exposed than the workers because the latter were shooting from the houses and mowed the others down with their machine guns. Don't imagine that the whole of Vienna was a battlefield and that you appear a coward because you weren't there; in the rest of Vienna we heard the shooting, young girls like you were not allowed to go into the street but had to stay at home for 3 days; that's all you could have done for us here; the centre of the city was immediately sealed with barbed wire by government troops; it never came to street fighting.

We were sitting unawares on a powder magazine and all the middle classes are happy that nothing worse happened. It is clear that the Social Democrats with their armaments were working towards a red revolution and soviet republic, and it's lucky that it was prevented in time.

From the outside it must naturally look as though we have been robbed of the last remnants of freedom here[26] and that a similar terror to the one in Germany is being imposed. Actually the government here finds itself in a predicament; it has been forced to resort to these measures by the extreme methods of Nazi propaganda (bombs, assassinations, etc.) and now challenged by an intolerable situation (an opposition party arms itself from taxpayers' money against the government). In our country it seems a democracy is impossible. That Dollfuss has forfeited English and French sympathy is very distressing of course.[27]

---

[26]Dollfuss had suspended Parliament in March 1933, thereby excluding the Social Democratic Workers Party from any say.

[27]Max clearly regarded Dollfuss not as a fascist in league with Mussolini, whose invasion of Abyssinia in 1935–1936 outraged him, but as a buffer against the Communists on the one hand and the Nazis on the other. Later in the year, Dollfuss banned both the National Socialist and the Social Democratic Workers parties.

To Evelyn Baxter, March 24, 1934

My friend Michel Benedikt[28] came to me saying I should do an analysis for him, a lump of coal, it's a simple one, he'd pay, I'd get 20 schillings for it. As it's already vacation time, I asked Oberkammer, the technician, whether I could do the work in his small lab in the courtyard. After working for two days I heated the substance with a burner and with the other hand I stirred it, suddenly a dreadful explosion, for a few seconds it thundered in my ears, I rushed into the courtyard like a maniac, noticed that I was covered in blood, people came running, flustered forms, I was taken to accident and emergency, the splinters were extracted from my hands and face, my eyes closed and I couldn't see anything, was taken to the eye clinic where they took glass splinters out, bandaged my eyes, and Gretl took me home a blind man; my eyes weren't damaged; they were just momentarily blinded by the splinters. News from the front: there's nothing to be seen anymore of the porcelain dish, and as little of the windows of the lab, they lie in tiny splinters in a wide area in the room and in the courtyard, tiny pieces of melted wire netting attached themselves to my coat, a heavy iron tripod was smashed and had been flung into the courtyard, the glassware hanging on the wall was smashed by the projectiles, my glasses were pierced and after 48 hours, healthy and able to see, I could already go for a walk thanks to quite unbelievable and fantastic luck (touch wood!). The technician assured me that in his 8 years of servicing the Institute of Chemistry he'd never experienced such an explosion.

Touch Wood! I still always carry your charming old drawing "Maximiliana Peruzuni" in my briefcase and believe that the symbolic picture brings me luck; just as the monkey hangs on the rotten bough and it doesn't break, so my life has already hung by a thread several times[29] and the thread held it, Touch Wood! Instead of earning 20 schillings, I had to pay about 70, but apart from an ear suffering badly in sympathy, everything is fine. The whole thing had little effect on my nerves, everyone said that I was as calm and slow as usual; there's no talk of shock; it's mainly other people who were shocked.

---

[28]Max had met Benedikt at the house of a school friend in the Swiss Alps. Benedikt was studying chemistry in Zurich and they compared notes: Max concluded that the difference between the Zurich and the Vienna labs was "as big as that between our lab and an alchemist's box."

[29]In German, the word is "bough" not "thread."

To Evelyn Baxter, May 26, 1934

I am writing to you because I have spoken to Leo Perutz about the translation of his book[30]; that was a couple of weeks ago; in the mean time I've been too busy to write to you about it. He says the book is to appear in a few days in England; he was terribly nice; thanked me for having already sent it to you, really seemed pleased that you liked it so much that you'd like to translate it, and said that his next book will probably appear in the autumn and that you should translate it. I am so sorry that nothing has come of your plans, but must point out that you got the book for Christmas and only looked into it in April, so that the extraordinary outcome, that in the meantime someone had translated it, was really to be expected.

To Evelyn Baxter, June 25, 1934

I am working here at the moment with an American writer and researcher on Africa. He wants to turn my short and dreary article on Lapland into a witty and very long piece of nonsense and to get it into the American National Geographic Magazine with which he has excellent connections.[31]

To Evelyn Baxter, February 21, 1936

Firstly I regrettably discovered that I can't write letters. A volume of the early letters of Hugo van Hofmannsthal has come out. Even by the most self-indulgent comparison, his letters are better. He writes so naturally and in such an unforced way just what he thinks. I can also do that if necessary. But there is a difference between what I myself think and what occurs to Hofmannsthal on the spur of the moment. What a pity!

Skiing is almost more beautiful than being in love on a brilliantly clear, icy, sunny winter day with powder snow and fast skis. It's an incomparable pleasure. Whizzing down, you feel as though you were flying as your skis slide through the soft almost frictionless snow.[32]

---

[30]The novelist was my grandfather's first cousin. *St. Petri-Schnee* appeared in 1933 and was published by Butterworth in 1934 as *The Virgin's Brand*.

[31]There are several references in earlier letters of attempts to perfect this article and get it into print.

[32]One of Max's worries about coming to England, expressed a few weeks later, was that he would unlearn a lot; this disturbed him greatly because he had observed that the thrills he experienced skiing were in direct proportion to his proficiency.

Max skiing

At home there are nothing but worries and anxieties. My father is so overworked that he's sometimes near a nervous breakdown. I'm a bit upset from time to time, that I have to sit here and look on and can't help; but I mustn't shift my destiny too to the Czech textile industry as, if something happens, such as war with Germany, we'll all be ensnared and trapped. One of the aims of my English stay is to search for a different path to the future.

To Evelyn Machin, April 21, 1936

I had to work from morning to evening and towards midnight the letters fluttered in front of my eyes, then you cannot get to sleep for ages and in the morning you wake up with a heavy head as though you'd drunk a litre of wine. Learning for exams is no joy. It goes on and on. In July I had to master the whole of chemistry from start to finish.

Here and everywhere people are unhappy with English politics. England is swaying in the wind. We should prefer to see England somewhat yielding towards Italy but unyielding against Germany. It would be good if you could see to the necessary. Otherwise I don't know if I can remain friends with you.

There's in fact a notable class of men, those whose convictions are always in perfect conformity with their wishes, passions and desires. Throughout their lives they are always right and act in good faith. Inner conflicts are unknown to them. If that's what business needs, today they are socialists and tomorrow National Socialist; they aren't hypocrites, liars, chameleons in character, but they are full of honest ideas. A whole people can show this same happy temperament if it comes to a war. Italians who previously laughed about the provocations of Abyssinia falsely engineered by Mussolini, will today lecture you about the holy right of Italy, the necessity finally to colonise the barbaric land of Abyssinia sunk by the slave trade, and once they have been talked into it for long enough, they will think that all the English are wicked devils and will smash the windows of their embassy with complete inner conviction.[33]

To Evelyn Machin, May 31, 1936

I completed a physical chemistry practical as fast as possible so as to be finished with my exams and definitely able to come to England in the autumn. It was a mad rush but also extraordinarily interesting. Physics really is the clearest and least ambiguous of all the sciences and if you occupy yourself with it a little more closely, you get a deep insight into how the world really functions and especially why you have done this in one way and that in another in chemistry. In chemistry you simply get to know what happens, learn the methods; physical chemistry teaches understanding of what happens. It's a wonderful feeling to penetrate ever more deeply the reason for and mechanism of what happens, to see how a theory by a genius allows you to grasp a dozen unexplained events mathematically in one go. In short, the six weeks have profoundly satisfied my boundless curiosity about the why and wherefore of things.

The people there were a distressing sight. They all represented the bad type of Austrian, uninterested, slovenly, lazy, trying to spare themselves any unnecessary chore, preferring to ask five times before thinking once themselves and cheating their way through where they could. It sickened me.

---

[33]After hearing of the Italian atrocities in Abyssinia, Max lost his faith. He had prayed fervently that Italy would not invade that hapless country and was revolted when the pope blessed the departing troops.

They were bad sorts. By contrast the head of the department was a very ugly Jewish lecturer, particularly nice with an illuminatingly clear grasp, who to my delight got at the crowd of students with the most biting irony.[34]

"In 1936, after four years of chemistry at Vienna University, I took the train to Cambridge to seek out the Great Sage.... The Great Sage was John Desmond Bernal, a flamboyant Irishman with a mane of fair hair, crumpled flannel trousers and a tweed jacket. We called him Sage, because he knew everything from physics to the history of art. Knowledge poured from him as from a fountain, unselfconsciously, vividly, without showing off, on any subject under the sun. He was the most incredible, magnetic and interesting character I'd ever met. In fact in my native Austria I never knew that anyone like that existed. His enthusiasm for science was unbounded. He became my Ph.D. supervisor. I could not have wished for a more inspiring one."[35] Bernal's brilliance turned his "dirty" laboratory, that "really was a terrible slum" into "a fairy castle." The laboratory "was also unbelievably unsafe. Nowadays officials of the Health and Safety Executive would have their hair standing on end to see how the high tension was taken from the transformers to the X-ray tubes on overhead wires which anybody could have touched by raising his hands, so that at one stage I nearly got electrocuted there."[36]

Max spent his first year in Cambridge learning crystallography by solving the structure of a mineral called rhodonite. To his disappointment, Bernal had had no crystals of biological interest to give him, but in his second year he embarked on the study of haemoglobin, the molecule that was to occupy him for almost 60 years. Max entitled his thesis, which he submitted in late 1939, *The Crystal Structure of Horse Methaemoglobin*, that is, haemoglobin, which has been stabilized by the oxidation of the iron in its haem groups. Of course he had only taken the first small steps toward the solution of the structure. "My colleagues, the other graduate students, thought I was crazy to tackle such a complex problem, and experienced crystallographers thought I was trying to solve an intrinsically insoluble prob-

---

[34]Hermann Mark, who does not look ugly in photos, was professor of physical chemistry.

[35]Perutz, M. 2003. *I Wish I'd Made You Angry Earlier*, expanded edition, p. 245. Cold Spring Harbor Laboratory Press, Cold Spring Harbor, NY, into which I have incorporated two sentences from a taped interview made 24 May 1980 for the Imperial War Museum.

[36]Taped interview made 24 May 1980 for the Imperial War Museum.

lem, but it was only Bernal who egged me on, who was an optimist."[37] In the autumn of 1938 a second enthusiast had appeared on the scene, W. Lawrence Bragg, who had won the Nobel Prize for demonstrating that it was possible to deduce the arrangement of the atoms in a crystal from an X-ray diffraction picture. Bragg had succeeded Ernest Rutherford as Cavendish Professor of Physics and he took over as Max's supervisor because his appointment coincided with Bernal's move to a professorship at Birkbeck College in London. Bragg was to collaborate with Max until Bragg moved to London in January 1954 where he became Director of the Royal Institution.

"One day I burst into [Bragg's] room announcing proudly, 'I have received an honour you can't match, I have had a glacier named after me.' 'I have one that you can't match' retorted Bragg, 'I have had a cuttlefish named after me.'"[38] In early 1937 a wealthy amateur glaciologist and founder of the British Glaciological Society, Gerald Seligman, had walked into Max's laboratory in search of a crystallographer who could ski. There was only one! His task was to join a team in the summer of 1938 on the Jungfraujoch in the Bernese Oberland in Switzerland to tackle the problem of "how the tiny snow crystals that drop on a glacier are eventually transformed into the huge crystals that you find at the end of the glacier tongue."[39] This assignment gave Max a second research topic, broadened his experience, and proved a cheering interlude in a bleak period. It also paid his expenses for four months and gave him a little pocket money, which he saved.

My grandfather's firm had gone bankrupt, although not the textile factory which my grandmother and her sisters had inherited, and it is clear from a letter of 21 March 1938, that Max knew that the £500 he had been given in the autumn of 1936 would be insufficient to see him through his Ph.D. even before the dreadful news reached him of Hitler's entry into Austria on 12 March. This had instantly changed Max's status from visiting scholar to refugee and filled him with anxiety about where his parents and his sister could find a home. Thanks to the Czech number plates of their factory car, they had escaped from Vienna to Prague with no questions asked, but when Hitler invaded the Sudetenland, where their factories were located, they fled once more, this time to

---

[37]Max Perutz interviewed by Katherine Thompson, 2001, National Life Stories, British Library Sound Archive catalogue reference C464/22.

[38]Perutz, M. 2003. *I Wish I'd Made You Angry Earlier*, expanded edition, p. 339. Cold Spring Harbor Laboratory Press, Cold Spring Harbor, NY.

[39]Max Perutz interviewed by Katherine Thompson, 2001, National Life Stories, British Library Sound Archive catalogue reference C464/22, tape 5.

Switzerland, where they had no right to remain. A stipend that Max received from the Rockefeller Foundation in New York enabled him to guarantee his parents' support and so bring them to England. Bragg had asked the Foundation to fund a post to assist himself and David Keilin, the Professor of Biology, with their research into the structure of haemoglobin, the topic of Max's Ph.D. As the reader will see, the generosity of the Foundation to scientists in Britain, which continued well into the 1960s, was extraordinary. Franz and Lotte, Max's brother and sister, decided to emigrate to the United States. This was particularly difficult for Lotte, who could find work only in a children's home in New Orleans; her Viennese doctorate had been in medieval English. Eventually she found a job with a family as a nanny; her boss became a close friend and helped Lotte to train as a psychiatric social worker.

All of the following letters were written in English from Cambridge unless otherwise indicated.

To Evelyn Machin, May 31, 1937

In the course of reading a Textbook of Biology, I came across a most remarkable definition of science: "Science does not deal with values, but with relations between objects of our external world." These words reminded me of a question you asked me in connection with [Max] Born's book; "What is Electricity actually?" This is the first of a series of futile questions, which will be worrying you often, if you continue your studies of science. They cause trouble to me or anybody else, who finds difficulty in realising any qualities not associated with familiar things of our world. I would like to tell you some more of these unanswerable questions and to explain the reasons why the problems cannot be solved or why some of them are only apparent problems. I can do this much better in a letter than by telling it to you. I like to write it down in any case and I know that you will be interested.
The main questions:

1. Why do masses attract each other, why does the earth revolve around the sun, being kept at a constant distance from it in obedience to Mr. Isaac Newton?

2. Why are electrical charges of different sign attracted and charges of the same sign repulsed?

3. Why does the electron spin around the atom and what actually is spinning?

4. What are waves and what is matter?
5. What is life? I think the question belongs to the same order.

Now the intelligent reader (thank you, Max) will ask why these apparently simple and natural questions are principally unanswerable, why they are banned from the field of science to the heights of metaphysics?

Somehow or other they are all going beyond the abilities of our direct observation and experimental verification. This fact can be shown most clearly by question 4.

In any experiments dealing with the ultimate nature of matter, we have to employ some device for registrating [sic], we must take a photograph (cloud chamber with radioactive track) or we must do something else which will enable us to see or hear or feel what has happened. We have to use light or sound or heat, which means that we cannot make any observations without the use of waves.—On the other hand if we want to find out about the properties of waves, we can only observe them by the material changes produced on a photographic film or in the nerves in our eyes. We have to use silver atoms, mercury column, membranes, etc.

We can only describe matter by its effect upon waves and we cannot observe waves without using matter for the experimental apparatus. This fact implies that we can choose deliberately whether we want to describe matter in terms of waves or whether we want to employ material ideas for realising the properties of waves. Both have been done at a time when physicists were profoundly confused, because the electrons, which had been believed to be particles suddenly behaved like waves whereas the waves showed a discontinuity hitherto attributed to matter alone.

But none of the two descriptions can bring you any further to the answer of your question 4, if you keep in mind that you cannot help describing one thing by another thing, whose nature you can only determine by expressing it in terms of the former.

If you should ever happen to read *Relativity: The Special and General Theory* you will understand that the impossibility of discovering whether the light from the stars is travelling in a medium called "Ether" or whether it is just travelling in "Nothing", is a rather similar one.

As to questions 1, 2, 3, obviously our abilities are exhausted after establishing the facts and the laws which rule their relations; if we continue to ask why, we arrive at a point as the following: "Why is the sun hot?" "Because the atoms in the sun are moving with high velocities." Why are they moving with high velocities? "Why shouldn't they?"

As to question 5 I do not deny the possibility that the simpler phenomena of life will be fully described by mathematical formulae after some generations of research. That these mathematicians will prove that the Free Will of Man only exists because the mechanism of the brains which *produce* the above formulae is too complex to be expressed *by* those formulae. But will those formulae answer our question?

Critical minds will continue to ask for the reason of phenomena, unless by that time critical minds are abolished altogether in some future Super-Fascism or Communism.

To-day I finished the most tiresome part of research I have ever done and consequently I am in high spirits. Too high, you will say after this letter. Some time ago I saw *French without Tears* [by Terence Rattigan] at the Criterion in London. Pricelessly funny, go if you can. You will laugh for another three days. Practically I am in high spirits all the time, these days—whenever I look into one of the Examination Halls and see crowds of perspiring undergraduates squeezing their brains over their papers I rejoice in the pleasant fact that I will never have to do anything of the kind.

To Felix Haurowitz. Reichenau, August 1, 1937[40]

As my father said to you, I'd very much like to visit you in Prague in order to seek your advice on a number of questions.

First, during my stay in Cambridge it became apparent that there's hardly anyone competent in crystallography and organic chemistry and that just through combining these two fields there's a prospect of success.

Second so far no-one has used crystallography to examine a compound from the haemin area and such an investigation seems rather promising, if it is possible to find two isomorphic, well crystallised porphyrins.[41] As I don't know anyone in England who has even touched those compounds, I would value a meeting with you very much.

---

[40]Translated from the German.

[41]Felix "pointed out to me that Fischer in Munich had already synthesised [the haemin] and everything was known about it and there was really no point in determining its structure. But he said 'why not work on haemoglobin itself?' and the idea appealed to me." Max Perutz interviewd by Katherine Thompson, 2001, National Life Stories, British Library Sound Archive catalogue reference C464/22. Felix knew that the Cambridge physiologist, Gilbert Adair, had crystallised haemoglobin and advised Max to approach him for help.

Felix Haurowitz

To Evelyn Machin. Grindelwald, September 6, 1937

Ages and Ages and Ages—since I have not written to you and there is ever so much to write, probably a very un-English letter, all about myself and far too melodramatic.

I had a fortnight's climbing which I enjoyed thoroughly in spite of persistent bad weather. We started in the good old Peugeot of Edi Schaar—*e pur si muove* [and it even moved]—it was big fun to squeeze the rattling, dilapidated wreck through the Rolls Royce-filled streets of Salzburg; we felt very superior and considered everybody else nouveaux-riches. The number of our party increased steadily and we ended as seven—family Eirich, Dehne, etc. They are all very nice and we were refreshingly vulgar, a very agreeable contrast to my usual life in England.

Many unpleasant news awaited me in Vienna; a friend of mine had killed himself on his motor-cycle in France. Weissel and I had to see his family and to try to cheer them up while we felt more like crying ourselves.

The second news was that I had to meet [Gerald] Seligman in Grindelwald on the 30th, which brought my holiday at home to an abrupt end.

However, I managed to see all the friends again. First of all I saw Gretl, who is as pleasant and lovely as ever. She is going to marry in October. We had only 4 hours to spend together and had great difficulties in telling each other everything we wanted to—I had to increase the speed of my speech by a factor of three and we talked all at once most of the time. We were so frightfully pleased to see each other again and to realise that we had not become strangers during all the long time, which had seemed a century to me after we had spent three years almost continuously together and I nearly fell in love with her over again.

And I met Gusti [Schultz] the darling who was always in love with me and admired all the qualities I have not got and she had not changed at all. She is going to be married, but she was so sweet that I regretted not to be able to run away with her before.

And I met the three boys, Weissel, Granichstaedten and Hoefft and compared them with the many people I had met during the past year and I thought they were nicer than most of them.

And in general I remembered the words of the Dutchman, who had returned to Holland from an expedition in the Karakorum after having seen half the world: "And then I realised that Holland was the most beautiful country in the world."

I left Vienna on the evening of the 29th and felt more homesick for the next 24 hours than I had ever been before in my life.

Grindelwald is an English colony. I arrived in the evening and had drinks with Seligman and our collaborators.

We started on the Jungfraujoch the next morning and had four days of creeping about glaciers, climbing into crevasses and endless discussion of snow and ice. They were three superb days of continuous sunshine; the position of the laboratory is most imposing and beautiful and the mountains are alluring. Unfortunately there was only time to climb the Jungfrau itself, as Dr. [Philip] Bowden, a Cambridge don, and I observed with much regret, that it might look rather funny if we went away on our climbs after Seligman had paid all our expenses. Consequently we had to pretend a fierce interest in glaciology and to make sweeping and final statements on the mechanism of glacial movement, which were substituted by other final theories half an hour later.

At the moment I am staying in Grindelwald because we have to wait for Bernal's arrival on the 9th. Most likely everything we have done up to now will look completely childish in the bright light of his incomparable brain. I am looking forward to seeing him again. Grindelwald after the season is full of awful English middle-class families, partly even with cockney accents. Their daughters are utterly indigestible and they are spending their days keeping themselves to themselves and looking very bored.

To Evelyn Machin, September 26, 1937

I started a love-affair with the lady who now prints my photographs and who is most amusing and intelligent and pleasant. When I found out that my predecessors were Bernal and all the more brilliant Cambridge scientists, I was rather bucked at first about the good company I had joined, but later I thought the company was rather too numerous and decided to withdraw gracefully. However, it was highly entertaining and I learned more about the soul of Cambridge in an evening than in a year.

I am continuing to read *The Search* [by C.P. Snow] and becoming rather fascinated, as it must be if you are discovering that somebody else had written your own autobiography. Many incidents and certainly all the reactions to the more significant events of life in general and Cambridge Science life in particular are almost as if they were irrelevant modifications which have to be allowed for in view of my different upbringing and education. As I will probably send you the book and you will consider myself very conceited after having read it, I am bound to say that my brain has none of the alert efficiency and mathematical gift of the hero in *The Search*, the resemblance I mean being more in kind than in quality.

My work is unfortunately not too well, the damn crystals are not growing, the usual misery of the crystallographer.

To Evelyn Machin, October 17, 1937

Yesterday I spent my time at the Institute of Parasitology; not, as you will believe, as the object of investigation, but actively engaged in watching other people doing some work for myself. However, the name of the place reminded me that I had asked you some weeks ago whether I could bring Meta Steinschneider to see you in your Schloss [country seat] Sunday next.

I am having a fairly good time and am thoroughly enjoying Cambridge this term. Last year I did not know enough people, this year there is rather embarras de richesse in girls, invitations and interesting work, and once again I feel that life in Cambridge is well worth living. The variety of interesting characters coming across your way is probably longer than anywhere else. There are pages more to write, but I am sitting in the lab and have to do some work.

To Evelyn Machin, November 6, 1937

I am doing a strictly crystallographic work with Dr. [Peter] Wooster which helps me in learning all the theory I should have learned last year. I am supposed to do another work on Haemoglobin (the red colour of the blood) with Bernal, but I have not got any time to do it. And I have to attend "glaciological" meetings with Seligman now and then and to write elaborate reports on the programme of our research party which, unfortunately, nobody reads. And I have to give lectures. Just imagine me standing in front of an audience consisting of 4 university professors and four other learned people and talking about a subject which I scarcely understand myself. I put in as many jokes as possible and they did even condescend to laugh at them, but they never understood the theories until I had explained them for the third time. It is a horrid feeling to watch the completely blank faces of an audience which does not really grasp what you are saying. And it is nice to hear the same people whom you have watched sleeping for over an hour saying afterwards how immensely interesting they found the subject of your talk. However, after the sweeping success of this first lecture I am going to give another one to the University Mountaineering Club on Glacier, Snow and Ice on Friday next. The subject is much simpler but the audience probably more difficult. Actually I am rather glad I have got hold of that opportunity to get some practice of talking in public.

The girls: well, there are only two and these have left Cambridge again. There was Meta, who is a most pleasant companion. Neither of us was in love with the other and consequently we got on very well indeed. Her presence helped me to dozens of invitations as nearly all my friends asked us to dinners, teas, sherries, lunches, but we got rather fed up with talking "Comparative Ethnology"—as I have called the discussions about how the lavatories work in different countries and how...

I attended [Ernest] Rutherford's funeral in Westminster Abbey. I am rather sorry I never tried to meet him last year. It would have been quite easy to get an invitation to one of his house parties for his research students, but I thought to postpone it until I become "somebody." Now I regret that I never knew him personally. And somehow you never realise that a person is on the same level with Newton if you see him passing your window every other day and hear him telling little stories in his lectures.

On the whole, Cambridge is rather less exciting but much more pleasant than last year. Of course there is always plenty of excitement on the road to success in science as in any other occupation. The profound wish to achieve something spectacular, to remain with science for the rest of my life and to remain in England provides plenty of thrill. Of course the atmosphere in the Crystall. Lab is more friendly than in most of the other labs in the world. There, at least, I have not got to fight my way through a hostile camp, but just got to make use of all the opportunities offered to me. Bernal is as friendly and encouraging as ever, our teas in the lab have become much more inspiring since Professor [Paul] Ewald has joined us (I think I wrote to you about him before.)[42] At times I am rather worried because I am wasting too much of my time on side-tracks, such as glaciology and lectures, instead of getting on with my main work. But under the present circumstances this is inevitable.

I am really going to be sent to Davos by Seligman.[43]

I am leaving England on 1st of January. Are you going to Austria at Xmas?

To Max Machin, Evelyn's Husband, undated

As I wrote in my letter to Eve, I am trying to bring Lotte to Cambridge. The arrangement is that she will stay for three months and try to make a living. If the attempt fails she will go on to New York where she has got several friends and would probably find something. She would rather come to England, because there are more chances of finding an intelligent occupation and perhaps an opportunity of using at least some of the things she has learned in the past. Besides she, like myself, has a liking for the English atmosphere and none for the American.

In my official invitation to her I wrote that she should keep house for me and have an opportunity of improving her English and continuing her linguistic studies at the University library (Bob Eichholz's advice).

In her application for a British visa to the Prague consulate she has to name two referees in the United Kingdom. I wondered whether you would find it very objectionable to act as one of the referees for an undesirable alien. Seligman consented to act as the other.

Lotte's application is sent from Prague to the Home Office. From there, enquiries will be made at the referees both about Lotte and myself. You

---

[42]No such letter survives. Paul Ewald was one of the founders of X-ray crystallography and a refugee from Stuttgart. He befriended Max at a difficult time.

[43]Max sought advice from and later collaborated with members of the Swiss Federal Institute for Snow and Avalanche Research in Davos.

would probably have to give a certificate of good character, say that we are descendants of a respectable and wealthy family (important because the Home Office must not get the impression that we are refugees) and that to the best of your knowledge my means are adequate for the support of both myself and my sister. They really are, only the money belongs to my parents and we do not want to spend it. They might ask you whether Lotte is looking for employment in England; it would be best to give a non-committal answer that you know nothing about her having such intentions.

I am very sorry to bother you with this. I wish there was no need for such a ridiculous fuss if you want to shift from one spot on this planet to another quite close by. It would be very kind of you, if you let me know whether you could do this for me.

To John Desmond Bernal (Sage), March 21, 1938

I have recently been measuring the cell of Horse Met Hb at pH 8.5. Furthermore I examined the absorption of visible light by crystals of Horse Met Hb in different vibration directions of polarised light.

After showing you these pieces of fundamental research I return, as usual, to the question of financing the highly ingenious worker who carries

Desmond Bernal

them out. Peter [Wooster] suggested that the University might create a job for me by making me an assistant who acts as a connecting officer between the biological and the crystallographic departments, and thought that Bragg, Keilin, Hopkins and Adair could bring the question to the Senate. This only in case you haven't come to a satisfactory settlement with Bragg already.

To Evelyn Machin. Jungfraujoch, June 19, 1938

I was rather surprised at the nasty end to your translation efforts. I am rather sad it failed because I had been so pleased with the idea to have helped both of you. You write that it will be good for your character—if failures do you any good I ought to be a positive saint by now; humiliations, disappointments are all along the road and yet I often wonder whether they make me any wiser. Perhaps they have. The people who fail now and then always seem to be more charming than the successful ones, unless they develop a minority complex.

My latest disappointment was meeting with my brother in Paris. You know that I never thought much of him, but that my own brother should have become such a miserable hypocrite, dripping of vanity, more tactless than any American[44] and a criminal fool altogether, that was rather a blow to me. He told me all the unpleasant facts he could possibly think of—I think he must have learnt them by heart beforehand, otherwise he could not have remembered them all during the 30 hours I spent in Paris. I loved Paris and its light-hearted atmosphere and thought it was the most beautiful town I had seen—yet under the circumstances I was glad to get away.

Up here my life is luxurious and quite pleasant, though rather confined for the lack of climbing company. Seligman does not allow my climbing alone and there is none of our party who likes to join me. The Party is quite a success, we are not yet getting on each others' nerves and the researches are making some progress. I have got a pleasant room to myself, magnificent food, a fairly intelligent occupation, a good wireless set, plenty of books, grand surroundings and considerable peace of mind. I never read any newspapers and try to forget about my numerous worries. Lotte is the big problem for the moment. I failed to get the scholarship for £350 a year

---

[44] I suspect that Max's view of Isidore Fankuchen, with whom he worked in the crystallography department, was probably the origin of this slur on the American people. This was not the first time or the last that Max vented his fury about his brother but he never blackballed him; on the contrary he made an effort to stay in touch and keep their relations cordial.

for which I had recently hoped and as far as I can see my income will be rather meagre. There are small hopes that I shall be able to keep her at Cambridge. However, there are hopes that she can go to U.S.A.

To Evelyn Machin. Jungfraujoch, July 10, 1938[45]

I must write to you once more in German as I'm in a German country and am in the mood to. Above all, I must write to you because I'm feeling so cheerful, as I normally do only at Amlet's Hill [Evelyn's home], and as my last letter was so gloomy that you will have become downcast from reading it, if you weren't anyway. My good mood is by no means without foundation. First, I feel terrific here. It's true that the weather was such that it could only be described by frequent use of popular expressions for animal excretions, but today it was glorious and for the first time I went skiing in earnest. Secondly I'm feeling fine because I have buried my head literally and metaphorically in the snow, and read the last newspaper on 29 May. Thirdly Lotte is coming here on Wednesday for a fortnight.

I got permission for her to stay free of charge at the research institute— for that she undertook to cook for me and to climb mountains with me. Apart from that I'm happy to put her down as Seligman's secretary and that's the official reason that she's coming here.

My glaciological work is finally not only advancing but is giving very nice results, that is, I've found just the effect that I took in Cambridge as a working hypothesis and am absolutely delighted. The colour of my face has greatly changed towards the red end of the spectrum, I'll soon be able to plait my hair and my condition after 6 weeks' stay at 11000 feet can only be described as damned good.

We still get on very well especially as one of us has a nearly inexhaustible fund of dirty jokes at his disposal, which I'm memorising for later recital in the Machin/Baxter family circle. I read *Poet's Pub* [by Eric Linklater, 1929], very charming.

I get lots of letters from Vienna from friends who could never rouse themselves to more than a picture postcard. Suddenly all have been seized by an irresistible need to communicate and take a childish pleasure in every letter they receive from abroad, and which sounds as if it is more reliable than what the people who surround them say. Aryans and Jews from the good bourgeois and intelligent circles with which I was friends are equally

---

[45]Translated from the German.

Max collecting crystals of ice from a crevasse, "cathedrals of ice, spectacularly beautiful with the blue sky at the top" and no more than a mere 30 m deep![46]

enraged, the Aryans perhaps more so, as the Jews expected nothing better, while the Aryans never imagined it would be so bad to be ruled by this insufferable, humourless corrupt rabble, who from the God-Führer right down to the least public servant see the path to success in servility, strident enthusiasm for the Nazis and above all in uniforms.

I can't be bored here because, as you know, I've a talent for occupying myself and then there's lots of work if we want to reverse all glaciology in four months and prove that all our predecessors were idiots and ourselves the only clever ones, so I'm mostly busy till midnight.—In addition despite my seclusion from the world or perhaps just because of it, I'm daily getting measurably cleverer as you will doubtless have gathered without difficulty from this letter.

---

[46]Max Perutz interviewd by Katherine Thompson, 2001, National Life Stories, British Library Sound Archive catalogue reference C464/22.

Max with his airman's outfit and polarising microscope on the Jungfrau. A mountain guide had "renovated an ice grotto that had been a tourist attraction so that there was a little tunnel into it. In there the temperature was just below freezing point ~minus 4 to 5°C."[47]

I now have a fur-filled airman's outfit in my igloo and my feet in large sacks filled with wood shavings. In this outfit I look like one of the 7 dwarfs going to a fancy dress ball as Colonel Lindbergh. Yesterday a Zurich professor came to our igloo who was so enchanted that in the autumn he wants to make a film there about meteorology and glaciers.

The second main subject of our scientific activity, "fornication at high altitudes," has unfortunately fallen by the wayside due to the indigestible nature of Swiss womanhood; the leaders of the expedition decided to collect the non-existent results in a series of balloon ascents in Paris. I hope you are as well as I am.

---

[47]Max Perutz interviewd by Katherine Thompson, 2001, National Life stories, British Library Sound Archive catalogue reference C464/22.

To John Desmond Bernal (Sage). Forschungsinstitut, Jungfraujoch, Switzerland, July 12, 1938

The optical work on glacier ice has yielded some very surprising results:

1. There is a certain place in our ice-cave, where plastic deformation of the ice is evident. Samples taken from this place show precisely the orientation we anticipated, i.e. the c-axes all lie in a plane perpendicular to the direction of flow.

2. The blue bands form from deposition of melt water of wind- or sun-crusts. When covered up with snow they show greater capillarity than the rest of the firn and consequently retain melt water. This melt water freezes in large single crystals with vertical c-axis. If this orientation is maintained throughout the glacier—I have only examined blue-bands from the accumulation area so far—then the blue bands would show greater plasticity than the rest of the ice and might become the slip planes they were often supposed to be.[48]

The weather has been playing us tricks during the last few weeks—it has been snowing for 10 days with little interruption—and consequently we are rather held up with some parts of our work. The crevasses are getting filled up with snow again and we cannot at the moment penetrate to the depth we want. In general, our work makes very satisfactory progress, thanks to a pleasant atmosphere, our good equipment, to the excellent management of the research station and last, not least, to the inexhaustible stock of dirty stories with which [Tom] Hughes keeps us in good humour.

To Evelyn Machin, May 17, 1939

This is just to wish Noel many happy returns of the day. Although you always said as a precautionary measure against disappointment that you

---

[48]For the benefit of the layman in 2001 Max explained "When the crystals fall on the glacier they are very small and their orientation is higgledy piggledy, but then the sun comes and it melts the snow during the day and it refreezes during the night. And we found that in this process the crystals oriented themselves with their hexagonal axes parallel to the temperature gradient; so there was a strong preferred orientation as you went a little way down. But then the ice begins to flow; so with that the crystals start gliding over each other and they lose this orientation again. But then something else sets in: initially as the snow melts in the summer the water trickles down but it can trickle down only so long as the ice is porous, because as it settles it becomes more and more compacted and then the water can no longer penetrate, and the temperature of the ice is no longer determined by the melt water and after that the ice takes up the mean ambient temperature quite a bit below the freezing point. So Tom Hughes and I got a very good picture of the way a glacier develops." Max Perutz interviewed by Katherine Thompson, 2001, National Life Stories, British Library Sound Archive catalogue reference C464/22, tape 5.

don't mind whether it will be a boy or a girl, I am sure you and Max will be frightfully pleased with the son and heir. [They already had a daughter.]

I do look forward to the time when I shall be playing railways with him, not to speak of meccano!

To John Desmond Bernal (Sage), December 6, 1939

I finished the text of the thesis today. I hope to have it typed and bound within a week. I shall let you have it for inspection as soon as I can. Bragg and Adair have been appointed as my examiners. I am sorry that you will miss that pleasure, and besides there are many points in my thesis which I wrote especially so that I can discuss them with you at the oral.

1940s

"So in the end I thought: in Vienna life is good and work's bad, here life's often bad but instead work is wonderful."

MAX'S LIFE IN THE EARLY 1940S WAS CHARACTERISED by dramatic reversals of fortune. No sooner had he received his doctorate than he was interned, that is to say imprisoned, as an "enemy alien" and transported first to Bury St. Edmunds, then north to Liverpool, on to the Isle of Man, and finally to Canada. The letters reveal his increasing desperation and then his joy eight months later in January 1941 when he was finally liberated and reunited with his parents and friends. From a letter written in November of that same year, we learn that Anne Hartridge, the girlfriend to whom he had written from internment, had rejected his proposal of marriage. Instead he had become engaged to my mother, Gisela (pronounced gheezela) Peiser, whom he married in March 1942. It was to prove the happiest and most harmonious of marriages.

During these months Max had been back at the Cavendish Laboratory hoping to contribute to the war effort but barely able to do so. Then out of the blue, in the spring of 1942, came a call to work on a top-secret project code-named Habbakuk [sic]. His first task was to make ice stronger. He had no idea why, "but gradually the secret leaked out, like acid from a rusty can."[1] The secret, the brainchild of Geoffrey Pyke, who worked at the U.K. Combined Operations Headquarters, was the Allies' plan to make an airfield out of ice in mid Atlantic. Work on this project was to take Max to North America again, now as a member of the British High Command, equipped with a large blue trunk embellished with his new status as a British army officer! Realising that, like his earlier trip to Scandinavia, this would be an adventure, he began to keep a diary. This one survives and is reproduced below. With its coded abbreviations, it reads rather like a spy story, but it also records his impressions of the United States and Canada.

The chief interest of the later letters of the 1940s seems to me to lie in the many revealing remarks about daily life in Britain and the descriptions of Max's return to the Continent and especially to his native Austria. This was a period of building both at home and at work. First I was born and

[1]Perutz M.F. 2003. Enemy alien. *I Wish I'd Made You Angry Earlier.* Cold Spring Harbor Laboratory Press. Cold Spring Harbor, NY, p. 87. First published in 1985 in *The New Yorker.*

then my brother Robin 5 years later. Max acquired funding to hire assistants and, as explained on p. 163–164 below, in his quest for the solution to the structure of proteins, he was joined by some remarkable men. In 1947, he also decided to return to glaciology in order to determine how glaciers flow. To prepare his expedition to the Jungfraujoch and the Aletsch glacier, he established a committee to which he recruited a geophysicist, Teddy Bullard; a solid-state physicist, Sir Geoffrey Taylor; an expert in metal flow, Egon Orowan; and a geographer, Vaughan Lewis. He applied to the Royal Society for funding to pay for apparatus, a supporting team, and a laboratory cold room in Cambridge.

During the 1940s, the advances towards a solution of the structure of haemoglobin were limited, and Max travelled up blind alleys for several years at prodigious cost in man-hours. Yet the letters reveal the indomitable optimism that enabled him to pursue a problem most scientists thought insoluble. Early funding came from several sources, notably the Rockefeller Foundation. From October 1947, the Medical Research Council became the chief funder of Max and his colleagues, while the Rockefeller continued to provide additional income. Max recognised that both organisations relied on Lawrence Bragg's judgement that he and his colleagues were worthy of support, and for that he was eternally grateful.

Internment

Why was Max interned? In Max's words, "The story begins in the autumn of 1939, when the Home Office and the War Office were anxious to avoid a repetition of the wholesale internment of nearly 30,000 mostly harmless Germans in squalid camps, which had taken place during the First World War. The Home Secretary, Sir John Anderson, therefore established tribunals that classified Germans and Austrians as refugees from Nazi oppression and ordered the internment of only those thought to be loyal to the Nazi regime.

On 9 April 1940, German forces invaded Norway, supposedly helped by a Fifth Column of Norwegian Nazis and by German spies posing as refugees. A month later, the Germans invaded Holland and Belgium, and Winston Churchill replaced Neville Chamberlain as Prime Minister. Churchill held his first Cabinet meeting on 11 May. At the insistence of the Chiefs of Staff, the reluctant Anderson was asked to abandon his enlightened policy and to intern all male Germans and Austrians living near the coasts that were threatened with invasion."[2]

To Hugo and Dely Perutz. Huyton?, May 20, 1940

I am terribly sorry to have left you without news for such a long time. We have not been allowed to send or to receive any letters until now. Even now our letters from friends and relatives have not been given to us so that I am without news from you.

We were first transported to a temporary camp where we stayed for a week. Conditions there were quite pleasant, we slept in comfort and got plenty to eat. My stomach behaved very well and I am still eating the butter I took with me. Please send another pound through the Cambridge Refugee Committee. Today we moved to somewhere else and then we shall be moved again. The duration of internment cannot be foreseen at the moment but our position is by no means hopeless!

The last camp was made pleasant by an extremely nice officer (20 years old undergraduate from Cambridge) who got for us all the comforts on his own initiative.

There is assembled among us the most distinguished crowd of people I have ever seen together, all the refugees from Cambridge University, undergraduates, research students, lecturers, fellows of Colleges. We have already started a kind of university consisting of lectures and courses. I am secretary of the Natural Science Faculty. The people are really most pleasant. I have acquired some very nice new friends. All University people are keeping together.

There is, I think, nothing you can do for me at the moment. I shall tell you when there is. Please send butter, cold-cream, 1 towel and 2 pounds of sugar. And there is a good chance that things are not as bad as you may think.

Keep well and don't worry too much. Written in a hurry.

To Hugo and Dely Perutz. Huyton?, May 21, 1940

There is nothing new to report from here since yesterday, but I thought I might write to you when I am in no hurry and can describe life at leisure.

---

[2]Perutz M.F. 2003. Enemy alien. *I Wish I'd Made You Angry Earlier I Wish I'd Made You Angry Earlier*. Cold Spring Harbor Laboratory Press. Cold Spring Harbor, NY, p.96. First published in 1985 in *The New Yorker*.

If the internment were not such a wretched waste of time as far as my research is concerned (plus a few other ifs) one might regard it as a good school of human companionship. It is most interesting in this respect. There are alternate waves of general depression and optimism going through the camp; apart from these, the opinion of individual people as regards the future is much more dependent on their individual temperament, the state of their health, their age and, most important, the amount of food which they have eaten than upon actual reasoning. This is, of course, partly due to most of the factors influencing our future being completely unknown to us. In this camp we are not even allowed to read papers or to listen to the wireless—things which were allowed to us in the last. So we have to depend mostly on more arguably less reliable rumours.

The longer I know these people here, the more I am impressed by the depths of the tragedies which have afflicted these poor men. Many of them have been in German concentration camps, have lost all they had in their former homes. Now they were just beginning to build up a future, one was just about to make an important discovery, another had just got a nice job, a third had experiments interrupted and spoiled which took years to prepare. Most of them have families and are worrying that they might lose the means to support them. Some had only come to Cambridge for the Whitsun Week-end, and were arrested by mistake and have not been able to have their cases considered. Another is already naturalised and only came with us because he did not protest energetically enough when arrested. There are a Jewish Rabbi and several evangelic pastors here. Many small school-boys who think it all great fun.

We are not suffering any great hardships except that we are not allowed to receive any mail but the fate of each of us is greatly afflicted by the loss of time the internment involves. Some, for instance [Walter] Ripper,[3] were doing work of the utmost importance, but failing an authority of appeal they cannot do anything. We hope that this will be different when we get to the next camp and that then we shall also be allowed to receive the mail which has arrived for us.

At the beginning the attitude of our guards was rather hostile, because they thought that we were all spies. But by now they have convinced themselves that we are homeless refugees and are quite friendly. There are many

---

[3]Dr. Walter Ripper had founded Pest Control Ltd., which provided scientific advice to farmers, sold the chemicals for pest control and hired out the equipment. He was in fact quickly released and proved crucial in saving the sugar beet crop from an infestation of aphids, as his daughter, Vanessa Bertram, informed me.

young students here who have been brought up in English public schools and whose speech and outlook can in no way be distinguished from real Englishmen. Some of them have been here for 6 or 7 years. I shall write again as soon as I can and hope that you are as well as can be under the circumstances. You can forward letters for me from abroad if you do not open the envelopes and send them through the Cambridge Police. These are given to us because they have already gone through a censor. Other letters are not given to us apparently because there is nobody available to censor them.

To Hugo and Dely Perutz. House 7, Central Promenade Camp, Douglas, Isle of Man, c/o The Chief Postal Censor, Liverpool, June 17, 1940

Thank you for your letters of 16, 18, 21, 26, 30, 31 May and 3 June and for 2 parcels with shirts and trousers. Send *food*, razor blades, toothbrush. In future, if you tell people that I have been interned, don't forget to add that all men in the area have been interned and that my only offence was my address. Also please work hard for my release, don't hesitate at any expense, take decisions and send parcels without awaiting my instructions. Try to arrange collaborations between Kemball Johnston,[4] [Lawrence] Bragg, Walter Ripper, and urge them to hurry up and secure my release at all costs. For heaven's sake shake my professors (Bragg, [David] Keilin, [J.D.] Bernal) and friends out of their complacency and impress on them that I don't want futile safety and degrading idleness but active work in our war effort, and that unless they make a real effort for my release I shall in all probability remain here for years, that you will starve and my career will be ruined without having rendered the country any service by my sacrifice. I made an application for release giving as reasons National Importance of helping Bragg and securing Rockefeller Grant, also fulfilling guarantee to maintain you. The application will be useless without outside help, as there is no sign of any machinery for reviewing individual cases here. Show this letter to Tom [Hughes],[5] and Anne [Hartridge], and ask her to find out from Dean of Barts[6] how he got release of Reichenheim (ordinary medical stud.). Hope to be allowed to write to my friends soon. Thank Tom for two letters and Anne for 2 short notes and give her my love. Ask them to write, even if I cannot reply yet. Wire any decisive developments.

---

[4]The husband of an Austrian friend, a barrister, working for MI6.

[5]His friend from the Jungfraujoch expedition.

[6]St. Bartholomew's Hospital.

To Lotte Perutz, August 12, 1940

Civilian internee M.F. Perutz has safely arrived at Camp 'L.' Internment Operations, Canada, and is well.

To Anne Hartridge. Camp L, Internment Operations, Canada, August 14, 1940

I was suddenly deported to Canada together with an age group to which I belong. I have not heard from anybody since I left and could not write before. We are interned as Prisoners of War, Class 2, Civilians and hence have to use this stationery.[7] It is with great reluctance that I write to you on this, but after 7 weeks I feel I cannot wait any longer. Four weeks ago the chances of our return appeared infinitely remote, but now things do not look quite as black. In optimistic moments I often believe I shall see you before Xmas. Much may depend on Prof. Bragg. Only my body is in Canada. When I don't work my thoughts

Anne Hartridge

are in England and I think of you and my people and friends and I dream of all the marvellous things I shall do when I come back.—As camps go this one isn't bad. I spend my time learning Physics and Maths. I am still together with several very nice friends. I don't know what I should do without them. I wish I knew what happened to my parents. Please inform either or both of them of the contents of this. I dare not write to my mother on this stationery for fear of getting her into trouble. Please write to me all about yourself, family, [what followed has disappeared off the edge of the card]. I wish I could be there to shield you from any dangers just as a year ago when your grandmother sent me through London with you.

---

[7]The postcard is headed "Prisoner of War Mail."

To Lotte Perutz. Camp L, Internment Operations, Canada, August 19, 1940

On 3 July I was suddenly deported to Canada. The vast majority of us are refugees from Nazi oppression and we do all in our power to get this recognised. I have not received any news from anybody since I left England. Mother's last letter dated from 29 June, yours from June. We are very well treated here in the way of food, clothes and hygiene and I am very fit. We set up a camp University. I lecture on X-rays and crystals and I study Maths and theoretical physics with excellent teachers.[8] We are, of course subjected to all restrictions applying to Prisoners of War, so that you are not allowed to send me books or periodicals. We have papers in the camp and quite a good library between us. I am very worried about the parents' fate. When will they be able to immigrate into the U.S.?[9] Please write to me a complete account of all that happened to them since the end of June and all you did since the beginning of June. How are Franz and family? Letters to us are in no way restricted in length and don't reach us a day earlier if they are short and bare of contents. So please write me a long one *at least* once a week. Political and military information is now allowed to be sent to us. My future is quite uncertain, but I have all sorts of hopes. There is nothing you can do for now except inform the family, T.P. Hughes and Anne Hartridge of the contents of this and send them my love. Please send me Lux, toothbrush, metal mirror, thin socks and woollen ones to wear with plus fours. I firmly believe that England will hold out and that we shall yet beat the Nazis. So don't get depressed.

To Lotte Perutz. Camp L, Internment Operations, Canada, August 23, 1940

Today I received your letter of 14/08, the first news since I left England and the first hopeful one since my internment began. I was terribly pleased to hear of all the efforts on my behalf. Since my last letter to you I could apply for release to serve England as a scientist. I also appealed to Bragg to sup-

[8]They included Klaus Fuchs, the atomic bomb spy, who had recently got an appointment at the University of Edinburgh, and two brilliant Cambridge undergraduates, Hermann Bondi, later chief scientist at the Ministry of Defence, and Tom Gold, who ended his career as professor of astronomy at Cornell.

[9]Max did not yet know that his father had also been interned and deported to the Isle of Man.

From M.F.PERUTZ, CIVILIAN INTERNEE, CAMP 'L', INTERNMENT OPERATIONS, CANADA.

PRISONER OF WAR MAIL   **FREE**

FRANC DE PORT

SEP 3
7³⁰ PM
1940

EXAMINED BY CENSOR

Miss L. PERUTZ, Ph.D.
~~Jewish childrens Home~~ 4542 Calhoun St.
~~5342 Street Charles Avenue~~
NEW ORLEANS, La.
U.S.A.
5342 St. charles ave

23-8-40.

Dear Lotte, To-day I received your letter of 14/8, the first news since I left England + the ~~first~~ hopeful one since my internment began. I was terribly pleased to hear of all the efforts on my behalf. Since my last letter to you I could apply for release to serve England as a scientist. I also appealed to Bragg to support my application. I don't understand in what way you imagine the Rockefeller could help, as I don't see how to get on a preference quota. Anyway I don't intend to join you unless all efforts for my return to Engl. fail. Your letter was partly unintelligible to me, as I don't know the antecedents. Most important is to get father released + both parents over the ocean. I can't write to either of them directly on this stationary for fear of getting them into trouble. Please send india rubber, shoebrush, brown shoe cream, thick woollen scarf. Did mother send you or Franz my books, etc? Did Fankuchen get my thesis? Any news from Fritz? What happened to Josef + Vally? Please send my love to Fan, Kraus, Anne. Heini is with me + sends you his. Yours MAX

---

port my application. I don't understand in what way you imagine the Rockefeller could help, as I don't see how to get on a preference quota. Anyway I don't intend to join you unless all efforts for my return to Engl. fail. Your letter was partly unintelligible to me as I don't know the antecedents. Most important is to get father released and both parents over the ocean. I can't write to either of them directly on this stationery for fear of getting them into trouble. Please send india rubber, shoebrush, brown shoe cream, thick woollen scarf. Did mother send you or Franz my books, etc.? Did [Isidore]

Fankuchen get my thesis?[10] Any news from Fritz [Eirich]?[11] What happened to Josef and Vally [Perutz]? Please send my love to Fan, Kraus, Anne. Heini [Granichstaedten][12] is with me and sends you his.

To Tom Hughes. Camp L, Internment Operations, Canada, September 15, 1940

During the last 10 days I received the 1st letters from England, amongst them all my mother's up till 19 Aug., except those she sent to Douglas [Isle of Man]. I never got her money order nor the authorisation form. I hope you can draw on my account. Otherwise please could you send her what she needs until I or father return. It seems as if you have looked after my mother as if she were your own. I find it impossible to think of any words to thank you; they all sound so foolish if addressed to you. Moreover, your efforts have been quite beyond what one could thank anybody for in a letter. I hope you and your people are well. Believe me, in my posi-

Tom Hughes
(around 1953)

tion it is much worse to read of events in England than to be on the spot. I suppose you can well imagine my feelings.—There are many queries from my mother to be answered: My luggage should stay with you, because I hope to return as soon as Bragg's release application [for me] is granted. There can be no question of release in Canada, nor of emigration to the U.S.A. I should have to wait 3–4 years for the latter. My mother acted on incomplete information when she undertook steps in that direction. It is inadvisable to transfer money to me or to send me clothes. We get well clothed and fed by the army and there is really nothing I need. When will mother's U.S. quota be due? From my own experience I consider voluntary internment and transfer overseas inadvisable for her. Conditions are entirely unfit for parents' age. I received very nice letters from [W.

---

[10] He had been a member of Bernal's laboratory and had returned to New York.

[11] His very old friend from Vienna, nine years his senior, who had played a part in teaching him rock-climbing and who had persuaded Max's father to allow him to study chemistry and then to do a Ph.D. in Cambridge. He had been deported to Australia and was released only in 1943, because, according to Max, he was less circumspect than he should have been in replying to questioning.

[12] Heini Granichstaedten, fellow chemistry undergraduate and companion on the trip to Lapland.

Lawrence] Bragg, [Desmond] Bernal, [Peter] Wooster, [Hermann] Mark[13] and hope to reply one day. I was glad to hear from mother that Bragg wants me back. Could you tell him that and thank him in the meantime.—I am very fit and reasonably comfortable. I enjoy a certain amount of peace to study. I lecture once a week on Crystals and X-rays and hear excellent lectures on Vector Analysis and Mechanics. Perhaps I shall even learn math one day. Hoping to see you again soon. Keep well and give my love to mother.

To Lotte Perutz. Camp L, Internment Operations, Canada, September 22, 1940

I got your letters of 7 Sept. and 22 Aug., your parcel and $10. They will last me for months. I was terribly pleased with all the letters. Parcel was grand. Don't send me food. Mother should send me the Min. of Labour letter. My luggage should stay in Cambridge, as return for scientific work is my only chance. The following will make this clear. The Brit. Gov. transferred us to the custody of the Can. Mil. Authorities who classified us as Prisoners of War, Class 2. Our status as Refugees from Nazi oppression and our fervent support of the British Cause does not concern them. Competent for our release is solely the Home Office, London, who has no authority to release us here, but can *only* order our return. We cannot communicate with foreign consulates, solicitors, refugee organisations, but only with the Swiss Consul as representative of our "Protecting Power." Some men's emigration papers are complete and ready for them at the U.S. Consul, London. He refuses them

Hugo and Dely Perutz in 1943

---

[13]Peter Wooster was a lecturer in the Laboratory of Crystallography; Hermann Mark, formerly professor of physical chemistry in Vienna, had a post at Brooklyn Polytechnic University.

visa without a personal interview, or to forward their papers unless the internee himself sends a request to the Consul, Montreal. The latter sent us a message that he does not accept letters from internees who have not been released by the Home Office. The latter does not order the release of emigrants before they have the U.S. visa. My passport has been impounded and I don't know where it is. I have my other documents but cannot send them out of the camp. Please tell Mother to do all in her power to get me back; never mind the dangers. In the old climbing days we used to take greater risks for smaller gains. If there were a 70% risk of death in my return, I should take it at once to regain my freedom. Actually the risk is about 1%. I should add to this letter that our officers here fully realise our difficulties and are very kind to us. They do all in their power to help us. It is only due to the understanding and personal kindness of our Commandant that I am able to pursue my studies here.

To Anne Hartridge. Camp L, Internment Operations, Canada, September 25, 1940

The other day I got your letters of 22/7, 3/8, 11/8 and your mother's very kind letters. You can hardly imagine how pleased I was to hear from you and to know that you and your family are well and cheerful. I was terribly worried about you. I try to study but sometimes it's rather hard. I make desperate efforts to be sent home; everything moves at snail's pace. I wish we would at least not be kept in one category with Nazi Prisoners. [The censor deleted the following two and a half lines.] Keep well and think of me sometimes.

To Anne Hartridge. Camp L, Internment Operations, Canada, October 8, 1940

Thanks for your pleasant letter of 25/8 (also for those previously acknowledged). I am so glad you had a peaceful holiday. I saw a grand aurora borealis the other night. I couldn't observe it for long though, as we get locked up in the barracks at 9.30. I sleep with [figure deleted by censor] men in a room; as none of them snores, it isn't too bad. Please tell my parents: a) *I don't want to go to the U.S.A.* b) *I want to return to England as soon as possible.* c) Could they make every conceivable effort to that end. I should like to swim across the ocean if there were so much as a 1 per cent chance to reach England alive and I should be glad to have seen the last of this continent where, as far as I am concerned, the only unlimited possibility is the duration of my internment. It will be 5 months this week. Please remember me to the family.

To Lotte Perutz. Camp L, Internment Operations, Canada, October 13, 1940

I got your letter of 24/9, Father's of 25/9, Tom's of 1/9. Please acknowledge them as mail to Engl. takes 7 weeks. I was shocked that they still believe release in Canada or to the U.S. to be possible. Release orders for some have arrived, but the Can. Govt. will not consider releasing anybody here, not even a specialist who would be useful to the country, as they don't want to set a precedent. There is no intention to create a machinery whereby men possessing U.S. visa could proceed there directly. I am fully informed from newspapers, and from letters we received from Refugee Committees. The sole way to freedom leads to England. It is extremely urgent that the parents should realise this. They should discredit English news stories to the contrary. Father will appreciate that I'd rather be dead than remain a prisoner. The supply of stationery has stopped, so don't worry if you don't hear from me. The parents' efforts for me are grand.

To Anne Hartridge. Camp N, Ottawa, November 17, 1940

Recently I got your letters of 20 Aug., 5 Sept. and 1 Oct. They were so nice and I was terrifically pleased to get them and to know that you are well and cheerful, that you had a pleasant holiday and that you stopped working in London. You have been terribly nice to my people and they praise you in almost every letter and always give me the latest news about you. I had quite an exciting time recently. I spent 5 days in a local police prison (real Sing Sing steel cage—I shall never go to the zoo again) and amused myself listening to local drunks etc. in neighbouring cells.[14] The days were rather dull except for some talks with local policemen. When I told them that I was a refugee they were unimpressed. So I changed my policy and related fairy tales of how I had blown up 5 bridges, 7 powder factories and 3 police stations in England and then I was treated with awed respect. On my return to the camp I found that I had been appointed associate Professor of Biophysics at a New York College and two days later received a cable informing me that my release and return to England had been granted. You can imagine what this news meant after 6 months of utter hopelessness. So

---

[14]Sing Sing is a maximum security prison in the United States. When the decision was taken to separate the Protestants and Jews from the Catholics, Max lied about his religion so as to remain with his friend Heini Granichstaedten. He was sent to gaol on being unmasked.

now I await anxiously to be sent back. I am told that it will be soon and there may actually be a chance that my dream to see you by Xmas comes true.—I am rather amused to see how my scientific reputation rises in proportion with the length of my internment; "eminent scholar" being just about the least epithet used by Americans who were overwhelmed by the cumulative effect of recommendations from my Professor and friends. If I remain behind barbed wire for another 5 years the Nobel Prize is certain to be awarded to me. In case I don't see you before then I wish you many happy returns of your birthday and to all the Hartridges a merry Xmas and a happy New Year. But I do hope that I'll see you. I am very homesick. Let my people know that I am well, please.

To Hugo and Dely Perutz. Camp N, Ottawa, November 24, 1940

Your last letter is dated 21 Oct. but I got your telegram dated 11 Nov. We can all write on this blank paper now and send it by airmail.

You can imagine how pleased I was to get simultaneously the news of my release and the appointment in New York. My release order arrived, but on the whole my position is not much more hopeful than before. As you know my release order has no effect in Canada and I am subjected to the same restrictions and military discipline as all the other prisoners of war—this being still our legal status.

Whether and when I shall be sent back I don't know. Some got their release order last September and are still here.

I can do nothing about the professorship in New York, because we are forbidden to communicate with the U.S. consul who, we are told, will have nothing to do with us. The official comment was "for the time being Prof. Perutz will have to take his chair in this camp." I have written to the president of the New School for Social Research [in New York City] accepting the job and suggesting ways to help me, but it is doubtful whether he will be able to help, since strong forces seem to be opposed to anybody's direct emigration, or indeed to any form of release. Please ask Mr. Pickthorn M.P.[15] to urge that I regain my freedom and Prof. Bragg to keep me a job.

As I don't know whether I fulfil requirements for a non-quota visa, I wonder whether the London Consul would grant me one.

I am in good health but rather dejected at these constant disappointments.

---

[15]Member of Parliament for Cambridge University.

To Lotte Perutz. Camp B, Ottawa, Canada, November 29, 1940

I got your letter of 11/3. I hope you are clear about my job in New York now. I heard nothing of endeavours of local committees to get me into the States. Meanwhile things started to move slowly. My release order arrived and I was transferred to another camp where I shall no longer get mail which will be forwarded straight to Cambridge. It is not known when we shall leave, it may be days, weeks or months. I informed Prof. Johnson of the New School of my impending departure and told him that I shall take matters up when I come to England. A man whose case was similar to mine asked whether he could stay here until the matter of direct emigration to the U.S. was cleared, but was told by the Military that he might forfeit his release by not going and that there was no hope of direct emigration. In the train I met Dr. Granichstaedten who had been promised that he would be sent to Camp N to join Heini and was sent here with me by mistake. There is hope that Heini will be sent here too. You can't imagine what Dr. Granichstaedten has had to go through. Compared to his sufferings I felt like a little boy making a fuss about having cut his finger. He bore his ordeal heroically and his wit, humour and interest are unbroken. He has become a bit of a queer old gentleman though and has rather aged in his looks. He sends you his kindest regards. This is a purely Jewish camp, in a way the best I have seen. However, I am sick of waiting and fed up to the brim. I just can't understand how a man with a 10 years imprisonment term does not commit suicide. But the fact that the Home Office ordered my release does not give me any privileges or relaxation of any of the restrictions imposed on Prisoners of War.—I am so tired of it all and so homesick that I nearly cry when I think of it.

Cambridge

To Dr. Warren Weaver, of the Rockefeller Foundation. January 26, 1941

I returned here a short time ago and want to take this opportunity of thanking you for all your generous and kind efforts in connection with my release and entry into the U.S. I should have liked very much to come to the California Institute of Technology as you suggested to Prof. Bragg, especially so since Prof. [Linus] Pauling's laboratory has now become the focus of all research on the molecular structure of proteins.

You may have heard from Prof. Alvin Johnson how I was sent off to England before anything could be done. I was told by the Canadian Authorities that there will be no possibility to enter the U.S. directly.

Prof. Bragg asked me to continue my work with him and I am really very happy to do so. I know that I did not yet stay long enough with Prof. Bragg to gain all I could from his vast knowledge and experience, and moreover I feel that his bold intuition may one day help us to find the clue to the fundamental problem of protein structure.

In conclusion I should like to thank you as the representative of the Foundation for all the help you have given me not only on this particular occasion, but throughout the last few years. Without the research grant from the Foundation I doubt whether I should ever have been able to follow up those first few results on X-ray diffraction from haemoglobin crystals.

To Evelyn Machin, January 29, 1941

I postponed writing to you several times because I wanted to wait until I could write a real, long letter. There was so much to do in the first rush of my newly acquired freedom and I spent most evenings just talking to my parents. Well to begin with you can't imagine how immensely happy I am to be back again. I had spent days and nights imagining what coming home would be like, but the real thing surpassed all expectation. People seem to have forgotten all the grudges they ever had against me and to remember just nothing but what a jolly good fellow Perutz had always been. Besides they all had such trouble getting me out that the successful conclusion of their labours alone would have provided them with sufficient satisfaction. I believe the past fortnight has certainly been one of my happiest and perhaps also the most successful I ever had.

Bragg (now Sir Lawrence) is taking me back again and cabled to the Rockefeller Foundation for continuation of my grant with increased salary. I started to do some teaching and have become part-time demonstrator in one of [Peter] Wooster's classes. I insisted with Bragg that I want to do some war work besides the continuation of my haemoglobin research and I have already picked up some problems. Bragg has a very bad conscience that he did not get me out earlier and moreover appears to be genuinely pleased to have me back and to have that weight off his mind and he is extremely nice to me. Of course, he always has been, except during the months of May and

June when he believed all he read about dangerous foreigners in the papers and was very reluctant to take any steps for my release. It was only when public opinion had changed that he went into action after much deliberation and with devastating effect, somewhat like a battleship. He not only secured my release but also, at my mother's suggestion, provided me with a job in the U.S.A. I don't know whether you got any letters from Canada or not, but anyway I received an appointment as Associate Professor of Biophysics at a New York college and a safe promise of an even better job (without professor) at California University once I come to the States. (The Professorial title is necessary to get a so-called preference visa to the U.S.A.)

It all came to nothing because of the obstruction by the Canadian Military Authorities and American Consul in Montreal. If I had refused to return to England (which was beyond my will power because I wanted to return with all my heart) I might eventually have reached the States after staying in hell for another 6 months or more, but at the same time I should have risked to remain interned for the duration had it come to nothing, because I should have forfeited my chance to return. In Canada I had a thoroughly unpleasant time and for all I care I don't ever want to see that country again. I was so disgusted with most of the officers and soldiers I met and particularly with the average attitude of the press. I never imagined that the dominions would be so different from the mother country. Democracy and its principles have none of the vigour and conviction there that one finds here.

"At Christmas, we were finally taken to Halifax, where we were met by one of Britain's prison commissioners—the shrewd and humane Alexander Paterson, sent out by the Home Office to interview any of the internees who wanted to return to Britain. . . . Paterson explained that it had been impossible to ship any of us home earlier, because the Canadians had insisted that prisoners of war must not be moved without a military escort, yet had refused either to release us in Canada or to escort us to England, on the grounds that our internment was a British affair. The British War Office had now fulfilled the letter of the regulation by detailing a single Army captain to take us home."[16]

I had a most pleasant return journey. I actually spent over 3 weeks on the boat, where we were practically free and acted as part of the crew. After what lay behind us the journey was most luxurious and a real holiday. There were no incidents of any kind, and if you are by yourself, potential dangers don't worry you. I was actually released within 3 hours after leaving the boat

[16]Perutz M.F. 2003. Enemy alien. *I Wish I'd Made You Angry Earlier.* Cold Spring Harbor Laboratory Press. Cold Spring Harbor, NY, p. 80. First published in 1985 in *The New Yorker.*

at Liverpool. I needn't describe to you how pleased my parents were. They had known nothing of my return and the first thing they heard of it was when I rang them up from London. My mother really did admirable work during these months. She spent all her time working for my father's and my release and her success speaks for the efficiency with which she has gone about her task.[17] My release was actually ordered in October, but the Canadian brass-hats took no notice of the Home Office's requests until a Home Office official appeared over there and made a row about it.

To the Aliens War Service Department, March 17, 1941

I should be obliged if you could send me an application form for the Aliens Auxiliary War Service Permit. I am of Austrian nationality (Home Office File No. 7685/2) and work here as a Research Assistant to Professor Sir Lawrence Bragg. Before his recent departure for Canada Sir Lawrence arranged with Professor E.K. Rideal that I should take up research on certain problems connected with lubrication together with other members of the Dept. of Colloid Science. Under existing regulations I am not permitted to enter that Dept. except by special arrangement in each case. The work is now expanding beyond our expectations and would be greatly facilitated if I could be given official permission to carry out research in Colloid Science.

To Miss Esther Simpson, Secretary of the Society for the Protection of Science and Learning, September 14, 1941

For some time past my father has been trying to find employment and recently volunteered to join a Government Training Centre for War Workers in the Engineering Industry. In the course of his endeavours he ran up against countless difficulties. The sum of these appears to me to be more than accidental and I thought that perhaps you might know the appropriate authority who could help my father to overcome the obstacles that are being put in his way.

My father (Hugo PERUTZ) is 63, quite fit and anxious to help this country in any possible way. Between 27 Jan. and 14 Aug. of this year he visited the local employment exchange 12 times.

Now he received the following letter dated 11 Sept.: "With reference to your application for training in the Engineering Industry it is desired to

---

[17]My grandfather had been released in September 1940.

inform you that there may not be an early opportunity for you to enter training as some delay is likely to occur before a final decision is reached regarding your eligibility." On receiving this my father went to see the man who had accepted his application and asked for the reason for the delay. He was told that only 25% aliens are accepted. On the other hand the man admitted that the Training Centre is half empty. It looks to me rather as if someone in the Ministry of Labour here does not like the idea of employing aliens, and by means of dilatory tactics tries to put them off as much as possible.

I really can't understand the idea behind it. On the one hand, my father has to register for war work, has to listen to speeches by Government spokesmen telling him how desperately short we are of labour, proclaiming that every man and woman in the country is wanted for the fight against Hitlerism. As soon as he tries to put into practice what he is, in theory, supposed to do, his enthusiasm is damped [sic] as tactfully as possible and he is given to understand that he isn't really wanted.

Please excuse my bothering you with this problem but I thought you might possibly know what to do about it.

To Lotte Perutz, November 16, 1941

There has been one great event in my life, overshadowing even the excitements of research. I got engaged, and not to Anne. It's a long story how this came about, and I shall not start at the beginning, but rather at the end. She is called Gisela Peiser; I mentioned her and her brother, a research student in Crystallography in my last letter to you. She is nice, of course, but it's hard to give you a vivid description of her and I have no photograph. She has lovely features and a great deal of pleasantly brown hair, beautiful teeth and a fascinating smile and kindly eyes coloured like a rainbow. She is 26 and born in Berlin which is rather a blow. She left that cursed place when she was 17 though, and polished her education first in England and then in Paris. In 1933 her father moved his business to Switzerland and Gisela joined him there. Later she went back to Berlin to liquidate her parents' belongings and finally entered the Polytechnic in Zürich to read photography.[18] She went to

---

[18]Neither Gisela nor her brother could remain in Switzerland because they were refused work permits. While my grandparents educated my uncle at St. Paul's School and the University of Cambridge, they arranged for my mother, who had hoped to complete her schooling and study medicine, to do a diploma in medical photography, because with that qualification she would not have to take a job as a maid in England. As a precaution, they also sent her to learn secretarial and basic accounting skills.

London and got a job as medical photographer at Bart's Hospital. Finally in the spring of 1940 the grant for that job was stopped because of the war and she took on a job at the Society for the Protection of Science and Learning which she still holds. There she is official translator from any language into any other (she seems to know most, including Swiss), accountant and general understudy of the boss. Her parents are still in Switzerland. Her brother is younger, went to school in this country and has become naturalised. Now so far the description was easy, but to give you an idea what kind of person she is will be much more difficult. She has

Gisela Peiser:
engagement photo

none of the evil characteristics of her Nationality and few of the external ones. She has a sense of humour, though a bit different from ours in some things and she has a sense of proportion which I greatly admire and an extraordinary amount of common sense. She is very intelligent and also intellectual, but in a nice, unpretentious and unobtrusive way. Altogether she is damned clever and in a pleasant constructive kind of a way. She seems to

Max: engagement photo

have a genuine interest for science, which she had before she met me. She has a social conscience to which is added a great deal of experience as a social worker at that Society. Finally I think she is efficient and industrious in her work. I know few of her friends and liked the ones I met so far. One rather serious snag is that as soon as we talk German her northern accent makes me freeze up; there are so many unpleasant associations connected with it and I couldn't get over it yet. So we gave it up and stick to English, which Gisela talks very correctly (she has a scientific way of learning languages with grammars, and dictionaries and idiom books) but with an accent that sounds quite pleasant. A less serious snag is that her life in Zurich seems to have had a decisive influence on her taste as regards clothes. She also has Swiss legs. Apart from that our tastes harmonise very well; she is enterprising and likes the same kind of books, pictures, music, mountains, people, landscapes as I do. She also seems to have the same kind of temperament, unruffled and yet not phlegmatic. We certainly get on marvellously together. When I read all this again I find that the description is quite inadequate and makes her look terribly priggish and virtuous which is far from the truth. As Gisela pointed out when I proposed to her, it would of course be better for my career to marry an English girl, but then it's no good running about and crying for the moon and saying I want a girl as nice as this one and she must also be a British subject.

All this looks as if I had callously deserted Anne, who was so good to me when I was in Canada and gave me a tremendous welcome on my return. Actually she could never make up her mind whether she was or was not in love with me. But somehow we were too different in temperament to be a good match and finally last July Anne made up her mind that it wasn't any good and that she couldn't marry me. I was very sad about that at the time, but I am glad now it didn't come off. I saw Anne last Saturday in town and told her all about it. Altogether I am very fond of her and hope that Saturday wasn't the last I saw of her.[19]

I managed to bring Gisela together with Wopp [wife of Fritz Eirich] who has no suspicions so far and Wopp's spontaneous comment on Gisela was that she is "clever and natural and unpretentious and good-looking on top of it." Although I had found that out for myself I was quite pleased to have it confirmed from Wopp who has a sound judgement of people. We want to get married as soon as Father will have found a job and provided we can find a place to live in.[20] This town is fearfully overcrowded and it's a devil of a job to get a flat or lodgings. Financially we ought to be quite well off as Gisela gets £4 a week and our combined income would be in the neighbourhood of 600 pounds a year.

I have to write to Gisela's parents now and I haven't the faintest idea how to start.

Gisela to Herbert and Nelly Peiser, November 18, 1941

You always told me not to expect a prince—I never really did, but I found one. He looks a bit like F.D., not very tall, dark, very young looking—he is actually only a year older than I am. He is very quiet—I mean in his behav-

---

[19]They remained lifelong friends; Anne was one of Max's few wedding guests.

[20]Max's father had just completed a course qualifying him to operate a lathe in the hope that he could take the place of one of the many men who had been called up. He quickly found a job working for the local railway company, the LNER (London and North Eastern Railway), and later a rather better job working for a Cambridge ironmonger, Mackays.

iour, we can talk enough all right! But his most striking characteristics seem to me, Sensible and Sensitive. He has an amazing amount of common sense, of cool and sober vision of any person or situation coupled with great sensitiveness for other people's feelings and reactions. His own actions seem to be dictated by a marvellous mixture of intelligence, feeling and warmth. I should not think that his feelings will run away with him easily, but they run deep.

I got hold of a statement about his work describing him as a brilliant man.[21] I think the result is probably what strikes you as brilliant—applied to his personality it seems the wrong term.

To Herbert and Nelly Peiser, November 19, 1941

Gisela has told me much about you. Even so it is difficult for me to form a picture of you sufficiently vivid to prevent this letter from becoming an impersonal statement. I feel it is so unfair on you that you cannot even see the man who wants to marry your daughter, that the least I could do is to try and make this a personal letter.

You cannot imagine how proud and happy I am to be engaged to Gisela. I had never dared to hope that I should get a wife as nice as this and sometimes it still seems too good to be true. Whether it is not foolish of Gisela to want to marry me is hardly for me to say and it is difficult to take the objective view where oneself is involved. Nothing is certain these days, but it is at least probable that a citizen of this country could have offered Gisela greater security. I shall try to do my best in this direction, but I don't know whether it will be good enough. I can just hope that the good luck which has carried me so far will continue.

Judging from my own parents' reactions in a case like this I expect you will want to know something of my background. Both my parents come from families of textile manufacturers in Bohemia. My father was born and brought up in Prague. After having spent three years in England he settled down in Vienna where he became partner of a cotton printing mill. My mother is Viennese; she got married to my father in 1904. They lived in Vienna until March 1938. I went to school in Vienna and learnt a great deal about skiing and mountains and little else that I have not forgotten since. In 1932 I entered Vienna University as a student of chemistry and read this subject with much enthusiasm. After 3 years, however, I felt a great urge to go

---

[21]Letters of recommendation, which Gisela would have seen at work, from both Bragg and Bernal had called Max "brilliant."

abroad in order to escape from the stagnant atmosphere which then prevailed in Austria generally and at the universities in particular. I finished my studies at Vienna with a kind of general exam which one had to pass before starting work on one's dissertation and left for Cambridge in Sept. 1936. By an odd coincidence I became research student in the Dept. of Crystallography which is part of the Cavendish Laboratory (Physics) and was then under Lord Rutherford.[22] During the first year I worked on a variety of subjects without hitting on any particularly promising line. Late in 1937 I found that X-ray methods could be applied to crystals of haemoglobin, the substance which fills the red blood corpuscles. With the exception of 6 months' glacier research on the Jungfraujoch I have been working on haemoglobin ever since, and favourable circumstances provided, I shall continue on this problem for some time to come. In 1938 the Rockefeller Foundation became interested in the haemoglobin research and in January 1939 appointed me research assistant to Prof. Sir Lawrence Bragg (Rutherford's successor) a post which I have held ever since. I took my Ph.D. degree here about 20 months ago.

I rather fear that to you this kind of work must appear hopelessly academic. I believe I can allay your anxieties on this point at least. My research concerns the very general problem of protein structure which is of topical interest for nearly all branches of physiology and pathology. If I should manage to solve it completely—which is unlikely—the rewards would be great indeed. If I only bring it some steps nearer to its solution I shall still have reasonable prospects in the scientific world here or in the U.S.A. I should add that in the course of years I have become very attached to this country and that I feel completely at home here.

I should like to tell you again how I sympathise with you for having no opportunity to judge for yourself whether or not Gisela made the right choice. Anyhow it must be something of a blow to be presented like this with an accomplished fact. I do hope that I shall meet you one day.

To Lotte Perutz, January 5, 1942

I had wanted to write to you for ages, but never did, having always waited for my temper to improve. The low level of this temper was not due to any shad-

---

[22]The coincidence was this: Max had asked his professor, Hermann Mark, who was visiting Cambridge, to arrange for him to do a Ph.D. with Gowland Hopkins. When Max questioned Mark, it emerged that he had quite forgotten, but all was not lost because Mark remembered that Bernal had told him that he was looking for a research student. The additional coincidence was that in 1942 Gisela's brother was a research student in the same department.

ows on my relationship to Gisela—on the contrary the longer we know each other, the more I see of her the happier I am with her and about her. She is a marvellous girl really and much as I love her I cannot but admire her and the way she does things with a minimum of fuss and maximum of efficiency.

Well, telling the parents was quite a job and when at last I managed to bring Gisela along a couple of times our engagement was already a month old. I couldn't bring her before because Mother had 'flu and couldn't have any visitors around. Father likes Gisela a lot and I think Mother would if she wouldn't want to marry me. Mother objects to her nationality and believes it would be harmful to my career, and she also thinks that at 26 Gisela is too old for me. She is pleased about her "good family" and her good manners and upbringing. On the other hand she feels hurt and left out, when it becomes obvious that I tell Gisela much more about everything and that altogether she is much nearer to me already than Mother ever was. And she objects to not having been told earlier which is really not my fault and was done purely out of consideration for the parents. In a fit of anger she actually told me that I had done exactly the same thing to them as Hans Oppenheim to his parents. If I had known that Mother would feel that way I could easily have invented a few lies and made it appear more recent. It was one of those occasions where frankness decidedly did not pay.

Mother's chief worry seems to be economic, though. She fears that life for them will be more expensive if I don't live with them any longer and that they won't be able to manage on what Father earns. Now you know that the parents have consistently refused to accept any help from me but I hope they will allow me to make up for this difference, at least. Gisela and I will be comfortably off with our combined salaries and in addition Gisela expects to get some allowance from her parents who seem to be quite wealthy. I was very surprised when I discovered she was rich in addition to everything else. That I never suspected.[23]

14 January Gisela came to Cranleigh over the week-end to see Max and Evelyn and they liked each other a lot. This is a very good thing as often such friendships go to pieces when one marries. I also went to Oxford to talk proteins and returned very satisfied with my trip.

Approval from the Peiser parents arrived at last to-day. We both wrote to them last November shortly after the letter to you and received a wire in

---

[23]It emerges from one of Gisela's letters that the offer of considerable financial assistance depended on the sale either of some nice pieces of furniture or of Gisela's father's life insurance policy, neither of which Gisela would countenance.

return last night. It is obviously penned by Gisela's father:

> "Your charming two letters so keenly awaited
> Arrived but last night therefore badly belated
> To say we consent this would hardly be right
> What we feel is far more it is joy and delight."

Which is sweet of them I think. Gisela's father lived here and in the colonies for about 15 years, hence the perfection of the English.

To Lotte Perutz, February 1, 1942

[My engagement] has now progressed so far that we are contemplating to get married soon, possibly on 21 Feb. It all boils down to flats, and we now hope to have found a place where we would have to move in fairly soon. It's not ideal, it's sharing a house with a woman whose husband's been called up (no children), but there are practically no unfurnished places going. Besides it's really absurd to buy furniture now when it has increased in price by about 300%. The place is cheap and that is most important. All the time I lived with the parents the bulk of our money has gone up in rent.

All your advice to me was much to the point. Being engaged has already become more of a burden than a pleasure and delight. The only time, in fact, when it has been delightful was when it was all secret and that time one [i.e., Max's mother] grudged us. At the moment it's wearing us down and we feel the shorter it lasts the better. Your warnings as regards Mother were even more topical—probably unconsciously she has a marvellous instinct for poisoning the atmosphere between us, just by harping on any point that is most likely to hurt me in this connection. She loathes the idea of my getting married to Gisela—or perhaps merely my getting married—and it often looks as though everything in her revolts at the idea.

Father is desperately looking for a job and I do hope that he will find something. If he doesn't our marriage will probably be a washout, because I can't leave the parents without any regular income. Still I believe that after some time he will find a job.

I am getting better though terribly slowly.[24] It is a shame that I am not well because it is such hard luck on Gisela in many ways, as I can't help being bad-tempered sometimes and can't do much in the way of going out

---

[24]Max was suffering from undiagnosed coeliac disease and food intolerance; stress always aggravated his condition.

and running about. The work is getting on too slowly, again on account of my not putting as much energy into it as usual.

You were quite right about Gisela being a strong personality. She always knows very definitely what she wants which is a great thing and is unruffled by most crises—usually family troubles on her side or mine.[25] We have not had a row so far, probably because we are both people who don't much go in for rows. The worst period so far was when I was ill and felt very unaffectionate towards (or against) everybody, and a lover being a sensitive thermometer on these things, Gisela noticed it and began to fear that I didn't love her after all. Apart from these minor troubles it's all a success so far.

To Lotte Perutz, March 16, 1942

[This letter opens with a passage advising Lotte to move away from New Orleans.]

I always belittled the effects which people alleged the Cambridge climate had on you, and now I see that suddenly, from one day to another, the cold and dampness become insupportable evils, particularly if you sit here all year without interruption. Mother can hardly move for rheumatism which never leaves her, Father has had a cold for over two months, and my troubles are not least due to the climate.[26] Even Gisela who is the very picture of health gets terrible attacks of rheumatism. All this is to show *not* what a terrible life it is here, for Cambridge is a marvellous place in many other ways, but that one might not feel the effect of bad climatic conditions for years and then suddenly they beset one, particularly so if one has not the means to spend longish holidays in a better climate.

Now about us: Gisela and I are marrying on the 28th. We are going to marry at the Register Office here, with only the parents, Wopp and Steffen (Gisela's brother) in attendance. We are then going to London and having a small party of friends at Gisela's aunt. We then want to stay in town for a couple of days and see a play and a film and then go to the country for a week. We still haven't managed to find rooms, though.

---

[25]In fact, Gisela's mother acquiesced less readily than the poem implies. She had misgivings about Max's origins in the lax society of Vienna and worried that his digestive problems and his general ill health might be hereditary.

[26]Whereas central heating or large tiled stoves and well-insulated houses were the norm in middle-class Austrian houses before the war, in Cambridge, private houses were heated with either open coal or gas fires; these were so ill-designed that 90% of their heat was lost to the chimney. Walls and roofs were uninsulated and double glazing was unknown.

Family life at home is still a strenuous affair. Although I admire Father more and more for his patience and tenacity and his unfailing good temper in adversity, Mother is terribly difficult. Your contribution of $20 per month will be extremely welcome and will make the parents' position much easier. You see the position is this: Gisela and I earn together over £600 a year. After payment of income tax and some laboratory fees less than £400 remain. The very minimum which we shall need for the two of us is over 300. So that I can let the parents have not more than ~70–80. There is a chance that the income tax for married couples will be reduced as we have to pay about £70 more after we marry than the sum total of our income taxes while we remain single. I asked Franz 6 weeks ago to repay his debt to the parents at the rate of $20 monthly and appealed very strongly to his conscience. I hope he will do it. I didn't ask you for anything as I did not think you had any money to spare and thought you had had a bad enough time already and really deserved a more comfortable life.

My work went well these past few weeks. I gave quite a successful lecture on my recent findings—Bragg was there and made very appreciative remarks about my work afterwards and also told me that he liked the lecture. I also wrote a short paper summarising my findings on the molecular structure of haemoglobin up to date, and the paper is going to *Nature*. It's quite an important one and contributes the first step in the solution of the great problem. In peacetime it would have made a certain amount of stir, but now very few people remain who still devote themselves to academic problems.

To Franz Perutz, March 16, 1942

Father has a job at the moment, but it is a rotten one and he is trying to be released from it and to get a better one. The difficulty is that one is not allowed to change one's employment without permission of the Ministry of Labour. Father worked on night shifts for 6 nights running last week and for some stupid reason was cheated of his overtime pay. After the night shift he had to walk home 40 minutes at 6.00 am. So you can imagine how exhausted he was by the end of the week. Now his employer agreed that until he gets the Ministry's permission he can work on day-shifts from 9–5.30. This is a blessing, but he doesn't earn nearly enough (£3.12.0 weekly).[27] So I still hope he will get a job with a firm paying better wages; this particular one does not pay trade-union rates.

---

[27]Before decimalisation, there were 20 shillings to a pound and 12 pence to a shilling.

To Hans and Annemarie Wendon.[28]
Hartley Wintney, Hants, April 1, 1942

After reading through Gis's enthusiastic lines I am at a loss to give adequate expression to my gratitude for all you did for us. The show looked as though you had a magic ring which makes a djinnee [sic] obey your commands and produce the food you desire out of his sleeve—or French Champagne for that matter. But this is not all. After all this frantic preparation I would have expected the family Wendriner to be at the brink of a nervous break-down, switching a forced smile on as the bell rings as the first visitors arrive and knowing that after bearing the ordeal for another two hours they could at last go to bed. But nothing of the sort happened, the family Wendriner seemed as happy and unconcerned and giving out of the full [sic] as if the aforementioned Djinnee had brought it all in on an enormous tray. Really we enjoyed it tremendously and it was grand to see happy faces all around. Speaking for my friends and family I am quite certain that they loved it from beginning to end. I only hope you liked them as much as they liked you.

To Herbert and Nelly Peiser. Hartley Wintney, Hants, April 1, 1942

[Max wrote a very similar letter to Lotte Perutz on 12 April. I have integrated a couple of sentences from that letter into this one but the remainder of that letter appears below.]

Months have passed since my last letter to you. I should have written before to thank you for your letters and for the wholehearted approval which you gave to our engagement, although I know that this was not, and in the circumstances could not have been, any compliment to me, but only the expression of your profound trust in Gisela's good sense. The trouble was I did not know what to write. I had no desire to present you with an account of all the obstacles which Gis and I had to overcome before we could marry and which made our wedding date appear like the top end of some very long Swiss glacier. These are slightly convex and as you go up hour after hour the end recedes further and further in the distance above. So instead of sending you an account of the crevasses lying ahead, I rather waited for the time when I could write a post-card from the top.

---

[28]Their surname was anglicised from Wendrina to Wendon; they were Gisela's uncle and aunt, whom Max addressed as "My Dear Vice-in Laws."

Well, the Wedding was a great success and really everybody, including ourselves, enjoyed it immensely. The ceremony at the Register Office was simple and unpretentious and yet in a way impressive. Gisela looked very nice, Steffen was terribly excited, more so than any of us. Wopp was sweet and the parents quite enjoyed it. It was even quite solemn at various moments. After the wedding we all went to the station and took the train to London. We had lunch on the train which eased the situation, as we didn't all have to sit in a row and gape at one another. In London we went straight to Gisela's relations, consisting of uncle, aunt and two boys aged 15 and 18 and the celebrations there were really the climax of the show. They outstripped everything conceivable in the way of hospitality and generosity. There was no trouble they did not go to in order to provide all the traditional trimmings of a wedding, not even the French Champagne was missing—the devil only knows how they managed to procure it. On top of it all they were not the nervous wrecks you would expect to find after all this frantic preparation but the most cheerful and congenial hosts imaginable. There was an astonishing quantity of marvellous food.

The guests consisted exclusively of people we were particularly fond of. Our only grief was your absence, and that of my sister in the U.S.A., and then there were also two friends of mine in Britain who live too far away from London. Steffen read your magnificent speech. It made a great impression on us all. As time went on we all felt gay and happy and excited, particularly Gis and I. We forgot about the graver issues and just enjoyed the moment.

To Lotte Perutz, April 12, 1942

Father Peiser sent a speech which Steffen read. It sounded a bit long and solemn, but it makes good reading. After 2 hours or so we vanished on the quiet and then we stayed for 3 days at a hotel in London which was extremely comfortable and not too expensive. We went sightseeing to Hampton Court on Sunday and shopping on Monday and at last found and bought the two pieces of furniture which we need most, a wardrobe and a writing desk, and all sorts of necessities. It is terribly difficult to buy the things you want, no matter what it is, and most articles which are not subject to government price control have gone up by anything between 30 and 300 percent. Furniture in particular is hopelessly expensive. For the money we spent on the two pieces we could, in former times, have furnished a whole room. Both are second hand, but particularly the desk is very nice.

Steffen Peiser (about 1942)

I cannot conclude without telling you again how proud and happy I am to have Gis as my wife. I hope our marriage will be as perfect and happy and successful as the wedding was.

On the 31st we went to a village in Hampshire and stayed for a week at a little pub. The place had all the charms of the English countryside. Hills and woods and fields and beautiful estates. There was a castle nearby built in 1612, one of the most magnificent early English Renaissance houses I have come across, and a gorgeous estate around it. We also went to Salisbury and Winchester. The latter is the prettiest town I ever saw in this country with a magnificent Norman and Gothic cathedral. Salisbury is nice too, but not as impressive as Winchester.

We returned last Wednesday and on Friday a conference started on: "The Application of X-Ray Crystallography in Industry." About 300 people attended from all over the country; I never knew that so many crystallographers exist. Of course the majority were not crystallographers, but merely interested and many used the opportunity to leave their dreary factories in the Midlands and the North to come here at their firms' expense. The result was that dozens of friends and acquaintances of mine converged and I had two hectic days talking to everybody and exchanging information and listening to lectures. I learned a great deal, partly from the public discussion and partly in private talks and made many valuable contacts. Steffen came here with people from his firm,[29] Tom arrived full of beans; Dorothy Crowfoot [Hodgkin] from Oxford, Bernal, [Dennis] Riley and many others whose names you don't know.

The parents are also much better than when I left them. Father has been without a job for 3 weeks and that did him a lot of good. Mother isn't so frightfully worried now about their living expenses because I found a good formula for supporting the parents as much as they need at any time, without hurting mother's pride. I guaranteed the parents an income of £6 a week, i.e. if Father earns nothing I give them the full amount, if Father earns say £4 a week I make it up to £6. If I give the parents the full amount I have to take most of it from my savings, of course, but 1–2 pounds a week I can manage on current income. Your $20 will be very welcome in this connec-

---

[29] He had left Cambridge to work at I.C.I.

tion, of course. Mother takes my money not as a gift, but as repayment of the £500 the parents gave me in 1936 for my studies in Cambridge. I am glad I reached this settlement in the week before we married, because I left the parents without having the feeling that I had done them a bad turn, Mother had no grudges and didn't threaten anymore that she would start work in a factory. Father has prospects of another job with reasonable working hours. I hope this one will be alright.

If the war wouldn't be in such a dreadful state, things wouldn't really look bad for us just now. Still, I hope that one day the Americans will really start doing something and then maybe the position will improve again.

To Evelyn Machin, April 28, 1942

Gis and I are very happy, in fact I cannot remember having ever been as contented as I am now. Apart from the happiness of being married, I am terribly glad to have got away from home. The views of Mother and me are diametrically opposed on most subjects and her increasing despondency drove me nearly crazy. You must imagine that every word she says, practically, is a complaint against her fate. While I felt terribly sorry for her being homesick and tired and overworked and suffering from constant rheumatism, I felt I couldn't do more than help her to the limits of my capacity in time and money, and when she used the smallest opportunity to have another attack of despair, I just didn't feel strong enough to cope with it month after month. Either you have to harden yourself and give up all feelings of pity or sympathy, or you are driven to melancholy yourself. I always find it much easier to get on with Father who takes things as they come and never complains against things that can't be helped.

To Mr. H.M. Miller of the Rockefeller Foundation, August 8, 1942

I should like to take this opportunity to thank you for all the help you are giving to me. The research on the crystal structure of haemoglobin would never have got beyond the initial stages without the help of the Foundation. Now I hope it will be greatly accelerated by the enlargement of my team.

You may be interested to hear that Sir Lawrence [Bragg] has called together a small conference for the end of September in order to discuss the structure of the globular proteins generally and of haemoglobin in particular. Most of the attendants will be people whose research is funded by the Foundation. Professor [Gilbert] Chibnall of London and Mrs. Hodgkin (Crowfoot) of Oxford have promised to come and we are hoping that Dr. [Gilbert] Adair, Dr. [Kenneth] Bailey, Professor [David] Keilin and Professor Bernal will join us. We chiefly want to persuade the biochemists to devote more energy to the amino-acid analysis of haemoglobin because it would be of great help to the crystallographic research if we knew more of the chemical composition of the substance which we are investigating. Finally I hope to persuade some people here to investigate the splitting of haemoglobin by various agents in the ultra-centrifuge and by measuring the diffusion constants.

To Herbert and Nelly Peiser, September 17, 1942

To begin with I want to wish Father many happier returns of his birthday, and that there will be better years again without constant grief and worry and misery and war. We have been very much upset by all the frightful news and the feeling of helplessness it gives one.

Life continues to be pleasant for ourselves. My research flourishes and is as fascinating as ever. As long as I am in the laboratory it is easy to forget the war and all outside troubles. I just published another short paper and made arrangements that a reprint should be sent to you. The summer is nearly over now and with it the most favourable time for experimental work. I am quite pleased with the progress achieved. In the winter there is always a lot of teaching to be done. There is going to be a pleasant interruption on 29 Sept. My Professor has called together a small conference to discuss some problems relating to proteins in general and my work in particular. People are coming from Oxford, London and Leeds and the show promises to become very interesting. Our idea is to persuade biochemists to undertake research in a direction that will help to solve the problem of protein structure—which is what we are after.

I don't know whether Gisela told you about the Rockefeller Grant and she can't remember either. Anyhow one morning I received a notification that a grant of 684 pounds had been awarded to Cambridge University in order to pay the salaries of two collaborators for me and to extend my own grant until September 1943. Although I had rather expected it, it was very pleasant when it came. One of my two collaborators has been working for nearly three months now and is a great help to me. She is most accurate, conscientious and quick on the uptake. I try to apply all my principles about how one should treat one's employees—but of course the matter is easy when one's own money is not involved and the employee is an enthusiastic physics student.

Our own home looks quite attractive now, especially with some pictures friends of mine from Edinburgh recently sent us—prints of old Vienna. There is a continuous supply of roses from the garden and lots of other flowers which all helps to make us forget the dismal wall-paper.

To Herbert and Nelly Peiser, November 28, 1942

Pressure is being brought to bear on us by you and Annemarie [Gisela's aunt] to have a baby. We should like to have a baby; we like children and agree with many of the arguments which speak in favour of having one. There are, however, a number of grave drawbacks. Conditions here at the present time are such that quite apart from all financial considerations it would involve terrible difficulties for both of us and particularly great hardships for Gis. You might reply that the British nation is having thousands of babies every day and why should it be impossible for us, of all people? British people have to a large extent at least their own homes, while we have not. We live in furnished rooms, at the mercy or otherwise of capricious landladies, who can turn us out at any time at a moment's notice, which is indeed what is happening to us just now.[30] To start our own home we lack the most primitive necessities; we haven't even our own blankets. On the other hand people are reluctant to take couples with small babies as tenants in lodgings. Where is our equipment, for the home, which is the first condition for starting a family, where is it going to come from? This nation is keyed up for total war and civilian goods are not being manufactured.

The news from us is good. We are as happy as ever and are getting on well with the world. My work continues to make progress and my two assistants are proving their worth. I am really lucky to be able to continue this work which is extremely pleasant and interesting in itself and constantly brings me together with the nicest type of people. Gis wrote to you that we had a small conference here last September to discuss problems of protein structure, and that this was very successful. It turns out that it had considerable after-effects. Not only did it stimulate the biochemists who attended to undertake work in the direction which will help my own

---

[30]This was the only time it happened to Max and Gisela once they were married, but it happened repeatedly to Max's parents.

studies most, but I also derived some personal benefit by being asked to deliver a course of lectures at this University next term on "Methods of X-ray Analysis and their Application to Biological Problems." If successful, Professor Keilin who arranges them believes they would become an annual feature.

To Evelyn Machin, March 21, 1943

We had to move, because we were turned out of our rooms at Gilbert Rd. After a dreadfully long and tedious search we found a charming little place in the middle of the town. It's called the "Green Door" (a euphemism for the back door), The Old Vicarage, Thompson's Lane. The house is hundreds of years old (~400). Our flat is on the second floor, a sort of attic with beams running across the ceiling. All the lines are crooked and all angles oblique and it looks as though it's going to fall in quite soon. Yet with some nice pieces of furniture, flowers in the window boxes, pleasant pictures and a spot of redecorating here and there, our flat looks most gemütlich[31] and attractive. We both love it and are very happy to have found it. We even inherited a char from the previous occupiers so that Gis's life is a bit easier now. The flat is self-contained, with all modern conveniences, including a bath in the kitchen.[32] The parents regard it as too bohemian and were a bit shocked at first, but they will get used to it alright.

As you probably heard through motherly channels, I am engaged on war-work now and am very pleased with it, as it's something that will really help to win it. For me, it is a great change and has widened the scope of my activities. I have more to do than I can cope with, as usual; I meet many interesting people and am enjoying myself on the whole, although the experimental work itself is most strenuous. The only drawback of it is that my present job is in London and I can only see Gis on week-ends.

I gave a course of lectures at the University for the first time on "Methods of X-ray Analysis and their Application to Biological Problems." This was quite a success. The interest for the subject was much greater than we had anticipated, about 80 people turning up for the first lecture, much more than the room could accommodate. After the first two this had shrunk to

---

[31]Very hard to translate here: the German word implies that you feel comfortable in it, that it is unpretentious and homely.

[32]Unlike many Cambridge houses, it had electricity and an indoor toilet. A wooden board across the bath served as the kitchen table.

The Old Vicarage. We lived in the attic, which lay at the top of a steep and narrow spiral staircase, just beneath all the chimneys, which shook the entire building every time the wind blew.

about 50, who stayed to the end. I did manage to make them understand what the subject is all about, although few of them knew any more physics than you do; but it was probably I who learnt more than anyone else. I had to read a good deal beforehand and I gained much valuable experience on how to present a difficult subject so as to make it both palatable and intelligible. The war permitting it is to become an annual feature.

All this kept us both busy and we feel quite like a holiday by now. We had our first wedding anniversary to-day. It's been an eventful year for us, so the time seems very long since we got married. Also it's quite inconceivable how we could ever have lived without each other. We are certainly as happy if not happier than a year ago. This year has been the most successful one I ever had for me personally, which is probably closely connected with the "happy home." Yet it sometimes frightens me that all this is too good to be true and that something will destroy it suddenly. It is not the house which is built of cards, but the foundations on which it is built; the world where undisturbed happiness [reigns] is a thing that hardly exists anywhere. Still one shouldn't think too much these days.

War Work: Habbakuk

Max told the story of Habbakuk a number of times, most fully in "Enemy Alien."[33] Here, by way of introduction, I am reproducing the story as he told it to an interviewer from the Imperial War Museum. "I was drawn into the war effort by a strange character, ex-journalist, ex-educationist, ex-speculator, Geoffrey Pyke, a tall man with a gaunt face and a goatee who looked the very picture of a secret agent and who received me [in the spring of 1942] in a flat in the Albany to ask me whether I would be prepared to work on ice trying to find ways of making ice stronger [and] freezing it faster. And all this [was] for a mysterious project by the name of Habbakuk, which he would gladly have revealed to me as one great man talking to another but which he couldn't disclose lest the enemy or, worse, that collection of fools, on whom Churchill had to rely for advice, would get to hear of it. So I started work on ice in an underground lab established for me in Smithfield Market at the bottom of a meat store and there worked on a mysterious substance which we called pykrete, which was a mixture of water and wood pulp, the wood pulp having the function of abolishing the brittleness of ice. So this pykrete was weight for weight as strong as concrete." Although named after Max's new sponsor, pykrete was in fact the brainchild of Walter P. Hohenstein, the assistant of Max's former teacher Hermann Mark, now at Brooklyn Polytechnic. They had published a report, which Pyke had given Max, on how the addition of wood pulp alters the properties of ice. On reading of their findings, Max switched his attention forthwith to the new compound.

"The project went under the code name Habbakuk and was under the personal direction of Lord Louis Mountbatten, the chief of Combined Operations . . . Churchill's idea was that the navy should go and cut an ice floe out of the Arctic pack ice, tow it to the middle of the Atlantic where it should serve as an air base. So Churchill's general directive was 'let nature do the job' and my task was, though they never told me what the job was for, to try and find out whether this was feasible. But, alas, I soon discovered with my colleagues at the Admiralty that an ice floe suspended on the crest of two waves in the Atlantic in a storm would snap in the middle. So could one make it thicker? . . . Even at the North Pole the ice is only 10 feet thick. Churchill thought you could thicken it as you would make an ice rink

---

[33]The project, named after Habbakuk's book in the Old Testament, was always misspelled. Perutz M.F. 2003. Enemy alien. *I Wish I'd Made You Angry Earlier.* Cold Spring Harbor Laboratory Press. Cold Spring Harbor, NY. First published in 1985 in *The New Yorker.*

. . . and that way you might make an ice floe 100 feet thick. . . , but unfortunately it would have taken much too long to produce. . . , because water sprayed on a surface freezes first at the top, and the heat that has to be dissipated to freeze the water underneath takes such a long time to go through the crust . . . that a layer only a few millimetres thick takes a long time to freeze even in the coldest weather, and an ice floe 100 feet thick would have taken about a year to produce and would have been broken up by the forces of the waves in the meantime . . . It had to be done by artificial refrigeration and that eventually brought its downfall." There was also another "grave snag," as Max wrote in "Enemy Alien." Although superior to ice in many respects, pykrete resembled ice in being "soft to the pull of gravity, which makes glaciers flow like rivers. . . . A ship of pykrete would sag more slowly [than ice] but not slowly enough unless it were to be cooled to a temperature as low as 4°F."

When Churchill, Roosevelt, Mountbatten and Bernal, as Mountbatten's scientific advisor, met in Quebec, as Max told his interviewer, "it was decided to build one of these bergships with the highest priority. The building was supposed to be done in Newfoundland and the British team was ordered to go to the United States forthwith to help with the planning of the construction. . . . When I went to the American Consulate with my invalid, outdated Austrian passport, they said 'nothing doing'; they said they wouldn't admit enemy aliens even if urgently required for the war effort. Now that was my good luck. Mountbatten thereupon asked his chief of staff, Sir Harold Werner, to request the Home Office to make me into a British subject forthwith. But rather like a parson who is asked to perform a shot-gun wedding without calling the banns, the Home Office insisted on at least the semblance of its usual naturalisation ceremonial. . . .

Having been ordered to the United States with the greatest urgency, I found myself twiddling my thumbs when I got there because the Habbakuk project had been referred to the American Navy department for examination and pending the results of their enquiry, there was nothing for us to do. So I decided to visit the Canadian physicists and engineers who had done experiments on pykrete and ice in parallel with my own and paid a second visit to Canada. The project proved impractical because the amount of steel needed for the refrigeration plant . . . was so large that one might just as well have constructed the entire floating island of steel, and also by that time the range of land-based aircraft was increasing rapidly. . . . Finally Portugal gave the Allies the use of the Azores as an airbase and that made a great deal of difference in the anti-U-boat campaign."

Diary of M.F. Perutz, Project Habbakuk, Naturalisation and a Journey to the United States and Canada

Key

B.A.T.M. = unidentified acronym
bird = Admiral Byrd
C.O.S. = Chief of Staff
D.S.I.R. = Department of Scientific and Industrial Research
F = Franz (Max's brother, whose name was anglicised during the war to Frank)
God Almighty = Churchill
gods = chiefs of staff
H = Habbakuk, or Hohenstein
Mahomet = General Mountbatten, Head of Combined Operations (?)
N.O. = New Orleans
N.P.L = National Physical Laboratory
N.R.C. = National Research Council
P = Pykrete
Q = Quebec
R = Roosevelt
R.F. = Rockefeller Foundation
R.I. = Rockefeller Institute
R.M. = Royal Marines
S = Senta (Franz's wife)
Sage = John Desmond Bernal
W = Washington
Wren = member of Women's Royal Naval Service
i, ii, iii = pykrete, steel, and concrete models
[*Editorial note:* To preserve the chronological sequence, two letters have been interpolated into the diary.]

24 August 1943, Tuesday   Yesterday the famous cable had come from Mahomet that P had won in a canter, against everybody's expectations that an assembly of ancient Generals and other brass at Q would prefer steel or wood.

However P seems to excite the imagination and by to-day a message arrived to the effect that P had been approved by the gods and that [Jon] Rivett, [E.S.] Green, Wright and I are to proceed to America forthwith. I never saw the message, but to-night Rivett informed me that I am going to be naturalised and sent overseas as fast as possible. I spent the morning

making out an endless list of things to be done before my departure and trying not to listen to my heart beating at twice the normal rate.

25 August 1943, Wednesday   Slept very badly and woke up at 6.00 am,
most unusual. Felt the discomfort and dreariness of my digs in 73 Holland
Park more than usual and felt a pang inside me every time I wondered
whether my naturalisation would really go through, and whether no obstacles would distract the official procedure from its purpose.

Spent most of the day unable to do any of the things I had put on the
list the night before, for one reason or another. Rivett asked me to hang on
lest the Home Office should want me. Nothing actually happened.

I went home to tell Gis. She asked me whether I had good news or bad.
When I said that depends on how you look at it, she asked me when I was
leaving. She took it much better than I had expected and was brave and
thoughtful as usual. I felt very miserable by the time I came home but calmed
down after an evening with Gis talking things over quietly. We both decided
that it was impossible to know for how long I shall have to stay away.

26 August 1943, Thursday   Returned to London by the 9 o'clock train.
Nothing new at H.Q. except the news that we are to go by sea, probably.
C.O.S. (Maj. Gen. Wildman-Lushington) described the journey as faster,
safer and more comfortable.

Later in the afternoon the Home Office informed me that an official
wants to visit me at my digs between 7.30 and 8.00 pm. I rushed home without any supper and waited in my room from 7.30 until 8.00. When I went
down I learned that the bell wasn't functioning so I cursed Mrs. Anderson,
the slovenly landlady, more than ever and imagined the official to have
gone home peeved as no one answered the bell. While I thus reflected on
my misfortune a gentleman in a blue serge suit and black hat turned up—
a Whitehall official from top to toe. When he had settled himself down
comfortably he pulled my application out of his pocket and began asking
me questions in a pleasant cockney accent. He didn't want to know my
secrets he said, but he wants to know all about me. I was excited and in
good form and told him the story of my life as best and briefly as I could.
He seemed gratified with all he heard, only frowned at Gis' birth-place. Told
me all about the bombs that nearly hit him, the plane that came down in
his back-garden, the 15,000 egg deal on the black market which he discovered, the diamond merchant and the glass blower. Of course he had lots of
stories that would stagger me if only he could tell them. I shall always

remember him as Sgt. Smith of Scotland Yard, Special Branch. He only departed after two hours.

27 August 1943, Friday Slept very badly after Sgt. Smith, although I had nothing to hide and all had gone well, it had been most exciting, knowing that all my future life and career hangs on the shoe-string of the naturalisation. Had a busy day. Letter from [Douglas] Grant [a naval architect] arrived with telling story of P at Q. How he was hit in the thigh and Mahomet in the tummy. And how P was stewed in the presence of the Almighty gods themselves. Concrete outcome: the great chief ordered to set up Anglo American Canadian Committee to speed P and the whole project to the utmost. It was decided that iii had insufficient scope as opposed to smaller objects while i had all the drawbacks of wood and was too slow. In the balance of operational requirements versus economic needs and technical problems ii had won: I should have liked to assist in the boiling of P and heard the comments of the Almighties. Very busy day with Thompson, Store etc.

28 August 1943, Saturday Went home with the assurance that naturalisation would be through by Tuesday night. Saw the parents and the Eirichs. Both were thrilled with the news. Mother kept on telling me of all the things I have to send her, such as almonds, suspenders, pearl string, lemon juice, stockings etc.

29 August 1943, Sunday Spent pleasantly in Cambridge making preparations for the journey, sorting my belongings.

30 August 1943, Monday Went to London at 9.00 a.m. Did odd jobs in the morning. Everybody at H.Q. excited. Rivett and [Geoffrey] Pyke inaccessible and in constant conference on questions of policy and money. Green pleasant as usual and Wright talkative. In the afternoon a message arrived from the Home Office that my papers are on the way and would I swear the oath and return them straightaway. I announced myself at Eichholz the solicitor, jumped into a taxi to London Walk. Eichholz was surprised but short as usual. I had to swear the oath at another solicitor's next door (cost 2/-); instructed Eichholz to draft a will leaving everything to Gis, took a taxi to the Cold Store to give some instructions to the sailors and to see Mrs. Hussey about the Monitor experiment, dashed back to H.Q. and off again to the Home Office to see Mr. Seaborne-Davies, the head of the Nationality Division. He was most amenable, assured me that my naturalisation was the quickest job the Home

Office had ever done; the record was that they gave me the certificate before I had paid the fee (£9), against the advice of his clerk. Seaborne-Davies thought that Mahomet's fortune was good enough for £9. He told me that less than 50 naturalisations had been granted during the war; so I felt prouder than ever. Gis' naturalisation was promised to follow shortly.

When I thanked Rivett and Pyke they were very nice about it. They seemed genuinely pleased about it, strangely enough; perhaps because they had so obviously made me happy with it. Muff beamed when I told her, [Kenneth] Pascoe vaguely understood that it was something important for me. I stood drinks all round and everybody was very friendly. I felt to-night that I must be popular amongst these people who all share my happiness.

Had supper at the Wendons and let the big news out during the meal. They were thrilled to the bones and full of enthusiasm. Luke kept on saying: "I am quite excited." He looked as though it were the first time that something really thrilling happened to some one quite close to him. Port was drunk and innumerable questions were asked until I went to bed tired and happy. Thus ended one of the happiest days of my life.

31 August 1943, Tuesday   Rang Gis in the morning to tell her. She was thrilled. Spent all day waiting for Rivett to get moving on the passport and other formalities. Saw the Hartridges in the evening. Anne was in bed with Bronchitis. George and she[34] made a nice a little home for themselves on the top floor of the house. Mrs. H was out unfortunately. Told them proudly of my naturalisation, but they did not quite grasp the significance of it for me.

Went out to the Fronde Laboratory at N.P.L. to see models of i and iii tested. Very interesting. The testing seems to be more a craft than a science.

1 September 1943, Wednesday   Spent the morning waiting for Rivett who was busier and more excited than ever. The financial squabble over the rate of compensation in America is still going on. Went to the passport office in the afternoon. Sgt. Cohen mentioned that my visa will probably require sanctions from Washington. Rivett rang up C.O.S. and asked him to get in touch with the U.S. Embassy so as to speed my visa. Left for Cambridge in the evening. Heard that we were sailing Saturday morning.

2 September 1943, Thursday   Spent the day packing and taking leave of as many people as I could in the short time. Had lunch with the parents who

---

[34]Anne had married George Corden.

were crying with one eye and laughing with the other about my going. Also saw Keilin, Fritz, Alex, [Charles] Burkill. The parents saw me off at the station and Gis accompanied me to London. We had supper at the C.O. Club and stayed the night at the Alwyn Court Hotel.

In Cambridge I saw the managers of Midland Bank and arranged that £12 monthly should be paid to Father's account during my absence. Also saw the University Treasurer (Assistant) Mr. Macdonald and persuaded him with some difficulty to ring Mr. Brundret Ass. D.S.R. Admiralty to arrange for 1/3 of my salary to be paid to me in Canada and 2/3 here in Cambridge to Gisela.

3 September 1943, Friday Woke up early and spent the morning dictating letters to Gis, so as to arrange everything with Bragg and other University people. Collected the rest of my belongings from 73 Holland Park immensely relieved not to have to see that place again. Took leave of Annemarie and the Wendons, rushed to H.Q. took my books to be censored, gave detailed instructions to Pascoe, had lunch with Gis at the Club, went to buy £10 worth of U.S. dollars which is all you are allowed to take and got that at the last minute with some difficulty because I didn't have my passport yet. Collected my books from the censor, all sealed up in a big parcel, dictated all the necessary letters to confer powers to Pascoe, attended a long meeting with Pyke, and all the engineers on two of his minor schemes. Phoned up the passport office at 5.45 and heard that my visa had not arrived. Had to wait until the seemingly endless meeting finished at 6.30 and told Pyke that I couldn't go. He took me straight up to Sec. C.O.S. (Lt. Cmdr. Mason) who assured us that cables had gone to the British Embassy from our end and the State Dept. in Washington from the U.S. Embassy asking for my visa. I was to follow the others by air.

Gis came in for supper looking rather excited and miserable, but soon cheered up with the farewell celebrations for Green, Rivett and Wright. They left that night to cross on one of the Queens and took my trunk along with them.

Gis spent the night at the Wendons and I at 73 Holland Park in my room which was as dirty as ever.

4 September 1943, Saturday Returned home and staggered the parents by my reappearance. Recovered slowly from the shock of plans changed at the last minute and enjoyed talking to Gis most of the day.

5 September 1943, Sunday Saw the Eirichs and Peter Wooster.

6 September 1943, Monday Arrived at H.Q. to find that there is more trouble about my visa. I went to the U.S. Embassy and heard from a very indifferent Mr. Chaffey that he knows nothing about me and was never asked by anyone to cable for my visa and had never heard of Combined Operations. He started by carefully putting down all my particulars, asked me whether I or Gisela had any relations in Europe, winced at Gisela's birth place, and wanted an official letter about me from H.Q. So I dashed back to see Sec. C.O.S. and told him the kind of letter the Embassy wanted and asked him to stress the security aspect.

Returned to the Embassy after lunch and was pleased to see Mr. Chaffey brighten up perceptibly on reading the letter from C.O.S. He looks like a Prussian official par excellence, but is quite friendly if treated the right way. Obviously a machine, though. He promised to cable Washington the same afternoon; expects a reply in between 3 and 12 days. What a waste it would be if my journey were really as vital as it is made out to be.

After tea Pyke introduced me to C.O.S. whom I thanked heartily for his help in my naturalisation. The reply was: "That's alright. If I don't do one thing I do another, that's what I get paid for." A creditably unpompous remark for a general. Seemed of the good-natured shy type. Pleasant ENSA [Entertainment National Service Association] concert at night. Had great trouble finding a room for the night.

7 September 1943, Tuesday Spent the night at the Bedford Hotel, Southampton Row, very grimy.[35] Took the first train to Sittingbourne, Kent to see Mr. Thompson at Edward Lloyd's pulp and paper mills, Kemsley. Was first received by Mr. Underhay, chief chemist of the company who wanted to know whether there will be any business arising for the firm arising from our project. I was as non-committal as I could. Drove by car to Kemsley where Thompson called in two senior technicians, one of them a Canadian. They were pessimistic at first and proposed Heath Robinson schemes for laying P, but were later persuaded that my basic plan would work. Made some tests of a rotary filter (vat machine) and found that a sheet of 10–14% P could be produced. Was led for an extensive tour of the factory including insulating and hardboard making machines, with intricate automatic conveyers. Most interesting.

Had supper at the Wendons and stayed the night there.

---

[35]Max refers repeatedly to the filth in London. This was the era before the first Clean Air Act passed in 1952, which imposed smokeless fuel. The Meteorological Office website notes that during the fog of December 1956 the pollutants emitted per day were 1000 tonnes of smoke particles, 140 tonnes of hydrochloric acid, 2000 tonnes of carbon dioxide, 370 tonnes of sulphur dioxide and 14 tonnes of fluorine compounds.

8 September 1943, Wednesday Waited for my visa, tried to get home after lunch but was kept by Pyke who then did not want me after all. Spent evening with the parents who are disconsolate, because they will have to find a new home once again.

Was thrilled and pleased to tears by Italians' surrender announced tonight.

9 September 1943, Thursday Returned to London. No sign of visa. Had a meeting with Carrol at Fanum House to discuss future of Pascoe, Sailors, Cold Store etc. Carrol was more affable than usual, but kept on talking at length without leaving me or Pascoe time for much comment. Offered Pascoe a fine job investigating stress distribution in welded merchant ships by X-ray diffraction methods. Apparently many of these rapidly welded ships break in two in mid-ocean under wave stresses. The cold store is to be "kept on ice" for the time being and the sailors returned to their units.

Spent evening at the Club.

10 September 1943, Friday Spent a good night at the Alwyn Court Hotel. Actually got a fried egg for breakfast, and jam. Arrived at H.Q. late in the morning, found no sign of visa. I am getting tired of spending my days in continuous suspense. Yesterday Carrol mentioned that a message had come in from Washington to the effect that from the strategic point of view iii is now being preferred to ii. So I am beginning to wonder whether maybe they don't want me there after all. This would be most awkward as most of my clothes are already there.

Negotiated with Mr. Hussey and Mr. Bundy at the Union Cold Storage Co. about reducing the rent for the stores. Did a spot of work in the Cold Store.

Thrilling news is continuing to come in from the war front. The Italians are surrendering to whoever is handy, either us or the Germans. The Russians have freed the Donetz Basin and are pushing the Germans back in ever growing strides. The landing of our forces at Taranto is announced tonight. For the first time one felt during the last few days that the German defeat is sealed and merely a matter of pushing them back into Germany itself from all sides. Still it will take some pushing. Hitler made a speech denouncing Italian treachery and extolling Mussolini's virtues, not mentioning either the Russian front or the allied air-raids or any other of Germany's problems. It is quite obvious that he is finished.

11 September 1943, Saturday Received my visa this morning and saw my British passport for the first time. Kept on admiring it. Sec. C.O.S. is trying to book an air passage. Returned home happy and spent afternoon cycling about with Gis.

Italian fleet surrendered and sailed into Malta. A great day for the Maltese.

12 September 1943, Sunday Heini came out for the day. Joy [Boyes-Watson, Max's research assistant] came to lunch and we all had a most enjoyable day. Had supper at the Eirichs.

To Dorothy Hodgkin, September 12, 1943

I have rarely been as pleased and proud of anything as I was and still am of the naturalisation. I love this country and want to stay here after the war. I was rather terrified of having to leave and start afresh elsewhere; even Austria has become a strange country for me where I don't know the people any more, and whose outlook is diametrically opposed to my own. I liked this country right from the start and to become a British subject is a great thing for me. This is difficult to appreciate for you who are born here and have never lived anywhere else and see more the drawbacks than the advantages. Having a home again and some measure of security for oneself and one's family makes all the difference.

I am very lucky to get it as the total number of naturalisations during the war is less than 50, while there are thousands of applications.

13 September 1943, Monday Saw Bragg who wrote 7 letters of introduction in his own hand. (Warren at M.I.T., Commander Bitter, U.S. Navy at Washington, Mr. N.P. Pitt at Montreal, Professor Shaw at Cornell, Professor Murdoch at Cornell, Professor Smyth at Princeton and Wykoff). Promised to help to get me recalled if necessary and was as kind to me as usual. Told me not to criticise the countries I was visiting.

Heard this evening that I have to report in London tomorrow and leave London tomorrow or Wednesday. Said good-bye to the parents once more. Met Norman and Dennis in the lab who were most envious. My Austrian friends envy me my naturalisation and the English ones my trip. I am quite looking forward to it myself by now.

14 September 1943, Tuesday Went to London in the morning, and had the company of Adrienne Weill[36] in the train. She said of a helpless person "Elle s'est noyeé dans un verre d'eau."[37] Kept talking all the way.

Heard in London that I have to leave tomorrow morning. Rushed around all day getting tickets, censoring of papers, writing last minute reports and letters, etc. Spent lots of money on taxis, but when Gis arrived at six I was practically ready.

Took leave of Pyke who was rather pathetic. I think he is afraid that he is losing his job. He has done his bit, of course, and is not wanted anymore. With Mahomet leaving without even saying goodbye to him, poor Pyke is left in a vacuum. He told me to "wash it out of my mind" when I thanked him again for the naturalisation.

Had supper at Freddie and Hilde [Himmelweit] and spent the night with Gis at the Wendons.

15 September 1943, Wednesday Left the Wendons at 8.45 am by duty car, drove to Airways House and left for Poole in a Pullman train. I am already getting the impression that we are travelling in outrageous luxury. My two fellow travellers are Grant and Ascoli, one army, the other R.M. Quite pleasant and honest chaps with a Sandhurst outlook on social affairs. The other passengers are mostly U.S. officials and officers travelling in mufti because of neutral Eire. Also some Canadian Officials.

Arrived at Poole at 12.20 and had to undergo innumerable war-time formalities. Everything very smooth, pleasant and efficient though. Embarked on "Golden Hind" 4 engined flying boat and left at 3.15. Unfortunately the blinds are drawn and locked, so that there is nothing to see. Flight uneventful but bumpy, particularly towards the end, when we ran into rain and fog.

Arrived at Shannon Airport, Foynes at 6.45 and immediately saw impressive looking Clippers. Went on shore to neutral Eire for perfunctory

---

[36]She was a French Jewish physicist who found refuge in Cambridge. In 1979, in a letter of condolence to her daughter, Max wrote, "The crystallographers at the Cavendish [in 1941] were nice people, but provincial and unbelievably dull. In the dreary setting Adrienne appeared like a fairy from a vanished world of cultured, well-bred Europeans. Gay, outgoing, widely read and travelled, warm-hearted and witty, she was one of those people with the rare gift of making you feel cheerful as soon as she came through the door."

[37]Literally, she has drowned in a glass of water.

passport and luggage examination which seems rather unnecessary. Asked what my government Dept is, I reply: "Min. of Home Security": I don't want to be interned as a naval officer!

Nothing of any interest can be seen at Shannon, apart from the flying boats. So I am pleased when we go aboard the Clipper after less than an hour. The Clipper, built by Boeing and commissioned in July 1941, is most luxurious, particularly compared to the "Golden Hind" which is stripped of all unessential fittings. The walls of Clippers are padded to reduce noise. The seats, beds and all fittings are both ingeniously made and perfectly comfortable. Kitchen, cloak-rooms, etc. all streamlined and dove-tailed to economise space. Yet the air-craft is enormous and moves with majestic grace.

We take off just after 8.00 pm (BST), the weather has closed slightly. In any case the Clipper is more quiet than the "Hind." We are all very hungry, but finally a splendid supper arrives at 11.00 pm. I enjoyed my first "off the ration" meal—two large slices of beef, plenty of butter.

The fare from Shannon to New York is $525. I can't help feeling that my importance in the war-effort is being much overrated. Surely it can't be worth all this luxury and expense!

16 September 1943, Thursday Went to sleep at midnight and slept fairly comfortably rolled up on my seat. The berths were rightly given to the older men. Woke up at 8 BST [British Standard Time] still in the middle of the night. Beautiful moonlight amid stars. Had a breakfast of melon, shredded wheat, plenty of [the next word is illegible], milk and butter.

Dawn found us travelling over a sea of fleecy clouds while the horizon turned first yellow, then crimson, with gorgeous clouds above us. Later we leave the cloud bank underneath and travel over a calm-looking sea at about 6000 feet. Nothing conveys the impression of speed more forcibly than the many different kinds of weather we are passing through. In contrast to yesterday's bumpy start, the ship now progresses with stately smoothness.

Most of the elderly Americans seem to have done the trip before and are indifferent to these sights, probably indifferent to Nature anyhow. Fortunately there are a few less sophisticated British and Canadians aboard.

First group of islands sighted at 11.45 BST or 15 hours and 30 minutes after taking off at Shannon. Mainland of Newfoundland sighted at 11.55. Alighted at Botwood 12.30 BST.

Botwood [Newfoundland] is certainly a dreary place. A small wooden village with houses painted in different colours provides the only cheery sight. The sky is grey, rain pours down every few minutes on the rocky hills where only small pine trees and shrubs grow. It can't be fun to be one of the United Nations soldiers[38] who man this outpost. Huts, hangars and nowhere to go to except for walks in the woods around here.

Had my first American breakfast in the Imperial Airways restaurant and sat about in their Club to await departure.

Took off at 2.45 BST and travelled over Newfoundland through thick cloud.

We crossed the Atlantic with 22 passengers on board, but now we take on some more among them 3 women with two small children. With the berths transformed into seats there is now room for 48 passengers.

Flew over Prince Edward Island. Pleasant farm country with neat look-ing rectangular fields, roads and villages, interspersed with woods and moors. All villages very small. The whole population seems to be almost evenly dispersed over the countryside. Very flat country, soil is red clay which gives the sea around the beaches a beautiful colouring.

Crossed the [Northumberland] Straits to New Brunswick and landed at Shediac at 6.35 BST. Trim little village typically the same as most Canadian places I have seen. Had tea and was stared at by the local beauties. Took off at 7.45 BST for the final lap.

We are having a flight in glorious weather above cumulus clouds over the forests of N.B. Altitude about 7000 feet. After a long journey above the clouds at about 10,000 feet we emerge over the open sea. Pass Cape Cod at 11.00 BST. Very beautiful clouds all the way.

Touched the water at New York at 12.40 am BST (La Guardia Air Port).

Endless passport examinations. Had to pass a hair-raising cross ques-tioning by the intelligence officers who were shocked to learn that I was nat-uralised only on 30 August. I didn't believe they would let me in. There is nothing like a good conscience and letters from D.S.K. and C.O.S. In the end the mind of one of officers was put at rest by the fact that Lotte lives in the same street where he used to live. That settled it and I was admitted. Customs were very friendly and did not examine my bags in view of my official status.

Left La Guardia and drove by bus to the Ambassadors Hotel where we arrived at 3.30 a.m. BST on 17 Sept or 41 hours and 31 minutes after leav-ing London. Put clock 5 hours back.

Rang up Frank who took 5 minutes to take in the fact that I was ring-ing him. Wired to Gis and Lotte. Went to bed dead tired at 12.30.

P.S. My total expenses from London to New York—five shillings!

---

[38]Chambers Encyclopaedia states that Allied Soldiers were referred to as United Nations Soldiers.

17 September 1943, Friday Woke up early and didn't feel too well. All the excitement of last night came out to-day. After a luxurious breakfast I rang up Mark and fixed an appointment. Set out to find the Rockefeller Foundation. The morning was rainy. I soon got to the Rockefeller Centre which I recognised from photographs and took a lift to the roof of the R.C.A. [Radio Corporation of America] building. The trip over Ireland was nothing but a rocking chair compared to the way in which that lift turned your stomach upside down. However the view was worth the shake-up. Tried to find 49 West 49th Street on coming down to earth, only to discover after 20 minutes search that it was identical with the R.C.A. building. The R.F. occupy the 55th floor. Mr. [Warren] Weaver is on war work and Mr. [H.M.] Miller in South America. Mr. [Frank Blair] Hanson received me and invited me to lunch.

Went to the Brooklyn Polytechnic by sub. Can't compare with London Tube in comfort, but the Expresses are faster. Also you can get anywhere with a Nickel. Had a glorious reception by Mark and Fan. Both got fatter and heartier, and were extremely nice to me. Had a preliminary talk about work and people. Went back to the R.F. Hanson, an elderly man with a thinker's face grooved and rugged, took me up to a magnificent lunch room situated on a corner of the building and overlooking most of N.Y. Most impressive, dignified and tasteful modern

Hermann Mark in 1950

room I ever saw. The whole Rockefeller Centre is a magnificent piece of modern architecture, completely original and its design, a symbol of the power of modern architectural engineering. Over a staggering lunch I had to give a complete report of myself and the two girls, of my plans for the future, of the way work is conducted in the Cavendish, of the way in which Bragg runs the lab. Hanson was anxious to know whether I had any prospect of ever becoming independent of the Foundation. I assured him that my recent naturalisation had made this a more attainable goal than it had been before and that Bragg had once mentioned the possibility of giving me a job at Cambridge after the war, independent of the R.F. I said that I loved Cambridge and very much wanted to stay there. Hanson replied that I shouldn't refuse a job at another university if I could get one, as many of them were very good. We discussed scientists on the Foundation in England and here. At my request Hanson gave me introductions to Bergman at the

R.I. and Northrup at Princeton, and he promised me any other introductions I might wish to have—he mentioned that Miller now covers South America, to foster research in the Natural Sciences. He explained that when the Foundation's research schemes in Europe broke down in Europe in 1940, they had to look around for other parts of the world where small and medium scale research in natural sciences could be started. The only possible countries were China and South America. All possible aid was already being extended to China. R.F. money in South America was princi-

Isidore Fankuchen (Fan)

pally being spent on agricultural research schemes—the large scale public health and medical schemes were of course quite independent. The grant for my girls is ok.

Mr. Hanson also explained that the R.I. for Medical Research was quite independent of the Foundation and possessed separate funds. After a trip round the windows overlooking the slanting Normandie and other big ships I left, full of gratitude for all I had heard, seen and eaten. I also met Mr. Weaver who asked me to see him again when he is less busy. Mr. Miller will be back in October.

From the R.F. I took a bus along 5th Avenue to the Washington Bridge. The Avenue's elegance is proverbial and impressive. You see few ugly buildings. Throughout the trip the town made a very clean and pleasant impression. The weather had cleared up and rain had given place to a brilliant afternoon. The Bridge is the most impressive engineering feat I ever saw. It looks forceful from a distance, powerful when you approach it and awe-inspiring when you walk across it. The view down the Hudson River and towards Manhattan is an unforgettable sight.

Returned to my hotel, repacked and took supper in a café in the RCA building and went to Fan's flat. This is in an elegant apartment house overlooking the East River. Diana received me in pyjamas and a dressing gown. Reason: she is getting a baby in January and had been upset this afternoon. She had a miscarriage some time ago, so this time the doctor forbade her to move about. After the morning's experience I thought that one ride in the R.C.A. lift should be enough to turn any baby upside down in the womb.

18 September 1943, Saturday Waking up in Fan's flat was as good as Zermatt. The view across the East River towards Manhattan, the Statue of Liberty far away in the morning mist under a cloudless sky was one of the best I have seen. Ships were slowly sliding up and down the harbour, Liberty Ships, trawlers, war ships while two freighters were being loaded up in the docks underneath our windows.

Had breakfast in a restaurant because Diana was still in bed at 9 o'clock and it would be too much work for her. What a fuss these people made about a little meal in a streamlined flat with every labour saving device. They should try the "Green Door."

Fan showed me some of his work at the lab. He has a very good set of pictures of ribonuclease, and of γ-chymotrypsin. Also pictures of many other interesting substances. But he never seems to have the time and I suspect the patience to work out any structure. It broke my heart to see stacks of ribonuclease pictures, both wet and dry, without any attempt being made at analysing them. Fan later offered to hand over the pictures to me to work out the structures in England. He has a monoclinic and an orthorhombic variety. The former has 2, the latter 4 molecules per cell. I shall certainly accept that offer, as the monoclinic variety looks most hopeful. Mol. Weight only 10, 000!

Later Sage arrived from W. He was clean-shaven, with his hair nicely cut, and looked younger and fresher than for a long time past. He was most cheerful and nice to me. Mark soon joined us and we had a discussion on P, i.e. I explained the material I had been making and the reasons which were responsible for the particular percentage used. Fan was jealous and impatient that he didn't have Sage's attention and interrupted Sage every two minutes until I shut him up. Later Sage, Mark and I had a private talk where Sage explained the new set up in W. An Anglo-American H Agency has been set up with naval officers on the U.S. side and Rivett and Sage on the British side. Apparently there had been a terrific row about the composition of that Agency, the Americans insisting on naval personnel only, and the British on civilian experts. Sage seems to have had some arguments with Admiral King. The Agency has the direction to set up production plants for P and to make a very large chunk of it next winter. It is all in its embryonic stage. No structural engineer has as yet been appointed, nor any person responsible for P. Sage is going to England for 3 weeks on Monday and has nightmares that they will all resign in his absence. I am to act as Sage's representative on that agency whilst he is away. Later Sage told the story of Q. Apparently Mahomet smuggled Sage and Grant on to the boat going to Q and suddenly produced them to the gods. They presented our baby and everybody was most interested. Sage said that at Q the combined gods finally agreed to H ii and P so as to avoid having to witness further revolver experiments and being shot by Grant. They shot into a chunk of P made up of small blocks sealed together with water and cooled with CO_2. Later they were suddenly summoned to God Almighty and his American counterparts. They nearly worked themselves to death trying to tidy up the P block and to saw it to pieces. When they finally brought it to the Citadel the Butler asked whether it was for the kitchen. It was carried up by the footman on a silver tray and put into a silver bowl together with a chunk of the pure material and boiling water from a silver bottle was poured over it. The pure chunk vanished, while the boiling water made no impression on P. Then R tried to hit it with a hammer and God Almighty smashed at it with his usual vigour but made no impression. God Almighty did most of the talking and R agreed to everything he said—said that ii was approved chiefly because it is unusual and original. The gods were not interested in iii at all because it is just an ordinary object, only much larger. Of the Gods themselves he said that they were just pleasant old country gentlemen except for the bird who is really good.

Had lunch with Sage, Fan, Mark and Hohenstein. After lunch saw two dentist brothers Klein who developed a most ingenious methods of stereoscopic X-ray photography with obvious applications to the war effort. The object is photographed by the same camera at two different angles. The two pictures are printed on two emulsions on the same film. One emulsion contains polaroid oriented in one direction. The other contains polaroid oriented in a direction normal to the first. The two images are displaced from each other by an amount which the brothers worked out from their own theory of stereoscopic vision. When viewed with polaroid spectacles where the polaroid in the two glasses is oriented at right angles, each eye sees a different picture—a perfect stereoscopic impression is obtained.[39]

Incidentally Fan developed a method for finding the orientation of quartz crystals. One reflecting plane is oriented so that it is permanently in reflecting position by being in the plane of rotation of the crystal. The crystal is then rotated until a reflection from another plane is picked up in the ionisation spectrometer. This gives all the data needed.

Went with Sage to the British Passport Control at the Rockefeller Centre, was introduced to Miss Gormer. Sage dictated a letter to confirm my

---

[39]The extraordinary illusion the dentists' equipment produced clearly sowed a seed. See Max's letter of May 14, 1963 and Tom Steitz's e-mail quoted in the footnote.

position in relation to the H agency. Took leave of Sage who promised to ring Gis when he returns.

Went to Grand Central and took the train to New London. Air-conditioned carriage; working class districts on the outskirts of N.Y. not nearly as dreary as London. There are large brick tenement houses with washing hanging outside, pretty close together, but not as bleak and grimy as London. The train is electric and very fast. The countryside pleasant.

Summing up the most vivid impressions of the first two days: The country is the engineer's paradise. New York one of the cleanest and most beautiful cities I ever saw. The large population of negroes.[40] The leisurely manner of working of the people in contrast to the speed of the machine.

Met Frank, Senta, Jimmy and Lad[41] at New London station. New London is a port and submarine base. Nevertheless Frank is allowed to drive along the waterfront. The meeting was most cheerful. We talked until I was dead tired and could not sleep for a long time after the many thrills and excitements of the day.

19 September 1943, Sunday F in a trim looking wooden house on a pleasant hillside. The house is painted white and is built in colonial style with porches on each side. There are 2.5 rooms downstairs and three rooms upstairs, all of them spacious and sparsely furnished as yet. There is one good-sized kitchen with fridge, a washing machine and mangle, gas cooker. There is a large basement below. Upstairs there are three bed-rooms and a bath-room. The house is extremely light, cheerful and clean. Coal operated central heating.

Both F and Senta are very thin although they eat as well as any Americans. F got very grey and looked pale. Senta looked quite well. Both were very cheerful. Around the house is a garden which is not in any way divided from neighbouring gardens. There are similar but *not* identical houses all around. They are spaced well apart. Nor are they all arranged in one line, but scattered over the hillside in a haphazard sort of way. The houses all belong to middle class people corresponding to say Gilbert Rd., Cambridge. But in spaciousness, comfort and attractiveness they can't be compared with their English counterparts. Only the gardens are not as well-groomed and charming. All houses have garages for two cars. The whole town of Norwich looks very clean and lively and cheerful under a cloudless summer sky.

---

[40]This designation had not yet become unacceptable.

[41]Their dog.

The family: they seem very happy because although they are by no means rich, they really have nearly all you could wish for. F has a good job, though he would like a better one, and gets on well with his supervisors and colleagues at the factory. His marriage is obviously a happy one. Jimmy is a sweet little boy. Although very tall for his age, he is perfectly normal child of 4½ in all other ways. He looks the spitting image of F, is very lively but I don't think quite as unmanageable as F used to be, though Senta says he is difficult sometimes. He is a very good mixer both with grown-ups and other children. I can't judge his intelligence at all or whether he is able to occupy himself.

We discussed the parents' finances in a very friendly way and he was quite sensible about it all. Apparently they are putting some money aside and F agreed to send contributions to England if Father has to stop work. Don't know what will happen when it comes to paying though.

In the afternoon we went for a ride in F's Ford V8 around the countryside. Most noticeable:

(1) People live mainly in openings and in the primeval jungle. 90% of the countryside even here in New England consists of forests, mostly leaf trees, few pines, which are inaccessible because of poison ivy. There is no cultivated land because the soil is rocky and extremely poor. There are farms scattered widely through the hilly countryside, but they are exclusively concerned with dairy and poultry farming.

(2) Farms, cottages, homes of industrial workers all look clean and comfortable. Plumbing and heating everywhere are up to the proverbial American standard.

(3) We looked at F's mill from outside. It consists of very large red brick buildings clustered along a railway line and river. The buildings look old and shabby.

(4) We parked at a very pleasant lake with a few cottages dotted along the wooded shores. An ideal place for bathing.

(5) There are no bicycles. People either use their car or stay at home. The ban on pleasure driving was lifted on 1 September, hence our drive was not illegal. F's factory is 3 miles from his home, but cycling would be too hot in summer and too snowy in winter. Buses are scarce—I never saw one and imagine all the workers have cars.

(6) The country is thinly populated and yet this is one of the most densely populated districts in the U.S.

After more talking went to bed dead tired at 11.45.

Second thoughts: Frank and S have no friends and few acquaintances in Norwich. Hardly any books, but they can get books from the library. Frank keeps his professional knowledge up to date by belonging to the Society of American Engineers from where he can get books.

F mentioned that the people round his place accused Britain of having dragged them into the war. When you see this peaceful little town you are not surprised that it is difficult for them to realise that their very high standard of living would just collapse like a house of cards if Hitler ruled the rest of the world.

20 September 1943, Monday   Took the 10 o'clock train to N.Y. In New London subs go in and out under everyone's eye, a thing unheard of in England. On the way back we passed some rather dirty looking industrial districts. The country is not a second Switzerland after all.

Arrived at Grand Central at 1.00 pm and went straight to the Brooklyn Polytechnic where I had another talk with Mark. He does not consider that the project would ever materialise. On the other hand he thinks that one must have wild projects of this nature in case anything goes wrong and the improbability of its realisation should not prevent one from working on it with all possible enthusiasm. He warned me again that matters in W will move very slowly and that much hanging about will be my fate there.

Missed my train because of general slowness of service at hotel and station. Caught the 5.30 to W. Saw many industrial towns on the way, some clean some dirty. Was impressed by the tremendous size of the industrial district of Philadelphia and the magnitude of the factories themselves. Countryside wooded but less wild and very pleasant.

Arrived at 9.10 and was met by the entire gang—Grant, Wright, Rivettt, Green and "Gill." They were all homesick and keen to see someone fresh from England. Terribly disappointed that I had brought no letters—I am sorry that I didn't do it in the rush of the last day. Went to a small hotel (Benedicks Hotel, 1808 Eye St. N.W.) where I got a room for 3.50. Had to go out for drinks and answer hundreds of questions about home and again got to bed very late and very very tired.

21 September 1943, Tuesday   Went to the office amidst an army of beautifully set out, white, perfectly built Government buildings. We are housed in the Public Health Building. The inside is more like a hospital than an office. Very trim-looking Wrens in tropical kit about the building and a lot of officers of all grades, denominations and sexes. There is nothing to do as

Mark predicted. I had to go about getting my passes and being registered and everybody was keen to accompany me in order to idle away the time.

The day was grey and damp, rather oppressive and Washington didn't look its best. It is a most beautifully planned town with tree-lined Avenues, plenty of gardens and nicely built houses. The gang thinks it is so perfect that it has no character. This may be so. It is perhaps too perfect to be interesting, but certainly not too perfect to live and work there. It has all the characteristics of a well-planned model town.

Took lunch and tea in our nice canteen and supper in a restaurant. Stood Green and Rivett a good supper in return for taking my trunk here.

22 September 1943, Wednesday   Went to the British Embassy to collect Lotte's letter, read that she was willing to come next week-end, rang her up (the connection can be got in 30 seconds) and fixed that she would come on Friday. It seems too good to be true [after doubting in 1939 whether they would ever see one another again].

Spent the morning at the office writing home. Went sightseeing with Wright in the afternoon, first to the army exhibition, where we were most impressed by the array of formidable weapons displayed. Ascended the Washington Memorial Obelisk. As you go up a loudspeaker shouts the history of the obelisk into your ear. On top you get a fair view of the city. Going down the loudspeaker shouts a discourse on the significance of the memorial as a symbol of the power of democracy. Went on to the Capitol and passed the charming National Gallery. Its pink marble has almost the colours of Athens marble and its proportions are perfect. The style of building here has obviously much improved and grown up in recent years. They don't try to make buildings imposing any longer by adorning them with masses of ornamentation, but they now try to impress by simplicity of design and beauty of outline. By contrast the capitol is dignified but hideous. It is a pathetic symbol of the failure of man that he builds a house like the Capitol and then sends his representatives there to throw ink-bottles [sling mud?] at each other. However, in another 100 years maybe they will live up to the dignity of the building.

Had supper with the Hendricks. The house is in the wood on the outskirts of the town. I could see little of its exterior, but its interior might well have belonged to the Woosters who gave me the introduction. The people too were very kindred to our kind of University folks and I got on very well with them. I had come with the intentions of pumping them for information. Instead they pumped me and I had to tell them about England and our English friends most of the evening.

Heard many interesting facts about American education though. School-teachers apparently are almost exclusively women. Reason: No man would go in for the teaching profession, since they are all brought up with the idea that it's easy to become a millionaire. Reason why there are no bicycles: you get run over. Hendricks is a friend of [Bradford] Washburn's and his house is full of Washburn's beautiful photographs of Alaska's mountains.

23 September 1943, Thursday Felt miserable all day, as Mrs. Hendricks' supper had disagreed with me or I had caught cold in the night. Went to bed after lunch and read Trollope's *Warden*.

24 September 1943, Friday Went to meet Lotte who arrived with the "Southerners" at 9.30 after a 25 hour trip. Was struck by her changed appearance. Her features have become more pointed, her face is grooved and her eyes are sunk almost as deeply as Father's under her bushy eye-brows. She is not changed otherwise. She found that I had an awful English accent and I was amused by her Southern American one. She has some grey hair and looks very thin.

We had lunch together and did a spot of shopping afterwards. In the evening our search for a riverside restaurant landed us at the "Stables" a modest looking but very expensive place with a negro band. Got a very good supper which disagreed with me and listened to the negro band playing the "Blue Danube." One negro sang "Spirituals" very nicely. Lotte and I talked about so many things that it is hard to record any of it. Each of us seemed to be even more anxious to tell his own story than listening to the other one. Lotte was pleased to be in an elegant restaurant with music, a pleasure which she had not had for many years.

25 September 1943, Saturday Put in a short appearance at the office where there is still nothing to do. Sent a parcel with stockings to Mother which took me most of the morning. Had lunch with Lotte, did more shopping, bought present for Jimmy, stockings, etc. Went to Mr. Mellons's National Gallery again and got in this time. Very fine collection, though not as complete as a really good museum. Many beautiful Rembrandts and Filippino Lippis, quite a representative collection of 19th century French.

Went out to supper with the gang in the evening. Had drinks and dessert at a Bar at the Carlton in semi-darkness with stars blinking, elephants, negro masks, banana leaves and other features suggestive of Hollywood jungle. [In a letter to Gisela, Max added: "American girls have a habit of living up to the occasion by pressing their temples against their partner's cheeks and keeping their eyes fixed on him with an ecstatic air. I was glad to have a simple Wren from a farm in Kent who danced rumba as badly as I did."]

Had supper at a restaurant called Bonnets which pretended to be a log cabin. Very pleasant evening on the whole. Wound up at own hotel where they all impressed Lotte with their bombing stories.

26 September 1943, Sunday Started out early for Hendricks' house. Lotte, Hendricks and I set out in a beautiful Pontiac and drove towards Cabin John and up the Potomac River. About 3.5 miles beyond Cabin John we crossed a canal by a foot-bridge, waded though a river with sub-tropical forests on either side up a large island in mid-stream. Walked through a beautiful forest on the island for about 15 minutes and arrived at the other shore. Here cliffs of 50–60 feet height rise straight from the river and provide a very good climbing garden. Hendricks and another man named Donald Hubbard whom we had picked up on the way led us up some very stiff climbs. I had little strength in my hands and feet. Nevertheless I did not do too badly and only fell off on the most severe of the climbs. Had a pleasant bathe in the river and sun-bathe on the lovely rocks and under an almost cloudless sky. Went home very satisfied with hope for more. Spent the rest of the evening talking to Lotte.

27 September 1943, Monday Went to see the Lincoln Memorial. Very attractive white marble temple on a small hill and powerful statue of Lincoln inside. Saw Lotte off at the station and was sorry to see her leave. Next meeting either in N.O. at X-mas or in England after the war. Was amused to see how leisurely the departure of the train was handled in the country of bustle. Returned to the office where there was nothing to do. Spent the evening writing.

28 September 1943, Tuesday Spent the morning buying a food parcel for Gis and various articles of clothing for myself. Then went on to the Library of Congress and spent the rest of the day exploring it. Beautiful science library in the annexe which can hardly be more than 5 years old. Most of the more well-known text-books of science are actually available in the reading room. The rest can be obtained on order after about half an hour's waiting. The reading room has no windows and is very well air-conditioned and lit up.

Went swimming to a nice indoor pool at the Shoreham Hotel in the evening and was glad to get more exercise.

29 September 1943, Wednesday, and 30 September 1943, Thursday Little to report. Spent my days reading and writing. Got fed up with [Jon] Rivett making disagreeable and tactless remarks at me and told him off with good effect. Got homesick.

1 October 1943, Friday It was decided to send me to New York to contact Hohenstein to find out more about his work. After lunch at the Allies' Mess, a most charming place, I took the 2.55 train to N.Y., travelling very comfortably by Pullman. Was amused by my neighbour who told his pretty neighbour all about himself, his family, the number of employees in his factory, etc. by way of casual conversation after 15 minutes' acquaintance.

Rang up Elfi [Carrol] on arrival in N.Y.; she took a long time to take in who I was but eventually asked me to dinner for tomorrow. Went to see Fan at the Polytechnic. He is so rushed with doing dozens of different things in daytime that he has to do all serious work in the evenings and on Sundays. Spent the night at Fan's.

2 October 1943, Saturday Went to the lab and had preliminary discussions with Hohenstein, interrupted by constant telephone calls. Attended a colloquium given by a member of research staff. The paper was poor both in quality and delivery. Subject: volume concentrations of polystyrene during cooking. Mark discussed the paper single handed and displayed much knowledge of literature. Had lunch with the whole research gang. Met one interesting man, a Dr. Harold P. Lundgren of the Western Regional Laboratory, Albany near San Francisco, Calif. There are four of these Regional Laboratories in different parts of the country. They were obviously created during the depression, with the purpose of finding alternative uses for natural products such as wheat, cotton, soya beans and wood, of which there may be a surplus at one time or another. Lundgren who worked with [Theodor] Svedberg in 1926/27 is working on the production of artificial fibres from plant proteins.

After more talking I went to Downtown Manhattan to see Fan's X-ray tube at 45 Fulton St. It's nicely designed. I liked the filament contacts which are an improved version of the Philips tube. Main advantages are shock proof cable and compact designs around the target, enabling camera to be brought within 1″ of target. Beryllium windows are incorporated. There is a triple focus which the firm is trying to eliminate.

Went to collect a document BNLO in Federal Offices building, a lavish Govt. building where policemen challenge you at every corner to countersign your pass.

Was impressed by the canyons of Wall Street. Took the subway to Elfi Carrol and took an hour to get there.

They live in a nice little flat in a pleasant flat-house in Forest Hills, Queens. Elfi looked quite unlike the round flirtatious beauty she was when I knew her 7 years ago. Much thinner, still attractive, more serious with harder features. Had a sweet little boy of two. Husband is pleasant and reserved business man, obviously intelligent, but apt to run things and people down. They were mildly interested in Heini, not too pleased to see me at first, but warmed up later on. They were well assimilated despite imperfect English, and seem [to] have American friends rather than immigrants. Got home very late and tired.

3 October 1943, Sunday Spent the morning talking to the Fans. Took the Staten Island Ferry in the afternoon and was very impressed by the harbour teeming with ships of all kinds. New Brighton on Staten Island has pleasant garden suburbs; nothing much to see. On return to Manhattan took a Broadway bus up to 34th Street. Most of the parts between Downtown and Uptown look just like the Salzgries[42] in Vienna, the houses are mostly old, low and dirty.

Went to see the Empire State Building which looks most impressive from below. By a succession of 3 lifts you reach the top at the price of $1.10. I saw a nice sunset over the city. The observation platforms are crowded with soldiers and sailors who get the trip free.

Walked up to Times Square which is crowded with soldiers and did not impress me much. Walked about Broadway and 6th Avenue where there was little to see except pornographic book shops. Back at Fan's I found Mark who was leaving for Boston.

4 October 1943, Monday Started off by taking a train to the East Rocks where Hohenstein's store is located. Passed through crowded and dirty dock areas at top speed and arrived at the store where H has a miserable little corner in a large room amongst piles of meat. They work without adequate clothing. I couldn't stand the cold for longer than 10 minutes. After our return H showed me their testing equipment and I was persuaded to the view that their very high strengths were perfectly correct. Most of the work seems to have been done by collaborators of H's who were never mentioned in the reports, while Mark never wrote a word of the reports. Was very

---

[42]The name of a street.

impressed by all the work that has been done with very poor equipment and facilities. Parted from H who is anxious to help but wants proper authority and collaboration with the Canadians.

Met [John] Edsall of the Harvard Medical School who was very pleasant. Fan suggested that I should write a chapter of a book on proteins. Immediately after I accepted Fan was overcome by jealousy, as he realised that this would give publicity to my haemoglobin work and began a violent, tactless and unjustified attack on my two-dimensional Fourier. He is like a 5 year old child in many ways. I fear Fan won't make much propaganda for me here, unless it flatters him to have me under his protection.

Took the 6.30 back to W and spent the time writing to Gis.

5–9 October 1943, Tuesday–Saturday   No great events. Wasted most of my time sitting at the office, unable to do anything useful, because of noise, overcrowding and incessant talking. Had lunch with Cmdr. F. Bitter of the Aeronautics Sections in the Navy Dept. Pleasant middle aged man who evidently works extremely hard.

Most interesting morning of week was spent with Cpt. W.H. Smith, U.S.N. to whom Green and I had to explain the project. He was sympathetic and extremely quick on the uptake and seemed to have a general education in science. Made excellent impression.

On Friday I received a very unpleasant letter from Fan, accusing me of trying to "take over" the writing of Edsall's chapter from him. I was a fool not to get out of the whole affair as soon as I noticed Fan's rising jealousy. Was very upset by the letter—personal troubles always do seem to get me down quite out of proportion with their importance. I do so hate having a quarrel with anyone. To make matters worse I felt very ill that day and had to move from the hotel into my new lodgings with Mrs. Minnex, 3712, Garfield Street, N.W.

I took these over from Grant and like them very much indeed. I have a charming room which contains all and more than the necessary furniture. The house is a fairly new brick house, with front and back garden and porches on each side. Coming in from the street you walk straight into the sitting room. The house is furnished with imitation "antique" furniture of indefinite design, but nevertheless looks pleasant and harmonious. The owner runs a photographic shop, has two boys in the army. Everything is kept very clean and tidy.

Letter To Gisela Perutz, October 8, 1943

Now before I come to the usual report of my activities during the past two days I'll give a picture of the general situation. We have only started work yesterday. Before that we just killed time. Consequently I know just about as much about the duration of my stay as I did when I started from home. I don't even know whether things will move fast from now on or slowly or not at all and whether I shall act in an advisory capacity or actually do something. This is very sad, but then I only arrived 3 weeks ago and I mustn't expect too much.

I sent you two pairs of stockings, a lipstick, two cigars for Father and two packets of lifesavers in a parcel yesterday. I'll send another similar parcel next week. I am also sending you and Mother some soapflakes. There are endless regulations about the way parcels have to be sent, boxes have to be below certain dimensions and weigh under 5 lbs, etc. Besides you can't get everything by any means. Half the goods in stores are often just sold out. There are no silk or nylon stockings to be had; I bought you rayon stockings which Lotte helped to choose and I hope that they will be better than the ones you can buy at home.

9 October 1943, Saturday On Saturday morning Mrs. Minnex drove into town with her car. She has little petrol she says but "having her own car does make her feel such a lady."

Green and I caught the 4.30 p.m. to Montreal. We are having a sleeping car compartment to ourselves. They do send us around in extraordinary luxury. While having supper in the dining car Brian Roberts walked in. I was very thrilled to see him here. He was travelling to Ottawa with a party of U.S. and Canadian Officers. He later came to our compartment with a Mr. Paul Siple, a member of Byrd's successive Antarctic expeditions, who told me of testings in glaciers down to depths of 50 m revealing bulk temperatures of $-25°$F. They used electrically heated borers. Notwithstanding that, temperature plastic flow produces pressure ridges rising to 40'. I thought Siple would invite me to come and see him in Washington, but in the end he didn't.

10 October 1943, Sunday After a comfortable night in the train which seemed to be moving at top speed whenever I woke up, we arrived at Montreal on an icy morning, changed trains at an attractive station not nearly as sumptuous as the American ones and took a train for Ottawa. The town itself and the villages on the way all looked poor and dilapidated compared to the U.S., the countryside pretty with the leaves turning. Had another talk with Brian who told of his experiences at the Quartermaster General's office. Apparently nobody there was at all interested in his own work, but he was allowed to pry into all their activities. Everybody is feverishly engaged in writing reports and nobody reads anyone else's, so that numbers of people do the same work in ignorance of each other. Americans use 30 people to do the same work for which we use 3—still Brian had to admit that they are very good technically.

Arrived at Ottawa and found palatial rooms reserved at the Château Laurier, a typical luxury hotel probably post-last-war.

We went around the Government buildings and Houses of Parliament and then took a tram trying to get to some inviting hills across the river. The tram took us to a park instead where we walked along the river and woods. The air was as clear as I had not seen it since the Alps and the sky cloudless. The different shades of yellow, red and green were magnificent.

Got very sick on the way home and had to spend the rest of the evening in bed.

11 October 1943, Monday Green and I arrived at the N.R.C. (Sussex Street) at 9.00 am for our appointment with Cook. The building, a large plain uninteresting institute, was deserted and we learned that we had happened to come on a National Holiday, Thanksgiving Day. [W.H.] Cook turned up at 9.30. He is a youngish man, director of the Biology Division. N.R.C. incidentally is a combination of D.S.I.R., N.P.L. and Agricultural Research Council. Cook spoke at length about the great difficulties of the proposal and obviously has lost interest as he thinks it is doomed. He spoke at great length and liked to hear himself talk, but after an hour with him we had heard little of any interest. He then called in Steeves who produced some samples of P that were most interesting and whose consistency explained entirely the discrepancy between English and Canadian optimal percentages.

Very interesting demonstration of the principle of "Hingreifen muss man" [you must seize the opportunity]. We might have written letters about this for another 6 months.

Later on Dr. Niven joined us and after lunch told us the story of his model. I felt very miserable by way of a hangover from yesterday and was unable to follow his long and detailed story. He is an Aberdonian with all the slow plodding along characteristic for this race. Slowly, without letting anything deflect him from his path he showed us the entire pile of his data and photographs. He felt very bad about his having been marooned at Jasper for all that time and thought it had been done to have him out of the way. We assured him that the delays and procrastinations were not due to anyone's ill will or inefficiency, but merely to the inevitable delay in making decisions by two democracies where many people have to be asked. We had to be very diplomatic and not allow ourselves to be drawn into critical discussions about other members of the lab with possibilities of reports of anything we said reaching the other fellow. Useful suggestions of Niven's: cork and diatomite, paper tubing.

At 5.00 pm Niven had the good idea of taking us out in his car and drove us to the Gatineau Hills, the very hills we had not been able to reach yesterday. The drive went through hills of Wienerwald dimensions covered with foliage trees displaying all the colours we had admired yesterday. We passed golf courses and a lake where Ottawa people keep summer cabins. Farms and villages look unkempt and dreary. Farmers are very poor, so Niven tells us, and have a hard time to make a living. On the way home we picked up three girls who had been hiking all day. They were lively and quite pretty. Green and Niven brightened up remarkably as soon as there were females around. At first I thought that all the boys are in the army because there are so many unattended girls around, but Niven says that boys and girls keep apart and don't go out together. They usually marry boys they met at school. Niven is a bachelor; it seems he could not find a wife out here; he seems a lonely soul.

We had supper together and talked shop most of the evening. He knew little about the details of the proposal or its history and we had to do most of talking.

12 October 1943, Tuesday   We started by calling at B.A.T.M. where we called on Mr. Champion who was fully informed and sent us on to CE Cpt. Stanton. The latter took a great interest in the proposal which he had known from its beginnings. He kept us for a long time and told us many interesting facts about Canada's ship building programme. At the beginning of the war Canada was building one ice-breaker at Quebec. Now her merchant ship building is on the same scale as the U.K.'s. Shipyards have sprung up on the sea coasts and on the great lakes. Some skilled labour was obtained from Tyneside ship builders who had emigrated to the Prairies during the depression. Ships can be taken out from the Great Lakes to New York or down the Mississippi. Stanton is a convert to welded ships, says they are doing very well now. Stanton remarked that "some of the scientists out here had not fully appreciated the difficulties of the project."

Went to get visa at the U.S. Embassy and got it without any difficulties, much unlike London. After that we had our appointment with Dean [Jack] Mackenzie.[43] Green was so disarmingly friendly and cheerful that the Dean could hardly help to fall in. We talked mostly on generalities. Mackenzie described the American way of organising a new enterprise. They take much longer to get started, because they set up a rigorous organisation with water-tight directives and definite responsibilities before anything is done. He contrasted this procedure with the English way of setting up a variety of ad hoc committees whose executive authority or lack of it nobody ever is clear about. One committee suddenly vanishes and he finds Mahomet appointed a different one in its place, etc. Of course his picture of the English way was exaggerated, but there was much in what he said. I wonder whether the American organisation will not be too rigid for H.—Only at the end of the interview the Dean remarked pointedly that Mark had invented P. I replied that Hohenstein did. Apart from this there was no backchat.

Did some shopping after lunch and had another session with Niven during which he produced various interesting materials, such as spun [?] rock. Niven's speciality is heat and he seems to be Griffith's counterpart at N.R.C.

Spent the evening writing home.

13 October 1943, Wednesday After reading [Prof. G.M.] Williams' report I decided that it would be useful to see him. So I spent most of the morning at B.A.T.M. fixing up my journey to Saskatoon. Mr. Williamson, one of their Canadian officials, did all the work efficiently, not without using "American efficiency" manners in the tone and economical way he talked. Saw ladies drinking beer, just after 4.30 pm in a restaurant!

There was little more to do. Green left at 4.00 for Montreal. I just managed to squeeze in a swim in the sumptuous hotel pool and had to leave at 7.20 for the aerodrome.

Ottawa is an unattractive town built in a splendid spot. If the houses were not quite so dingy looking it would be quite a pleasant town. There are surprisingly many pretty girls.

At the Aerodrome I found a Lockheed two-engined plane—the civilian model of the Ventura, with a capacity for 14 passengers and a crew of three:

---

[43]Dean of the College of Engineering at the University of Saskatchewan.

two pilots and a pretty stewardess with a fixed smile. The plane is covered with polished aluminium sheet and looks most attractive but small after the Clipper.

The plane is filled to capacity. We start at 8.00 pm for Toronto. There is a slight haze on the ground, but the weather is clear with bright moonshine. Nevertheless I found it impossible to pick out any features on the ground except water. Even though the cities are fully lit up it is impossible to make out any buildings. It must be quite impossible for a bomber to hit a definite target at night and quite difficult enough to find the right place.

After a short stay at Toronto we took off for North Bay. There was little to see on the way. At North Bay, a small town on a little lake off Lake Huron, we had to interrupt the flight because of bad weather further ahead. We were driven to a hotel which was quite good for such a little place. There was a bible in the room, just as at the Château Laurier. This still is a religious country. Got to bed at 12.30.

14 October 1943, Thursday Was woken up at 5.50 and told to be ready to go at six. Actually about 40 minutes were spent having breakfast in a nice little restaurant which was open at this hour of the day. We took off at dawn and soon saw a bright red sunrise flying above a sea of clouds. At 9.00 we landed at Kapuskasing without having seen much of the country in between, because of continuous cloud. Kapuskasing is a large village built around a pulp mill. The houses look much neater than in Province Quebec, the old ones are wooden, the new ones made of brick. There are hardly any gardens either flower or vegetable. One has the feeling that it's an effort to live here and that keeping a garden is more than people can manage. Besides the climate is probably too severe for most things.

Went for a walk around the town and looked to the edge of the waste of woods. It's a desolate place, though possibly better than Eastern Europe or Lancashire slums. I wonder if people are happy here or if their one thought is to get away—provided they have known something else.

Took off again at 11.00 and flew over expanses of wood, red rocks and water—most desolate looking country. It must have needed courage to trek across these wastes to the West. No sign of human habitation can be seen for hours of flight. After 3.5 hours—the longest stretch—we landed at a primitive air field in the forests for refuelling (Kenora). There was snow on the ground, it was icy cold and we had to scrape thick layers of ice from the plane. We took off after half an hour and flew over more forests and lakes. Suddenly the scene changed as we entered the great plains and you could see nothing but wheatfields as far as the horizon. Arriving in Winnipeg at 4.00 pm. It looks nicely planned from the air. Heard that there is no more connection between Regina and Saskatoon to-day and that I shall have to stay the night at Regina. Arrived at Regina 6.45 Eastern time (4.45 Western).

15–17 October 1943 Spent one day and one night at Saskatoon with Professor G.M. Williams. Detailed description in Gis' letter. At the University met Professors Spencer, Thorvaldsen and E.L. Harrington, heads of Engineering, Chemistry and Physics respectively.

Visit was quite a success as far as H is concerned and I very glad I made up my mind to come. Williams has done excellent work and is obviously the man to take over from me. He spent 9 years testing concrete at the Bureau of Standards; is an American and will be on easier terms with the U.S. Navy.

Note in the Diary The remainder of my story until 18 Nov. is well covered by my letters to Gis. On the H side little more happened as far as I was concerned. Everybody was well pleased with the results of my Canadian trip as set out in the Canadian report. I had but one more discussion with Capt. Smith reporting on the manufacture of P in the light of the Canadian results. Shortly afterwards, i.e. towards the end of October, it became a practical certainty that P would not be used. I was satisfied with this development, as the technical difficulties had become formidable, the concrete had many obvious advantages, and finally I was getting very homesick and tired of travelling, hanging about waiting and living by myself to no particular purpose.

To Gisela Perutz. Regina, Saskatchewan, October 16, 1943

We were 10 hours late and had missed the connecting plane to Saskatoon, so I had to stay the night at Regina. As the delay was the company's fault, they paid for my room. Hotels in all the principal Canadian towns belong to the big railway companies and are built without regard of cost. Some are over-luxurious, others very nice, all are very comfortable and up to date and not necessarily expensive. At the Saskatchewan Hotel I got the first really nice tea since I arrived on this continent. There were a lot of local society ladies having afternoon tea, whereas at Ottawa I stepped into a respectable restaurant at 4.30 and found ladies having BEER, just beer!—with their kids looking on and getting nothing. This just shows you how tolerant the Empire is now.

Regina is a prosperous looking town, quite unlike the towns in Eastern Canada. Houses are built in the same style as I have seen them in the States, they look well kempt with trim little gardens in front, without the monotonous uniformity of English suburbia. The people both here and in Saskatoon are strikingly good-looking—many of Icelandic and Scottish stock, some Eastern European. Every other girl you see is pretty. Nearly all have healthy complexions and beautiful teeth. You rarely see the shrivelled, worn-out, pale-faced kind of women which is so frequent in industrial cities at home, nor is there any similarity to the nondescript crowd around New York. The climate and life must be healthy out here, despite the extremes of hot and cold. There are no slums, of course, though life on the farms must be far from comfortable.

Yesterday morning there was fog on the ground and the plane could not leave until about noon. So I arrived at Saskatoon over 30 hours late, but still much sooner than I could have got there by train. Professor Williams was waiting for me and we spent the afternoon at work.

In the evening we were joined by Professor Spencer, the dean of the Engineering Faculty, a tall stern looking man with a little red wig covering the bald patch of his head (I hope it won't come to that with me). Williams treated us to dinner at the hotel—he is a bachelor and lives there. Both Williams and Spencer are middle-aged hard-working men whose lives turn on teaching at the University and who have few outside interests. They were interesting to talk to and kind in answering my endless questions on conditions and life at their University and the country in general.

The wealth of the country depends on wheat and wheat alone. Farms are very large, not because farmers are rich, but because they need very large farms to make a living. They get a poor price for their wheat because it has to be transported for thousands of miles by rail and then compete with prices elsewhere. During the depression prices were down even further and in addition several years of drought added to the farmers' plight. The University nearly had to close down. Now they are doing well, but Hitler's theories about the great living space in this country are so much rubbish, because all the arable country is already under the plough, and the wheat would have to be transported by rail at so much cost whatever the economic system. The large farms depend of course on mechanised farming and the engineering department of the University trains students in theory and practice of agricultural machinery.

The University has about 3000 students. Before the war there were few scholarships, yet students did not come up at their parents' expense; the great majority take jobs during the holidays and pay their fees from their saved up money. If they run out of money then they just interrupt their studies, take a job for a year and save up enough to return to the University. Now the State gives scholarships to bright high-school boys so as to relieve the shortage of doctors, engineers and scientists.

I asked what people quarrel about at the University and was told they don't. There are no differences either political or religious and the University runs smoothly and as a happy family, thanks to its founder who was president until a short time ago and the present head, both universally respected. Students live in hostels if their homes are outside the town. The proportion of boys and girls is about equal, with "too much" social life in the way of dances and games.

The staff spend most of their time teaching and are doing a tremendous job for the war effort in turning out masses of engineers and physicists. Some research is being done, mostly directed towards the War Effort, some on wheat, milling, vegetable fats, etc.

I spent this morning looking over the Departments of Chemistry, Physics and Engineering and was introduced to everybody from the Professors (Dean of the Department) downwards. All the people are proud of their departments, particularly the professor of chemistry, a charming Icelander called Thorvaldson, who showed me every detail in the building. There is obviously not the wealth of equipment here which you expect to find at the very rich American Universities. Classes, laboratories all are on a modest scale and research equipment is very scarce indeed. Yet the teaching seems to be well organized and most of the teachers received their training at famous schools. The interior of the buildings is not quite up to standard. Obviously there was not enough money to use the best materials and laboratories are more worn-looking than they should be after 30 years. There is a complete lack of outside stimulus as regards research, the best of which seems to be concerned with the problems of a farming community.

Of political parties in this part of the world there were only conservatives and liberals until a short time ago, with little to choose between. Recently the Commonwealth Cooperative Party, a labour movement, which wants to nationalise the railways and basic industries, is gaining much ground among the farmers. Spencer and Williams regard it as just another party, don't think it will help to solve the farmers' problems. Interest in politics is very lukewarm. On the other hand the country is nearly 100 percent in the war which affects life in every way. Naturally food is not short here, but other things are more expensive—most of the young men are in the forces. Cost of living is about half that of Washington.

Cultural life consists of pictures and radio, outdoor life of games, there is no countryside that is not covered with wheat, no hill for hundreds of miles. Yet people look happy and exceedingly healthy. My plane is due to leave shortly, so I shall have to stop.

Kapuskasing, Ontario, 17 October 1943 We are snow bound here, goodness knows for how long. We took off at Regina late last night, first stop Winnipeg, where we had to wait for a couple of hours. We then flew on through fine weather all the way, with one more landing for refuelling until we arrived here and found 6 inches of snow on the ground. About 5 minutes after we landed a blizzard started carrying wet snow, the kind that is most effective in icing up wings. The wretched thing is that if only the blizzard had started 20 minutes earlier we needn't have landed here and might have flown on to the west air field. I had hoped to be back in Washington this afternoon which is out anyhow. If we can't get away by plane it will take me about 48 hours to get there by train. While I am duly concerned about my work, what I am really anxious about is that I might miss the Philadelphia Philharmonic Orchestra concert in Washington on Tuesday night. It's snowing lustily in big flakes and I wish I had snow-skis and a hill to use them on. As it is I have only a dark blue suit and town shoes. There is no train before tomorrow and no room in the local hotel either so I wonder how it will work out. At the moment we are all hanging about in the lounge of the hotel which the pulp mill built for its employees (they make the paper for *The New York Times* here), and various amateurs are trying their skill or otherwise on the piano. For most of the morning I could hardly keep my eyes open, but a nice lunch has woken me up temporarily.

After a walk in the snow I got an unexpectedly good tea in the club which the paper mill built in the town. A homesick London waitress was touchingly pleased to talk to someone from home. (Nobody out here notices by my accent that I was not born in England.) After more writing and hanging about we got a posh supper and beds to sleep in—I had expected nothing better than the dining room carpet. Today *18 October,* the weather isn't much better, but I had 10 hours sleep in a comfortable bed so my personal outlook is brighter. We drove out to the airfield in the morning and waited hopefully only to drive back to the hotel again for lunch. The Company's policy is to take no chances; they'd rather send their passengers home by rail than risk an accident. The pilot fears that the aircraft will ice up in the sleety rain before he can rise above the clouds.

Toronto, 19 October 1943, 9.00 am   In the end it was decided to send us here by train. Getting here took us just 18 hours, but was quite pleasant and comfortable. Just now I am investigating how to get to New York and from there to Washington without travelling another three days. Although I have been living as the guest of Trans Canadian Airways most of the time I have run out of money, very nearly, and out of shirts, handkerchiefs, razor blades, etc. So I wouldn't mind getting back from this trip which has been most interesting and worthwhile and took me much longer and further than I intended when I set out from Washington 10 days ago. I am looking forward to finding some letters from you there.

To Gisela Perutz. British Admiralty Delegation, Washington, D.C., October 10, 1943

I was terribly pleased yesterday morning when "Safe Hand" appeared with your letter No. 3 and two hours later brought in No. 4. "Safe Hand" is an elderly gentleman of petty officer rank who always offers you all kinds of letters and brings many disappointments. Hope rises in my heart whenever he opens the door only to sink again when I find that it isn't for me after all. You made me feel pleased and ashamed of myself by telling me how much you loved me in so much nicer words that I even could find for you. I do love you very much though even if I never managed to say it so nicely.

To Gisela Perutz. British Admiralty Delegation, Washington, D.C., October 28, 1943

My life is easy to describe. I leave the house at about 8.00 am, take a bus to the centre of the town and have breakfast at a cafeteria. After the usual half hour I trot to the office to read the paper and any letters that may have arrived. Later on we go for elevenses in one of the canteens and chat about people and America. From 11.30 to one I either read a book or write letters. Lunch takes us to another cafeteria where you usually have to queue up for 15 minutes or so, but this doesn't matter as time is no object. The afternoon is spent similarly as the morning. We make tea in a coffee percolator. We leave the office sometime between 5.00 and 6.00. In view of this description

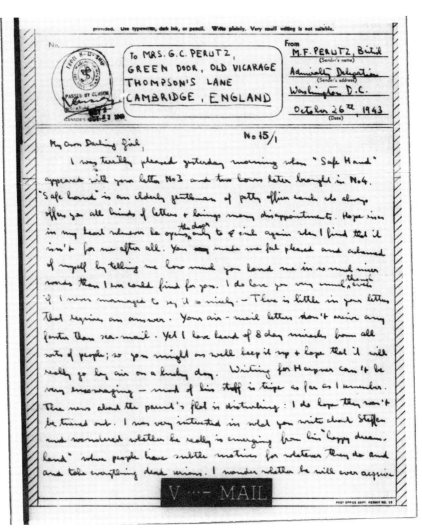

"V, or Victory mail, was a valuable tool for the military during World War II. The process, which originated in England, was the microfilming of specially designed letter sheets. Instead of using valuable cargo space to ship whole letters overseas, microfilmed copies were sent in their stead and then 'blown up' at an overseas destination before being delivered to military personnel." (Source: http://www.postalmuseum.si.edu/exhibits/2d2a_vmail.html). Original size

you might think we could spend the time more profitably, but then we usu-ally are wanted for some five minutes per day and there is no telling when these five minutes will be—so we just have to hang on or around. All this waiting isn't really anyone's fault or due to lack of foresight on somebody's part. It just happened that way and we have to make the best of it.

Breakfast, 29 October 1943 Last night I was invited at Commander Bitter's. I met him at his office in the Navy Department, which is so huge that messengers ride about its corridors on tricycles. There is a saying that any work that is being done in Washington is done *at least* twice over which may account for some of its size. Bitter is really a Harvard physicist who donned uniform for the duration. This seems to be a general habit here, and there are countless professors and engineers running around in the disguise of naval officers. The very big ones are Admirals and the lesser ones Captains and Commanders.

There are three Wrens sitting behind me who have been talking about nothing but hens ever since they got here. One of them sounds like a great expert and I found on inspection that she looks just like a hen. How unfortunate some people are in the choice of their hobbies.

I am very keen to go home soon. You will have gathered from this account that my contributions to the War Effort here are slight. I am longing to do some proper scientific work again.

To Gisela Perutz. British Admiralty Delegation, Washington, D.C., October 31, 1943

I managed to get down to work yesterday afternoon and today, and actually started to compose my Harvard lecture (invitation from Dr. John Edsall). I find it very hard to concentrate on haemoglobin suddenly. My mind wanders away across the ocean imagining what it would be like coming home, thinking of when it would be and how to get there soon without offending any of the people to whom I owe so much. Or I wonder what would happen if Fan were to attend my lecture, intent of running down the work out of jealousy rather than for the sake of truth. It's very hard to answer criticism that is not objective, but pretends to be, particularly if the person concerned has no control over his mind and is always totally unaware of his motives. However, there is little chance that Fan will be there and I can only hope that he will not do too much harm to my reputation in my absence.

More spotlights on America: Advertisement in a tram "Why not try God—Come to the Baptist Congregational Church on Sunday." On the other hand I saw inscriptions in a service department which are well worth adoption. One said "In an emergency any quick intelligent action is better than delay in search for the ideal." The other read "Nothing is impossible, it just means that it hasn't been tried."

To Gisela Perutz. Norwich [i.e., Franz's home], November 10, 1943

I made various calls on Saturday, amongst them Dr. Bergmann who is one of the great lights in protein analysis. He is a rather grumpy and morose old chap who has a permanent position at the Rockefeller Institute for Medical Research. He had read my papers, but holds the view that X-ray analysis of proteins has been begun 50 years too early and that there is no hope of finding out anything very useful before the chemists have vastly extended their knowledge of the constitution of proteins. He thinks that [Bill] Astbury is a charlatan—a view with which I sympathise—and does not think much of [Albert Charles] Chibnall [Professor of Biochemistry at Cambridge]. Bergmann himself certainly has done magnificent work and every progress he made only went to prove that the problem is vastly more complex than anyone anticipated. He is all against people who get sensational results without having a complete and satisfactory basis for them. I tried to persuade him that we are not after stunts but slogging away hard after solid facts—but I doubt whether I convinced him. It was an interesting interview, certainly a candid one, and I am glad to have seen the man.

I also saw Fan who had quite forgiven me for all the insults he had hurled at my head. I don't think I wrote to you that I managed to withdraw gracefully from the mess I had gotten myself into and to reconcile everybody concerned.

Having Jimmy around makes me think again how nice it would be to have one of ours, even though he is a pest at times.

To Gisela Perutz. British Admiralty Delegation, Washington, D.C., November 18, 1943

I went to Boston last Monday and proceeded straight to the Harvard School of Medicine where Dr. Edsall received me at the Department of Physical Chemistry. I arrived at 2.00 pm, and my talk was to take place at 4.30, so I had to start straight away preparing illustrations and drawings. There was a real tea before the lecture and I was introduced to about two dozen people in as many minutes and all of them made little speeches how extremely pleased they were to make my acquaintance. This is a most embarrassing habit in Boston which made me blush every time and mumble some quite inadequate reply about my considering myself fortunate to have come here. Edsall introduced me to the audience of about 30 people at the lecture. My own talk went off without any hitches but also without producing much response on the part of my listeners. I had the impression that many of them know so little about crystal-lography that it was hard for them to follow even though I left out everything that is at all difficult to grasp such as vector diagrams and reciprocal lattices. There was a discussion which was not particularly lively or productive.

After the lecture I drove home with Dr. Edsall who had asked me to stay with him. He has a very charming house some 10 miles from the town and an exceptionally charming and educated wife. They had asked another haemoglobin worker and his wife and we spent an interesting evening, one of the best I have had in this country. Edsall is one of those people who is interested in the whole of science and knows something about it and his wife, while not a scientist herself, takes a genuine and intelligent interest.

On Tuesday morning I was conducted through most of the Phys. Chem. Department and was very impressed by the crowds of bright and able work-ers, by the high standard of research and excellent workmanship displayed on all the instruments. The latter is far superior to anything we have at home. Moreover these people are not just gadgeteers, they really know how to use their ingenious and well-constructed tools and produce results. In the afternoon I just managed to pay a very short visit to Dr. [Martin Julian] Buerger of Mass. Inst. of Technology and again was impressed by his mag-nificent instruments. Buerger, however, *is* a gadgeteer who spends most of his time improving his instruments and produces few results of general value. I wouldn't have minded taking some of his gadgets home with me. I had a somewhat difficult time, because he accused Bragg of stealing his ideas and it took me a long time to persuade him that he was mistaken. By the way, the entrance door to MIT opens automatically as you approach it. Both MIT and the Harvard Medical School are attractive and dignified, though not new buildings. Boston itself looks more like an English town than anything I have seen here. Most of the houses were built in the last century and are made of bare bricks. The streets are narrow, traffic unregulated and wild, few points of attraction that I saw. This university has one great attraction though— people go skiing to the mountains on Sundays, at least they used to.

Return to Civilian Life

Research in This Decade
Max published a number of short papers on the X-ray analysis of haemoglo-bin, chiefly in Nature, *and later three major papers, two in the* Proceedings

of the Royal Society. *The X-ray results published in* Nature *in 1942 suggested an ellipsoidal shape for haemoglobin with dimensions of 64 x 48 x 36 Å (not greatly different from current textbook values of 65 x 55 x 50 Å). From his experiments with crystals in different concentrations of salt solutions, Max demonstrated that swelling and shrinkage are purely intermolecular processes, which means that there is no effect on the internal structure of the haemoglobin molecules themselves. This was important because crystals were dried to varying degrees when prepared for X-ray analysis, and even after the structure of haemoglobin had been solved, there were those who questioned whether the structure of the protein in crystals was the same as that of haemoglobin in red blood cells. From the crystal form, he was able to conclude that the molecule was composed of two identical subunits (corresponding to the αβ dimers).*

Over several years, Max collected data from 135 X-ray photographs of crystals of horse methaemoglobin at different stages of hydration and measured the intensities of over 7000 reflections. This was followed by many months of calculations, all of which had to be done manually, although in later years, some of the calculating work was contracted out, as is evident in the following correspondence. In the first of the papers in the Proceedings of the Royal Society A *(191: 83–132, [1947]), Max provided evidence for rod-like structures that are now known to be α-helices. He had hoped to obtain a molecular structure from the three-dimensional Patterson synthesis published in 1949 (*Proceedings of the Royal Society A *195: 474–499). In this paper, he produced the erroneous model that he called his "hatbox model," with the molecules arranged in layers in the crystal, and within each molecule, the chains were folded backwards and forwards to give a compact structure. The correspondence shows Max's ceaseless enthusiasm throughout the many years of hard grind collecting data and calculating results, but as we now know, it would be another 8 years before the critical breakthrough afforded by the isomorphous replacement method using heavy metals would make it possible to solve the structure.—AW*

Attracted by the challenge of discovering the molecular structure of proteins, a few remarkable individuals joined Max, who continued to receive financial support. In October 1947, under the auspices of the Medical Research Council, he became the director of the Research Unit for the Study of the Molecular Structure of Biological Systems. Initially the unit consisted only of Max and John Kendrew, who was supported by a fellowship he had won at Peterhouse in 1945. While in the Royal Air Force,

Kendrew had met Desmond Bernal, and he had fired Kendrew's interest in the problem of protein structure. Kendrew and Max would share the Nobel Prize in Chemistry in 1962. Francis Crick and Hugh Huxley joined them at the end of the decade. Like Kendrew, Crick came as Max's Ph.D. student in name at least; Huxley came as Kendrew's. After demobilisation, Crick had decided to move from physics into biology. He had been recommended to work on the viscosity of the cytoplasm of cells, but he soon dismissed the problem as trivial. By contrast, Max's problem was really important. As is well known, Jim Watson's arrival in the unit in 1951 directed Crick's attention to DNA, and together with Maurice Wilkins, they would win the 1962 Nobel Prize in Physiology or Medicine.

"Using his much better mathematical knowledge than my own, the first thing [Crick] did was to examine the validity of a model of haemoglobin which I had proposed in 1949 on the basis of my, I don't know how many years, probably at least five years' effort at what is called the three-dimensional Patterson synthesis of haemoglobin; and he demonstrated that it was nonsense." In fact Crick's disproof must have postdated Max's paper on the α-helix of September 1951. "You can get some information about the structure from the intensities of the diffraction pattern, which doesn't give you the structure itself but gives you the distribution of the vectors between the atoms, that is, the distances and direction of the links between the atoms, all projected to a common central origin. That means to say, supposing you had a structure that consisted of parallel rods, then the vector structure would also show parallel rods and would tell you the distances between them. Or if the structure consisted of parallel layers then again the vector structure might tell you. So my hope was that the protein structure had some simplifying features which would actually show up in this vector structure, and to obtain this I had to take about 200 or 250 X-ray diffraction pictures, each taking 2 hours' exposure and each containing several hundred spots and all these spots had to be measured. That is, one had to measure the intensities of the spots and their positions and index them. So I did years of work myself and I had two assistants who helped me with it, but it was tedious to a degree but all [done] hoping that it would provide clues to the structure." Crystals took about a month to grow and then they had to be mounted in the capillaries in which they could be X-rayed and X-ray diffraction pictures analysed.

"Now when it came out in 1949, I thought I did indeed see a rod-shaped distribution of vectors, which suggested that the structure might consist of a zigzag of protein chains all running parallel to the same direction, and I also had some ideas about the shape of the molecule and I produced a model, which was known as the hatbox, because that's the shape it had, and the proteins were arranged in a parallel zigzag, and I did publish that in *The Proceedings of the Royal Society.*" Max also concluded from Kendrew's results that the structure of myoglobin was similar. "I was very disappointed but I wasn't angry at Crick for disproving it because in a way it was my own fault. . . . The evidence which he produced was convincing."[44] To Harry Kroto Max said: "Having put this tremendous effort into the work, I think I just couldn't face saying it was all in vain. It told me nothing. It's just more than you are capable of to admit to yourself that this was useless and you had to throw it all away, and of course, as you can imagine, I was very unhappy because I didn't know what to do next and how to find the true solution."[45]

Luckily Max also had a glaciology project. The 1938 expedition to the Jungfraujoch "had got me interested in the mechanism of glacier flow. . . . It wasn't quite clear how a crystalline body could flow at all. After all, a glacier is solid, so how can it flow? When the snow has melted, the surface of glaciers shows regular dark lines [across the direction of flow], lines where ice has become dirty, and those are the annual lines like the lines on tree growth. They are curved so that the centre is more advanced than the sides, which shows that the glacier flows faster at the middle than at the sides, and the problem was: how can a solid body flow like this? And again there were theories that it flows by melting and refreezing which didn't seem very likely." Max learned from Egon Orowan, a colleague at the Cavendish, about the way metals flow, as happens, for example, when "you draw steel into tubes or wires." Because metals are crystalline, Max imagined that crystals of ice might behave in a comparable manner. "I thought if I could measure the vertical velocity distribution in the glacier, so actually measure how much faster or otherwise the ice at the surface flows than the ice at the bed, that would provide information about the physics of flow, and especially if I could correlate that with the mechanical properties of ice measured in a laboratory cold room."

To make the measurements, in the summer of 1948, his team drilled "a hole from the surface to the [glacier] bed, lined it with a flexible steel tube and surveyed its inclination after one and two years." This demonstrated that the glacier "flowed faster at the surface than at the bottom and that it behaved just as a crystalline solid ought to behave. That is, ideally crystalline solids . . . are rigid up to a certain stress and above that they become ductile, and we

---

[44]Max Perutz interviewed by Katherine Thompson, 2001, National Life Stories, British Library Sound Archive catalogue reference C464/22.

[45]Vega Science Trust 2001, www.vega.org.uk.

realised that it behaved just like that. . . . But now the trick was to relate our measurements in the field to the mechanical properties of ice in the lab, and to do this the Royal Society provided me with the money to install a cold room in the Cavendish," where Max and two postdoctoral students whom he had recruited worked. "Between us we actually managed ... to produce a physically sound theory of glacier flow based on the physical properties of ice."[46] That is to say, at the end of the 1940s, his sideline, in contrast to his main line of research, had given me one result of lasting importance.

To Herbert and Nelly Peiser, May 21, 1944

It would be tempting to hint that I sent letters at frequent intervals which were all suppressed by the censor. I believe I always wait for a particular occasion when there would be something special to write about. However, this time there certainly is something special. I hope you will be pleased that an offspring is on the way. We are both delighted and very much looking forward to it. Many things have changed for the better since I last wrote to you on this subject. The war is approaching its final phase and our day to day dangers here have very substantially diminished. My change of status[47] has given me a home and confidence in my own future, whereas two years ago there always loomed the fear in my mind that my position after the war might not be any more favourable than before. Finally we have a flat to ourselves; admittedly it is tiny and will become too small for us as soon as our baby reaches the crawling age, i.e. by the end of 1945; but on the other hand there is no likelihood that our land-lord will suddenly take it into his head to turn us out or to double the rent or to declare that he objects to children. In fact our landlord is a sweet good humoured little man who looks rather like a rabbit, plays the piano and disapproves of ever profiteering in a practical way—a very rare virtue. We are not particularly worried about the cost but there are many essential items which are hard to come by and can only be bought at prices quite out of proportion with their value. The trouble is that a large

---

[46] All quotations on the glaciology project are from Max Perutz's interview by Katherine Thompson, 2001, National Life Stories, British Library Sound Archive catalogue reference C464/22.

[47] That is, naturalisation as a British subject.

part of the population earns more than they ever did before and that these people will pay any price for almost any piece of rubbish thus boosting prices of all goods that don't come under control of the State. So we hope that our friends will lend us some pieces of equipment.

Last night I had a session with Sir Lawrence Bragg which went on until late. I discovered a new type of crystal just after Easter which suddenly transformed the whole aspect of my protein research and gives rise to high hopes. It was an unusual honour and a great pleasure to discuss my problems with the great man for several hours. He has an extraordinarily clear vision and a powerful imagination, coupled with a boyish enthusiasm and spirit of adventure; he also has a most useful ability of putting me on the right track. I owe much to him for the success I have had so far and I very much hope to stay with him for several years to come. I also presented him with a long list of proposals for expansion of the laboratory after war. I was surprised by his attitude towards these which can be summarised with the words: "Why not do it now?" He is a man with great drive who likes to get things done and a very efficient administrator.

As you can see from this account we are very happy and look forward to staying here for a long time to come. When I saw my brother I could not fail to be impressed by the comfort and luxury in which he lives. Still we would not exchange the stimulating and delightful company of our friends for all the spacious houses, refrigerators and washing machines over there, with a life that is dull and monotonous. I believe that there is no place like this, with its congenial atmosphere, its absence of petty rivalry and intrigue and the broad-minded tolerance that is almost universal.

To Mr. Frank Blair Hanson of the Rockefeller Foundation, August 1, 1944

On the personal side I am sorry to report that Miss Davidson has accepted a demonstratorship at the Royal Free Hospital in London, and is leaving Cambridge at the end of September. I am disappointed to see her go as she proved a very conscientious and industrious worker and has done very well indeed. She made her appointment conditional on being allowed to continue the protein work at the Davy Faraday Laboratory, and Sir Henry Dale, its present director, has kindly agreed to let her use its facilities. Seeing that collaboration with us would involve a certain amount of travelling expenses which would be more than Miss Davidson could pay out of her own pocket, I wonder whether the Foundation would be willing to provide a fund of, say,

£30 to cover these extra expenses, with the balance to be returned to the Foundation at the end of the year.

There is little apparatus that can be bought at the moment for any research not connected with the war. We did, however, manage to obtain a Philips X-ray tube which is intended to replace the tube bought for me by the Foundation in 1939. The new tube costs £88, and we should be grateful if the Foundation could cover that sum. There is other apparatus that will probably be needed, apart from mathematical tables of a certain kind, which may involve a major expense, but all these projects are still uncertain, and some depend on whether the war in Europe is going to end this year or not. I therefore propose not to ask for more than the above-mentioned £88 at this stage.

To Lotte Perutz. Wastwater Hotel, Lake District, September 3, 1944

We arrived here yesterday after an all night journey from London.

I have had two months of most successful work, in the course of which I obtained a wealth of experimental results. I think I might as well give up worrying that I ever reach deadlock in my protein research or run short of ideas. The more I work, the more ideas occur to me for more research and the more people I employ, the more work I have to do for them. I had a prolonged talk with Bragg about my position at the University and was pleased to hear that he wants me to stay there after the war and to make my position more permanent and secure. What form this will take is not settled as yet, but there is every hope that a position will be created for me in the next 6 months. What I should like is to become a lecturer in physical biology and a fellow of a college; I don't know whether this will be feasible just now, but there is no doubt that something is going to happen. I am planning to enlarge my team to about 6 people after the war, with improved facilities.

The article[48] in the *Scientific Monthly* (issued by the American Association for the Advancement of Science) has appeared in the July number. I rehashed the article some weeks ago and made a number of improvements which suggested themselves to me when I discussed the article with some people who read it; Professor Keilin, in particular, criticised many points and made a number of useful suggestions; in the end I sold the improved

---

[48]Proteins: The Machines of Life.

version to an English periodical called *Discovery*. The article is a good proposition financially and will bring in about as much as a month's salary.

Some amusing stories. There are many West African students in Cambridge just now. One has lodgings in the street where our char lives, a street of small working class houses populated by women who have never been far away from Cambridge; so the negro is the talk of the street and we hear all about him. He is ever such a gentleman, they say, and wants a bath every day. Seeing that his landlady could not provide this and did not like his washing in the kitchen he proposed to have

David Keilin

his bath in the back yard. When his horrified landlady remonstrated that there all the neighbours could watch him, he retorted with surprise: why not, there is nothing private about me? On the other hand when the landlady went out to pay rent, he was horrified that people have to pay rent for the house they live in. Nobody pays rent for his house in Africa, he remarked. He was also shocked at the frequent murder stories in the papers—wondered why people kill each other here. Nobody ever kills anyone in Africa he said. Which made me wonder which are the savages, we or they?

Speaking of savages I thought on the way here that this nation has unfortunately lost much of its former charm under the stress of war. Wherever you go people are unfriendly or downright rude to you. In the shops they serve you with a sort of take it or leave it attitude. At Euston on the way here the porters were drunk and so rude that it was hardly possible to find out where which parts of the train were going. On the way up a ruffian of a guard turned everybody out of the carriage at about 10 sec. notice. War profiteering is rife everywhere; it is impossible to leave a bicycle anywhere in Cambridge without it getting stolen. There is an appalling amount of petty theft and fraud going on all over the country, of a kind that would have been unthinkable before the war. The University is a sort of island where people are still as nice as they were and most of the people we have friendly contact with have preserved their moral standards and decent manners. One can only hope that this will improve again after the war. Much of the lowering in the moral standard—such as public love making with American soldiers in parks and streets, of a kind which would be unthinkable in the U.S.A.—is probably due to the breaking up of family life. It will be difficult to make decent citizens of these people after the war.

These gloomy aspects recede to the background after to-night's wonderful news—Brussels taken, Antwerp reached, nearly all the German army in Northern France trapped and facing disaster, no army to man the Siegfried line, and the Gothic line in Italy broken. Perhaps the European war will be over by the time this reaches you. By the way, people here are well aware that we still have to fight the Japs, though none is pleased at the prospect.

To Lotte Perutz, December 1, 1944

Speaking of babies, Gisela is getting on very well. As the great event is due just about the time when I hope this letter will reach you, I shall try to send you a cable.

I believe I told you that I had to give a new course of lectures this term on the submicroscopic structure of cells and tissue, to advanced physiology students. There were 6 lectures and 6 hours of practical demonstration. Both of these were new features and had not been given before by anyone else so that I had to spend a great deal of time in reading and preparation. I had the nicest lot of students I have ever come across; eight boys in their 3rd year, all of them outstandingly intelligent and very pleasant indeed. Only medical students who do their exams at the end of the second year with particular distinction are allowed to specialise on a scientific subject—the others have to go through the routine medical course as fast as possible and are called up for the forces as soon as they become qualified. I shall give my usual course again next term and hope that it will be better than last year when I felt too feeble and miserable to put enough "pep" into it.

Priority No. 1 just now is to get some experiments done before next term starts. I am very anxious to collect the material still needed for the first of my long papers on the crystal structure of haemoglobin. One day I might try to write a book on the lines of my protein article, that is to say on the submicroscopic structure of living matter. But if I think of the amount of work that the small article entailed, I am horrified at the idea of a book. On the whole it is more profitable to do original work than to write books—popular or otherwise.

By far the larger part of the baby's equipment is borrowed from many friends who were kind and helpful. Without them we should be in a terrible plight as the majority of articles are unobtainable. Altogether the shortage of civilian goods is now becoming very acute. Even food has been more difficult for the past month or so than it has ever been, but I gather that this particular shortage is purely local. On the whole, I think this Government got the food distribution better organised than any other. You must know that during the whole of the war, with blitz, flying bombs, blockage and all, it never happened once that we did not get our weekly rations nor have I ever heard of any one else who failed to obtain them, nor have rations been changed substantially since 1941. Food may be monotonous and "standing in line," as you call it, is a shocking waste of time for women who are in jobs and sometimes the unrationed things get very short, but no one in these islands actually had to starve because of the war.

We have been looking for an Xmas present for you, that is, to send a book, which is the only thing one can send, but the situation is very dreary. Any good book is out of print within a few days or weeks of its appearance and all the old stocks have either perished in the big Blitz or have been sold out since.

You speak in your letter about post-war plans for the weather. A man I know thought the thing to do here would be to build a very high mountain in Ireland. This would (a) improve the English climate (b) create employment (c) bring winter sports within our reach (d) solve the Irish problem.

To Evelyn Machin, December 10, 1944

Life is going on much as usual. I teach and do research and enjoy both very much. There has been much progress during the summer and that spurred me on to further efforts. The nice thing about research is that one gets a little nearer to the truth all the time and can build up new work on what's already been done.

We had a very nice holiday in Wastwater in the Lakes where I started rock climbing again and enjoyed both it and the knowledge that I could still do it after all these years. I also became an almost expert tennis player during the summer and I've now started to play squash. I had previously believed myself to be hopeless at all such games but with a little perseverance I managed to learn them after all. I had the great asset of possessing four balls of Gisela's, and the use of a court at Peterhouse, by means of which I tempted various expert players who lacked such riches to play with me. Anyhow these various recreations help to keep me in good health and I hope will avert my succumbing to the rigours of the Cambridge winter as in previous years.

To Herbert and Nelly Peiser, January 15, 1945

This was the first day when I went for a walk with Gis and daughter [born 26 December] and took them for lunch in a restaurant. Vivien was left in a pram outside, much to the waitresses' amusement, and we continued our custom of not cooking a big meal on Sundays. I wonder how much longer we can do it. The nurse was with us. She is a good old soul, works very hard and is quite good to the baby. We are a bit unhappy about having a stranger with us all the time, but apart from that very glad to have secured her services, particularly so as Gisela was turned out of the nursing home after only ten days.

I decided that the war was approaching its end and submitted to Sir Lawrence Bragg a programme of research for the next year or two; I had a lot of fun drawing up that plan which served to impress upon people my need for increased assistance both as regards personnel and apparatus; moreover Bragg seemed to like it and asked me to stay on at the Cavendish Laboratory after the war which I am happy to do and which relieves me of the anxiety of many of my colleagues who are wondering what to do when their war-time jobs get to an end.

As soon as this research plan was finished I found myself very busy collecting the material for my new lectures to medical students on the "Molecular Structure of Cells and Tissues." There were only six lectures altogether, yet it takes a very great deal of time to prepare them if the subject is not standard textbook matter—actually one week's work per lecture is not uncommon. I was, however, rewarded for this labour not only by having learnt many interesting things myself, but also by having the nicest lot of students I have ever come across.

January 20, 1945 I always have to write these letters in instalments. In the meantime I have been to London for a short visit, to buy some microscopes for the laboratory, to hear a lecture at the Chemical Society, and to have a talk with Sir Henry Dale, the President of the Royal Society. I had tea with that august body on Thursday and saw your old friend [the chemist Sir Alfred] Egerton. Sir Henry Dale was as nice as these people here nearly always are, expecting the best from everybody and never wanting to impress you with their authority except by virtue of their natural grace. I had to tell him about my research and found him a kind and interesting listener.

To Franz and Senta Perutz, February 27, 1945

The baby is extremely well and gaining weight. Gisela manages to get through all the work without having to rush. It is not easy, though, in our minute little flat, where we have no room for the baby who sleeps in our bedroom in daytime and our sitting-room at night. Besides you must remember that we possess no washing machine and no bath-room—everything has to be done in the tiny little kitchen. Of course there is also no refrigerator, vacuum cleaner or telephone and none of the shops delivers goods to your house. There is no proper garden—the baby is put into a sort of no man's land between the church yard and the synagogue, and the people from the synagogue complained once that Vivien interrupted their service by her crying. Nevertheless we have much to be thankful for. For we do have enough to eat—Gisela gets 2 pints of milk per day for the baby and herself, concentrated orange juice and cod liver oil; the baby also gets the full fat ration of a grown-up and many other rations in smaller quantities. We also have enough fuel to keep ourselves warm.

To Lotte Perutz, March 11, 1945

We have not been out of Cambridge since I last wrote to you, but lots of people have come to see us here. There was also Edna Davidson, another of my former collaborators, who was so very nearly killed by a rocket that her escape is nothing short of a miracle. A rocket fell just outside the room she worked in, shattered her window but threw her on the floor without injuring her except for a few cuts and bruises. She is so pleased to be still alive that she hardly minds the shock.

In the lab we had visitors from France and Holland. They thought life here was really perfectly normal compared with France. They have not had gas or electricity in their laboratories for about a year; fat ration is 100 grams total per month, bread very severely rationed, meat rations minute. Things are much worse now than during the German occupation when most families got food parcels from relatives in the country; now rail traffic is so badly cut about that this parcel traffic is no longer possible.

Our Dutch visitor was the director of the Philips Lamps research laboratories in Eindhoven. He told us a story of the Germans packing up the entire contents of their very large research laboratories during the British advance through Belgium. After the Germans had stripped their lab and had all their equipment loaded on railway trucks, British parachutists dropped in the neighbourhood, the Germans fled in a hurry leaving the trucks behind, and the Dutch recovered all their equipment. When this man saw us, production at their factory was still at a stand-still, because they had no gas for glass blowing; the gas works were some distance away and still in German hands. Conditions in liberated Holland are worse than in France—those in *occupied* Holland must be ghastly. Many of us would be willing to cut our own rations to help the liberated countries; we are actually storing up food for the time when the sending of parcels will be allowed. I hope soon.

There has been a little progress with my job, though it is exasperatingly slow. Bragg told me that there may be two Royal Society Research Fellowships going, which will be established by discontinuing a professorship and dividing it in two. Bragg will try to get me one of these with the support of Prof. Keilin (Biology) and Chibnall (Biochemistry). So I drew up a research programme which has still to get Chibnall's approval before Bragg is going to send it in. I really wanted a lectureship, but if Bragg and Keilin think that this is a better idea, I don't want to stop them, seeing that they have been the kindest and most consistent benefactors which I ever could hope for. I have just finished my usual course of lectures, without being entirely satisfied with them; many of the biologists always find the initial theoretical part so difficult that they are frightened off and don't stay to hear the remainder. I think I shall change things round a bit next year and make it easier for people to understand, give them less theory and more application.

We have been extravagant lately and went to the theatre three weeks running. Speaking of extravagance you may be interested in the cost of a baby in this country. The bills for the nursing home which was first class, the doctor and the home nurse for 6 weeks amounted altogether to $200.[49] I wonder how this compares with your standards. Perhaps I ought to add that my monthly salary amounts to merely $160 and that a quarter of this is taxed away.

To Lotte Perutz and Franz Perutz, April 8, 1945

Thank you very much for your letter and for the wonderful parcel. The toys for Vivien are grand and just the very thing for her; we were very pleased

---

[49]My birth predated the National Health Service, which provides free medical care and dates from 1948.

because all modern baby toys like that are unobtainable here. Thank you also for the hot water bottle.

I have been asked to give a lecture on the "Application of X-rays to the Study of Colloids" to a summer school for industrial chemists. This gave me a lot of work lately and will bring in 10 guineas [i.e., £10.10.0]—apart from enlarging my knowledge again.

We are all thrilled with the progress of the war and of course with the prospect that it may end any day now. The only event which spoils thoughts that the Hitler nightmare will shortly be over is the siege of Vienna. I had hoped until a short time ago that the war would be over before the Russians reach Vienna, or that the Germans would abandon the town. Instead Hitler put that scoundrel Dietrich in charge of the defence. Tonight the BBC announced that the Russians had taken the Arsenal and Klosterneuburg [a town just east of Vienna]. According to other BBC reports and others from the Austrian resistance movement the town is already ruined morally and materially. There has not been any gas, water, or electricity for weeks, most of the men were killed fighting the Russians in Hungary, air-raid damage is said to be very severe. The middle classes are said to be bankrupt and sharing their flats with crowds of evacuees from Germany, the working classes mostly lethargic. Will Vienna rise again from such fearful calamities in our life time? Will it be the capital of the Austrian Socialist Republic or part of the Confederated Danube States? Will any of our friends there still be alive, I wonder?

Well it's a week since I started this letter, and a very eventful one at that. Vienna is free, without the fearful struggle which we had been led to expect, and the Allies are 65 miles from Berlin.

On Tuesday night we went to see the film Wilson,[50] on your recommendation, and found it very interesting despite all the adornment with sentimental trash. The film does bring out the greatness and the tragedy of the man who failed to persuade the American nation to take the step which could have saved them from this war. How terrible that Roosevelt, who would have succeeded where Wilson failed, should have left us at this crucial moment.[51] Or do you think that his message has taken firm enough root in the minds of the American people to make them remember even in the triumphant hour of victory that the safety of the world

[50]The film of 1944 starring Alexander Knox as U.S. President Woodrow Wilson.

[51]President Franklin Delano Roosevelt died on April 12, 1945.

depends on their protection and that there is no safety for America in a world of war?

On Wednesday a cousin of Gisela (there are dozens) arrived here on embarkation leave; a nice boy, potentially, whose life has been completely messed up by emigration and the war, who is quite alone in the world, without having received any adequate education to make him fit for civilian life.[52] I went to the annual conference on X-ray Analysis of the Institute of Physics which was held in London this time. It was very interesting in parts. One of my friends there is Mrs. [Kathleen] Lonsdale, a physicist who has just been elected a Fellow of the Royal Society, the first woman to receive that honour during the 300 years of the Society's history. She is a Quaker and conscientious objector to all forms of compulsion, and went to prison a couple of years ago for refusing to register for fire-watching. The extraordinary thing was that she actually did regular fire-watching duty at the time, and it was only to the act of registering that she objected. The judge did everything he could to avoid sending her to prison, but she refused to pay her fine and wrote specially to say that she still refused to register, so that she had to be summoned again for the same offence. She is a most resolute little woman of about 45 with two daughters of about 14–15, and an amazing output of interesting research. *The Manchester Guardian* wrote that she and Bertrand Russell, the philosopher, were now the only two fellows of the Royal Society who had been to prison—Russell having been a conscientious objector during the last war.

A lot of family assembled for Vivien's christening. Mother put all her jewels on and looked extremely elegant. She always still manages to look as though she had just emerged from a shop in Paris, and is by far the smartest dressed woman in Cambridge. Afterwards we had the whole little party for tea and Mother told Gisela's aunt about all the things she used to have and all the people she used to know in Austria, father admired me because I looked after the baby, a thing which he could never do, and Viven thought I wish there wouldn't be so many people and I could play with Mummy as usual.

Next Friday I shall go to N. Wales with Heini and I look forward to it.

---

[52]This must be Dennis Palmer (Dieter Peiser). After his demobilisation from the army, he joined the Control Commission for Germany as Chief Interpreter of the Supreme Court in the British Zone and read for the Bar in his "spare" time. He ended his career as Commonwealth Public Defender in Australia and then in "retirement" as Lord High Justice in Fiji.

To Mr. H.M. Miller of the Rockefeller Foundation, June 22, 1945

First of all, I should like to clarify a point in Sir Lawence's [Bragg] last letter concerning the future finance of my research programme. While I am hoping to get a research fellowship for myself, personally, we have no alternative source of support for my research programme as far as apparatus and assistants are concerned.

As concerns the finance of the two pieces of apparatus which we asked you to purchase for us, we should be very glad if you could consider this as a grant in aid, supplementary to our grant for the year 1944–5.

We are now trying to find the appropriate channels for obtaining import licences for these instruments, and we shall let you have these at the earliest moment. I am afraid the prospects of having apparatus made in this country are now more remote than ever, so that we are extremely glad to have your help in getting the two instruments from the United States.

To Herbert and Nelly Peiser, July 17, 1945

My father wondered whether I shall now have the letters F.I.C.I [Fellow of Imperial Chemical Industries] after my name; but though this would be decorative no doubt, there is no precedent for it so far. My new job has many advantages: the first of these is that it merely gives my old job a new and better name, with a certain prestige attached to it, and a slight financial gain. My duties, such as they are, will be the same as before, and I shall largely be free to do what I please. The job entails no obligation towards the I.C.I. and is purely a University appointment; whether it will lead to contacts with that firm in addition to those which I have already, remains to be seen. The research fellowships, 60 in number, are a gift from the I.C.I. to the universities which was made last year in order to foster research; 12 were given to Cambridge and eight of these have now been awarded for the first time. I am of course very pleased to have it and hope that it will help me on the road to better things, i.e. I regard it as an opportunity rather than an end in itself.

We are going to make every effort to come and see you as soon as ever permission can be obtained, but I fear it will take until the autumn before the authorities will let anyone go. This by the way is purely a guess of mine—so far no one is prepared to give any indication at all. Travelling anywhere these days is pretty frightful, but travelling with small children is a nightmare. I have just returned from a week-end with Steffen in Derbyshire.

I travelled up a large part of the way jammed into a luggage van and back standing in an overcrowded corridor, missed my connection and had to stay the night in London. I can hardly think what it must be like in Europe.

To Lotte Perutz, August 4, 1945

I got the I.C.I. Research Fellowship for which I had applied. It is very nice, because it gives me a definite status and a certain prestige, judging at least from the number of congratulations I received. The Fellowship lasts three years with a salary of $2400 a year; this used to be a lot in this country, but now the cost of living has risen so much that we shall hardly save anything on it. The financial improvement over my previous salary is in any case very slight. I hope that I shall have either the Royal Society Research Fellowship or the lectureship before the three years are up.

You may have heard of the astonishing outcome of our elections. We were as much surprised as anyone else, but also very pleased. It may seem strange to you over there that we should have voted against Churchill, but over here the matter appears in quite a different light. The conservative party hoped that by switching the limelight on Churchill and by exploiting his immense popularity they could stave off the defeat which the disastrous results of the pre-war policy would bring about. But we and the majority of people saw that by voting for Churchill we should put into power a party which is against social progress and against taking any of the radical measures which will be needed to pull this country through the post-war years. You see while attention is focussed on Churchill people overseas forget that the leading men in the Conservative Party today are still the same as those who supported Chamberlain. On the whole I think that most newspaper comment on the reason for the surprising swing was off the point. The first and most important reason why the masses voted Labour was their conviction that they were the only party who could stave off unemployment after the war. In any worker's family the reminiscences of unemployment are indelibly printed into people's memory; to vote Conservative for them means to vote for the dole. It is also widely believed that only the Labour party is willing to take drastic enough steps to solve the desperate housing problem. The younger scientists are in favour of Labour to the extent of about 80–90%, because Labour stands for an economy planned on a rational basis. Finally many of us fear that Churchill's preference for constitutional monarchies in Europe and his discouragement of leftist governments within the British sphere of influence would have led those countries back to fascism even though he might not have intended that to be so.

The Labour Party has, of course, no monopoly of virtues. It is much under the thumb of the trade union bosses, and it is to be feared that they will force up wages and reduce working hours without ensuring a corresponding increase in productive capacity, a move which would further increase the danger of inflation. Also [Clement] Attlee [the new Prime Minister] cannot be compared in stature with Churchill—as a matter of fact I hear that he is rather mediocre; they seem to have a tendency to distribute Parliamentary seats and Government offices among worthy and meritorious trade union secretaries, whose qualifications for the offices they hold are not always obvious—I gather that the first American reaction to the election results was a fear that Britain would now line up with Russia and leave the U.S.A. without an ally. There is no question of that; the Labour Party is strongly anti-communist, though less anti-Russian and more sincerely in favour of collective security than the Conservatives.

May I put one request to you for something we shall need very badly next winter? Do you think you or Franz could buy us three rubber hot water bottles and send them to us. I shall repay you when an opportunity offers itself.

To Felix Haurowitz. Wastwater, English Lakes, September 13, 1945

I was glad to hear that you and your family are well and got through the war unscathed, even if difficult times are not yet over. I was amused to hear of your mountaineering expeditions—I had not realised that such high mountains are within easy reach of Istanbul.[53] I am at the moment climbing about in hills of a much more modest height—3000 *feet* is the best we can do here. On the other hand they are not without charm and beauty and offer some very good opportunities of rock climbing of a high standard.

Work is going quite well. I got some interesting data on haemoglobin crystals this summer and hope to start writing the first of a series of larger papers this autumn. We determined the unit cell of haemin, but so far have no information on the structure, on account of great technical difficulties in getting a sufficiently strong X-ray photograph of a certain type from our rather small crystals. But no doubt we shall succeed to overcome these

---

[53]Haurowitz had taken a professorship in Istanbul.

snags, and the structure analysis itself will probably not prove unduly hard. I shall let you know if we get anywhere.

I was extremely sorry to hear of the terrible fate of Leo[54] and Gina's mother—that is to say I heard that they had vanished without trace. It must be very hard for Gina to be completely powerless to find out anything about them and to have been helpless during the war to avert these frightful happenings. We are all very upset about Uncle Arthur[55]—particularly Father who can't get his fate out of his mind and broods over it when he lies awake at night. I did not show Father your letter because it contains a remark that Arthur was killed. I presume you just refer to the information we all have, namely that he died either at a concentration camp on the border of Austria and Hungary or on removal from that camp with the approval of the Russians. Father thinks he just died of exhaustion, cold and hunger, but was not actually killed. I should just like to have a confirmation from you that your remark implies no more than this.

To Dr. H.M. Miller of the Rockefeller Foundation, September 28, 1945

The apparatus which you are purchasing for me will be of immense help. All my efforts to obtain suitable X-ray tubes and cameras in this country have failed, and without your assistance much of my experimental work would inevitably have come to a standstill.

To Evelyn Machin, December 27, 1945

There were lectures, demonstrations, an exhibition at the Royal Society Soirée in November, two students to train in research, a new laboratory to organise and equip, visitors from overseas, conferences and discussions—I wonder why the life of a University don was ever regarded as leisurely. There is always so much more to do than can conceivably be squeezed into one day. Our laboratory has now moved into a grand new building, finished in 1940,[56] where I enjoy the nicest room I have ever had, and have every opportunity of building up the X-ray lab as I like it—which of course implies that I shall also be blamed for any of its future shortcomings. There

---

[54]Leo Perutz, Felix's brother-in-law, not the novelist.

[55]My grandfather's brother.

[56]The Austin wing, financed by the car manufacturer.

are crowds of students back from the forces and from government research, and the total research staff of the Cavendish has swollen to 100 people, distributed over a variety of research projects and divided up into numerous teams. My own team will number three next term and will include one man, back from operational research with the R.A.F.[57] and another of those "dreadful Viennese"[58] who is very interested in protein problems.

We are contemplating a journey to Switzerland next spring, as Gisela's parents are pressing us very much to come. I may poke my nose into glacier research again, interest in which is gradually reviving in various countries, though I don't contemplate spending any more weeks working in ice caves.

To Herbert and Nelly Peiser, January 6, 1946

This is just the end of the Xmas vacation and perhaps the last chance I shall get of writing one of my long epistles to you before I shall see you in person. As time goes on, each term seems to become more hectic than the last; yet I feel that a scientist's life should be leisurely and much of it devoted to quiet thinking—for which one hardly ever finds time.

Perhaps I'd better get down to the main business which concerns our proposed visit to Switzerland. First of all the date: I propose that we leave here on 1 May and stay until the end of June. I hope you will not mind if I contradict you on one point, namely, in your opinion that May and June are unsuitable months for skiing and climbing. You see I am really a very old hand at this game; apart from my wide experience in mountaineering in all seasons, I call myself a glaciologist, and have spent, for instance, the entire spring and summer of 1938 doing research on the Jungfraujoch. While places like Engelberg or Lenzerheide have comparatively little to offer during that time, the Bernese Oberland, the Wallis and the Engadin have their best season for combined ski and climbing expeditions. June is too early for the Matterhorn, I admit, but it is ideal for the Monte Rosa, Piz Palü, Piz Bernina or the Finsteraarhorn. To make quite sure that I don't underestimate the difficulties of that season I consulted an acquaintance of mine, [Noel] Odell, one of the greatest living English mountaineers, who has been on Mt. Everest both in 1924 and 1936, and knows the Swiss Alps inside out. He actually confirmed that there is no better time than spring for many of the Alpine giants. What I like so much about this season is that you start at

---

[57]John Kendrew.

[58]Herbert (Freddy) Gutfreund, the other, of course, being Max.

the crack of dawn, you reach the summit, in the early morning you ski down to the valley just as the hard crust of firn melts and by the time the sun gets really warm you pick crocuses and narcissi on the green fields below the snow line. By midday, you might reach a lake and bathe. It has been an old dream of mine to ascend the Piz Bernina from Pontresina and to descend to the Italian Lakes hardly feasible next spring yet, I fear.... [I plan] to go to the Avalanche Research Station on the Weissfluhjoch in Davos, where I should like to pick up the threads of research which we started together with the Swiss in 1938, and which the Swiss have apparently carried on and greatly extended during the war. I should like to meet Gisela and Vivien and stay with them in the mountains for about 4 weeks. This may seem a somewhat immodest request to you and I'd better tell you the reasons why we have set our hearts on that project: I have grown up in the mountains and have missed them very badly during the war; neither Gisela nor I are as fit and tough as we were four years ago, not to speak of 1939. Life has been and still is a great strain here, and we have been looking forward for years to a real, long thorough holiday in the mountains.

A few days before the wedding [of a friend of Gisela], I had been to Oxford where some people in the Ratcliffe Hospital had crystallised human haemoglobin. I collected these crystals and took them here for X-ray analysis; they have already yielded some very interesting results. I must say that while I am rather overwhelmed with work, and actually had to work during most of the vacation, I have recently realised many of my ambitions. I now have, at last, two very good collaborators, plus one girl for routine work; our laboratory has been moved to a fine new building where I have a very nice room, and a free hand to equip the lab with the apparatus I want. Some of the equipment should arrive from America in 2 or 3 months' time; after some protracted negotiations I have arranged that the Rockefeller Foundation will buy the apparatus in the U.S. and have it shipped to us, so that I avoid having to use any dollar exchange. As you can imagine, both the negotiations for apparatus and the training of my new collaborators take a great deal of time. The jobs that are now waiting to be done are these: I have hitherto only published short summaries of my protein work in *Nature,* and it is time that I wrote up at least the first part of my researches into a more comprehensive paper which would then be published in the *Proceedings of the Royal Society.* I shall try to get this written before we go to Switzerland. There is also a tremendous calculating job to be finished off, probably the most extensive that has ever been attempted in X-ray analysis. This job has gone on for some three years and is nearing its conclusion—it will be exciting indeed to see the result. It is one of those great gambles which one sometimes has to risk; the results of these calculations might get us no further than we are already; or they may lead to the discovery of the molecular structure of haemoglobin. One of my collaborators, Gutfreund, is working out the crystal structure of an ordinary organic compound, merely in order to acquire a knowledge of the technique of X-ray analysis. The other, Kendrew, who is only just joining me, will work on an ambitious project which Sir Joseph Barcroft and I want to embark on. Barcroft, who is a physiologist, discovered a difference between the oxygen affinities of adult and foetal sheep haemoglobin. We now want to try whether that difference can be detected and interpreted in the X-ray diffraction pattern of the two compounds. Besides these large projects, I have my fingers in various little ones, which might, with luck, come off and yield some interesting results. I have great hopes that my new collaborators will raise the general working standard of my team and the next few years will be very fruitful.

There would be quite a few more pages to write, as my life is always full of interest and excitement and I meet a lot of brainy people from many countries, but it is getting late and there are still many jobs to be done before the end of Sunday.

To Franz and Senta Perutz, January 15, 1946

Last week all the parcels arrived and we were very pleased to have them. The soap situation has actually improved since we made our request, i.e. the ration is being honoured again, but it makes all the difference to have a little extra. The quality of your soap is also so much better than ours. The meat came in handy on the very day it arrived, when Gisela found the shops empty, so we could have spam.

I like the work in the new lab which is much better equipped and intelligently laid out. We also have a much nicer director [of the Crystallography Laboratory] than the previous one, in many ways. I can get more done and get less tired than in the old place.

To Felix Haurowitz, February 3, 1946

It appears to me that the sharp contrast between the crystal structures of Hb and HbO_2 can only be explained on the basis of a considerable molecular reorientation on oxygenation and reduction, involving not only the haem but also the protein components. The implications are obviously most exciting and I hope to follow this work up at the earliest moment.

Just recently I have had an opportunity to study human HbCO. The structure of those crystals differs considerably from that of HbO_2 of horse. The wet crystals are pseudo-cubic, indicating nearly spherical molecules. a = 85 Å, b = 79 Å and c = 85 Å in the wet crystals. I have yet to examine them dry.

My main work is still concerned with MetHb of horse. After years of work I am now sorting out and correlating the data for a complete list of the intensities of all these reflections from that crystal. There are 8700 of them. These will then be used to calculate a three-dimensional Patterson vector synthesis. There is also a certain amount of work on the composition and swelling properties of the crystals, giving information about the hydration of the protein.

To Franz and Senta Perutz, April 11, 1946

We are already actively preparing our departure for Switzerland. We shall stay in Zürich for a fortnight, and then have a few weeks in the mountains where I hope to get rid of my tummy troubles completely. Bragg was a little staggered when I asked for 2 months' leave, but I don't think he will raise any serious objections, seeing that I am one of the more hard-working members of the department. I am already enjoying myself studying maps and planning trips!

In the lab I have just completed one of the worst and most tedious jobs that has ever been done in my subject, a piece of work which just wore me down. Now that it is over I feel much better all round and life more worth living again. At the moment I spend my days writing comfortably the first of a grand series of papers on protein structure.

We have an interesting Norwegian with us now who knows Arne Naess quite well and told me all sorts of stories about their common work in the underground movement. My friend made wireless transmitters in the physics department, while Arne ran a courier service to Sweden. Arne was apparently just as careless in his secret work as he used to be in the mountains; owing to luck and to his innocent air of Weltfremder [stranger to the world] philosopher, he was never caught. One of his pupils was caught on the trip to Sweden, though, and tortured to death by the Germans, obviously without giving Arne or my friend away.

To Hugo and Dely Perutz. Lenzerheide, May 25, 1946

[The first part of the letter below describes the delight of travelling through the Swiss countryside and picking edelweiss out of the new snow, a pleasure not yet outlawed.]

I had spent the previous week in Zürich mainly in visiting people and laboratories, received a lot of information on snow and ice research and saw a few interesting pieces of work. There was the Wasserbau Laboratorium where I saw [R.] Haefeli—the avalanche expert, the Mineralogical Laboratory whose professor, [Paul] Niggli, is one of the great men in Crystallography, and where there is also a small X-ray laboratory. Finally I visited Paul Scherrer, the Professor of Physics who asked me to give a colloquium on haemoglobin to the combined Physics Departments of the Poly' and the University. This I did *in German,* much to the admiration of the audience who curiously enough did not suspect my origin, though I told one or two of them afterwards. (I expect they thought: Dafür könnt sein Deutsch ja besser sein [in that case his German should certainly be better]). They seemed quite interested but there was little discussion; no one except the Ordinarii [professors] said anything. I suspect that most people are too shy to open their mouths in the professors' presence. There was a second colloquium after mine, by a Dutchman, on low temperature physics, and again very little comment.

On Tuesday I visited René [Jaeger][59] in Bern. We had lunch at the Casino and exchanged our war experiences. René had been attaché at the legations first in Budapest and later, during 1944–5 in Berlin, where he had to work during the worst Allied bombardment. Apparently the Berliners "took it" much as the Londoners did; though the official machine was evidently much disorganised, the bombardment definitely helped to maintain their morale. René looked a little older, as I expect we all do, but as nice as ever.

There exists now a parcel service for Austria which is run by the Delegation of the Austrian Red Cross. We have ordered 6 parcels for various people already and probably shan't have enough francs for more.

To Lotte Perutz. Coaz Hütte, June 6, 1946

I do wish you were here. I am longing to do the Bernina, Rosegg and Palü, and have no company at all; so I can only do the little peaks which I can safely do alone and hope that someone will take me along to one of the big peaks at Whitsun.

A word or two about the family at Zürich. Gisela's father is a perfectly charming old man[60] with a subtle wit and humour, an immense knowl-

---

[59] A Swiss school friend, the son of the ambassador to Austria.
[60] He was 65!

edge, a fabulous memory and many other enviable gifts. Gisela's mother has some artistic gifts, but is a very difficult person to get on with, as she suffers from a neurosis which has never been diagnosed or treated, and which makes her turn against Gis or her husband, suspect everyone of slighting her, have her heart full of grievances and makes her unable to concentrate on any subject. It meant that Gis had a terrible time in Zürich.

Herbert Peiser

Nelly Peiser

To Herbert and Nelly Peiser, undated

I just had the sort of trip I have been hoping for, going up a ski mountain on a magnificent morning. It was as good as I had imagined it in my dreams during 8 mountain-less years. I was also pleased that I can still ski as though I had done it this winter. I thought this morning that I should like to continue mountaineering to the age of 70 at least.

To Evelyn Machin, July 20, 1946

As soon as you have got over your troubles and Blaise is big enough, there is nothing that I could more warmly recommend than a Swiss holiday. There is something about the mountains and the flowers, the pine-woods and the tidy little villages, the hot sunshine and the delicious food that turns a nervous war-weary middle-aged feeling 'flu-ridden lowlander back into a vigorous youth full of pep and ideas. In fact I felt like 40 when I arrived and like 20 when I left. Primary purpose (or excuse) of our visit was to see Gisela's parents and to introduce Vivien and myself. My own prime purpose was to become once more an active mountaineer instead of having to live on the glory of the past, and of course to get fit. Gisela's parents live in a charming flat on one of the hills overlooking the lake of Zürich where we spent a luxurious fortnight. After that we cycled to the Engadine, spent

some time in Pontresina and one week at a hut right in the heart of the
Bernina mountains. I did a lot of skiing, and was thrilled to find that I was
still able to master that art as well as 8 years ago. In fact I never noticed any
difference. I went up quite a few mountains, sometimes alone, sometimes
in the company of Swiss acquaintances—Gisela likes the views but can do
without the 4–6 hour ascents which most of the high mountains require.
Later we had over two weeks of continuous rain which was rather a pity—
but in the end there were a glorious ten days which amply compensated us
for all the shivering in the wet. I cycled from Zürich to Lugano, from there
to the Lake of Como, to Chiavenna and up again to Pontresina, met an old
friend there, donned my skis and climbed the Piz Palü, a famous and beautiful mountain from which we had a 4000 ft descent on skis on 2 July. I thus
realised a very old plan of mine, admittedly in reverse order which consisted in skiing in spring in the Engadine, followed by a tour of the Italian
lakes. There is an exquisite contrast between the southern landscape and
the summer heat at the lake of Como, the spring in the Engadine with its
glorious flowers and the winter of the glaciers. The Italian lakes, particularly Lake Como, were a great experience for me; there is a quite unique
charm about the combination of mountains, vineyards, picturesque and
dirty old villages and the blue lake. A friend and I thought the other day that
only catholic countries are truly picturesque, a quality that requires a mixture of conservativism, devoutness, easy forgiving of sins and an absence of
birth control and puritanism. Getting into Italy was quite easy by the way.
The villages there look even more derelict than before the war and the people mostly unspeakably poor and shabby, particularly after Switzerland.
Nevertheless there is still the old charm about the place.

Switzerland is incredibly rich; everyone goes about in new clothes, on
new bicycles, wheels his children in new prams, lives in houses which are
newly redecorated and sometimes also new. The shops are absolutely as pre-
war, prices up by about 50–100%. Some things are much cheaper than here,
though, and the quality of most goods is very superior indeed. All Gisela's
friends live in flats such as we haven't even started to dream about; and
some of them aren't really richer than we. The Swiss were generally very
nice and hospitable to us—even in the shops we were treated with courtesy
and consideration. People there actually try to sell you something when you
enter a shop, and insist on making a beautiful parcel for you even when you
explain that you are not going to carry fish home in your pocket. On the
other hand, you only have to hear the inside story of Swiss university life to
realise what a paradise Cambridge really is. Professional jealousies and sus-

picions are common, social life is practically lacking, wives are treated as household slaves, the prospects for a career in university teaching are very restricted and in academic research practically nil. Altogether most Swiss still live on the principle to expect the worst from your neighbour and lack the easy going ways which make life among the English so pleasant.

Here life is full of international conferences at present, and our work gets interrupted by endless streams of visitors who want to be shown over the laboratory. Last week I had to give four identical lectures lasting five minutes each to four relays of Newton Anniversary Celebrators of average age 75. Most of them didn't understand English anyway, so it didn't really matter what I said; besides a large proportion seemed too deaf to understand me in any language. I know all about rations everywhere by now—the most common theme of conversation. There are, of course, a few really interesting people who radiate inspiration and ideas and with whom it is a pleasure to converse; but the lesser breed of continental scientist is frequently a dull bird, resembling the dry as dust picture of the German Professor of the *Fliegende Blätter*.[61]

To Linus Pauling, August 5, 1946

I wonder if I may ask your advice in the following matter. You probably know that I have been engaged for some time on the X-ray analysis of haemoglobin. Part of this work is concerned with an intensive study of horse methaemoglobin crystals which proved particularly favourable for analysis. Some time ago we decided to try and push the methods of structure analysis to the limit in this case and to extract the maximum possible information on the molecular structure of this protein. One point on our programme involved the measurement of the intensities of all 6000 reflections, with a view to calculating the three-dimensional vector structure. The work of indexing, estimating and correcting those intensities has now been completed, and we are faced with the formidable problem of calculating the three-dimensional Patterson-Fourier synthesis.

Although there exists a Hollerith machine in this country which could be used for the job, there is no organisation whereby it could be put at the disposal of crystallographers; insurmountable difficulties have so far prevented its use for our job, and there is little prospect that the situation is going to improve.

---

[61]A comic weekly.

After the X-ray conference last month Dr. [David] Harker came to visit us and we discussed this problem with him. He mentioned that you had the use of a Hollerith machine and that some members of your laboratory were actually doing Fourier synthesis work with it; he suggested that I might ask you whether there is any possibility of your doing this three-dimensional Patterson synthesis for us. I do this somewhat hesitatingly, since it really is a tall order; on the other hand, the inherent interest of the problem is very great and we can be certain that this sort of job would have to be done sooner or later, if the molecular structure of the proteins is to be worked out. It would be of immense help to us if the synthesis could be carried out in Pasadena.[62]

To Herbert and Nelly Peiser, August 8, 1946

I am so glad you enjoyed John Kendrew's essay. This and his fellowship thesis which it was meant to accompany, are both very well written accounts of a first-rate piece of research which K carried out last winter. He knew no X-ray Crystallography when he came last January, learnt the elements of the subject in two weeks, set to work on his problem which required great experimental skill, and solved it in a few months' concentrated work. Besides, he is a charming fellow, and it is a pleasure to talk to him; so I consider myself very lucky to have him with me. My second collaborator, Gutfreund, has just gone to Sweden to work with Professor [Theodor] Svedberg for two months; Svedberg is one of the great men in the physical chemistry of Proteins, he is director of a famous laboratory where Gutfreund is going to perform some special experiments. I tried to get rather involved in the problems and calculations which occupy me all day and Gisela finds me more absent-minded and useless than usual in the evening.

To Herbert and Nelly Peiser, December 26, 1946

I got a copy of Bertrand Russell's [*A History of Western*] *Philosophy* from Annemarie [Nelly's sister]. It looks good. I was very impressed by the introduction. Russell always manages to dig out a wealth of illuminating detail and to show you old and well-known ideas from a revealing new angle. Besides, I like his epigrammatic style.

---

[62]The reply came back from Professor Pauling that he had "had to reach the reluctant conclusion that it would not be wise for us to attempt to do this job." The grounds he gave were that "the nature of the calculations depends on the progress of the investigation"; hence, even had he someone to do the calculation in a routine way it would not be "wise."

I envy you the snow and ice just now. We are living very well, one might even say luxuriously, here with Annemarie, but what a hideous place London is. It turns you into an introvert because all your surroundings are so ugly and dreary that you try not to notice them. For the first few weeks after Switzerland it was almost unbearable. Perhaps this is why I am a scientist in England and merely a vegetable in Switzerland. Over there it's so nice just to take in one's surroundings and feel happy, there is no impetus to think.

To Franz and Senta Perutz, February 26, 1947

Your letter to me of 27 January arrived at a very opportune moment, because Father received the news that you and Lotte were both willing to co-operate in my pension scheme on the very day when he got notice of his dismissal. I consulted Otto Harpner about finding Father some occupation, no matter whether paid or unpaid, in order to prevent Father's getting too depressed. Harpner very kindly offered to let Father do some work in connection with a food parcel service to Austria which he has organised through the Anglo-Austrian Democratic Union. The job will be unpaid.

I then went to London to console the parents, explained our pension scheme again in great detail and showed them that they won't have to fear destitution, assured them that everything will be alright, etc. I think I managed to comfort them a little.[63] One difficulty is that Father, being over 65, gets no unemployment assistance because he qualifies for a pension; but the Ministry who pays the pensions takes several months before they react to an application. Mr. Wendriner[64] kindly offered to pay Father an equivalent amount as a pension until the state pension becomes operative, and Father has accepted that.

In the long run it will certainly be necessary to find the parents a cheaper place to live in but just now is not the time, because we are in the middle of this dreadful fuel crisis and I am thankful that they are reasonably warm and comfortable where they are. *There are so many places which are entirely unheated.*

---

[63] It emerges that Max and his siblings were to give them £150 per annum. The result, according to a later letter was "a great relief for me not to have to be depressed every time I see them and to feel guilty about not being able to help them effectively."

[64] My grandfather had lost his job as a lathe operator with the return of men who had been in the forces and from September, 1945, had worked, but far from competently, for Gisela's uncle, Hans Wendriner, wiring the lamps he made.

This country is in an appalling mess, as you know. At least 10% of National Income this year will be lost through the crisis. At the University all experimental work has been stopped. Our domestic troubles have been variously concerned with frozen drains (one week), frozen gas mains (several days), frozen water pipes and now a burst pipe. We have to carry all our water up in buckets from the basement to the 2nd floor.[65] I shall leave for Switzerland on my "Alpine Ski Course" on 21 March.

To Gisela Perutz, March 13, 1947

I got out a draft for our application to the Royal Society which secured general approval [for the expedition to study glacier flow]. The Committee meeting went off very well and it looks as though we have a reasonable hope of getting all the work started as planned. While I was in Oxford I secured the collaboration of [Geoffrey] Hattersley-Smith for the field work in Switzerland in the summer of 1948. This should be a great help.

My job: Keilin saw Bragg last week and they pretty well decided on MRC [Medical Research Council], because Ass. Dir of Research provides no security. Bragg said that he would, of course, be delighted to have an MRC team at the Cavendish, but he had never thought he would get it. Keilin practically forbade him to discuss it with anyone—even me—because he thought Bragg tackles Chibnall the wrong way and one wrong move might spoil all. Apparently departmental jealousy is the one and only obstacle to this scheme and success depends on convincing [Alexander] Todd and [Albert] Chibnall that the Cavendish is the only Dept. where this work could be successfully carried out.[66] It looks rather as though the previous attempts at getting me established here broke down over inability to decide on the Department to which I was supposed to be attached. It's a nuisance, but I suppose it's better this way than if everybody wanted to get rid of me. Keilin's plan is that at the right moment, i.e. when [Sir Edward, chairman of the M.RC] Mellanby returns from the States, Bragg should make the application to the MRC, and that Keilin would wangle the supporting moves on the part of Chibnall and Todd. I am to write up a comprehensive programme of work on the structure of substances of biological importance for the next five years, covering a field much wider than proteins so that Chib-

---

[65]The flat was heated with a gas fire, the water with a gas heater, and had a gas cooker. Electric kettles were unknown.

[66]Keilin, Chibnall and Todd held the chairs of biology, biochemistry and chemistry, respectively.

nall cannot claim that it must come into the province of his Department. What a game!

I received a letter from *Penguin Books* to-day asking me to write a 5000 word article on glaciers or crystallography for £4.4.0 per 1000. I shall accept, of course.

To Lotte Perutz and Franz Perutz, April 19, 1947

You will be issued with ration cards here and you will find rations reasonably adequate.[67] If I were you, I would take 2 or 3 lbs of Kraft cheese and possibly 2 or 3 tins of butter, otherwise some cooking fat, of which people are short. You will also be issued with soap, and you will be quite alright if you bring 3 or 4 cakes yourself.

If you don't fly, bring a bicycle so that you can get around. If you don't fly, bring your tennis things.

My "Course in Alpine Skiing" was a roaring success in the end. After having had all conceivable varieties of appalling weather and snow for the first 10 days, the second ten were perfect. We were in training by then and able to go at the first sign of clearing up. As a result, the last week was one of the best I have ever experienced. I explored some superbly beautiful new regions of the Bernina group, climbed 8 high mountains in almost as many days; I led my party without a single mistake, incident or accident of any kind and I got a great kick out of the feeling of their confidence in my leadership. I got on extremely well with them all and some were as charming and delightful people as I have met anywhere. Without the help and cooperation of the Swiss, the planning and supplies of our trip would have been difficult. One of my difficulties was the very low skiing standard of my pupils. It was impossible to think of skiing on a rope with them and I had to adjust my programme so as to avoid all skiing over dangerously crevassed glaciers. Nevertheless, we managed to get through quite an ambitious programme.[68] All my people were thrilled and by the end enthusiasm was at a high pitch; they had also learnt a lot of skiing.

Zürich was very pleasant indeed after the cold of the high mountain, hot and summery. I visited various glaciological friends ... and the exhibition of Austrian Art. There was one exhibition of contemporary Art which was enough to make any sane person with normal colour vision sick.

---

[67]Lotte was due to come to England from the States.

[68]Max lists all the peaks climbed, the lowest being 3350 m, the highest 3900 m.

Lotte Perutz in 1947

Incredibly perverse and revolting. Negation of all accepted ideas of art and beauty for negation's sake.[69]

In Zürich I found the very agreeable news that my salary has been raised from £600 to £700 dating from October *1946*! Very welcome indeed. By the way, about 2/3 of the expenses of my holiday were covered by money received for the Ski Course. Gisela's expenses were partly defrayed by her parents.

In Cambridge I found no news of any importance. We were rather overwhelmed by a stream of visitors as soon as we arrived. They are a curse sometimes. People drop in at all times of the day and evening; they never bother to ask whether their presence happens to be convenient, and as we have only one room where one can sit, they stop us from reading or writing anything. It would be sad if no one came. What gets me down most is the kind who say they now have to go and then stop and talk for half an hour on the stairs.

To Herbert and Nelly Peiser, May 29, 1947

You will naturally be interested in how the plans for my future job are shaping. Since I saw you, Bragg, Keilin and I have definitely decided to approach

---

[69]By contrast, Max wrote enthusiastically about the Renaissance drawings and the wooden Baroque madonnas and saints.

Max's party ascending Piz Corvatsch.

the Medical Research Council, rather than go for a University job. The reasons are purely financial. Owing to the interminable delays in deciding the amount of additional grants which the University is to get from the Treasury, all decisions relating to increased salary scales of University staff had to be postponed. Just the job (Assistant Director of Research) which was to be assigned to me is still paid on a pre-war scale with the addition of a small bonus, and would not entail any significant salary increase above my personal research fellowship (in fact the pensionable part of the salary would be lower). There is no possibility of foreseeing either when or on what scale a salary increase will be decided by the University.

After a series of discussions Bragg has now approached the Medical Research Council with the proposal to create a "research unit" in the Cavendish Laboratory under my direction, to work on the "Molecular Structure of Biological Systems." In the first instance, the Council is asked to provide salaries for myself and Kendrew, and to put aside a sum of the order of £3000 for capital expenditure on equipment. I put forward a detailed research programme to go with Bragg's letter, and Keilin (a former member of the Council) supported the application. The next step will probably be a discussion between Bragg and Sir Edward Mellanby, the chairman of the Council. The salary proposed for myself is £900 per year (my present one is 700); and Keilin assured me that he would see to it that the salary would be pensionable and include annual increments. I am very satisfied with these developments so far and I am reasonably hopeful that the Medical Research Council will approve the scheme. The greatest difficulty is apparently the fact that no grant has ever been given by the Council to a Physics Laboratory, and the Council might consider that other bodies such as the Dept. of Scientific and Industrial Research, should support my work. Unfortunately, their salary scales are rather lower and their conditions of employment altogether less favourable, although both draw their funds from the State.

The results of the vast calculations which I mentioned to you have been plotted now, and are very satisfactory. They give a clear picture of certain fundamental features of the arrangement of the atoms in a haemoglobin molecule. Although these results have only been obtained at prodigious cost, and have taken nearly 5 years to work out, they do provide information about the fine structure of biologically important substances which could not have been obtained by any other existing method.

My glacier project for the summer of 1948 is also progressing well. The members of my Glacier Physics Committee are delighted with my proposal to collaborate with the Swiss, and our preparations are reaching a more definite and concrete state. I have not heard yet whether I shall get the £1200 which I applied for from the Royal Society, but I hear from "usually well informed circles" that there is every likelihood of my application being approved. This summer I propose to arrive in Zürich on 25 August or 26 and then go to meet Mr. [Gerald] Seligman in Zermatt.

I am considering going to Vienna after my glacier tour with Seligman. Surprisingly the Russians have withdrawn their garrison from Reichenau and Felix Perutz very kindly offered to take the restitution of the house in hand. I just received a very nice letter from one of my former teachers at Vienna University who has now become Professor of Biochemistry there. His letter includes the statement: "Especially now one needs to feel that one has no share in the guilt for the appalling events of recent years. For only thus can you cope with the psychological and physical demands with which we are now faced."[70] It is nice to know of people who have preserved their sense of moral values and who do not take their innocence for granted.

Life here is much easier since we have come back. When I was in Zürich I almost dreaded the return to the endless difficulties of our drab existence of last winter. But with the spring and warm weather the outlook is much brighter. It is hard to be gloomy when the sun shines and you are well fed and healthy. Even the food has much improved with the spring weather. So what with tennis, the river, good health as a result of our holiday, the success of my work and hope for a decently paid, secure job we feel altogether much happier than we did 3 months ago.

To Herbert and Nelly Peiser, July 26, 1947

I am still very busy with a variety of jobs and working most evenings. At the laboratory there are far more results than I can cope with, and I shall soon have to start writing another long publication. Just now I am preparing a major paper together with Kendrew on adult and foetal sheep haemoglobin—I believe I told you about this work. I am also putting the finishing touches to an article on glaciers which is to be published in *Science News*, a Penguin Book.

You will remember the enormous calculations I told you about; the firm who did it have now complained that their costs were more than double of what they estimated and asked us that we should meet some of their additional expenses. After a long conference it was decided yesterday that we would pay £450 which still leaves the firm with a loss of about £200 as far as I can see. Staggering though this price may seem to you it may in the end prove worthwhile, because the results look as though they would really lead to a solution of the problem of protein structure. My working time is somewhat reduced these days by a continuous influx of foreign visitors; some very interesting, like Mark, others less so; for instance two days ago I was told to show the laboratory to four *extremely distinguished* Russians, without being told who they were or what made them so distinguished. Fortunately, in the end, one of our more ardent communists took the job on and I could continue to work in peace.

With a certain amount of regret I cut out all the recent international conferences, as I decided that I should never get through my enormous programme of work, unless I sat down and got on with it.

---

[70]The extract from the professor's letter has been translated from the German.

To Gisela Perutz, undated (late summer 1947)

I am writing from your bedroom, looking out over the Zürichberg which is green and neat and peaceful as ever. Lotte saw me off at Charing X. At Folkestone I had no difficulty in getting a boat ticket and had a lovely swim in the sea amidst huge breakers. The beach was crowded with local working-class families, women standing in the shallow water with their skirts rolled up and playing with their kids, Punch and Judy shows and countless children. On the whole beach you couldn't see one pretty face over the age of 10. The crossing was beautiful, lovely sunshine and eggs and bacon for tea. At Calais I found that my train had one rear carriage with unreserved seats. The people with reservations were herded together, 8 to a compartment in the rest of the train. Actually I had a bench to myself for the whole night and the whole journey to Bâle cost me £8.

To my surprise I found that Swiss cooperation will be forthcoming alright. There had been no difficulties except Haefeli's illness which made it impossible for him to write to me. I left him with a clear course of action ahead, and with a definite decision to work on the Jungfraujoch. I saw Niggli yesterday morning to discuss financial help from the Swiss, and this interview too was satisfactory. I also visited the professor of geophysics to discuss collaboration.

To Gisela Perutz. Montreux Station, undated (September 1947)

I sit here with a slightly pricking conscience, because my better self tells me that I ought to have left yesterday and gone up to look at the Aletschgletscher [Aletsch Glacier] on the way. But the persuasive powers of Werner and Daria [Weissel], combined with a convenient break in the otherwise perfect weather, were too much for the better self—the spiritual vitamin tonic of the Oxford Group notwithstanding.

I stayed in a little pub. It was a bit schlampig [slovenly] and dirty (in French manner) so that it was shunned by the priggish Oxford Grampians and served as a convenient refuge for Werner and Daria. Criticising the Oxford Group and discussing the moral problems they try to solve was of course one of our occupations. We thought their ideas were childish and inadequate, but we had to confess that we had really nothing else to propose in their stead that would stop the moral breakdown and disillusionment.

Shoes are their worst problem. They have only Fr.30 between them and have to resist all the shopping temptations that offer themselves here so that they can buy shoes for the children.

Like all Austrians they are terrified of a future war, but none of the reasons why it might break out seemed very convincing or alarming to me. The horrors of the last war are terribly real and vivid to them; they still get very upset when they talk about air raids. They dislike the sound of planes even here and the memories of the war years seem to play a much greater part in their lives than in the lives of English people. I heard little new about conditions in Austria as far as fundamentals go, but I was supplied with a wealth of vivid and often very funny detail.

We saw another Oxford Group Play, called *The Forgotten Factor* (meaning God) which was really very good, and is as striking an appeal for people to stop fighting each other and to co-operate instead, as any I have seen.

Seligman's research programme really is very meagre and his methods quite inadequate. It sounds conceited, but I really did collect the only worthwhile results obtained on the whole of his trip on my few days at the Findelengletscher [Findelen Glacier]. Even these consist only of scrappy notes because he had left his photographic apparatus behind at Grindelwald.

The child psychology book I took along is very good indeed and helps one to explain much otherwise unintelligible behaviour of Vivien, as well as one's own child fears and fantasies. You will have to read it too.[71]

To Lotte Perutz, September 21, 1947

I was not quite as thrilled with Switzerland this time. The most enjoyable part of my trip were the three days at Caux; Werner and I were friends again immediately as though we had parted the previous week, except that we had more to tell each other—mostly about the intervening years—and his Russian born wife is an emancipated Natasha [the character in *War and Peace*] tempered by Viennese charm, and one of the most vivid personalities I have met.

At the lab I found an official invitation to join the Anglo-Norwegian-Swedish Antarctic Expedition 1948–50 as senior glaciologist. Start October 48—return spring 50. This is of course quite out of the question, because it would be tantamount to giving up my job here; it would also imply turning down Mark's invitation to the States. Much to my regret, therefore, I shall have to refuse, though I'm extremely pleased at having being asked, with all the recognition of past achievements that this implies.

I feel very rested from my Swiss trip even though it was not an ideal holiday and I can tackle the great variety of jobs at the lab with renewed

---

[71]It emerges from another letter that it was a book by Susan Isaacs.

Daria and Werner Weissel

vigour. There is also the good point about going away that one tends to get into a cul de sac if one works on some jobs for very long (sich festrennen) [one gets bogged down], and after an interval one can usually see an easier way out of the difficulty.

To Lotte Perutz, September 26, 1947

[In this letter, I have cut Max's analysis of the precipitating factors in the antagonism between Franz and Lotte and between the two of them and their parents.]

As regards the state of our family when we were all grown up, I think we all had much to learn from more civilised families that I have come across since. That tact and consideration for other people is a thing which has to be practised at home, though it should not end at home, as it does with many Jewish families, was unknown with us. The same applies to friendliness and the general helpfulness which I first found here and which you like so much in America. Also I believe you and I were so disgusted with all the sham friendliness and hypocrisy that we saw within the wider family that we came to regard *any* expression of friendliness or warmth as hypocrisy—which made it difficult for us to get close contact with other people. I think there is no doubt that we were unfriendly to people in general or at any rate not friendly enough.

One final point: over the short comings of our upbringing I think we are liable to overlook its virtues, which also struck me of late: through both

Father and Mother being busy within their own spheres, and also thanks to a certain liberal and tolerant outlook of theirs, we were left pretty much to do what we liked and to develop our own interests. We were never sat upon, and our activities supervised and directed from hour to hour, or had to give detailed accounts of all our doings. I think compared to most other children we enjoyed an immense amount of freedom, and I for one came to love and appreciate freedom more than anything, and am never at a loss what to do with it either. And as long as the money was there, we were also given the means to enjoy our various and varied pursuits to the full. I had a bit of an argument when I wanted to read chemistry—but really not much compared to what might have happened in a more autocratically run family. And I believe it is largely due to the freedom we enjoyed in our youth that we became the independent and self-reliant people that we are.

On reading this, Gisela thought you might still be worried about having made the parents unhappy by your row with them. As I mentioned in my last letter I don't think that this is the case, but I still think that some nice letter from you saying how glad you were to see them again . . . and that you admired the way they managed things in their single room would be a wonderful tonic. You can put a lot of things very convincingly in a letter even if you don't really believe in them yourself, and it would help a lot to cheer the parents up, if you told them a few things they would like to hear.

My general guiding principle with them is that, since I cannot help their fundamental troubles which are inherent in their character and habits of thought, the best I can do for them is to try and keep them happy in little ways, and be as nice to them as I can, and this is the only thing I can recommend to you. Of course, they drive me to despair occasionally, and I would probably also explode if I had to live with them for long with nothing to do. But even if I sometimes fail, I usually try to work according to this general principle.

To Herbert and Nelly Peiser, November 16, 1947

Very many thanks for your congratulations and for all the kind things you said in your letters. You can imagine how pleased I am myself to have found a job that is made to measure, as it were. Whatever other job (with higher pay) I would have taken would have meant giving up a large part of the work which I want to continue. The MRC appointment fulfills all the essential requirements, i.e. an adequate salary and financial security, freedom in my work and the necessary resources for collaboration and instruments. I have the resources, in fact, to set up a new sub-department of the Cavendish Laboratory. Whether I shall succeed in finding the people to man it is another matter—so far this is one of the most difficult tasks.

Since Gisela wrote to you we have had the official letter giving the detailed conditions of my appointment. I start on 1 Oct 1947 with an initial salary of £917 which rises to £936 on 1 April 1948 and from then onwards rises in annual increments of £35 to £1005. The MRC pays an additional 10% of this sum for a pension fund and I have to contribute 5% of my salary. This means that the amount of my life insurance policy will be raised substantially.

Kendrew, as an independent member of the team, gets £500 in addition to his college fellowship, and money for two assistants with salaries of £500 each is provided. They are also willing to give grants to as many good research students as we can find and to bear the cost of heavy capital equipment. Current running costs and smaller items of equipment are to be paid out of laboratory funds.

Incidentally I shall get separate pay for my University lectures and supervisions, of which I do a fair amount this year and this should provide another £100 to [sic] my income.

I am glad that the days of student penury are over at last. I am sorry for Gisela that they have lasted so long. One reason was that due to the rise in prices the value of the I.C.I. fellowship was much lower than it had been when these fellowships were first founded. In 1942 £600 a year was still quite a good salary by University standards. There were two reasons why it proved so difficult to find me a permanent job: one reason was that I am neither flesh nor fish, i.e. my subject which lies on the borderline of physics, chemistry and biology really fits into neither so that I could not be given any of the existing posts. The creation of a new post, on the other hand, requiring additional funds and the consent of large numbers of people, proved very difficult.

The work just now is going exceptionally well and we continue to get very interesting results.

We had a great surprise to-day when your fat parcel arrived with its wonderful treasures. It seems to contain the equivalent of our bacon ration for at least 5 years, quite apart from the butter, meat and cheese. We really feel we don't deserve it. But the additions are a great help to Gisela as they make the shopping so much easier.[72]

---

[72]The queues for the different ration coupons were long and slow-moving, and then there were queues at all the separate counters of the shops. Supermarkets or self-service outlets were unknown.

To John T. Edsall, December 12, 1947

It is said that the number of people who read a paper decreases in proportion to its length, which made me fear that this number will approach zero in the case of my lengthy screed. You are already the fourth person who positively asserts to have read the whole of it since it appeared, thus proving the inaccuracy of the above rule and cheering me a great deal.

The results of the three-dimensional Patterson do not in any way contradict the results of the earlier work set out in my long paper. The synthesis shows rod like structures running along the X direction. The rods are about 10 Å apart and seem to fit in a hexagonal close-packed pattern. The repeat of the fundamental pattern along the rods is 5 Å. It is reasonable to interpret the rods as polypeptide chains which are in the α-keratin configuration. The rods lie in the plane of the "four layer structure". Presumably we have a short-range fold of the α-keratin type in combination with a long-range fold. Thus to show one layer:

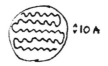

During the past four weeks Kendrew obtained some very significant results of myoblobin which confirm this structure. Myoglobin (horse) is a circular disk of about 60 Å diameter; the disk is only one polypeptide chain thick, and the zig-zag of the chain clearly shows up on the Patterson projections. Again the spacing between neighbouring chains in the zig-zag is 10 Å. The haem group lies normal to the plane of the plate and near normal to the length of the chain. The biochemists (Sanger) find that this protein has only one amino-acid end group and probably consists of just one polypeptide chain. If the crystals were a little better myoglobin might yield to complete X-ray analysis.

To Felix Haurowitz, January 20, 1948

I am very amused about Fankuchen's remarks concerning myself [that Max "should leave the Hb crystallography theme because it seemed exhausted"], especially so as they just came at the moment when our work here has more than justified the labour spent on it.

I do of course intend to branch out beyond haemoglobin, and possibly beyond crystallography. Since you were here I have been made head of a research unit on "Molecular Structure of Biological Systems" under the Medical Research Council (a government agency) and have been given ample funds to build up a larger research team and get better equipment.

To return to the question of haemoglobin, it is not that I am tied body and soul to that substance, but that I am aiming to find the structure of the crystalline proteins as completely as possible by X-ray methods. Horse methaemoglobin is still one of the simplest cases among all protein crystals which have been examined by X-rays. The great majority of proteins seem to have structures like the human CO haemoglobin which I recently described in *Nature*— where literally no information about the molecular structure can be derived. Myoglobin is probably the simplest of all protein structures so far encountered in X-ray analysis, but has the drawback of a very unfavourable crystal habit.[73] Hence my continued concentration on haemoglobin.

To Herbert and Nelly Peiser, March 17, 1948

I was touched by Father's charming letter and very glad that you liked my broadcast [on proteins]. As you can well imagine I approached this task with some trepidation. To develop a worthwhile idea in ten minutes without using any technical jargon beyond the absolutely necessary and without dropping into a string of meaningless platitudes is not easy in my subject. Atomic physics is fundamentally simple; the entities with which it deals any intelligent schoolboy can understand. But these large biological molecules, their chemistry, structure and function merely seem dull and senselessly complicated to the intelligent layman. Hence my stress on their fundamental biological significance rather than on what they are. I am glad if you think I succeeded in making the talk interesting.

As to my Royal Society paper, I am afraid that X-ray Crystallography is a very difficult subject which few physicists really grasp and even fewer chemists and biologists. It is one of those things which you have to *do* yourself to see how it works. I only say this to show that you are in good company if you find my paper a little indigestible.

I am glad that my glacier article amused you. The fluent style does not come quite as easily to my pen, though, as you may think after reading it. "Easy reading means damned hard writing" someone said—I spend hours polishing these articles and papers of mine before I send them off to the

---

[73]Kendrew's crystals of horse myoglobin were very fine needles and diffracted poorly. Only later, with sperm whale myoglobin, was Kendrew able to obtain good crystals that diffracted well.—AW

press. Every piece of writing I publish is generally twice re-written. I have a great admiration for the people who can put a piece of polished prose straight down on the typewriter and never alter another word.

Just at the moment I am reading a delightful little book by Max Beerbohm: *Zuleika Dobson*, a satire written about Oxford in 1911, and I wonder if you know it. One of its many merits is a style of quite exceptional brilliance and wit.

To Herbert and Nelly Peiser, May 23, 1948[74]

Your kind letters appeared with Peiserish punctuality on the morning of the 19th. I'm embarrassed when I remember birthdays only on the day itself. It was terribly nice of you to write so much about my successes, because it was already high time that my many years of work resulted in a proper result. Whether I am happy with it myself, that's a difficult question. First, research is an art; hence its results are never as beautiful as you might wish. But there's also a deeper reason. What's unknown is always interesting. What you uncover delights you only for a short while; soon it becomes trivial and familiar to all. Locke, I think, said, "felicity consisteth in prospering, and in having prospered." The researcher is always happy only if a new observation beams from the fog of the unknown. That brings me to Father's observation in wishing me many happy returns [in German, you wish people luck].

Certainly one would like to think that success comes thanks alone to one's own cleverness. But you can't imagine how much in research depends on luck. Just one example. Over the years I have superficially investigated a large number of different proteins. Among them, till now, only one was suitable for systematic research, and remarkably that was the first that I investigated. That is, had I begun with human haemoglobin rather than horse haemoglobin, I'd still have no results now. This doesn't prevent you from helping luck along occasionally, as for example by founding the Glacier Physics Committee which will transplant me again to your wonderful country. I am already enjoying myself greatly, anticipating skiing on the crisp snow on the Jungfrau, climbing the Mönch at dawn, and of course all the other small pleasures like breakfast in Basel, the clean train, the green valleys, the flowers, the atmosphere of confidence and stability that you still have and last but not least our happy reunion in the Toblerstrasse or even earlier in Basel, Olten or Wengen.

---

[74]Translated from the German.

Now for some personal news. Yesterday I got galley proofs of my 2nd article in the *Proceedings of the Royal Society*. The third and most important article is finished and should be sent off in two to three weeks. In the week before our departure there's a big haemoglobin congress here (Barcroft[75] Memorial Conference), at which with much pomp and circumstance I will announce my discoveries.

To John Edsall. Research Station, Jungfraujoch, July 18, 1948

To my great regret and disappointment my visit to the States has fallen through, having been vetoed by my employers, the Medical Research Council. I had been so very pleased when [Warren] Weaver and [Gerard] Pomerat [of the Rockefeller Foundation] offered me a travelling fellowship, so that my disappointment was even greater when the Medical Research Council informed me that it would not be in order for a member of its staff to accept such a fellowship. They say that they would have no objection to my going to the States to fill some visiting lectureship, but they are not in favour of my going for the purposes of study.[76]

I am spending my holiday running a glacier research party at this station 11,000 feet up in the Swiss mountains, but so far our work has been largely stopped by almost continuous blizzards.

To Herbert and Nelly Peiser, October 24, 1948

I don't know whether this was what Humpty Dumpty in *Alice* calls an "Un birthday present"; it reminded me of a custom in one of the labs here that the persons having birthdays are compelled to provide a large cake for the company assembled at tea (that was at the time that one could still get large cakes). In any case it revealed what psychologists call the "Feier Inversions Komplex" [celebration inversion complex] in Father who far from accepting his role as hero of the day, tends to regard himself of the victim of such cel-

---

[75]Sir Joseph Barcroft, who studied the oxygenation of haemoglobin.

[76]To Sir Edward Mellanby Max had explained, "What I am most anxious to see is the work on proteins which is being done at the Department of Physical Chemistry at Harvard Medical School, and the structural investigations of F.O. Schmitt and his school at the Department of Biology of M.I.T. There are other places which I should like to visit, some because they have developed new methods in X-ray analysis, and others because they have made great advances in one or the other method of studying macromolecules."

ebrations, and in order to "sublimate" his complex, to use the psychologists' jargon once more, presents his celebrators with far more magnificent gifts than they have provided for him. Not enough, therefore, in having presented us with a charming antique candlestick, in anticipation of the Day, he gives his son-in-law a magnificent wallet, whereas he himself had to pay excess postage on the son-in-law's birthday letter. But whatever the motives, whether it was due to the "F.I.K" or to Christian forgiveness over the excess postage, the gift was most acceptable and I want to thank you for it very much indeed. It really was a sweet thought.

Now some of my news. L'Energie de l'Ouest Suisse are really paying me Frs.3000 for the boring tripod, so that I shall be able to pay all my debts and still have a handsome sum left over for future operations on glaciers. Here I am rather glad to have wound up most of the expedition work now—except for a great deal of permits and letters needed to get all our gear back into this country. André Roch[77] was with us last week and told me the results of the second lot of inclinometer readings done in September which were quite satisfactory. Roch showed his magnificent Himalaya Film here—if you get a chance of seeing this in Zürich you should go. It is a colour film—the official record of the Swiss Himalaya exp. 1947—and one of the loveliest films I ever saw. Roch's commentary was perfectly charming and extremely witty and his visit here was a great success. I felt very pleased about this, as I had invited him and arranged for the showing of his film to a large student audience.

I am very glad that you liked my play.[78] An incredible number of people seem to have read it by now, and I am having to meet demands for more copies all the time. I did enjoy writing this, you know, and I am still deriving a lot of fun from it. I am going to give the members of my lab an illustrated account of the expedition next week, with readings from the play and slides.

To Herbert and Nelly Peiser, December 28, 1948

We did enjoy Xmas. There is no greater happiness than celebrating Xmas in the company of small children, sharing the intense delight which Xmas brings at an age when the previous one is an event that took place in the timeless past, to be remembered only by hearsay and a few odd details. My own childhood memories do not go back as far as that, yet in a way I think

---

[77] Head of the Institut für Schnee- und Lawinenforschung (snow and avalanche research) in Davos and an outstanding mountaineer and photographer.

[78] On the Jungfrau expedition.

Vivien's lot is better than mine ever was. Xmas was never so intimate. The presents were laid out on the huge table in the dining room next to a tree that reached to the ceiling. There were the presents for the large family and half a dozen servants and a few hangers on. Bliss was diffused by large numbers and dimmed by a governess telling one not to. One's parents had lots of people to attend to besides the children. Later on skiing became the dominant purpose of our life and we even bullied our poor parents into arranging the Xmas celebration a day or two earlier, so that we could rush off to Kitzbühel and try out the new pair of skis that we had just been allowed to buy. The departure was preceded by an agony of suspense whether the snow would fall in time, and be followed by a journey in a miserably overcrowded train among ill tempered people deter-

Max with me (Vivien), spring 1948. I am dressed in one of the outfits that would appear as from a fairy godmother in parcels sent by a Swiss friend of my mother.

mined to assert their own rights to whatever everybody else also happened to want. It was only in England that I discovered the joys of Xmas in a family with small children. Vivien behaved as a model child all through these days. Thrilled though she was with her presents, she examined each of them thoroughly and methodically before she passed to the next.

It is very nice of you to be so pleased with my success at the Royal Society, I was rather surprised that my lecture was so much acclaimed. I had shown my results to scores of people and lectured about them on two occasions. A few people had been thrilled and others merely sceptical. To many they did not mean much. In any case I thought that most people in the appropriate circle know about my work by now. But as it happened the President of the Royal Society who is Professor of Chemistry in Oxford, seemed to have been unaware that this work had been going on and was taken completely by surprise by its results. Incidentally Bernal was one of the people who, though very familiar with my work, made many nice remarks about it.

To Gisela Perutz. Kühtai, March 29, 1949

I arrived here about an hour ago after quite a comfortable climb with S. . . and A. . . and a nice snooze on the way. The weather is as perfect as ever, with just the right amount of cloud at lunch time to provide a much-wanted bit of shade for our climb. The place is a 16th century hunting lodge built by the Emperor Maximilian and is largely unchanged outside. Inside his ghost is at the present moment being haunted by an atrocious jazz-band which drowns your voice and almost kills your thoughts.

Our party consists of the six people you know and a Cambridge party of 2 girls and one man. One of the girls is a psychologist who used to look glamorous during the war when she sported a flight lieutenant's uniform in Cambridge.

I had often imagined how I would cross the frontiers of my native land after 12 years' absence with a lump in my throat and tears in my eyes. As it happened all emotion was drowned in the laughter over Rob Hill producing a 1000 Schilling note just as the train arrived at Buchs and getting flustered over trying to find a hiding place for it. In the end he hid it in his sock, getting red under the collar and looking furtively at his leg to see whether it showed. There was also an American lady in the compartment who "really knew the place inside out." She had just been at Zürs [where Max had spent happy skiing holidays], you see, which "is the most desolate place she had ever seen—not a tree or an animal only snow and ice—just like the Antarctic you know not a living thing for miles—just 3 hotels in the whole place. The sun sets at 3.30 there and once it goes the place turns into a night club. You just have to sit and sip cocktails because there is just nothing else to do. Oh dear there is another party of these displaced children—poor things— well I wish our Congress would do more for them, of course you English let in about 1000 children a month which is really awfully good of your 'liddle' island. You meet the most interesting people in Zürs, I was buying a picture-post-card when a man next to me said, I want another card just like that, and when I turned round, who do you think it was—Count Bernadotte— that happened when I was there last year. Oh would you like to borrow this *Reader's Digest*? It really is a first rate magazine, my brother is one of the editors you see. Oh I think Austria is a lovely country but what these poor people have been through."[79] At this point I got out into the corridor to watch the train slowly wind its way down from St. Anton to Landeck. The sun was blazing and it was hot and dusty as we stepped out of Innsbruck station. The Station Square is a shambles with bomb damaged houses and ruins all around.

Then I walked through dusty streets with dismal looking battered houses to the Theresienstrasse, that loveliest street in all Austria, where snow covered peaks seemed to rise straight above the cheerfully painted houses leading to the Goldenes Dachl [house with a golden roof], with a baroque church thrown in here and there, that street that symbolised all the happy traditions of Tyrol. I found the churches bombed and in ruins, the houses looking gray and drab, dust covered, rather like stage props after the show when the company has gone bankrupt.

Walking round the streets I found a cheerful looking place: "Haben Sie Zimmer?" "Na leider, mir san requisiert." ["Have you got rooms?" The reply in broad dialect is "sadly no; we've been requisitioned."] Next to it a large building which serves as the French barracks showing French soldiers in American uniforms, radiating boredom from the windows. Jeeps with carefree vacant-looking youngsters driving in and out.

[Finally, Max was advised to try the Weisses Kreuz.] There I find some pleasant clean rooms for a reasonable price but not the warmth of welcome that I used to love in Tyrol. The menu for supper is fully up to pre-war standards, but next to the price a ration coupon value is printed for each dish. [At this point, Max goes into German again.] "What shall we do then, we have no ration cards?" "Oh that doesn't matter, we simply add something to the price."

Down in the Theresienstrasse I saw an elderly news vendor who I thought would make a good foreground for a picture. His accent—Austrian civil servant or the like. An ex-Nazi? Or some other political casualty? The post-bus was a ramshackle 1935 model, the paint dropping off outside and the woodwork inside. I caught it just in time I thought, but at starting time the driver—who called me Herr Professor—disappeared for a quick one which took him half an hour. When the drive started the road felt as though it would shake the bus to pieces any minute.

As soon as we got into the countryside the scene got more cheerful. The houses were trim and friendly, the little churches freshly painted and the

---

[79]This vignette reminds me of the characters created by one of Max's favourite actresses, Ruth Draper. I still have his long-playing records of her solo performances. It is just the kind of story he himself loved to recount.

people did not bear that air of fed-up indifference they had in Innsbruck. Not that people look ill nourished and they are only slightly more shabbily dressed than the English.

In the country inn at Gries im Sellrain we seemed welcome enough and had a large second breakfast in grand style. The woman would not charge me anything because I was the "Reiseleiter" [party leader].

Walking up to Kühtai I found the Tyrol of old quite unchanged. At St. Sigmund I found a little church on a hill placed at the loveliest spot where two valleys meet; at Haggen, further on I dropped in at a farm for a lunch of Erbsensuppe und Schmarrn.[80]

Asking the farmer's wife where she got the electricity from was like opening a tap. She talked for the rest of my stay while ironing an unending succession of pillowslips. "Now, during the war we earned well but with the putsch we lost everything again because the Schilling was revalued. If only we got summer visitors but the English and French don't go to a small village like Haggen, they want chic places. Now the Germans were the best visitors, so cheap to feed, they always eat potatoes at every meal."

When I got to Kühtai I found we were the only foreigners in the hotel which is surprising in view of all the propaganda one can see in England. I suppose the 3 hour walk discourages the English.

To Hugo and Dely Perutz. Vienna, Friday, undated (April 1949)[81]

As I wrote before, Innsbruck is really sad. On the journey through Tyrol you notice the many destroyed stations but the small villages and farms are still very nice. At dusk the train arrived at Kitzbühel; in the new snow in the evening light it looked as charming as ever and awakened many happy memories. Then the train chugged on—after the Arlberg no question of its being an express—until Hochfilzen, the frontier between the French and American zones, which was celebrated with another 10 minute stop. At Schwarzach St. Veit I had to change into the train to Villach and in Villach into the Rome-Vienna "express," then as a British citizen the Russians allow me only to cross the Semmering but not to enter Vienna via the western line. At the Semmering the Russian official woke me up which was brief and painless. There was also snow on the Semmering; otherwise

---

[80]Pea soup and a cake-like Austrian pudding doused in icing sugar and flavoured with liqueur and fresh or dried fruit.

[81]Translated from the German.

it looked unchanged and the Südbahnhotel was still standing in unaltered imperial splendour. On the journey down you can still see traces of the allied bombing of the viaduct. You can imagine how excited I was as the train approached Peyerbach. What I'd have liked best was to leap out there, but first I was still in my underpants—in Villach I got a sleeper—and secondly it was too risky as my permit was only for Vienna. Around the viaduct the bombs had damaged many houses, otherwise from the train it looked shabby and a little dilapidated. I could still see the Wessely villas but ours was hidden and the Rax, alas and alack, was hidden in fog as it was still snowing.[82]

Well, the entrance to Vienna would be shocking if you weren't used to London, but compared to that it still looks relatively good. The South Station is being rebuilt and the train drew up outside.

Your heart starts to ache as you drive through Wieden into town. I would never have thought that a city could become so dilapidated in ten short years. In London the bricks get blacker every year, but in Vienna the dirt on the houses and the paint on the windows gives you the impression of unutterable shabbiness. Mother would have wept as the taxi drove through the Augustinerstrasse—the bomb damage was not as bad as the so-called undamaged houses. I stopped at the Theresianum,[83] where a morose porter told me that it is a Russian club and that I was not allowed to go in. Most of the windows are missing and the building is decayed.

Then we reached the inner town where it already looks much better. The Michaelerplatz has scarcely changed nor has the Herrengasse. But in the Währingerstrasse and the Billothstrasse you still see a lot of bomb damage; and everything looks unspeakably changed. As the Viennese have assured me in the meantime, much has already been done to set the city to rights. But all the same your first impression is a shock. I drove directly to Felix [Perutz, his second cousin] who has a charmingly furnished and comfortable flat. Sadly all the family and the servants were sick so my visit came just at the wrong moment.

So at lunch time I drove to the Weissels in Neuwaldegg. They are camping in 3 rooms in a large and totally neglected Art Nouveau villa. Their style of life is reminiscent of ours in Cambridge—no bathroom, no hot water—but they do have plenty of space. Werner and Daria were as delightful as ever and we chatted away all afternoon. I went back to Döbling to fetch my

---

[82]Max had spent many happy hours with Lotte on the Rax learning rock climbing.

[83]Max's secondary school, housed in a 17th century royal palace.

toothbrush and returned to the Weissels where I'll sleep till Gisela arrives. Then we'll move to the Steinschneiders.

Tuesday   What astonishes me most is how little the Nazis really did for Vienna. They introduced driving on the right. But that's all. You see no new trams or buses, nothing new on the town railway, no new buildings, nothing. Everything is as it was in 1936, except that in the mean time it's rusted, the worse for wear and dilapidated. Some things are quite unchanged, for example the smell in the tram which now seems much more antediluvian than before the war. The Nazis expanded some industries but that's not part of the picture you have of the city.

If people tell you that Vienna is more elegant than London, that "all" the women are wearing the "New Look," all these tales are fabricated by people for whom "all" means only the wives of industrialists, bankers and men with large businesses. The average Viennese man or woman is unspeakably shabbily dressed and wears the most impossible combinations of town and country wear. Most of the people you see in the tram look pitiful. On the Käntnerstrasse and the Graben here and there, but rarely, you see a well dressed woman.

There's lots in the shops and things which were traditionally made in Austria are very fine: fashionable clothes, leather goods, porcelain and goods produced by the Wiener Werkstätte. A good man's coat costs S.2000, while Werner's salary is S.900 a month, his total revenue S.1800. A worker earns S.600–1200, a meal out costs 10–20. To put fresh paint on a door costs several hundred Schillings. An arm chair costs S.180, a lady's handbag S.400, a nice dress S.100–1000. So you see that it is really people like Felix[84] who are doing well, but for the average Viennese it's not easy.

Food is wonderful. Every meal is a treat. People cook marvellously and eating is only limited by the high cost of food. You can buy everything with ration cards; without them it's more expensive, but not much. The displays in the shops are a delight. The flats with double glazing wonderful, even if, as for example at the Weissels, the ceiling is about to fall in.

That's all for the external impressions. My conversations with people are harder to describe. Everyone's really nice and I had a touching welcome. I get on famously with Werner as always and his wife is charming. I went into town with her yesterday afternoon and we strolled around while she showed me the sights—bombed buildings and those still standing; she told

---

[84]He ran the firm founded by his grandfather manufacturing textiles and clothes.

me the tragi-comic incidents that happened in various places: for example the bomb that hit the balcony of the Hofburg on which Hitler announced his 1000-year empire.

Daria Weissel looks just as one imagines Natasha in *War and Peace* and is a very amusing person. On the other hand, she's a very English housewife; the chaos and dirt in her flat just can't be put down to the ruinous state of the house. The children look a bit neglected. Werner and Daria need a new flat but Werner especially needs a consulting room, but that costs S.5000. At the moment they are negotiating the acquisition of one in the Russian zone where the danger of its being requisitioned reduces the fee to S.3000.[85]

At lunchtime I was invited to Meta Steinschneider. She's just as smart as 12 years ago, with a great zest for life, and is full of enterprise. She's stinking rich and enjoys life. Her house, that is, her father's, is quite unaltered with a nice view over the Wienerwald; she's got a small Tatra and drives everywhere. "Yes, it's marvellous, my boss has just gone away so I don't have to go to the office. You must come to Heurigen[86] with me and invite all the people you want to see and you must go the theatre with me and come to supper with me on Thursday." Her father is "an old bore." That doesn't stop him being director of a pharmaceutical firm and earning pots of money.

This morning I visited Prof. [Friedrich von] Wessely, one of my lecturers, now head of the II Chemical Institute and [Ernst] Späth's successor. He received me very nicely in his flat in Pitzleinsdorf. We had a nice chat although scientifically and personally we lack common interests. Like all Viennese he told me his adventures on being "liberated," which are impressed on their memories as a quite unforgettable and terrifying experience.

At lunchtime I went to a charming beer hall in town with Werner. In his hospital there's still a great shortage of medicines, not because there aren't any to be had but because the state can't afford them. Wessely too complained of a terrible shortage of money at the Institute. For instance, there was not enough money to enable him to come to the International Congress of Biochemistry in Cambridge. The outgoings of the Austrian state (excluding the burdens of occupation) nowadays consume 53% of GDP [gross domestic product], mainly, it seems, because there is an enormously overblown number of officials whom they can't get rid of for political reasons.

---

[85]Werner was a cardiologist and had both a hospital position and a private practice.

[86]A country-style wine bar selling new wine from the local vineyards.

To Lotte and Franz Perutz, April 29, 1949

On Wednesday evening I had another long talk with Felix and Hilde and really got to know them a bit better than on my previous meetings with them. Felix himself is an extraordinarily restless individual—I must say I admire his enterprise. At home he acts the part of a little Mussolini, but no lady really takes him seriously, least of all his children. Hilde has grown very well into her part and makes a sensible and efficient wife; she has also developed a fine taste in art and furniture and keeps a perfect home.

That evening Felix told me quite a few interesting things about Hungary.[87] The ruling clique there, Felix said, consisted entirely of Jews. He knows most of them personally. Those who are now "Textile Controllers" were small textile employees before the war, who spent the war in various German concentration camps and joined the Communist band wagon in 1945. There is a continuing revolution in the sense that the underlings push out those above them to get to the top themselves. [The remainder of this paragraph and all of the next is translated from the German.] The Jew who was only a clerk denounces the Jew who was a book-keeper as a capitalist who lives in a large flat. Thereupon the Jew who's the Minister of Justice informs his friend the book-keeper that he has been fingered and the book-keeper hires a Russian who takes him across the border. Smuggling over the border is operated principally by Russians. The book-keeper then comes to Felix's office where Felix helps him to organise his onward journey to the west or to Palestine.

Austria is full of "Poor Refugees" from the East, mainly from Hungary, at whose luxury people poke fun. The "Refugees" are much more elegant than all the Austrians. Many of them go to Salzburg. However, you rarely see Jews among them. Altogether you don't see Jews anywhere in Austria not even in Leopoldstadt[88] or the Vienna coffee houses.

Next morning Meta Steinschneider took me in her car to meet Gisela at the station.

Thursday We had lunch with René Jaeger, who is now—by sheer accident—attaché at the Swiss Legation in Vienna. The Coburg Palais being occupied by the Russians, the legation is now housed in the Palais Wolf on the Prinz Eugenstrasse. René was nice as always—not quite so good looking as he used to be as a boy—and there was no gulf to be bridged between us. He

---

[87]Felix spent the war in hiding there; Hilde and the children were safe because she was a not of Jewish extraction.

[88]Formerly a Jewish working-class district.

took us to lunch into the Schwarzenberg Palais—this surprised us at first, as the Palais is badly damaged by U.S. bombs allegedly meant for the Süd-bahnhof [South Railway Station], the portal and the western wing being largely in ruins. It is a great surprise when through a series of wooden passages more appropriate for a coal mine one arrives at a suite of palatial Baroque rooms with all their frescos, portraits and tapestries untouched. This part has been transformed into a restaurant, where superb food is served to a select public accompanied by discreet music from an able pianist. The view from the windows was disappointing though—the park at the back is still in a mess with sculptures lying on the ground and potato fields disfiguring the lawns. At the front the view is marred by the Monument to the Red Army which stands between the Springbrunnen and the Rampe—an erection very much in the Nazi style. I suppose you heard that the Schwarzenbergplatz has been renamed Stalinplatz. After our delightful and delicious lunch we departed from René and had a look into the Belvedere which I must confess merely reminded me of all the dull mornings spent there with Cilli.[89] The Schloss Belvedere is little damaged and mainly needs a new coat of paint, as do all public buildings, especially the Hofburg. They look terribly dilapidated so that I always had to preface my explanations to Gisela with the words: "You can imagine, how nice this would look, if. . ."

From the Belvedere we made a pilgrimage and shed some tears in the Jaurèsgasse which actually carries this name again, but we merely saw a large heap of rubble on the site once occupied by No. 10, so that I could only point to the house opposite to explain to Gisela what kind of place we lived in. She loved all the nice gardens around—I really know no town where there are so many charming public gardens as in Vienna.

We then met Daria Weissel for another round of shopping mainly to buy a wedding present for Gisela's brother. We got a perfectly charming coffee set at Augarten for the equivalent of £3. We were very pleased as this purchase alone really paid for our journey to Austria—in England we would have had to spend above £25 to get anything decent.

We were invited to dinner by Meta Steinschneider followed by a Heurigen in Grinzing[90] with the Weissels and Wolf Kurzel, another of my former schoolmates. [The remainder of the letter is translated from German.] It was nice and funny to see how little it had changed; the same absurd couples, the

---

[89]The grounds of the Belvedere were the largest green space near the Perutz family's apartment; Cilli Jetzfellner was Max's nanny.

[90]One of the little villages within Vienna that appear quite rural.

same music, the same songs, the same hawkers of every kind who wanted to sell everything imaginable or make your portrait. Kurzel, who was attaché in London for a while and is now at the Foreign Office in Vienna, had a whole store of funny stories. In government offices the Christian People's Party rules now and their orientation is increasingly right wing; as Kurzel says, he's putting out feelers to see if it's possible to join the party retrospectively because it's so advantageous for one's career in Austria.

After consuming countless 1/4 litres of wine (also expensive now) we went back home on the last blue tram filled with good-natured tipsy people, all in the best of moods. Here the typical scene was acted out between the order-loving conductor and the tipsy public (among whom was also an American sergeant in front of us who was winding his way down the Peter Jordanstrasse in spirals), during which Gisela saw the typical crowd of Viennese locals all chatting with one another. It was all good-humoured; as everywhere, people were friendly and welcoming to us. The general tetchiness which must have been unpleasant immediately after the war has really disappeared thanks to better nutrition. Gisela was very struck by her initiation into Heurigen.

On Friday we were invited by Prof. Wessely to lunch on the terrace of the Hochhaus. The Hochhaus is still standing undamaged. It was a gorgeous clear spring day with a view over the Vienna woods and the Danube. I took lots of photos from up there. Beforehand we had a look at the interior of the St. Stephen's Cathedral which is being restored and which is quite changed. All the mysterious solemnity has gone, the west wing [nave?] is open to the public again and is as light as a Protestant church. You can now see a lot of fine sculptures that were formerly hidden by the darkness, but also much that upsets the harmony. All in all, I'd forgotten that so many Austrian churches were marred by ugly Baroque and imitation Baroque altars. Now, in place of the destroyed high altar, there's an attractive Gothic polyptych. After this visit we still bought ourselves two lovely framed prints at the Albertina, a Raphael Madonna and a red chalk drawing of a child by Rubens for our flat. After all it's Gisela's birthday.

Our programme of entertainments was still not over as Meta took us through the Hohenstrasse which the Nazis developed to the Wienerwald. It was so charming that it really made my heart ache at the thought that I could no longer live in Vienna. The trees, the fresh green, the charming view over the town and the really blue Danube got to me.

On Saturday morning Meta drove us to the Prater, where the violets had just come out. Much of the Würstelprater has disappeared because all of it was burnt in the battle between the Russians and the Germans. The giant wheel has been re-erected. On the other hand, the Prater is as pretty as ever, even the House of Pleasure is being rebuilt in the old style. On the way back we had a little incident in the car and could hear the many nice remarks of passers-by in the old style: "Off home with you and darn your socks if you don't know how to drive" and similar. What was touching was that a policeman came and demanded a 2 Schilling fine—all prices have quintupled at the very least, but the 2 Schilling fine is still the same.

On Saturday lunchtime we ate with the old Weissels. Then the younger and youngest Weissels had an Easter egg hunt and finally to conclude our Viennese stay we went to a performance of the Bettlelstudenten[91] at the Volksoper. You can't imagine how charming it was. The music, the costumes, the actors, the scenery, the ballet—everything was charming, so effortlessly cheerful, so full of the joys of life and humour, as really only the Viennese pull off. Also the colourful vivacity of the whole stage set was inspired and properly thought through. We'll feed on this experience for a long time still.

Touchingly, next morning Meta still drove us to the South Railway Station. I must say I was really unhappy to leave and would gladly comply with the urging of my nice friends to return every year henceforth. But it was probably high time that I left, before I really felt too much at home there.

The journey to the Semmering looked much friendlier in bright sunlight than it did the previous week in driving snow. This time I even saw our house from the Peyerbach viaduct.

We boarded the next train at 1.00 in the morning; when we woke up tired and exhausted at the Wörthersee, we were already an hour late, and in Villach our connection had long gone. As the next train to Zürich was leaving only late in the evening, I proposed to use the day which was a brilliant one for a visit to Salzburg.

We reached Salzburg in the early afternoon of Easter Monday. Salzburg and the Bettelstudenten were really the high points of our journey. I'd often been to Salzburg but never in spring. The combination of Salzburg Baroque and spring blossom really carried me away. You can suddenly understand the inexhaustible gaiety that flows from Mozart when you see what inspired him.

The beautiful Baroque bridge over the Salzach has gone and has been replaced by a modern concrete construction but otherwise the old town is unharmed and in almost perfect condition. The contrast between Innsbruck

---

[91]Literally the beggar-students, an operetta by Carl Millöckers.

The landscape near Reichenau looking towards the Semmering, the Schneeberg, and the Rax.

where the French suck money out and Salzburg where the Americans pump it in is amazing. Innsbruck is shabby and decayed while in Salzburg the bomb damage is already mostly repaired and the majority of houses renovated. In Innsbruck the people look sullen and apathetic. In Salzburg they are cheerful and confident. In Innsbruck they go about in old rags and look hungry. In Salzburg they are nicely dressed and well fed. There is now a Lotte Lehmannstrasse and a Max Reinhartstrasse!

The American occupation is a chapter in itself. The luxury has to be seen to be believed. Every soldier has a new American car—usually with a bird. Only a few drive Jeeps. The town is full of American restaurants and clubs, the majority of which are only a 1/4 full. The American women and children stand out from the natives because of the fine quality of their clothes. The prices in Salzburg are higher than elsewhere in Austria—I think the Salzburgers profiteer at the Americans' and perhaps also the Hungarian refugees' expense.

In Döbling[92] most of the nice houses are occupied by the Americans who all have their own cars. So that no American ever needs to take a tram, they have introduced their own bus service in Vienna. These buses regularly travel without there ever being a soul inside them and are a thorn in the side of the Viennese who aren't allowed to board them.

Austria would be wonderful if politics there were more sensible. But firstly there's the occupation, then the Socialists and Christian Socialists fight one another as before and finally the latter are still infected by Nazis. All professional life is messed up by and made precarious by politics. So in the end I thought: in Vienna life's good and work's bad, here life's often bad but instead work is wonderful.

To Lotte Perutz, June 30, 1949

Gisela is expecting another baby in December. The imminence of No. 2 brought the housing problem to a decisive point. After this housing problem had driven both of us to the point of distraction, we have at last found a house to buy and the money to buy it with. The house is a small semi-detached one in a little street built in 1935. It is typical of the English mass-produced small house. Its outside is plain light brick and what style there is to it is ugly English suburban. But it's in a pleasant green street and has a nice little garden. The rooms are minute.

At the lab one of my problems is space. My team is swelling up to six or seven in August and we are still crowded into one room—I have to make great efforts to persuade the University to give me a proper lab. My team includes some really excellent people. I think this space problem also means that my ultimate aim—an independent laboratory for the study of the fine structure of biological systems—is not so far off now.[93]

Did you ever read the Harold Nicholson book I sent you for Xmas? It really is damn good and very topical. Do you ever read Thurber? I find him very funny. I am being pestered by various publishers to write a textbook, but I cannot make up my mind to start. Sometimes I think of writing a funny book—i.e. a novel and amuse myself thinking out plots and characters. I wrote a children's story last March which I must send you sometime.

---

[92]The suburb where Felix lived.

[93]In fact, that took nearly another 13 years.

To Felix Haurowitz, August 5, 1949

Great changes have come over us. We bought a house 3 weeks ago and have already moved in. It is small, but very pleasant and a tremendous improvement for us, not to have to live in our cramped flat any more. I do hope we shall see you there quite often and then we can show you what it is like. [To Evelyn Machin he wrote: "It's the first time since 1936 that I don't live in digs, with other people's hideous furniture around me and the first time since 1943 that we have a bathroom. It is lovely to have one's own home again."]

It is very good of you to offer to bring us something—although I don't know why you considered last year's gifts useless—they were really very nice and much appreciated. After some consultation Gisela and I have come to the conclusion that you would please us most if you brought us *a little meat* in some form or other. Though we find our food rations quite adequate on the whole, it is often difficult to entertain visitors to meals because of the lack of meat. It would be so nice if we could invite some of the Congress visitors to our house (including yourself obviously) and a little extra meat would help us to do it. I hope that you won't have too much bother getting it in.[94]

To Herbert and Nelly Peiser, September 12, 1949

Charles Jason who has been staying on the Jungfaujoch since the beginning of August in order to carry out the second survey of our borehole got into serious trouble last week. He tried to get some ice out of the tube with a scraper, and the scraper got stuck at 13 m below the surface. Jason hired guides to dig a shaft in order to extract it, but the guides found the work too hard and did not go below 7 m. Jason had to leave the Joch and the whole experiment seemed abandoned. So I thought the only thing to do was to go out and pull the confounded scraper out myself. But André Roch, that deus ex machina, appeared on the scene first, put life into the guides and dug the scraper out. So at the last minute I put the journey off again. Since then Roch sent a wire that the inclinometer is not functioning. Jason is returning to the Joch at the end of the week to put it right and then I hope the final (and crucial) experiment will at last be successfully done. But further excitements may be in store for me yet.

This excitement came suddenly after several weeks of quiet and happy life at our new house which I still enjoy immensely. Perfection is a long way

---

[94]In the spring of 1949, Felix had left Istanbul to take up a professorship at Bloomington, Indiana.

off yet, but it is gradually looking more presentable. From the outside it will never be a beauty, though we may improve it by growing creepers on its walls, but the rooms will be pleasant enough. Mutatis mutandi, the letter which Steffen sent you describing his domestic occupations apply to me too. Labour has become so expensive that any man has to be his own bricklayer, plumber, decorator, carpenter, electrician and I don't know what else. What nonsense all this talk is about specialisation in the modern world. Never had a single man to be a Jack of so many trades. My father never even folded up his own napkin, because the only thing he could do was textile business.

Just now the laboratory is officially closed and my students are away on holiday. The closure came after a hectic week when 1700 people visited Cambridge for the International Congress of Biochemistry. It was an interesting and stimulating meeting. I read a paper, i.e., gave a lecture, which was well received and provoked much discussion. Altogether I was pleased by the intense and widespread interest among biochemists in my work. It makes one feel that one is doing something worthwhile.

Publishers are pursing me like wolves and I expect that an American go-getter called Johnson of the *Academic Press Inc.* will get me in the end. He offers good dollars, no income tax deducted at the source, and a large market in the U.S. Incidentally Johnson is a metamorphosis of Jollawitz. *Academic Press Inc.* used to be the Akademische Verlagsgesellschaft, once a firm of high repute in Germany. My book [which Max never actually wrote] is supposed to be part of an International Series in Physical Chemistry.

To Herbert and Nelly Peiser, November 22, 1949

For the past few months you suggested in various remarks that I am not looking after Gisela properly, i.e., that I am not letting her have enough money. Now the fact is that I give her all I earn.

Of course there are my parents who receive an annuity of 50 pounds a year. There can be no question that we stop this annuity. The support which my parents receive from their three children, together with the tax repayment they get under the Deed of Covenant which I contracted (and which costs me nothing), constitute about 70% of their total income. Without our support they would literally be starving.

Now to come back to my other point, that Gisela gets all the money I earn. This literally means all. I don't buy the most essential scientific books, I don't buy new clothes unless the old ones are in rags, I don't take any holidays unless they are financed from an outside source, I don't even travel to

London unless I get my expenses officially paid. As I neither smoke nor drink nor spend my money by betting on horses, my vices, if any, cost me no money. We married as two people who felt that they had supported themselves for several years, that they were both completely independent and that marriage for them was a partnership on equal terms particularly as far as finances were concerned. You may conclude from all this that obviously my income is quite inadequate and that I should never have married Gisela anyway. It was small indeed in 1942. But it is really quite substantial now. During the past financial year I earned *1100 pounds*. Unless I had my own business, I doubt that any other form of career would have provided me with a substantially bigger income at the age of 35. My income is in fact exactly four times what it was when I got my first job in 1939. With income tax rarely less than one quarter of one's income, with prices soaring far ahead of salaries I think you could look far and wide to find a young couple who have done better than us.

If Gisela were not modest, if she did not do her utmost to keep expenditure within the limits of our income and if possible to save some money as well, we should not be better off—as you sometimes suggest—but very much worse. Our debts, instead of diminishing, would be increasing and there would be no question of our even having a second child.

To Lotte Perutz, December 27, 1949

The baby at last. A boy arrived this afternoon. Obviously we wanted a boy and are happy to have one. He is to be called ROBIN NOEL, the former because we like it very much and the latter because he is after all a Xmas baby.

1950s

"Don't worry about my holiday. Playing with my Fourier on the Pepinsky machine will be like working the organ of King's Chapel for another sort of man."

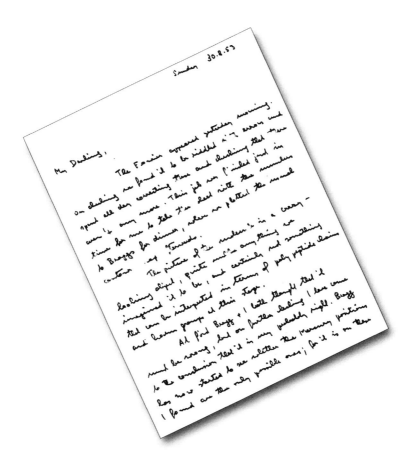

THE LETTERS OF THIS DECADE GIVE THE FLAVOUR OF MAX'S daily life as a scientist. This introduction is a bare historical summary lightly spiced with Max's later recollections. Unlike the 1940s, the 1950s ended in triumph for Max: "Imagine sailing for years through uncharted waters and then suddenly you see land rising on the horizon and this model [that of haemoglobin reproduced in on page 275] emerging was like this. So one morning in September 1959 our results came out of the computer of the Cambridge University Mathematical Laboratory, 1000s of numbers which we plotted on sheets of paper, and then we drew contours round them, and there emerged a landscape of peaks and valleys. So I built this model and suddenly saw this thing, which I'd been working on for 22 years, and it was a fantastically exciting moment. And I always say it was like reaching the top of a mountain after a very hard climb and falling in love at the same time, the intensity of joy and jubilation and admiration, which perhaps you find only in science when nature reveals one of its great secrets. So that was marvellous."[1]

This was the last of Max's triumphs of the 1950s: the first came in 1951 when he thought of a way to prove Linus Pauling's α-helix model of polypeptide chains. Anger at being pipped at the post by Pauling had provoked him, but he was delighted all the same. The next triumph came in 1953 with his discovery that the phase problem could in principle be solved. "By phase we mean that when you look at the X-rays as a wave, what you have to know is whether this wave has a maximum crest or a trough or some intermediate value at that particular point in the crystal and that has to be determined for each of the thousands of reflections that you get from a protein crystal."[2] Back in the 1930s, Desmond Bernal had proposed that attaching heavy atom derivatives to the molecules might solve this problem, a suggestion that Francis Crick repeated when he demolished the hatbox model. The prevailing view, however, was that application of this method to protein crystals

---

[1] Interview with Harry Kroto, Vega Science Trust 2001, www.vega.org.uk.

[2] Max interviewed by Katherine Thompson, 2001, National Life Stories, British Library Sound Archive catalogue reference C464/22.

would definitely not work. After reading of an experiment Austin Riggs had conducted, Max started to question that assumption, and, in 1953 in a few exciting weeks, documented in letters to my mother, he demonstrated that in principle the solution was possible. In this same year, Hugh Huxley, who had left for a spell at Massachusetts Institute of Technology, and Jean Hanson, who was also working there, demonstrated the sliding mechanism of muscle. The most astounding discovery to come from his unit in 1953 was that of Francis Crick and Jim Watson: the solution of the structure of DNA.

As for haemoglobin, the discovery of how to overcome the phase problem in principle was not enough. It required two different heavy atom derivatives, and finding a second took a dispiriting four years. In the meantime, assisted by Howard Dintzis, John Kendrew succeeded with myoglobin. He proceeded to develop the computing methods needed to manage the prodigious quantity of X-ray diffraction data, and in 1957, the results emerged enabling him to build a model of whale myoglobin. This protein is the substance that acts as an oxygen store in the muscles and makes them red. The solution of the structure of haemoglobin depended on the computing methods that Kendrew had developed. When it came out, it was revealed to be uncannily close to that of four myoglobin molecules locked together. Before Kendrew's low-resolution model of myoglobin came out, there was another significant discovery, as the letter of 24 August 1956 explains. In 1956, Vernon Ingram showed how sickle cell anaemia, a genetic disease, changes haemoglobin.

During this decade, the wartime hut into which the unit had moved in 1957 became increasingly cramped. The exciting discoveries had brought many new people: graduate and postdoctoral students, foreign visitors and permanent staff. Among them were David Blow, Gerhard Bodo, Sydney Brenner, David Davies, Dick Dickerson, Howard Dintzis, Vernon Ingram, Hilary Muirhead, Alex Rich, Michael Rossmann, and Bror Strandberg. The arrival of a new Cavendish professor in 1954, Nevill Mott, further accentuated the need for a new laboratory, since he wanted the space that the unit occupied for real physicists. Max's strategy was to lobby for a completely new institute for himself and his colleagues.

"We were a lot of chemists and physicists but were weak on the biochemical side, and so I approached Fred Sanger [and asked] if he would join us in such an enterprise. He agreed "and then I realised that we were strong enough scientifically and put the proposal to [Harold] Himsworth [the secretary of the Medical Research Council] who asked me to write a paper to submit to Council. So I . . . finally produced a paper on recent advances in molecular biology which I submitted to Council." Asked to present the paper to Council, "I spent a sleepless night wondering how this was going to go but when I came into the MRC one of the men there said to me that it was the most interesting document that he'd ever read."[3] As the letters show, however, the MRC's backing was only the first hurdle.

The Medical Research Council Laboratory of Molecular Biology (LMB) finally opened in 1962. Fred Sanger did indeed join the new laboratory which was still further strengthened by other new arrivals. Hugh Huxley, who had spent the later 1950s at King's College, London, returned to work on muscle. Rosalind Franklin had intended to join the laboratory but tragically died of cancer in 1958. Nonetheless, her group, consisting of Ken Holmes, John Finch, and Aaron Klug, then working on the structure of viruses, did come from Birkbeck College. Before the laboratory opened, Sanger won the Nobel Prize in Chemistry in 1958. He would win it again in 1980. His first prize was for determining the amino acid sequence of insulin, and the second was for sequencing DNA. Huxley won the Royal Society's two most prestigious medals, the Royal Medal in 1977 and the Copley Medal in 1997, both of them for his work on muscle. Klug won the Nobel Prize for Chemistry in 1982 for his "development of crystallographic electron microscopy and his structural elucidation of biologically important nucleic acid–protein complexes." He became the director of the laboratory in 1986 and in 1995, President of the Royal Society. Sydney Brenner directed the laboratory from 1979 to 1986 and won the Nobel Prize in Physiology or Medicine in 2002 together with Robert Horvitz and John Sulston. Many more outstanding scientists would join the laboratory, among them the winners of two further Nobel Prizes, César Milstein and John Walker. As Walker remarked, the concentration of talent Max and his colleagues had assembled drew young scientists like "bees to a honeypot."

To Lotte Perutz, January 25, 1950

I am fearfully busy as always, but I have just got my life well organised now and get through my work without getting worn out. Of course I should really be doing less and thinking more, which would be better for my research. In general good research workers are killed by kindness, i.e. they are given so many responsibilities, put on so many committees, asked to give so many lectures that the time available to think quietly about their research is gradually eliminated. I am determined to resist this process strenuously.

---

[3]Interview with Harry Kroto for the Vega Science Trust 2001. www.vega.org.uk.

I have just entered a field that you have contemptuously forsaken as part of your shady past. There is a general feeling that scientists tend to become narrow minded specialists, devoid of a cultural background and ethics in the wider sense. To help them become human beings of a more desirable kind, our laboratory has started a course of Culture for Physicists which I am attending together with about 250 enthusiastic undergraduates. This term we are having a series of lectures on English Literature. Of course they cover a wide field in a short time—we have to gather in 8 lectures the information it would take a less intelligent audience 3 years to absorb. These people lecture in a most stimulating manner and arouse one's interest in treasures of past ages which one would otherwise not touch. In principle I object to lectures about literature—I like to read the books rather than be told about them, but these lectures do help me to select what to read.

I am sometimes surprised that your interest has become confined to psychological and sociological books—don't you get tired of reading these things? I have become interested in writing as such; the presentation of a scientific discovery is, or at least it should be, a work of art. Scientific papers ought to be written so that they grip the interested reader, to be so clear that you don't have to read each sentence twice, and to explain to the reader not only what you have done but also why. Apart from scientific papers themselves I have long been toying with the idea of writing a book about research conveying the fun and excitement of it, the triumphs, the disappointments and the blunders, and to destroy the popular misconception that research is always done with some utilitarian object in view (to cure diseases, to invent things, to predict what is going to happen) rather than for its own sake, to discover the strange workings of a wonderful world.

Instead of writing such a book, however, Academic Press Inc. at N.Y. and half a dozen other publishers are on my tail pressing me to write a textbook or monograph on the "molecular structure of biological systems." I shall no doubt have to do this, partly to fill a gap which needs filling and partly to earn money and repay my large debts. How I shall combine writing this book with my many other activities is still obscure.

To Herbert and Nelly Peiser, February 26, 1950

I have some good news to report. I have been invited to attend two conferences and give some lectures in the United States next Easter. An American named Pepinsky has invented an electronic calculating machine promising to revolutionise the subject of X-ray analysis, by speeding up the time taken for computation enormously.[4] With the machine, work which would normally take months to complete, can be done in an afternoon. Pepinsky has now asked six European X-ray crystallographers to attend a conference on calculating method, and to work on his machine. I have the privilege to be one of that half dozen. My journey is being financed by the Rockefeller Foundation who are putting $1000 at my disposal, so that I can fly there and back and spend some time at one or two other laboratories.

A further help was the receipt of another grant from the Royal Society towards my glacier work. This enabled me to recover some out-of-pocket expenses. Of course it is also nice as a recognition of the success of the work.

I got the grant a few days after I had given an account of our experiment to the Geophysical Section of the Royal Astronomical Society. They had organised a meeting on glaciers where [Gerald] Seligman, [Egon] Orowan and I, and one or two others spoke. I came home rather depressed, because not one single piece of intelligent comment emerged at that meeting, but I later heard that one member of the audience, at any rate, gave a favourable report of my work to the Royal Society afterwards. I shall be talking about it on the BBC (Home Service) on 23 March and also to the University at the Scott Polar Research Institute next Friday. This is all very nice, except that my weekends tend to get rather busy with the preparation of all these talks. My weeks are crowded with activity: research, lecturing, supervising undergraduates, administration of my research unit and interminable discussions about work with my colleagues Kendrew and Crick. My unit remains a happy and quite successful family—certainly an extremely lively one.[5]

I see Steffen wrote some peculiar information to you about [Klaus] Fuchs. In the first place I am surprised that after having lived in this country for 17 years, he can write that prisoners get tortured. After all, if he believes that, what is there in British ideals that is worth preserving? I am sure Father knows the very elaborate safeguards provided under British law, whereby a

---

[4]Pepinsky's computer, built to calculate three-dimensional Patterson maps, did away with hours of manual calculations or the punched cards used for the Hollerith machines. Pepinsky's computer produced the output as contour maps on an oscilloscope screen, but it was soon superseded by new electronic computers just becoming available in the 1950s.—AW

[5]John Sulston in an interview with Harry Kroto remarked of the later Laboratory of Molecular Biology: "Max had engendered this atmosphere, a kind of family atmosphere. People didn't feel inhibited about going to talk to their elders and betters." Max himself remarked to Kroto: "I liked to have people around who were cleverer than I because I learned something from them usually, and they produced astonishing ideas, and they were fun to talk to and sometimes would help me to understand my own problem better." Vega Science Trust interviews 2001. www.vega.org.uk.

man who is charged with a criminal offence and arrested is asked if he wishes to make a statement, and told that he need not make one unless he wants to. The continental "Voruntersuchung" [preliminary investigation] does not exist in British judicial procedure, and the accused if he so chooses need not talk to anyone except his own solicitor. Fuchs made his confession long before he was arrested, partly apparently because he was disillusioned about Russian policy, and partly to avert suspicion from his own colleagues—who incidentally include scores of German and Austrian refugees. The other point I wanted to make clear is that Fuchs will be neither hanged nor shot; he did not pass information to an enemy but to an *ally*, and is therefore not a traitor. He committed an offence against the Official Secrets Act, for which the maximum penalty is 10 years, I believe.[6]

What a tragic figure he is! Apart from the more obvious effects of his misguided action, he has done irreparable harm to the cause of freedom in science and to the standing of political refugees in this country. How fortunate that he is not a Jew.

To Gisela Perutz. On board R.M.A. Contour Speedbird, in flight B.O.A.C, Gander–New York, March 24, 1950

I have seen the sun rise slowly out of the Atlantic mist. At first all was black. A little later I saw tufts of white cloud over the dark abyss that soon revealed itself as the sea, like pieces of cotton wool scattered over a black polished table. A red glow in the east spread all around the horizon and reflected in the western mist as a purple glow; bits of white surf showed that the blackness 18,000 feet below really was the sea. Gradually all the scene beneath came aglow, beginning with the tops of the highest cumulus clouds and spreading over the sky slowly and in patches until the whole immense horizon was brilliantly lit, while above us the starlit sky had changed to a deep blue. All this performance was drawn out over more than an hour as we moved away from the rising sun at great speed. Later the clouds beneath came to an end sharply where the pack ice border began, vast areas of broken ice floes with water channels between. We are still fly-

---

[6]Fuchs worked first on the British A-bomb and then on the American Manhattan Project, where he devised the implosion trigger for thermonuclear devices, and subsequent H-bomb project. He passed information on these matters to an agent for the USSR and was prosecuted as a result. The maximum penalty for his crime—violation of the Official Secrets Act—apparently was 14 years, which was his sentence. However, he only served 9 years and was released on 27 June 1959, was stripped of his British citizenship, and went to the German Democratic Republic.

ing over it now after we spent most of the day at Gander for some engine trouble to be mended.

It was good to have the *Churchill*. In addition I bought the book reviewed in *The Observer* last Sunday, *Ill Met by Moonlight* about the kidnapping of the German General commanding Crete by British officers—a great thriller which stood me in good stead while waiting at Shannon until 2.00 am for another engine defect to be mended.

I have next to me an American businessman of the would-be Clark Gable kind—described in Hollywood blurbs as "men who hate" to be matched by "women who love." After the smoothest and swiftest of customs procedure ever at London he boarded the aircraft with a scowling "I have been on many flights in my life but I've never been through so much fuss before." He has also never been so uncomfortable in his life as on this Boeing Stratocruiser's super upholstered luxury arm chair; which makes one wonder at the remarkable absence of discomfort in a life of at least some 45 years' duration. A prolonged stay at the bar sweetened his temper, though, and he is quite tame today.

To Gisela Perutz, March 28, 1950

I had my most profitable day just now seeing fascinating electron microscope and X-ray work at [F.O.] Schmitt's laboratory at MIT. This alone made my visit well worth while.

Monday night dinner with [John] Edsall followed by an interesting meeting on the anti-Communist loyalty oath which is being forced on the Californian State Universities. I was much cheered by the courage and vigour of the opposition to encroachments on academic liberties in this country. The trouble is of course, that the Boards of Governors of the Universities tend to be composed of wealthy businessmen to whom the ideas of academic freedom seem foreign and irrelevant in the face of the imagined Communist threat. Among the academic people I have yet to meet anyone whose outlook is in any way dissimilar to our own.

On the other hand, I witnessed one of those examples of American unbalanced behaviour at the Medical School on Monday when a well-known crystallographer who has discovered a new and in my view largely phony method of determining phase factors, tried to persuade [Edwin] Cohn and Edsall to set him up a large laboratory for solving the crystal structure of proteins by his new method. He had already collected a large sum of money from some mug or other and proposed to solve the structure of proteins forthwith. The prospect of having this fanatical and not too pleasant fellow set up over her head frightened poor Barbara [Low] out of her wits. I do hope for her sake that the whole proposal will fizzle out, because the man is obviously developing into a crank—he even refused to try his new method on a reasonably complex structure like penicillin—he is determined to go straight for proteins.

To Gisela Perutz, undated

What a time I am having, darling. It is a thousand pities that you are not here with me. I have not had a meal in my own company for days now and the longer I stay the more invitations arrive. My lectures all went off well and aroused great interest. One of my useful functions was to tell people at Harvard what goes on at MIT and vice versa.

To Gisela Perutz. Cambridge, Mass., April 4, 1950

I am just waiting for my party to collect me to go to Pennsylvania. I really had a wonderful time and am very pleased with the results of my visit. Social life beat all records on Sunday when Lotte and I were invited to all meals including breakfast. We had lunch with the Edsalls who inhabit an early 19th century house in a charming New England village 30 miles from Boston. Mrs. E is an interesting and highly educated woman of great charm. Lotte diagnosed the Edsalls as typical of liberal New England aristocracy. They impressed me because they practise what they preach: civil liberties are things to be fought for.[7] These people are close to the ideals Eleanor Rathbone and Alec Paterson stood for—talking to them makes one feel stronger and happier about "Western Civilisation" because they show that

---

[7]These words were prophetic, as I learned from the speech Max gave on the occasion of Edsall's 80th birthday. Edsall defended Robert Oppenheimer protesting in *The New York Times* against the court of enquiry's verdict in 1954. "It is in the interest of national security that controversial issues should be thrashed out freely and that no man should be throttled in expressing his opinion even if it seems counter to prevailing doctrine." This was that the United States "cannot in the interests of security have less than the strongest possible offensive capability in a time of national danger." In 1955 Edsall stood by academic colleagues who were attacked by McCarthy. To *Science* he wrote that he would refuse grants from any Government agency that withheld "research grants for unclassified research on grounds unconnected with the scientific competence and integrity of the investigated." Max's final example was a recent one. Edsall had publicly opposed the suppression both of the "investigation into the possible genetic factors that may influence intelligence and behaviour" and of sociobiology. "I believe that the advancement of scientific knowledge, though it might cause temporary distress in some quarters, will actually serve to dissipate false views on such matters as racial differences and lead to increased wisdom in dealing with social problems." As for E.O. Wilson's ideas, they should be subjected "criticism and debate" not "emotional attacks."

it is something positive; they are pillars of strength among the aimlessness and shallowness of the "American Way of Life" particularly when set against the [Joseph] McCarthy scandal[8] which shows unscrupulous American party politics in its most degraded form.

From the Edsalls we were driven to the [Paul] Dotys who live an equal distance out of town in another direction and who drove us to a historic village named Concord where the first battle between the "bloody English red coats" and the American Revolutionaries took place. It's a charming place, delightful, built of wooden houses, white with green shutters and classical doorways or porches scattered around the village green. Most of the houses date from pre-Revolution days and are associated with famous names. It was strange to see a place in this country so soaked in history.

To Gisela Perutz. State College, Penn., Easter Sunday, 1950

My story starts when we left Montclair to drive across New Jersey and Pennsylvania to State College. There was little to see except the anthracite coal fields where opencast mining has transformed a vast stretch of country into a scene of black desolation, a desert of coal and soot which has to be seen to be believed. The miners live in dreary villages amidst this waste and drive to the pits in their shiny limousines which are the only cheerful looking objects on the scene.

We left this man-made desert to emerge on rolling hills of woods and farming country, and arrived here late in the afternoon. It's a pleasant little town amid soft hills and contains a vast University Campus. There are 10,000 students here!

Ray Pepinsky is a nice fellow, full of vitality and incredibly hard working. His machine is truly miraculous—I look forward to using it next week. The conference time-table was arranged in accordance with his own ideas of a working day. Meetings from 9–12.30, 2–6.30, 8–10.30 pm. Of course people get tired of listening and never kept to this theoretical time-table. The conference was interesting though terribly theoretical in parts. There is a sharp contrast between the English crystallographers who do beautiful work in solving ever more complex structures by improvements in existing methods and the American School whose thought is concentrated on the discovery of new methods which they try to test on the simplest kind of

---

[8]This must be Senator McCarthy's assertion that communists had infiltrated the U.S. State Department.

Lindo Patterson, Easter Sunday, 1950

structure, or sometimes on the development of purely abstract theories. The latter applies especially to [Lindo] Patterson, who is a perfectly charming character, tall and Scandinavian in appearance, with a roguish twinkle in his eye, a wit full of delicious surprises and a lot of common sense.

My own lecture took place yesterday afternoon. I looked forward to it with some trepidation, since I had to contend with, on the one hand, the entire lunatic fringe of American crystallography, comprising [Dorothy] Wrinch, [J.M.] Buerger and [David] Harker; on the other hand Fan [Isidore Fankuchen] who does not believe in my work anyway. Harker had kept quiet during the conference and not mentioned a word of his new method of protein analysis. I was determined to bring this out into the open and to force a discussion, so that we could all judge the validity of his claims.

I did this with great success. Harker had to explain his method to us, and it became perfectly clear that it was devoid of any physical basis. I had the entire meeting behind me—even Fan on my side and Barbara [Low] shook me warmly by the hand afterwards—she would have kissed me if it had not been for the company. Wrinch never opened her mouth and Buerger was absent, having left State College in a temper a few hours before, because Ray would not calculate a Patterson synthesis for him on the machine. I expect Harker will still get his million dollars, but his shares have dropped a lot in value. I gather that Brooklyn is going to take him on.[9]

Apart from this success, my talk went off alright and I managed to arouse some interest even among the rather exhausted audience.

To Gisela Perutz, April 13, 1950

Fan also launched a stupid attack on my work after my lecture here yesterday, violent in words, but unsubstantiated in substance. I gather that most people considered it in very poor taste. Caroline MacGillavray, the Dutch crystallographer, made a gallant speech in my defence, saying that any sensible person would draw the same conclusion from my data as I had done. She is hideously ugly, but a brilliant and very nice person—immensely popular with the people with whom she has worked. Fan's attack was followed by a florid speech from Dorothy Wrinch who praised the beauty of my *data* in eloquent terms and launched an emotional appeal that I should make them available to all the world. What a madhouse! How fortunate that I was prepared for all this, so that I never lost my temper and managed to gain the sympathy of all the house by being amiable to all my assailants. I told D. Wrinch in private afterwards that she had better not send the Office of Novel Research to chase after me again.

It was nice after this to be complimented on my lecture by a lot of friends and strangers, and to be told by Ray that no one really takes Fan seriously—a view that is shared by Patterson among others. I heard, for instance, that people at the Calif. Inst. of Technology had 2 colloquia on my haemoglobin papers and that they (incl. Pauling) considered them sound. Yet how I wish I could get convincing proof for my conclusions.[10]

On the whole, lecturing to a Congress like this is most unsatisfactory. Since Crystallography is a method rather than a subject, you always feel that you are talking to the wrong people anyway. Besides, the programme was so overcrowded that the best people were much too tired or overburdened with their own duties to listen to anyone else.

---

[9] I wonder whether Max did not have to eat his words about Harker; see letters 10 September 1953 and following. As Max acknowledged, he was later to draw on Harker's work: in 1956, Harker published a paper proposing "Argand diagrams as a convenient graphic method of solving the phase triangles for more than one heavy atom derivative" and "a way of finding the relative coordinates of the heavy atoms in the absence of three centrosymmetric projections." Perutz M.F. 1997. *Science Is Not a Quiet Life*. World Scientific and Imperial College Press, London, p. 69.

[10] It would take the use of the isomorphous replacement method from 1953 onwards to solve the phase problem and thereby provide real structural information.—AW

To Gisela Perutz, April 17, 1950

I had my first day with *The Machine*.[11] It was interesting although there were quite a few interruptions, because The Machine suffered a slight cough and had to gargle at intervals and once or twice a doctor had to be called in to soothe it. Once it went into a tremor, but the complaint turned out to be purely nervous in character; nothing organic could be discovered. So we took note and it stopped doing it. No idea yet whether I shall get any results.

Your letter of 12 April arrived this morning—how lovely that Robin was such a social success. I am looking forward to seeing all his new tricks. I am very pleased that Vivien was such a good girl. . . . What a business it must have been coping with the children and the household and looking after your mother. I am looking forward to hearing a full account of all the dramatic events. Did you have to defend me all day long you poor darling?

To Herbert and Nelly Peiser. State College to Minneapolis in flight, April 21, 1950

American hospitality surpasses anything ever known by man and puts the Caliphs of Baghdad to shame. I have never yet managed to spend an evening alone or even had a meal by myself. People really are touching in the lengths to which they will go to look after you, but it is quite an exhausting business for the guest in the long run.

I am so pleased that you managed to see Gisela and the children. They were so delighted to have you.

I really had a very interesting time here and a most profitable trip. I met a great variety of nice people and actually did some good work on that remarkable electronic computing machine.

My impressions of America are so varied that I find it hard to write about them. It is a country of great contrasts and you can find almost anything in it. Infinite variety of scenery, of architecture, of human character, of atmosphere, both in the literal and figurative sense and of culture. Perhaps their motorcars are the Americans' only common denominator—they all seem to lead an unhealthy hothouse life, stepping from their overheated houses into their stuffy cars which take them to their sweltering offices—nobody ever gets a breath of fresh air. But they like it that way and their cars are nice to

---

[11]Max worked on the machine again in September 1953 and got a Fourier out in 24 hours.

ride in. It is quite an experience to go along their roads in a column of cars 2 deep and spaced no more than 50 meters apart at 80–100 km an hour.

I am still overwhelmed by their generous hospitality—after all it really is touching of them that they pay me all this money to come over here and then treat me as though I were a royal guest. I don't see how we can ever live up to their standards when our American friends come to us to return the visit.

To Gisela Perutz. Minneapolis, April 23, 1950[12]

What a place this is, like the uglier parts of Hammersmith or Shepherd's Bush spread out over a hundred square miles. In the suburbs there are nice houses and gardens and a great many lakes where ice is still piled up against the leeward shore. The snow has only just melted, an icy wind blows over the plains and the rain pours down at intervals.

I got here by plane in a few hours from a small town near State College where the Pepinskys drove me. The plane just touched down, picked me up and buzzed off again, as informally as a country bus at home.

 The last 5 days had been spent in exciting work on the machine which yielded quite promising results, mostly on Kendrew's myoglobin data. It was extremely interesting to see what could be done on the machine—its possibilities are immense.

The Pepinskys really were touchingly nice to me. Everything possible to help me was done at the lab, and at all other times they looked after me as though I were an Eastern Monarch on a State visit. These Americans put themselves out for their guests to a quite fantastic extent, and they enjoy doing it which makes you feel at ease.

I am taking a night tram for Chicago now and will go on from there to Philadelphia tomorrow after trying to extract some crystalline protein from the laboratories of Armour Meat Co.

About my plane. It is scheduled to arrive at London airport at 6.45 on Sunday morning. Now everyone tells me that the times of arrival are quite erratic and planes may be as much as 24 hours late.

To Herbert and Nelly Peiser, August 25, 1950

I have been given a task so fascinating that I could not face refusing it, however pressed I am. There is to be a grand Science Exhibition as part of the

---

[12]Max went there to lecture on his glacier work.

Top of the bore hole for the inclinometer

Festival of Britain in 1951, where the present state of fundamental knowledge is to be represented in popular form. The climax of this exhibition is
to be a hall dealing with "Growing Points of Science": one of these is to be
on the "Nature of the Universe" and the other on the "Problem of Life." I
have been asked to do the second of these and to present the problem in its
chemical and physical aspects. Linking these two exhibits will be one on the
"Origin of the World and the Beginnings of Life" (which I suggested) and
where I shall again deal with the living aspects. Isn't this a wonderful opportunity for applying one's creative imagination? It's a nice subject to think
about night and day. I hope you will come and see my exhibit next year.

To Gisela Perutz. Jungfraujoch, September 7, 1950

Things are going well here. Today we laid the cable from the Station to the Tube and took the inclinometer with its 7 core cable down. The weather was quite reasonable. My 3 companions let the inclinometer down the tube and found it to be ice-free. So far things could hardly have gone better.

[J.W.] Glen and [John] Nye will be up tomorrow morning and want to be present at the inclinometer run. If the inclinometer behaves we should finish the job tomorrow—the site is completely housed in now, so that we should not be dependent on the weather. I am much relieved that the pipe is clear of ice and has no bends around which the inclinometer refuses to go. Still, I am waiting anxiously how the crucial experiment will go tomorrow. Will we get over the last hurdle, and will the results make sense?

To Linus Pauling, December 14, 1950

I received a message to say you were annoyed by an article in *Nature* by Mitchison and myself; in this article we suggest crystallisation as the cause of sickling in sickle cell anaemia, and you say that we over-looked the fact of your having made this suggestion without using the term as such.[13]

Actually you will find a remark in our introductory paragraph which reads "They (i.e. Pauling et al.) suggested that the disease may be caused by a change in the composition or structure of the haemoglobin molecule, leading to molecular aggregation of haemoglobin in the de-oxygenated state."

I am very disappointed that you should have been annoyed with our paper, particularly because all the new experimental evidence we report seemed to fit in so beautifully with the basic ideas set out in your first paper.

I am sorry that this misunderstanding between us should have arisen, particularly as I have spent much effort trying to convert unbelievers to your scheme. [Fritz] Eirich still thinks that sickling is caused by the presence of an unknown substance, rather than by a structural change in the haemoglobin molecule in which he does not believe. [David] Keilin considers that the change in the haemoglobin molecule, even if genuine, may be no more than a secondary accompaniment of the disease, which may be caused partly by the absence of whatever substance inhibits crystallisation inside normal red cells (for instance crystallisation of the very insoluble oxyhaemoglobin inside the red cells of rats) and partly by a change in the properties of the stromatin.

---

[13]This paper was Perutz M.F. and Mitchison J.M. 1950. State of haemoglobin in sickle-cell anaemia. *Nature* **166:** 677–679. See page 261 in this chapter.

To Herbert, Nelly and Steffen Peiser, June 17, 1951

We have some extremely interesting and exciting news for you. I have made a discovery of decisive importance which changes the whole outlook of our work.

I am going to tell you about the details of the discovery in somewhat technical terms knowing that you have Steffen with you who can explain to you in more detail than I could do in a letter. For many years research workers including ourselves have tried to discover the way polypeptide chains are folded in proteins like hair. We have all tried to build models of different kinds, but none of them seemed entirely satisfactory. A few weeks ago Pauling published a new and very promising looking model and produced some striking arguments to show that his model could explain the observed X-ray pattern of hair and muscle. Pauling's arguments were most suggestive but not conclusive because of the extreme paucity of the experimental data. Thus Pauling's model was still one of many which were advocated by their different inventors and though it looked nice, one could not be sure that it was really right. When thinking over this problem two weeks ago yesterday, I thought that each of the models that have been proposed should give rise to a certain diffraction effect observable on X-ray photographs and that this effect could give us decisive information on the correctness or otherwise of the different kinds of models. (For Steffen: I was looking for a reflection from planes perpendicular to the fibre axis which would give away the distance at which amino-acid residues repeat along the direction of the fibre and together with the length of the fibre axis would give away the multiplicity of whatever screw axis the fibre might contain.) I found a reflection at a spacing of 1.5 Å which is extremely powerful in all fibres of the α-keratin group including hair and muscle and which dominates the diffraction pattern of the artificial polypeptide recently investigated by F. Happey. This reflection has never been observed before because no-one looked for it. It fits in exactly with Pauling's model and with no other and provides complete proof that Pauling's chain configuration is right.

As you know my long and laborious research on the structure of haemoglobin has led me to the tentative conclusion that haemoglobin consists of a bundle of parallel polypeptide chains having the keratin configuration and that these chains extend along the crystallographic x-axis. The diffraction pattern of haemoglobin fades out at a spacing of about 2.5 Å so that isolated strong reflections at 1.5 Å would have gone unnoticed. Two days ago I started to search for the 1.5 Å reflection on the assumption that my model of haemoglobin was right. I found it this morning in the exact place where I had expected it.

This discovery vindicates my interpretation of the haemoglobin data and the long labours and dispels all doubts about the years of labour spent on what seemed to practically all my friends and colleagues a problem of hopeless complexity. The field of protein structures is thrown wide open and the next few years will see the solution of many of these structures. By my new method one can find the chain direction in any protein and, given that, the structure can be solved.[14] Another aspect of this discovery will be its effect on the interpretation of fibre diagrams. It seems that most fibres give rich and revealing X-ray diffraction patterns if only one looks at them in the right way, and that structures like silk and cellulose which have eluded us for so long will now become capable of solution.[15]

As regards proteins, the greatest share of the glory will of course go to Pauling whose solution of the chain problem is a true stroke of genius. It is a terrible shame that we missed this model through a combination of unfortunate circumstances and blunders for which we shall never forgive ourselves. It is particularly sad for Bragg as it is part of the work in which he collaborated and which has now proved in vain. But all this disappointment is forgotten over the intense thrill of having removed all doubts and having my ideas of the structure of globular proteins vindicated. My discovery has had an electrifying effect on the work of the Medical Research Council Unit and has produced a surge of enthusiasm and intense activity which will, I hope, culminate in a long series of interesting discoveries and will have a profound effect on our understanding of chemical processes in living cells.

To Linus Pauling, August 17, 1951

I am sending you a reprint of my recent paper[16] together with my warmest congratulations on your 3.7 residue helix. As you know, your first paper

---

[14]This was all wildly optimistic.

[15]Proteins such as keratin (α-helical) and silk (β-sheet) can be oriented in fibres and give relatively simple X-ray patterns that can be interpreted in structural models. Pauling's (and Max's) work was a real breakthrough in understanding protein structure, something very much needed by Max after years of frustration and disappointment.—AW

[16]Presumably Perutz M.F. 1951. The 1.5-Å reflection from proteins and polypeptides. *Nature* **168**: 653–656.

with Corey and Branson[17] led me to predict that your helix, if present in all fibrous proteins and artificial polypeptides of the α-keratin type, should give rise to a reflection at 1.5 Å spacing when the fibre axis is inclined at an equal angle to the incident and diffracted rays. The fulfilment of this prediction with the discovery of this reflection in haemoglobin has been the most thrilling discovery of my life. The reflection has now been found in a variety of substances in addition to those mentioned in my paper, and there is no doubt that it is a universal feature at least of all fibres of the α type. Whether all crystalline proteins show it remains to be seen. Ribonuclease apparently does not.

To Herbert and Nelly Peiser, September 14, 1951

I have never lived so intensively before, and I do not know whether I like all the excitements that my discovery brought with it. But whether I like it or not, I am the prisoner of my own doings and must let their consequences shape my life. So far, nothing has happened to shake the conclusions which I drew from my discovery and announced in *Nature* last June,[18] but a lot of people have been very cross with me, because I upset their ideas so much, and did it too bluntly. I hope that all the dust which it stirred up will settle down now and that we shall be able to settle down to a long period of fruitful research.

To Gisela Perutz, Autumn 1951?

"Shall I wear the haemoglobin or the insulin dress tonight darling?" The Pattersons of proteins are definitely being turned into textile patterns for the Festival [of Britain] and I am getting the easiest £10 ever earned. Haemoglobin Pattersons will decorate the curtains in the Bailey Bridge Restaurant of the Festival Gardens.[19]

---

[17]Pauling L., Corey R.B., and Branson H.R. 1952. The structure of proteins: Two hydrogen-bonded configurations of the polypetpide chain. *Proc. Natl. Acad. Sci.* **37:** 205–2110.

[18]Perutz M.F. 1951. The 1.5Å reflexion from proteins and polypeptides. *Nature* **168:** 653–656.

[19]For Max's explanation of Pattersons, named after their inventor Lindo Patterson, see page 164. They resulted in the contour maps, the patterns of which were reproduced in the textiles. See Jackson L. 2008. *From Atoms to Patterns: Crystal Structure Designs from the 1951 Festival of Britain.* Richard Dennis Publications, Somerset, UK.

To Harold Himsworth, April 6, 1953

I am writing to tell you that Watson and Crick in this unit have found the structure of nucleic acid which agrees with chemical and X-ray data and which has every appearance of being right. The most attractive feature of this structure is its suggestion of a possible mechanism of duplication of genetic material during cell division.

The structure is that of deoxyribonucleic acid (DNA) which is the variety found in chromosomes. It consists of two chain molecules coiling round each other in a regular helix. If the structure is pictured as a spiral staircase, then the purine and pyrimidine bases form the central supporting pillar, the rings form the steps and the phosphoric acid residues provide the outer banisters. The two chains are held together by specific bonds between certain purine bases in one chain with complementary pyrimidine bases in the second chain.

A molecule of DNA may consist of several hundred or thousand "nucleotides" strung together in a chain. Each nucleotide consists of a base, a sugar and a phosphoric acid residue. The sugar and the acid are the same in all nucleotides, but of the bases there are four different kinds, and the sequence of these four bases along the length of the chain is now thought to constitute the code which characterises a specific gene. It is the most beautiful feature of Watson and Crick's structure that it suggests a mechanism by which this code can reproduce itself. Suppose the bases are given numbers from 1 to 4, then the structure shows that base 1 in chain A can combine only with base 3 in chain B, or vice versa, and similarly base 2 in chain A can combine only with base 4 in chain B. Such an arrangement is shown below.

Chain A	Chain B
3	1
1	3
4	2
3	1
2	4
4	2
1	3
4	2
3	1
2	4
2	4
3	1

If the two members of the pair were to dissociate during nuclear division then chain A could serve as a template for the formation of a new chain which must have the specific sequence B. And similarly chain B could serve as a template for the formation of a new chain with the specific sequence A. In this way two pairs of AB could be formed from one. The structural basis of this mechanism is easier to explain with the help of the models than in a letter.

You will see from the picture on the foregoing page that the structure of Watson and Crick allows an arbitrary sequence of bases along any one chain, which is in accord with chemical results. On the other hand it predicts that in any sample of nucleic acid of the DNA type the number of bases of type 1 should equal that of type 3, and the number of type 2 should equal that of type 4. This is in fact what the chemists have recently found, and it is one of Watson and Crick's achievements to have provided a structural explanation for this hitherto puzzling observation.

The structure was built by Watson and Crick on the basis of stereo-chemical and genetic arguments. They also used the published X-ray data of Astbury and of the MRC unit at King's College London, plus a certain amount of unpublished X-ray data which they had seen or heard about at King's. All these X-ray data were either poor, or referred to a different form of structure, and while they indicated certain general features of the structure of DNA they did not give a guide to its detailed character.

While Watson and Crick were building their structure here, Miss Franklin and Gosling at King's obtained a new and very detailed picture of DNA. Watson and Crick only heard of this photograph when they sent the first draft of their paper to King's, but it now appears that this new photograph confirms the important features of their structure. In fact, had the structure not been found, this photograph would probably have led Miss Franklin and Gosling to build much the same model; though it is hard to say whether they would have hit upon the ingenious chemical and geometric relationship between the two complementary chains which led Watson and Crick to the solution of the problem.

I believe that this discovery will provide a great stimulus to the structural and chemical interpretation of genetics. I am also very pleased on personal grounds, because this discovery justifies the Council's continued support of Crick in spite of initial failures and upsets.

The structure and the X-ray data supporting it will be published in the form of three letters to *Nature*, one from here and two from King's. However, to appreciate the beauty of the idea you have to see the models in the flesh. I wonder if you would like to come here and look at them;

Watson and Crick would be delighted to show them to you. If you are too busy to come up, I shall be in London on Friday, April 17th and again on the 20th and I could show you some pictures and models, if you happen to be free.[20]

To Felix Haurowitz, July 28, 1953

We are very sorry that Bragg is going[21] because our collaboration proved most fruitful. I have been appointed a lecturer at Cambridge and should like to stay here, and if at all possible keep the Protein Unit together here. On the other hand, Bragg would rather like to take Kendrew and myself to London and start a new unit at the Royal Institution. I am strongly in favour of keeping the whole unit together as the stimulus, facilities and brain power that we have got together here is unique; and because it will take many years to build up anything on a comparable scale somewhere else.

To Gisela Perutz, August 22, 1953

The Fates have been kind these last few days and I have not yet got used to their New Look. This morning's news was wonderful.[22] I had so much feared that Father might not live to see the better days and now they have actually come. A comfortable old age and independence; who would have believed it would yet come to the parents? Let us hope it will last and no cruel blow is in store for them.

The progress of my work is unbelievably fast.[23] There were some puzzling changes among certain low order reflections which appeared to overthrow Bragg's interpretation of the "salt-water diffraction pattern" and which were anomalous in other respects also. This afternoon a possible interpretation occurred to me which cleared the whole problem in half an hour. The fit between my intensity readings and those predicted from the

---

[20]The contentious issue of Watson and Crick's use of Franklin and Gosling's work has been the subject of several studies. See particularly Judson, H. 1978. *The Eighth Day of Creation*. Simon & Schuster, New York, pp.147–195. Klug, A. The discovery of the DNA double helix. *J. Mol. Biol.* **335**: 3–26, an article based in part on a re-examination of Franklin's notebooks. Olby, R. 1994. *The Path to the Double Helix*. Dover Publications and Constable & Co., New York and London. On this particular letter, see Ferry, G. 2007 and 2008. *Max Perutz and the Secret of Life*. Chatto & Windus and Cold Spring Harbor Laboratory Press, London and Cold Spring Harbor, p.153.

[21]He had been appointed Director of the Royal Institution in London.

[22]Almost certainly, Max's parents' receipt of reparations for their wartime losses.

[23]Max was busy with experiments and calculations that would finally solve the phase problem.

mercury positions is thereby further improved and is now getting better than in most normal crystal structure determinations. Bragg's diffraction argument is right.

I told you on the telephone that the difference Fourier (which Eric [Howells] and I got out in a day) is just perfect. David Green has worked out the exact mercury position now, so that the preparation for the main haemoglobin Fourier can start on Monday. David has volunteered to postpone his holiday by a week and is now staying here to help me until

Lawrence Bragg

I go away. Bragg has also offered his services, and Mrs Davidson who works the Hollerith machine will be available when we are ready. Let us hope it will show something interesting when we get it, the Fourier that is.[24]

To Gisela Perutz, August 25, 1953

Progress continues to be rapid. Yesterday the imidazole haemoglobin cleared up quickly and I expect that we shall now solve this puzzle too. Despite checking and rechecking there are still two uncertain points among my waves, and I am now trying to clear these up by a further experiment. Meanwhile preparations for the Fourier are well advanced and calculation should start tomorrow afternoon, omitting the two doubtful bits of the waves. It should be ready Saturday or latest Monday.

---

[24]The atoms in crystals diffract X-rays giving rise to spots on an X-ray film, but the positions of the atoms in the crystal cannot be determined from the intensities and spacings of the spots on the film. All Max's work in the 1940s failed to solve this problem. The essence of isomorphous replacement is to attach a heavy atom derivative (e.g., mercury ions or compounds containing mercury) to the protein without affecting its overall structure (isomorphous means same shape). Comparison of the X-ray photographs of the normal crystals and those of the derivative shows measurable differences caused by the presence of the heavy atom. Fourier analysis of the intensity difference maps, called Patterson maps, allows the atomic arrangement of the heavy atoms to be determined, and from the positions of the heavy atoms using several different derivatives, it is possible by complex calculation to determine the structure. It took Max several years to obtain the necessary heavy atom derivatives to solve the haemoglobin structure; see also the introduction to this chapter.—AW

On the whole everything goes well and smoothly, but yesterday and today I got a bit worried again at the amount of work there still is to be done before I go. I expect it will look less formidable as I clear it out of the way one by one. David Green is helping me very actively, and Bragg drew a beautiful set of waves last night.

The rose is all tied up; the weather was so pleasant last night that I fixed some electric lights outside and worked at it until 10.30. I may be able to keep the beans for you in the lab deep freeze; also some of the corn. In the meantime Mother is profiting from my garden produce.

To Gisela Perutz, August 28, 1953

I do hope that the present exciting days will not be unique in my life. The present discovery should start a new era in Crystallography of Proteins, i.e. in future I hope one will actually try to determine structure, instead of trying to make reasonable (and often erroneous) guesses, and being harassed by doubts from within and criticism from without. If this hope is fulfilled there are many exciting discoveries yet in store for us.

After all the Fourier, which I may get tomorrow, will have only a low resolution and its interpretation may be difficult. It is by now almost certain that a Fourier at full resolution can be obtained, and this will be a much greater event than the present one. There is about a term's work required to get that out. The really thrilling discovery would be if we get structural information which explains the biological activity of proteins, and that I fear may be a long way off yet.[25]

I am angling for the service of one of Crystallography's lady computers to help draw Fouriers and waves for me next week.

To Gisela Perutz, August 29, 1953

In the lab David and I calculated the new structure features for the mercury positions derived from last week's Fourier. Nothing exciting happened and all went well.

---

[25]In fact, the first low-resolution structure of haemoglobin came out only in 1959. In 1968, with his colleague Hermann Lehmann, Max was able to correlate structural changes in the haemoglobin molecule with specific genetic diseases and finally in 1970 to propose a molecular mechanism for the molecule's take up of oxygen and its delivery to the tissues.

To Gisela Perutz, August 30, 1953

The Fourier appeared yesterday morning. On checking we found it to be riddled with errors and spent all day correcting these and checking that there aren't any more. This job was finished just in time for me to take the sheet with the numbers to Bragg's for dinner, where we plotted the usual contour map afterwards.

The picture of the molecule is a crazy-looking object quite unlike anything we imagined it to be, and certainly not something that can be interpreted in terms of polypeptide chains and haem groups at this stage.

At first Bragg and I both thought that it must be wrong, but on further checking I have come to the conclusion that it is very probably right. Bragg has now started to see whether the mercury positions I found are the only possible ones; for it is on these that the validity of the picture depends.

I should like to try a number of other checks. One or two simple ones this week, and some lengthier ones next term. Everything must be checked many times over before one really believes this sort of thing and is satisfied that it is right.

In the circumstances I want to postpone my departure until the 8th. I know that this shortens my holiday, but on the other hand my holiday is of little use if I worry all the time whether the evidence I have collected is really convincing. Peace of mind is what I really need.

I rang Dorothy [Crowfoot Hodgkin] last night and asked her if she would like to come and see the Fourier and she proposed to come on Tuesday. An hour later she rang again and asked if she could spend the night here. I duly warned her that I would be all alone, but she said she did not mind. I hope the neighbours won't be scandalised.

To Gisela Perutz, September 1, 1953

After a day brooding over my results and trying to do his worst, Bragg came in this morning, just as I was explaining my results to Dorothy [and confirmed] that he found my arguments inescapable. The mercury positions I had found are the only possible ones, he found, and hence we have to accept the Fourier even if we don't like it.

Dorothy gazed at it here for an hour last night, without being able to get any sense out of it, but thought that it might improve as more terms are put in. I had the whole Fourier recalculated by the Hollerith ladies and the new result agrees with the old, as corrected for computing errors by David and me. I also spent Monday going over all the preparations of the data once more to see if no slip had occurred and found none. It may still have a few terms with wrong signs in it, but the major features must be correct.

Nevertheless I am glad that I postponed my journey a little longer, to be able to improve the evidence to be presented at Pasadena.

I felt rotten yesterday when the whole correctness of the Fourier was in doubt and thought I was getting a fever, but now that the doubts are stilled I feel quite well once more. It was also very nice to talk to Dorothy about things and to hear her comments concerning applications of this method to simpler structures where anomalies similar to those I observe occur.

Bragg is off tomorrow. It was very nice to have his friendly criticism and enthusiastic encouragement all this time, and to be breathlessly plotting the first haemoglobin Fourier with him.

To Gisela Perutz, September 3, 1953

In the lab I am carrying out a policy of consolidation. By taking a picture of one of the swollen lattices of the mercury haemoglobin I hope to double the number of points where the signs of the transform are fixed by the mercury, and thereby make the evidence stronger. I have already got two beautiful pictures—which incidentally finishes my experimental work before I go—and shall analyse them tomorrow and Saturday. I hope all will go well and there won't be awkward contradictions. Another swelling stage I tried to make would not work.

I received a welcome invitation from Pepinsky yesterday. Welcome because there may be some Fouriers and Pattersons still to be done which I cannot carry out here any longer and which could be done on his machine in no time.

Bob [Parrish] has thought up a new and ingenious way of attaching iodine atoms to the haem groups on which he is working like fury. I hope that it will work. He and Anne [Cullis] would like to join the Xmas party to Austria; they liked it so much last spring. I had offered to take anyone from the lab who wants to come.

I am much better because the main excitement is over, and it is clear that the method works. Bragg's satisfaction that my conclusions are cast iron was a tonic. I am not so tired any longer, sleep better and have few tummy aches. I am not worried about the Fourier being difficult to interpret—obviously it would have been nicer if it had been easy—because it is very likely to improve with further work next term.

To Gisela Perutz, Sunday night, September 6, 1953

As to your worries about the correctness of my conclusions: the main body of the signs assigned to the waves are cast iron. We have now recalculated the difference Pattersons putting in all the observed differences in intensities regardless of whether they are within or without the experimental error, and the result is astonishingly favourable. The map shows one huge peak in the mercury position; one very much smaller spurious peak and much less general "muck" than the first difference Patterson. I believe that this will be convincing in itself. Then there are still two further, independent, methods of demonstrating that the mercury atom can only be in the particular place chosen.

The agreement with the waves is most impressive, and the great bulk of the signs is fixed without any doubt. There were, however, one or two little wiggles where evidence was uncertain.

To get over this I made an expanded form of the mercury crystal last week, and hoped that this would supply the lacking evidence. The method worked as far as this was concerned, and actually confirmed the few doubtful signs which the first crystals had indicated but not proved. On the other hand this expanded form shows complications which do not make these results quite trustworthy yet. A new difference Patterson will have to be made of the expanded form, the mercury position re-determined and this cannot be done before I go. I shall not discuss these last minute results at the Conference but show a second Fourier with all the terms now indicated by the two methods, together with the first Fourier. There should only be small changes, though perhaps they will make the picture of the molecule look more sensible.

There is no doubt that the picture needs refining, as every Fourier in X-ray analysis does, and everyone at the Conference will realise this. There is no danger that anyone else can think up the little additional terms that have to be added to make the Fourier look right. As Bragg admitted to me many times since I worked out the signs: "You are absolutely right that every sign has to be determined directly," i.e. by direct experiment and not, as Bragg tried, by intuition. I do not think you need to worry. The thing cannot be solved by thought but only by experiment. The armour of methods now at my disposal is immense, and I can fix most signs directly I believe. So eventually I hope that a sensible picture will emerge.

What I should like to try out on Pepinsky's machine is how much the picture is altered by changing the signs of some of the smaller terms. Does it change the picture completely or is it hardly noticeable? In Cambridge this question can only be answered by long calculations, while at Pepinsky's it can by done by flicking a few switches. Don't worry about my holiday. Playing with my Fourier on the Pepinsky machine will be like working the organ of King's Chapel for another sort of man.

I shall spend tomorrow getting my material prepared for going away. David Green is still helping me most efficiently. I hope to have 2 or 3 difference Pattersons, a difference Fourier, the picture of the waves with the mercury signs, the haemoglobin Fourier, with I hope slight variations on those done on the Pepinsky machine.

To Gisela Perutz. September 8, 1953

After many difficulties Lunn's secured me a passage for tomorrow night. This suits me very well, as we can get all our preparations ready by then. I shall travel with my bags full of nice results, confident that they are correct except for one or two details, and drawn out in presentable form. I have not yet written my lectures and shall have to do that in America, but this should not prove too difficult.

Your sweet letter imploring me to come to Lenzerheide arrived yesterday morning and tempted me sorely. But then I imagined how disappointed I should be if Lotte came to Europe and stopped to see me for just 24 hours on each way, and that's what my going to Switzerland would have meant.

I think we must organise our summer more sensibly next year. There is no question now of my organising a glacier research party, and I look forward to a proper holiday with you and the children, if possible in Austria.

To Gisela Perutz. Upper Montclair, New Jersey, September 10, 1953

While you have visions of your husband tearing round the grilling pavements of New York, I am reclining in a deck chair on Franz and Senta's cool veranda on a perfect day, sunny but cooled by a faint autumn breeze.

Here I found (a) an invitation from Harker to visit his laboratory—a great relief. (b) a message from Pepinsky that his great machine will be at my disposal.

To Gisela Perutz. New Haven, September 13, 1953

Blitz résumé of my activities: Friday: visit to Harker, Francis and Ewald.[26] All very friendly. They knew my news from a letter by Bragg to Ewald. Harker engaged in experimental work—no mention of glabs. Fan was out.

---

[26]Francis Crick was doing a postdoctoral stint at Brooklyn Polytechnic with Harker. Paul Ewald had moved from the Cavendish to Belfast and thence to Brooklyn.

I am just off on a two day mountain trip with Lotte. We had a long walk on the beach yesterday.

To Gisela Perutz. Berkeley, September 19, 1953

I gave my first lecture here yesterday and it went off quite well. I had a large audience of biochemists, even though it was only announced the same morning, and people were interested. Talking about my Fourier and how to find the signs I made a brave effort to explain the physical principles involved, but I don't know how successful I was. I found afterwards that people had not really grasped the difference between a Fourier and a Patterson, that they were unfamiliar with the idea of contour maps and projections, so I shall have to try to make things clearer next time.

From conversations I gather that we shall have a hard job convincing biochemists here of our X-ray results, because they stoutly maintain that they cannot understand how these results are derived. "Do you really believe that globular proteins consist of α-helices?" Watson and Crick[27] is regarded as an interesting hypothesis, but the power of the X-ray and stereochemical proof eludes people. Even Edsall has not really taken it in yet.

To Felix Haurowitz. Pasadena, September 21, 1953

I have some really exciting new work. I succeeded in getting a compound of haemoglobin with Hg-benzoate which is isomorphous with normal haemoglobin. Thus the isomorphous replacement method which is the mainstay of the structure analysis of complex organic compounds can now be applied to haemoglobin. I have already determined the phases of 100 reflections and have a projected electron density map (not a Patterson) of the haemoglobin molecule at 4 Å resolution. The picture looks very complex indeed and quite uninterpretable at this stage, but I am nevertheless very thrilled to have a picture of the haemoglobin molecule which is derived by methods free from any arbitrary assumption and can be proved to be right.

To Gisela Perutz. Pasadena, September 25, 1953

The conference is over. It was a great success and well worth coming here for. My paper was well received and most people realised the achievement

---

[27] That is, their model showing the structure of DNA as a double helix.

as well as the potentialities of the new approach. There was much interesting discussion, but no bickering, and this applied throughout the conference. There was a general atmosphere of soberness, and a realisation that no-one's solution of the protein problem was complete, and every approach still fraught with complications. Cambridge made a brilliant show I think and I was very proud of us. [Maurice] Wilkins from Kings and F.O. Schmitt from M.I.T. also did very well; so did [A.] Elliott and Ian Trotter from Courtaulds. John K[endrew] gave a beautiful paper even if he had no conclusion at the present stage.

Bragg introduced the discussion of globular proteins by comparing haemoglobin to a mountain climb on which he and I had been firmly roped together and taken the lead in turn, with myself having just led the way up the last pitch. It was charmingly put and a very fair description of our respective parts. My only quarrel would be with describing my present struggle as the final pitch. It may well open up the view to further stiff obstacles ahead. Bragg gave a brilliant lecture on the X-ray optics of the protein problem, which all enjoyed hearing.

The Paulings went out of their way to be nice to me, Mrs. P sending her boy down to fetch me after one of the meetings for a swim in their garden. They live in a beautiful modern house far up on the mountainside with a grandiose view over the city which is particularly enjoyable at night.

To Gisela Perutz. Denver to Chicago, September 29, 1953

Salt Lake City and Denver are as beautiful as they are reputed to be, though Denver is still on the flat prairie with the mountains rising suddenly from the plain 30 miles away. The town has 15 or 20 large and beautifully kept public gardens, apart from all the gardens around everyone's houses.

California is so unlike anything we know that it would take me some getting used to. Let me describe a Californian village. There is no town hall, no market place, no inn, no church in any prominent position and above all no pedestrian. Imagine King and Harper's Car Service Station on Hills Road just beyond the railway station. Imagine a string of 20 or 30 of these, only newer and brilliantly white, strung out on both sides of a road 50 or 60 yards wide. Interspersed between them Motels (a motor-car hotel—it has a string of bungalows each with a garage and rooms adjoining), Drive ins (a restaurant where you eat in the car), Liquor Parlors, Drug Stores and Super Markets, all built in incongruous modernistic sprawling bungalow style.

Imagine alongside these, rows of telegraph poles and gigantic advertisements, mostly for various brands of beer. This is the village. It is scrupulously clean. The shops and restaurants will be air-conditioned. Everyone will be friendly and treat you as an equal. The food sold in the super-market will be displayed with a hygiene unknown anywhere in Europe and its diversity will dazzle you. There will be no soot, no dirt, only dust blown in from the desert outside.

This, the desert, the fundamentally inhospitable character of the landscape, is the most striking impression of all. The only comparable place familiar to us by hearsay at least is Palestine, a poor country where wretched Arabs managed to scrape a miserable living from the soil. It is amazing that the Americans made California the richest country in the world.

To Professor Nevill Mott, the new Cavendish Professor of Physics, February 19, 1954

I am very sorry about my misunderstanding. I told Bragg several times, while he was still here, that I should like to discuss the future of the Unit with you, but he insisted that he had already settled it all with you. I was rather surprised myself that you should have agreed to keep us before having seen anything of our work.

I am grateful for your agreement to keep us, at any rate until July 1955, and hope that some modus vivendi will be found after that. I am of course extremely keen to carry on. For the first time the subject of biological structures has entered the stage when the results obtained can be proved, and the solution of the great problems really seem within our grasp. Nearly all the methods of attack were developed by my friends and myself in this Unit, and I am naturally proud of this. Kendrew, [Hugh] Huxley, Crick, [Vernon] Ingram and [Tony] Broad are as gifted a band of enthusiasts as you can find. By our different abilities and training we all supplement each other in a hundred useful ways, and by staying together our chances of getting results are greater than if we all worked dispersed in different laboratories. This is why I should like to keep the Unit together.

It is often thought, especially by the General Board [of the Faculties] that we are carrying out work for the MRC. The truth is quite the contrary. We were fortunate in convincing the MRC that our work is of fundamental biological importance even though most of it seemed to them to be physics. It was due to their support, and to Bragg's within the Cavendish, that we were able to carry on the work on the scale needed to get results.

To Lawrence Bragg, May 10, 1954

I am not sure if Kendrew made it clear to you what Ingram's achievement in attaching a heavy metal to myoglobin implies. If his method works, and we cannot be absolutely sure of that yet, it means that it is of general application to proteins and that it should now be possible to attach heavy atoms in definite positions to most of the proteins that have been examined by X-rays. This would render it much easier for you to develop an original research programme of your own at the R.I. [Royal Institution], quite apart from the wider implications that X-ray analysis of proteins may become as fruitful a field of research as minerals were thirty years ago.

To Vivien and Robin. Gronigen, May 23, 1954

This is a funny country. The cows wear rain coats and chocolate blanc mange is sold in milk bottles. You pour it out for your pudding. The trains are electric, very fast and shaky. I saw a newborn calf in a field being licked clean by its mummy, ships going along canals which look as though they were steaming right through the fields. The bridges over the canals can be turned round to let the ships pass.

To Gisela Perutz. Paris, July 24, 1954

I am having a pleasant time and am not working particularly hard. Bragg's and my paper went off all right yesterday afternoon, thanks to careful preparation, and was well received, with Sage [Desmond Bernal] and Dorothy singing my praises afterwards. Dorothy gave a brilliant lecture on Vitamin B12 last night. As Adrienne [Weill] said, she is divine the way she guesses the right answer invariably and talks about it with irresistible charm.

I had dinner at some French scientist's flat on Thursday—Wilkinson's mess multiplied and compressed into a small volume, but an excellent practice for my French. They spoke no English. Yesterday I lunched with Alfonso [Liquori] in fluent Italian[28] and afterwards impressed a Swiss by my faultless German. I was very proud.

To Gisela Perutz. Lenzerheide, March 1955

One great help for me here is freedom from inner conflict. At home giving in to my laziness or taking care of myself can never be done without hurt-

---

[28]This is said tongue in cheek!

Max with Robin and his puppets   *Gisela*

ing you, neglecting my lab, disappointing the children, making trouble all round, so that I feel unhappy not only about the fact of feeling sick, but about the consequences for other people. Here these conflicts do not arise and this has an excellent effect on my nerves. True, I use up the family's money which ought to be used for better ends, but this aspect worries me least, as I can easily earn it again once I am well.

A further good thing for me, of which you should reap the benefit, is that I have to organise myself and be responsible for myself, so that such silly things as my blaming you for pushing me into this or the other activity does not arise. I make mistakes, of course, both in doing too little some days or too much on others, but at least there are no scape-goats, and I don't have to be miserable afterwards for having upset you as well as myself.

To Gisela Perutz. Lenzerheide, March 28, 1955

A sweet wedding anniversary letter from you this morning. I hope you will forget all the silly complaints made under the stress of illness. Instead of grumbling I should be (and am) grateful for all your care and help which have enabled me to keep reasonably well for so many years, despite my unfortunate constitution. Indigestion puts grey glasses on my eyes. Sometimes your sweet face or the sparkle in Robin's eyes cheer me up for a while, but soon the heaviness, the never ending tiredness pull me down to my own black thoughts or more often just to a dull stupor, in which external impressions are hardly registered. [Wilfred] Noyce[29] describes how at high altitudes the higher layers of his brain were never engaged. To appreciate the scenery he had to switch the oxygen on. This is the way I often feel now, and why I dislike myself so; only I have no oxygen to resort to.

To Gisela Perutz. Lenzerheide, March 30, 1955

My impression is that there are 2 factors involved in my troubles. One is an organic illness for which a definite cure is required and which cannot be surmounted by distraction, patience and energy alone. The other is nerves caused by the first.[30]

To Dr. G.R. Pomerat of the Rockefeller Foundation. Hope Cove, Devon, August 8, 1955

I was very pleased to get your letter. I was hesitant so far to write to you, because the University is still undecided about our future accommodation. However, Professor Mott will write to you that we can stay where we are until new quarters are found for us, and I hope that this guarantee, together with the previous one from the General Board [of Cambridge University], will allay any possible fears that the Unit might find itself homeless.

I think you ought to go to this lovely spot if ever you go on holiday in England. Blue sea, wild rocks, rare birds and exquisite food all combine to give you a wonderful time.

---

[29]Noyce W., 1954. *South Col: One Man's Adventure on the Ascent of Everest 1953*. Heinemann Publishers Ltd., Oxford, UK.

[30]Later that year, a medically trained research scientist, Werner Jacobson, who had read the relevant Dutch papers, diagnosed coeliac disease, thereby dramatically improving Max's health. In Max's case, the disease was complicated by the damage inflicted on his digestive tract during the years it went unrecognised and by intolerance to many foods and inhalants, intolerances that continued to develop over the rest of his life and that always led to more diarrhoea or sore throats and even the loss of his voice for several months in 1977. In 1954–1955, his illness had become so bad that he suffered continual diarrhoea, overpowering fatigue and mental cloudiness, all characteristic symptoms of coeliac disease and food intolerance. Further features of this condition which plagued him for the rest of his life are poor absorption of essential nutrients, hypoglycaemia and greater than normal susceptibility to infections. Although the medical profession was only beginning to recognise coeliac disease in the 1950s, it is so widespread and well-recognised nowadays that UK supermarkets have separate sections of gluten-free food and most food labelling indicates whether the product contains gluten (gluten is a protein in wheat that is the principal allergen).

To Dr. G.R. Pomerat of the Rockefeller Foundation, August 15, 1955

Kendrew, Bodo and Dintzis have made a heavy atom compound of myoglobin which looks as though it would solve the phase problem in this protein. Alex Rich and J.D. Watson have obtained excellent X-ray photographs with RNA and are building models of the structure. Huxley's muscle work continues to make good progress. The chemical work on heavy atom substituted proteins has greatly increased our

Hugh Huxley

expenditure on glassware, chemicals and other small items; the photometry and calculations involved in working out the X-ray pictures will in due course require a photometer and a second calculating machine, in addition to the one already provided by the Foundation. More technical assistants will be needed for chemistry and computing.

Below is a list of items for which we should like support during the coming academic year; this comes to about £3000. It is always difficult to estimate the needs for future years, because so much depends on the progress of the work, but perhaps it would be reasonable to assume that our needs in 1956–7 would be much the same; there will probably be some further expansion after that, bringing expenditure up to £4000 a year in 1957–8 and 1958–9. Please let me know if you would think this proposal reasonable and tell me what changes, if any, you would advise me to make in my final application.

To Dr. G.R. Pomerat of the Rockefeller Foundation, August 30, 1955

I should now like to ask the Foundation for a grant of £14,000 over a period of four years to support the work on the structure of large biological molecules carried out in this Department by my colleagues and myself. Of this sum about one third would be spent on permanent equipment such as machine tools, calculating machines and X-ray equipment, one third on general supplies of glassware, chemicals and small items of equipment, and the rest on technical assistants.

In the course of the next four years the main task of Kendrew and myself will be the further analysis of haemoglobin and myoglobin.

You are familiar with the work on muscle structure of Huxley and [Jean] Hanson, and their discovery of the structural basis of the striations in muscle. They intend to find the exact structural relationships of actin and myosin and the part played by these two proteins in muscle contraction, using X-ray diffraction, electron and optical microscopy. There will probably be collaboration with Professor Randall's group at King's College, London.

It appears probable now that the discovery of the structure of DNA by Crick and Watson will soon be followed by that of RNA. This is turn should provide the clue to the structure of certain plant viruses, notably the mosaic virus of the tobacco plant. Much more important will be the relation between the structure of these molecules and their biological function, but any forecast about the path which this research will follow seems still premature.

To Harold Himsworth, Chief Executive of the Medical Research Council, September 20, 1955

Gerhard Bodo in 1956

Research in the Unit has been very exciting lately. Kendrew and Dintzis, an American Postgraduate Fellow, have prepared several heavy atom compounds of myoglobin and have solved the "phase problem" of this protein now. The first pictures of the molecule are emerging and look very interesting.

Crick and Rich, another American, have found a structure of collagen which looks highly promising. Crick, Rich and Watson have also made great progress towards the solution of the structure of RNA, the second form of nucleic acid, which had so far escaped solution. Bodo, the young Austrian chemist whom the Council allowed us to engage, has succeeded in crystallizing for the first time cytochrome C. Since its discovery by Keilin in 1926 many workers all over the world have tried unsuccessfully to crystallize this enzyme so that Bodo's success is evidence of great skill.

Tony Broad developed the first successful rotating anode X-ray generator. Not only did it produce X-ray diffraction patterns sharper than those produced by earlier machines, but it also reduced the time to produce an image from 2 days to less than 1 hour. With four generators, two of which could be expected to function at any one time, the crystallographer could hope to get 50 X-ray diffraction patterns a week, rather than two as had been the case hitherto, as Broad explained to me.

You remember that last July I appealed, successfully, to Sir [Arthur] Landsborough for a raise in salary of our technician [Tony Broad], because this man had built us an X-ray tube more powerful than any other in the world. It was the existence of this tube which caused Rich to come to Cambridge with his specimens of RNA and it was his presence that triggered off the structural work both on RNA and on collagen. I mention this because it shows how the help you are giving us often pays in unexpected ways.

Sir Harold Himsworth

To Dr. G.R. Pomerat of the Rockefeller Foundation, October 12, 1955

I was delighted with the good news. Will you please express my warmest thanks to the Executive Committee for their approval of the grant, and also accept my gratitude for your own personal efforts in ascertaining our needs and giving them such sympathetic consideration. The grant comes as a great relief to me. Progress of our work has been so rapid during the last few weeks that our needs have far outstripped the financial support which we can reasonably expect from the Medical Research Council. I must tell you that great credit for this belongs to Howard Dintzis[31] whose discovery of an HfI4 [hafnium tetraiodide] complex of myoglobin has solved Kendrew's phase problem and has already produced a first Fourier projection looking far less enigmatic than mine of haemoglobin or Harker's of ribonuclease. Dintzis believes that he and Kendrew have all the prerequisites for three-dimension work on the protein. This means calculating machines, computers and chemical laboratory assistants whom we shall be able to afford more easily now.

---

[31] In Cambridge on a Rockefeller Foundation fellowship.

To Harold Himsworth, August 24, 1956

I am writing to tell you of exciting developments in the work of our unit.

The first news is the discovery by Dr. Vernon Ingram of a definite chemical difference between the globins of sickle cell anaemia and normal haemoglobin. Ingram has devised a new and rapid method of characterising proteins in considerable detail. This consists in first digesting the protein with trypsin and then spreading out the peptides of the digest on a two-dimensional chromatogram, using electrophoresis in one direction and chromatography in the other. By applying this method to the two haemoglobins Ingram finds that all the 30 odd peptides in the digest are alike except for a single one. This peptide is uncharged in normal haemoglobin and carries a positive charge in haemoglobin S. The size of the peptide is probably of the order of 10 amino-acid residues. Ingram is now going to set about to determine the composition and sequence of the residues in the two peptides.

Vernon Ingram in the early 1950s

This discovery is particularly interesting, because the change in structure from normal to sickle cell haemoglobin is thought to be due to the action of one single gene, and the action of genes is thought to consist in determining the sequence of residues in a polypeptide chain. We have long wanted to know how large a section of chain is affected by one gene and Ingram's work will enable him to find out. Moreover the many other abnormal haemoglobins offer interesting field for further study.[32,33]

Crick is particularly interested in this work. He and Brenner, who is shortly going to join the Unit under an appointment from the Council, plan a wider programme of work both on the reproduction of genes and on their mode of action, which means in effect the biosynthesis of nucleic acid and protein.

---

[32] See the letter of 18 June 1968.

[33] Sickle cell anaemia is an inherited disease found mainly in people of African origin because it increases resistance to malaria. Its cause is a single mutation in one of the two haemoglobin chains. Vernon Ingram identified the single amino acid substitution when compared to the same peptide in normal haemoglobin. This was the first demonstration of a structural change in a protein correlated with a single mutation in a gene: this substitution greatly reduces the solubility of the haemoglobin and, as a result, deforms the red blood cells, thereby causing them to break with consequent severe anaemia in the patient. In the 1950s, African children inheriting the defective gene from both parents rarely lived for more than a few years, but with good medical care, close to 50% will now survive well into adulthood. Nevertheless, the disease is both debilitating and disfiguring.—AW

The abnormal haemoglobins offer one way of studying the action of genes. Another is the study of the tail protein of bacteriophage. This has the advantage that phage has only one chromosome consisting of a single chain of DNA, so that changes in the amino-acid composition of the tail protein caused by a certain mutation could be related to changes in the sequence of bases in the DNA chain. In this way a correlation between sequence of bases and DNA and the sequence of residues in a polypeptide chain might gradually be established.

There is also a proposal to study haemoglobin synthesis by rabbit reticulocytes. Evidence is accumulating that the "organs" which carry out protein synthesis in cells are the microsomes.[34] These are particles comparable in size to small viruses, which look spherical in electron micrographs and consist of 50% RNA [ribonuclease] and 50% protein. Crick suspects that they may have a regular structure like the viruses, and wants to try and verify this idea by X-ray analysis of microsome crystals. Together with Brenner he therefore wants to try and crystallise them and of course study the mechanism by which they synthesise protein.

I think that this programme looks exciting, all the more so as recent experiments carried out in America suggest not only that the Watson-Crick structure of DNA is correct, but that the mechanism of duplication which they proposed may also turn out to be right. This programme does however need additional equipment.

Returning to scientific news Kendrew and I, in collaboration with Dr. David Ingram, a physicist at Southampton University, have used electron spin resonance, a spectroscopic method of employing radar waves, to determine the orientation of the haem groups in myoglobin and haemoglobin. This still does not give us their positions which would be much more interesting, but it is at least one definite piece of structural information.

To Felix Haurowitz, September 20, 1956

We have two successes to report. 1. David Ingram and I found the orientation of the haem groups in haemoglobin by paramagnetic resonance. This is a most powerful new spectroscopic device by which one can determine the angular orientation of each of the 4 haem groups separately with an

---

[34]Reticulocytes are premature red blood cells which were used for experiments on protein synthesis in the test tube. The "microsomes" described here were pellets centrifuged from cell homogenates at very high speed: They contained mainly ribosomes, later identified as the biological sites of protein synthesis.—AW

accuracy of ± 2°. 2. Vernon Ingram in my lab has discovered a definite chemical difference between the globins of normal and sickle cell haemoglobin. It is located in one small section of one of the polypeptide chains.

We are getting rather short of hands which is sad in view of the interesting stage of the work. We have had a great batch of American post-graduate students, but they are now leaving and at the moment we have no one to replace them with.

To Felix Haurowitz, April 19, 1957

Most exciting news: Ingram has found the nature of the chemical difference between sickle cell and normal haemoglobin. A glutamic acid residue in normal Hb is replaced by valine in sickle cell Hb. It is fascinating that the effect of a single mutation in one gene appears to be a change in just one amino-acid residue in a protein, and that this change should have such far-reaching effects on the physiological properties of the protein.

To Vivien and Robin Perutz. Approaching New York, April 21, 1957

I saw the comet.[35] It had a striking very long tail, pointing away from the rising sun and could be seen for a long time, because we were flying away from the sun so fast. I was the only man on board who spotted it; the navigator was unable to find it, and yet it was as brilliant as Venus. The comet appeared on the star-board side, and when I looked out on the port side the moon was up and I could also see what at first looked like a strongly lit cloud of greenish colour. When I watched it for a while I noticed that some of the cloud suddenly seemed to vanish and other patches appeared as from nowhere. Then I realised that I was watching the Aurora Borealis which lights up the sky like strange curtains of cloud in the neighbourhood of the magnetic poles.

Now this was just where the aircraft was flying to. It went in a great circle from England north to the Southern tip of Greenland and then touched Labrador at Goose Bay and flew south across Canada, past the St Lawrence River and so to the United States.

One of the prettiest sights appeared right at the start when the plane rose over London and we could see the lights in Parliament and Trafalgar Square and all the lovely lighted bridges across the Thames.

---

[35]This seems to be the comet Arend-Roland C/1956 R1, which was visible until July of 1957.

John Kendrew

To Dr. G.R. Pomerat of the Rockefeller Foundation, September 16, 1957

Kendrew completed the first three-dimensional Fourier of myoglobin a few weeks ago and we are all very thrilled with it. It shows the position of the iron atom with the haem group together with several long stretches of rods of high electron density which clearly represent polypeptide chains. Their configuration cannot be seen directly but judging by the distances between these rods one would guess them to be α-helices. The structure of the molecule as a whole is most complex and intricate, and quite different from anything anyone had ever imagined, the haem group being attached to a kind of basket work of polypeptide chain with many different kinds of contact between protein and prosthetic group. The resolution (6 Å) is still too low to make out details but at least the shape of the molecule, general layout of the polypeptide chains and the position of the haem group are clear.

I am immensely encouraged by Kendrew's success and am redoubling my efforts to try and get a three-dimensional Fourier of haemoglobin at a comparable resolution. Kendrew meanwhile is already going ahead with plans for a second three-dimensional Fourier at twice the resolution of the present one and so far as we can see there are no fundamental obstacles in the way of this being achieved.

I am very pleased that the long-continued support of the Foundation for this research is now beginning to bear genuine fruit.

To Steffen Peiser, undated[36]

In my opinion nothing matters so much to a scientist as the interest and stimulus of his work, and I hope that you will consider your difficult choice first and foremost from that point of view, without letting yourself be swayed too much by considerations of position, finance and personal loyalties.

To Steffen Peiser, Easter Sunday, 1958

We received the news of your intention "mit einem lachenden und einem weinenden Auge" [with one smiling and one weeping eye]. We had no one else in this country to whom we felt as closely linked by family ties and bonds of affection.

To be set against all these losses are the gains in your professional life. I have often felt that your talents were not used to the full. You have an enthusiasm and energy which inspires people around you. Your meteoric rise at the NBS is a magnificent achievement and shows that your gifts are appreciated in America much more than they were here.

You were quite wrong when you wrote that we might jeer at you, as though you had become a disaster. Science is as international today as scholarship was in the Middle Ages, and a scientist must go where people will allow him to blossom out and do great things. It is true that this country had given you asylum, and that you felt you had to give your best to it in return, but I think you have repaid your debt in about 17 years of good work and should feel free from all guilt when you decided to change to a post with wider opportunities in the States.

My own position is quite different. After the repeated and spectacular successes achieved in my Research Unit, the Medical Research Council is prepared to do anything we ask for, and research workers are coming to us from many countries. It looks as though we are only at the beginning of the discovery of the molecular basis of living processes, and fascinating prospects of scientific revelation stretch out in all directions.

On April 18th I am to address the MRC on the scheme of building a Laboratory of Molecular Biology, and I think the prospects for its acceptance are good. On the other hand, the University may well put insuperable difficulties in our way, even if the MRC is prepared to build and maintain such a laboratory.

---

[36]Steffen was taking a year's sabbatical in Washington at the National Bureau of Standards and had written that he was debating whether to accept a permanent post at the Bureau.

Despite these bright prospects the first 3 months of 1958 have been most worrying and difficult for us. My father's illness looked hopeless at times and I never thought that we should be able to get him on his feet again.[37] Then there is your mother's hostility against Gisela which always haunts her dreams both by day and night.

Finally my own work on haemoglobin (3D Fourier) went through a crisis, now happily overcome, when it looked as though we had got to a dead end. There are still great difficulties ahead, but none as intractable as that which foxed us for the best part of 4 years, until a chance observation led me to discover its cause.[38]

To Linus Pauling, April 21, 1958

There are moves afoot to put both Crick and Kendrew up for election to the Royal Society. The arrangement is that Bragg will propose Kendrew and I shall second him, while Crick will be proposed by me and seconded by [Alexander] Todd. We wondered if you would be willing to sign either or both of these certificates?[39]

To Nelly Peiser, May 25, 1958[40]

In the lab I also had to struggle with tremendous scientific problems, which I've solved at least in part. They only concerned my own work. My labora-

---

[37] He died later that year.

[38] In *Science Is Not a Quiet Life*, Max explained that his aim was to put into practice Bijvoet's method of phase determination by double isomorphous replacement. "Bijvoet's method required a second heavy atom derivative with different heavy atom positions, but I had no idea how one could be made. I obtained a variety of mercurials from colleagues in the United States and Germany, but none of them solved my problem. Even worse, I was unable to reproduce the original crystals of the parmercuribenzoate derivative without introducing a lattice defect which ruined their isomorphism with the native crystals and made phase determination impossible. For several years I tried in vain to find the cause of this lattice defect, until one day I happened to take an X-ray diffraction picture of a crystal and was surprised that it was perfect. When I examined the tube from which I had taken it, I noticed that its stopper was leaky. It now occurred to me that evaporation from the tube might have lowered the pH and I soon confirmed this. I guessed that this must have cured the lattice defect." Later that year, Max solved the problem of finding a second heavy atom derivative: see the letter to John Edsall of 26 November 1983. Perutz M.F. 1997. *Science Is Not a Quiet Life*. World Scientific and Imperial College Press, London, p. 67.

[39] Pauling replied "I may say that I would be delighted to sign a certificate of nomination of Kendrew and of Crick to the Royal Society. I would put them in this order—that is, Kendrew first."

[40] Translated from the German.

tory as a whole is a tremendous success and our reputation with the Medical Research Council constantly rising. From the human point of view the lab also works brilliantly as we've succeeded in keeping a number of extremely gifted scientists all of the same age who work together harmoniously without jealousy or feuds. That is only possible in England where there's the most remarkable trust in the personal decency of others.

To Harold Himsworth, October 24, 1958

As regards the site, our first aim is to have a laboratory in which we can solve some of the key problems of molecular biology by the methods we have developed. Moreover, we want this laboratory to serve as a focus and model for the development of the subject in this country and overseas. If this aim cannot be realised in Cambridge we should certainly be willing to move elsewhere, and I have no hesitation in assuring you that we are all anxious for an enlarged Laboratory of Molecular Biology to be set up under the Council, even if this has to be done independently of the University.

I do not think that at this stage any of us are vitally concerned over the matter of Ph.D. students, because we have no difficulty in staffing our laboratory with post-doctoral graduates. Moreover, the number of first class B.A.s wanting to take up research in a borderline subject for their Ph.D. thesis is small. Therefore rather than abandon our proposal for a laboratory, we would abandon our right to have Ph.D. students.

However, we still retain our hope that it will in fact be possible to retain the cooperation of the University and that the University will do its best to let us have a laboratory on a central site, associated with one or more of the existing departments, and that it would be acceptable to the University as a place where Ph.D. students might be trained.

It would help me greatly if our document "The Case for a Laboratory of Molecular Biology" could be "declassified," leaving me free to send it to interested members of the University.

To Steffen Peiser, Easter Monday, 1959

You probably gathered from Gisela that the General Board of the Faculties has approved the plan to set up a Laboratory of Molecular Biology jointly with the MRC and that the University is offering us a central site for the building. If it is all right, there are only minor disagreements between the

University and the MRC to be settled. If we are lucky a Grace for the establishment of the laboratory might be passed this term.

Gisela will also have told you of the £100,000 which were left to the MRC by the widow of an Indian cotton magnate who died last year at Monte Carlo. The money was left mostly in the form of jewellery which has to be sold at Sotheby's. According to the will it is to be spent by the MRC for the support of research in the University of Cambridge. Is it not an extraordinary piece of luck that this money should have appeared at this vital moment, given under conditions which are tailor-made to our purpose? I have no notion what made the old lady or her husband, Sir Cudrow [Wadia], do it. Himsworth believes that this will cover 2/3 of the cost and that it would not be too difficult to raise the remainder from the Treasury or elsewhere. We intend to put up a building of about 18,000 square feet with room for expansion if possible.

To Gisela Perutz, May 1 [?], 1959

Yesterday morning seems an age ago. I found the vacuum of our X-ray tubes had begun to leak and by this morning both had to be shut down. With Tony [Broad] in hospital this is a calamity. We are sad about this as our next 3D series of pictures is nearly finished and we might have got to the end in another 2–3 days. We shall consult Tony in hospital tomorrow.

This morning I found the enclosed letter from Fort [?] and decided to see Himsworth this afternoon. After nearly 2 hours with him I believe I have convinced him of the need for a speedy agreement with the University, regardless of the complications. But there is still a fearful struggle ahead, with the University Financial Board (a new difficulty), the Hospital Board and finally the Ministry of Health who own the land. [By this time the site in question must have been that adjacent to the relocated hospital on the southern edge of the city.] I told Himsworth again and again not to give up and emphasised my belief that with one more great heave the battle can be won. I am sure it can. This is chicken feed compared to the 3D Fourier of Hb.

At the RI [Royal Institution] I found the X-ray spectrometer which had broken down several weeks ago still not repaired. Here again a great push is needed to get the measurements completed.

Don't think I am depressed. These setbacks are unavoidable and part of life. In a week's time most of them may be overcome and you may find me wondering how to cross the next hurdle.

I can hardly believe what life will be like when haemoglobin is solved and the Laboratory has been built. Will I be able to resist complacency? Let us hope that we shall continue to live happily through all these difficulties. They matter little as long as there is love and affection at home.

To Gisela Perutz, May 3, 1959

As you see from the children's letters, we are all well. I enjoyed Robin's enthusiasm when I worked with him in the garden yesterday and found it a tonic after the tension of the previous day.

Yesterday morning I mobilised Mott, Todd and Noel Annan against the Financial Board and hope that they will all bear down on it next week.[41] I have told Himsworth that the scheme will collapse unless we can push it through by 10 June which is the last General Board meeting, and I hope that this will induce him to deal with matters more expeditiously. If only I could move these various officials out of their offices where they write nasty letters to each other and get them to discuss matters in person, everything could be settled in one afternoon. A summit meeting is what we want.

To Harold Himsworth, May 3, 1959

[Mott and Todd] were also most indignant about the scandalous business of Taylor offering the Council a site which the University does not have, and I do not think that the last word has been said about this.

When you asked me on Friday whether Crick would agree to a laboratory on the outskirts of Cambridge, I ought to have remembered that he was actually asked that question at the hearing of the General Board Committee last November and replied that he would prefer to accept a post abroad. Moreover Kendrew is dead against the entire scheme unless the Laboratory can be part of the University. There is little doubt therefore that the whole scheme will fall through unless it is pushed through in the form now contemplated.

I am confident that it can be done, especially if we enlist Mott and Todd's very willing help to iron out difficulties rather than try and do it through the cumbersome official channels. [On 13 May, senior members of the proposed laboratory agreed to a hospital site with the proviso that the agreement on the general relationship with the University should remain intact.]

---

[41]The Board was making administrative difficulties which would have entailed a delay of years. Among its few members, as a representative of the colleges, was the bursar of King's College; hence the appeal to Noel Annan, its Provost. Todd was the head of the Chemistry Laboratory.

To Dr. G.R. Pomerat of the Rockefeller Foundation, October 1, 1959

Kendrew, Dickerson and Strandberg have completed a three-dimensional Fourier of myoglobin at 2 Å resolution, three times better than the resolution of Kendrew's first attempt. M.G. Rossmann, Ann Cullis, Hilary Muirhead and I have a three-dimensional Fourier of haemoglobin at 6 Å resolution. The four units fit together in a most beautiful way, so that the surface contours of one part of the chains match those of the other. The model is a remarkable thing, and I shall send you some photographs when I have them ready.

What is most exciting, perhaps, about our results are their wider implications. If the myoglobin of a whale is like the haemoglobin of a horse, then the structure of these two proteins is probably much the same throughout the animal kingdom. There must be certain standard sequences of amino acids which all these proteins have in common and which determine the characteristic loops and turns of the chain. These must have developed from a common primeval gene which provided the physiological basis for the development of the higher animals, by making possible the storage and transport of oxygen.

Looked at from the point of view of protein chemistry it makes one suspect that proteins are probably grouped into broad classes, and that within each class the main structural features are similar. In other words, one will probably discover a natural history of enzymes which will give one an insight into the biochemical development of the species.

All this is for the future.

These advances owe much to the far-sighted support by the Foundation, especially during the long, lean years when the problem seemed complex almost beyond hope. Please assure the Trustees of our gratitude for their long-continued support and accept my thanks for your own kind interest.

To Dely Perutz, October 2, 1959[42]

I am working on the construction of the haemoglobin models suitable for publication. It is really difficult to present this huge molecule effectively but I am enjoying it.

---

[42]Translated from the German.

To Felix and Gina Haurowitz, December 13, 1959[43]

I have spent some of the happiest weeks of my life this autumn working out the results of my 3D Fourier of haemoglobin. It gives a clear and most satisfying answer. There are 4 chains and each has a configuration very similar to Kendrew's whale myoglobin. They are arranged at the corners of a tetrahedron. The haems lie in pockets on the surface of the molecule as shown in the picture and are far apart from each other.

To Gisela Perutz. Near Munich, December 27, 1959

I had a stormy but comfortable passage and a good night under my cosy eiderdown. So I feel quite well and refreshed and have started to read my *Scientific American*s. One of the books you gave me, *The Catcher in the Rye*, is very good and highly original. I much enjoyed it last night. *The Wrong Set* is the usual "people are no good" satire which we deplore in modern art. Writers must spend most of their time in the company of good-for-nothings.

The train is full of parties of schoolgirls going to Kitzbühel. I share the compartment with their dear old teachers to whom you have to say everything twice before they take it in. One never referred to her coat, but always carefully to her fur-coat. She is called Millicent and wears a dark red beret and a pink scarf tied under her chin with the fur coat. I thought V[ivien] would be all agog to hear these fascinating details.

---

[43]Glued to Max's Christmas card was a photo of his model of haemoglobin.

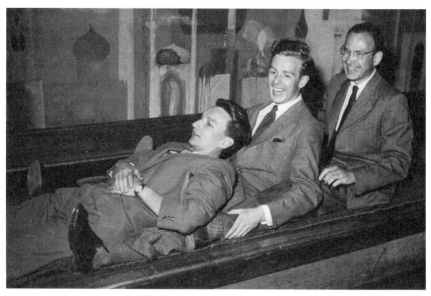

From left to right: *Gerhard Bodo, David Green and Howard Dintzis taking time out from a conference, 1956.*

1960s

"As I said to Lady Bragg the other day,
we owe it all to you!"

THE SOLUTION OF THE LOW-RESOLUTION STRUCTURES of myoglobin and haemo-globin, and the move of the expanded unit into a brand new laboratory opened by the Queen and chaired by Max, transformed his life. The sight of these strangely coiled molecules caused a tremendous stir. First, long articles appeared in all the broadsheets as well as the scientific press, and then Raymond Baxter interviewed Max and John Kendrew for BBC television. Invitations to give endowed lectures followed: the Weizmann lectures in Israel in 1961 and the Dunham lectures at Harvard in the spring of 1963. Last but not least, one evening in November 1962, the telephone began to ring: reporters had received wind of the imminent announcement of the Nobel Prize. Knowing what had happened to Dorothy Hodgkin, my father warned us that the rumours might be false, but the next day brought the official news that he had indeed won the Nobel Prize in Chemistry jointly with John Kendrew.

Max with Raymond Baxter in 1960 with the complete model of haemoglobin in front of Max, to the left probably a model of one section, and beside it an atomic model of the haem group, that is, a porphyrin ring with the iron atom, to which the oxygen molecule attaches, at its centre. Behind Max is one photograph of haemoglobin crystals taken under the microscope and another showing the spots that the atoms of a haemoglobin crystal create when they diffract X-rays. (From BBC Eye on Science. © BBC.)

The pride the University of Cambridge now takes in its offshoot slowly grew over the years, but as Max wrote to Harold Himsworth's successor, John Gray, in 1994: "When the Queen came to open the new Addenbrooke's Hospital, neither Himsworth nor I was invited to lunch with the Queen, because the University administration continued to ignore our existence. When Kendrew and I won the Nobel Prize we received congratulations from everybody we had ever met in all corners of the world, but received no congratulations from the Vice-Chancellor or any of the other University top brass who were clearly displeased."

Max took the whole family including my grandmother to Israel via Cyprus, Lebanon and Jordan. As always, when embarking on a novel adventure, he kept a diary. Because in part the diary is simply a travelogue, I have cut it extensively, but not so radically as to destroy its continuity and character. What makes it particularly interesting today is that he saw this region before the 1967 and later wars. Moreover, what he saw and heard shaped Max's views on Israel and the Palestinian problem. The occasion of another diary, again partially reproduced here, was the International Congress of Biochemistry in Moscow where Max lectured on protein structure to an audience of 1000 and chaired the symposium on molecular biology. Our trip to Stockholm prompted him to write the third diary of the decade.

The journey to the Middle East, hot on the heels of a move to a larger house and garden near the new laboratory, had squeezed our family finances; the Nobel Prize put an end to all the financial worries of the previous 25 years and boosted my father's self-confidence. It also transformed his status in Cambridge: his old college, Peterhouse, elected him an Honorary Fellow, that is, to a fellowship without any of the duties the office normally carries. Not being a fellow had often made him unhappy because the Cambridge colleges are a little like clubs. Without a fellowship, he felt excluded from the "clubs" to which everyone else seemed to belong. From 1963 Max took Saturday lunch in college, where he made new friends. Among them were the historians Lord Dacre (Hugh Trevor-Roper), master of the college from 1980 to 1987, with whom he later corresponded, and Brendan Simms, a contributor to this volume.

The leaps and bounds by which molecular biology had developed led to the foundation of the European Molecular Biology Organisation (EMBO) in 1963. At its inaugural meeting, held in the romantic castle of Ravello on the cliffs above Amalfi, Max was voted chairman, an office that gave him new and often very interesting international duties.

Scientifically, Max and his team were as active as ever. The award of the Nobel Prize coincided with the first evidence that haemoglobin changed its structure on taking up and shedding oxygen. One half of the molecule rotates relative to the other as it switches from the oxy to the deoxy state. The next step was to refine the structures of the two states, that is, to map the precise positions of the ~10,000 atoms of carbon, nitrogen, sulphur and oxygen of the polypeptide chains that cradle the four haem groups.

The more exact structures finally allowed Max to begin to tackle the problem he had set himself in the mid 1930s, namely, precisely how the atoms move and what triggers their movement as the molecule first takes up and then sheds its four oxygen molecules. Most excitingly, the atomic models opened two new fields he would continue to explore: evolution at the molecular level and haemoglobin diseases. At the close of the 1960s, together with Hermann Lehmann, he was able to explain some of these diseases in terms of the molecular mistakes that induce them, so raising the possibility of specifically targeted drugs. Although drugs have taken a long time to materialise, the principle was to become a cornerstone of molecular medicine and drug development.

To Gisela Perutz. MIT, June 3, 1960

I spent the morning in [Paul] Doty's lab and found a wealth of fascinating work there. He obviously has lots of good ideas. I lunched with John Edsall at the Club, had my lecture in the afternoon, dined with 6 or 8 people afterwards and then went with Edsall to attend a lecture of Hans Bethe on the Cessation of Nuclear Tests. He gave a fascinating account of the technical problems of test detection, of the Geneva negotiations and of the attitude of Congress. He left me with the feeling that the present administration and Congress are unlikely to sign a test agreement; their aim is to drag on negotiations by making progressively stiffer demands for inspection. Bethe himself impressed me immensely by his combination of fervent convictions for what is right and calm reasoning power which seems inexhaustible. He talked for 2 hours without either exhausting himself or the audience, and never said a word too much.

To Harold Himsworth, January 25, 1961

During Lord Hailsham's visit[1] last week the question of high speed computers came up. We mentioned to him that Cambridge University had applied for an "Atlas," a computer under construction by Ferranti's which

---

[1]Hailsham was Minister of Science in Harold Macmillan's cabinet.

is to cost £1.5M and is to be comparable in performance with the fastest American machine under way.

We told Lord Hailsham about Kendrew's present arrangement with Aldermaston,[2] but stressed that this was not really satisfactory as development of new types of work really required a computer nearby; the proximity of a very fast computer acts as a stimulus for attacking problems which could never be solved on a slower machine. Such new programs need so much trying out that they can hardly be developed unless one has continuous access to the computer.

It is true that our Unit would not occupy such a machine for more than 10% of its working time, but there are many other, equally interesting problems at the University ranging from theoretical chemistry to astrophysics, for which an ultra-high-speed computer is vital.

It would certainly be of great help to our work, and we would be grateful for anything you can do to support the University's application.

To Harold Himsworth, February 9, 1961

Sydney Brenner

I am writing to tell you about a major advance made in this Unit by Brenner, in collaboration with F. Jacob at the Pasteur Institute and M. Meselson at the California Institute of Technology.

The work is concerned with the mechanism and genetic control of protein synthesis. It is known that in bacteria, most and perhaps all protein synthesis takes place in the cytoplasm, located in small particles called ribosomes which consist of ribonucleic acid (RNA) and protein. It used to be thought that the ribosomes contained permanent templates for protein synthesis, each ribosome being a factory for the production of one specific protein. In Brenner's words, the current scheme could be epitomised by the "one gene—one ribosome—one protein" hypothesis.

Certain inconsistencies prompted Jacob and Monod at the Pasteur Institute to suggest instead that the ribosomes themselves are non-specialised structures which receive information from the gene in the form of an unstable intermediate or messenger.

---

[2]The location of the headquarters of the UK's Atomic Weapons Establishment.

The experiments of Brenner, Jacob and Meselson were done to test this hypothesis. They used coli bacteria infected with T4 bacteriophage and employed tracer techniques to follow the course of events in the ribosomes after infection.

When growing bacteria are infected with a virulent bacteriophage such as T4, DNA synthesis stops immediately, to resume seven minutes later, while protein synthesis continues at a constant rate. However, after infection many bacterial enzymes are no longer made. In all likelihood the new protein synthesized after phage infection is genetically determined by the phage.

According to the old hypothesis the infecting phage particles should have produced new ribosomes which would in turn produce phage protein while the production of bacterial protein in the existing ribosomes would be inhibited.

The new experiments have proved this scheme to be wrong. The new protein, made after phage infection, is in fact synthesized in the old, existing, ribosomes. In addition a new RNA, made after phage infection, is added to these ribosomes. This must be the messenger envisaged by Jacob and Monod. New ribosomes could be detected. The new RNA "turns over" rapidly which means that the RNA molecules are continuously being destroyed and replaced by fresh ones.

It was recently discovered by Volkin and Astrachan in the States that after a phage infection a new RNA is made, with a base composition similar to phage DNA and different from bacterial DNA, a fact which proves this new RNA to be a genetic product of the infecting phage and not of the bacterium. The messenger RNA now found in the bacterial microsomes is identical with the RNA detected by Volkin and Astrachan.

The importance and novelty of the results of Brenner and his colleagues lies in their direct demonstration of the transfer of information from the gene to the site of protein synthesis by a messenger RNA. Its rapid turnover suggests that perhaps each molecule of messenger RNA makes only one protein molecule and is then destroyed. For continuous synthesis of a particular protein, messengers would have to be made continuously by the gene. An infecting virus apparently inhibits the production of host messengers and substitutes its own, while still using the host's existing apparatus for protein synthesis.

Members of the Unit continue to be pressed to accept posts in the United States. Brenner has been offered the directorship of the Carnegie Institute of Genetics at Cold Spring Harbor, Kendrew the chair of biophysics at Ann Arbor and another one at Los Angeles, and Crick the directorship of a new laboratory of Molecular Biology at the N.I.H. [National Institutes of Health]. Luckily they have all turned deaf ears to the Sirens' calls.

The Middle East, April 1961

Easter Monday, 1961, Flight to Cyprus Our plane touched down at Athens at 4:00 am. It was still dark and only shadows of distant hills could be seen from the airfield. We flew off again an hour later, turning east to meet the dawn over the Aegean. At 550 mph the day starts with a bang: the sun pops over the horizon with ridiculous speed. From 35,000 ft the Aegean islands are merely blue green patches in a black sea. We reached the Turkish coast in less than an hour and had our first thrill when we saw the snow-capped mountains of Anatolia. A few minutes later Cyprus appeared out of the mist and we looked down on the cape where Venus is said to have been born fully grown, floating on a sea shell (see Botticelli).

Kyrenia When we got to Kyrenia, the little hill town where we had decided to stay, we deposited Mother at the best hotel and ourselves in the worst. It was a little "Beisl" [pub] somewhat to our taste, run by a Greek and his English wife or mistress, not very clean or comfortable, but very cheap and quite cosy.

Imagine Cannes 150 years ago as a sleepy little town with only one big hotel, with a small fishing harbour at the side of a formidable medieval castle and all this surrounded by olive, orange and lemon groves. In the town men at work in open shops along the street, and a limpid blue sea gently splashes up on the shore. Dilapidated buses and cars of all ages race through the town honking their horns. A few miles inland to the East of Kyrenia and about 800 feet above the plain stand the remains of a 12th century abbey called Bellapais, a corruption of the original Cloître de la Paix, a very apt name This is one of the loveliest places I have ever seen.

From the Greek village of Bellapais a path leads down through olive and orange groves to a Turkish village where you find a quite different culture, untouched by Kemal Ataturk's reforms which changed mainland Turkey. Women still wear veils and this place and other Turkish villages are much poorer than the Greek ones. The old people are mostly bandy-legged showing that rickets must once have been rampant. We were touched by the Turkish children running into their gardens to pick bunches of flowers for us without expecting baksheesh, just a gesture of friendly welcome.

Next day we went for a drive to the south coast which took us over the mountains and the monotonous plain to the remains of a big Graeco-

Roman town called Salamis. We had read about this place, but no one had told us that we would find acres upon acres of ruined town overgrown with shrubs and largely untouched by the archaeologists. It used to be a flourishing port, which got sacked by Arab invaders and never rose again.

Cyprus: Economy and Politics The economy of Cyprus is peculiar. Inherently the country is agricultural and lives on olives, wine and fishing. Poverty of farms, simple mud huts without windows. However, since the withdrawal from Suez, Cyprus has become the main British base in the Near East and 20,000 troops are now stationed there. Their presence has given towns on the island a wholly artificial boom and sent prices soaring. Since the end of hostilities and especially the joining of the Commonwealth, the Greeks are officially pro-British again, and everybody was very friendly to us, perhaps partly for commercial reasons, but the former pictures of the Queen are now replaced by the twin portraits of Archbishop Makarios and General Grivas, the guerrilla leader

Dely Perutz at Salamis

who directed the heroic campaign of shooting British soldiers and civilians in the back and liberated Cyprus from the colonial yoke. Under the surface there is still much tension. An old Peterhouse friend now stationed in the army there told us of gang warfare resulting in 2 murders a week in the port of Limassol and of a continuing vendetta against Cypriots thought to have helped the British. However, to the visitor Cyprus has an air of peaceful unspoilt beauty.

Flight to Beirut A Viscount whisked us to Beirut in an hour. I had written to the only 2 people I knew there to tell them of my visit. One, Hanania, is an Arab, a former research student at Cambridge and now chairman of the chemistry department of the American University, and the other a French

Jesuit Father and former crystallographer, until recently dean of the medical faculty at the French University. Professor Hanania came to meet us. He drove us to our hotel, which was modest but one up on the Cyprus Beisl, and immediately afterwards took us to his flat where we found quite a party to meet us. There was Mrs. Hanania, a slight young woman of rare beauty. She charmed us all by her wonderfully delicate features and sweet expression. We discovered later that she was an accomplished linguist and highly educated in many fields. Her English was immaculate and she worked as an English teacher at the local high school. As a hostess, she had warmth, tact and a native dignity, without any of the ingratiating Eastern manner which I expected to find in these parts of the world. The hospitality of the Hananias was so charming that we never found it overwhelming or embarrassing even though they lived up to their promise of devoting the entire time of our visit to us.

From them and from the other people we met at their home we learnt much about the Lebanon. Its population is half Christian and half Muslim and it is governed by a coalition, rather like Austria, if you equate Catholic = Christian and Socialist = Muslim, so that for each job given to a member of one community an equivalent job has to be found for one of the other. It is the only democratic, free-trade country in the Near East and is flourishing economically. Beirut is an architect's paradise, a mosaic of ultra modern hotels, offices and apartment houses, and offers more varied and exciting new ideas in building than any city I know in Europe or America. Shops are well stocked, smart and always open, prices reasonable by Western European standards, traffic dense, noisy, chaotic and dangerously fast, cars mostly American.

Arab View of Israel   To come back to our hosts, we had had to tell them of course that we were en route for Israel. Imagine our consternation when we learnt that they were all, except the Jesuit Father, refugees from Palestine. I felt like sinking into the ground. This included the professors of chemistry, physics and biochemistry and Mrs. Hanania. They had all come from patrician Arab families long established in Jerusalem or Haifa, and what made the situation even more poignant, they were all *Christians*!

This put our minds into a state of divided loyalty from which we have not recovered. Every time we think of them, and of the fearful refugee camps which we were to see later on, we feel that the State of Israel is a terrible wrong. And then we think of the stories we heard from the Jews to whom Israel was the haven from the concentration camps and of their fabulous achievements, and we feel if only this could have been accomplished without another, and equally great, tragedy.

However, if our hosts felt any animosity towards us, they betrayed no trace of it. On the contrary they said how disappointing it was to them that Israel had become the scientific centre of the Near East, and was visited by scientists from all over the world, while Beirut lacked the funds for inviting people, and how pleased they were that we were visiting the Arab countries as well as Israel. At both universities only undergraduate teaching is done, but at the American University there are at least plans for starting Ph.D. students and the professors all seem very able. I was asked to give a lecture, although the vacation was still on, and gave an informal talk about protein structure to a small group.

Drive out to Byblos   The Hananias had of course planned to show us the sights. This meant two trips by taxi, the general and cheap means of transport in the Lebanon. There are 2 kinds: Christian ones who drive madly and put their faith in a Madonna, and Muslim ones who carry a rosary to protect themselves from their even greater folly. Hanania picked a Muslim one who scared the wits out of me by getting into the wrong lane on a two lane motor road and continuing unperturbed to drive straight against the

oncoming traffic for a mile or so until he found a crossover to the correct lane. Altogether drivers have an endearing habit of going straight at each other and waiting to see who will get out of the way first.

Beirut seems to have fewer slums than many Western towns, but on the way out we saw some terrible wooden shacks, resembling those in the coloured slums of Chicago, where Armenian refugees from the First World War still live. Also some very poor quarters inhabited by Palestinian refugees. We drove out northwards along the coast to see Byblos, claimed to be the oldest continuously inhabited town until the recent excavation in Jericho.

Professor Hanania (right) and our driver beside giant column drums of the Temple of Jupiter at Baalbek.

American University   The American University in Beirut where I lectured in the afternoon lies in a beautiful park overlooking the bay, with a private tunnel connecting the campus with the beach. How lucky these students are compared to those in Sheffield or Newcastle where they work in mostly hideous buildings in a grimy cold town under a grey sky.

The Temples of Baalbek Next morning Hanania and our Arab driver reappeared to take us to Baalbek, a great temple to the Sun god [Jupiter Heliopolitan] built in the first century A.D. It beats all expectations. The grandeur of its design and the workmanship of its execution are both remarkable. Admittedly it lacks the grace of the temples on the Acropolis and its style is a little Baroque but it makes up for this by its imposing scale. The columns of the main temple are about 7 feet across and 60 feet high. These support a marble cornice decorated with boldly carved and expressive lions' heads. I worked out that the individual column drums must have weighed 80 tons. The basalt and marble are not found locally but came from Aswan. To be able to ship these colossi over large distances and transport them over the Lebanon and erect them to these colossal heights the Graeco-Romans must have had much greater technical resources than we generally imagine. Again they must had had an efficient transport system to be able to feed the thousands of workmen engaged on the temple construction in that inaccessible place. The temple was obviously built to attract pilgrims by the thousand and there must have been good roads and inns and an efficient supply system to look after them all.

We talked some more politics to our hosts at night. While Hanania takes the uncompromising line that Israel must be wiped off the map, his wife feels that the Jews and Arabs are cousins and that an understanding must be reached. Contrary to reports in the English papers, news about Israel is accurately reported in Lebanese papers and Arabs here seem to be well aware of the achievements there. We later heard that clandestine trade between Israel and the Lebanon was actually going on, Lebanese cattle being exchanged for Israeli textiles.

We left Beirut rather regretfully as we liked the town and the people we had met.

Flight to Jerusalem (Jordanian side) We took an early plane from Beirut to Jerusalem. It first flew out to sea to gain height, then crossed the Lebanon and Anti Lebanon towards Damascus and finally flew south via Amman. We were courteously treated at the Jordanian customs; indeed nowhere on the entire journey was our luggage ever opened. Our hotel, though new, looked shabby but was reasonably clean. It formed part of a new town which has sprung up to the north of the Old City since the division in 1948 and was not far from the wall which now divides Jordan from Israel.

The Old City Entry into the old city was perhaps the most vivid and dramatic experience of our journey. We had seen a few oriental types in various places, but here we suddenly entered the heart of Arabia and found ourselves surrounded by a colourful jostling crowd pressing through steep streets too narrow for motor traffic. There Bedouins in traditional dress, Arab women shrouded in black veils, Muslim Sheikhs with short beards, Greek orthodox and Armenian priests with long beards, monks and nuns of all denominations and of course that staunch and unmistakable figure, the English clergyman: "You come from Cambridge do you? I am Queens'." Armenian women in prettily embroidered dresses, attractive Arab children begging for baksheesh and rogues of all kinds trying to sell you things and to guide you around the sights. Even asking the way costs you money.

Church of the Holy Sepulchre In the middle of the city is the Church of the Holy Sepulchre, supposedly built on the site of the Crucifixion by Helena, mother of the Roman emperor Constantine, to whom a cross had been revealed in a dream. The Church is a shapeless and labyrinthine conglomerate of

Roof of the Church of the Holy Sepulchre showing the chapels of the Armenians

shabby chapels belonging to a multiplicity of different Christian sects and it repelled me as a place of organised and commercially exploited superstition, full of poor old women shuffling around on their knees to kiss the greasy stones where this or that is supposed to have happened to Jesus, and polyglot parties of pilgrims conducted along dark passages by glib Arab guides shouting "mind your heads." The walls of the Church are propped up by a system of ugly steel struts erected 30 years ago by the Royal Engineers after an earthquake had brought the church close to collapse. And not all the churches in Christendom seem to be able to agree on who is to repair it.

The Dome of the Rock   While the Church of the Holy Sepulchre stands as a lament not only to the Crucifixion, but to the division of Christendom, the Dome of the Rock symbolises the glory and unity of Islam. It is built over a strange rock which is anchored at one end and slopes upwards like a cantilever; from here the Prophet is supposed to have ascended to Heaven on his favourite steed. It was built in the 7th century on a magnificent open site where King Solomon's temple stood until it was destroyed by the Romans, and it shows the great flowering of Islamic art at a time when Europe went through the Dark Ages. As at Baalbek, the grandeur and beauty of the design and the perfection of every detail delights the eye.

The Mount of Olives   We rose early and drove to the Mount of Olives, a hill some 400 ft high which overlooks the city from the north east. Here on this hill it was possible to conjure up in one's mind's eye the picture of the city 2000 years ago, and the agony of Jesus' last days. It would have taken him only half an hour to walk here from the Temple and the soldiers who came for him would not have had to look far. Below the Mount lies the Garden of Gethsemane with olive trees so old that they might have stood when Jesus went there to pray. In the garden of the Russian Orthodox Convent immediately above, the wild spring flowers delighted us again. Two Russian nuns who came to turn us out surprised us by being English and let us stay.

Bethlehem   In the afternoon we drove to Bethlehem on a new road constructed since the war, as the old one passes through Israel. The countryside is truly biblical, except that it was probably more fertile 2000 years ago. The hills are rocky and have scarce grass cover. One can see little terracing except near villages and no attempt at reforestation in contrast to Israel. Farming methods apparently have not changed since Biblical times. In the villages people mostly live in windowless mud huts. It all contrasts strangely with the American cars carrying tourists along the road.

We had been warned that Bethlehem was entirely commercialised and overrun by tourists. To our surprise we found it much more genuine than the Christian shrines in Jerusalem, with only a few tourists about. The Byzantine Church of the Nativity is simple, dignified and well preserved,

Bedouin camp between Jerusalem and the Dead Sea

and the underground manger at least must be very near to the true site of Jesus' birth. The Church and the little town around are all built in the same yellow stone characteristic of the district. It looked warm and golden in the evening sun driving back to Jerusalem.

Jericho   Having seen the excavation from Jericho [at the Archaeological Museum], we next took a taxi down to the place itself. In Jerusalem at 2600 ft above sea level the air is fresh even at midday, but as the road winds its way down to the Dead Sea, the heat gets oppressive, the green hillsides get brown and barren and make one wonder how the Bedouin tribesmen camped there in their black tents can extract a living from them. There hardly seemed food for a flock of sheep and no water was to be seen. The road goes down and down, past a notice saying "sea level" until finally the valley opens out into a wide arid desert plain.

Suddenly we entered the oasis of Jericho and the scene changed abruptly. The desert gave way to banana plantations, beautiful gardens and flowering trees. The bougainvilleas, trees as tall as a medium sized chestnut all covered in deep red flowers, delighted us especially. The town looks untidy but moderately prosperous.

Just outside the oasis, to the west of the present town, lies Tell el-Sultan where excavations have uncovered the walls, and not only of the Jericho which Joshua's trumpets blew down, but of many earlier settlements going back to about 7000 B.C., further than Troy or any other built up settlement yet found.

Refugee camp at Jericho

Arab Refugee Camp   As you walk across the Tell, a camp for refugees from Palestine housing over 100,000 people comes into view. It is built, not in the oasis, but in the desert; for several miles as far in fact as one can see, stretches a town of miserable mud huts, mostly without windows. A barbed wire fence surrounds it. Near the entrance are a few well-constructed army huts put up by the United Nations which serve as schools and workshops. Think of it. To have lived in this desert cauldron for 13 years without work or hope or a single relieving feature. The total number of refugees is about a million. I do not know how many live in camps like this one. It was the most terrible sight I have ever seen and cast a shadow on all the achievements we later saw in Israel.

Crossing from Jordan into Israel   We were terribly sorry to leave as there was so much we had not had time to see and we would have like to spend many more hours just strolling around Jerusalem and looking at all the varied types and races. However, I had told my hosts at the Weizmann Institute to meet us at 5.00 pm on 14 April and our time was up. We had been warned that the crossing from Jordan into Israel through the Mandelbaum Gate would be grim. Tanks would be guarding the gates and machine guns pointed at us from each side, while we carried our luggage across no-man's land.

   In fact nothing could have been gemütlicher [more relaxed]. A couple of policemen on the Jordanian side invited us into their hut while they filled in the forms. We saw another couple across the road playing cards. Successions of cars of United Nations personnel waiting to cross the barrier were stopped by a pair of British officials aged 4 and 5 who had taken over the job of lifting the barrier for them. Meanwhile an Arab porter carried our luggage half way through no-man's land. When he had got his baksheesh and vanished, an Israeli policeman came with a car and the Weizmann Institute's driver to pick up our luggage and take it to the Israeli police post. Here we got a very warm welcome from my old friend Gerhard Schmidt and Judy Bergman. At the police post we were treated as VIPs with a minimum of formality, and the customs examination was a great joke. When we drove away into Israel in 2 cars we found ourselves back in Europe, in a totally different world from the one we had left half an hour before.

First Sight of Israel　At 5.30 on Friday afternoon the Sabbath had begun and the City had closed down like Aberdeen on Sunday. The shops were shuttered and the streets deserted. Gerhard wondered about taking us through the orthodox quarter, but the driver thought the barriers which stop sinful drivers disturbing the peace of the Sabbath would be down.

As we left Jerusalem through ordinary looking suburbia and drove down the hill towards the coastal plain, the countryside amazed us. The same stony hills which were covered with sparse grass in Jordan had here been turned into fertile gardens. At this moment the Israelis are planting at the rate of a million trees a year. If necessary soil is carried from the plains up to the hillsides and water is pumped over great distances where necessary.

We discussed the [Adolf] Eichmann trial which our host considered a thoroughly unnecessary affair.[3] We had found it reported daily in the English-language Arab newspapers, but in Rehovoth, the *Jerusalem Post*, Israel's one and only English paper, was not on sale, and we read or heard very little more about the trial until we returned to England. Most people we talked to took the same view as Schmidt. The trial merely stirred up their old pain over the dreadful happenings.

The Weizmann Institute　The prevailing ugliness gives place to beauty immediately when one enters the campus of the Weizmann Institute through an impressive gate which bears the nickname Brandenburger Tor. The Institute started in the thirties with a chemical laboratory built by Israel Sieff, the chief of Marks & Spencer, in memory of his son. Weizmann himself actually

---

[3]Secret Mossad agents apprehended Eichmann in Argentina, who was tried and hanged in Israel for his role in the Holocaust.

worked there. It expanded later into a great "Advanced Institute of Science" employing some 250 graduates on pure research. It is built and maintained entirely from the contributions of wealthy Jews abroad, mostly British and American. Every single building is designed with taste and imagination and one or two are outstanding feats of modern architecture in a tropical setting.

The only lavish villa we saw belongs to the Chairman of the Executive Council, a Mr. Weissgal. He is a colourful figure retired from New York music hall and theatrical world where he had worked as a writer, actor and producer. He is literally a man of many parts, friend of Reinhardt and Epstein and acquainted with leading Jews throughout the world and has the sole job of collecting money for the Institute. He obviously discharges his task most effectively and is justly proud of it. At his house we met a mixed company of Zionists, but it was not clear who was being milked by whom. There was a German gentile and his family who professed to philistinism and told us that he went around lecturing to German audiences about Nazi times and the achievements of Israel. In his presence it was evidently tactless to blame the Germans for everything which led people to discourse on Austria as the cradle and hotbed of Nazism. This annoyed me as I knew how many stood aloof from Nazism there, except perhaps during the period 1938–40 when it was a national power.

Jerusalem (Israeli Side) We were driven to Jerusalem in a ramshackle old Chevrolet over terrible roads, as I had to give a talk at the Hebrew University. We found the City flag-bedecked and thronged with holiday crowds and soldiers in preparation for tomorrow's independence celebrations. There were also masses of armoured cars and tanks concentrated for the great military parade to be held despite the protests of the Jordanian Government. People from all over the country were being brought into the city by coach, and parties of schoolchildren in their Saturday best were being conducted along the streets to see the army tanks (not, as one well-meaning guide tried to tell us, on natural history excursions). She was very disappointed that we would not attend tomorrow's parade. I told her that we were pacifists, to which she replied that the army's sole task was defence. In fact the Government's attitude strikes the observer as ultra-nationalist and aggressive. They would certainly try to push Israel's frontiers back to the Jordan and the Suez Canal if they got half a chance.

The Hebrew University The original buildings of the Hebrew university are now isolated on an island of Israeli territory on the Jordanian side of

Jerusalem, and are unusable except for the library. The University we saw has been built since 1948 and again entirely from gifts provided by Jews abroad. The administrative block was built by Sherman, the owner of a football pool in S. Wales, and is outsize and absurdly lavish for a university of only 3000 students, while physics is housed in shabby single storey buildings. Most of the university buildings are beautiful pieces of modern architecture.

We were received by a Dr. Frankl, a physicist applying X-ray crystallography to solid state problems, and shown around the department. They have beautiful apparatus all built by their own workshop, which is run by an elderly German mechanic and kept as clean as an operating theatre. Research is financed by grants from the U.S. Air Force on the principle of not looking a gift horse in the mouth. The Israeli Government merely provides staff salaries.

Research problems struck me as sensibly selected within the limited means available, though nothing was exciting.

Tel Aviv and Nathania By way of a pourboire [gratuity] each Weizmann lecturer is given a tour of the country; by a generous extension of that customary act of hospitality, all five of us were included in this tour on which we were taken by Judy Bergman in a large new American car hired for the purpose.

Tel Aviv has the looks of a shabby Balkan town with occasional attractive houses. In Nathania, on the other hand, these predominate and there are some inviting-looking hotels. As it was Independence Day the entire population was out on the Esplanade or the beach. I told myself how marvellous it was to see all these people liberated from the oppression of the ghettos in eastern Europe and holding up their heads in their own country. Yet their appalling ugliness oppressed me, and I had only the one wish to get away from them, out into the hills.

Mount Carmel: Arabs in Israel We next drove up to Mt. Carmel above Haifa only just in time to see the sun drop into the Mediterranean and settled down for the night in a picturesque hotel built by a former Arab lawyer in Haifa. It is built in the style of what I guess to be an Arab country house with rooms opening out on to loggias and a drawing room full of beautiful oriental rugs. It was run by the widow of the lawyer and his handsome well-educated daughter. She told me that her father had had the strength of mind to stay behind in Israel when the Arab press and radio advised everyone to leave. He had been arrested several times by the Haganah [Jewish paramilitary organization], but was eventually left in peace and tried to develop this hotel on Mt. Carmel as a place where people from Haifa could go on hot summer nights. He died tragically as a result of a knife attack by an Arab servant who had gone insane, and now his widow and daughter find themselves isolated as Christian Arabs in a Jewish state. All their friends and relatives have fled and they could follow only by giving up all their possessions, as Israel will not allow any export of capital. The girl wants to go abroad to study political science thinking perhaps that this will teach her how to put the troubles of her people right.

Haifa, Nazareth and the Sea of Galilee   We finally emerged from the hot and noisy town into the hills of Galilee. The ground was thick with spring flowers. Soon afterwards we arrived in Nazareth which is still a wholly Arab town. The Christian churches and convents all seem to carry on as before. We found the Church of St. Joseph supposedly built on the site of Mary's and Joseph's house closed, but a French nun whom I asked for the way to another church took us into her convent and showed us some interesting underground dwellings which fitted biblical descriptions of Mary and Joseph's house, and were in any case dwellings of that period.

Night at a Model Kibbutz   We finally arrived at the Kibbutz Ayalet Hashahar, north of the Sea of Galilee where we were to spend the night in a charming guest house, built on the lines of an American motel. All the houses, furniture and fittings were done by local people in exquisite style and workmanship. The kibbutz itself was nicely laid out among attractive gardens; people lived in middle class houses with curtains, books and good furniture. However, we learnt that nevertheless it was still run on communist lines. The children slept in houses separate from their parents, and all meals were taken in a communal canteen which incidentally was an architectural masterpiece.

   We heard that this particular kibbutz was exceptionally wealthy partly because its members had helped to drain a great swamp in the Jordan valley which had been turned into a fertile farm, partly as a result of German compensation to many individuals. The Israeli economy as a whole was much helped by German reparations, and people were worried how they would manage after 1962 when the reparations are due to cease.

Upper Galilee   We first drove to a small remnant of the former swamp which is being kept as a bird sanctuary. Our boatman was a former businessman from Shanghai who had had to leave because of the Communists and had fled to Israel with his Chinese wife. He now works on a kibbutz.

Haifa and Home   We drove into Haifa where I had to give another lecture. Meanwhile the family visited the Baha'i shrine and temple and were cheered to find a sect proclaiming that all faiths were one and all peoples one.

In the afternoon we embarked on a German-built liner of the Israel Shipping Line (given to Israel as reparation) and sailed through the night to Cyprus.

Moscow Diary, August 9–17, 1961

Our Comet[4] left London at 3.30 and took us over the Hague, Amsterdam and the Zuidersee. I always enjoy flying over familiar places even if they look like coloured maps from 33,000 ft.

The International Airfield lies in the midst of a great forest with no sign of any big town around. The airport building is small by our standards, but lavishly decorated with marble, stucco and gilded chandeliers: this was my first meeting with Stalin Baroque. Formalities at the airport were disorganised but easy.

I found the Congress Bureau well organised and friendly. They had expected me and had everything ready for me, including an allowance of 6 roubles a day during my stay (£2.8.0).

My hotel is enormous. My room was small and dirty but was changed for a much nicer and cleaner one next day. Luxury suites have TV and piano and walls hung with oil paintings.

A pleasant young girl called Nina introduced herself to me and told me that she had been assigned to the British guests of the Soviet Academy.

At first people in the street seemed terribly drab to me. Especially women seemed worn out from cares and hard work and everybody shabbily dressed. However, there were no hungry children, no beggars, and in fact everybody looked well fed. Shops of all kinds are well stocked and though some goods are shoddy, especially paper, by no means all things are. Food is about the same price as here, clothes more expensive, optical instruments and cameras, gramophones and especially records much cheaper.

In the evening Boris Vainshtain, a Russian crystallographer who visited us here on two occasions, came to meet me at the hotel and took me out for

---

[4]de Haviland jet airliner.

a meal. He is a very bright, hard-working, friendly and generous man, and wants to start protein crystallography in Russia.

The University lies 10 miles from the centre of the town and is a magnificent complex of buildings dominated by a skyscraper. The lecture rooms are well lit, air-conditioned but have poor acoustics. The entire building is lavishly decorated with marble, sculptures and chandeliers. It even has decent toilets, usually a sad chapter in university buildings.

A friend told me that there was to be a press conference held by the Soviet Academy in honour of Major [Gherman] Titov, and that there would probably be an invitation for me, as a guest of the Academy. The press conference was held in the grand marble assembly hall of the university which holds over 1000 people. I was lucky to get a seat near the front. The conference was opened by the President of the Academy of Sciences, an applied mathematician who is said to have contributed to the success of the space programme. He looked intelligent, determined, tough, unyielding and humourless, and made an orthodox Communist Party speech not worth listening to, to introduce Titov. Titov himself is a fighter pilot and looks it. [He had returned from orbiting the earth, only the second person to do so, on 7 August.] A daredevil of the absolutely fearless kind, and a romantic who will climb the north face of the Eiger or perform any other great feat calling for exceptional courage, skill and endurance. He introduced his speech by saying that he had been aware during every second of his flight that the eyes of the heroic Soviet people, the glorious Communist Party and of Nikita Sergeyevich Khrushchev were turned upon him and that he must do his duty by them. This sounded like the start of another party speech, but to my relief it was followed by a spontaneous account of his great adventure. Most fascinating to me was his account of the view from his space ship. How he could see not only continents, but rivers, fields and mountains, and how he could distinguish clouds from snow-capped mountains because the former cast shadows on the ground and the latter did not. And how beautiful it was to be flying through the night side of the earth, with the brilliantly lit stars above him and to look down to see the borderline between night and day lit up in all the colours of the rainbow at the line of sunrise. He told us that he was in complete control of the space-ship, and would turn it in any orientation and determine himself the moment of descent. The condition of weightlessness made him a little giddy at first, but after a night's rest he felt this much less. Otherwise he felt no discomfort and the air in his space capsule was excellent throughout.

Titov's story was followed by a lecture by a physiologist who told us about all the observations made on Titov both during and after the flight. So far there had been no ill-effects. There was a further talk and finally answers to press correspondents' questions. Most amusing were the questions from the *Soviet Children's Newspaper:* whether he used a knife and fork to eat, whether he stayed in his space helmet or took it off and whether he slept sitting up or lying down. The answer to the last question, amid roars of laughter, was that it's all the same when you are weightless. When asked about future passengers he admitted that an excursion into space was still a tough affair and had required months of training.

We visited the palace of former Princes Lisnitzky [?], a noble family of several hundred years' standing. The palace was built by serfs in the 18th century and contained a fabulous display of wealth in regal style, with ballroom, theatre, innumerable salons, inlaid floors and painted ceilings; the style and scale was similar, perhaps to the Palais Schwarzenburg in Vienna. The last room contains some interesting statistics drawn up by the Soviets on the accumulation of wealth by the family. The number of serfs owned by them rose steadily until it reached the number of 97,000 in 1800. The domestic staff alone numbered 1000. Just to show that people can never make ends meet, however rich they are, they exhibited graphs of the family's debts which rose to several million roubles in the 19th century.

A couple of pleasant girls came to take me to the Institute of Crystallography, an old-fashioned laboratory across the river. They do excellent work on X-ray analysis and electron diffraction, but nothing very good yet in the biological field. Russian built equipment looked excellent. They are presently moving to a new institute.

We next went to a new Institute of Biophysics at the other end of the town. This was shoddily built and looked shabby, even though it was brand new. Here I had to give a lecture on methods of protein crystallography in a badly designed colloquium room with a rough wooden blackboard and a noisy lantern. The room was lit by brass chandeliers. No fluorescent lighting anywhere in the building. The audience consisted only in part of crystallographers, and I heard afterwards that my lecture, in which I had been told to concentrate of methods rather than results, was lost on the majority of those present. Vainshtain did a brilliant job of translating it sentence by sentence and was usually able to explain my slides in Russian without my having to say anything in English. The people at this Institute seemed of mediocre calibre and I doubt that they will do anything brilliant.

We next went to visit the workshop in the Institute of Crystallography which lies in an area of research institutes run by the Academy. This shop employs 200 people: about a dozen graduate engineers and a horde of highly skilled men. To my mind this number is quite out of proportion to the work done at the Institute, but even so the workshop, run regardless of expense, seemed a symbol of the importance attached to scientific research in the Soviet Union. It also showed the abundance of skilled manpower.

[Paul] Doty and I went home early [from a dinner]. He recounted how he had reproached the Praesidium of the Academy about the failure of the Nuclear Test Talks. He told them that he had persuaded the American Government to accept all the main conditions on which the Russians had insisted earlier, and expressed his great disappointment that these conciliatory proposals had met with a flat rejection. These reproaches, however, merely met with an embarrassed silence. No explanation was given. He himself believes that the Chinese must have vetoed the nuclear test agreement, but this is just a guess. (Paul Doty is a member of Kennedy's Scientific Advisory Committee.)

After an hour or more queuing at various counters I finally boarded the Russian jet which was to fly us home. The exterior design is marvellous and its two jet engines must have a bigger thrust than their Western counterparts. The interior, however, is fitted out with brass railed luggage nets and gilded table lamps like one of those antiquated dining cars of the Companie Int. des Wagons Lits on the Continent of Europe.

Summing Up   All my generalisations faded away as the days in Moscow passed. Life there is not as hellish as I thought at first when I saw the dreary barrack-like blocks of apartments lining the streets of Moscow's suburbs, or the drab crowd of people in the streets.

There is much to enjoy life with: woods, swimming, sports of all kinds, books, records, the arts. Material progress is terrific and every man and woman is made to be extremely proud of it.

People are not really conscious of the lack of correct news about the outside world. No foreign, non-Communist paper is obtainable anywhere in Moscow. It is clear that everybody feels himself watched and is guarded in his conversation, but they take this as part of the nature of life.

They are all convinced of the iniquity of the Capitalist system and of the superiority of theirs. They all fervently hope that there will be no war.

Foreigners who had known Russia in the thirties told me that material progress and progress in personal freedom were tremendous, and this is clearly what keeps people's enthusiasm going.

It would take a much longer stay to discover what an individual's life is really like.

For me the trip has been a great adventure, and I am very pleased to have come.

Perhaps I should still add that the Congress itself was extremely well organised in every way. This was quite a feat as it had 6000 members. My only criticism concerned a tendency to leave things to the last minute.

To Dr. G.R. Pomerat of the Rockefeller Foundation, July 21, 1961

I note that the Foundation wishes to cut down their commitments in Europe, but I am glad if you think that they might nevertheless continue their association with us.

Sir Harold Himsworth is against our applying for grants from the National Science Foundation or the U.S. Public Health Service, because he believes that the British, rather than the American tax payer, should support our work. Indeed the Medical Research Council are providing us with all the staff and equipment needed for our work, so that we do not require massive support from outside.

We should like to ask the Foundation for support on a modest scale, just to do some things for which the MRC cannot pay. This is mainly payment of travelling expenses and lecturing fees to visitors from abroad, and payment of travel expenses to young research workers from our own laboratory to attend scientific congresses abroad. Sometimes we also need money to support a promising young man or girl who failed to secure a scholarship.[5]

To Nelly Peiser, April 26, 1962[6]

Many thanks for all your touching presents and your offer in addition to give me a moving-in present for the lab. Your idea of pictures of those on whose shoulders I stand, pleases me greatly. I would love to hang pictures of [Lawrence] Bragg, [Desmond] Bernal, [David] Keilin and Dorothy [Hodgkin] in my office. It is these 4, who from the first recognised the significance of my work and supported me in the period when it looked hope-

---

[5]Max cites two research students who won scholarships after doing excellent work in their first year.

[6]Translated from the German.

less. Keilin's name is possibly unfamiliar to you. He is now the retired professor of Biology here in Cambridge, in whose lab for many years I did the biochemical part of my work.

I only knew [Max] Von Laue fleetingly and in my active years as a scientist he was occupied with a very different branch of physics. On the other hand I would love to procure a picture of his Ph.D. student and my old friend P.P. Ewald. In fact it was Ewald's thesis that in 1912 gave Von Laue the idea that crystals could bend X-rays.

To Gisela, Vivien and Robin. Harwich July 23, 1962

As I am now v. famous I have asked Anthony Scooper, special correspondent of the *Daily Tripe*, who follows my every step, to report to you on my movements so far.

"Dressed in dapper grey suit (not new) MFP arrived at Cambridge Station with bulky, but unassuming, luggage. Prolonged search produced a long-haired young man who introduced himself as a porter (ex Eton and Trinity perhaps) and volunteered to take his luggage. Pleased by generous tip, perhaps not Eton after all.

"MFP settled in empty carriage immediately, unpacked various coloured files and proceeded to work on manuscript of world shaking discovery relating to *Secret of Life*. Looked over his shoulder to obtain news for my readers; read Hashimoto, M. See Motohashi, H. and Hashimoto, M. 1960. Cannot understand it. Must spin it out for benefit of my readers.

"On arrival at Bury St. Edmunds MFP settled on luggage trolley, still working on *Secret of Life*. Ventured a few words by offering to help with his luggage. Declined charmingly. Delightful personality.

"MFP entered boat train, baby in first compartment had one look at him and screamed. Personality must strike people in different ways. After finishing *Secret of Life* MS, MFP proceeded to dining car and ordered mixed grill with colourless liquid. Left 14 peas, explained they tasted like last year's crop. Sipped colourless, clear liquid. Explained it was neat Vodka, habit he had acquired in Moscow.[7]

"On arrival at Harwich MFP had correct passport and tickets actually ready, not absent-minded professor after all.

"Disappeared into pleasant single cabin. Offered to share same with

---

[7]Max's allergies meant that he had become teetotal as of course we knew.

Max with the Queen at the opening of the laboratory (© The Times)

charming Scandinavian lady who arrived at boat without reservation, but surprisingly lady declined. Shock for professor.

"Ascended on deck where he was immediately joined by three cronies from Manchester specialising in crystal gazing and bound for same destination.

"Now have to dive for bar before it closes. Look for report 'On the Spot with MFP' or 'The Secret of Life' in tomorrow's column by Anthony Scooper."

After this fascinating account which I trust you will enjoy I send you lots of love and kisses.

To Lawrence Bragg, November 3, 1962

As I said to Lady Bragg the other day, we owe it all to you! I never believed we would get the great Prize as quickly, and have no doubt that your enthusiasm and authority, vouching for the correctness of our results, turned the scales. As you can imagine, we are all overjoyed. I had hardly dared to hope that my long odyssey would come to such a happy ending. Many many thanks for all you have done for us!

I am very excited by the 3D Fourier of reduced human haemoglobin which Miss [Hilary] Muirhead and I have obtained. It shows that the black chains move relative to each other by 7 Å in the reaction with oxygen, while the movement of the white chains is less than 3 Å. There is also suggestive, but still shaky evidence, that the helical segment which is linked to the haem group changes its angle of inclination, and that the dyad symmetry of the molecule is lost in the reduced form. I wish that I would not have to leave for America just now, but could continue working on these fascinating results, which show that the molecule changes its shape as it breathes.

Lady Bragg tells me that you are really getting better now. I hope that your rate of recovery from now on will be exponential and that you will soon be restored to your old health and vigour.[8]

To Gisela, Vivien and Robin Perutz. Mid Atlantic, November 4, 1962

I was lucky again. Owing to adverse winds we had to refuel near Reykjavik in Iceland.

Next, we flew over Greenland, my dream for many years, and had a superb view of its spectacular mountains flanking the great icecap and of the gigantic glaciers flowing out from it, all bathed in soft sunshine with long silvery shadows cast over the ice by the craggy peaks. It was wonderful.

I noticed the picture of F, J and me[9] in *The Sunday Time*s as a woman next to me was reading it. I asked her for the paper and she gave me permission to cut the picture out; I am glad to say she never noticed it was me on the picture. In fact no one on the aircraft spotted it. No Sherlock Holmes aboard. I am glad, as I like my anonymity.

Telegram to Gisela Perutz from Washington, November 9, 1962

Loving greetings from united family. Lunching with ambassador. Your haircut vindicated. Your swollen headed Max.

To Steffen Peiser, November 16, 1962

I visited the Rockefeller Foundation on Monday, and they let it transpire that they too had proposed John and me for The Prize.

---

[8]In an interview in 2001, with tears in his eyes, my father told of visiting Sir Lawrence in hospital and being told by a nurse that it had been touch and go; the announcement of the Prize, she said, had been the turning point in his mentor's recovery.

[9]Francis Crick and John Kendrew; Francis Crick, Jim Watson and Maurice Wilkins won the prize in Physiology or Medicine in the same year.

At the Brooklyn Poly[technic] later that afternoon I had an uproarious welcome from Mark, Fankuchen and others, with party, press conference and a lecture on how to win the Nobel Prize.

What follows is the diary my father wrote for the relatives who did not accompany us to the Nobel prize-giving.

Stockholm, December 1962

The Journey, December 7th I felt gay and happy as we started off from Cambridge on 7 December—Gisela, Granny, Vivien, Robin and I + 15 pieces of luggage. Gisela had helped me the previous night to pack my starched shirts, dress suit, dinner jacket (the same that my father bought me before I left Austria in 1936), dark suit, white ties, black ties, studs and the rest, and I had gone to sleep while she packed hers and Vivien's finery for all the parties at Stockholm. Before I had left the laboratory a French television team, 10 strong, had appeared straight from Paris, tired and delayed by the fog, to record an interview with a colleague and me about "life." So I still cycled to the laboratory early on the 7th to speak about living molécules in my best French, having practised by reading *Bonjour Tristesse* to Gisela for two evenings.

The interview went quite well and earned me the compliment that I had been much clearer than all the French savants they had interviewed for the same science programme before. These had used many long and complicated words to explain matters which I, in ignorance of more sophisticated terms, had to express in words of one syllable.

In London the fog of the last few days had just cleared, but the chaos caused by it had not. At the station no porters were to be seen and the trolleys were all laden with accumulated mail. At West London Air terminal the counters were beleaguered by people whose reservations had to be changed, and so it went on. When we at last boarded the Scandanavian Air Lines Caravalle, it was 5.5 hours after our arrival in London. However, Mother had stood up (literally) to it all.

The Arrival The plane was smooth and luxurious. It gave Gisela and me the first chance we had had for some weeks for a quiet talk and, as we were soon to discover, also the last of this trip. By the time we arrived in Stockholm all my cheerfulness of the morning had returned. We were, as always, the last to leave the plane. As I stepped, unsuspecting, out of the door, I found myself blinded by a host of floodlights and heard camera shutters clicking all around. When I arrived at the bottom of the steps I was overwhelmed and deeply moved by friendly faces giving me a tremendous welcome, as though I were a traveller returned from space, or the saviour of their country come back from a victorious campaign. I soon realised that here in Sweden my friends and I would be national heroes.

But this was not all. Our own glory was reflected on our families who were accorded as much honour as ourselves, and our children were spoilt and admired like fairy princes.

After the Cricks, Wilkins and Perutzes had told the Swedish Press all about themselves and their great work in the VIP lounge of the airport, they were whisked into luxurious limousines and driven to the Grand Hotel, I in the company of two distinguished-looking gentlemen. The older one of them was Rudberg, the Secretary of the Swedish Academy of Sciences, and the younger was Wahlquist, First Secretary at the Swedish Foreign Office; Wahlquist was to be my Personal Attaché throughout my stay, while his beautiful and charming wife looked after my family, especially the two grandmothers. Both men had manners to make any old Theresianisten [alumnus of Max's school in Vienna] feel like a country bumpkin, combined with warmth, charm and a keen sense of humour. I could not have been luckier in my companions.

When we arrived at the Grand Hotel we found Gisela's mother with more Swedish colleagues to welcome us and another bunch of pressmen eager for a conference. It was midnight before we found a meal in a crowded and noisy dance hall.

Preliminary Parties   During the succeeding two days we were invited to a series of parties and receptions which introduced us to Swedish Scientific Society and those associated with the Nobel Foundation. First came a luncheon at the British Embassy. It was characteristic of the thoughtful arrangements that both grandmothers were included in this invitation, and that a simultaneous party was given by one of the Councillors for the children. Vivien was in some doubt as to which party she should attend, but on learning that the Councillor had a 16 year old son, decided in favour of the children. (British Ambassador: Sir John Coulson).

The first evening Gisela and I, and John Kendrew, were asked to a dinner at the Rudbergs, given at the Secretary's official residence in the Science Academy's grounds. About 30 people sat at a long table in a room lit only by candles. It seems that in Sweden crystal chandeliers were never converted to vulgar electricity but left with the candles for which they were originally intended. The effect is charming.

The dinner, like most of the meals that were to follow, was opened by a solemn speech on the part of the host, in praise of John and me. I always tried to relieve the embarrassment which these speeches caused me by telling funny stories in reply. The meals themselves were good and comparatively simple, consisting of no more than 3 courses; even at the Royal Palace there were only 4. It pleased me to find that these very cultured people considered sumptuous meals, which I hate, vulgar. The company was mostly older than ourselves; people were remarkably good-looking, extremely well bred and spoke immaculate English. They were a little formal, perhaps, but full of a genuine warmth and friendliness which made us feel welcome and happy.

On Sunday all the Prize Winners and their families were taken on a conducted tour of a beautiful exhibition of Venetian art arranged in celebration of the King's 60th birthday. Afterwards we were shown the Wasa, a Swedish battleship which sank in Stockholm harbour on her maiden voyage in 1628, and has recently been dug out of the mud and raised. This was the most interesting thing we saw on our trip. It is a ship of nearly *1500 tons' displacement*, carrying 48 guns under elaborately carved gunwales. The bows and stern were decorated by magnificent wood carvings, and the hull was constructed of oak beams more massive than any I have seen. I had no idea that ships of such size existed at that period. It gave me quite a new conception of the naval battles that must have been fought, say in Queen Elizabeth's reign, and of the engineering skill that must have been available at the time of the Renaissance.

I saw little of Stockholm this time, except for what I could observe from the window of the car driving us from one engagement to the next, but what I did see refreshed the impression gained on previous visits. Many graceful buildings of all periods and far fewer ugly ones than in any other modern city I know. Spacious vistas across the water showing parks, palaces and attractive houses. A soft winter light casting a romantic halo over the town.

The day ended with another dinner, given by one of our Swedish colleagues in the Naval Officers' Mess, a simple and attractive 17th century building first intended as a soldiers' barracks. The party included the Scientific and Medical Prizewinners, the British and American Ambassadors, Swedish Service chiefs and scientists and wives. A most unlikely mixture at any English party. I found myself opposite the Chief of the Swedish Defence Staff and the beautiful wife of the American Ambassador, Mrs. Parsons.

The same evening the grandmothers and Liesel Frank [Max's cousin] (who came from Paris by kind invitation of the Swedish Technical Academy for whom she had done some service) took the children to the ballet. On arrival there Robin noted the absence of press reporters and remarked sadly "Without Daddy we are just nobody!" In fact the children had their fair share of publicity, pictures of their doings, and interviews with them, appearing in the papers every day.

The Prize Giving   Monday December 10th was the day of the Prizegiving at the big Concert Hall, followed by the State Banquet in the Town Hall. All the prizewinners were taken to rehearse the ceremony in the morning. It was there that I made my first acquaintance with [John] Steinbeck,[10] a great burly man with a chest like a sailor and a deep husky voice. We found him the opposite of a man of the world, and rather nervous of the part he had to play that day.

Shortly before 4:00 pm the Prizewinners and certain Swedish Academicians who had acted as referees to the Nobel Committee assembled backstage, and listened while the National Anthem was being played. Then, preceded by 2 students carrying decorations, we marched on to the stage in procession. I felt gay and happy as a lark and was surprised to find Gisela in the front row of the stalls with tears streaming down her face as though she were attending my funeral. Robin luckily was unaffected by all this solemnity and exchanged some cheerful winks with me.

The Perutzes and Cricks combined were so numerous that they occupied all the right-hand side of the front row; the King and his family were in the middle, while the Wilkins, Watsons, Steinbecks and the Soviet Ambassador (recognisable by a simple peasant woman who was quite obviously his wife) were on the left. The Prize Winners and all Academicians sat on the stage. The Concert Hall was crowded to the last seat, everybody who is anybody in Sweden being present. This surprised me because the ceremony must have been deadly dull to anyone not directly involved.

Each Prizewinner was introduced by a 10 or 15 minute speech in Swedish, which explained the reason for the award. These speeches were read and judging by the English translations and the faces of the audience were unrelieved by humour. The first speech referred to [Lev] Landau, who was being presented with the Prize at that moment by the Swedish Ambassador in a Moscow Hospital. Next came the speech for me, delivered by a crystallographer, Gunnar Hägg, whom I have known for many years. When it ended I had to walk down from the stage to the stalls

---

[10]Winner of the Nobel Prize in Literature that year.

Max with Ivar Waller
(© Scanpix/Sipa Press)

Gisela on the arm of the King of Sweden at the Nobel ceremony (© Scanpix/Sipa Press)

where the King presented me with a diploma, a gold medal and an assignment for the Prize Money. He did it in a charming, informal and fatherly manner, talking not to the public, but only to me; he congratulated me, told me how pleased he was to be able to give me the Prize and wished me every success for my future work. Then I had to return to the stage, bow to the King and sit down.

Kendrew, Crick, Watson, Wilkins and Steinbeck came next, in that order. I forgot to mention that after each Prize a piece of music was played, or sung, in honour of the winner. I had hoped that they would play a nice piece of Haydn, Mozart or Schubert for me, but the music was all dreary stuff by Scandinavian composers.

From this account you might think that, as far as I was concerned, the great ceremony was an anticlimax. Not at all; I felt cheerful and extremely happy throughout, but never solemn, because ceremonies never affect me that way. What made me happy was the warmth and friendliness of all around me, the happiness of all my family, the reflection that Hägg and many other Swedes had been just as nice to me on my first visit in 1951 when nobody could have foreseen that I would win the Nobel Prize. And finally the thought that the Prize was only the final expression of the great enthusiasm aroused all over the world by John's and my research and that judging by reports that had reached me, the scientific community at large considered the Prize justified.

After the ceremony I asked my colleagues to sign letters to Landau, telling him how sorry we were that he could not be with us, and to Bragg and Himsworth, thanking them for their long-continued support.

The Stockholm Town Hall might be described as the first modern building in Europe. It was designed before the first world war and completed in the early twenties. It has an originality, grace and beauty which delight me every time I see it.

All the Prizewinners and their families assembled in an anteroom, to be presented to the King and his Court; from there we were to walk in procession into the Great Golden Hall where dinner was laid for 830 people.

The precedence of the Prizewinners is arranged in the order in which the subjects are mentioned in Alfred Nobel's will: Physics, Chemistry, Medicine, Literature and Peace. Since Landau was absent, chemistry had first rank, and I had the great pleasure of seeing Gisela, looking beautiful and regal in a magnificent black velvet gown, walking into the Banqueting Hall on the arm of the King.

I took Odile Crick who sat on the King's left, and on my left sat Princess Christina, a girl of Vivien's age, with much the same interests and little more sophistication. I was pleased to learn from her that she went to school like other girls and that she was determined to attend university afterwards.

Opposite us sat John between the Queen and the lovely Princess Margareta. During the dinner Odile Crick remarked to me, with a glance at the Queen: "I had always thought that diamonds were overrated. Now I see how they sparkle when they are really big!" Which gave me a clue as to what Crick's Prize money will be spent on.

At the end of the dinner Steinbeck had to make a 15 minute speech, and Watson, Kendrew and I each a 2 minute one. Steinbeck and Watson said some nice things, but neither spoke into the microphone so that only the people nearest them could hear. John spoke very well and charmingly, and so that everyone could hear him. My own speech was also audible; its text is attached to these notes. Many people seemed to like it. The King was impressed by the fact that John and I were able to speak fluently without notes, a trick which I should have thought monarchs and politicians ought to be able to learn too. It is so easy to memorize a short speech.

The banquet was followed by a ball in a hall resembling the court of a medieval castle. The ball was opened by students of both sexes swinging colourful flags and singing. Then John had to make a short speech on behalf of the Prize Winners thanking the students for their reception, which he did humorously and charmingly. After that the dancing started with a Vienna waltz and I took Gisela off into a happy spin.

We got back late, tired, but very happy.

The Nobel Lectures On Tuesday morning I had to visit the Nobel Foundation to be given my Prize for the second time, and to hand over the manuscripts of my lecture, biography, dinner speech, list of publications and a photograph of myself. All this was done in a leisurely manner with a great deal of chat. Next Wahlquist took me to the Scandinavian Bank to arrange the transfer of the money to Cambridge, not with the clerk at the counter, of course, but with the Managing Director. In the afternoon John and I had to deliver our Nobel lectures to a scientific audience at the Technical High School. Mine went well for the first half, but I had put so much drive and enthusiasm into it that I flagged in the second half.

Dinner at the Palace This evening all the winners with their wives were invited to dine at the Royal Palace. We were told that this would be an intimate affair involving no more than 20 guests, but it turned out to be 120. The Palace is a graceful and simple Baroque building, but sumptuously decorated inside. We assembled in a huge drawing room, and this time it was for me to lead the Queen to dinner.

She is an Englishwoman in her seventies, a sister of [Louis] Mountbatten under whom I worked during the war. I had been told by the British Ambassador that conversation with her would present no difficulties. She is intelligent and forthright, and my brief acquaintance with her brother, with the English Queen and with Prince Philip [her nephew] provided plenty of topics for talk. On my other side sat Princess Margareta, a very tall and lovely girl in her twenties, with whom I talked mainly about skiing.

There were no speeches this time, and dinner was followed by an informal party. Great care was taken by the King to talk at length to all the Prizewinners. He is an active archaeologist and a highly educated man; I found him simple and straightforward without the slightest show of pomp, making one forget that one is talking to a King. Gisela was taken to talk to the Queen and the various princesses, while I chatted to various members of the Cabinet and Ambassadors, without being put in my place, as often happens in not so exalted society nearer home.

The rooms were nicely decorated with flowers, and the tables with very precious silver, but the gallery where we dined was too sumptuously baroque for my taste, and the rooms in the Palace not as tastefully furnished as some Swedish homes we saw.

All the same, Gisela and I felt a little sad as we left the Palace because that was the last of the celebrations and from now on we would be ordinary people again.

Uppsala Next morning Gisela, John, the children and I were driven to Uppsala, some 50 miles away, for more meals, receptions and lectures. However, it was different from the Stockholm festivities because we found ourselves back in a research atmosphere. We spent the morning discussing protein crystallography with old friends and some colleagues new to the field. We had lunch at one of the Students' Houses, a luxurious club house donated by one of Uppsala's wealthy alumni, where we were entertained by the Rector's wife and the Pro-rector with more speeches. Then John and I lectured in the Chemical Laboratory to a small and bright audience of staff and research students. This was followed by tea with all the people who were at the lecture, and immediately afterwards by dinner at the house of our old friends who had invited us in 1951. Again the people were cultured, well-mannered and terribly nice to us all. It was touching to notice on all these occasions the immense pleasure the Swedes take in bestowing their supreme recognition, and the warmth and friendship they feel towards the recipients of the Prizes. This really was the most wonderful thing of our stay.

The children were excited and talked all the way from Uppsala back to Stockholm. At the hotel both mothers and Liesel were waiting for us eager to hear all about our outing. It took us a long time to put them all to bed, and Gisela and I were dropping with tiredness when we were allowed to retire.

Santa Lucia's Day We were not as thrilled as we ought to have been, therefore, when were woken up at the crack of dawn by a tall and beautiful girl in white, wearing a crown of lighted candles and followed by her smaller satellites, who walked into our room singing a refined Swedish version of the Italian organ grinder's "Santa Lucia." They sang very nicely and gave us coffee and cakes, rather than hot grog as custom would have required, but we were too sleepy to appreciate their beauty or their offerings!

After another nap it was time for me to start on a visit of laboratories where I saw some interesting biochemical work. I joined the staff of the Biophysics Laboratory for their Santa Lucia lunch at a restaurant in the old town, and managed to reach the hotel just in time to set out for the studio of the Swedish Radio, where Crick, Watson, John and I were to take part in an informal discussion. (Wilkins failed to appear, and had been so nervous throughout his stay that he never spoke in public at all, except for the obligatory Nobel lecture which he read from a prepared manuscript.)

The Radio Discussion was great fun, as we held contrary views on a variety of subjects related to science. At the end I told the anecdote of a distinguished lady visitor to whom Himsworth had tried to explain our models. When at last he imagined that he noticed a spark of comprehension, she said delightedly: "How fascinating, I never realized we had all these little coloured balls inside us." Kendrew and Crick looked horror-struck, because they thought that this had been said by the Queen (our Queen). However, I was able to reassure them that it had only been her lady-in-waiting.

That night all 3 generations of us were invited to the Santa Lucia Ball by the Stockholm Students' Union. It started with an endless dinner during which I was wedged between two dull Professors' wives with little knowledge of English. Then followed the apparition of another Santa Lucia and later a host of student songs. Then came a charming ceremony at which John and I were knighted with the Order of the Humping and Ever-smiling Frog. This was done by an immensely tall man, masked like a member of the Ku Klux Klan, who later turned out to be an old glaciologist acquaintance of mine. We had to kneel down and to the accompaniment of some Abrakadabras, had a lead frog on a green ribbon hung round our necks.

Next came a play, written and produced by a girl student, which I enjoyed even though I could not understand it. After eleven the actual ball began; Vivien had a number of partners whom she enjoyed, and one very nice girl student danced with Robin.

I tried to dance with some nice-looking students rather than my neighbours at the table. Among the many people I chatted with was one man who had handed the Prizes to the King for the past 40 years: he told me how the late King, when he was very old, had once by mistake conferred the Nobel Prize on him instead of the proper candidate.

We got home ever later and more tired than on the previous night, but had to pack my things as I had to fly to Denmark next morning.

To Harold Himsworth. Stockholm, December 12, 1962, from Max, John Kendrew, Francis Crick, and Jim Watson

It is wonderful to get this supreme recognition but we all remember that you supported us even though there was nothing to show you.

To Steffen Peiser, January 20, 1963

I founded the Molecular Biology Skating Club last Monday and took my laboratory skating most afternoons. Result: 2 broken arms! I shall get into trouble with the MRC if their staff gets incapacitated through my passion for winter sports.

To Robin Perutz. In flight, April 4, 1963

When one's son goes abroad for the first time one should give him some fatherly advice.[11] Famous men have always done this. There are Lord Chesterfield's letters to his son which you will no doubt have to do in English one day. So why should there not be Lord Haemoglobin's letters to his son, to be preserved for a grateful posterity. But more about this later.

Now the important thing is always to check if you have got all the luggage before you leave the house. I didn't and Mummy's got left behind, and if you had been with us and I had given you this advice it would never have happened.

The other things to mind on the journey are all written up anyway, such as: "Ne pas se pencher en dehors"; "Ne pas tirer. . .," "Ne pas cracher dans le wagon." So I need not bother about them.

Now I come to the things you must do and avoid when you get there. I know that you are there already, but good advice is never too late.

Always change your socks dear when you come home with wet feet and never go out without an umbrella when it is raining and never wear the same shirt (or socks) for more than a week and remember to wash in your bath.

When you decide to ask Dominique's hand in marriage don't go to her and say "Will you marry me?" It is not done like that in France. No. You must wait until Sunday morning after church. Even if the idea occurs to you on Monday you have to wait for another 6 days, keeping a poker face and not telling anyone of your intentions.

Then on Sunday morning you put on your best suit, don kid gloves, put a white carnation in your button hole and buy a bunch of roses (I have forgotten what colour). After church, then, you ask to be received by Mme. M in her drawing room. On entering you bow and say: "Madame, permettez moi, etc." I have forgotten what the rest is in French but any phrase book will tell you.

---

[11]Robin was staying with a French family on an exchange visit.

When Madame has agreed she will call Dominique and tell her of your proposal. Dominique thereupon will faint (s'évanouir in French) but don't worry this is the custom. You have to offer smelling salts—I have forgotten to tell you that you must buy them beforehand. They are cheaper if you just ask for ammonium chloride.

Now I come to the final piece of advice, to preserve this letter. Don't use it to wrap your cake in or stuff it into your shoes when you travel home, but put it among your most precious possessions, whatever these are.

And now in earnest I am sure that everybody will like you if you are just your usual cheerful self, but none more than your loving Daddy.

To Gisela Perutz and Family. Cambridge, Mass., May 11, 1963

What's all this? What are you proud of now? Have I been made Lord Haemoglobin of Reichenau at last or have I merely been made an Honorary M.A. of the University of Cork? Has the French Academy given me the Prix Goncourt for my book [*Proteins and Nucleic Acids*] or have I merely been made a Corresponding Member of the Portuguese Academy of Sciences?

Why do you send me telegrams putting me into such a state of mental anguish? Governor [Nelson] Rockefeller got his divorce for that, mental anguish I mean, inflicted by his first wife (though this was probably for not wanting him to marry the second).

So what do I do now? Flourish Mother's telegram in front of my friends here saying "You can also be proud of me, but I can't tell you why until next week?" Or do I keep it under my pillow or hat or whatever it is and say to myself at the Dunham Dinner tonight if only these people knew that I have been made whatever it is they would be proud of having me as their guest.

As it turned out I am supposed to wear "Black Tie" at this dinner which they luckily had forgotten to write to me. At first I was going to wear my dark suit, but now having been made into something that you are all proud of I thought I'd better go out and hire what they call a Tuxedo here, made of a horribly shiny cloth with purple lining and a cummerbund or Bauchbinde [a belly sash] for which I have the wrong figure and then do not have a suitably dignified Bauch to stuff underneath it—I expect a theatrical shop would have been the place for that—so I finally persuaded them to let me have a waistcoat instead which they said was midnight blue but by lamplight nobody will notice that it is not black.

So now I better settle down and prepare my speech, though I feel handicapped by having become a mystified and suspended Daddy.

To the Family. Cambridge, Mass., May 12, 1963

Your letter with the CBE[12] has just arrived. As you say, nothing to get either worried or jubilant about.

To Gisela Perutz. Cambridge, Mass., May 14, 1963

My first lecture yesterday afternoon was a great success. 700 people turned up! When I showed what they call here a "3D Spectacular" making the myoglobin model come out in space on a 9' screen the audience burst into applause. It really looked marvellous, as though you actually had a 7' high model in the room.[13]

I think Realist Inc., the firm who makes it, can look forward to a great sale of their projectors.

To Robin Perutz. Dana-Palmer House, Cambridge, Mass., May 17, 1963

I asked you when your exam will start because I still wanted to tell you not to worry about it unduly. Luckily it no longer matters to us financially whether you get a scholarship or not.

Success in examinations is often a matter of being slick, and neither you nor I possesses that quality. However, there is much to be gained by being well organised and prepared for any kind of trap.

But whatever happens, don't let anybody tell you that because I have won the Nobel Prize, it is your duty to win a scholarship. Nobody expects it of you, and I shall love you just as much whether you succeed or fail.

---

[12]Commander of the Order of the British Empire.

[13]I cannot resist quoting from an e-mail to Richard Henderson from Tom Steitz on the occasion of my father's death: "Probably the moment that no one who was in that room will ever forget came when Max showed us the first stereo slide that any of us had ever seen. . . . We had all been given stereo glasses and watched with great anticipation as the two stereo images were being adjusted and the picture of the skeletal model of myoglobin jumped into three dimensions for everyone in the room at the same time. . . There in front of us was the modest sized Max Perutz who appeared to be standing under an enormous myoglobin molecule, two or three times the size of Max, that had popped out from the screen. We were all entranced as Max, with his pointer stick uplifted described the intricacies of a protein structure that none of us had ever seen before; and Max was just as excited as we were." (Cited from Finch J. 2008. *A Nobel Fellow on Every Floor: A History of the Medical Research Council Laboratory of Molecular Biology.* Icon Books for the MRC-LMB, Cambridge, p. 332.)

To Gisela Perutz. Cambridge, Mass., May 19, 1963

I always spent the entire day of the lectures preparing them, so that I spent only Tuesday and Thursday visiting colleagues, but I shall be doing this all next week. However, you are told many things no matter whether you want to hear them or not. Many people here are obtrusive and thick-skinned to a degree and "Herr Doktor ich hab ein Resultat, das wird Sie interessieren" [Professor, I've got a result that will interest you] is a common opening gambit. People will stop you in the lift or when you are just about to lecture to harangue you with a long tale without so much as asking whether you want to hear it. They also provide you with other interesting material. For instance, over lunch in the Medical School, on hearing of my disability, a colleague presented a fascinating account of the appearance of the intestine in the post-mortem of a man who had died of coeliac disease!

Holding 700–800 people for an hour with a closely argued lecture is a terrific effort for me; luckily, perhaps, people don't notice this and think I can just go on listening and talking to them afterwards as though I had been sipping tea in a café for an hour. I was so annoyed to be taken off to a dinner party immediately afterwards. The dinners and parties were well-meant, but often turned into ordeals for me, because I wanted nothing so much after the effort of my lectures as being left in peace. Also most of the houses were pretentious and the women artificial. Unlike in Sweden, most of the people left me cold. I enjoy being with my friends, The [John] Edsalls, [Vernon] Ingrams, [Paul] Dotys, Jim [Watson], [Bill] Lipscomb, but most of the others können mir gestohlen werden [can get lost as far as I'm concerned].

To Linus Pauling, July 15, 1963

We try to decorate our new laboratory with portraits of scientists who have made fundamental contributions to molecular biology and wondered if we could have a picture of yourself to be hung up near a model of the α-helix.

To Lawrence Bragg, December 20, 1963

I should like to let you know that we have now cleared up the remaining doubts about the structural change accompanying the reaction of haemoglobin with oxygen. I am enormously thrilled that this doubt has been cleared up. I hope that the rearrangement of the four subunits in haemoglobin will lead us eventually to an interpretation of its physiological properties in structural terms. It looks as though the idea that such rearrangements can occur will have wide implications in enzymology.

To John T. Edsall at Harvard, January 15, 1964

I was afraid that all the interesting things John [Kendrew] and I showed you might whet your appetite for that review in *Advances* [*in Protein Chemistry*]; we should have kept them under cover.

John and I discussed your letter, but feel reluctant to pledge ourselves to any definite date. Even if John's myoglobin refinement can be completed

John Edsall

this year, he has an immense task in front of him in getting the work published as a paper or series of papers. I have a steep uphill job in getting high resolution data for haemoglobin. The experience of the last two years has taught me that it is vain to hope that my collaborators will get these data out unless I help them actively most of the time.

My main purpose now is to discover the structural basis for the physiological properties of haemoglobin. This problem is so important that all other activities ought to come second.

You will be pleased to hear that I managed to find the positions of the mercury atoms in reduced horse haemoglobin just before Christmas. The distance between two pairs of mercury atoms attached to one molecule is 37.5 Å, in agreement with human reduced haemoglobin and different from that in horse oxy-haemoglobin, which is 30 Å. This is strong evidence indicating that the structure of horse and human reduced haemoglobins are alike and that the difference between horse oxy- and human reduced which Hilary Muirhead and I discovered last year is truly due to the oxygenation.

To Vivien Perutz, April 19, 1964

My first week at the laboratory was difficult. A tremendous pile of paperwork awaited me, then a day was wasted with. . . . And a third with action over EMBO [European Molecular Biology Organisation] at Mill Hill. This was to initiate some collaboration between EMBO and a Foundation with somewhat similar aims started by Princess Lilliane, wife of the ex-King of the Belgians (father of the present one). In this connection I am supposed to fly to Brussels today fortnight to have lunch with her and certain Belgian ministers, but have little "envie" [inclination] to do so. It will be inconclusive chat I fear, and I will feel ill at ease.

I have been elected a member of another academy, a German one, called the Leopoldina. Matters are complicated because the real Academy is in East Berlin and has been Sovietised. The Leopoldina is supposedly neutral and embraces scientists of both Germanies. Anyway, it is nice of them to think of me, and who would have thought 20 years ago that I would receive honours from that quarter one day!

See as much of Italy as you can with your friends and forget all about schoolm'ams, Newnham, Classics, The Future but NOT of course about your dearest Papa who sends you much love.

To Vivien Perutz. Domaine d'Argenteuil, May 4, 1964

I was wrong not to want to come here. It was quite an experience, beginning with my staying the night at the Medawars (Head of the Nat. Inst. For Med. Research). They acted on me like champagne, like the characters in those plays who converse with unnaturally quick repartee, quite the liveliest and brightest family I have met. When I wondered after 11 if any of them would still go for a walk on Hampstead Heath with me they all came!

On arrival at Brussels Medawar and I were met by a green Jaguar which drove us at 90 mph to the Château, a lovely fake Empire mansion built by an American businessman in the twenties, situated in a beech forest a few miles south of Brussels. The Princess is about my age, well preserved and very chic. She has a Ph.D. in Psychology and Philosophy from *Vienna* and speaks excellent Viennese as well as English. She went to school in England. The King went to Eton. She is lively and charming, but with all that she is no Queen. Her bearing, her occasional tactlessness, all her being is that of a society woman rather than a Queen. The ex-King is a great sportsman, but a bit of a sad figure, being no king now and lacking his wife's intellectual powers. He goes on expeditions, plays golf, climbs rocks and is very good at playing host to all the intellectuals his wife invites.

Our meeting was a much greater success than I thought it would be, mainly thanks to the Princess having persuaded the Prime Minister to pay

UNESCO some money which can serve to start off our new-born Molecular Biology Organisation.[14]

Apart from Medawar, the outstanding man of the meeting was a Russian. So quite unlike the popular image of "the Russian" was he that I find him hard to describe. A gentle scholar sincerely devoted to science, at the same time a skilful diplomat with a quick wit. When asked what he and the King were doing after dinner, bent over a map of the Soviet Union, his prompt reply was "plotting the restoration of the monarchy in Russia"! His name is Kovda and he is the director of Natural Sciences at UNESCO. I hope to see more of him.

Of course all the trimmings were superb. The furniture, the views, the food, including that specially prepared for me, my suite of rooms, the service. Medawar and I flew out on Sunday morning and returned first thing on Monday morning so that I shall be back in my lab before noon.

The Princess accepted my invitation to return the visit with alacrity and will come to our lab in June.

To Vivien Perutz, June 1, 1964

Vivien

We had vicarious thrills following your visits to Siena, San Gimignano and Pisa in your postcard serial. I have never seen any of these places but remember getting excited like a little boy and exhausting myself until my head spun when visiting Florence for 18 hours in 1952. One never believes that men were capable of creating such beauty that it keeps its freshness for ever. Seeing it in pictures and learning about it is nothing—it is something to be experienced, and the experience enriches one's life. Also you will see more in it every time you look at it again.

I had my own thrill in Scotland when some mountaineers took me rock climbing on Sunday; I found it hard going and noticed that I was not 30 but it was grand all the same and made me feel the reverse of staid. My lecture next day was not up to the usual standard, perhaps because I was a bit tired still. This embarrassed me.…

---

[14]The European Molecular Biology Organisation (EMBO) had been offered a site at Waterloo for the proposed laboratory. The laboratory was eventually sited in Heidelberg.

[Sandro] Vacciago was here, deeply troubled over the impending trial of [Giordano] Giacomello and [Domenico] Marotta (the former head of the Istituto di Sanità) on charges of misappropriation of public funds. In a way they are being made scapegoats for a system under which a dynamic scientific policy can hardly be pursued without breaking the law. As a result of Vacciago's visit I am trying to help, mainly by organising the sending of a letter of protest, signed by Nobel laureates and others. The Italian scientists themselves have formed a Society for the Defence of Scientific Research which is to help the 2 accused as well as try to reform Italy's antiquated and cumbersome administrative system. I am terribly sorry for the Giacomellos. Luckily the Minister of Education is on G's side so that he still has his post of University Professor to live on.

How lucky we are in England to have an honest and efficient civil service and judiciary.

To 21 Colleagues for Signatures, July 16, 1964

I wonder if you heard that Marotta, the former head of the Istituto di Sanità in Rome, was arrested, though later released on health grounds, and Giacomello, the present director, suspended from his office. Both face a trial next October for alleged irregularities in the use of public funds.

I have copies of the charges against both men. Neither of them is seriously accused of personal corruption, but rather of evading fiscal regulations in administering the Institute.

Here are some examples. 1. The staff of the Istituto included internationally known figures such as [Daniel] Bovet and [Ernst] Chain. In order to keep the services of first class scientists, the directors paid them salaries in excess of those approved for the Italian Civil Service. The excess was apparently paid from outside grants provided by the NIH, WHO and other bodies. 2. The purchase of major items of equipment had to be approved by a government Office which took many months to reach a decision. In order to cut through this procedure firms were asked to present their invoices split up into smaller sums which did not require approval by a higher authority.

The practices of which the two men are now suddenly accused have been common knowledge for some time. In the view of the Italian colleagues with whom Kendrew and I have recently spoken, Marotta and Giacomello are being made the scapegoats for an administrative system under which a dynamic scientific policy cannot be pursued without infringement of fiscal regulations.

This situation has led Italian scientists to form an Association for the Defence of Scientific Research. This group is anxious to gain the support of scientific colleagues from abroad. I have therefore drafted the enclosed open letter to the President of Italy, for which I should like to obtain the signature of a number of friends of Italian science. This is to be communicated to *La Stampa* and *Il Corriere della Sera* some time after it has been sent. Would you be willing to sign it?[15]

Telegram to Dorothy Hodgkin on the announcement of her Nobel Prize for Chemistry, October 29, 1964

Of corrin rings[16]
All England sings,
And Stockholm's choice
Lauds every voice,
But no one's song
That swells and waxes
Is quite as strong
As your old Max's

Dorothy and Thomas Hodgkin on the occasion of the awarding of her Nobel Prize (© Scanpix/Sipa Press)

To George Beadle, December 10, 1964

Thank you for your letter in connection with Warren Weaver's book. I do not think it would be too much to say that this outfit owes its existence to the Rockefeller Foundation. In *Les Prix Nobel* (1962) you will find a short biography of mine in which I recount my start in Cambridge as a research assistant to Bragg on a grant from the Foundation in Britain. At that time there was a great deal of unemployment among scientists and in Britain, and universities were not allowed to give posts to foreigners if British subjects were available to fill them. It was only because the money for the post was provided by the Rockefeller Foundation that the Ministry of Labour agreed to give me a permit to work with Bragg. The Foundation supported me personally, with various interruptions due to the War, until 1945, when Kendrew joined me and I obtained a Fellowship [from the ICI] at this university. Even then dollars were so short that we would not have been able

---

[15] I note that there is now a lecture hall called after Marotta.

[16] Corrin is the central ring of vitamin B12, the structure of which Hodgkin discovered.

to buy the apparatus for our X-ray studies but for the help of the Foundation. This kind of difficulty persisted over many years, even after we were taken on by the Medical Research Council in 1947.

We have received support from the Foundation continuously until now. On many occasions it has enabled us to do things on a bigger scale than we might have been able to do with Medical Research Council support alone. Now the Foundation provides no more than 1/2 per cent of our total budget, and this is used to invite lecturers from abroad; to extend fellowships of visiting workers who are unable to finish their research in time, before the termination of their grants; and to send our own research students abroad to meetings. It has also enabled us to give scholarships to several gifted young people who have failed to get enough marks in their final examinations and thus failed to secure state scholarships. In other words, the Foundation's grant allows us to pay for things which the Medical Research Council, being a State supported body, is not allowed to do.

Jim Watson arrived here with an Eli Lilly fellowship which had been given to him to work at Copenhagen for two years. The Fellowship Board was so incensed about his changing over to Cambridge after only one year that they deprived him of the fellowship. Again, I believe it was the Rockefeller Foundation that came to our aid and helped to support him. Otherwise the collaboration between Watson and Crick might never have taken place.

I am always deeply touched when Pomerat from the Foundation turns up here once a year or once every other year, like a benign Father Christmas, asking me whether there is anything they could do for us, and whatever it is that we happen to be asking for, they invariably agree to it. Finally you might find some interesting information about the decisive part played by the Rockefeller Foundation in Karl von Frisch's autobiography *Erinner ungen eines Biologen* published by Springer.

I hope this gives you the information you need.

To Dr. Falkner, March 15, 1965

I am writing to you concerning the proposals of the European Molecular Biology Organisation. The formation of this body was prompted by the contrast between the massive development of molecular biology in the United States and its feeble and reluctant development in most European countries, causing many of the gifted young European workers in the field to emigrate to the United States.

It is widely felt that molecular biology will revolutionise not only fundamental biological concepts, but also the scientific basis of much of medicine and agriculture. It would be tragic if, through present neglect, Europe would have to depend for future developments entirely on the United States.

EMBO aims to foster the development of the subject in Europe by (a) a programme of fellowships, scientific collaboration and exchange and (b) the creation of a European laboratory of molecular biology.

The case for the creation of a European laboratory does not rest, like that for CERN, on the creation of any one experimental facility which no single country can afford, but of a combination of facilities and approaches which is beyond the resources of any country: financial resources not so much as specialist resources.

Let me illustrate this by an example: at present, if a young man wants to become acquainted with the field of molecular biology in its broad sense he should spend a period of work on (a) control mechanisms at the Pasteur Institute at Paris; (b) chemical mutagenesis at Tübingen; (c) reaction mechanisms of enzymes at Göttingen; (d) protein structure and molecular genetics at Cambridge; (e) the higher nervous system at London or Harvard. Several other fields could be mentioned, but this is enough to illustrate the point.

EMBO wants to create a laboratory where young scientists can become acquainted with, and trained in, at least several of the important disciplines of molecular genetics in one place, in order to make them fit to teach the subject on a broad basis at a university in their own country. At present no such graduates are available in Europe and very little of the subject is taught at universities.

The Laboratory is not intended as an "Institute of Advanced Studies" where distinguished European molecular biologists can enjoy American salaries and experimental facilities in combination with the good life of Europe, but as the seed bed for the fertilisation of European universities and research laboratories.

To John T. Edsall, December 12, 1965

I am writing to ask for your help to redress an injustice to Herman Watson, and to a lesser extent, to David Phillips over John Kendrew's failure to publish the myoglobin results. My suggestion is that you ask Watson and Phillips to write a joint article on the conformation of globular proteins for *Advances in Protein Chemistry*.

No-one outside our laboratory quite realises how overwhelmed John was by his success. On solving myoglobin at 2 Å resolution he became famous overnight, and has been showered with invitations of all kinds ever since. As a result, the actual scientific work on myoglobin, since the building of the original model, has been carried out by his collaborators. Phillips extended the resolution from 2 to 1.4 Å. Watson helped him with the Fourier programme and has since refined the Fourier by a series of calculations which have proceeded as far as it would be profitable to go. Some further refinement may yet come from a least squares programme developed by [Bob] Diamond, but this is not expected to change the present results appreciably. There is no reason for holding up publication.

Phillips has made his reputation independently with lysozyme, but Watson has nothing to show for his years of good work, except for a few papers on peripheral problems on which his name appears.

I find myself in a state of conflict. On the one hand, I do not like being disloyal to John and want to do nothing that would impair our good relations. On the other hand, I regard it as my duty as Chairman to ensure that members of my laboratory get due credit for their work.

Quite apart from these personal questions, I believe that protein chemists at large have a right to see the myoglobin results in print. Conceivably John might start writing them up himself one day, but his life consists of an unintermittent succession of committees, conferences, appointments and travels which leave him no time to make the concentrated effort required. I hope that I am not causing you too much heart-searching and embarrassment by raising this matter. You may not want to be drawn into this difficult situation and prefer to wait for time to resolve it. However, please consider it and let me know how you feel.

To Jeffries Wyman, February 23, 1966[17]

Thank you for the copy of [Ephraim] Katchalski's[18] letter of 9th February. I agree with every word he writes, and I hope you will forgive my saying that I am not happy about your minutes of our last council meeting which refer to Israel's position. What you put into the minutes and what you subsequently wrote to Katchalski was essentially what you told council about the Swiss Gov-

---

[17]Written in Max's capacity as chairman of the European Molecular Biology Organisation to Wyman who was a member of its council.

[18]He later changed his name to Katzir.

ernment's attitude. But, as far as I can recollect, council said quite clearly that Israel was a full and equal member of EMBO and they wished Israel to be included in any diplomatic initiative made by the Swiss Government. If you feel doubtful, I could send a circular to council and ask them once more.

I don't like the proposal "that Israel would be brought into the picture as soon as possible after the initial diplomatic approaches"; I am sure that they ought to be included in the initial diplomatic approaches and take part in the preliminary meeting. I do not think the Swiss Government can easily refuse to do so, if we are firm on this point.

To Jeffries Wyman, February 2, 1967

Thank you for your letter of 30th January. I think you must have misunderstood my resolution. It does not ask the Swiss Government to include Israel as a participant in the forthcoming conference—on the contrary, it says that we appreciate the difficulty in doing so but that all we are anxious for is that Israel be included in any scientific activities that may be decided on by the conference. I hope this explanation will remove your objections.

To Sir Lawrence Bragg, April 4, 1967

I thought you would like to know that [David] Blow and [Paul] Sigler have a 3-dimensional Fourier of chymotrypsin at 2 Å which shows the complete course of the polypeptide chain and many of the side chains. The active site is clearly visible. The Fourier is not yet as good as Phillips's of lysozyme was, but I am sure it can be further clarified by the inclusion of another heavy atom derivative. The correctness of the Fourier is proved by the correlations between the electron density map and the known chemical sequence. This includes five cystine bridges, four of which are clearly visible, a number of bulky side chains which are easy to identify, and one short stretch of α-helix. As you can imagine, I am very thrilled about this success.

To Vivien and Robin Perutz.
Geneva to New York April 7, 1967

The Conference When I met my colleagues of the EMBO Council for dinner I was amazed, as I often am, how fast men take for granted what has been accomplished and become dissatisfied because the next jewel is not yet within their grasp. That first day's speeches, which had revealed a wide measure of agreement on the need for putting EMBO's present activities on a more permanent footing, seemed to them like the conquest of the Mittagshorn. The Matterhorn, in the form of the European Laboratory was the only object worth discussing now and they were disappointed at seeing it put off.

The Conference had asked EMBO for financial estimates to cover the three years after the end of the Volkswagen grant. Unfortunately I left this job to a party of my colleagues meeting over liqueurs at midnight. Without showing them to me they wrote the results of their calculation on the blackboard of the Assembly Hall next morning. This blackboard was hidden behind curtains during the opening remarks. When Wyman got up to discuss them the curtain was drawn back to reveal a set of astronomically high numbers which were so unrealistic as to confirm the civil servants' worst fears about the financial irresponsibility of scientists. All the good of the first day was very nearly wrecked, and I had a terrible time arguing with my EMBO colleagues that night. We had been to a cocktail party given by the Swiss Government which had sent my Swedish and Italian colleagues into a euphoric mood. The Swede kept repeating that to governments these figures were "peaca-ca-caca-canuts"! And that he as the head of the Swedish Defence Research Council could authorize them at any time without causing a single eyelid to be raised; the Italian talked in even more grandiose terms.

But I know that Government expenditure, like housewives', is made up of long sums of mostly small items, and the Treasury officials learn to scrutinize the small ones just as much as the big ones. If your estimates are exaggerated they feel that you want to cheat them and would rather give you nothing.

The President of the Conference was a brilliant man, a Professor of Greek at Geneva who deserves much credit for the success. Some of the civil servants, Swiss, French, German, Swedish and British, also stood out for their quick grasp and ability to formulate their thoughts with fluidity and precision. The scientists' often voiced arrogant view of civil servants as lesser breeds did not seem borne out by performance there.

We had a morning off while an inner circle drafted the resolutions of the conference and I used this for a sight seeing trip of CERN. I was unable to see the big accelerator ring, because it was running, but I was lucky enough to see the hydrogen bubble chamber disassembled. I had had no notion of its great size and of the formidable engineering problems involved in its construction and operation. Nor of the problems of automating the scanning of the 1000s of track photographs taken of nuclear collisions in the chamber. Their analysis seems to provide material for Ph.D. theses for most of the nuclear physics research students in Europe.

To Vivien and Robin Perutz. New York–Seattle, April 10, 1967

The spectacular sight of the day was Fred Richards' and Hal Wyckhoff's atomic model of ribonuclease, an enzyme that splits ribonucleic acid, and one of the smallest enzymes known. They have a beautiful, detailed and very accurate 3D Fourier, which aroused my admiration and envy. The structure is most interesting, a feast to the protein crystallographer's eye, and, incidentally, splendid ammunition for my lectures at Stanford.

The passengers include many young men in the forces, or just called up, the first visible sign that this country is at war. Lotte reminded me how lucky we are to live in England. If we lived here, Robin would be called up next year. Of my 2 neighbours, one is joining the National Guard, in the hope that he will not be sent to Vietnam. He is a homesick young farmer, just married, with a wife expecting a baby. The other is in the Coast Guard, I suspect for similar reasons, and wants to read oceanography at Woods Hole when he comes out.

To Robin and Vivien Perutz. San Francisco–Los Angeles, April 20, 1967

My stay was scientifically interesting. [Dick] Dickerson has a 3D Fourier of cytochrome C, the respiratory enzyme discovered by Keilin in 1925 for which he should have, but never got, the Nobel Prize. Seymour Benzer showed me sections through the eyes and brain of a fruit fly and told me of his ideas for discovering how the connections between nerve cells developed. He is a most ingenious man for whom I have the greatest respect, and I was interested to see how he is feeling his way forward in a biological problem more complex by far than the one I am trying to solve.

To Robin Perutz, January 29, 1968

After you left me I found a huge lecture room packed with about 500 students all eager to hear the latest about protein structure. [Hans] Zachau introduced me by telling the students what an important guy I was and how grateful they must be to me for tearing myself away from my administration of the Cambridge laboratory to condescend to lecture to them. With my usual tact I refrained from telling them not to believe a word of that rot, but plunged into the strange world of enzymes.

I had to wait until Saturday's lunch in Peterhouse before hearing the outcome of the Geneva Conference. John [Kendrew] stayed until almost the end and tells me that it was a great success for EMBO. The Draft Convention giving us government support for our Fellowships and Summer School for 5 years after the end of the Volkswagen Grant was approved by all the delegates except the British.

To Robin Perutz, February 5, 1968

I finished my model yesterday. One of the deficiencies of our electron density map is the absence of clearly marked traces of the first and last residues of the chains. Having built the rest of the structure following the density on the map, I let my fancy play yesterday and connected the ends of the α-chain so as to build what I thought would be electrostatically the most stable structure: constructing a network of +ve and –ve charges. I then measured the coordinates, looked back on the map and found to my great pleasure that it contained little peaks exactly where I had placed the COO^- group which being the heaviest, would be expected to produce the largest peaks. Next I put 2 [groups; see diagram] near the central symmetry axis and 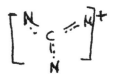 found another 2 peaks just there. Finally there is a peak on the symmetry axis itself which could be neatly accounted for by an SO_4^{2-} group sandwiched between the 2 +vely charged ones. So I cycled home very satisfied last night.

Earlier in the week I listened to Andrew Huxley speaking on muscle research in the 19th and 20th century. He was interesting as always and told

Model of deoxygenated haemoglobin, which magnified the molecule 850 million times.

us how a 19th century German physiologist called [Ernst] Brücke had correctly inferred the existence of rigid rods in the A-bands of the sarcomeres,
from the fact that their birefrigence was high and their length independent
of the length of the muscle fibres. So the evidence for the sliding filament
theory was there, but was later forgotten and buried under a heap of contradictory evidence by inferior observers. Even more astonishing, people
also detected the network of submicroscopic capillaries through which Ca^{++}
is now known to be transported from the outer membrane into the centre
of the muscle fibre, simply by staining it with carbon black. The capillaries
showed up as black threads.

I was interested in Hoyle's new theory of planetary development,
because it seems to be the first to predict correctly their chemical composition. Finally I was excited by a news item in *Nature* that a super-conducting
electric motor had successfully been built and that another of 3000 hp is
being constructed for the Fawley power station.

To Robin Perutz, February 18, 1968

Through the Peterhouse Book Club I received a volume of essays in memory of the physicist Niels Bohr. Some of them are very vivid and give a picture of what it is that makes a very great man. The outstanding feature is
his towering strength and *stamina*, which makes him capable of arguing
not just for hours, but for days and even weeks to hammer out a new theory. When [Erwin] Schrödinger came to Copenhagen to talk to him about
his new wave mechanics, Bohr found a flaw in the theory and continued
arguing "Aber Sie müssen doch zugeben, Schrödinger. . . ." [But you must
admit Schrödinger] until the poor man got ill. The inconsistency in question was finally resolved by Heisenberg's Uncertainty Principle (Heisenberg
was also working with Bohr at the time).

Other impressions of mine are of the terrible agony that is involved
even for the greatest minds in making advances in thought, such as Bohr
arriving at the atomic model which explained the spectrum of hydrogen, or
Heisenberg at the Uncertainty Principle.

Finally the moral for you and me is that to make a mark in science one
must go and work with a great man. One cannot learn to be as intelligent

as they are, but can learn from them how a difficult problem has to be approached and sometimes, what the vital problems are.

Jim Watson's book [*The Double Helix*] is out as a serial. I have the impression that it is better than the draft we saw, but I still have quarrels with it, one being that it fails to picture Francis' tremendous intellectual strength and imagination, which puts him in the class of great men, even if he lacks that other quality of thinking deeply about human matters.

To Robin Perutz, February 25, 1968

Last week brought two letters from you, one about your reactions to Fitzroy Maclean's book[19] and the other describing your skiing around Innsbruck. I can see the similarity between the Serbian Partisans and the Vietcong, and understand your sympathies. Yet my own sympathies are always ambivalent, especially towards people fanatically devoted to one cause. My feelings are best expressed by [Bertrand] Russell's reaction to Soviet Russia in the early 1920s. In his book *The Practice and Theory of Bolshevism* he writes "Contact with those who have no doubts has intensified 1000 fold my own doubts, not as to Socialism itself, but as to the wisdom of holding a creed so firmly that for its sake men are willing to inflict widespread misery." In Serbia and now in Vietnam men are not only willing to die, but also to commit murder of innocent people. They do it in order to liberate their country from foreign dominion, to impose a dictatorship, not as they believe of the proletariat itself, but a gang of ruthless politicians ready to exploit their sacrifices. I find this heart-breaking.

The Indians have shown that a foreign oppressor can be got rid of by non-violent means. I believe that the same would probably have been true of Vietnam. The present war, in which the prestige of the two superpowers is involved, is calamitous for the people of Vietnam and terrifying for the world as a whole.

To Robin Perutz, April 7, 1968

Only the news from my laboratory is good. Hilary [Muirhead] at last discovered the trivial error which has prevented the working of the model-drawing programme for the past months. We now have a magnetic tape

---

[19]Possibly *Eastern Approaches*.

with coordinates of all protein atoms in haemoglobin (alas still not the haem groups!) and our computer will produce stereoscopic drawings of any desired part of the structure on an oscillograph screen, whence it can be photographed as in the enclosed picture.

To Robin Perutz, April 15, 1968

After the encouraging picture I sent you last week of "haemoglobin drawn by computer" Hilary and Bob Diamond still experienced fearful difficulties before they could actually get the pictures we need. The magnetic tape with the coordinates would not get read, the whole programme would get erased from the memory, the tape would wear out and a new one had to be prepared in London, etc. However, by the time the lab closed down for Easter they had got several very good pictures of the contacts between subunits. No haem groups yet.

To Robin Perutz, May 19, 1968

Here is a lock of Vivian Dreyfus's lovely black hair which she secretly asked me to send you when she had lunch with us today. Or is it?

It was Jim Watson week in England. [*The Double Helix*] has received a chorus of acclamation from scientists and laymen alike. Lay critics are delighted to see scientists at last with their pants off, making me feel sick at all the nonsense that gets talked and written, as if all scientific activity took place in an atmosphere of personal competition and recrimination. Some good points emerged though, from the remarks of Bragg and the more intelligent and adult critics. That the creative process in science is not based on "scientific method," but is an erratic human activity like artistic creation. This realisation has done something to bridge the gap between the two cultures.

I saw some interesting exhibits [at the Royal Society soirée]. Did you know that nuclei of uranium and many other heavy atoms are whizzing around in space? The enclosed are enlargements of their tracks in nuclear photographic emulsions recorded in balloon flights over Texas. Did you know that the R.A.E. [Royal Aircraft Establishment] at Farnborough discovered that graphite whiskers, made by slow oxidation of nylon fibres, are weight for weight 100X stronger than steel? They are single crystals with the graphite carbon layers normal to the long axis, so that they cannot slip over each other. If the carbon fibres are embedded in plastic they give a kind of reinforced concrete which is to be used for turbine engines. Now you will guess what the lock of hair really is. More in your present line was a sound-film showing a courting pair of haddocks; the male's dance was graceful enough, but his love song a bit monotonous. However, his girl liked it.[20]

The students' revolution in Europe is probably all too justified and yet terrifying. What will it lead to? Parliamentary democracy is an inefficient and often corrupt form of government, but is the only alternative to tyranny that society has devised. Democracy can be reformed from within, but its overthrow is fatal!

To Robin Perutz, June 2, 1968

Robin

2 days ago Andrew MacLachlan came up with an idea of how haemoglobin might work. It is so ingeniously simple that I believe it must be right. It is based on the observation of a large hole in the place where the oxygen goes, which exists both in myoglobin and in the 2 kinds of haemoglobin chain. Andrew suggests that in haemoglobin the helices surrounding the hole are flexible and movable relative to each other so that, when the dissociation of the oxygen molecule leaves a vacuum or hole, this is par-

tially filled by amino acid side chains moving into it. The resulting local movement causes a slight rearrangement of most of the helical regions within any one chain, and that this in turn causes the substantial rearrangement of the chains relative to each other which we can observe. In myoglobin, on the other hand, the helical regions are firmly interlocked, so that the structure remains rigid on combination and dissociation of oxygen.

To substantiate his idea, Andrew built space-filling models of the β-chain and of parts of myoglobin, and actually tried to show me the flexibility of the one and the rigidity of the other. He also did another experiment (which had actually started him off): you may or may not remember that I drew a set of maps superimposing exactly the chains of horse oxy and human deoxyhaemoglobin, drawing the former in red and the latter in blue on a series of perspex sheets, in order to see if there is any change in the folding of the chains. I could see none of which I could be sure that it was greater than the experimental error.

---

[20]Between school and university Robin worked at the Max-Planck-Institut at Seewiesen studying imprinting in ducks.

Andrew viewed these contour maps through 2 adjacent strips of red and blue celluloid, so that he would see only one image, the red or the blue, at a time, but could switch rapidly from one to the other. By this method he thought he could distinguish slight, but consistent, movements of several helical regions. These movements actually formed the starting point for his attack on the problem.

At that stage I was sceptical, because I regarded the movements as too slight to be significant, and this may still be true; but the general idea to which his experiments have led him seems most convincing to me. The concept of the vacuum or hole created by the dissociation of the oxygen molecule being the driving force for the structural change and all its associated effects is much simpler than all other proposals that have been made, such as movements of the iron atom in and out of the plane of the haem group, or polarization of the periphery of the haem group by the electronegative oxygen or other ligand, or fanciful long-range interaction. I am doubly keen now to get out the structure of deoxy at high resolution to see if Andrew's exciting idea is correct.[21]

I told you that Keith [Moffat] discovered how one of the inhibitors of the cooperative effects works. Last week Bill Bolton found the solution to the workings of another, which, though somewhat different chemically, seems to produce its effect in the same way, namely by displacing the 3 residues at the carboxyl end of the β-chain from their normal positions. His result is doubly interesting because the X-ray results show that the reagent has become linked to a quite different group on the β-chain from that which the chemists thought they had found it to be after hydrolysis.

To Robin Perutz, June 9, 1968

I do not share Mummy's depression about [Robert] Kennedy's assassination. One must think of America not as Western Europe, but rather as Sicily. A country in which you find the most sophisticated and civilised people at

---

[21]Overlaying the structures of oxy- and deoxyhaemoglobin revealed small differences between them, which might have helped elucidate the mechanism of the structural transition. Max was very excited about the slight differences revealed in Andrew's observations. It was later discovered that the fitting of the density data and superposition of the two structures were not quite correct and as a result Max concluded that the small changes observed could not be trusted. Max then turned to chemical approaches, using cross-linking agents and inhibitors, also enzyme digestion of the terminal residues of the β-chain (below), which modified oxygen binding. Only later with much higher resolution was he able to detect the 0.4 Å movement of the iron atom into the plane of the haem group, which triggers the structural changes observed on oxygenation.—AW

one extreme, and at the other, a polyglot, uprooted people without even the culture of an African tribe. A crude barbarian society where each man fights for himself. Governed very loosely, leaving people to fight their conflicts out among themselves. Since possession of firearms in this kind of society is still widely regarded as a man's right for self-defence, it is difficult for the police to protect prominent persons from attack by political fanatics, paranoid maniacs or habitual criminals.

However, all this having been said, it is terribly tragic that two brothers, who were both bent on public service to improve American society, should have fallen victims to its lunatic fringe. One must feel deeply sorry for them and their families.

To Robin Perutz, June 18, 1968

[Hermann] Lehmann appeared next morning to take me at my word about our long-promised collaboration on the abnormal human haemoglobins. There are now over 80 different mutants, the great majority of them giving rise to the replacement of one amino acid in either the α- or the β-chains. I had a most interesting time with Lehmann sorting them out on a stereochemical basis and relating the stereochemistry to the clinical symptoms. It turned out that nearly all the replacements of residues on the protein surface were harmless while all the others are harmful, especially those of residues which touch the haem group or those which occur at contacts between subunits. The data contain a mine of information

Hermann Lehmann was the world authority on genetic diseases of haemoglobin. Max and Hermann, who returned to Cambridge in 1963, first met in 1936 and had been interned together.

concerning the relationship of protein structure and function.

Having finished the survey of the data on Friday, I began writing the next paper for *Nature* on Saturday. I want to call it "The Molecular Pathology of Human Haemoglobin."

I also wrote to the Prime Minister today, supporting [Fred] Sanger's and [Maurice] Wilkins's initiative on biological warfare and asking that Porton[22] should be transferred to civilian control and its work made public.

---

[22]Porton Down is a British laboratory under the Ministry of Defence which has specialised inter alia in research into defence against biological and chemical warfare.

To Robin Perutz, June 30, 1968

The most interesting information I gained at the Conference concerned the structure of the "Thick Elements" of [Hugh] Huxley's muscle picture. It used to be thought that these consist of the single protein, myosin, forming a molecule of 2, or possibly 3, very long polypeptide chains. It now turns out that there is a long straight segment consisting of 2 α-helical chains, possibly intertwined, and a head made up of the long and 2–4 short chains.

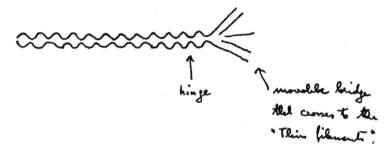

The head is the part which bridges the gap to the thin filaments and actively moves to and fro during contraction. So it must change its structure in response to chemical stimuli, rather like haemoglobin does in response to oxygen. It is marvellous that this is being unravelled now, at least chemically, although it may be very difficult to find its 3-dimensional structure.[23]

I expect Mummy told you about the Royal Society Conversazione where I exhibited my model again. Someone brought Sir Mortimer Wheeler, the President of the Royal Academy [the national academy of art], and I was burning to offer it to him for the Academy's Summer Exhibition, but he merely stared at the model with a glassy eye and asked where he could get a drink.

To Gisela Perutz, Vivien, and Robin. Cornell, April 29, 1969

Mrs. Leopolski is a pet! She knows what every one of her students likes and no trouble is too much for her. She used to be the chef in the Statler Hotel, she proudly told me after I said that the students were very lucky, but now she has cooked for students for 15 years. Her kitchen is like home where the children can come and help themselves to anything they fancy, either at

---

[23]It would not be until 1991 that Ivan Rayment and his colleagues would solve the three-dimensional structure of the myosin head, and subsequent X-ray and other studies have elucidated the molecular mechanism of muscle contraction.—AW

mealtime or any time of day and night. It is always open. So are all the rooms at this fraternity (and sorority) where only specially gifted students are given free board and lodging. They run the place themselves and entertain me as their guest, without formality and fuss, but proudly. I have a large ugly dark room with 3 beds (why the 3rd?) and a bathroom which I share with a Professor Crystal whom I have not set eyes on yet. No one makes my bed and I must find out where to empty my waste paper basket, but there is a huge HiFi set in the lounge with a collection of classical records which any one can play and where this letter is being written. And then there is Mrs. Leopolski who cooks everything just right.

Cornell is in a state of upheaval caused by 60 negro students. A few of them were reprimanded for I don't know what by a disciplinary board of dubious status. By way of protest they occupied one of the fraternities on Parents' Weekend, turning the outraged parents out of their beds. On being threatened by extreme right-wing toughs they had guns brought in by the anarchist "Students for a Democratic Society" and prepared to fight a siege battle. The stage was set for bloodshed, when the President of Cornell wisely negotiated a truce, annulling the reprimands, and promising not to prosecute. He got them to agree to leave the building peaceably but *not* to surrender their guns. Whereupon a string of conservative professors accused the President of capitulating and threatened to resign. Other professors refused to teach until all guns (right and left) on the campus are surrendered. Most lecture halls were occupied by students' and staff meetings the day I arrived, but they found one where I could give my lectures.

I believe that the President is to be congratulated on avoiding bloodshed and any kind of violence in this very difficult situation; so do most of the sensible dons I have talked to. The students in this house do not seem to sympathise with the revolutionaries, but there is no doubt that they are extremely dangerous. The "Students for a Democratic Society" stand for the opposite; i.e. to smash up the universities which form the basis of existing society, and they have no positive programme. Yet the SDS is not made up of fools but includes gifted students. They are excellent speakers, arguing with great persuasiveness, and compared to them most dons sound feeble. They are also accomplished in revolutionary tactics. At this moment the crisis has subsided, but I fear it will flare up again in another form.

When you look around this gigantic and luxurious campus and watch the crowds of students the University looks, solid, contented, friendly and peaceful. You have to talk to the professors to realise how vulnerable a fabric it is. If the SDS decided to smash up the central computer, the administration and much of the research could be paralysed. They could do this under the pretence that it is used for military research. Or they could smash up labs that have defence contracts, most of which are for fundamental research of no military interest. (Congress is too stingy to vote enough money for basic research, so the government tries to circumvent their restrictions by financing much basic research through defence departments which get plenty from Congress.) There is no police to stop the SDS in a small place like this from turning the University from a place of learning into a "Base for Social Action."

I doubt that you would have enjoyed it here, Gisela. Most of the wives I have met here are pretty awful; the students are really the best company around. One French student threw a champagne party last night to celebrate De Gaulle's departure.

To Robin Perutz, June 18, 1969

I went to the Senate House with a dual purpose yesterday: to look for your results and to vote for the Medical School.[24] Over lunch at Peterhouse I tried to persuade one of the historians to vote for it. He raised all kinds of doubts and then suddenly burst out: "We don't want to train a lot more Harley Street abortionists!" When I explained that I expected our laboratory to benefit he said, "I expect you want human guinea pigs." What fantastically cock-eyed views people have about science and medicine.

Your letter about German politics is heart-breaking. Hitler played on the solid German citizen's fear of communism, which the Weimar Government was unable to check. In the same manner I expect Herr von Thadden solicits support from those who fear and detest Cohn-Bendit's gangs.[25] And in their efforts to defend themselves against student extremism, the Germans succumb to fear of the constructive reforms urged by the moderates, which would save the universities. How fortunate we are in England that political extremism is confined to the lunatic fringes. May this continue through your lifetime.

---

[24]Hitherto students had only been able to undertake preclinical study in Cambridge; the new Medical School was designed also greatly to expand medical research.

[25]By the summer of 1969, Daniel Cohn-Bendit, a German student of the sociology faculty of Nanterre and the most prominent of the leaders of the French student rebellion of May 1968, had been banished from France. The rebellion had swept across France, spreading from university to high-school students and also to blue-collar workers, an uprising so powerful that for a short while it looked as if the rebels, whose key demand was direct democracy as opposed to centralised power, would succeed in bringing down De Gaulle's government.

Last week I went to vote for the Social Sciences Tripos [i.e. the introduction of a B.A. in Social Sciences]. We won by about 450 against 320. I was very pleased until I read the *Shilling Paper* which regards the new tripos as an instrument to destroy the University.[26]

To Robin Perutz. Berlin–London, June 22, 1969

The best part of our visit to Hannover was a tour of the VW works. Strictly capitalist principles could be seen to be applied. As you know American laws now require cars to have various safety devices; these are incorporated only in cars for export to the U.S. and not for the rest. The power plant is heated with American coal because it is cheaper than German, when German miners are unemployed. I was amazed at these things, because a large part of the VW shares belong to the Federal Government and the State of Niedersachsen.

At the dinner of the Foundation I found academics despondent about the student revolt: "Die deutschen Universitäten liegen im Sterben" [The German universities are dying] was a typical comment. The estrangement between the generations of which your colleagues at Seewiesen told you was described to me by their fathers. A student seen to talk to a professor is treated by his mates as a traitor. Sizable reforms can no longer be discussed, because the atmosphere has become so embittered. It all sounded tragic.

In Berlin Mummy's friend Otto von Simson who is Dean of the Philosophical Faculty sounded a similar note, but my scientific colleagues were more hopeful, saying that conditions were not bad in the science faculties.

To Robin Perutz, August 1, 1969

I have not written to you since you left us, having been overwhelmed by work and events. Of the latter, the best is Hilary [Muirhead's] and Jonathan [Greer's] Fourier of human deoxyhaemoglobin, which is surprisingly clear, considering the relatively low resolution of 3.5 Å. I was anxious to see whether it confirms the links I had predicted in the paper on the Bohr effect. The link between the 2 α-chains is beautifully confirmed, though it is more intricately designed than any of us had realised. The link between

[26]The last issue before October of this student newspaper which I was able to find dates from 6 June. It presents those spearheading opposition to the new tripos as a small cabal of right-wing dons. The paper also carries an article about the ultimate aim of the French student revolutionaries, namely, the destruction of bourgeois capitalist society. The majority of their leaders were students of sociology.

the C-terminal histidine and aspartate 94 of the β-chain also appears, but not too clearly. We hope to see more of it on a difference Fourier of an abnormal haemoglobin which Jonathan will have ready next week.

At first I thought that I could also see a shift of one of the histidines near the haem group which would explain the low oxygen affinity of deoxy-haemoglobin, but this now appears to have been an optical illusion due to the different angle of view. So at this moment the problem of the low oxygen affinity, and the trigger which releases the change from the deoxy to the oxy form, is still unclear.

Coming back to my London visit, my first job was to ask the MRC for a computer that would allow Sydney [Brenner] to digitize the information on the neural system of his nematodes, and eventually to compute the behaviour of the worm from their "wiring diagram." I found the MRC sympathetic, as always. Next I had to attend a Press Conference on the occasion of the publication of the Annual Report to Parliament. As expected, nobody wanted to ask me any questions about my article, since it is not news. [John] Gray made an appallingly dull statement about Council's Policy, talking meaningless generalities which not even the best-intentioned journalist could turn into a piece of news. This was followed by questions from journalists about expenditure on mental illness, causes of coronary thrombosis, adverse effects of the pill, answered very competently by various members of the Council or scientific staff. However, no one gave them any item of news about advances in medical research which would have fired the journalists' imagination; to me this would have seemed the obvious thing to do on such an occasion.

To Robin Perutz, August 10, 1969

This week's great event was a phone call from Dorothy [Hodgkin] that insulin was solved! So 6 of us drove to Oxford on Tuesday to celebrate the happy conclusion of 35 years' research on this most refractory of all protein structures. Dorothy looked radiant and so did all the young chaps who had slogged out the solution in recent years.

After a disappointing 2 weeks of slipping crystals and troubled diffractometers I have had a marvellous day today. Bill Bolton's Fourier of horse deoxyhaemoglobin at 2.8 Å is being plotted now and looks beautifully clear. This proves that he must have done his measurements and calculations very carefully. I looked at about 8 sections which included the haem group and the C-terminus of the β-chains. To my delight I found my postulated

link between the C-terminal histidine and aspartate 94 beautifully confirmed. So my proposed mechanism of the Bohr effect is proved! This is
marvellous.[27]

To Robin Perutz, August 25, 1969

I am having a marvellous time labelling the amino acids in Bolton's Fourier,
which allows me to see many of the differences between the structures of
the oxy and deoxy forms. One of the problems that has long puzzled us is
how the oxygen gets into the haem pocket, because space filling models
show that amino acid side chains block the entrance. Going through the α-
chain I noticed that the electron density which corresponds to the histidine
at the entrance to the haem pocket in deoxy haemoglobin is blurred, while
in oxyHb it is sharp. When I examined the blur more closely I found that it
corresponded to the path which the histidine side chain would trace out if
it swung open and closed in turn. In other words, in deoxyHb there is a
door swinging back and forth which lets the oxygen in, while in oxyHb the
histidine probably stabilises the oxygen molecule by forming a hydrogen
bond with it.

The more I think about haemoglobin, the more I come to regard it as a
complex organ of molecular size, capable of a variety of movements in
response to chemical stimuli, and of transmitting interactions through different parts. So I feel as some of the early microscopists must have felt
when their exploration of the cellular structure of different organs gave
them a first understanding of their workings.

We have just heard Janet Baker and [Dietrich] Fischer-Dieskau recite
Lieder at the Queen Elizabeth Hall on Saturday night with V[ivien]. Very
beautiful. We also admired Leonardo's sketches in the Queen's Gallery.

To Robin Perutz, September 3, 1969

Having confirmed that the mechanism of the Bohr effect I proposed is correct, I tried to see whether the molecule contains any other ionisable group

---

[27]The Bohr effect describes the decrease in oxygen affinity under more acidic conditions as occur
in muscles compared to the lungs. The link between histidine and aspartate 94 will occur only if
the histidine has attached a proton (i.e. under more acidic conditions). Thus, conditions in the tissues favour the formation of the link and thereby facilitate the unloading of oxygen. In a later letter to Robin (3 September), Max confirms this by showing that there is no other ionisable group
that might be responsible.—AW.

that might contribute to it, but found none. So this part is ready to be written up.

I next turned to haem-haem interaction. I had often feared that the X-ray analysis might not tell us anything about it, because the changes in the structure of the individual subunits might be too small to be detected. I was very relieved, therefore, when I discovered, on comparing horse oxy and deoxy, that this was not so. The angles of inclination of the haem group relative to the protein chain containing them change markedly, and so do the position and orientations of several amino acid side-chains. As I had expected, the pathway of interaction lies along the lines joining the 2 haem groups which are nearest together. It looks as though the mechanism is purely mechanical, rather than electrical, and triggered by the bulk of oxygen which requires a rearrangement of the haems whenever it combines with, or dissociates from, the iron atoms. This is all highly satisfactory.

On the other hand, my idea of the swing door of which I wrote to you last week is wrong. I misinterpreted the electron density map and the relevant feature must be either a water molecule or the end of another amino acid side-chain.

To John T. Edsall, September 7, 1969

Work has been exceptionally interesting this summer. First Jonathan Greer and Hilary Muirhead obtained a 3D Fourier of human deoxyHb at 3.5 Å resolution, and shortly afterwards Bill Bolton's long-awaited Fourier of horse deoxyHb at 2.8 Å resolution emerged. The two structures are closely similar and tell the same story. It proved especially useful to have 2 Fouriers, because if any difference between oxy and deoxy appears in both, one can be confident of its being genuine.

Naturally I had my heart in my throat wondering if the linkages I had postulated to explain the Bohr effect would show up. They do indeed, exactly as predicted, only that they are more beautiful and elaborate than I had anticipated. By now I have examined the environment of all ionisable groups in oxy and deoxyhaemoglobin and reached the conclusion that no others can contribute significantly to the Bohr effect.

I am afraid this letter contains little of interest to Margaret [John's wife], but I hope to bring *some* non-scientific news with me. Newton is right when he says that one makes discoveries by keeping the subject constantly in one's mind, but it does make one rather a bore to non-scientific company.

1970s

"I hope that the Queen will enjoy Charlie Chaplin's autobiography. Walking all alone through the crowds outside, past the changing guards, across the great Palace Yard, to be received by Her Majesty in private audience, made me feel rather like Charlie Chaplin myself."

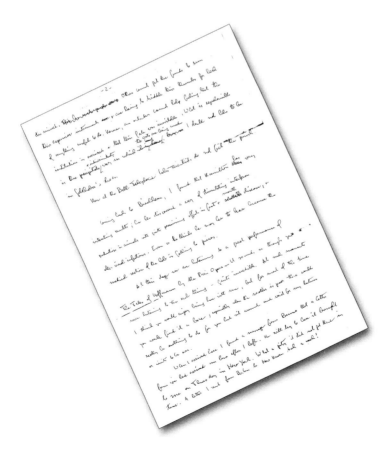

SCIENTIFIC PRESTIGE BROUGHT MAX INVITATIONS to lecture, membership of academies and other honours, which took him away from home for a few weeks a year. In this collection, we reap the benefit of his travels through letters describing his experiences. On the other hand, prestige did not bring acceptance of his work—on the contrary. At the outset of the decade "by a brilliant series of insights,"[1] he finally realised his dream and was able to publish a paper that charted the mechanism that makes haemoglobin function as a "molecular lung." The disbelief that the paper engendered and the subsequent attempts to refute it cut Max to the quick. It is true that initially it was unproven in many details, but he had put forward arguments in support of his proposed mechanism, the force of which he thought his opponents had failed to grasp. Consequently, he devoted much of the next two decades to disproving the purported refutations until finally all doubts were laid to rest. In the process, Max refined and elaborated his explanation of nature's subtle design, showing in detail why in its deoxygenated state haemoglobin is hungry for oxygen, and, once sated and transformed, it is equally eager to disburse oxygen to the tissues. I owe the following explanation to Alan Weeds.

Haemoglobin has evolved to have a high affinity for oxygen in order to bind it efficiently in the lungs, while in the tissues, where the oxygen concentration is lower, oxygen is released. This change in affinity (binding strength) depends on structural differences between the oxy and deoxy forms. Based on a comparison of the two structures, Max proposed a mechanism to explain the structural changes and relate them to the process of oxygen binding. The deoxy structure is stabilised by strong electrostatic bonds (salt bridges) between the subunits. These are broken when oxygenation occurs. When oxygen binds to the iron atom, there is a very small movement of the iron into the plane of the haem ring. This small movement drags with it parts of the protein on the other side of the iron atom, thereby amplifying the movement into a change of protein structure. The bonds that stabilise the deoxy form are broken, resulting in formation of the high-affinity oxy form. This process must be reversed in the mus-

---

[1] David Blow, page 19.

cles and organs. The lower oxygen concentration in tissues helps reverse this process, but in addition, carbon dioxide generated from oxygen promotes acid-ification. It had been known for a long time that haemoglobin has a lower affin-ity for oxygen under more acid conditions and this further facilitates oxygen release (the Bohr effect). When the oxygen is released carbon dioxide can bind to haemoglobin and is thereby transported back to the lungs and exhaled. Using high-resolution X-ray structural analysis and chemical modification as well as the study of a variety of haemoglobin mutants, over a number of years, Max defined the molecular interactions that stabilise the two structures and proposed mechanisms to relate the structural transitions to the physiological properties of haemoglobin.—AW

To John T. Edsall, May 6, 1970

I was as pleased with your letter as with my election[2]: it conveys so much of the warmth of your friendship. No doubt it was you also who proposed me, so that the honour on which you congratulate me was partly of your own making.

Not that I feel a peer of your Olympians. When people see my name along with [Paul] Dirac's and [Manfred] Eigen's, it disappoints them to find that I hardly understand Maxwell's let alone Schrödinger's equations. But it gives me enormous pleasure that my work on haemoglobin should have aroused such wide interest and generous recognition. I only hope that I find out how it works.

To Cyril Clemens, Editor of the Mark Twain Journal, May 7, 1970

Thank you for your letter of 14 April announcing my election to the Knight-hood of Mark Twain. What is the initiation ceremony? Do I have to swing a dead cat by the tail in a churchyard at night?

To Gisela Perutz. Pittsburgh, June 3, 1971

Did you know that this place was Duquesnes until the British captured it from the French and named it after Pitt? It smells like a locomotive shed

---

[2]J.T.E. had written to him to congratulate him on his election as a foreign associate of The National Academy of Sciences.

and has made no concessions to non-productive amenities. The steel mills flank the Ohio River belching forth smoke while barges carry in the coal and iron ore and take away the steel. A haphazard crop of massive towers, crowded as in San Gimignano, but graceless, has grown up in down town, and all around are motorways and smaller towers. One oversized Gothic spire has under its roof the office of the president of Pittsburgh University. It has no campus, but crowds in with the rest of the city and the hospitals that are part of its medical school.

George Jeffrey, the English crystallographer, and Chien Ho met me at the airport and took me to the University Club, where the faculty eats, and its guests sleep, in neo-Victorian splendour. Cambridge colleges are Spartan by comparison; if I were a student I might well look upon the faculty as a bunch of social parasites.

Luckily no feelings of guilt disturbed my sleep, nor was my internal clock upset by the sudden transfer. Next morning I talked to young people in Jeffrey's lab who are doing excellent work on structure analysis of small molecular compounds. They told me of a particularly tricky structure. How long did it take to solve? One week was the startling answer! X-ray analysis has made fantastic strides. The lab was crowded with visiting workers from all parts of the globe who radiated enthusiasm for their research.

To Gisela Perutz. Detroit to Notre Dame, April 30, 1972

Senta's eyes are cured after a visit to the fountain of St. Odile in Alsace. At this shrine the short and the long sighted, the sufferers from cataract and glaucoma are all cured. They throw their spectacles into the fountain and never need them again. Knowing Senta's careful disposition, I asked "What did *you* do?" "*I threw in an old pair*" was the answer. Even so, the miracle worked and Senta's trouble with the unoperated eye has gone. I suppose forgiveness is in the nature of saints!

To Gisela Perutz. Morris Inn, Notre Dame, Indiana, May 4, 1972

Notre Dame is a rest cure and would be a good chance of learning some theoretical chemistry if I did not have to be so polite to all the people coming to see me to tell me this and that.

They are proud of their president here, a Catholic priest called Hesburgh, who is also President of the Civil Rights Association.[3] When I arrived, my host announced that I was invited to dinner with him, but when the night came, I discovered that I shared his honour with 800 faculty members and their wives, all assembled in a huge hall to celebrate a sort of Speech Night, where an orgy of mutual back patting was followed by a sinister Jesuitic speech of the President, admonishing the faculty to face the oncoming university crisis in a spirit of mutual love and affection—by which he really meant that they should accept whatever measures he ordained without protest. All his talk of love and affection made me conclude that the entire faculty must be at each others' throats for most of the time, but my colleagues here strongly denied this. He may be a pillar of Civil Liberties abroad, but I could not help the impression that he is an autocrat at home.

To Robin Perutz, October 4, 1972

Today I drew up the programme for the lab symposium which is to begin in a week's time. [John] Gurdon, and his people will have pride of place, but there will be other exciting new things: Fred's [Sanger] DNA sequences; a precursor for immunoglobulins; differentiation in a blue green alga; structure of chromatin; control of muscular contraction, etc. I have tried to mix the divisions up so that people don't come only to listen to their own special fields. Selection has become a problem. When we started the symposia, nearly everybody spoke. Now there is time for no more than 1/4 of the scientists in the lab. Nor does the lecture room hold everyone. About 1/3 have to watch on closed circuit TV in the canteen.

John Gurdon and his Oxford group were invited to join the lab in 1972 with the aim of enhancing research in the area of cell biology. "Gurdon had been the first to clone an animal. Working on Xenopus laevis . . . , he had destroyed the nucleus of an unfertilised egg with UV, and replaced it with the nucleus of an intestinal cell of another frog and the egg developed, generating a fertile adult frog—a genetic twin of the frog that donated the nucleus. In this way, numerous male and female adult, fertile frogs were obtained." Cited from Finch, J. 2008: A Nobel Fellow on Every Floor: A History of the Medical Research Council Laboratory of Molecular Biology. Icon Books for the MRC-LMB, Cambridge, p.196.

---

[3]Father Theodore M. Hesburgh was Chair of the U.S. Commission on Civil Rights from 1969 to 1972.

To Robin and Sue Perutz. Salzburg, November 9, 1972

The meeting [of the European Organisation of Molecular Biology in Heidelberg] was fun as a reunion of old fogeys of Mol. Biol., and it included some good lectures, but many lecturers were handicapped by their instructions to treat the general development and future potentialities of their research, especially their methods, rather than discuss their latest results. This had a dampening effect.

I gave a talk in the Max-Planck-Institut for Physiology and was surprised to find all the bigwigs of German biochemistry there, because they were just having a meeting. My lectures are fated with technical snags. This time the microphone had a loose contact so that my voice bellowed or faded every time I moved.

The new Max-Planck-Institute at Martinsried looks like a battleship beached in a pine forest. In the lecture room scaffolding still barricaded the blackboards and my colleagues were battling against the vicissitudes of half finished labs. When I quoted Pope's dictum "Be not the first to try the new," I touched the right note.

[Robert] Huber has a marvellous new Fourier of the trypsin-pancreatic trypsin inhibitor complex which actually shows for the first time the structure of a tetrahedral intermediate in an enzymatically catalysed reaction.

The honorary degree ceremony in Salzburg droned on like the citations on Speech day. The Cardinal Archbishop König of Vienna got up to thank the University on behalf of those honoured. When my host introduced me to him before the ceremony, he slipped up and called him by the name of his politically compromised predecessor. The cardinal didn't bat an eyelid, but I was reminded of an episode during the war when Churchill sent [Geoffrey] Pyke to the Canadian Prime Minister to sell him the iceberg ship. When Pyke came into the presence, the elderly P.M. greeted him warmly with the words "Mr. Chamberlain has told me so much about you." The Cardinal, instead of just saying a few polite words of thanks, treated his audience to a pompous 10 minute sermon. This stung me to ask for permission to add a few words. I began with, "I don't much like solemnity. Here I feel like a young man, who has long been captivated by a charming girl, and suddenly realises that she isn't indifferent to him."[4] I ended with a eulogy of Salzburg and expressed my delight that my love had at last embraced me. Half the audience rushed up to me to say that I had spoken the first human

---

[4]Translated from the German.

words this morning, but when I ran into the Cardinal afterwards he looked the other way.

The Salzburg students to whom I lectured afterwards were a cheerful and responsive audience. Which reminds me of a remark made by Michael Levitt, a brilliant student of ours who has just finished his Ph.D. When we were having a meeting at Heidelberg to discuss the organisation of the future EMBO lab, he got up to say that at the MRC lab everyone, Chairman, scientific staff, postdocs and students, were equal. To this one cynic replied that he expected some of these people to be more equal than others, but Michael retorted: "It's the students who are more equal." This, coming from a student, is the nicest tribute I've ever had.

To Gisela Perutz. Nearing Montreal, May 25, 1973

I got my second glimpse of Greenland today, viewed off its southern tip. Saucers of widely spaced ice on the sea in the foreground and crowding up against the shore further back. Deep fjords cutting into the land which is covered by range upon range of black mountains. Further back banks of mist hid the ice cap from our view which was a pity. A spectacular scene all the same. At the departure gate the Air Canada stewardess, on perceiving my distinguished appearance (even before she saw your nice haircut at the back) at once changed my economy boarding pass for a first class one. So here I am turning down smoked salmon and champagne, but much enjoying the luxury of a wide and comfortable chair. I sit next to a chatty old Irish lady. When she saw that I lived on a diet she proceeded to tell me of all her friends' diets. However, more interestingly, she was struck how prosperous the countryside in Southern Ireland had become since her childhood there.

We are just flying over Quebec City reminding me of [Hermann] Bondi's and [Klaus] Fuchs' lectures and Heini Granichstaedten's tactful and considerate companionship and [Heinz] Meyerhof telling me that I will become a great scientist one day, which had never occurred to me, and lying on my back on hot starlit nights watching the beams of Northern Lights flashing up and extinguishing in the sky.

To Gisela Perutz. Baltimore–Seattle, June 2, 1973

My progress all this week consisted of preparing a lecture, going to a lab, listening to accounts of people's work, giving the lecture, listening to accounts of people's work and back to preparing a lecture. However, it is still far more profitable to visit American universities than it is to travel to European ones. At every place I heard of interesting new work, had useful comments on my own work and fixed up collaboration on one problem or another. Away from the centres of the big cities, life is outwardly as peaceful as in Switzerland and you are still struck by the American genius for making things practical and easy. People complain of inflation, but no worse than they used to. The market for chemists and physicists is improving again but many have found they can make better money by servicing household gadgets. As in Hungary, plumbers are the new aristocracy.

To Gisela Perutz. Battelle, Seattle Research Center, June 4, 1973

Now I must tell you about my marvellous weekend in the mountains. We drove for about 1.5 hours through wooded hills, and real meadows with real cows (not factories making the imitation cream powder now used for coffee) to [Hans] Neurath's cabin which lies in a tall pine forest just inside Rainier National Park. Next morning we drove into another valley and then started climbing up a little forest trail. It might have been in the Alps but for the size of the trees: massive firs stretching 100–150 ft into the sky. After an hour and a half of climbing through the wood we emerged on a promontory from which I could see range upon range of wooded mountains about 2000–2500 m high, some wooded, others topped by spectacular volcanic rock pinnacles and to the west of us hung a large cloud covering Mt. Rainier. We now got into snow and I found myself bricking steps up a long steep slope to a ridge and finally making my way to the top at about 1900 m. As we sat by the fire services' observation hut, the clouds parted revealing a glacier behind where I expected the sky to be. On the way down the curtain lifted first in one place and then in another until it finally showed us the whole of this incredible mountain, like a Mont Blanc in the Steyermark, towering 2000 m above every other one around. Imagine standing on top of the Loser and having the Dachstein twice as close and 1500 m higher, its icy apron glistening in the sun.

To Gisela, Vivien, Sue, and Robin. Battelle, Seattle Research Center, June 8, 1973

I gave a lecture on my spectroscopic work this afternoon and was pleased that [Martin] Gouterman did not tear it to pieces, but then he is not fiery and temperamental like [Bob] Williams and clearly had never pinned his own hopes on solving haem-haem interaction. Earlier today I talked to the local haematologists who are part of a medical genetics group. They have just discovered that 1/5 of patients hospitalised with coronary attacks have a genetic trait that makes for high cholesterol and triglycerate (fat) content in the serum, and so makes them more prone to such attacks; this could be discovered early and the attacks prevented by a suitable diet. Yesterday was spent with the protein crystallographers who have solved several interesting structures and have also developed new methods of refining atomic positions. It really is worthwhile to go and see people's protein models because it makes me notice features which I had never spotted in their published pictures. One of these models gave me an interesting new idea which I hope to take up when I return.

To Robin Perutz, October 21, 1973

Following your advice I think I geared my lecture to the CU Chem. Soc. just right. The general discussion continued until after 10.00, and then a few indefatigables still argued with me until 10.30. People made some very good comments, especially one young man who looked Malaysian, and said to me, "if the change in spin state of the iron provides the trigger for the RT transition, then it is obvious thermodynamically that the RT transition in turn must change the tension at the haem."[5] He must be a very brilliant young man to see immediately what I have been unable to drum into the heads of any of my thick-headed colleagues in the haemoglobin field. The only other person who saw the force of this argument has been Michael Levitt.

To Felix Haurowitz, December 8, 1973

Recently I had occasion to read all your old and not so old papers on denaturation of haemoglobin by alkali, because I had an idea which explains why haemoglobins of different species are denatured at very different rates even though they all have the same structure. The answer is quite simple, and I have written it up for *Nature*. I shall send you a preprint presently—I was

---

[5]Max based his theory on the two-state mechanism of Monod, Changeux and Wyman, where haemoglobin could exist in one of two structural states, T (tense, the deoxy state) and R (relaxed, the oxy state). The structural change was termed the RT transition.—AW

terribly pleased when I discovered that your own findings and those of others were all consistent with my idea.[6]

At the moment I am in the middle of a piece of detective work aimed at finding the still missing Bohr group in human haemoglobin. Following in [David] Keilin's footsteps I find optical spectroscopy a useful tool. Combined with a detailed knowledge of the classic structure of a protein it is very powerful indeed. So with any luck I might send you another preprint before too long.

To Felix Haurowitz, December 26, 1973

We are having a very gemütlich [pleasant/relaxed] Christmas with all our children at home—fortunately some at least of our trains are still running so that Robin and Sue were able to come down from Newcastle. Luckily the MRC is exempted from the 3-day week work order, provided we reduce our electricity consumption by at least 35%, which we just about managed to do by switching off the elevators, air conditioners, ovens, etc. However, the general situation is still very unnerving, not because of the oil shortage, but because the mineworkers' union and the Government by failing to reach a compromise are forcing the country to commit economic suicide.[7]

I gravely fear that scientific research will not survive the poverty which this will inflict on the country. However, everything around still looks so normal and cheerful that it is hard to imagine the magnitude of the disaster beyond the abyss or to believe in it.

---

[6]Max noted that the rate of alkali denaturation in bovine haemoglobin is slower than that of human foetal haemoglobin, which in turn is dramatically slower than that of human adult haemoglobin. He postulated that the differences arise from buried side chains that can become charged in alkali by loss of a proton. Human adult haemoglobin has three such groups at the contacts between α- and β-chains, human foetal has one, and bovine has no such groups. He also looked at other primate species and found that their sequence was also consistent with his theory.—Robin Perutz

[7]When the Conservatives came to power in June 1970, they had hastily put through an ambitious but flawed industrial relations bill, aimed at encouraging legally binding agreements and strengthening union control over their rank and file, while preserving individual liberty. Heath and his colleagues had hoped to win consensus. Instead, hostility to this bill played a part in provoking a series of strikes by key workers, who won wage increases of 9–20% with no compensating productivity deals. That induced the Government to revert to the statutory pay and price controls they had hoped to avoid. Max's letter dates from the union response to this, a second strike by the miners with its consequent threat to power supplies. Economically Britain was on its knees: there was rising unemployment and galloping inflation, the pound had been floated, and Rolls Royce and the Upper Clyde Shipbuilders had been bailed out at huge cost to the exchequer, and now production was lower than ever.

To Lotte and Franz Perutz. Syracuse, Sicily, April 16, 1974

We read several books about Sicily last winter, but none of them prepared us for what we were going to find. We expected sunshine, warmth, Greek temples, Baroque churches, Norman mosaics, a barren landscape, beggars and hungry faces, and at Palermo University, provincial mediocrity.

Only the architecture and the mosaics conformed to our expectations; as they are what attracted us in the first place, I shall begin by telling you about them. When you look at pictures of Greek temples or theatres, they all look much the same, but the reality has a grandeur that touches your heart. Each of them is built in a position where you could imagine that a god would want to live: on a hill overlooking a range of lovely valleys and mountains, or on a promontory on a beautiful stretch of coast. The best of them has proportions that even Michelangelo could not have improved upon: there is something absolute about its perfection and simplicity. I have never been to Delphi, but its theatre could hardly be in a more beautiful position than the one at Segesta on a hillside some 2000 ft up and overlooking the coast. It must have been marvellous for the Greeks to see their tragedies enacted against this setting.

In the 1950s archaeologists uncovered the remains of a luxurious imperial residence [Piazza Armerina] of the 3rd to 4th century AD high up in the interior of Sicily. This has become one of the prize attractions, better in some ways than Pompeii. It contains perhaps 25 rooms, the floors of which are covered with an exuberant wealth of mosaics, depicting hunting, chil-

Roman mosaic at Piazza Amerina of girls in bikinis playing ball. (Source, http://commons.wikimedia.org/wiki/Image:Casale_Bikini.jpg.)

dren at school and at play, girls in bikinis playing ball, African animals being taken on board galleys and unloaded, presumably for the circus at Rome, and scenes showing the layout of the villa itself with its gardens and ornamental ponds. I found this of great historic as well as artistic interest.

The Baroque architecture dates from the late 17th century when many towns were rebuilt after a terrible earthquake. It is quite unlike Austrian and German Baroque and at its best, most graceful and original. Only at Syracuse has a real effort been made to restore historic buildings to their former splendour. This is a terrible pity, because many of the towns lie in superbly picturesque positions, having been built, fortress like, at the top and around the flanks of steep hills, dominated by a cathedral on the summit. So you drive up the steep road to the town filled with expectations, only to find a gigantic slum, a labyrinth of narrow lanes with outwardly decayed houses, broken rusty balconies, peeling paint, dogs sifting through garbage that was not collected, or collected in so slovenly a way that half of it was left to litter the streets and blow about in the wind; it putrefies and stinks to high heaven. Suddenly you come upon the remnants of a palace with a graceful portico and beautifully carved balconies beneath its broken windows. Your disappointment mounts until, turning a corner, you see a church that has been restored and through a hole in the racing clouds is lit up by the sun; the beauty of the scene instantly changes your mood and you feel that it was worth coming after all, because here is something quite uniquely lovely.

I said *outwardly* decayed houses, because a glance through the window may show new furniture and modern appliances; each roof sprouts its TV aerial, everyone looks well nourished and dressed. Palermo has 1 car for every 5 inhabitants. Yet in the towns that were destroyed by an earthquake in 1967, the people still live in army huts, not because there is no money to rebuild them, but because the money that was collected for the purpose had never been spent, the Italian administrative machine being totally paralysed by a labyrinth of antiquated rules that nullify the intentions of Parliament and Government alike.

To Robin Perutz, December 1, 1974

Bob Ladner has at last finished his refinement of horse met[Hb] and HbCO [carbonmonoxyhaemoglobin],[8] the continuation of Betsy [Heidner's] work,

---

[8]Heidner, E.J., Ladner, R.C., and Perutz, M.F. 1976. Structure of horse carbonmonoxyhaemoglobin. *J. Mol. Biol* **104:** 707–722.

and came out with a startling result. In the high spin metHb the SH group of Cys93β lies as indicated in black on the attached picture, but in the low spin HbCO it swings about the α-β carbon bond and now lies in the tyrosine pocket. In this position it would come within 1 Å of the phenolic ring of Tyr-145 whence the ring must be out of the pocket.

This proves a vital part of my *Nature* 1970 mechanism for which I have been seeking evidence for the last 4 years, namely that transition of the haem to lower spin is directly coupled to the expulsion of the penultimate tyrosine and rupture of the C-terminal salt bridges. It also explains certain anomalous ESR and NMR results obtained by [Harden M.] McConnell and [Michael A.] Raftery which have been quoted as evidence *against* me, which now turn out to be *for* me. You can imagine how pleased I am.[9]

To Robin and Sue Perutz, January 19, 1975

Another development which pleased me is the thwarting of a general MRC Technical Officer strike, which ASTMS [Association of Scientific, Technical, and Managerial Staffs] tried to order for tomorrow, by our own staff. They got wind of it, held a meeting at which they passed a resolution that they were not prepared to strike and sent David Battison (my electronics engineer) to a national meeting of the technical officers' delegates in London last Thursday. David's was the only written resolution brought to the meeting, and he won for it a majority of the votes, against the official leadership. The official leader explained to the meeting that their policy was to set the technical officers against the technicians and then to call them out on strike in turn. David B retorted that the technicians were his friends and that he would resist such an attempt to sow discord between them.

Never have I heard it so blatantly confirmed, that it was the Union's official policy to poison the atmosphere in order to win power for them-

---

[9] The 1970 mechanism emphasised the importance of the positions of these Tyr residues, because a chemical reagent that blocked their access to their binding pockets in the protein inhibited the cooperative effects in haemoglobin. As a result, the salt bridges that stabilise the deoxy structure could not be formed. The high-resolution structures reported here provided proof that was missing in the earlier paper. Max also needed physical and chemical experiments to validate his conclusions from X-ray work. One was to investigate the "spin" state of the iron (using a technique called ESR spectroscopy). There is a change of spin on the iron when oxygenation occurs reflecting the movement of the iron atom into the plane of the porphyrin ring. Hence, the number of references to spin in these letters.—AW

selves. I was quite surprised by the character and skill shown by David Battison in defeating this nefarious plan, and greatly pleased that my policy of always being nice to people should have turned the scales at a decisive moment. However, it will be a continuing battle, and the personnel officers at the MRC are not really helping me—they are a bunch of small-minded clerks.

When I was peacefully mounting crystals of human foetal Hb for Jim Frier the other day, Margaret [Brown] rushed in saying Buckingham Palace wanted me. After telling her to say I had no time, I managed to extricate myself from my nitrogen box, to hear that the Queen would receive me in private audience on 12 Feb and give me my CH.[10] Since then I have asked Alan Hodgkin[11] and Dorothy what it was like to get the OM [Order of Merit] and have been reassured that the Queen made it extremely nice and easy. [Peter] Medawar said it was one of the pleasantest 20 minutes he has had. The Palace also instructed me to wear a morning coat; this is a pity because I shall feel foolish in such fancy dress.

To P. Moore, Deputy Private Secretary to Her Majesty the Queen, February 14, 1975

Please thank Her Majesty for receiving me so graciously on Wednesday morning and for taking so much interest in my work. Only after I had left her did I realise that she had made me talk away like an excited little boy about my own doings and that I never asked her anything about hers.

I hope that the Queen will enjoy Charlie Chaplin's autobiography. Walking all alone through the crowds outside, past the changing guards, across the great Palace Yard, to be received by Her Majesty in private audience, made me feel rather like Charlie Chaplin myself.

To Robin and Sue Perutz, March 28, 1975

At the lab my technical officers came to tell me about another meeting of the ASTMS Committee where the Union leaders reported deadlock in their negotiations with the MRC over technical officer salaries. In the mean time the MRC technicians have won a huge wage award which has eroded the

---

[10]The award of the Companion of Honour had been announced earlier.

[11]Alan Hodgkin was the cousin of Dorothy's husband Thomas. Alan and Dorothy were both OMs.

differential between them and the technical officers, to the latters' resentment. The technicians now get nearly as much as the scientists and the top of their scale almost equals a university professor's pay. The [scientists'] pay is linked to the university scales which the AUT [Association of University Teachers] is vainly trying to raise. I am also faced with a revolt of my younger scientific staff.

Scientifically all is well here. Bob Ladner showed me his new 2.0 Å Fourier of the old horse metHb. It is beautifully clear and solves most of the stereochemical problems which the 2.8 Å Fourier had left in the air. My Japanese student [Kiyoshi Nagai] had done a crucial experiment demonstrating the effect of spin state of ferric haems on the oxygen affinity of ferrous ones in valency hybrids. However, I was upset by two papers by [Quentin H.] Gibson et al., submitted on the heels of my *Biochemistry* papers and scorning all my conclusions: IHP [inositol hexaphosphate] does not convert metHb to the T state, does not affect tension at the haems, etc. It's mostly nonsense, but why are people so venomous about my ideas? My

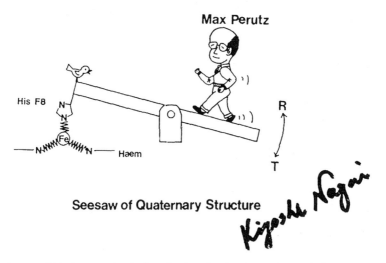

A caricature of Max's stereochemical mechanism showing the tension at the haem as portrayed by Kiyoshi Nagai. As Max wrote in his letter of 21 October 1973, the high spin state pushes the iron atom out of the haem plane triggering the transition from the relaxed oxygenated state to the tense deoxygenated state. This in turn changes the tension at the haem; in other words, the mechanism resembles a see-saw. This letter explains that Max believed correctly that IHP changes tension at the haem. (Courtesy of Kiyoshi Nagai.)

mechanism is so obviously right and intellectually satisfying that people who try to disprove it only stand to lose, yet they pour their gall on it as though I had proposed something obscene.

To Gisela, Vivien, Robin and Sue Perutz. Riverside, California
February 25, 1976

We arrived at Riverside to find a neat well-kept university campus with delightful architecture. All the buildings are in warm pink brick and white concrete, designed imaginatively, so that no two of them are alike, yet they all harmonise. They are scattered over a park and partly hidden by trees, so that the sites never look crowded. I must try and get pictures. Every building is well proportioned—I wish Oxbridge college architects would come here to learn—but probably they wouldn't notice the difference between their clumsy buildings and these graceful constructions—certainly my architect [Edward] Purefoy wouldn't.

To Gisela, Vivien, Robin and Sue Perutz. Santa Barbara,
March 1, 1976

The night before I had the more difficult task of making the formal after-dinner speech in honour of [Linus] Pauling to 250 guests, mostly former students and associates plus wives or husbands. Max Delbrück also spoke, because they had asked him to take over, on the principle as he put it, "that one Max is as good as another." I went to visit Pauling in the afternoon at the beautiful house on a mountainside above Pasadena which he had built in the shape of an amide group [see Max's diagram], the wings being set at the exact angles of the chemical bonds that allowed him to predict the structure of the α-helix (lächerliche Schmocherei [a ridiculous conceit]). I asked him why he missed the accompanying change in radius of the iron atom, to which he replied that he never thought of it! On rereading his book *No More War* I had been struck by his faith in human reason. Later I wondered whose spirit his book reflected and suddenly, early one morning, it came back to me: Bertrand Russell's. As soon as I thought of it, I was struck by other similarities between the two men, which again you

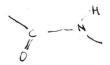

will find in my speech—except for their common vanity which I discreetly omitted. So I asked Pauling about his relations with Russell. He told me that he tried to read *Principia Mathematica* as a young man, but soon gave up and decided that this kind of mathematical logic was not for him. He then described how they both came to London for the sit down in Trafalgar Square against atomic weapons and later how they sat together outside the Old Bailey trying to testify for the people who had been arrested there, but were frustrated because the judge ruled against their being called as witnesses for the defence. As happens so often, his talks with Russell had been mostly concerned with the practical matters of the anti-bomb campaign, and they hardly touched upon the fundamental outlook which I believe they shared.

I then told Pauling how sad it was that the disarmament campaign had run out of steam. What he says in his book is as relevant today as it was in the fifties, yet everything that can be said has been said so often that people have become indifferent to the sound and the words themselves have died out.

One of the people attending the celebration was Lynn Hoard from Cornell, a crystallographer who does beautiful X-ray work on small haem-like complexes. I had a useful talk with him yesterday morning, talking about a strange contortion which [Tsuni] Takano found in myoglobin and was relieved to hear that this was not unique.

Today I had hoped to spend at the University here where a geophysicist, Michael Fuller, possesses the supersensitive magnetic balance on which I want to do my measurements.

Linus Pauling's 75th birthday party. Pauling (left), Max Delbrück (centre), and Max (right).

To Gisela, Vivien, Robin and Sue Perutz. University of California, Riverside, March 3, 1976

My lectures are much appreciated which encourages me to make them even better—the main trick is not to lecture at, but to talk to the people. Tomorrow night I shall give a party for my students so that they can talk to me—as I do in Cambridge.

To Robin and Sue Perutz, April 4, 1976

We listened to [Aleksandr] Solzhenitsyn's speech on the BBC and were most disappointed. Most of it is a diatribe about the moral decline of Britain which consists in not stemming the advance of socialist tyranny in other countries. He even blames Britain for being one of the first to recognise the Communist regime in China. He has no idea about Britain's comparative success in building a socialist society which has preserved personal liberty. His speech is fodder to all the reactionaries who bolster up fascist regimes as bulwarks against communism. Any more of his speeches and I shall become an active member of the Labour Party! Like so many other moralists S has no set of values to put in place of the ones he deplores.

To Gisela, Vivien, Robin and Sue Perutz. Rome, June 26, 1976

Perhaps because she is so unfussy, Gerda [Blau] is a most agreeable and easy-going hostess who never makes her guests feel guilty. The evening I arrived we went out for a walk on the Campidoglio, but found the approaches blocked by hundreds of cars blowing their horns. Up on the hill Marcus Aurelius[12] carried the red flag as his banner and a crowd of youths milled around singing what I took to be the Internationale and chanting: "Rome is red today and Italy will be tomorrow." This is a new kind of proletariat which has more to lose than their chains—most of them got to the Campidoglio "in macchina" [by car], but Gerda remarked sadly "they think that they will get jobs now but [Enrico] Berlinguer[13] can't create them either." She gave me a lucid account of party politics. To you the most interesting facet may be the Communists' success at attracting some of the most brilliant and respected people here by offering them safe seats as *indepen-*

[12]The equestrian bronze statue of the Roman emperor.
[13]Secretary general of the Italian Communist Party.

dent members of parliament. In this way they have persuaded many intelligent people to vote for them as the party of reform rather than revolution.

To Robin and Sue Perutz. Dahlem, March 17, 1977

At Schering I had a disappointingly small audience for what I expected to be of big interest to the hundreds of scientists employed there, but most of the people who did attend looked attentive. In a way the talk was most interesting to me, because I found that evidence in favour of the analogy between the mechanism of mutagenesis in bacteria and carcinogenesis in animals has strengthened since I wrote the *Nature* article. In addition, a unity has emerged between several apparently disconnected micro-biological phenomena which I found very exciting, because they point to a common mechanism and begin to suggest what kind it might be. So, as so often, I groaned at having to prepare yet another lecture, but then found the subject so fascinating that I enjoyed getting to know it and having to chisel it so as to make it clear to others.

At Schering's I found scientists worried about the future of pharmaceutical research. The cost of research per marketable product is rising all the time, which increases the pressure to which the scientists are subjected by the management. This is partly due to the increase in sophistication, and partly to the public's demand for safety, which you and I regard as justified, but which our colleagues inside the fence find paralysing, because it is absolute. They point out that no drugs are absolutely safe, that their risks must be balanced against those of not using them, and they feel that the public's demand for absolute safety is impossible to fulfil and puts their profession at risk.

To Robin and Sue Perutz. Bellagio, April 25, 1977

All the gardens in Rome are beautiful at this time, with chestnuts and other trees in flower and the grass looking fresh and green. Here the hotel has a subtropical garden in which tulips, peonies, clematis and roses are all flowering at the same time, not to forget azaleas. Rome is marvellous. Wherever you walk you come across some picturesque alley or some lovely square or a marvellous church, and you can easily get away from the din of traffic if you keep off the main arteries. On Sunday morning even these were relatively quiet.

As far as my throat is concerned I should have stayed in Cambridge, but as far as the magnetic work is concerned my visit was essential. It turns out that none of the results reported in the draft paper is quite right or quite complete; I would never have gathered this without coming here. The effects, when correctly presented, will turn out to be even more spectacular than they had appeared in the first draft. I also rewrote the paper on the magnetic effects entirely before starting off from Cambridge comparing the behaviour of haemoglobin with that of synthetic compounds in thermal spin equilibria. My Italian colleagues had never read the modern literature—neither would I have done if you had not sent me some of the key references. My colleagues have built these marvellous magnetometers, but they lack chemists to supply them with interesting compounds, so that their instruments are under-employed.[14]

On my last evening Gerda kindly asked all my friends and colleagues for drinks. My friends were much upset by the shooting that had taken place at the University the previous evening, perpetrated by left wing extremists whose main object is said to be violence for its own sake. I was interested to find a poster issued by the Italian Communist Party here in Bellagio this morning condemning the murder of the policeman by the left wing extremists and avowing the Party's opposition to all forms of violence.

To Robin and Sue Perutz. Bellagio, April 26, 1977

This afternoon I went for a heavenly walk up on the hills behind this little town. Through deciduous woods full of fresh green leaves or catkins and even flowering shrubs, through meadows thick with forget-me-nots and cowslips and anemones and violets including some flowers I have never seen before. And each opening of the trees affords views over the lake and the snow-capped mountains behind. I rested by a farm with cows eating the grass under flowering fruit trees and felt the warm sun dissolving the blockage in my left ear which had kept bothering me. It was perfect bliss.

I walked up though the steep woods and down steep paths without feeling my hip. This cheered me enormously. The walking, the hot sunshine and the gorgeous scenery have all conspired to shake off the depression that has

---

[14]In a letter of 26 June 76, Max had written: The magnetometer is a huge, complex, home-built machine, designed by Massimo Cerdonio, a delightful and really excellent young Associate Professor of Physics at the University of Rome, and run by Callogeno Messana, a tall, burly Sicilian with curly black hair and black stubbles who looks like a brigand but does his work with gentle meticulous care. The measurements occupy Messana and his two technicians continuously. I am very lucky to have encountered such enthusiasm for my problems that these people are willing to work all out on them for two weeks.

hung over me and given me hope that I shall also regain my voice before too long. Being unable to talk is almost as frustrating as not being able to walk.[15]

To Robin Perutz, May 10, 1977

Your letter about the NO_2 MetHb arrived just in time for a visit by W.S. Caughey, the ir [infrared] spectroscopist from Colorado who did the NOHb at my suggestion. I would not be able to measure the ir spectra of the NO_2 at Norwich because the spectrometer there lacks a temperature control, and this derivative must be kept at 0°. So Caughey's visit was most welcome and he was delighted to take up the challenge of finding the NO_2 bands, since he had after all found the O_2 stretching frequency at approximately 1150 cm^{-1}.

Messana's results from the measurements done after I left Rome arrived this week and fulfil my most sanguine hopes. I never expected such large magnetic differences between R and T states as have now shown up. For instance OCN MetHb in both the R and T states of human Hb is almost pure low spin, which is why I could not find any difference in χ [symbol for magnetic susceptibility] by NMR with [Chien] Ho in 1975; the T state of carp is largely high spin.[16]

To Robin and Sue Perutz, June 9, 1977

During the weekend I read another chapter that Horace[17] has produced on the French school of molecular biology. It's a real scientific thriller; it is quite astonishing how he has mastered the intricate web of experiments which led to the discovery of the operon and the feedback control of enzyme biosynthesis. He presents the science with all its disappointments, false clues, initial misunderstandings and often totally unexpected experimental results, yet conveys the powerful logic of the French group that kept them on the right trail, uncovering the mechanism step by step. Also

---

[15]The improvement did not last and Max decided he had to return home next day. He had strained his vocal chords by lecturing with laryngitis brought on by an allergy to cigarette smoke which he had developed. His problem was eventually diagnosed as "parson's throat" and cured with the help of a speech therapist who taught him to speak using his lips: he had endlessly to recite "many miners make more money." In the summer of 1976 Max had injured his back which gave him pains in his hip and often made walking painful.

[16]See the cartoon by Kiyoshi Nagai, p. 16.

[17]The draft of Judson's *Eighth Day of Creation*.

the people are very well portrayed and of course emerge from the transcripts of Horace's interviews which he skilfully intersperses with the accounts of the work.

To Robin Perutz, June 15, 1977

I sent you the magnetic results. They don't really need any explanation: aren't they fantastic? But how odd that whatever spin state is reached at about 200° K remains frozen in.

What put me on the track of my present experiments on the acid Bohr effect were reports of a diminished acid Bohr effect in foetal human Hb. I then guessed that of the 40 odd amino acid differences between adult and foetal, one specific histidine was likely to be responsible for the effect and checked 2 abnormal Hbs, one in which that histidine is replaced and another in which a neighbouring lysine is replaced, to test my theory. As a final check I decided to repeat the experiments in foetal Hb reported in the literature and asked [Hermann] Lehmann for a sample which he promptly provided.

Yesterday I started the measurements which showed immediately that the acid Bohr effect of Hb is normal. So all my fabric of theories was in shreds and I spent an unhappy night. This morning I remembered that there was a characteristic difference in O.D. 290 nm/O.D. 538 nm between adult and foetal human Hb. So I measured those ratios and found that Lehmann had given me the wrong Hb! I hope to sleep better tonight.[18]

To Robin and Sue Perutz, August 8, 1977

I enclose H.G. Wells' biography which I found very interesting from beginning to end. I have now begun to read Einstein's correspondence with [Max] Born which [Manfred] Eigen gave me last winter and was disappointed to see that Einstein's opposition to quantum mechanics stemmed from his own failure to develop a theory to account for quantum effects.[19]

---

[18]Max needed to account for the Bohr effect (enhancement of release of oxygen by carbon dioxide and acidification) by identifying the residues in the protein that were implicated and his work had suggested a particular histidine residue.—AW

[19]Einstein famously defined quantum entanglement as "spukhafte Fernwirkung" or "spooky action at a distance."

I have found so often that failure to discover the right solution turns scientists into cranks: that is to say they do not have the strength of character to admit that they were wrong or that someone else succeeded where they failed. Rather than admit it, they withdraw into lifelong opposition to the new advance and so cut themselves off from the mainstream of scientific thought. I had always believed that Einstein was a great enough man to see through and overcome his emotional bias and am sad to find that this is not true.

There is some basic similarity between this story and one about H.G. Wells. In 1915 H.G. Wells lived with Rebecca West. At about this time he wrote a book which contained a vicious attack on Henry James as an artist. There was some truth in Wells' criticism, yet James had been Wells' lifelong friend, patron and counsellor, and was deeply hurt, but too much of a gentleman to retaliate. Dickson relates that this episode coincided with Rebecca West's writing an admiring biography of Henry James. Incidentally, that book is much recommended by Dickson and is one of the next ones I want to read.

To Robin Perutz, August 9, 1977

After I had written that note about Einstein and Wells, I received a preprint from [James P.] Collman telling of an experiment designed to test my tension theory of haem-haem interaction. So Collman concludes that his experiments "provide evidence on a molecular level that the Monod-Perutz mechanism is viable."

I am thrilled by this result, as it does corroborate my ideas in a model system which any chemist can understand, and should convince many of the neutral sceptics of the validity of my mechanism. I doubt that it will cut any ice with [Brian] Hoffmann, [Robert] Shulman and other active opponents of mine for the reasons set out in my note about Einstein.

By the same mail I had a letter from Chien Ho about an experiment that confirms my ideas about how the stereochemical change at the iron atom is transmitted to the penultimate tyrosine. So yesterday was a red letter day.

To Robin and Sue Perutz, June 23, 1978

Next morning we took the train to Brussels [from Paris], an ordinary 2nd class express but very luxurious by our standards. We shared our compart-

Selected Letters: 1970s   *363*

ment with 2 Walloon Belgian couples returning from Spain who spent a large part of the time abusing the Flemish. We were shocked at their bitter groundless hatred. Why are men no better than rats who murder any rat that does not smell like their clan?

To John T. Edsall, August 22, 1978

I also complained to you about not having heard from *Science*, but had a letter today that my lecture had gone to press. However, they deleted the first page with my tribute to you and put it as a note at the end of the article—I suppose it would have detracted from the dry as dust atmosphere of impersonal science. Their decision reminded me of the one time editor of the *Journal of Glaciology* who wanted to delete a joke in one of my articles, because it would debase the scientific tone of his journal.

One night Gisela and I boarded an overcrowded compartment of a train in Vienna when a man jumped up and introduced himself as the editor of the *Journal of Irreproducible Results.* We had a hilarious evening with him—I wish he were on the editorial staff of *Science,* but alas, his home was in Israel.

To John T. Edsall, October 29, 1978

Here we had a dinner to celebrate [Fred] Sanger's 60th birthday. Rod Porter made a nice speech describing his early work with Fred who never calculates anything and would produce sheets of paper with smudges, say-

ing this spot is this, and that spot is that, and being invariably right. Fred got up to say how pleased he was that all these professors came to honour him, because *he was just a chap who messes around in the lab!*

Fred Sanger had won the Nobel Prize in Chemistry in 1958 for determining the sequence of the amino acids in a molecule of insulin, thereby inventing a method that could be applied to other proteins. He would win a second time in 1980 for finding a method of sequencing DNA.

To Vivien, Robin and Sue Perutz. Hawaii, April 4, 1979

UCLA and Pasadena were most interesting and stimulating. In the middle of the afternoon somebody asked me if I was not tired after listening to so many people. I replied, truthfully, that I tire only if people bore me. The drive and brilliance that go into research here are fantastic.

To Gisela Perutz and Family. Pasadena, April 15, 1979

I wish you had all been with me last night to hear [Carlo Maria] Giulini conduct at the Los Angeles Music Center. It's one thing to see him on TV and quite a different order of experience to be there. For a start, the Music Center is such a marvellous piece of modern architecture that it gives you a great thrill just to approach and enter it. I now appreciate what you had kept telling me, Vivien, the great difference between hearing these pieces at home and in a concert hall. Just the sound of the music was tremendous, and I enjoyed [Paul] Hindemith evoking the temptation of St. Anthony with sinister discords in a way I would never have done at home. When it came to the Emperor Concerto, tears of emotion came to my eyes. E.H. . . , whom I had invited to the concert, uttered not one word of appreciation. I am not sure whether the concert failed to lift him out of his stupor or whether he was unable to express any enjoyment he might have felt.

Max Delbrück dropped in for a chat. He seemed well considering his illness and quite delightful to talk to as always. I told him the *Nature* story of Einstein and Paul Valéry, and to my surprise Delbrück did not even smile. Instead, he told me the real story which he had heard immediately afterwards (in 1927) from an attaché of the German Embassy in Paris who had been a former student of Delbrück's father, the historian, and who had witnessed the conversation. Paul Valéry tried to explain something to Einstein and asked him for a notebook so that he could write it down. When Einstein said that he carried no notebook, Valéry asked whether he did not need one to write down his ideas. Einstein replied: "Je n'ai jamais des idées; je fais des calculs." ["I never have ideas; I do calculations."]

To Robin and Sue Perutz. Naples–London, October 16, 1979

This time I taught molecular biology to a cardinal! As Mummy and I walked through the streets of Rome on Monday morning we saw posters on the walls announcing a symposium on Medicine and Morals at the Italian National Research Council, with myself as the first speaker on the Medical Implications of Molecular Biology. When I got there at the appointed hour I was collared by a man from the Vatican Radio who asked for my wisdom on the present hopes and dangers of science for mankind, and then by the Italian Television on the dangers of molecular biology. He was disconcerted when I replied that I could not think of any. To their further embarrassment, I then proceeded to eat my usual cheese and banana to stoke up for the lecture ahead.[20] When I had swallowed these, they conducted me to another anteroom where I was introduced to Cardinal Poletti and Bishop Angelini who chaired the meeting for the Catholic Medical Foundation. By now it was long past the starting time and I insisted on going into the lecture room to arrange my papers. It was huge and to my consternation about a third full of nuns. I wanted to start my lecture but we were still waiting for the Minister of Education or one of his minions.

When at last he arrived, I thought that after a few introductory remarks I would be launched on my lecture, but instead I had to listen to three long speeches, the first by the education guy, the next by the Cardinal and the third by the Bishop. I couldn't understand them, but afterwards an Italian student remarked that he couldn't either—he could understand the words, that is, but not their meaning. I found both these clerics "unsympatisch" [i.e. he did not take to them]. When I told an Italian friend about them afterwards, he said that the Cardinal was even talked of as a candidate for the papacy. At that time someone said: "If Cardinal Poletti becomes pope, I shall believe in the Holy Spirit." "Why?" "Because no man would have chosen him."

Anyway, having been told the meeting would start at 5.00 pm, I was finally allowed to speak at 6.15, by which time the audience was tired. I talked in Italian, because I suspected that few of the medical men or nuns would understand me in English, but having arrived in Rome the night before I found it hard going, and I bored the audience by being much too slow. The Bishop, a Machiavellian-looking man, remarked afterwards that I deserved another Nobel Prize for my courage in addressing the audience in Italian! I doubt that his was meant as a compliment. I wanted to talk last about the use of genetic manipulation for the diagnosis of hereditary diseases, but the Bishop stopped me because it was getting too late for the audience. My Italian friends interpreted that move as a deliberate act of censorship.

---

[20]Max suffered from low blood sugar and had to eat at regular intervals.

To Jim Gowans (Secretary, i.e., the Chief Executive, of the Medical Research Council), October 31, 1979

[Max wrote the following letter on his retirement as chairman of the MRC Laboratory for Molecular Biology. The official retirement age was 60, but Max exceptionally had been allowed to continue in post a few months beyond his 65th birthday.]

There were a few more things that I should have said to you and your colleagues in the office. Everybody has been surprised that I managed to combine my chairmanship with intensive experimental work. I owe some of this to the assistance I have received here and much to the way your office is run. Your colleagues have helped me to solve my administrative and financial problems and have always given their help in a friendly, personal way, so that I never felt I was dealing with an impersonal machine. By not inundating directors with unnecessary paper work, making them sit on futile committees, MRC Headquarters are so much more considerate to them than are university administrations to their heads of department. Finally, and perhaps most importantly for their morale, MRC Headquarters give directors the feeling that they are interested in their research and that science comes before regulations. So I should like to thank you and your colleagues for helping me to remain a working scientist throughout those 32 years, also for letting me continue to remain one now.

1980s

"I dislike any machine coming in between me and the sheet of paper. By some magic, thoughts come when I grasp my pen."

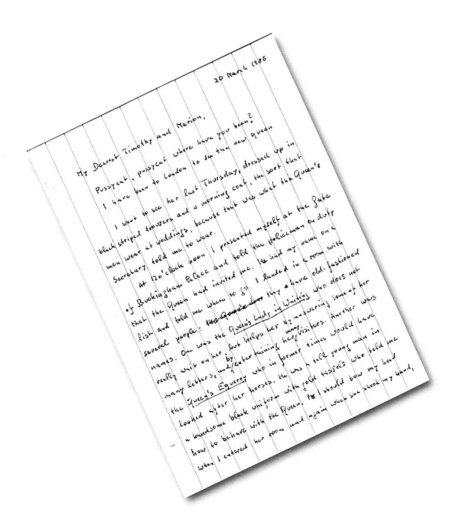

20 March 1985

My Dearest Timothy and Marion,

Pussycat, pussycat where have you been?
I have been to London to see the new queen.

I went to see her last Thursday, dressed up in black striped trousers and a morning coat, the sort that men wear at weddings, because that was what the Queen's Secretary told me to wear.

At 12 o'clock noon I presented myself at the gate of Buckingham Palace and told the policeman on duty that the Queen had invited me. He had my name on a list and told me where to go. I landed in a room with several people. One was the Queen's Lady in Waiting who does not wait on her but helps her by answering some of her many letters and/or entertaining her visitors. Another was the Queen's Equerry who in former times would have looked after her horses. He was a tall young man who told me a handsome black uniform with gold tassels. He told me how to behave with the Queen; that I would bow my head when I entered her room and again when she shook my hand,

As revealed in the letter Max wrote to Sir James Gowans on retiring from his post as chairman of the Laboratory of Molecular Biology, the Medical Research Council allowed Max to continue to work in the lab as a research scientist, which he did until 6 weeks before his death on 6 February 2002.

As before, Max continued to travel to lecture, one trip fascinatingly coinciding with the last days of the East German regime. Honours also continued to arrive. Without his administrative duties, however, he found time to write the story of his internment and of Habbakuk for *The New Yorker* and to start reviewing books. As Max's circle widened, descriptions of the people he encountered become prominent in his letters and among their most interesting passages. Fewer duties enabled him to amuse himself by corresponding at length, for example, with John Edsall, whose interests in scientific history and contemporary politics he shared, and with Lord Dacre, Master of Max's college, Peterhouse.

At home his family had expanded: he had become a grandfather and during the 1980s he began to write to his grandchildren, Timothy and Marion. Politically, the world had also changed: Margaret Thatcher had come to power in Britain in 1979 determined to get a grip on public finances, to emasculate the unions, and with a belief in top-down management. Like Ronald Reagan, she regarded military might as the best defence. Although she impressed Max, as the letter that he wrote to her on 14 January 2002 reveals, many of her policies were anathema to him and he began to protest about her policies in those cases where he thought his voice might be heard.

Alan Weeds, in the following paragraphs, gives a brief account of Max's research, which remained his top priority thoughout this decade.

In "retirement" Max's already prolific publication record accelerated: 47 papers as compared to 39 in the 1970s. Drawing on molecular structures at ever higher resolution and on spectroscopic and magnetic measurements, he continued to explore the subtle mechanics of haemoglobin, allowing him to prove its mechanism of action, as originally proposed in his 1970 papers. He also took up earlier threads to develop four novel fields of study, all originating in the ability of the haemoglobin structure to accommodate many variations in its amino acid composition. First, he demonstrated that it was possible to correlate the specific pathological symptoms arising from inherited errors in sequence with structure change at the molecular level. Second, he examined variations of haemoglobins in different species and showed how some of these changes enable the animals to adapt to their habitats and life styles. Third, he determined how particular chemicals attach to the haemoglobin molecule and modify its action, opening the way to developing drugs by this method. Finally, Kiyoshi Nagai and he began to study the effects of artificial changes in the amino acid residues on the structure and action of haemoglobin.

Many genetic mutations had been identified in human haemoglobin sequences, and Max related these to structural changes in the protein and demonstrated how they might relate to abnormal behaviour in terms of oxygen binding. He wanted to understand how genetic variants of haemoglobin give rise to specific symptoms in haemoglobin diseases. Analysis of amino acid sequences of haemoglobins and myoglobins from a wide variety of species had shown enormous variation: there were only a few amino acid residues that could not be substituted by others without harming the molecule's oxygen binding properties. Max was able to demonstrate why particular residues were critically important, while others could undergo considerable variation with negligible effect on protein structure. Since it was axiomatic that the three-dimensional structure of a protein was determined by its amino acid sequence, it was revolutionary thinking at the time to show the extent to which sequence variation was possible without loss of biological function. In the 1980s Max broadened his investigations to explore species adaptation. For example, he studied the haemoglobin from crocodiles because they are able to remain underwater for more than an hour without resurfacing to breathe, and he discovered new properties of crocodilian haemoglobin that might explain this adaptation.

Max was particularly interested in sickle cell anaemia and other diseases related to haemoglobin abnormalities; therefore he undertook experiments on haemoglobin as a potential drug receptor in the hope that this might lead to cures for some of these diseases. The development of techniques to express human proteins in bacteria led him to create mutants that could be used as tools for studying not only the haemoglobin mechanism, but also protein folding and the molecular evolution of protein structure. From the "fat innkeeper" worm to the brine shrimp, the blood clam to the earthworm, he showed how each of these species must have evolved different ways to achieve cooperative binding of oxygen, employing totally different proteins from haemoglobin, thereby as he wrote "illustrating the outstanding inventiveness of nature even at the molecular level."

To the Repository for Germinal Choice, October 7, 1980

Thank you for your letter of 7 October. I have no time to fill in your questionnaire and in any case I don't wish to donate sperm, first because I do not want to father a child by a woman I don't know and secondly because I believe that a child needs to know his father.

Apart from these scruples, let me tell you that I am small, bald, shortsighted and cross-eyed, that my testes have been exposed to X-rays these 44 years through my profession of X-ray crystallography, and that I am plagued by multiple allergies and crippled by back trouble. This shows that the winning of the Nobel Prize does not necessarily go with other desirable genetic traits.

To Steffen Peiser, October 12, 1980

Your story about [Boris Vainshtain] disgusted me. The time-serving wretch would never have got into protein crystallography but for the massive help I gave him for many years. We have been "friends" for over 20 years and he has received no end of hospitality both at my laboratory and at our home. His attempt to cut you deserves nothing but contempt and made me sign another public protest about the treatment of Russian dissidents. Another Russian friend has told me another shameful story of Vainshtain's behaviour. Vainshtain, who is half-Jewish himself, did in a Jewish crystallography student.

To Felix and Gina Haurowitz, December 6, 1980

This year I have to give one of the Christmas lectures for children at the Royal Institution which are televised nationwide. I want to start with the circulation of the blood and show the children a dynamic model of the two ventricles of the heart with their valves. In racking my brain for suitable valves, I remembered your operation and went to the local chest hospital where they have provided me with a variety of valves of the kind implanted in you and also shown me all the machinery of their heart lung device. It was all very impressive, but it also convinced me that you must have a very sound constitution to have recovered so well from it all. So next week I shall have to construct my demonstration heart and on 30 December I shall try to teach them all about that and haemoglobin in one hour. I find that Hewlett Packard now make a spectrophotometer that shows absorption spectra instantly on a CRT screen so that one can show spectral changes directly to an audience. I hope it will all work on the appointed day.

Gisela Perutz to Nelly Peiser, April 3, 1981[1]

Windsor was a really unique and a great pleasure for both of us. In the excitement my misgivings vanished. Everything right down to the tiniest details was wonderfully organised for the guests, and yet it was so tactfully and expertly managed that it felt relaxed and natural; nothing was too formal.

The first few minutes were somewhat overwhelming and very comic especially in retrospect. We weren't allowed to drive through the main gate until 10 minutes before the reception. As we drew up, the Master of the Household and several other men welcomed us, and our car was driven away. Then we were led to our suite—separate bedrooms with a sitting room in between and a bathroom and a toilet each. Two housemaids and a manservant threw themselves onto our luggage, which was not actually prepared for this, so knickers, combs, powder, etc. landed in the wrong room. Moreover, I was supposed to change into a cocktail dress in 10 minutes with all the servants milling around me.

The official reception was in a salon beautifully decorated with flowers overlooking large gardens shrouded in mist. After a while the Q appeared with her 5 dogs which lay down quietly while she and Prince Philip conversed in an informal way with a number of people. They both have particularly likeable expressions, talk in a relaxed way and like laughing. The Master of the Household decided on the right moment to present people and gave Max an opportunity to talk to the Queen.

Between the first reception and the dinner we had half an hour to get changed. My soft, delicate georgette dress with long wide sleeves was appropriate for the occasion. Only the Queen wore a formal evening dress in silver lamé. After the dinner and more conversation we were conducted through the State rooms. The most interesting things were the documents and books in the library. The librarian had prepared something of special interest for each of the guests. For Max there was a diary of Queen Victoria noting that a Professor Hoffmann had come from Göttingen and had given a most interesting lecture on chemistry on which she had made some notes. Only at 1.30 in the morning did the Queen and her husband take their leave. The next morning after a luxurious breakfast in our private apartment we drove off to resume our daily lives.

---

[1] Translated from the German.

To Lotte Perutz, April 4, 1981

I am terribly worried about the arms race, and about the gaining ground of the idea, in the USA, that a nuclear war may have to be fought, never mind if half the human race and all civilisation perish. We saw a harrowing BBC programme about Edward Teller, who clearly favours a preventive strike and has the ear of the new administration.[2] This reminds me of my conversation with the Duke of Edinburgh who did not realise that radioactivity cannot be turned off by some antidote, put out as you put out a fire. Perhaps your senile politicians don't realise this either. Here the main initiative for nuclear disarmament comes from the left, whose motives are suspect and who consequently have no influence with our government, let alone the American one. I am still searching for an organisation which does not suffer from this handicap. The Church? But which one? The head of the Methodists had quite a good letter in *The Times* on this subject.

Gisela has just written a very nice and vivid account of Windsor Castle which she let me send to you [see below].

I decided to take Iris Origo's *Merchant of Prato* to the Queen. The Master of the Household took us by the sleeve and presented us to her, as Gisela described. I told her that last time she received me I had given her a paperback, so I wanted to give her a proper book this time. She asked us what it was about and I described it to her, and then told her what a fantastic success the lab was which she had opened 19 years ago. She has a very nice way of encouraging people to talk to her—Gisela also liked her.

The food served on Meissen 1740 china was excellent.

The Queen, Duke of Edinburgh and palace staff took us on a tour of Windsor Castle which Gisela describes. The rooms are nearly all hideous to a degree, but the paintings and mementoes marvellous. In one small room I found, framed, Marlborough's letter to Queen Anne announcing his victory at Blenheim. In a showcase Gisela found Winston Churchill's handwritten instructions to General Alexander to clear the Germans out of North Africa and Alexander's later telegram to Churchill saying that this task was accomplished and asking for further instructions. A medallion with the bullet that killed Nelson at Trafalgar, a letter from Gladstone to Queen Victoria telling her that the Treasury had run out of money and that the only way of carrying on the State's business was by asking the Bank of England to print more money. This exhibit had been put out by the Librarian for the amuse-

---

[2]That of Ronald Reagan.

ment of the Chancellor of the Exchequer. I found so many interesting
things to look at that I always lagged behind the main party. Finally we were
back in a large drawing room where I was asked to sit down next to the wife
of the High Commissioner of Guyana who was deadly dull, instead of being
allowed to talk to some of the interesting people around. Opposite us the
Queen sat down with the Chancellor of the Exchequer for a long and seri-
ous-looking talk; I hope she expressed her concern over the Government's
financial policies which will soon bring the number of unemployed to 3
million. Finally the Queen rose and said good bye to all of us in turn.

To John T. Edsall, May 19, 1981

Fankuchen received me in New York the following summer [1961] with congratulations, but after listening to my lecture about our results at Columbia
his jealousy got the better of him again and in the discussion he expressed
"grave doubts" about the correctness of John's and my structures. It was one
of his characteristics that he would be charming to me in private but attack
me in the presence of others.

I often think I owe it to his discouragement of protein crystallography
in the U.S. that I had no serious competitors in my efforts to solve the structure of globular proteins. So I owe him a debt for that unwitting help. But
none of this can be said publicly.

To Victor Weisskopf, December 21, 1981

Yesterday [Carlos] Chagas, [Hermann] Brück, the Apostolic Delegate to the
Court of St James and I called on the Prime Minister [Margaret Thatcher] to
deliver the Pope's message about the medical consequences of nuclear war
and his personal letter to the Queen.[3]

Chagas first outlined the academicians' initiative intended to arouse the
Pope's concern, and the steps that led to his decision to approach the heads
of government of the nuclear powers. He assured the Prime Minister that the
Pope did not intend to weaken the Western stand on defence. He then summarised the content of the Academy memorandum and emphasised several
times the inability of medical services to help a significant fraction of those

---

[3]Weisskopf, an Austrian-American physicist, who had worked on the Manhattan Project, had been
deputed to deliver the same message to Reagan. Weisskopf, Max and Brück, who had been
interned with Max as an "enemy alien" and was now Astronomer Royal of Scotland, were all members of the Pontifical Academy of Sciences of which Chagas was the President.

injured in a nuclear conflict. Nuclear war must be avoided like the plague.

The Prime Minister replied that she had studied [Solly] Zuckerman's memorandum on the consequences of a nuclear attack with its description of the breakdown of all services on which civilised life depends. She went on to stress that even the consequences of a conventional war would be horrific; Russia was prepared to use chemical weapons, while our preparations for chemical warfare were purely defensive. Our generation had learned that there are evil men in the world. Safety can be had only by remaining strong. She was delighted by President Reagan's marvellous speech offering Russia a zero option and she hoped that this would lead to sincere negotiations on arms reduction. Yet we must be sure that such reductions are verifiable and that Russia is willing to open her frontiers. According to her secretary's record, she added that she regarded the danger of nuclear war as remote, because deterrence was working, though I do not remember her saying this. The Prime Minister said that she would pass the Pope's message to the Queen immediately. She explained that under our constitution the Prime Minister advises the Queen on her reply to a political communication from the head of a foreign government, and this she would do when she sees the Queen next week. (I did not realise that the Pope is regarded here as the head of a foreign government, and that the Queen is not free to draft her own reply.)

So much for the record. I doubt that our message made much of an impression on the Prime Minister who is firmly wedded to the increase in nuclear armaments decided upon by the Reagan administration.

At the interview with the Prime Minister I had no chance to speak. I therefore sent the attached letter to the Prime Minister today. I was disturbed by the Prime Minister's insistence that Russia must open her frontiers for inspection, since this would preclude any agreement on arms reduction from the start. I hope that this does not reflect the attitude of your administration.

To the Prime Minister, December 21, 1981

Thank you for receiving me last Friday in the somewhat incongruous guise of the Pope's messenger.

I am not sure that Professor Chagas mentioned one of the vital reasons for the scientists' deep concern. The eminent physicists who advise the Pope believe that technical developments such as the increasing accuracy of missiles, the growing vulnerability of satellites and the probable develop-ment of methods of locating submarines are likely to make the present, rel-atively stable state of mutual surveillance and deterrence obsolete. Technically each of the superpowers is already moving from a strategy of deterrence to one of destroying the other side's nuclear arsenal in a first strike. On each side there are said to be strategists who believe that a nuclear war waged in this way could be won. The scientists fear that these technical developments will lead to a situation of mutual suspicion where in an acute political crisis one side may be stampeded into pulling the nuclear trigger by fear that the other side is about to do so.

The scientists therefore suggested to the Pope that he appeal to the governments of the nuclear powers to do their utmost to bring about an agreed reduction both in the scale and quality of nuclear arms now before that unstable situation is reached.

As I said to you when I left, all my colleagues here enjoyed your visit last year enormously and felt very cheered by your great interest in our work.[4] I hope that you will come again.

Margaret Thatcher's reply, January 12, 1982

Thank you for your letter of 21 December about technical developments in nuclear weaponry and associated systems, and the concern that such developments might jeopardise the present relatively stable nuclear balance.

This concern is shared by politicians as well as military strategists and planners. It is true that technical developments have led to an evolution in thinking about deterrence. In particular, the deployment of highly accurate missiles has meant that, for deterrence to remain credible, we must have the ability to respond to limited, as well as strategic, nuclear aggression. This makes the maintenance of deterrence more complex. But it does not mean that the United States or NATO in general entertain illusions about waging limited nuclear war. Indeed, the general effect is to make the nuclear balance more stable than in the past because deterrence now rests on a much wider basis of possible responses to nuclear aggression than was available in the 1960s.

The vulnerability of land-based missiles is of course much debated at present. But we are convinced that ballistic missile-carrying submarines will continue to remain immune to detection and thus invulnerable. They therefore provide an assured second strike capability and make it impossible to "win" a nuclear war by a disarming first strike.

In general, I believe one should be cautious in trying to deduce propositions about strategy merely from the particular characteristics of any

---

[4] As an undergraduate at Oxford, Lady Thatcher was Dorothy Hodgkin's student.

given nuclear system. Presumably the Russians must know—as the Western Alliance certainly does—that the outbreak of nuclear war would be an unimaginable catastrophe, and that to gamble the fate of civilisation on an assumed technical virtuosity in the strategic nuclear field would be irrational, to put it mildly. This does not mean that we can afford to let it go unheeded if the Soviet Union seeks to disturb the existing relatively stable balance to its own advantage. But I do not accept the view that the United States is moving to a strategy of a disarming first strike. As President Reagan said on 18 November: "No NATO weapons, conventional or nuclear, will ever be used in Europe except in response to attack." The concept of a preemptive first strike has never been and is not part of Alliance strategy.

At the same time, I fully agree with you about the importance of nuclear arms control. As you will know, negotiations on intermediate range nuclear forces are now under way in Geneva where the United States delegation has the full support of the European allies in proposing the complete elimination of long range land-based theatre missiles on both sides. We now look forward to the resumption of strategic arms reduction talks in the Spring. I welcome American statements of their intention to seek real reductions in strategic weapons. The achievement of verifiable and balanced measures of arms control is a major priority for the Government. I believe that these negotiations between the United States and the Soviet Union offer the prospect of genuine progress towards limiting and reducing the current levels of nuclear weapons.

To Karl Popper, March 7, 1982

It is some time since you sent me the reprint on the Rationality of Scientific Revolutions which I read with great interest. There was one point which seemed contradictory to me. On p. 79 you state: "I contend *there is no such thing as instruction from without the structure* [sic], or the passive reception of a flow of information which impresses itself on our sense organs." Quite generally you refute the belief that science proceeds from observation to theory. However, on p. 90 you describe Rutherford's reaction to Geiger and Marsden's α-recoil. The result was unexpected and led Rutherford to the nuclear atomic model. Was this not an example of instruction from without?

In my own field of protein crystallography, instruction from without is the rule. Though Kendrew and I had some ideas what the structures of myoglobin and haemoglobin should be like, these ideas were proved wrong by the structures that emerged from X-ray analysis. Similarly my ideas of the functional mechanism of haemoglobin proved off the mark: the structures of the oxygen-free and oxygenated forms told me how the molecule works. All I needed was open eyes to see the message; I had no preformed ideas.

In principle I like your and [Peter] Medawar's scientific method, because it stresses the imaginative approach, but in my field imagination was needed for the discovery of a method of solving the problems, but not in anticipating the nature of the solution.

Similarly I have some misgivings concerning your views about the preliminary nature of scientific knowledge, which applies to much of physics or biology, but not to most of chemistry, as I tried to point out in the extended review of Medawar's book.[5]

I believe that there are as many approaches to scientific discovery as there are varieties of human minds. Your method applied to relativity and quantum mechanics which could never have been developed by induction, but in my own field our imagination remains quite inadequate to anticipate what we shall find. We have to wait for Nature to instruct us.

I hope that you will forgive my raising the objections.

To Karl Popper, March 23, 1982

Thank you for your letter which made your lecture and your interpretation of the α-recoil story clearer to me.

I don't want to compare myself with Rutherford, but there is some analogy between his reaction to Geiger and Marsden's experiment and mine to the haemoglobin structure. You tell me that neither of them saw the meaning of the experiment, but that Rutherford "invented" the atomic nucleus to account for it.

None of my collaborators who saw the haemoglobin models had the imagination to draw any conclusions from it. It inspired me to "invent" a cooperative mechanism that accounted for its physiological function on a chemical basis. So you are right that I did not arrive at it purely by induction.

To Robin and Sue Perutz, June 29, 1983

My paper on species adaptation has been rejected by *Science*. The editor sent it to some old-fashioned fish-evolutionist to review who has written 5 pages of comments like the following. About my demonstration that the

---

[5]Perutz M.F. 1989. How to become a scientist. *Is Science Necessary?* Barrie and Jenkins, London, p. 189. This review first appeared under the title "True Science" in the *London Review of Books* in 1981.

switch from DPG to HCO$_3$ in crocodile Hb arises by only 3 amino acid substitutions, he writes: "This is a gross overstatement. There are many amino acid differences, yet he concludes the 'new function' arises by 'no more than three' and discusses the other 100 as conservative with little effect on oxygen equilibria. These two statements and others like them throughout this manuscript make Perutz look very naive and perhaps even foolish..."[6] Here are some of the general comments. They are so patronising they made me laugh: "I beg Dr. Perutz not to publish these naive statements. They will be a source of embarrassment that will haunt him for years to come."

I am not sure what to do next. Edsall is publishing the paper in *Advances in Protein Chemistry* but few geneticists and biologists will see it there. I don't want to compare myself with Darwin, but I do think he was lucky not to have had his manuscript of *The Origin of Species* reviewed by 3 referees.

To The Editor, The Times, August 15, 1983

Your leader on the How and Why implied that the dual support system of university research under which the research councils provided grants for most of the capital equipment and the universities paid most of the running costs was breaking down because the universities were deliberately "skimping on research support." Your leader conceals the real reason, namely that the Government has reduced the money from which the universities used to pay a major proportion of the running costs and buy some of their vital capital equipment.

Your leader also accused the research councils of not providing value for money under Rothschild's customer-contractor principle, under which ministries were to commission applied research from the councils. The system has proved difficult to work, not because of obstruction by the councils but because the ministries concerned were not able to provide enough ideas for new research. Such ideas rarely originate in ministries but spring from scientists working at the bench. This is why Soviet science, which is centrally planned, has proved largely sterile in spite of the vast number of scientists employed, while British science, which is funded in response to indi-

---

[6]Max had suggested that no more than three amino acid substitutions were needed to account for the very different behaviour of crocodile haemoglobin compared to human although there are well over a hundred amino acid differences between the two proteins. His later work was to show that these properties of crocodile haemoglobin could be transferred into human haemoglobin with as few as 12 amino acid replacements, i.e. a relatively small number.—AW

vidual initiative, has probably produced more original results per head of population than any other country's. Our flexible research council system is the envy of the scientific world.

The greatest recent advances in medical research, both fundamental and applied, have come from F. Sanger's methods of deciphering genes, and from G. Köhler and C. Milstein's invention of monoclonal antibodies; they were made at the Medical Research Council's Laboratory of Molecular Biology. Why could not the chief scientist at the Department of Health have commissioned these works of genius, as the Duke of Milan commissioned Leonardo to paint *The Last Supper?* The Duke chose Leonardo's theme from the Bible, while the Chief Scientist could not have opened the books of Nature and guessed in advance either the feasibility or the practical consequences of these scientific advances.

One of the research councils' difficulties lies in the relative allocation of funds to different subjects. For example, a major share of the Science and Engineering Research Council's money is spent on high energy physics, but projects in this field produce results whose scientific interest and potential practical value are no greater than those of many top-ranking and much cheaper research projects in other fields which the Council cannot support for lack of funds. A hard look at the relative merits of research in these different fields may lead to a better distribution of funds.

To John T. Edsall, September 27, 1983

I read Tolstoy much later than you, probably in my late twenties, and then reread *War and Peace* and *Anna Karenina* in my fifties. Each time I found them totally absorbing and lived with the characters as though they were my friends. Few of Dickens' characters have that marvellous quality. I found [Henri] Troyat's book revealing about the autobiographical aspects of Tolstoy's novels. Do you remember how in *Anna Karenina* Levin nobly looks after his brother as he lies dying of TB, regardless of the repulsive tart with whom his brother has chosen to live. Troyat relates how Tolstoy in fact had shirked his brother's tragedy and done little or nothing to help him. So Tolstoy makes his hero perform the noble deeds where he himself had shamefully failed in his elementary Christian duty. It always seems to me that charity begins at home, and Tolstoy was one of several men whom I have known, or about whom I have read, who pretended to love all mankind and lacked any human feeling for their kith and kin. Surely, Tolstoy lived in the 20th century and not in the

Middle Ages and could have set up a trust that assured his wife of an income from the royalties of his books during her lifetime, instead of leaving her destitute. I knew an old Princess Troubetskoy,[7] who had known him and described him as an unpleasant character. The most creative men are not always the nicest!

Troyat has also written a biography of Dostoyevsky, which forges the link between D's life and his fiction. Dostoyevsky's father was a brutal landlord whom D hated. He so maltreated his serfs that they eventually murdered him (rather as Joy Adamson is said to have maltreated her black servant until he finally killed her). So D makes Dimitri Karamazov perform the patricide from which he himself had flinched, but which the serfs performed for him.

Thank you for recommending [Abraham] Pais's *Einstein*. I am not sure that I want to read another book about him. To my mind, he belongs to the same category as Tolstoy: a cold character who supposedly loved all mankind (except the Germans) and especially all Jews, but treated those close to him without affection. Do you remember Einstein's heartless reference to his wife after [Max] Born had written him a letter of sympathy on her death? I got to dislike him more and more on reading his letters to Born, while Born himself emerged as a warm hearted and lovable man. I was also put off by Einstein's obstinate refusal to acknowledge the power of wave mechanics, engendered, it seemed to me, by a false pride that would not allow him to change his point of view. Nor could I go along with the collective guilt that he attributed to all Germans.

Reagan is a menace. People tell me that he is such an accomplished demagogue that Congressmen and Senators are scared to vote against him, lest this would cost them votes in their constituencies. He seems to have exploited the shooting down of the Korean airliner to get Congress to foot the huge bill for his rearmament programme. This is very disturbing.

I have not done any politicking lately, because I am up to my neck in haemoglobin again, with a long queue of interesting experiments waiting to be done and results emerging at the double.

A few days ago I received a letter from the Sloan Foundation inviting me to write an autobiographical book on the lines of Freeman Dyson's *Disturbing the Universe* or Lewis Thomas's book, but as long as my research is going so well I may find it hard to get down to writing down my life's experiences rather than describing my latest experiments.

---

[7] Daria Weissel's mother.

To Lotte and Franz Perutz. Milan Airport, November 16, 1983

Gisela and I are on our way home from a trip to Rome and Naples, and I am taking the chance of a long wait between two flights to tell you about our adventures.

We were invited to Rome for the annual meeting of the Pontifical Academy of Sciences who generously pay the expenses of spouses as well as participants. The members are a mixed bag: scientists elected for their scientific valour, others for being good Catholics, others for being the only representatives of science in 3rd world countries. The president, a good Brazilian neurophysiologist, claims rightly that it is the only *international* scientific academy. Our discussion was to be on Science and Peace, an inauspicious subject at this menacing moment, and it began with several hours of argument on the possible election of a member from the USSR. Some of us were not too keen, but were persuaded by those familiar with conditions there that most Soviet scientists felt oppressed by and had little sympathy with the Party, suffered from isolation from their foreign colleagues, and would be enormously pleased to be elected if they were allowed to come to our meetings.

Next we were received by the Pope [John Paul VI] in the pompous, baroque, grandiose and over-decorated Sala Regia, together with the Diplomatic Corps and our wives. It was all very formal. Our President delivered a speech to the Pope and he an address to us, in French, read off a typed pre-circulated text; the substance was printed in *The N.Y. Times* the next day where you may have seen it. The Pope made one suggestion which I liked, and which I have put forward in the past, namely that scientists should be made to take a kind of Hippocratic Oath when they take their degrees, pledging themselves that they would use their knowledge only for the benefit of mankind.

After the speech our President introduced us individually. I took the opportunity to tell the Pope how moving I had found his plea against violence in his sermon in Eire. He looked pale and worn as one has seen him on TV ever since the attempt on his life, but he was lively and went round the room talking to as many people as he could. He has a kindly and humble expression. Our Roman friends told us afterwards that he is more popular abroad than in Italy, on account of his reactionary views on most subjects, especially contraception and abortion, and of his constant search for publicity.

In his speech he made great play of scientists' duty to discover and publish the truth. I used this cue in my own lecture to the Academy for a plea to the Church to recognise the appalling prospects of famine with which the world will be faced unless underdeveloped countries take vigorous measures for birth control. I said in effect that, if the Pope asks us to speak the truth, we ask him also to listen to it. Alas, he was not present then.

Among the Diplomatic Corps I recognised [Lawrence] Bragg's son-in-law who is British ambassador to the Holy See, and Bragg's daughter Margaret. They kindly invited us to dinner at their embassy, a lovely old palace in a large garden shaded by fabulous old trees just above the baths of Caracalla. I told them about my involvement with nuclear disarmament, and my anxiety over the installation of Cruise and Pershing missiles in Europe which I regard as unnecessary because the American submarine-based missiles are a sufficient protection from Soviet nuclear blackmail. The Ambassador took the official Government line, not surprisingly as I was attending an international meeting, but afterwards he and his wife showed us a new book, written in the form of comic strips, which describes the bewilderment of a simple-minded couple attempting to protect themselves from nuclear attack following official British instructions. We spent a pleasant evening; their superb cook added to our enjoyment.

The Academy meeting was disappointing, since few of the great minds had anything to say on Science and Peace that has not been said before. One of the more eccentric suggestions, made by Alex Rich, an American, was that the U.S. and U.S.S.R. should mount a joint expedition to send a man to Mars. This would require scientific and technical collaboration on a large scale and an industrial effort that would direct the physicists and engineers who were now designing and building missiles to a peaceful task.

The men from 3rd world countries dwelt mainly on their countries' exploitation from what they called technical and economic imperialism by the Great Powers; their most moving complaint concerned the collapse of commodity prices which has plunged them into debt to the tune of 50 billion dollars. They also made great play of the enormous cost of armaments exported to 3rd world countries by the Great Powers. This made me tell the Indian and Pakistani members during the coffee break that I had just read the memoirs of President [Anwar al-] Sadat of Egypt. He complains about the Soviets' failure to supply his army with the most modern weapons. Exasperated, he finally travels to Moscow and speaks his mind to [Leonid] Brezhnev. When Sadat finds Brezhnev adamant, he orders all Soviet military personnel to leave Egypt and begins negotiating for arms with [U.S. President Jimmy] Carter instead. Which shows that it is not always the

Great Powers who press their weapons on the poor innocents of the 3rd world. Both my friends looked embarrassed and retorted that the British policy of divide and rule had left them with great tensions.

Weisskopf suggested that we should try to form a group or committee of scientists, churchmen and public figures who make it their task to bring home to the politicians the conclusions recently arrived at by [Carl] Sagan and others of the U.S. Academy of Sciences and their counterparts in Moscow, namely that the explosion of as "little" as 200 of the 20,000 megatons of explosives amassed by the Great Powers would bring about a global nuclear winter that would extinguish human and most other life on earth. I promised Weisskopf to support this initiative in Britain.

Some months ago I received a touching letter from one of Gerda [Blau's] former colleagues at the FAO [Food and Agricultural Organisation] telling me how much she was valued there. Gisela and I therefore asked him and his wife to dine with us at a restaurant. I was surprised to hear that Gerda was dismissed from the FAO in 1968 for expressing views opposite to those of the Director. It was official policy all over the world to tell coffee growers to diversify while Gerda said they should stick to coffee. Events, her colleague told me, proved her right, because the coffee price increased fivefold. But what an organisation where independent economists are sacked for not toeing the party line!

Later I asked him why we have surpluses of grain in the world when it had been forecast a few years ago that there would be a shortfall of 45 million tons of grain, or half the exportable surplus of the U.S.A. by 1985. The answer lies mainly in the fantastic success of the green revolution in India, Pakistan, Bangladesh, South Korea, the Philippines and China, but also in the reduced demand due to the world depression. In other words, fewer people can afford to buy the food that is waiting for them.

Cambridge, November 17, 1983   One of the more appealing suggestions made at our meeting was by a French geneticist: children should be taught that all humans have the same chromosomes, whence all men are brothers, and it makes nonsense to teach them to hate the Russians or the Germans. I could not help reflecting afterwards about Cain and Abel.

Today I feel like the morning after because we dined out nearly every night, two of them at the homes of Roman colleagues. One who had just returned from the U.S. told us how impressed he had been by the effectiveness of legislation that has opened State universities to the handicapped. Everywhere he saw students in wheelchairs, so crippled that they would hardly have ventured out of their homes before. He was shattered by the realisation of how many handicapped young people there are.

Roman and Neapolitan eating habits sometimes added to the stress of our stay. On Monday I rose early to prepare my lecture to the Pontifical Academy. After that Gisela and I caught the train to Naples by the skin of our teeth. When we got there I was taken to a huge lecture room with smooth bare walls and ceiling where every word drew a multiple echo. I could understand hardly a word that was said in the lengthy Italian introductions and decided that the audience would never understand me if I spoke in English. So I improvised in Italian, somewhat haltingly, interrupted by the constant blowing of horns from the cars passing under the windows and by the creaking of seats by people coming and going. You can't even say "How the hell do you expect me to lecture under these conditions?" but have to act politely as though nothing unusual were happening. After that ordeal I needed a rest, but when my host had brought me back to the hotel, he said "We shall come and pick you up for dinner at 9.30"! It started at 10.30 and continued until midnight, long past the hour when I was capable of entertaining the two ladies on either side of me in Italian or in any other language.

At dusk [another day] we went to St. Peter's Square which struck us again by its grandiose splendour. We were searched for arms before being allowed into the cathedral. Once inside we found the Pope presiding over two rows of cardinals at a memorial service for a deceased prelate. I could detect no Polish accent in the Italian sermon, which made me think that it must be someone else speaking, but I learned next day that it was the Pope himself. When he received the academicians he addressed them all in their own languages, including German, French, English, Spanish and Russian (to a guest of the Academy). The interior of St. Peter's was brightly lit for the occasion. Just as when I first saw it 31 years ago, I thought that it expressed the worldly grandeur of the popes rather than the teachings of Christ. They emerge solely, but movingly from Michelangelo's *Pietà*.

Which reminds me that my most valued privilege as an Academician is lifelong free access to all the buildings, collections and treasures in the Vatican.

In conclusion, here is a saying of Pascal's quoted by a French colleague at the Academy meeting: "Jamais on ne fait le mal si pleinement et si gaiement que quand on le fait par conscience." ["Never is evil done as completely and cheerfully as when it is deliberate."]

To John T. Edsall, November 26, 1983

Today I found a question in your letter of 3 October which I never answered concerning Howard Dintzis' part in the solution of haemoglobin. Howard's chief method was the soaking of protein crystals in a variety of heavy atom complexes about which he was very knowledgeable. This method worked wonders for myoglobin, but all his complexes spurned haemoglobin. I saw myoglobin advancing into 3 dimensions with great strides while haemoglobin remained marooned in flatland. Eventually Howard left bequeathing me only dimercuriacetate whose two heavy atoms proved too close to PMB [*p*-mercuribenzoate] to provide 3D phase angles.

Howard Dintzis in 1975

Sometime later Ann Cullis and I found a cupboard of his full of haemoglobin crystals which he had never mentioned to us, precipitated with a variety of heavy atoms. On going through the preparations methodically, I found one that showed intensity differences different from any I had seen before. This was prepared by first treating Hb with iodoacetate and then adding mercuriacetate. I discovered later that this treatment makes the hidden SH [sulphydryl] group reactive, though I have never understood why, nor what made Howard try this.

About a year ago Lizzie Hodgkin asked me to subscribe to an autobiography in verse by her father Thomas, Dorothy's husband. The other day the book arrived. Many of the cantos are as much fun as Thomas' company used to be. Curiously this fantastic work is dedicated not to Dorothy, to whom he was blissfully married for over 40 years, but to his first love to whom he was engaged as an undergraduate, which I find a bit tactless to Dorothy. Besides, when I visit my first loves, I thank my lucky stars that they refused to marry me.

To Don Abraham, February 3, 1984

I am writing to you to confirm that I shall be very happy to continue my collaboration with you and do X-ray crystallographic analyses of the binding sites of potential antisickling drugs that you develop. This work is now entering a very interesting phase. By determining difference electron density maps of a variety of known drugs and of new synthetic compounds, the various possible binding sites in haemoglobin are being mapped, and are falling into some kind of order. Your recent comparisons of the binding sites of bezafibrate with those of clofibric acid and parabromobenzyloxyacetic acid were particularly illuminating. I hope that we shall soon be in a position to predict where a particular compound is likely to bind, and whether it is going to enhance or oppose sickling.

Don Abraham speaking at the memorial for Max in 2002.

Your compound DG5 is the most potent potential antisickling drug that anyone has yet made. Since your visit, Dr. Claude Poyart, our haematology colleague in Paris, has tested it on homozygous sickle cells and found that it does indeed inhibit polymerisation of haemoglobin S in the cell, which is very encouraging. Your discovery that it shifts the oxygen equilibrium curve to the left implies that it binds preferentially to oxyhaemoglobin. Further X-ray work may reveal its binding site there and provide a clue to the stereochemical mechanism of its antisickling activity. Diffractometers and computing facilities are now so well set up for this kind of work that it may progress quite rapidly.[8]

To Lotte Perutz, July 29, 1984

Today Zhores Medvedev, the Russian biochemist who was exiled because he wrote a book about *The Rise and Fall of T.D. Lysenko*, came to see us together with his wife. They are charming and most entertaining people, free from any bitterness or the extreme views often found among émigrés. Did you know that the Soviets have recently passed a law making it illegal for anyone to *speak* to a foreigner without official permission? Mrs. Medvedev has kept her Soviet citizenship and went back there just now to see her son and his family, and to attend a meeting of the European Biochemical Societies. She told us that her old acquaintances were scared even to look at her. Her

---

[8] Max was very disappointed that he and his colleagues failed to find a cure for sickle cell anaemia, but their research did have positive outcomes. Max, Don Abraham and their colleagues were able to demonstrate for the first time how drugs bind to protein molecules. I learned from Abraham that the properties of an anti-sickling agent, clofibric acid, led to work on drugs for the delivery of oxygen for hypoxic diseases, resulting in his discovery of a compound that delivers oxygen to tumours for radiation therapy of brain cancer metastasis. Although this compound failed the last stage of clinical trials, it might still prove useful for hypoxic diseases, since it did release oxygen to the tissues, something that no other compound given externally has ever done, and behaves like the natural allosteric effector, diphosphoglycerate.

son dropped his economics studies and now makes puppets for a puppet theatre. There he does not need to worry about promotion being barred because of his exiled father. Mrs. Medvedev had also visited the U.S. recently and was shocked that, on learning that she was Russian, most people asked her "Why do the Russians want to invade us?" Your free press makes no difference to the lies people believe.

I enclose an article in the *Scientific American* on the appalling consequences of "deinstitutionalising" mental patients. It seems to me that Reaganism and Thatcherism are taking us back to Dickensian conditions of abject and unrelieved poverty for those who are down and out.

To John T. Edsall, November 12, 1984

I look forward to your article in [Giorgio] Semenza's series. Alan Fersht's and Greg Winter's work is superb and the most imaginative that is being done in this field anywhere. I had the pleasure of lecturing about it in Holland the other day. They combine great technical skill with profound insight into chemical mechanisms.

I have been through a "high" of discovery when every day brought new ideas and every prediction was confirmed by experiment. What set me off on it was an attempt to discover the basic mistake underlying Chien Ho's nonsensical work about the origin of the alkaline Bohr effect. The title of the paper that is now the fourth and *surely* the last but one draft is "The pK_a of two histidines in human haemoglobin, the Bohr effect, the dipole moment of α-helices, and the possible design of ion channels." Chien Ho, I found, had assigned the wrong NMR resonance to the C-terminal histidine and, by doing so, had believed mistakenly that he had disproved [John] Kilmartin's and my work on the Bohr effect. The correct assignment shows that the field created by the dipole moment of an α-helix can change the pK_a of a histidine by nearly as much as the field of a nearby carboxylate. This discovery brought home to me the reality of the dipolar character of α-helices and made me think about the significance of Nigel Unwin's and Richard Henderson's structure of the purple membrane protein, which consists of α-helices running normal to the membrane surface. It is a photo-activated proton pump. I wondered if the one-way traffic in this and other ion channels is guided by the field created by parallel α-helices. I'm too poor a theoretician to calculate the consequences of such a field and therefore showed my scheme to David Buckingham, the Professor of Theoretical Chemistry here, who specialises in the dipolar and multipolar character of molecules. I was delighted to find him encouraging and willing to collaborate. It would be marvellous if the idea worked at least in theory, but in the present state of knowledge of membrane proteins, it may be years before it can be tested experimentally.

In the field of protein crystallography the most exciting event is [Hartmut] Michel and [Robert] Huber's solution of the structure of the photochemical reaction centre of *Rhodopseudomonas*. When you ask Bragg's favourite question: "What is the structure trying to tell you?" you find it gives you a very good idea of how photosynthesis works. It is a fantastic achievement and I am thinking of Michel and Huber as my next candidates for the Nobel Prize in Chemistry.[9]

When writing the memoir on [Gilbert] Adair with [Paley] Johnson, I wondered why in all his work on the effects of salt he had never asked himself what influence it had on the oxygen equilibrium curve. Why did [F.J.W.] Roughton tell John Kendrew and me that the purification of haemoglobin spoils the equilibrium curve without asking himself what he removed by purification? Why did [Samuel] Rapoport, when finding a high concentration of DPG [diphosphoglycerate] in red cells, never ask himself whether it had a function? The older I get the more impatient I get with scientists who just measure things without using their imagination.

I thought your letter to *The Times* about the MX [missile] was excellent. Here there is no real debate on such issues. Mrs. Thatcher decides and that's that. It is true that there are letters to *The Times* and sometimes debates in Parliament, but they alter nothing, because the Tories have an overwhelming majority. You at least have an independent Congress. We are all deeply worried by the near civil war that is going on over the miners' strike. I enclose a cutting from today's *Times* which reports Church leaders expressing very well some of our feelings about Government policies. The Church used to be on the side of the rich but this is no long true. *The Times* reported salaries of top executives which are over £0.5M or ~100 times a workman's wage, while today a vicar of England told of a man who was unemployed and tried to commit suicide because he could send only one of his children to school, since there was only one pair of shoes for them both. Yet the government announced tax cuts rather than public works to create jobs. It is quite inflexible.

Basic science is in a bad way here. I am lucky to be supported by the NIH and NSF.[10]

---

[9]They won the Nobel Prize in 1988 with Johann Deisenhofer.

[10]National Institutes of Health and National Science Foundation, both in the U.S.

To Lotte Perutz. London–Munich, July 17, 1985

I shall talk about the new approach to the development of drugs that molecular biology has opened. The most spectacular is a human protein called tissue plasminogen activator, which dissolves blood clots. I have just read the results of two clinical trials, one American published in the *New England Journal of Medicine* and the other European, published in *The Lancet*. The protein was infused intravenously 5 hours after the first onset of pain in heart attacks. In 66 out of a hundred patients, the protein dissolved the clot in the coronary artery and restored circulation. The protein is present in human plasma in concentrations too small to make extraction practicable. One of the Californian biotechnology firms isolated the gene, cloned it and introduced it into *coli* bacteria. From a culture of these bacteria the protein can now be made in bulk. Since it is a human protein, patients have no allergic reactions and no side effects. It seems fantastic!

One advantage of being asked to give general lectures is that in preparing them I often learn about interesting new developments which might otherwise have bypassed me.

We have arrived.

To Lotte, Franz and Senta Perutz, August 28, 1985

My life has been fuller than ever. In the first place I have become a film producer! With the help of a young mathematician, Rod Hubbard, at York University I turned the story which I told at the Hanush Hospital into a movie. This will replace the 3D slides. Using the latest computer graphics machine, Hubbard conjured up pictures of the drugs binding to haemoglobin on a colour TV screen, where the atomic models rotate and thus give you the sensation of seeing them in 3D. This method makes the story more vivid than the slides do, and it will also enable me to tell it in a shorter time.

I first spent 3 days in York immediately after our return from Italy, but our film turned out to be under exposed. So I spent another 3 days there last week, and this time it came out beautifully. However, it was all a terrible rush. I took the developed films home with me on the 16th, a Friday, spent last Monday until late at night splicing it together from 60 separate pieces, had it driven to a processing laboratory in London to be copied on Tuesday. They declared they could not do it and sent it to another laboratory on Wednesday. I got the copies back by rail express yesterday afternoon, had it run and saw it properly for the first time half an hour later and was very thrilled with it.

Did some more splicing today and am taking it to the International Congress in Amsterdam to show in my lecture the day after tomorrow. Everything is always touch and go!

Getting *The New Yorker* article [Enemy Alien] ready for press was also exciting. Their "fact-finding editor," one Michael Green, was on the telephone with me from New York one evening while I was staying in York with Robin and Sue. He had done an impressive amount of research on my article and uncovered several inaccuracies. He consulted an oceanographer to find out if the waves in the Atlantic were really as high as I had written and was told that they were much higher.

In the midst of all this I also wrote a paper on the latest potential anti-sickling drug and refereed several papers that editors of scientific journals sent me. Finally the work of my Japanese collaborator Kiyoshi Nagai on mutants of haemoglobin made by genetic engineering in *coli* bacteria is giving exciting results, involving me in a lot of thought and discussion. On some days I feel I need 9 lives!

To Lotte Perutz, undated but presumably autumn 1985

Many thanks for your letter of 27 September and your welcome comments on my *New York Review of Books* article. While the reaction to my *New Yorker* article has been quite overwhelming, hardly anyone has commented on the review.

My life has been made more interesting than ever by *The New Yorker* article. You may remember my story about Merlin Scott, the young soldier who had to watch the Italian internees and survivors of the Arandora Star[11] being herded onto another ship and whose letter to his father at the Foreign Office turned the tide.[12] Later he was killed by the Italians in Libya.

On my return from a visit to Heidelberg last month I found the enclosed letter from a Mrs. Kierstead of *The New Yorker* with a transcript of a letter she had received from a Lady Scott, the second wife of the father of Merlin Scott, telling Mrs. Kierstead that her 98-year-old husband had been moved to tears by my mention of his son's compassionate letter. Lady Scott wanted to tell me this, but assumed that I lived in the U.S.A. Upon getting my address from Mrs. Kierstead, Lady Scott immediately phoned me to say

---

[11]The ship had been torpedoed in July 1940 killing ~1100 of its 1800 passengers and crew.

[12]That is, the Government came to appreciate that Britain had nothing to fear from most of those it had interned as "enemy aliens."

that her husband wanted to meet us. The Scotts live only 46 miles from here and I offered to drive there that same weekend, but she said that just for the past three days her husband had deteriorated and was too weak to see anyone. This was followed by a gloomy letter, making us fear that he was beyond recovery, which was very sad. However, last Friday Lady Scott phoned to tell us that he was better and asked us to tea on Sunday.

Her husband is Sir David Montagu Douglas Scott, Montagu Douglas being the family name of the Dukes of Buccleuch. He is the Duke's cousin and lives in a 25-room "outhouse" of the Duke's palace, Boughton House, in Northamptonshire. It looks like a French château of the 16th century with a beautifully proportioned, simple early baroque facade, set in grounds that are a scaled down copy of Versailles. The house is built of a local, warm greyish-yellow stone; the whole edifice and its surroundings radiate elegance and harmony. The "Dower House," where the Scotts live, is a fine old brick building, facing a walled garden full of beautiful flowers.

Lady Scott, whom Mrs. Kierstead described as a "dumpling in wellingtons, gardening at 90 miles an hour," greeted us with great joy. She seemed warm-hearted, cheerful, unaffected and tremendously energetic, managing an invalid husband, a huge rambling house and two gardens planted with a profusion of the most exquisite flowers, all growing higgledy-piggledy as if they were wild ones that had sprung up there by chance. That *Durcheinander* [confusion] was half accidental and half deliberate, and so different from the tidy regimentation you often see in professional gardens. It gave her garden a unique charm. And professional she is, because she grows batteries of plants for sale to the visitors of the Duke's palace and is on colleagial terms with the directors of several important botanic gardens.

In a way the inside of the house is like the garden, only less well tended. It has not been repainted in this century, but this hardly seems necessary because all the walls are covered with pictures. In some rooms family portraits dominate, in others the pictures range from minor Dutch 17th century masters to 19th century genre; collections of picture postcards and large frames full of small family photographs plaster the kitchen passage. The rooms are crowded with a medley of furniture of all periods in a state of greater or lesser disrepair. Lady Scott is trying to turn one room into a "museum" with Sir David's christening gown, his uniform of the First World War, his diplomatic uniform and a thousand other mementos, all mixed up like her flowers but not washed by the rain. There are boxes full of Merlin's letters, all unsorted, without lids, collecting the dust.

In one large room on the ground floor, next to a blazing wood fire, sat Sir David in an armchair. He did not look at me when I greeted him because he is blind, but he could hear quite well so that conversation was easy. His face has shrunk, but he is still 6'5" tall, and one could well imagine him the handsome English country gentleman personified. He told me that in 1940 he had been at the Foreign Office in charge of relations with the U.S.A., even though he had never visited that country; that was why he had been able to warn Halifax, the Foreign Secretary, of the bad impression which the treatment of the Italian and Jewish refugees would make there. I asked him how he got on with Halifax, to which he replied that he liked him because Halifax always attributed to him greater knowledge of affairs than he actually possessed. He told me that he is the oldest living Etonian and that he had received questions about his days there from boys now at Eton. When they asked him what things had been like there during the war, he told them that it was the Boer War! He also showed me pictures of Montagu House by the Thames, where the family resided in his younger days and related how the Duke would move from castle to castle in synchrony with the various hunting and London seasons. The Duke only had to tell the Steward, who would organise it all, while now the Duke was alone and his vast estates had turned into a burden and a worry. We met him later on. His legs are paralysed because a horse fell on him, and he moves around his huge palace in a wheelchair from which he can just raise himself into the driver's seat of a specially adapted Volvo; he seemed an enterprising, able intelligent looking man in his mid 50s.

Sir David never knew how his son met his death until last June, when on the 40th anniversary of Victory in Europe Day, a soldier who served under his son wrote the story to the Duchess of Gloucester, thinking erroneously that she was Merlin's sister. The Duchess forwarded the letter which opened old wounds in Sir David's heart. Loss of a child, and especially an only one, is something people never get over.

After we left, I felt at first as though we had visited figures out of an Oscar Wilde or a Chekhov play, but this was too simplistic; Gisela says it merely conjured up the unreality of it all. These people live in surroundings of a past age, but without complaining that they have no more servants to look after them and their vast mansions. Nor was there any kind of regret over the passing of class distinctions or any kind of snobbery. They were not incapable of managing their affairs and yet they were remnants of a bygone age. Sir David, a shrunken image of the ideal English gentleman, decent, handsome, well mannered, tactful, considerate, erudite in the classics and history, utterly devoted to the English countryside and to his own home and garden where his mother had lived since 1902. Lady Scott, not a socialite, but an able, straight, lively, warm-hearted woman whose love of their garden seemed to bond her to her husband and who referred to the Duke as tenants might have referred to the squire. We felt that we had witnessed the approaching death of a gracious way of life and seen a home that is beautiful without being showy; encumbered with all the bric-a-brac of past generations which piety had preserved for a future that no longer exists.

Lady Scott spotted a fellow gardener in Gisela. When I come home now vases full of exotic flowers she gave to Gisela remind me of our visit and next year we shall enjoy watching the growth of the many plants she gave us for our garden.

To John T. Edsall, January 18, 1986

I was very interested in your account of Edwin Cohn. I met him first in 1943 when you invited me to give a talk at Harvard and again in 1950 when he was very helpful and gave me an introduction to the plasma factory in Chicago from which I needed some substance or other. I remember him as enthusiastic but also as one of the scientific operators and empire builders to whom I never take. It is fantastic that he should have forbidden the members of his lab to attend Sanger's lecture. Does Fred know this?

We in Cambridge were aware of the conflict between you and Cohn, I seem to remember, and our opinion was that you were a better scientist than Cohn, and that you were too much of a gentleman to stand up to him. The parallel to Cohn and Fred Sanger at Harvard is Frank Young, who forbade his students to attend Sydney Brenner's lectures on molecular genetics, forcing Brenner to move them from an upstairs room in Tennis Court Road to his room in King's. The Biochemistry Dept. here has blossomed since Young left and [Hans] Kornberg took over.

Did I ever tell you my story of Frank Young? From about 1944 [David] Keilin made me hold an annual course of lectures on the structure of large biological molecules at the Molteno Institute. These were extra curricular until 1954, when I was made a University lecturer and they became official, but still held upstairs in the Molteno. So in January 54 I made the usual preparations for my first lecture to begin at 5.00. Old James, the ginger-haired Irish technician, was ready with the projector. We waited for the biochemistry students till 5.00, then until 5.15 and when none had come by 5.30, I went home like a dog with his tail between his legs. No one interested in my lectures!

Next day I tried to find out what happened. Frank Young had agreed to support Bragg's approach to the General Board of the Faculties for a joint appointment of myself as Lecturer in Biophysics, but when it came to my actual lectures, he had told his students to keep away because he considered them too specialised (the definition of that term must have been that he thought he would not have been able to understand them).

Bragg was exceptional in having no power complex. Occasionally he annoyed me by behaving like the squire to his tenant, as when we met at Liverpool Street Station and he would go into the 1st class and let me travel alone in the 3rd, but such lapses were relieved by his genial nature and because he always put scientific problems and ideas above his own ego. [Desmond] Bernal was marvellous in treating us all as equals, and his is the code that I set myself in dealing with people in my lab.

To John T. Edsall, February 17, 1986

About the Shuttle disaster.[13] Before it happened I read [James] van Allen's [sic] article explaining that anything men can do from the shuttle can be done better and more cheaply by unmanned vehicles. I also learned that the soaring costs and long delays of the shuttle forced NASA to abandon many scientifically valuable missions. Shortly after the disaster I had dinner with Hermann Bondi, who used to head the European Space Agency. He told me that earlier manned space rockets had safety devices designed to prevent this kind of disaster. The booster rocket was fitted with sensors to detect overheating and the spaceship itself was fitted with small rockets capable of shooting it off the booster, and with parachutes, to allow its safe return to earth. If the sensors detected overheating, the signal from them would fire the rocket that detached the spaceship from the booster. Bondi then told me that the same safety device had been planned for the Shuttle, but because of mounting cost and delays, and the technical problems involved, which would have entailed further delays, this plan was abandoned. Had it been followed, the Shuttle crew could have been saved.

To my mind the sending of people into space is pointless and the plans for colonising space, manufacturing things in space and collecting solar energy there are all unjustifiable. The romance of being there would wear off after the first day and be replaced by claustrophobic boredom. [Carl

---

[13]The U.S. Space Shuttle Challenger disintegrated 73 seconds into flight on January 28, 1986, killing all astronauts aboard and stalling the U.S. space programme for 32 months.

Friedrich] von Weizsäcker has said it best: "There's a curious fascination with technology, a bewitching of minds, that leads us to imagine that progress consists in doing everything that's possible. For me that's not progressive, it's childish."[14]

To Robert Silvers, February 24, 1986

I am not sure whether I should regard [Ernst] Chain as an enemy or a friend. He had an obsessional hatred of molecular biology and in the 1970s conducted a campaign to get the Government to close down this laboratory. He happened to be friendly with Edward Heath [Prime Minister 1970–1974] because they played music together and lost no opportunity to put the case to him. Consequently when my retirement as Chairman was looming, the Medical Research Council felt itself obliged to appoint a commission to consider whether the laboratory should be closed down after my retirement.

Now to the other side of the story. My wife came to this country before the War and became a medical photographer at St. Bartholomew's Hospital in London. After the outbreak of war, part of the hospital was evacuated from London and her job folded. In the spring of 1940 she heard that Chain was looking for an assistant and went to Oxford for an interview. She found him so unpleasant that she decided she would rather starve than work for that man and returned to look for a job in Cambridge which is where I met her. So, if Chain had been less disagreeable I would never have met her and for this I have always been profoundly grateful.

To Lotte Perutz, May 21, 1986

Granada was colder than Cambridge when we arrived there late one evening. It's a large, prosperous modern town high up on a plateau at the edge of the snow-covered Sierra, full of traffic and bustle. The Alhambra lies on a steep hill opposite the Sierra, so that the Moorish kings could look down on the town and across to the mountains on the other side. It's a marvellous monument of Arab architecture. I had imagined it grandiose, but there is an engaging intimacy and individuality about the different courts and a wonderful sense of taste and proportion This sense of intimacy and diversity is reflected in the gardens which have none of the pompous grandeur of the French, but consist of a succession of charming hedged-in

---

[14]Translated from the German.

courts, each with different waterworks or flower beds. They are built on a long terrace, one edge of which is lined with tall cypress trees, while the other edge looks over the town and the mountain. It's all suggestive of a splendid and civilised way of life, but on reflection my image of the Moorish king came down to a little man, surrounded by his harem and his eunuchs, all quarrelling among themselves, the man perpetually terrified of being murdered by one of his rivals; so that, if he did not murder his brothers, they would murder him. Which made me think Sedley Taylor Road[15] may be preferable after all to the Alhambra, quite apart from the absence of window panes; I don't know how these people managed to live with the icy blasts that we felt going right through their rooms. And that was on a fine day.

At Madrid we were welcomed by Mr. Gonzales, the director of the Juan March Foundation that had invited me to lecture as part of its aim to foster the sciences and the arts. Next day I came to give my lecture in the splendid hall of the Foundation. It was preceded by a heated argument among my hosts, in loud and voluble Spanish with the hard, guttural ch's echoing through the hall and sounding as if they would presently come to blows, but afterwards it transpired that they were just discussing the lighting. There followed a delicious dinner in really first-rate company. The same happened next night after I had given another lecture at the University. People were fantastically well educated, widely travelled and well read, and some of them were excellent talkers. It was all great fun and very different from the dreary formal dinners which I normally have to attend on such occasions.

Next day Gonzales drove us to Toledo. It also has two of the world's oldest synagogues whose splendour testifies to the wealth of the Toledo Jews before Ferdinand and Isabella drove them out. I was amused that synagogues are monuments of Moorish architecture. A colleague from the University took us to the mountains near Madrid. A two hour drive brought us to range upon range of rather dull mountains covered everywhere with the same bush (cistus) and totally deserted. A deserted village was so primitive that it could have dated from the Stone Age. On the other hand, all the mountain sides were recently terraced and on all the terraces the Spaniards had planted fir trees. The trees had only grown to a height of 2–3 feet, but in time all these bare hills will be thickly forested. I had heard about millions of trees being planted in Israel, but I had not known that Spain was also trying to make the country more fertile that way.

---

[15]The location of our home.

Madrid has the air of a great capital, with wide avenues, splendid buildings and hundreds of luxury shops, but it is full of beggars, because the unemployed get no benefit after 18 months. Unless they can find some odd jobs in the black economy, they have *nothing* and can only keep body and soul together by begging in the streets. Some of the beggars are said to be drug addicts but this did not make the picture any more cheerful. Spain was hard hit by the recession and unemployment runs at 20%.

We spent our last day at the Prado, where the Grecos made the deepest impression on me. When I first visited the National Gallery nearly 50 years ago I was deeply moved by Greco's "Christ in the Garden," and I have longed to see the Grecos in the Prado and in Toledo ever since. So this trip was a wish fulfilled. Greco's "Annunciation" and "Nativity" in the Prado are two of the greatest pictures I have seen. After them, most of the other painters' religious pictures looked trite.

I nearly forgot about the festival of flowers. One evening in Granada we found the streets cleared of traffic, bands playing and girls in gaily coloured frilly Andalusian dresses with flowers in their hair performing the national dance with arms above their heads and skirts swirling almost as high. It was like a scene out of Carmen, except that the ages of the girls ranged from four upwards, tiny tots trying to copy their big sisters' graceful turns. Even baby girls in prams wore national dress. Stalls were selling sweet cakes, boys rode about on horseback, and the entire population thronged the streets, only clearing a patch here and there to give the dancers a chance. Many girls were very attractive; in some the features of the Visigothic invaders predominated, while others looked Moorish. Ferdinand and Isabella expelled the Moors in 1492, but you can still see their genes strongly expressed to this day.

To Lotte Perutz, August 14, 1986

Two days ago I went to hear 83-year-old Karl Popper give a lecture at the Royal Society on A New Interpretation of Darwinism. To my surprise the auditorium was packed and people were queuing in the street to get in, something I had never seen before at the Royal. He did have something original to say on the subject, but was too dogmatic, because his ideas fit some aspects of evolution but not others. Nature is too diverse for neat logical minds. I was surprised by Popper telling us that biochemistry cannot be reduced to physics and chemistry. Since I have spent my life showing that it can, I put the first question asking him for his reason, to which he replied:

"If you think about it for an evening you will understand the reason."[16] This drew a great laugh from the audience. All the same I had a nice chat with Popper afterwards and was glad to have had the chance of meeting him, because in the past we had corresponded about the nature of scientific method, but had never met.

To Robin Perutz, August 20, 1986

Last month Braunitzer told me that he had sequenced a *bat* haemoglobin and found a closer relationship to human Hb than in any other non-primate. I happened to mention this to Francis Crick who told me that a neurophysiologist friend of ours, Horace Barlow, had similar evidence. Barlow referred me to an Australian, Jack Pettingrew, who came to visit me yesterday, looking as though he had come straight from the Australian bush, long beard, short trousers, sun-tanned hairy legs, sandals and tousled hair.

He found that flying foxes had a connection between the retina and the visual cortex that is found only in primates. He also told me that they were fruit eaters and had teeth like fruit-eating monkeys, whereas "microbats" were insect eaters and had sharp teeth to crunch their hard shells. Also the bones under the flying foxes' wings were more like those of primates' fingers. So the conclusion is that mammals evolved wings and learnt to fly twice: once when the microbats branched off, and more recently $\sim$20 $\times$ 10^6 years ago when the flying foxes evolved from the early primates.

To Timothy Perutz, October 6, 1986

On Friday morning, after I had told you about Mr Leakey[17] I put the book into a jiffy bag, pushed it into my black briefcase and carried it to my lab in order to post it to you. I always walk there across a playing field that is next to the lab and the big hospital. On Friday morning the field was shrouded in mist so dense that I could not see one end from the other, but the air was fresh and I felt like a walk. I therefore deposited my briefcase high up on the branch of a beech tree and circled the field twice, without seeing a soul. When I returned to the tree my briefcase had vanished. I was very upset. Besides *Mr Leakey*, it contained my notebook with the telephone numbers and addresses of all my friends, a nice woollen hat that Linda Wendon had

---

[16]See letter of August 17, 1987, where Max sets out Popper's argument.

[17]The reference is to J.B.S. Haldane's wonderful children's story *My Friend Mr Leakey*.

knitted for me, my best green scarf, an Italian cheese that Vivien had bought me the previous day and two very sweet bananas. What thief could have found the briefcase up on the tree in that mist? And what use would the contents be to him? I was perplexed and very angry.

A friend of mine in the lab always turns on the 1 o'clock news. I happened to be nearby when the announcer reported that someone had landed on a Russian satellite in space and was using its radio to transmit messages in a secret code. One of them read:

20 15/ 15 12 9 22 5 18/ 20 8 5/ 15 3 20 15 16 21 19/ 9/ 19 8 1 12 12/ 2 5/ 1 23 1 25/ 6 15 18/ 1/ 6 5 23/ 4 1 25 19/ 13 1 11 5/ 19 21 18 5/ 25 15 21/ 6 5 5 4/ 20 8 5/ 3 1 20/

12 5 1 11 5 25

A prize was offered to anyone who could decipher the messages.

Can you? I couldn't at first but the news aroused a suspicion in my mind.

I listened to the next news at 5:00. This time it said that the Russian ambassador had called on the British government. He alleged that the coded messages came from an English spy and demanded that he be recalled at once or else the Russians would blow up a British satellite. The British government assured the Ambassador that they did not know who the Englishman was. The British Government may not have known, but I realised that the invader must be Mr Leakey, who had flown into space on his magic carpet and taken my briefcase with him. I hoped at least that my hat and scarf would keep him warm, but I was concerned that his landing on the Russian satellite might provoke a war in space. How could I stop it? I must tell the Russians.

Why would Mr Leakey have wanted to go into space? What was he doing there? What did the coded message say? Perhaps I shall know more tomorrow.

[In Timothy's childish hand is the deciphered code: To Oliver the Octopus I shall be away for a few days make sure you feed the cat Leakey.]

To Don and Nancy Abraham, November 27, 1986

The other day when I rolled up at the lab after my morning walk I found that enormous parcel. Never having worked my way through Köchel I had no idea that Mozart had composed so many piano concertos, let alone that [Alfred] Brendel had recorded them all. After a while I found your card and finally Kiyoshi [Nagai] appeared and revealed himself as the special messenger who conjured your gift to my office.

I always think HiFi is one of the great inventions of the century. Not being musical enough to play an instrument, I had little appreciation and less knowledge of it until I acquired a gramophone and gradually discovered a new world. Having grown up in Vienna, you would have thought that I learned to appreciate music there. My parents were regular opera and concert goers, but, having hated my piano lessons, I decided music was not for me and would not accompany them. The first concert I enjoyed was that given by a young violinist in the Canadian Internment Camp where music made a romantic break from the dreariness and monotony of our existence.

Actually I remember just now being able to pick up Milan Radio at our house in the country south of Vienna in the thirties. I would listen to operas sung by exquisite voices, but just music alone usually bored me. On one occasion, however, it had that lucid quality that brought out the sound of every instrument and I listened captivated till the end when the announcer said that the orchestra had been conducted by Toscanini, the great conductor who later emigrated to New York in protest against Mussolini's fascist regime. On another occasion quite recently I went to a concert in Los Angeles conducted by [Carlo Maria] Giulini, and that had the same clarity.

All this long story just to tell you again how much I enjoy the clarity of Brendel and the orchestra of St. Martin in the Fields on those records you gave me.

To John T. Edsall, November 30, 1986

I am so pleased that you think I brought out a vivid impression of [David] Keilin whom I deeply loved and respected. Since my father's arrival here in 1939, he had become dependent on my help and advice in all matters large and small, so that the father-son relationship was reversed. As a consequence, perhaps, my relationships to Keilin and Bragg became filial. I was heartbroken when Keilin died, and for many years after Bragg's death, whenever I had an interesting result I would think "I must tell Bragg about it," and was robbed of some of the joy by no longer being able to.

I am pleased, also, that [Ernst Peter] Fischer's biography of [Max] Delbrück[18] appeals to you, despite the difficult German. I agree with you about his special qualities: was it clarity of thought that he radiated? Also warmth, and humour, and imagination, and some kind of magnetism.

---

[18]A first version of this biography appeared in 1985. The English-language edition is Fischer E.P. and Lipson C. 1988. *Thinking about Science: Max Delbrück and the Origins of Molecular Biology.* Norton, New York.

German "Kultur" [culture in its widest sense] has become an object of derision, but it saw a wonderful flowering among German academics and professionals around the turn of the century; it was largely ruined by the inflation after the First World War which robbed the bürgerlichen Familien [middle-class families] of all their savings. Life in those days is also charmingly described in Max Born's autobiography.

To Lotte Perutz, December 4, 1986

As to the Pope's attitude to sex and marriage, I wrote to Prof. Chagas, the President of the Academy, after our meeting that I regard overpopulation as the fundamental cause of poverty, disease and malnutrition in the Third World, problems with which we were supposed to be concerned, and implored him to use his influence with the Pope to change his attitude to birth control, but I doubt that my plea will have any effect. In fact, the proceedings of the meeting three years ago, where I spoke forcefully about that problem, have still not been published, presumably because the Vatican's censor is keeping them back.

I do envy you the Rudolf Serkin concert. That must have been a marvellous experience. Don Abraham has given us the complete collection of Mozart's piano concertos played by Brendel by way of thanking us for looking after him after his accident. They are marvellous, but no match for hearing the man in the flesh.

Last week Gisela and I attended a lecture at the Royal Institution by a great Oxford historian, Margaret Gowing, who has made a study of the history of the atomic bomb. The lecture was about Niels Bohr's attempts to persuade the American and British Governments during the war to share the secret of the bomb with the Russians so as to forestall the suspicions which secrecy was bound to arouse and also about Bohr's later efforts to prevent the nuclear arms race.

On 20 December we are giving a big party. Once in a lifetime! Coming here was the best decision I ever made.[19] Nothing would have become of me if I had stayed in Vienna even if Austria had remained free. I owe it to Cambridge that I have been able to do great things. The people who helped me here are no longer alive, except for the Tutor of Peterhouse [Charles Burkill] who admitted me. He is coming to the party. So is Evelyn Machin who made me feel part of her family.

---

[19]A celebration of 50 years in Cambridge.

To Patience Thomson, February 6, 1987

Thank you for your letter in response to my Planck review. It reminded me of the correspondence between Born and Einstein that appeared some years ago. After 1945 Born retired from his chair of theoretical physics in Edinburgh and returned to Germany, whereas Einstein remained at Princeton. He swears never to set foot in Germany again and reproaches Born for his decision to return as he regards all Germans as guilty, whereas Born tries in vain to convince him of the decency of many Germans who felt helpless in the face of Nazi tyranny. I agree with Born.

To come back to Planck: he was 75 when Hitler came to power and 81 when the war started, too old to realise that whatever had made him proud to be a German could only be resurrected after a military defeat of the Nazi regime.

To Lotte Perutz, March 27, 1987

Last Monday the head of the MRC asked me to see him in London. He requested me to chair one of the two committees set up by the MRC for research on AIDS. One for the development of a vaccine to be chaired by him, the other for the development of a therapy to be chaired by me. I suggested other people who might be more suitable, but failed to persuade him to another choice. His main reason: that I have no need to get any money out of his special AIDS fund for myself. I have mixed feelings about the job: I know too little virology; the problem is appallingly difficult; we would have to do something highly original if we are not to duplicate the American effort.

To Lotte Perutz, April 19, 1987

So far, the AIDS committee is not very demanding. Several of my crystallographer colleagues want to try and crystallise proteins of the virus and determine the structure, hoping that this might provide clues to the design of antiviral drugs. One of the biochemist/molecular biologists at my lab has ingenious ideas for a gene therapy that would introduce T-cells immune to the virus into the patients and so restore their immune systems. (T-cells are thymus-derived white blood cells essential for the immune response and are the targets of the AIDS virus.) All of the research will be in competition with American workers who are being mobilised for work against AIDS on a huge scale.

To Timothy and Marion Perutz. Brussels, April 28, 1987

Here is a story I read in a French paper. A millipede arrives late for a party. When his friends complained, he answered: "I am sorry, but there was a notice at the door *Please Wipe Your Feet.*"

To Timothy Perutz, May 20, 1987

I was so pleased to get your well-observed and accurate drawings of the emperor moth, together with your vivid description of it. It is a great marvel how these elaborate organs develop and grow during the metamorphosis from caterpillar to moth.

Many of my scientific friends are trying to solve this great mystery, not with moths, but fruit flies which multiply and grow much faster. So they ask questions such as "What determines the growth of wings out of the 7th segment of the fly's body?" You might have thought that this would be simple to answer, but No! Some of the best scientists have been at it for many years and have only advanced a small step closer to the answer, because life is so fantastically complex and likes to keep its secrets.

To Gisela Perutz. Cold Spring Harbor, June 2, 1987

Two or three years ago [Tom] Cech and [Sid] Altman in this country discovered that ribonucleic acids can act as enzymes. I did not realise until I listened to the papers at this meeting that this discovery sparked off speculation that life might have begun with ribonucleic acids acting as both genes and enzymes, catalysing their own replication; quite a bit of time was taken up with speculation on the possible chemistry of such a system. X... took part in this and presented a lecture whose obscurity was exceeded only by that of his collaborator. Next morning at breakfast I questioned X... about his lecture and gradually squeezed out of him what his theory really meant, and it was not all that complicated. Why can't people say what they mean, instead of presenting incomprehensible mumbo-jumbo! There were 10 other people at the breakfast table who agreed with me that X... had been incomprehensible before he came into the room, but none had the courage to question him about it. I often find this. People are either too timid or ashamed to admit that they could understand nothing.

To Gisela Perutz. Pittsburgh, June 8, 1987

Another morning was spent with Don Wiley [at Harvard]. I arrived just as his group had solved a vitally important structure of the immune system, called the histocompatibility complex. As so often, it tells you immediately how this hitherto mysterious protein works. That was a great thrill.

To Gisela Perutz and Family. Ottawa to Pittsburgh, June 8, 1987
[Misdated?]

Mr. [John Witney (Jack)] Pickersgill is quite a man. Born in Ontario, he went to the same one-room school to the age of 16, except when, aged 14, he looked after his mentally ill father's lumber business. After a year at high school he read history at Manitoba University, and after graduation, won a scholarship to Oxford from the "Imperial Order of the Daughters of the British Empire." There he stayed for two years and got an M.Litt. in history, went to Paris to study French, sat for the civil service exams in Canada and at an early age was given a job in the Prime Minister's office. He became a minister in several liberal cabinets. I liked him because a thread of humanity and common decency ran through all his talk. After the Russian invasion of Hungary in 1956, when thousands of refugees streamed into Austria, he was Minister of Immigration and flew to Vienna to arrange for as many as possible to be given Canadian visas; he then went to the Hague, Brussels, Paris and London to arrange for those who could not be transported to Canada and accommodated immediately to be given temporary asylum. He finally brought 35,000 Hungarians to Canada. His wife says to this day Hungarians stop him in the street to express their gratitude. Pickersgill looks back on this as his greatest achievement, especially as the Hungarians have done very well here.

The Pickersgills live in a modest-sized New England style two-storey house in a beautiful suburb of Ottawa. They have lived in the same house since they first came here in the forties. She is lively, intelligent, straight and cheerful; both are totally unpretentious. Mr. P has become a historian once more after his retirement and is widely read in history and politics which made conversation enjoyable. He said he resigned from the government when a prime minister younger than himself was appointed, because that would create an avuncular relationship which is an embarrassment to the prime minister. He has since edited Mackenzie King's diaries, commenting on the entries with his own historical account in a huge 4 volume work, where I found an interesting account of a conversation with De Gaulle, explaining to Mackenzie King the origin of his cool relationship with

Churchill with surprisingly little rancour. P has also written a biography of [Louis] St. Laurent in whose cabinet he served and whom he admired.

He is a true liberal in all his views and on the side of the have-nots. *For* Nicaraguan government, *for* equal opportunities of the Quebequois, *for* birth control, *for* a huge reduction in nuclear armaments and the use of the funds thus saved for the rehabilitation of Africa. *Against* Margaret Thatcher. *Against* Ronald Reagan! So we agreed on most matters.

To Robin and Sue Perutz. New York–London, June 16, 1987

The last day was the best! I spent the morning with two Iranians at the Montefiore Hospital in the Bronx; they are brothers, one a haematologist and the other a chemist [Parviz and Iraj Lalezari]. Stimulated by Poyart's and my discovery that bezafibrate, a drug against high blood lipid and high cholesterol, lowers the oxygen affinity of haemoglobin, the chemist set out to modify its constitution so as to increase the affinity for haemoglobin. He made some 20 compounds, none of them any better than bezafibrate. Finally he thought he might combine two reagents which he happened to have in his drawer and discovered that the resultant compound is 15X as active as bezafibrate not only in its effect on haemoglobin, but also in lowering blood cholesterol and lipid. It is non-toxic in rats. It looks as though it might turn out to be a very useful new drug and I am thrilled that my work provided the impetus for its synthesis.

The chemist was head of the school of pharmacy at the University of Teheran and a founding member of the Iranian Academy of Sciences when Khoumeni took over. He immediately fled with his family, leaving all his possessions behind; science is anathema to the fundamentalists. Moreover he is Jewish, so that he was doubly endangered.

I next went to see the editor of *The New York Review of Books* whom I found in a small suite of offices crammed with mountainous piles of books. Bob Silvers, the editor, was hidden behind a wall of books 3 ft high erected around his desk, with an array of extinct cigarillos higgledy piggledy like pick-a-sticks under his feet. He is there day and night, yet is the reverse of a neurotic workaholic, a tall expansive, jovial, relaxed man of 50 or so who knows and remembers everything he has ever published and gives his authors no end of encouragement. The best thing is he likes my writing. We talked about books and people. I told him that I should like to review François Jacob's marvellous autobiography which I got in Paris last March and which I have been reading on this trip, and described to him how most of it is about Jacob's experience as a youth at the fall of France and as a soldier in de Gaulle's army, how vividly Jacob was able to conjure up the atmosphere, people and his own feelings. So after a while I had enthused Silvers sufficiently for him to agree to publish a review as soon as the book appears in English. I shall enjoy that job.

I had spent Saturday afternoon and Sunday morning with Felix Haurowitz who is 91 and stricken with multiple myeloma, a horrible form of leukemia that destroys your bones. When I phoned him to announce myself, he replied that he would be pleased because he has some important matters to tell me. I found him in a wheelchair, badly emaciated and weak. He soon came to the point. He wanted to tell me how decent several Germans had been to him during the Nazi era, because he would like me to record this. For example, the editors of the *Zeitschrift für Physiologische Chemie* had continued to publish his papers at danger to themselves, even though publication of papers by Jewish authors was forbidden. After this he told me some moving stories of other colleagues' and strangers' behaviour. I was touched that this should be Felix's last wish in a world where most people are out for revenge, but I don't know yet what I can do to publish this.

To Lotte Perutz, August 17, 1987

Speaking of old people, I went to visit Karl Popper a couple of days ago south of London with two young friends from my lab. He immediately took us for an hour's vigorous walk across the heathland near his house, proudly showing us every old tree and rare plant as though it were his own estate. He talks very quietly, but with zest. His purpose in inviting me was to refute my criticism of him in my article in the *New Scientist*. Popper had argued that biology cannot be reduced to chemistry and physics, whereas I have spent my life showing that it can. His reason is that *in vivo* chemical reactions acquire purpose that they don't possess in the test tube. When he argued that the combustion of gas in a car is different from the combustion of the same gas in a laboratory because in the car it is burnt to a purpose, I realised that his point was philosophical rather than scientific. He then told us about his early development and his disagreement with the logical positivists in the Vienna Circle and how Einstein's papers led him to formulate his theory of knowledge. As we left he told us that he is 85. He had one or two slight strokes recently, but got over them by walking for at least an hour a day. Next day a friend told me that Popper had taken her for a 3-hour walk the previous week.

This morning I received the enclosed letter from Weizsäcker.[20] This is quite a rare honour. The "Orden" has 30 German and 30 foreign members, 10 each from science, the humanities and the arts. [Dietrich] Fischer Dieskau is one of the German members and Rudolf Serkin is one of the foreign ones. The only snag is that most of them are over 80 and probably will be reluctant to travel to the biennial meetings of the order.

Our holiday was great. Timothy's and Marion's enthusiasm was really sweet. A few grasshoppers made their day! They were thrilled with every butterfly, identified every flower, picked the odd strawberry and were full of mountaineering ambitions.

An important Government Committee has produced a report on the future organisation of research in British Universities. This proposed that research, instead of being spread thinly in many universities should be concentrated at a few big ones (15 out of 60). The rest should be downgraded either to liberal arts colleges where the staff only teach and do no research, or to intermediate institutions that carry on research in some subjects, preferably in collaboration with other universities. At the big universities some large new interdisci-

Marion in the Dolomites

plinary laboratories, on the model of my own, are to be built.

Robin is terribly upset about this plan, because York is a minor institution that will not be in the big league. If it is downgraded to a liberal arts college, everything he has built up will be destroyed, and even if it is put in the intermedia*e category, he would be unlikely to get research grants or attract good students.

Timothy in the Dolomites in 2007

The whole plan is a managerial monster made without thought about its effect on the people concerned. Robin has written an excellent letter

---

[20] An invitation to be a member of the German order Pour le Mérite.

of protest about it, pointing out that it would create an embittered staff at the affected universities. I discussed it with the head of the Medical Research Council who is a member of the committee responsible for the plan, but who had no share in drawing it up, and agreed with Robin's and my objections. I have long thought of myself as being out of the arena of scientific politics, but I shall have to try and use what influence I have to stop it being accepted. Our fear is that the Prime Minister will adopt it and push it through regardless of the consequences. I am trying to enlist Dorothy Hodgkin's help, who has her ear, to try and dissuade her.

To Lotte Perutz, September 13, 1987

We had quite a successful press conference at the MRC. [Oswald] Jarrett's vaccine looks very promising indeed, but still faces the difficulty of human tests. It won't help people who are already infected with AIDS, but should protect those exposed to risks. First, it will have to be established that it raises antibodies to AIDS in volunteers. To find out whether it protects people from infection, one will probably have to go to Uganda where the disease is spreading most rapidly, but it may be difficult to do a controlled double-blind trial there.

My next task will be to organise further tests of castanospermine, the substance from Australian oak trees that kills the virus in vitro. When I took over the chairmanship of the AIDS Therapy Committee, I did not believe that I would be able to do much towards the development of new therapies. In fact this position gives me that authority to take the initiative when any new lead turns up, to persuade people to take up the work and to get them financial support if needed. Though I have no formal powers, I can do a lot.

From what Jarrett said at our meetings, the American vaccine consists of the AIDS virus coupled to the baculovirus (a virus of butterfly larvae) but without the carbohydrate particles from the bark of the S. American tree that enhances the activity of Jarrett's vaccine.

I am also campaigning on Robin's behalf. I enclose a copy of his letter which has by now been widely distributed and is having an impact, and also one of mine that will be laid before a Royal Society committee considering the Report on the Research Councils.

At the same time I am fighting with difficulties in my crystallographic work which drive me close to despair. None of my instruments works properly and my crystals are giving me endless trouble.

Luckily I feel full of vigour most of the time.

To Hugh Trevor-Roper, Lord Dacre,
October 1, 1987

I met [Benno] Müller-Hill in Cologne last week. He told me how pleased he had been with the review of *Tödliche Wissenschaft*[21] that you wrote for *Nature*. I then asked him what reviews had appeared in Germany. None, was the answer!

To Lotte Perutz, October 4, 1987

Hugh Trevor-Roper
(Lord Dacre)

Many things have happened since my last letter. After weeks of struggle and frustration I got my X-ray machine and crystals to work by the middle of September and have splendid results on the complex of haemoglobin with the drug that the Iranian gave me on my last day in New York. I heard of my results by telephone in Düsseldorf, where I had been invited to lecture on 23 September. The main attraction there is a gallery of 20th century art housed in a beautiful modern building. They boast over 70 Klees, some lovely Chagalls and Miros, good Kandinskys and Kokoschkas and many other works.

Next day I lectured in Cologne where we had very interesting company: a cousin of Gisela's married to a blind survivor of Buchenwald.[22] They write radio plays and features that remind Germans what it was like to be a Jew in the 30s—unsentimental stuff, dry even, but all the more powerful for it.

On my return here I found piles of mail, an SOS from my inexperienced colleagues to revive the X-ray machine, and a lecture to prepare quickly for a high-powered meeting to celebrate the 100th anniversary of the NIH.[23] The president of the NIH was there and the heads of the Medical Research Councils of several European countries. The meeting's theme was "Prospects for Improvements in Health Care from Medical Research."

Some of the speakers played their stock gramophone records, but a few were really interesting. I talked on "Determining the Atomic Structure of Living Matter: What Use to Medicine?" and managed to produce some new results that made the point that it really is useful and will become more so.

---

[21]*Murderous Science: Elimination by Scientific Selection of Jews, Gypsies, and Others in Germany, 1933–1945*, originally published in 1984.

[22]Brigitte and Rolf Kralowitz.

[23]The National Institutes of Health in Washington.

To Lotte Perutz, November 22, 1987

Incidentally the Urania where I lectured [in Berlin] was also founded by Humboldt, for the enlightenment of the public, only a few years after Count Rumford founded the Royal Institution for the same purpose. The Urania seems to cover a wider spectrum judging by the man who gave the lecture preceding mine: a Japanese poet who spoke no word of either German or English and whose talk was translated sentence by sentence. His wife kissed Gisela's hand on being introduced to her!

I gave my title as "Ging's ohne Forschung besser?" [Would we be better off without research?] and was taken aback when I saw it announced as "Ist die Wissenschaft ein Risiko?" [Is science risky?] When I remonstrated, the Director replied that no one in Berlin would turn up to a lecture in favour of science and you could only lure them in under false pretences. I began by talking about science and health. After a while I heard someone leaving. He stormed into the booking office demanding his money back, because he did not hear what he had come for. After my talk I faced a barrage of questions from youngsters who had no idea what life used to be like for the common people in former centuries and who had swallowed all the nonsense about the dangers of science that the papers write. The discussion lasted for *90* minutes. In the end I was pleased by the Director's deception, because I had never talked on this subject to anyone other than the converted and for once I was able to address the Greens. They had a policeman on duty in case I needed protection but he never left the Director's office. The performance seems to have been a success because the Director asked me to come again.

To John T. Edsall, February 17, 1988

Very many thanks for your letter of the 10 February and for sending me the two articles from *Issues* which arrived today. I really ought to subscribe to it again. It is marvellous that your cataract operation is such a success.

I was interested in your 1939 note, but it does not say what you used to titrate the SH [sulphydryl] groups. Was paramercurybenzoate already available then? The rationale of my first attempt at isomorphous replacement with mercury is explained in the enclosed introduction to my *Proc. Roy. Soc.* paper in 1954, but in the concise way appropriate for such a paper. I do not think I discussed it anywhere else. I did not mention in this paper how I came to measure the absolute intensity of diffraction from a haemoglobin crystal; we needed it when Bragg and I tried to determine the shape of the haemoglobin molecule from the transform of the changes in structure amplitude by changing the density of the mother liquor from water to concentrated ammonium sulphate solution. In order to measure it, I borrowed a primitive Geiger counter spectrometer constructed by Bill Cochrane which was fitted with a monochromator. This allowed me to compare the intensity of the incident beam with that of the beam diffracted by my haemoglobin crystal and made me realise for the first time that, even in the strongest reflections, over 99% of the scattering contributions of the light atoms were cancelled by interference. On the other hand, the electrons of a heavy atom would all be concentrated at a point and scatter in phase; hence they would make a measurable contribution to the X-ray intensities of even a large protein. Thanks to the result of this experiment, my mind was well prepared when Austin Riggs' reprints arrived.[24]

To Patience Thomson, February 28, 1988

[The following letter was written to thank Patience Thompson for congratulating Max on the award of the Order of Merit, which is restricted to 24 people and given to scientists, artists, musicians, writers and people active in public life.]

Thank you so much for your charming card. I lead a Hans im Glück existence these days.[25] Everyone I meet congratulates me, like the Nobel Prize all over again. Gisela and Vivien and Robin are very pleased and so are the people in my lab. If I put my mind back 50 years, I find it quite fantastic that I should be given the O.M. Just think of my story "Enemy Alien."

To Lotte Perutz, February 28, 1988

Another *good* piece of news comes from the head of Robin's lab who is on leave and is Chief Scientific Advisor to the Ministry of Defence. Robin sent me a copy of a letter from that man to another one of the professors in

---

[24]When Riggs blocked the sulphydryl groups of human haemoglobin, he "found that in both normal and sickle cell haemoglobin, it changed the characteristic S-shape of the relationship between oxygen pressure and the affinity of the molecule for oxygen. . . . 'I jumped when I saw that, because it was clear to me that if it left the biological properties intact, then it would also leave the structure intact.'" Ferry G. 2008 *Max Perutz and the Secret of Life*. Cold Spring Harbor Laboratory Press, Cold Spring Harbor, N.Y., pp.158–159.

[25]A Lucky Hans existence. Max must have forgotten the Grimm fairytale because everything Hans divests himself of is worth less than what he gains in return.

Robin's lab that says the proposed three tier classification of the universities is "dying if not dead." Max Perutz's piece has probably been the most influential single thing.

I am delighted to have won that battle, especially because this has taken a heavy weight off Robin's mind.

To Timothy and Marion Perutz, March 20, 1988

Pussycat, pussycat where have you been?
I've been to London to see the new Queen.

I went to see her last Thursday, dressed up in black striped trousers and a morning coat, the sort that men wear at weddings, because that was what the Queen's secretary told me to wear.

At 12 o'clock noon I presented myself at the gate of Buckingham Palace and told the policeman on duty that the Queen had invited me. He had my name on a list and told me where to go. I landed in a room with several people: they have old-fashioned names. One was the Queen's Lady in Waiting who does not really wait on her but helps by answering some of her many letters, and by entertaining her many visitors. Another was the Queen's Equerry, who in former times would have looked after her horses. He was a tall young man in a handsome black uniform with gold tassels who told me how to behave with the Queen. I should bow my head when I entered her room and again when she shook my hand, and the same when I took my leave. Then there was a jovial, stout old gentleman who looks after the Order of Merit, the medal which the Queen was going to give me. And finally there was Professor [Ernst] Gombrich, the art historian who actually went to the same school in Vienna as I did and who was to receive the same medal from the Queen. Vivien had told me that he is very nice and knows a fantastic lot about art. He went to see the Queen first, because he is older than I am.

I was quite excited, because it is rare that the Queen asks you to see her, and even rarer that she gives anyone this medal. I had a present for her in my pocket. It was a card with a very pretty drawing that the nine-year-old daughter of friends of mine had drawn for her. I entered the Queen's room as her Equerry had told me. She greeted me with such a pleasant smile that I did not feel at all awkward talking to her. She asked me what made me come to England and how things were going in my laboratory 25 years after she had opened it. Of course, I nearly forgot, first of all she gave me the Order of Merit, a beautiful medal which I shall show you next time you

Max and Gisela lunching at the house of Jean Medawar (far left) with Ernst and Ilse Gombrich. A picture of Peter Medawar is on the wall. His death had vacated the place in the Order of Merit, which my father had now been awarded.

come here. Finally I told her about the research of some of my friends who are trying to make new and better medicines against AIDS and she was very interested in that. I had told her Equerry that I had trouble sitting on soft chairs and asked if the Queen would mind if I stood up. He went and asked the Queen, and told me she would not mind. In fact she received me standing and never sat down while I was with her, which was very tactful of her.

In case you wonder what she wore, no crown but a nicely cut wine-red dress with a lovely diamond brooch in the form of a crown and her initials ERII.

I found Granny and Vivien waiting for me at the gate and we all went to have chicken and mashed potatoes together at the house of a friend.

To Lotte Perutz, March 25, 1988

I thought you might like to see the letter I wrote to Timothy and Marion after my visit to the Queen. She looked young and attractive and has a charming, slightly diffident way of talking to you. Never condescending.

Next day I exhibited my medal in our canteen with a note saying that it had really been earned by all members of the lab past and present, because I sensed that it is the fantastic success of the lab above all that earned me this recognition.

To Franz and Gerda Perutz, May 21, 1988

About travel on Italian trains: I could tell you sagas. In 63 when Gisela and I and the children travelled from Rome to Naples, two men attacked each other with knives. Before your wedding [in 1986], I first stood in line in Rome endlessly for my ticket to Naples, then the porter had put me on a train that was so packed that I had to stand all the way with my luggage in front of the toilet; then I discovered that he put me on the wrong train which stopped at a different Naples station from the one where my Neapolitan friend was meeting me. Travelling may sometimes be hellish, but then there are heavenly places to reward you when you get there.

My college, Peterhouse, was so pleased with my winning the Order of Merit that they celebrated it with a party for all the Fellows of the College plus my family and any other guests I wanted to invite. After the lunch the Master, an ecclesiastical historian [Henry Chadwick], presented Gisela and me with a huge silver loving cup inscribed to both of us in memory of the occasion. I was very touched by all this.

To Lotte Perutz, May 21, 1988

Our main news was the marvellous party at Peterhouse described in my letter to Franz and Gerda. It is very nice for Gisela and me, the ex-enemy aliens, who felt a bit excluded from Cambridge society for many years afterwards, to be so fêted here now.

Vivien has bought a word processor. As to a word processor, I am very happy with my fountain pen and don't long for anything else. I dislike any machine coming in between me and the sheet of paper. By some magic, thoughts come when I grasp my pen. I doubt that they will in front of a keyboard.

To Robin and Sue Perutz, June 10, 1988

Mummy and I enjoyed our stay at Bonn. The order of the Pour le Mérite is a unique kind of club where you meet people from the sciences, humanities and the arts from many different countries. Where else would I have the chance of a long chat with the director of the Hermitage in Leningrad or even a short one with George Kennan, the American historian and former ambassador to Moscow, or with [Hansjochum] Autrum, the zoologist who succeeded [Karl] von Frisch (the bee Frisch) in his chair at Munich. He turned out to have been a close friend of [Nikolai] Timofeyev-Resovsky (of Timofeyev, Zimmer and Delbrück) who told me more about that legendary character.

[Michail] Piotrowskij [director of the Hermitage], the Russian from Leningrad, told me of his discovery of a road from Aswan to an ancient Egyptian gold mine and of a Babylonian (or Assyrian) fortress in Turkey that was burnt down so that the ashes buried all its contents and preserved them like the ashes of Vesuvius at Pompeii. This reminds me that a Russian geneticist has just brought me presents from Natasha, [Vladimir] Engel-hardt's daughter. He came to England to visit his aunt in London. Previous visits had been made conditional on his working for the KGB, who wanted him to give them a list of the people in his laboratory who had read Solzhenitsyn! He refused and was not allowed out.

The award is a solemn ceremony held in the Aula of the university in the presence of the Bundespräsident and about 700 guests. Manfred Eigen spoke for me and did it most charmingly with much warmth and humour. He asked me to stand next to him so that he could address me "Du hast dies und das gemacht."[26]

The ceremony was followed by dinner at Bundespräsident Weizsäcker's residence. I sat next to the sculptor's [Eduardo Chillida's] wife. We talked about Miró who was a friend of theirs. Before she had watched him, she said, she could not believe that Miró could draw the same little star with loving passion time and time again, but once she and her husband spent a fortnight with him and saw that he puts that loving passion into every one of his pic-tures and that's why they are such a delight. I talked about my hobby-horse that the Two Cultures are a myth, because art and science are both imagina-tive creations, but she disputed this because scientists stand on their prede-cessor's shoulders, while artists can learn nothing from them. The very fact that one artist has created a piece of art means no one else can do anything like it. What about techniques, I asked, surely you learn those from your elders. No, not even techniques. Vivien tells me that all this is fashionable nonsense. She is the mother of 9 children and still an attractive and very

---

[26]"You"—the familiar "Du" rather than the formal "Sie"—did this and that.

lively old lady. On my other side was the wife of a German jurist from Berkeley who has 8 children and 20 grandchildren. How would you like it, Timothy and Marion, to have 18 cousins? Wouldn't it be fun?

The President gave us an off-the-cuff talk on the international scene, in the course of which he chided Mrs. T. [Thatcher] for quoting Saint Paul about everyone having a duty to work; when he read Saint Paul carefully, he found that what Saint Paul means is that everyone has a *right to work.*

To Robin, Sue, Timothy and Marion Perutz. Zürich, September 1, 1988

Marion, I thought of *you* when the bus driver sounded his horn. Before I tell you why, let me explain. The Swiss Post buses have a special horn that sounds a little melody, the sort of melody the drivers of the horse-drawn post coaches might have blown on their horns before there were motorcars. You asked me once if one can weep for joy. The sound of that horn brought tears to my eyes because it evoked memories of all the happy holidays I spent in the Swiss mountains when I was young and of the war years when I wondered if I would ever hear that sound again.

Strap hanging in that crowded bus as it climbed the steep hairpins of the precipitous road made me feel that I am 24, just out again to explore another Alpine valley. Besides I felt young and strong after lifting all my luggage unaided. This morning I even tied *both* my bootlaces. Whence I no longer feel a handicapped old so-and-so but a grandfather back in his youth.

I took the bus to St. Luc, a village on a steep mountainside 400 m above Vissoie, which is down in the valley. There, an Italian-born geneticist who works in London built himself a chalet 34 years ago. [Guido] Pontecorvo made me think of you, because his hobby is the genetics of Alpine flowers. He told me that very similar flowers grow in high mountains all over the world. For example, he has recently been to Tibet to study the Alpine flora. He found that the flowers that grow in Tibet, the Andes, the Alps or on Kilimanjaro are different species, but they have evolved similar patterns, even though the climates in those mountains are very different. Pontecorvo cannot explain this. He wonders whether the spectral distribution of the sunlight at high altitudes has favoured the evolution of similar species in widely separated habitats. He told me that the near infrared is more intense at high altitudes and the distribution of intensity in the visible is also different. I had a very interesting afternoon with him. He is a charming character.

To Hugh Trevor-Roper, Lord Dacre, September 23, 1988

Dinner in the hall at Christ Church after you left me there was a treat, not for the food, which was frugal, but the magnificent hall with its great portraits. Millais's picture of Gladstone, Kneller's of Locke, Romney's of Wesley are all marvellous. I then spotted an interesting looking character high up on the left of the entrance. By climbing on a chair I then managed to read the inscription "Masterman," someone of whom I had not heard. I asked [Henry] Chadwick the other night and he told me of his exploits during the war. The Auden portrait also looks very interesting. Seeing them all was a great joy.

But what philistines most scientists are: for all the notice the people I dined with took of their surroundings we might just as well have eaten at McDonald's.

To Hugh Trevor-Roper, Lord Dacre, September 28, 1988

I have now read your chapter about Thomas More's *Utopia*, and was astonished how that man of the world could have thought up so naive a political system. It reminded me of Hermann Hesse's *Glasperlenspiel*,[27] where all these pious monks solve the world's problems by thinking about Bach's music.

To Gisela Perutz and Family. Brookhaven, October 3, 1988

The man sitting next to me in the British Airways plane recognised me and introduced himself as a former member of Bell Labs in New Jersey. I did not take in his name at first, but after he had told me of his ingenious discovery of a molecular switch, I asked him again: "Angelo Lamola." "You must be the author of the paper showing that computer switches of molecular dimension are unlikely to become practicable in the foreseeable future?" That was the paper I quoted in my *New York Review* of Feinberg's book on *Tomorrow's World,* supporting my contention that Feinberg's forecasts had no basis in scientific fact. Then Lamola told me that 20 years' work on the development of molecular switches lay behind that paper and that it was written in order to stop dubious scientists extracting millions of dollars for the development of biocomputers from a gullible Congress.

It was lucky that my visit [to Alex and Jane Rich] coincided with their party in honour of Francis Crick, which included the [Matthew] Meselsons. He is the man who proved that the yellow rain in Thailand consisted of bee

---

[27]*The Glass Bead Game,* published in 1943.

faeces and not biological poisons made in Russia. He has been working for the elimination of chemical weapons and has fresh hopes that this will now be accomplished.

To Robin and Sue Perutz. New York to London, October 26, 1988

At Boston Airport I bought Stephen Hawking's best-seller *A Brief History of Time*. I have just finished reading it and am convinced that no more than one in a hundred people who bought it read beyond the first 20 pages or so. It is heavy going for the likes of me. It is not nearly as readable as Stephen Weinberg's *First Three Minutes* and gets obscurely metaphysical in the final chapters. If it were not for Hawking's terrible affliction and the miracle that he was able to write such a book, I doubt that people would buy it. It is a fantastic victory of the spirit over the body.

To Hugh Trevor-Roper, Lord Dacre, November 12, 1988

I found your pursuit of Hitler's entourage very interesting and am still amazed to read "Johannmeier was easily found, living with his parents in Iserlohn." Allied intelligence must have been very efficient to find those wanted individuals in the chaos of defeated Germany before the days of computers. Rereading parts of your book[28] makes me wonder what it must have felt like to you, a young officer, not only to discover what happened, but to penetrate the mentalities of the men who had served in Hitler's court. Before that you would only have read about such characters in books; now you had them naked and reduced to size, as it were, in your hands. It must have been a fantastic experience and one that shaped your historical judgements.

Among your *Renaissance Essays* [published in 1985] I most enjoyed the Lisle Letters. They convey the impression that the seeking of privileges, enrichment at the expense of those who have fallen from power, bribery in the form of costly presents and every other kind of political opportunism were regarded as natural then as take-overs and asset stripping in the City are today. Your picture did remind me of good old Austria where advancement was through influence in high places, known as "Protektion" [patronage], an institution my mother firmly believed in. When I won the Nobel Prize, she proudly remarked to a cousin of mine: "Dabei hatte er keine Protektion." [It wasn't even due to patronage].

---

[28]*The Last Days of Hitler,* published in 1947.

I was invited to dine with the undergraduates last June. To my surprise and delight I was entertained by half a dozen attractive, lively and high-spirited young girls, a wonderful improvement on my days as a research student.

To Lotte Perutz, January 8, 1989

On the 27th I took the grandchildren to the Natural History Museum in London to see the Chinese dinosaurs—a fantastic sight. The largest is 22 m long, with a neck of about 8 m, but the numbers don't mean much until you actually see the skeleton of this immense beast that must have devoured a dozen trees a day just to live. It made me think that the dinosaurs died out because they had deforested the world, just as we are doing now. This seems more plausible than [Luis and Walter] Alvarez's idea that a meteorite killed them. . . .[29]

I have spent nearly all my time on a review[30] about proteins that change their structure in response to chemical stimuli, like haemoglobin. This subject came into focus last year because crystallographers have solved the structure of several of them and found out how they worked. So far no one has thought of looking at them as a whole to compare and, if possible, unify the principles underlying their function.

To Solly Zuckerman, February 3, 1989

I read your review of Talbott's biography of [Paul Henry] Nitze[31] with interest and sadness, because you show that our fate hangs not on what is really the case, but on what a bunch of self-serving people make those in power believe to be the case. Only Eisenhower and Kennedy were shrewd enough to see through them. It is ironic that Nitze, who was clearly picked as a disarmament negotiator to prevent any agreement being reached with the Russians, having been given that job, should have made it his life's ambition to succeed in reaching agreement.

---

[29]The impact theory explains the high levels of iridium at the geological Cretaceous-Tertiary extinction boundary and was supported by the discovery of the Chicxulub crater off the Yucatan Peninsula in Mexico.

[30]Perutz MF. 1989. Mechanisms of cooperativity and allosteric regulation in proteins. *Q. Rev. Biophys.* **22:** 139–236.

[31]Talbott, S. 1988. *The Master of the Game: Paul Nitze and the Nuclear Peace.* Alfred A. Knopf. Nitze was the architect of U.S.-Soviet cold war defence policy for 40 years.

To Timothy Perutz, March 24, 1989

I am reading a book by a German physicist who tells a story about the great mathematician [Carl Friedrich] Gauss. When he was 9, his school teacher told the boys to work out the sum of all the numbers from 1 to 100, thinking that this would keep them busy and give him time to twiddle his thumbs. To his astonishment Gauss got up in a few minutes and told him the answer: 5050. He then explained to the teacher that all one has to do is to add one after another the remaining smallest and largest number whose sum is always 101:

$$100 + 1 = 101$$
$$99 + 2 = 101$$
$$\cdot$$
$$\cdot$$
$$\cdot$$
$$51 + 50 = 101$$

Since there are altogether 50 such pairs of numbers, their sum is clearly 5050. Simple, after you have thought of it!

To Hugh Trevor-Roper, Lord Dacre, April 5, 1989

I read [Peter] Carrington's[32] autobiography and liked his attitude to people and events. I first met him when we both got honorary degrees here and later visited him at the Foreign Office when the Pontifical Academy put me on a committee to formulate a declaration against nuclear war, to be signed by the presidents of the world's scientific academies.

I heard that we were to ask for a pledge of No First Use of Nuclear Weapons, and I did not want to do this if it went against British Government policy.

I put it to Carrington that the threat of nuclear retaliation in the event of an attack by conventional forces was hardly credible, because the Russians knew that we knew that it would be suicidal.

Carrington argued that the Russians could not be sure that we would not use our nuclear weapons all the same, and that this uncertainty was the deterrent on which our security rested. I then asked him what my committee should press for instead, and he said No First Attack. I did persuade my Russian colleagues to incorporate some such phrase in our document. The

---

[32]Carrington, Peter. 1988. *Reflect on Things Past: The Memoirs of Lord Carrington.* HarperCollins.

chief Russian was [Yevgeny] Velikhov, now Gorbachev's scientific advisor, a brilliant and charming man with a disarming sense of humour.

So the presidents of the academies all went to Rome (I didn't because I had something else on) and spent 2 or 3 days redrafting what we had drafted, but then it did not get ready for the Pope in time because the Vatican's only Xerox machine had broken down.

It never made the headlines either, because the Vatican's press office is hopelessly inefficient, and they had not thought out that two things are needed, first to draft such a declaration and then to devise a way of publicising it.

To come back to Carrington, he impressed me by his good sense and I liked his book for its light on events, and for his way of seeing the good in the people he worked with. I was surprised that he found Henry Kissinger the most brilliant politician he had come across and also a great patriot—very different from the cynical comments one reads about him.

To Timothy Perutz, April 10, 1989

After the meeting at Edinburgh an Italian biologist visited me here and told me about fish in the Antarctic that have colourless blood—blood without haemoglobin![33] I had read about them, but had never seen a picture of one or heard how they live.

He showed me a colour picture of one that had very large gills, and he told me that it has a larger heart than other fish of the same size. It has no scales and many blood vessels close to the skin. It lives in very cold water at temperatures close to $0°C$ or a little below (seawater freezes below $0°C$ because it is salty.)

How does it get enough oxygen? Oxygen is more soluble in cold than in warm water, so more oxygen can diffuse into his blood through the large gills. Oxygen can also diffuse through the skin, and the large heart can pump it round efficiently. Even so I read that these fish are sluggish. I expect they run out of oxygen if they move fast.

They were first described in print by an American biologist in the 1950s, but the Italian told me that a biologist on Shackleton's expedition discovered one around 1913. He wanted to draw and describe it for a scientific journal, but before he had a chance to do so, the ship's cat had eaten it.

---

[33]Antarctic icefish; suborder Notothenioidei, family Channichthyidae, the only known vertebrates without haemoglobin.

To Lotte Perutz, April 19, 1989

When I received Mrs. Thatcher's invitation to lunch I sent her a copy of my book [*Is Science Necessary?*]. She welcomed me with the words "I have read your book and took it to Africa with me"! and told me that she had had no idea of my internment and deportation. 15 of the British Nobel laureates came to her lunch, plus the secretary of State for Education and two men of her scientific staff. She was a changed person in private. None of that school-mistressy, all-knowing hectoring manner. At lunch she put herself between Dorothy and me, and was very nice to both of us. I asked her to tell me about Gorbachev and was interested that he was a farmer's son and that his father had been expropriated by Stalin. Now I understand one reason why he wants to give farmers back their land. I also asked her to tell me about her African trip, and she gave an interesting and *compassionate* account of it. I only wish she would show the same compassion for the unemployed and homeless in the U.K.

My medical colleagues are concerned that clinical research will be adversely affected by the impending reorganisation of the National Health Service. As this is a subject about which I care very much, I had myself briefed, and composed a short memorandum about it. I found the Prime Minister very receptive. She is very keen on research and tells everybody that I convinced her that the support of young talent is the best way to get results. She listened to what I had to tell her, took my memorandum away with her and seemed determined to follow it up. I hope she will.

When the dessert came, she asked everybody to bring up whatever problems they had on their minds and seemed very open to ideas, whereas other people complain that she never listens.

She asked us, collectively, for suggestions how to spot and support young talent. I found my colleagues' response disappointing, probably because most of them have retired from active university jobs. When I came home I asked Robin, who told me the right answers which I shall pass on to her.

People tell me that she holds me in great respect and pays attention to my views. I am astonished to find myself in this fortunate position, seeing that I don't respect many of her views and publicly opposed the Falklands War. Now I must try to use my unique position of influence to the benefit of British science.

We did get an excellent lunch; even my special diet lunch was delicious.

To Noel Annan, May 3, 1989

I wonder if you can help me. Silvers has asked me to review a book *Mother Country* by Marilynne Robinson, an American novelist.[34] The book is written to warn Americans and the world that Britain is poisoning the globe by its radioactive effluents from Sellafield.

The book is written in three parts: a long introduction which summarises her indictment; Part I outlines British social history from the 14th century to the present day to show how a tradition of callous disregard for the social consequences of its actions has conditioned British society to perpetrate such a crime against humanity; Part II gives a lurid account of the negligent, money-grabbing accident-ridden running of the Sellafield plant, the National Radiological Protection Board, the venality of our MPs and the connivance of the British public. The author has drawn all her material from English newspapers. As far as I can see she has not consulted any scientist. Her book is written with an irate passion similar to Rachel Carson's *Silent Spring*. Its mixture of fact and nonsense reminds me of the judge in Kleist's *Der zerbrochene Krug* saying to the defendant:

> In eurem Kopf liegt Wissenschaft und Irrtum
> Geknetet innig wie ein Teig zusammen;
> Mit jedem Schnitte gebt Ihr mir von beiden.[35]

Venomous sneers at all aspects of British life and especially intellectuals abound. I think the book will be a great success in America.

To Hugh Trevor-Roper, Lord Dacre, September 27, 1989

When I wrote to you from the lab earlier today I forgot to congratulate you on your brilliant review of Toynbee's biography.[36] What extraordinary characters you bring to light! Toynbee is almost as good as Sir Edmund Backhouse.[37] Both are "on the borderline" in their different ways, in mistaking their fantasies for reality, in being egocentric to a degree, in being interested in other people only to manipulate them, though Backhouse hid his megalomania under a mask of humility, while Toynbee seems brazenly to sport it.

---

[34]The review in *The New York Review of Books* is republished in Max's book of essays, *I Wish I'd Made You Angry Earlier*.

[35]In your head knowledge and error are kneaded together as in dough; with every slice you give me both.

[36]McNeill, W.H. 1989. *Arnold J. Toynbee: A Life*. Oxford University Press, Oxford and N.Y.

[37]The chief character in Trevor-Roper's historical thriller *The Hermit of Peking*.

Do you have a copy of the original review in which you pricked the bubble of his scholarship? I should love to read it.

To Lotte Perutz. Berlin and East Germany, October 27–November 1, 1989

I retired to cook my supper and to an early bed, because the driver of the Akademie Leopoldina was to take me to Halle in East Germany next morning. I had last been there over 20 years ago when I had to carry my suitcase and stereoprojector 1/4 mile across Checkpoint Charlie, to be met at the other side in a ramshackle Russian car. This time the driver had a permit to pick me up in West Berlin in a smart Mercedes presented to the Akademie by the Max-Planck Gesellschaft and the frontier guards let us in without bothering to examine our luggage—a great change for the better. Last time any deviation from the prescribed route had been bei Strafe verboten [a punishable offence]. This time I had no difficulty in persuading the driver to take a detour to Wittenberg, a once pretty and now dilapidated town that contains the church where Martin Luther posted his 95 articles. Its exterior was black and crumbling, but the interior was nicely redecorated. It contains a collection of paintings by [Lucas] Cranach, father and son, including a beautiful triptych showing the last supper with Christ and the Apostles seated at a *round* rather than oblong table and an unusual disposition of the figures around it.[38] A young custodian took me round and made the pictures interesting by telling me who all the people were whose portraits Cranach had painted as apostles and other biblical figures. One painting shows Christ's parable of the vineyard: on the right, virtuous Protestants in simple clothes tend the vines; on the left the expensively attired Pope and Catholic clergy destroy them. The back of the triptych shows the Last Judgement, which students of former times had defaced with their names, those who had passed their exams signing on the figures ascending to heaven, and those who had failed them signing on those descending to hell, contrary to Christ's dictum: "Selig sind die Armen im Geiste, denn ihrer ist das Himmelreich."[39]

Halle had improved little since I last visited it. Few houses seemed to have had a face-lift since the thirties, or possibly not since the beginning of the century. Ruins of bombed houses added to the general gloom, but this

---

[38]Unusual only relative to the depictions in Italian refectories.

[39]"Blessed are the poor in spirit, for theirs is the kingdom of heaven." The German "Geist" means both spirit and wit and therefore intelligence.

was soon dissipated for me by a demonstration of 50,000 people, calling for freedom. "Wir wollen freie Wahlen," [We want free elections] "Weg mit denen, die 40 Jahre lang recht hatten," [Down with those who for 40 years were right] "Weg mit der Mauer" [Down with the wall] were some of the banners they carried. They chanted "Wir sind das Volk, wir kommen wieder" [We're the people, we're coming back]. Most of them were young. I was told that those young people who did not flee to the West are now demonstrating. It was a moving experience. A colleague from West Germany and the Vice President of the Leopoldina with his wife were to have dinner with me at 7.00, but we waited for her for nearly an hour. She finally arrived in a euphoric mood, having taken part in the demonstration, she, a respected paediatrician at the Bezirksspital [district hospital] and wife of a university professor with three grown children. She told us that past demonstrations had been preceded by a church service and most demonstrators carried candles that made the demonstrations even more impressive, but tonight had been too windy. No police were to be seen and a convoy of Russian troops passing by took no notice. The demonstrators often challenge party officials to discussions to demand radical reforms of the system. I asked about the army's attitude as that proved crucial in Peking, and was told that 9 October had been the critical day when the government posted troops on top of Leipzig buildings ready to mow down the demonstrators, but some of the soldiers declared that they would shoot the ones who shot the demonstrators. Since then no more troops had been called in. The paediatrician told us that she had been scared when the demonstrations started. It had always been dangerous to speak her mind lest an informer overheard her, but "Seit 8 Tagen kuck ich mich nicht mehr um." [Eight days ago I stopped glancing behind myself.] This was the most revealing remark I heard on my visit. My colleagues were concerned that the people's initiative might peter out, because East Germany has no Lech Walesa, nor anyone who is politically experienced outside the Communist camp.

My driver told me that 90% of the people were Kleinbürger [petty bourgeois] like himself and did not want a capitalist state but a free socialist one.

Next morning he drove me to Dresden.

The air is filthy with smoke around Dresden and Halle, because all the power is generated from soft coal and everything is scarred by enormous pits left after the coal has been extracted by open-cast mining. It is estimated to last for another 50 years, after which there will be no more indigenous fuel. There is hardly any nuclear power, although this would be the obvious source, since uranium is mined in the Erzgebirge nearby.

I gave my lecture to a packed and appreciative audience. I delivered it in memory of Kurt Mothes, the Akademie's late president with whom I had made friends: a man of great character and courage who contrived to keep the Akademie non-political in the midst of East Germany, with members drawn from East and West Germany, Austria and Switzerland and German-speaking émigrés like myself. I began my talk with a tribute to him, saying that he would have been pleased with the developments I had witnessed and remarking that "after being oppressed by dictatorships of the right and left people now realised that, despite its shortcomings, democracy based on free elections remained the best political system men had devised." This drew vigorous applause. I then switched to proteins.

By the way shops in East Germany were well-stocked with essentials. I saw no one standing in line for food or anything else, but I heard that any special item, like the odd screw you need, is unobtainable.

To Hugh Trevor-Roper, Lord Dacre, November 25, 1989

I was touched by your choosing *Is Science Necessary?* as the Book of the Year and delighted when I was told this afternoon that your recommendation had appeared. I rushed to buy the *Telegraph* and was particularly pleased by your last sentence, alluding to the human values I try to express in my writing about science and scientists.

I usually hate watching the news as it homes in on every place in the world where people are killing each other, but last night I was pleased that Gisela made me turn it on. The scene on Wenceslas Square was quite fantastic, literally so. Not in my wildest fantasies would I have imagined that something like that would happen. I was in Prague in August 1968 amidst the euphoria of the people who believed they had shaken off the Stalinist tyranny, and two weeks after I left the terrible blow fell. When I was next invited to the Soviet Union, I replied to the Soviet Academy that I won't set foot there as long as a Stalinist regime is imposed on Czechoslovakia. Not that this helped the Czechs, but it helped me to vent my fury. As you said to me in Peterhouse, it is fantastic that all this should have happened without bloodshed.

The Perutz family is rooted in Bohemia. My ancestors lived in a small town called Rakonitz (Rakovník). My paternal grandfather and his brother made their fortune by introducing English cotton spinning and weaving machinery into the Austrian Monarchy, and my uncles then ran the great textile firm Brüder Perutz in Prague. My maternal grandfather founded another cotton weaving mill, also in Bohemia. Some years ago my elder brother went to look at one of these, now nationalized mills. He found a window that had been cracked when he left in 1938 had not yet been replaced.

In short, events in Czechoslovakia touch me even more than those in Germany.

The news from Prague and the beautiful weather put me in a euphoric mood this morning, but when I tried to convey my joy to some of the fellows of Peterhouse I found that they could not have been less moved if last night's momentous events had taken place in Polynesia. John Adamson was the sole exception; he does have a sense of history.

I read "Clio Deceived" with the greatest interest.[40] It does not seem to have occurred to the German historians and officials that by trying to deceive the world about the origins of the First World War, they were deceiving themselves and laying the foundations for the same ghastly miscalculations about Germany's chances of gaining world domination by force of arms to be repeated. No one appears to have thought of the possibility then of gaining world domination peacefully, by superior technology and organisation as the Japanese and the West Germans have now done.

I was disappointed that none of the reviewers of *Is Science Necessary?* commented on my review of Weizmann and my quotations from his speeches: "One law and one manner shall be for you and for the stranger that sojourneth among you." "I am certain that the world will judge the Jewish state by what it does to the Arabs." My piece originally appeared in *Nature* and was met by stony silence on the part of my colleagues in Israel.

---

[40]Herwig, H.H. 1987. Clio deceived: Patriotic self-censorship in Germany after the great war. *Int. Security* **12:** 5–44.

1990s

"When I asked Margaret Thatcher what she thought of
[François] Mitterand she said that he promises you one
thing today and does the opposite tomorrow. It's a pity
she can't marry Gorbachev now."

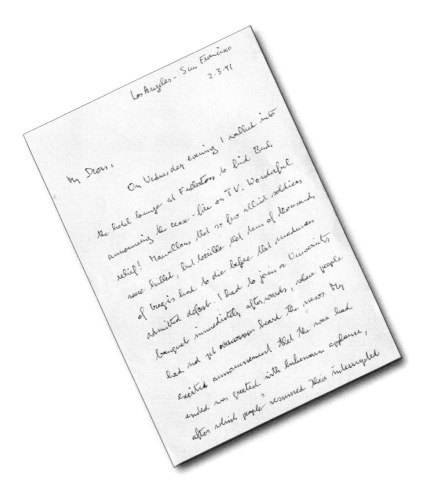

Like most people, Max enjoyed reminiscing as he aged, but in many ways, the character of the letters of this decade is similar to the last: his descriptions, his comments on people and his interests in scientific history and contemporary politics constitute their chief interest. His life changed in two ways during this decade: first, he became more active politically. He organised a sadly ineffective Pontifical Academy meeting on population control and served as the Royal Society's representative on the scientific academies' International Human Rights Nework, set up on the initiative of Carol Corillon at the U.S. National Academy of Sciences. Second, as documented in the letters, he moved out of haemoglobin research and turned his attention to the molecular basis of Huntington disease. Alan Weeds surveys Max's research interests in the 1990s in the following paragraphs.

Max's output remained prodigious: he published 46 articles during the decade. These show his increasing involvement with protein structures related to neurodegenerative diseases, principally Huntington disease. The severity and age of onset of this disease are correlated with mutations in the amino acid sequence of a protein called huntingtin. The mutations lead to the repetition of a particular amino acid residue (glutamine) and the greater the number of glutamine repeats, the earlier the age of onset. Evidence suggests that these repeats alone are sufficient to provoke the disease. Max wanted to understand the molecular mechanism and particularly to elucidate the structure of the polyglutamine repeats and show how their expansion related to changes in huntingtin structure.

Work on haemoglobin from the parasitic worm Ascaris *had led Max to propose a new kind of structure containing "β-strands," which he called a polar zipper. He went on to postulate the existence of polar zippers in huntingtin as a result of research on synthetic peptides containing glutamine repeats. Peptides containing extended repeats form rod-shaped particles that Max proposed might contain rolled-up sheets of these structures known as "antiparallel β sheets." With the normal length of repeats, huntingtin is soluble, but with longer lengths it forms aggregates. Indeed aggregates containing the protein have been detected in inclusion bodies (abnormal structures observed by light microscopy) in various types of cells in the brains of affected individuals. In later X-ray work published in 2002, he proposed that these longer sequences form helical water-filled fibres, which he described as "nanotubes." Max could account for the relationship between age of onset of the disease and the number of glutamine repeats on the basis of standard nucleation theory in physical chemistry. Because the formation of β structures is a feature of many neurodegenerative diseases, including Alzheimer and Parkinson diseases, this work was of considerable interest in the field and not without contention.*

Max published three papers on glutamine repeats in his final years, the last two being submitted the day before he was admitted to hospital in mid December, 2001. He was looking for a unifying theory that might explain a variety of neurodegenerative diseases. Inevitably there was controversy and uncertainty remains to this day. We cannot yet judge the extent to which he was right—only time will tell whether his ideas explain the cause and development of these diseases. The philosopher Whitehead observed "It is more important that an idea is fruitful than that it is correct." Even if some of the ideas do not stand the test of time, Max's enthusiasm and involvement greatly raised the profile of the work, stimulated others and helped increase funding for this very important research.

To Lotte Perutz, March 25, 1990

I am not sure if I told you or wrote about my involvement with the organisation of a workshop on population and resources to be held at the Pontifical Academy of Sciences next year. Fortunately I managed to recruit the Director of the Population Council of the U.N., a Hungarian called Paul Demeny, to join us in Rome [to draw up a programme]. He is said to be the top scholar in the field. The workshop's purpose will be to bring the horrendous population problem and the bleak outlook for the future to the Pope's attention and to persuade him to a more enlightened attitude towards birth control.

To Vivien, Robin and Sue Perutz. Richmond, VA, April 27, 1990

I have just finished the fourth and last of my lectures here and have half an hour before I have to attend a reception. This morning began with a visit to the chemistry labs where one of the professors was in the street to welcome me together with a photographer. We all repaired to his labora-

tory together where the professor pressed a flask with a brownish-red solution of his favourite enzyme into my hands to have himself photographed
~10 times in my company clasping his treasure. I was then conducted to a
room where reluctant graduate students had to take turns telling me their
projects. This was followed by a taped interview with a reporter for the
university magazine.

Lunch with two ex MRC friends, delightful people with a warm sense
of humour with whom I feel quite at home.

After lunch another interview with the science reporter of the local
paper, an intelligent widely read man with a physics degree, while his photographer clicked her camera shutter like a metronome. After spouting at
him for half an hour, off to another building to give the so and so lecture.
My heart sank when I saw an oversized silver bowl on the lecture bench,
but luckily it transpired that I merely have my name inscribed on it.

Last night there was a party for me and the faculty where each of the
men used the opportunity to present me with an unsolicited seminar on his
work, reminding me of the Japanese visitor who poked his head through the
door and asked, "Can I give you a lecture?" Only they never even asked.

April 29, 1990 [At yet another party I] was solemnly presented with a mini
edition of the big bowl, designed by Thomas Jefferson who, besides draft-
ing the American Constitution, also designed Richmond's handsome classical Capitol. They drew up a programme for a man of iron half my age, leaving me no time even to prepare my four lectures. I had to refuse to carry out
some of my tasks in order to get them organised. Yesterday's programme
lasted from 9.00 am to 8.00 pm.

At the party I met some nice people with whom I could have normal
conversations instead of being exploited as a captive audience. Which
reminds me that yesterday a departmental chairman used the opportunity
of having to introduce me to a multi-disciplinary audience to deliver himself of a eulogy, not of me, but of his department, telling the audience of his
$3 million grant income, the number of papers published, the number of
graduate students turned into Ph.D.s and tenured positions. After this Tonie
Wright got up and made a charming, light-hearted introduction of me.

Speaking of a sense of humour and what goes with it, a sense of proportion, which many people here seem to lack, one postdoc from Krakow
came up to me after the party to thank me solemnly in the name of the Polish nation for my lecture. Another visitor, Russian, I seem to remember, had
a sideline in philosophy and worked on "Humour." He showed me the pro-

gramme of a 4 day conference to be held at the University of Sheffield next August on Humour. He didn't think there was anything funny in it.

To Lotte Perutz, May 25, 1990

I also went to an AIDS committee 2 days after our return, but jet lag made it very hard for me to keep awake. Apparently clinical tests of the drug that was developed here, and on which I pinned high hopes, have run into the ground in the U.S. because of patient resistance. They all want AZT[1] despite its toxicity. I have asked Searle in Chicago to let the MRC have the drug for trials here, but Searle refused for complex patent reasons or because of FDA[2] objections. I have just written again to the chairman asking him to change his mind. It's such a shame to let it drop.

A British, Swiss-owned firm has made a compound that looks very promising in *in vitro* tests, but so far has not been tried on humans. I am sure that other drugs will come soon, but vaccination is still far away. In some ways I shall miss being on the committee, but I shall be pleased not to have to cope with the mountainous agenda, mostly in unfamiliar fields, with which I am supposed to cope each month.

To Lotte Perutz, June 17, 1990

I have sent off my review of the [Peter] Medawar book to *The New York Review [of Books]* and am waiting for the editor's comments. When I send (solicited) reviews to the English *Times Literary Supplement* or the *London Review of Books*, I receive the proofs in due course, but never a word of encouragement or comment. By contrast, Robert Silvers, the editor of *The New York Review*, tells me if he likes my work. He is marvellous. He goes through every review with a fine tooth comb, questions anything that is not clear, asking you to enlarge on points that make it more interesting, accepting additions and alterations until the last minute when it actually goes to press. It's so much better to work for someone who takes an interest in one's efforts.

I was upset last week by a TV programme, lasting 45', purporting to prove that AIDS is not infectious. The producers found a German-born virologist in San Francisco[3] who clings to this view, I suspect because oth-

---

[1] Azidothymidine, also known as zidovudine.
[2] U.S. Food and Drug Administration.
[3] Peter Duesberg.

ers rather than he isolated the virus, and they picked out a carefully selected lot of people (idiots would be a better word) who supported that crazy view, without interviewing anyone who would have presented proofs of its infectivity. The clear message was that sexual pleasures can continue to be enjoyed without fear and that all the warnings about AIDS are put out by a self-interested gang determined to secure money for their research and their own pockets. It was criminal, because the millions who watched and believed it, will throw precaution to the winds and many more will die as a result. Sometimes I wish there were censorship. Media don't care a damn how many people are killed as long as they can create a sensation.

Sorry to close on this gloomy note.

To Hugh Trevor-Roper, Lord Dacre, August 27, 1990

I thoroughly agree with your views about Germany. I found already in the 1950s that the post-war generation was free from the chauvinism that Fritz Fischer described so vividly, and I regard the attribution of genetically determined and inherited national character as humbug. I therefore disagree with the attitudes of some of my ex-German Jewish colleagues who believed in collective guilt and swore never to set foot in Germany again.

*The family at Feder. (*Left to right*) Marion, Vivien and Gisela Perutz; Gerda Grafström (school friend of Gisela); Roy (Mac) Stock; Gerda (second wife of Franz); Robin, Max, Sue, and Timothy Perutz; Alice (Liesel) Frank Stock (cousin of Max)*

We had a superb holiday in the Swiss Alps, with children, grandchildren, cousins and in-laws. There were 12 of us and nobody quarrelled! I did a lot of mountain walking and in the intervals read [Andrei] Sakharov's autobiography which the *London Review of Books* sent me just before we left. This portrayed a man very different from his public image, as you will see from the enclosed manuscript which I am sending you just in case you have any comments or corrections that I might incorporate at the proof stage.

To Hugh Trevor-Roper, Lord Dacre, January 1, 1991

About Sakharov [Nobel Laureate for Peace, 1975]: after I had drafted my review, I got worried that I might have misinterpreted his *Memoirs* and drawn a false picture of his personality. I therefore rang Zhores Medvedev, Roy's brother, the biologist who lives in London, and told him that I had written this review. Before I could say more, he interjected that there had been two sides to his person. When he had read my review, he reassured me that I had got it right and confirmed that Sakharov lacked all sense of humour (which Medvedev possesses in a high degree). The Medvedevs then came to visit us one Sunday and told us more about Sakharov's coldness to his children and about Elena Bonner's [Sakharov's wife] domineering ways. On the other hand, after I had sent off my own review, I read the one in the *The New York Review* and learned about Sakharov's key role in perestroika. It seems to me that his voice would be needed now more than ever to tell Gorbachev that the assumption of dictatorial powers will not solve his problems.

I read your "Uses of Fakery" with much amusement and interest, such as your account of Thomas J. Wise, the pure scholar who traded in his own faked first editions, but did not escape exposure. Was it the last year of his life, *because* he had been exposed? I had not realised that Erasmus demonstrated the forgery of the only biblical text that can be cited in defence of the Trinity. Your review, together with the German historian Horst Fuhrmann's book *Einladung ins Mittelalter*[4] have revealed to me that much of the Catholic Church's dogma rests on forgeries. What a gullible child I was to believe it, miracles and all!

To Lotte Perutz, January 6, 1991

Last November I assembled a programme committee for the Study Week that is to be held at the Pontifical Academy, next autumn on Resources and

---

[4]The title means "Invitation to the Middle Ages."

Population. I got some excellent people and also obtained good advice from outside the committee. The meeting was farcical because the President of the Academy, a genial, elderly chemist from a Catholic University in Rome, was not quite there. The Director of the Academy is a younger, vain, loquacious engineer-cum-padre who kept interrupting us in Italian, which only I could understand, and arguing over irrelevant trivia. I wondered if we would ever get there, but by the end of the day we had drawn up quite a good and ambitious programme. It then transpired that this would have to be agreed by the Vatican, possibly by the Pope himself, before invitations can go out. This was to be decided within a few days, but now, 7 weeks later, I am still waiting.

To Lotte Perutz, January 27, 1991

About Sakharov: Karl Popper phoned me last night. He was just reading Sakharov's *Memoirs* for the second time and was deeply shocked by his development of a hydrogen bomb that was thousands of times more powerful than the Hiroshima bomb. Popper pointed out to me that Sakharov put the super-bomb into [Nikita] Khrushchev's hands just before the Cuban missile crisis and he concluded that it was possession of that bomb that gave Khrushchev the confidence needed to challenge the U.S. Popper also quoted to me Sakharov's writing that in so doing "Khrushchev showed his mettle." Popper was particularly angry, he said, because he had given a lecture in honour of Sakharov's 60th birthday in N.Y. knowing nothing of his early activities.

I had lunch at Balliol the day before, having been invited by its new Master, the discoverer of the hepatitis B virus, Baruch Blumberg, a New Yorker who began his great work as a post doc at Oxford in 1955. I thought it was marvellous that this bastion of the English establishment should elect a New York Jew as their Master. After that lunch Gisela and I had tea with Trevor-Roper and Linde Davidson, Paul Ewald's daughter, at whose house we were staying. I raised my ambiguous feelings about the Gulf War. On the one hand, I still remember how the League of Nations' impotent protests against the Japanese invasion of Mongolia encouraged Mussolini's attack on Abyssinia, and how the Western powers' ineffective sanctions failed to stop Mussolini and drove him into the alliance with Hitler and encouraged Hitler's own aggressive plans. On the other hand, I have a horror of war and fear that it will not solve the problems of societies used to absolute rulers and military dictatorships, and will aggravate the Muslims' hatred of Western democracies. I am still hoping that the Allies will win without the appalling casualties for which the government is preparing. Addenbrookes Hospital has been asked to prepare for the arrival of 60 a day! A terrible thought.

I asked Trevor-Roper (alias Lord Dacre) what the feeling is in the House of Lords. Determination to see things through was his answer because Saddam Hussein clearly built up his formidable military machine for conquest, and he would have had to be stopped sooner or later. Hussein's great ambition is probably the obliteration of Israel.

I fear that Hussein's conquest of Kuwait and missile attacks on Israel will eventually make the Palestinians' lot in Israel much worse, because the U.S. government, which distanced itself from Israel's brutal suppression of the Palestinians, has now closed ranks with [Yitzhak] Shamir [Israeli Prime Minister].

Trevor-Roper reminded us of the origins of Saddam Hussein's accession to power. Roughly, his story was this: Hussein came to power by murdering all his rivals in the Baath party, which came to power by murdering General X, who came to power by murdering the king and his entire family.

Trevor-Roper talked about the problem of establishing an Iraqi government based on any kind of legitimacy. Jokingly, he suggested that King Hussein of Jordan be made king of Iraq, and Hussein's brother succeed him in Jordan.

The BBC treated us to an interview with Col. Gaddafi[5] sitting on a throne, attired in voluminous robes of what looked like sack cloths. A sly crook adept at evasion and demagogic double talk. His words were as ambiguous as the oracle's at Delphi, and delivered with a Roman emperor's air. Not a man I should like to encounter in a lonely street on a dark night.

This letter was interrupted by another telephone call from Karl Popper, for a further talk about Sakharov. Popper told me that the Soviets have still not stopped expanding their fleet which was capable of obliterating the U.S.A. He had suggested in an article in the *Welt* that the western powers should offer the U.S.S.R. economic help by buying their fleet and then sinking it. A splendid idea.

To Gisela, Vivien, Robin and Sue Perutz. Los Angeles to San Francisco, March 2, 1991

I was sorry that you, Gisela, were not here for Pauling's celebrations because it brought so many friends. My host, Ahmed Zewail, is an Egyptian who showed me his fantastic femto-second (0.000000000000006) resolution

---

[5]Muammar Abu al-Gaddafi, leader of Libya.

laser outfit that allows him to track atoms in chemical reactions. George Porter started his lecture with a slide of Muybridge's snapshot of a galloping horse, followed by a statement that since then we have learnt to follow molecular motions that occur a million times faster. Francis began his talk by recalling how thrilled he had been in the spring of 1953, just after the solution of DNA, to receive an invitation from Linus Pauling to deliver a course of three lectures at Cal. Tech. until Bragg gently broke it to him that the letter had been a hoax by Peter Pauling who was with us at the time and who had forged his father's signature.

Of course Pauling himself stole the show with a lecture on the early days of crystallography at 9.00 am and a speech about the early days at Cal. Tech. at 10.00 pm, having sat through the entire symposium in between. He stood up for both his talks. When walking, he likes to take your arm to steady himself, but gets along very well. Enviable!

I had stage fright but in the event things went very well and I received appreciative comments from everyone, including Francis, who is not in the habit of paying compliments.

Pauling in his talk had made fun of present-day crystallographers who are so busy determining structures at the double that they have no time to think about them. My last slide illustrated his scornful remark. It showed a striking example of "my" bond in the structure of an organic compound which the authors had not noticed, even though it constitutes that structure's only interesting feature.[6]

To Gisela Perutz and Family. San Francisco–Philadelphia, March 7, 1991

I spent a rainy and intellectual weekend with the Rosenbergs.[7] Finally two young collaborators of Rosenberg dropped in. One of them studied the relationship between secrecy, success, and profits among chemical and drug companies. To my delight, he found an inverse correlation between them. Openness pays, confirming my principle that science flourishes best in glass houses where everyone can look in.

I got first-hand confirmation of its validity two days later when I spent a morning at Genentech, the biggest and most successful of the new

---

[6]The papers are published in Zewail A. (ed.). 1992. *The Chemical Bond: Structure and Dynamics.* Academic Press, San Diego.

[7]Nathan Rosenberg, an economist, and his wife Rina.

biotechnology companies. They have 1700 employees, nearly a quarter of them scientists doing research who are free to discuss their work with outsiders and to publish it, because the directors agree that much more is to be gained by openness than is lost by other people sharing one's ideas. I got good views of the elaborate sophisticated machinery needed to produce kilograms of pure, sterile proteins for injection; I also sensed the constant panic and fear of the FDA inspectors who come several times a year and who have the power to order the shut down of any plant if they are dissatisfied with its safety standards. That was most impressive and reassuring. My host was Paul Carter, an English graduate student of Greg Winter and David Blow. Wherever I went in California expatriate English people abounded. He and others showed me most promising research on the development of a monoclonal antibody for the treatment of breast and ovarian cancer. All round, the level of science being done there is of the best.

To Robin Perutz, March 13, 1991

On Wednesday one of our biochemists, Terry Rabbits, gave me a paper on a new oncogene to communicate to *PNAS*. The paper contained the base sequence of the DNA, and hence the amino acid sequence of the protein coded for by that gene. Terry noted that it was rich in cysteines.

When I woke up yesterday morning I suddenly realised that the sequence of cysteines cys-X-X-cys-X-X-cys was the hallmark of ferrodoxins, with the fourth cysteine further down the sequence. This protein has a repeat of the three and one cysteines, plus two more pairs of cys-X-X-cys, suggesting the presence of 4 Fe-S centres: $2(Fe-S)_4$ and one $(Fe-S)_2$.

When I told him that his gene coded for a ferrodoxin, he was a bit sceptical but I soon convinced him. A few hours later he came back to me, having found a paper in *Science* that reported the presumed presence of a redox protein involved in the cooperative activation of two other oncogene products. They in turn activate other genes, but only when joined into a heterodimer, and dimerization depends on the oxidation or reduction of specific SH groups by that inferred redox enzyme. This may be it.[8]

---

[8]Patterns of residues in proteins are often "signatures" of particular structural features that relate to biochemical activities. Cysteine is a relatively rare amino acid so a repetitious sequence like this (where X can be almost any amino acid) is extremely unusual. Ferrodoxins use the cysteine residues to bind iron and sulphur (S), but unlike the iron in haemoglobin, this iron undergoes cycles of oxidation and reduction—hence a redox protein. The observation promoted speculation about a possible role of redox proteins in the function of cancer genes.—AW

Rabbits is now amending his paper which this discovery has made much more exciting. We discussed how we might use the cDNA of the gene to produce the enzyme in *E. coli*, crystallise it and determine its structure. This might be an interesting new project for me.

To Patience Thomson, April 17, 1991

Gisela and I were charmed by your account of life with your father [W.L. Bragg]. I saw him letting himself go only once when he and your mother acted a charade at a party with great panache. As a rule he was reserved with anyone outside the family.

I do remember how much your father enjoyed your exuberant terrier. You hit the nail on the head when you wrote: "There was never any free-wheeling of the mind. . . ." Nor did he ever say trivialities. I was so annoyed with the platitudes they put into his mouth in the DNA TV film, "Life Story," because he would never have uttered anything like it. It reminds me of Faust's dialogue with the Spirit of the World. Faust says:

> Da du die weite Welt umschweifst,
> Geschäftiger Geist, wie noch fühl ich mich dir!
> *Spirit*
> Du gleichst dem Geist den du begreifst,
> Nicht mir![9]

The script writer could never have fathomed your father.

Your story of the tide carrying you back to Yarmouth harbour reminded me of my first outing on a sailing boat. I went to Salcombe to recover after an illness and passed the time watching the sailing boats gaily tracking back and forth across the estuary. "Looks dead easy," I said to myself. I had never sailed before, but the spirit of adventure gripped me and I went and hired a dinghy.

I hoisted the sail and let the wind carry me towards the sea. It was exhilarating and I

Patience Thomson speaking at the memorial for Max in 2002.

---

[9]Faust: "Thou who dost roam the whole wide world, Spirit Ever-active, how near I feel to thee!" Spirit: "You are like the spirit you comprehend, not like me!" Translated by Ron Gray.

felt better than I had for a long time. As the afternoon drew to a close I decided to turn back. I seemed to be doing well, but when I looked at the shore it was moving landwards, not seawards. It dawned on me that the tide was carrying me out to sea faster than the sails were moving me back to Salcombe. I had oars on board and started to row, but lacked the strength to do it vigorously enough to reach the shore. Eventually a motor boat came to the rescue and towed me back to harbour; otherwise I would not be here now to sign my letter.

To Timothy Perutz, April 17, 1991

I watched a TV programme "Laughter in Russia" last night. One Russian to another: "A few years ago the communists took over the Sahara." The other: "What happened?" The first: "After a few years there was a shortage of sand!"

To Hugh Trevor-Roper, Lord Dacre, August 24, 1991

What fantastic times we live in! After I left you the other day, I regretted not having talked to you about [Mikhail] Gorbachev's[10] declaration that Communism had failed and should be discarded, but all this has been over-shadowed by the dramatic events of the past week.

The Roman Empire took centuries to disintegrate. It's unbelievable to see the Russian one break up in a week, not under external pressure, but by the very internal contradictions that were supposed to bring about the collapse of capitalism. Will [Boris] Yeltsin [Russian President] now inherit the vast military machine and become the Russian Napoleon? Will the EEC [European Economic Community] turn around to become the bulwark against American world domination? True to style, the French this morning snubbed its other members by recognising the Baltic republics on the eve of the EEC ministers' discussion of the matter. When I asked Margaret Thatcher what she thought of [François] Mitterand [French President] she said that he promises you one thing today and does the opposite tomorrow. It's a pity she can't marry Gorbachev now.

To Bernard Davis, January 7, 1992

First of all many many thanks for your thoughtful and extensive review of *Is Science Necessary?*, so different from the superficiality of most others. . . .

---

[10]General Secretary of the Communist Party of the Soviet Union 1985–1991.

May I take up one of your points? The public distrust of science. This originated with Hiroshima, and more recently it was intensified by Chernobyl. However, it has been fuelled enormously by unscrupulous publicists' realisation that there is money to be made by playing on public fears. The late George Pimentel told me that as President of the American Chemical Society he made a survey of all press headlines containing the word "chemistry." Nearly every one was pejorative. On one occasion a ship spilt toluene into the San Francisco Bay. Next day the headline read "The T in TNT spilt into the Bay." Drugs that work get little praise; dangerous side effects receive great publicity; there is no effort to teach the public that the genetic variability of humans makes some individuals hypersensitive to drugs that are well tolerated by nearly everyone else. In summary, most of those who complain about science in general lack any historical sense of the common people's lot before science, and any desire to understand science. Scientists are often blamed for not explaining their work to the public. There is some truth in this, but often the media give them no chance.

I was puzzled by your defence of [David] Baltimore. It seems to me that Baltimore lacked the scientific humility that continues to ask "Is my result really true?" If someone else produces good evidence to doubt it, the first thing I would do is to repeat my experiment.[11]

To Hugh Trevor-Roper, Lord Dacre, March 1, 1992

Did you watch last Monday's Horizon programme on the German atomic bomb project? Gisela and I had [Werner] Heisenberg at home to dinner on his first visit here after the war, when he assured us that he only pretended to work on the bomb and had no intention of letting this fall into Hitler's hands.

The real story was clearly very different. I hope that you will support Nicholas Kurti's campaign for the release of the original German transcripts as this is a matter where the nuances of language matter so much.[12]

---

[11]This is a reference to the controversy over his paper with Teresa Imanishi-Kari and alleged research misconduct and cover-up. Baltimore defended her against charges of falsifying data, although Baltimore himself was never accused of wrongdoing. He was criticised by many for his role in the controversy and, as a result of the furore, resigned as President of Rockefeller University. In 1996 a Federal appeal panel dismissed allegations of scientific misconduct against Dr. Imanishi-Kari.—AW

[12]In 1993, under the auspices of the Bristol Institute of Physics, Charles Frank was able to publish the taped conversations of the German physicists imprisoned near Cambridge as *Operation Epsilon: The Farm Hall Transcripts*, a book which my parents read with great interest. The transcripts were simultaneously published in German as Hoffmann D. (ed.), 1993. *Operation Epsilon: Die Farm-Hall-Protokolle oder Die Angst der Alliierten von der deutschen Atombombe*. Rowohlt, Berlin.

To Dorothy Hodgkin, March 2, 1992

Among the exhibits [on the history of Cambridge biochemistry] I found a paper from an annual publication of [Gowland] Hopkins' lab called "Brighter Biochemistry" dated 1931, where J.B.S. Haldane set the questions for a future undergraduate exam paper. His first question is as follows: "Write down the structural formula of human type C oxyhaemoglobin and briefly summarize the evidence on which it is based. (Structural formulae should be written stereoscopically. A stereoscope is provided.)"

Isn't that marvellous. JBSH really was the most imaginative of scientists.

To Lotte Perutz, April 12, 1992

This reminds me of Abraham Karpas and his passive immunisation of AIDS patients that helped Jim [Max's nephew] so much. The other day Karpas appeared in my room to tell me that it had been officially approved by the State FDA in California, after extensive trials. Karpas is an unconventional Israeli, a very intelligent and hard-working virologist who does all experiments

Kiyoshi Nagai

with his own hands, but he has the greatest difficulties in getting his work published because he has antagonised some influential people, foremost among them [Robert] Gallo at the NIH who claims to have discovered the AIDS virus, but in fact stole it from [Luc] Montagnier at the Pasteur Institute— you may or may not have heard about that scandal.[13]

Approval in California will probably be followed by approval throughout the U.S. When the British media get to know about this, there will be an outcry why a treatment developed in Britain

---

[13]This bitter dispute was resolved in 1987 when both scientists agreed to share credit for this discovery. Montagnier and his colleague Francoise Barré-Sinoussi were awarded half of the 2008 Nobel Prize in Physiology or Medicine for their discovery of the AIDS virus, HIV. Harold zur Hausen was awarded the other half for his work with human papilloma viruses.

has not been followed up here. I won't be able to offer any excuses for my colleagues' disdainful rejection of Karpas' work. It reminded me of Geoffrey Pyke's derisive motto: "In England nothing ever gets done for the first time."

I am not sure if I told you of another important development. Kiyoshi Nagai, my very able Japanese co-worker, together with a biotechnology firm in Colorado, has made a genetically engineered haemoglobin that can be produced in bulk in a culture of *coli* bacteria and may be suitable as a blood substitute. Publication of this work in a recent issue of *Nature* aroused great interest in newspapers, radio and TV. It has really made Kiyoshi quite famous. American venture capital is investing some 200 m dollars in the production of this haemoglobin on an industrial scale, and clinical trials have already begun. I have always been disappointed that my life-long work on haemoglobin has never cured anybody, but now there is real hope. The synthetic haemoglobin could not have been engineered without knowing the structure.

To Rita Levi-Montalcini, May 18, 1992

I am with you on a Magna Carta of Duties for scientists. Many years ago I suggested to a meeting, I believe at Harvard, that scientists should take a Hippocratic Oath, but my proposal was greeted with stony silence.

But you know, every idiot of a journalist now mouths concern for the biosphere and the Third World, and there are hundreds of conferences discussing these issues. When I think of the work done by the 250 odd scientists in this laboratory, I cannot lay my finger on any single person whose research would be influenced by adherence to the principles of the Magna Carta, because their problems lie outside its realm.

On the other hand when I watch the deterioration of scientific morals, especially in the U.S., I believe your Magna Carta should begin in people's own laboratory calling for

> Honesty
> Truthfulness
> Openness
> Loyalty and generosity to colleagues
> Treatment of juniors and technicians as equals

and after this

> Carrying out research for the benefit of mankind and the world we live in. Doing all in their power to preserve our environment, *civilisation and cultural heritage* for future generations.

But does this really need a conference?

Gisela (my wife) thinks that your Magna Carta may help to reassure a suspicious public about scientists' aims.

As to the Third World, the problems of our relationship with these countries are predominantly political and economic (the terms of trade, interest on loans) rather than scientific. Most grandiose schemes of technical aid have been disastrous failures.

I hope that you don't find this letter too discouraging.[14]

To Hans Mark, May 20, 1992

Christoph Kratky in Vienna recently sent me the news of your father's death [Hermann Mark]. I owed him a great debt for launching me on my career as an X-ray crystallographer in 1935, and for his lifelong friendship and encouragement ever since.

Your father possessed a unique combination of Old-World Viennese charm and New World dynamism. To be received by him as a visitor at the Brooklyn Poly was a heart-warming experience. He would immediately organise a seminar and afterwards press an, in those days, extremely welcome 50 dollar note into one's hands. With that warmth went a mind sharp as a razor.

I remember a visit by your father, and I think it was with you, to the Cavendish Laboratory in 1947 when your father offered to give a seminar on recent developments in nuclear physics in the U.S. When you heard that title you said to him: "Gee Dad, this time you've really overreached yourself."

My last meeting with your father took place at the Vienna Opera when we sat next to each other and when his conversation was just as interesting as always.

I had great affection for your father and I am sure you must feel his loss very deeply.

To Lotte Perutz, May 26, 1992

I corresponded with Mark's son Hans about his father. He sent me his own speech on Mark's 90th birthday. The final two paragraphs epitomise his greatness, which lay in his indomitable optimism, his determination that problems were there to be solved intelligently, his following of the Bishop's advice to Richard II that

---

[14]Compare letter of 16 February 1996.

"Wise men ne'er sit and wail their woes,
But presently prevent the ways to wail."

To Timothy and Marion Perutz, June 23, 1992

On Sunday morning Granny, Vivien and I were invited to the opening of a new laboratory called the Crystallographic Data Centre, built in splendid style with no expense spared by a great Danish architect.

On arrival a polite young lady ushered us into a shiny transparent lift that conveyed us noiselessly, together with several other visitors to the first floor.

Stepping out I found myself faced by a galaxy of famous professors and their wives in their Sunday best. Not wishing to turn my back on that distinguished company, I stepped slowly backwards to make room for the others getting out of the lift, when

S P L A S H

I fell into a pond! It was a scene worthy of Charlie Chaplin.

When I had clambered out, my new beautifully pressed summer trousers and freshly polished shoes soaking, the Great Danish Architect rushed up to me and offered his apologies for having placed an unprotected pond, lit from within, its edge level with the floor, at the centre of the Great Open Space of the new laboratory, merely to trap unwary visitors into an unpremeditated

P L U N G E

After this the Great Old Man, Lord Todd, told our hostess that before her next party she had better cover her pond.

To Robin Perutz and Family, July 9, 1992

We have just returned from Buckingham Palace where the Queen entertained all the OMs [members of the Order of Merit] and their wives or husbands to lunch. Mummy thought that Francis, tall, thin and grey-haired looked the most distinguished. The Queen did remember my letter explaining to her what DNA is when she was considering him for the OM, and she seemed pleased to meet him in the flesh.

By far the largest contingent came from Cambridge; only Alan Hodgkin, sadly, is so crippled that he could not come; incidentally Marni, his wife, told me last night that she too fell into the Great Danish Architect's pool, before we got to the party.

Francis Crick

I was thrilled to be able to exchange a few words with Yehudi Menuhin. Something made me remark that musicality was a rare talent; to my surprise he denied this vigorously, saying that musical talent was common and merely waiting to be brought out from early childhood. I am sceptical.

I also managed some chats with Isaiah Berlin who was the Queen's neighbour at lunch. When I told him that I had just begun to read the recently published book *Conversations with Isaiah Berlin* by Ramin Jahanbegloo, he told me rather indignantly that the man never informed him of his intention to make a book of them, and that he, Berlin, had not read it! I did not tell Berlin that I am reading it in order to write a piece about him so that he gets elected to the Pour le Mérite, where I would have more chances to talk to him. I regard him as the greatest advocate of the liberal ideals on which civilised life depends.[15]

We were all in the prescribed solemn lounge suit when a tall man walked in in blue and white striped cotton trousers and tennis shoes, to be greeted by Yehudi Menuhin with loud kisses on both cheeks. That was Michael Tippett [English composer]. I was pleased he had not been turned away.

To Claudio Cuello, October 5, 1992

May I just take this opportunity to make one more request? I always find introductory eulogies before my lectures most embarrassing. If young people are told what an honour it is to have me here, then I have the devil of a job to overcome the hostility thus engendered. People are also put off by a long list of my honours. The introduction I really like best is just: "Here is Max Perutz, he is going to talk to you about haemoglobin." That does not raise such high expectations and saves a lot of time!

---

[15]Sadly he was not elected. The Pour le Mérite is the order that inspired the foundation of the British Order of Merit.

To Lotte Perutz, December 29, 1992

A few weeks ago my colleagues at the lab read with alarm of yet another plan to reorganise British science, on the lines of Tory dogma that wealth creation is the supreme criterion, and that it is best served by handing all public institutions to private enterprise. To this end, research institutes would be taken away from the Medical Research Council and forced to compete for funds in an open market or sold off.

Having made my reputation by successfully fending off two such reorganisations in the past, my colleagues asked me to do it again. I concocted a piece that I handed to the Minister for Science when he came to visit the lab just before Christmas, and I hope that it will convince him. My main argument was that most of our successes, including those that resulted in commercially valuable inventions, are the outcome of many years of work, without any certainty that it will lead anywhere and that few commercial companies would take on such a gamble. I also tried to defend the Medical Research Council which is first class and does not need reorganisation.

Just before Christmas I heard on the morning news that the Israeli Govt. refused to allow the International Red Cross access to the Arabs deported to the Lebanese border. I was furious and decided to organise a protest which took the shape of the enclosed advertisement in this morning's *Independent*. I spent most of this morning on the lab's fax machine making sure that it reaches the Israeli Govt. Isaiah Berlin refused to sign on the ground that such protests are useless, but I disagree. It may just be this little push that helps to tip the scales.

Tomorrow I am giving a holiday lecture for local school children on "Living Molecules" telling them how Oswald Avery discovered in a lifetime's work that genes are made of DNA, how Watson and Crick solved its structure, etc.

To Lotte Perutz, February 7, 1993

I have just read a biography of [Giuseppe] Lampedusa, the author of *The Leopard*, which Gisela had given me for Christmas, a tragic figure, the last descendant of a noble Sicilian family who saw the family fortune dwindle, his country palace destroyed by an earthquake, his Palermo palace bombed by the American liberators. Yet he managed to live without ever earning a living and to devote his entire time to a study of English, French, Italian, Spanish and Russian literature. Only when he felt his health failing and his life having been wasted did he attempt literary work himself, but *The Leopard* was refused by publishers before he died of lung cancer aged 60, having been a chain smoker. After his death, Feltrinelli accepted the book and made a contract with his widow that cheated her of nearly all the royalties.

I nominated three members of my lab and one American for the Nobel Prizes. They have all done fantastic, very original work, leading to fundamental discoveries.

To Lotte Perutz, April 6, 1993

I did not tell you when you were here that my NIH [U.S. National Institutes of Health] grant would expire on 30 November, and that I had applied for an extension for another 3 years. Shortly after you left, I was told of opposition to approval of a foreign grant, insufficiently high priority, deferral of a decision to May or even next autumn, which made me conclude that I was unlikely to get it. To my immense surprise and pleasure I received a phone call last Friday that it had been approved after all. One of its benefits is the psychological one that the lab profits financially from my continuing to work there rather than being a burden.

Whether I shall have the energy to continue producing a stream of interesting papers is another question. It's getting harder, not only on account of my age, but also because science is so overcrowded with people that it is hard to find a problem that someone else is not already working on. I had a disappointment of this kind today; someone in St. Louis has already done what a young Belgian came here to do last week.

To Gisela Perutz and Family. Cosmos Club, Washington, D.C., May 18, 1993

The Academy meeting [that of the International Human Rights Network held at the U.S. National Academy of Sciences] was no bore. I sat between representatives of Jordan and Israel, but they showed no hostility. The American, French, Dutch, Swedish and Italian academies' human rights committees were strongly represented, while I had to confess that the Royal Society does not have one. But then it struck me that the SPSL [Society for the Protection of Science and Learning] fulfils exactly the function that these societies have shouldered, though the others objected that it lacks the requisite prestige. I'll tell you more when I get home.

The Americans wanted to limit intervention to cases of imprisoned scientists, but the Jordanian pointed out that governments have other ways of victimising scientists, for example by ordering them to do 18 hours' teaching per week which makes it impossible for them to do research! Vivien, you might tell your superiors that in Jordan this is a form of punishment. He is also a member of the Arab delegation at the Arab-Israeli Peace Conference, a very intelligent and genuine man of peace.

To Gisela Perutz and Family. Cosmos Club, Washington, D.C., May 21, 1993

I spent the morning of my birthday listening to Mrs. Sakharov, alias Elena Bonner, a Jewish granny who thinks herself as clever as her late husband, but talked meaningless drivel for about an hour.

Next came a likeable elderly physicist who knew Sakharov well, had fought for him when he was public enemy no. 1; he traced his career, told nice anecdotes about him, and made us realise what a remarkable physicist he was. At his Ph.D. exam, his examiners did not give him top marks because his answer to one of their questions in theoretical physics appeared to be wrong. On sleeping on the matter, [Igor] Tamm, himself a Nobel laureate in physics, realised that Sakharov had been *right* and the examiners *wrong*. He tried to get the marks corrected, but characteristically, they were already in the bureaucratic machine and could not be changed.

Another speaker was the president of Kyrgyzstan, a physicist turned statesman who seemed a cross between [Václav] Havel [President of Czechoslovakia and then the Czech Republic] and the president of Costa Rica whom we met in Goteborg. He made a thoughtful speech but aimed more at a Rotary Club than this sophisticated audience; he convinced us that many of Sakharov's ideals had been realised in his new republic where the rights of individuals really were respected; the press was free, people were free to change the government. The individual was above the state and the constitution was on a par with those of Germany or France. Afterwards, the knowledgeable foreign secretary of the Swedish Academy told me that Kyrgyzstan having no Soviet army to defend it was in grave danger of being swallowed up by China which had already started propaganda similar to that preceding the annexation of Tibet.

More about Sakharov. When he taught theoretical physics, the students complained to Tamm that he was too hard to understand. Tamm told S that he must not assume students to be as bright as he was. S retorted that he could not think of his students in any other way. I like that.

An American economist, Lawrence Klein, talked about the contrast between China's economic success and Russia's failure. China's is now the fastest growing economy in the world while Russia's GNP had declined sharply. Klein maintained that the Chinese did better, because they had liberalised the economy before allowing personal freedom, but this was vigorously denied by Yuri Orlov, the dissident Russian physicist now at Cornell who was the most impressive speaker by far; he had thought deeply about the dismal consequences of political freedom in Eastern Europe. He attributed them to a failure to think out the relationship between human rights and political demands, or between human rights and "the demons in our souls," or rights and mass psychology. Failure to teach people to compromise.

He warned us not to negotiate on human rights with the heads of the Russian Academy of Sciences. Some of these had been KGB agents. We should work, not through the Academy, but with human rights activists outside it.

The Swedish delegate gave me alarming reports about the rise of anti-semitism in Russia. He had been in Moscow just before coming to Washington and had witnessed a mass meeting of some 20,000 people who cheered a speaker when he attributed Russia's economic troubles to an international conspiracy of Jews. My Swede's interpreter followed the translation of that harangue with the remark that the speaker had been quite right. This popular movement is reflected (or led) by the blackballing of Jewish candidates for election to the Academy against which I asked [Michael] Atiyah [President of the Royal Society] some time ago to protest. While in Washington, I received copies of letters from Press, the President of the U.S. Academy, asking a Russian mathematician who had published a vicious anti-semitic tract to resign from foreign membership, which that man refused to do. It's a sinister development.

To come back to Orlov. He predicted that political liberalisation in China would lead to the break up of the country just as in the Soviet Union unless people were educated in the spirit of non-violence, compromise and tolerance.

To Gisela Perutz and Family. La Guardia Airport, May 25, 1993

At the laboratories of Paul Sigler, Spyros Artavanis and Tom Steitz I was given the customary interviews with all their collaborators. Exciting for me was a hospital radiologist who had asked for an interview. He told me that he was working with the compounds that [Iraj] Lalezari had made and had contrived to put them to effective use in animals. These compounds lower the oxygen affinity of haemoglobin. When we discovered this, clinicians said that they would be useful for improved oxygen delivery to tumours before irradiation (oxygen sensitizes tumours to radiation), but then their high affinity for another blood protein, serum albumin, prevented that action. The radiologist, Paul Fisher, takes red cells from the animal, saturates them with one of Lalezari's compounds, and transfuses them back into the animal before irradiation of its tumour. As a result he was able to kill the tumour with a lower dose of radiation than in the absence of the compound. I would be really thrilled if this work will eventually be of clinical use. On the other hand, I know it will take years before any firm undertakes to make the compounds and the FDA approves their use.

The new Picower Institute for Medical Research is financed in part by a friend of its director, Tony Cerami, a brilliant biochemist. He owes his discoveries to a fantastic ability for lateral thinking. Gisela, you may remember [Makio] Murayama, the paranoid Japanese-American who came to work with me in our hut and once complained to Dibden, the brash and often drunk ex Naval officer and administrative secretary of the Cavendish, that people were spreading derogatory and libellous rumours about him. Well, after he left me Murayama took up the discovery of a crazy Armenian doctor, one [Robert] Nalbandian, that huge doses of urea relieve sickle cell anaemia. It made the poor devils feel very sick, but they had to swallow it regardless. Cerami remembered that urea decomposes spontaneously into cyanate and ammonia, and that it always contains traces of these decomposition products. He showed that the beneficial effect of urea was due to its contamination with cyanate, which you can administer in small doses without torturing the patients. Sadly cyanate soon turned out to be a nerve poison, and that was the end of it. However, Cerami has made other discoveries of a similar kind since.

To Lotte Perutz, June 28, 1993

I wrote to you some time ago that I have won all the honours there are, but I was wrong. This month I was made an Honorary Fellow of the Royal College of Physicians and received honorary doctorates from the Universities of Paris and Oxford, each with pomp and ceremony.

Oxford was a really great occasion. My co-doctorands were a much more interesting lot, as you can see from the enclosed pamphlet. The ceremony took place in the Sheldonian Theatre, an impressive Baroque building filled with a great crowd of people for the great event of the year. The Public Orator solemnly read the citation in Latin for each doctorand, followed by the Chancellor, a liberal peer, handing you the scroll from his throne. I was pleased to be in the company of Father [Trevor] Huddleston and [Javier] Pérez de Cuéllar[16] and to note that the honours were awarded to champions of peace, the liberal ideal and the underdog. I managed a chat with Father Huddleston to whom I took a great liking and to Edward Wilson, the Harvard biologist and author of *Sociobiology*[17] who was full of fun and interest. Huddleston was full of hope for S. Africa.

In summary, Gisela and I had a good time this month and I got little work done, but I have had one new idea in relation to the recently discovered gene for Huntington disease which I am following up. No connection with haemoglobin!

To Lotte Perutz, August 7, 1993

I visited Father Huddleston in London before we went away. He had the conventional English upper-class education: public school followed by Oxford, but after graduating he joined an Anglican religious order and had to vow poverty, celibacy and obedience. The order sent him to a mission in a black township in S. Africa where he saw the despicable treatment meted out to the blacks at first hand and won their affection by treating them as equals. He is optimistic about the future there; on the other hand, I was alarmed when he told me that a whole generation of black children boycotted school in protest. They have now grown up into an unemployable lot numbering 1–2 million. How can any government cope with them? I cannot see any stable peaceful society emerging with such people in their midst. However, I found Father Huddleston a lovable man and hope to see more of him.

To Lotte Perutz. Vienna, August 24, 1993

Vienna was a treat! The morning after my call to you I walked out into the sunlit town and thought how beautifully laid out it was, and well kept, with flowers in bloom in the public parks. All the palaces and churches looked splendid in the sunshine, and I felt cheerful to be still alive and well to enjoy it.

---

[16]Peruvian diplomat and Secretary General of the U.N. 1982–1991.

[17]Wilson E.O. 1971. *Sociobiology: The New Synthesis*. Harvard University Press, Cambridge, MA.

Next Sunday, Marion [Turnovszky née Perutz] drove me to Kaiser-brunn where I took her up the path to the top of the Stadelwand, two thirds of the way up the Schneeberg.[18] I used to love that spot where we emerged after climbing the Stadelwandgrat, and I was thrilled to see it again, after an interval of 56 years. Marion had never been there and was in raptures about its beauty. When we came down, we still drove up the Höllental to the Binderwirt, another of my favourite spots. It was unspoilt and as lovely as I had remembered it. Finally I knocked at the gate of the Villa Perutz where the present owners, the second ones since I sold it, knew our name and received us kindly. The house and gardens are well kept. The Kachelofen [immense tiled stove] in the hall and the built-in Bie-dermeier cupboards in the dining room are still there, but the rest of the furniture is ugly. The old trees are very tall now and most attractive; the garden could be anywhere in England. I was very pleased to see the house again and thought how nice it was. Finally we still drove up the little road past Frau von Mandel's house and walked up the hill where I used to watch the sun set behind the Rax. It had already set, but it was a happy ending to a glorious day.

It's good that I can enjoy revisiting my much-loved old haunts without a trace of regret that I no longer live there.

To The Prime Minister, the Right Honorable John Major, October 13, 1993

In April I told your predecessor about my medical colleagues' concern that under the reorganisation of the NHS [National Health Service], clinical research would be squeezed out by the drive for cost-effectiveness in an internal market. These fears have now been reinforced by the imminent reorganisation of the Regional Health Authorities who fund the vital infra-structure for research and teaching.

The fundamental problem of clinical research in a market-orientated NHS is that research is strategic and long-term, while the market is driven by short-term concerns based on hospitals' annual contracts.

The finance of medical research affects not only the future quality of British medicine, but also the industrial exploitation of that research, much of which is too unpredictable at the outset to attract drug companies' sup-port.

---

[18]See photo on p. 218.

Britain has led the world in medical advances. Vaccination, antiseptics, antibiotics, hip replacements, the connection between tobacco smoke and lung cancer, combined drug treatment for tuberculosis, effective drugs against stomach ulcers, monoclonal antibodies and many others originated here. Discoveries made by members of this laboratory have revolutionised the intellectual basis of much medical practice. Yet excellence in research is a fragile flower. Early in this century my native Vienna had one of the world's leading medical schools. Financial neglect and bad politics killed it, and no amount of post-war prosperity could revive it.

To Lotte Perutz, October 27, 1993

This past week saw our annual laboratory symposium. Again, the standard was very high and the laboratory continues to live up to its great reputation. I gave a short paper on my new work on Huntington disease which suggests (vaguely) what the molecular mechanism or mechanisms responsible might be. Strangely, these ideas developed from my work on the haemoglobin of a parasitic worm.

Running a laboratory taught me the paramount importance of taking an interest in people's work. It's what makes them tick.

To Lotte Perutz, February 5, 1994

Last Sunday Archbishop Trevor Huddleston came to visit us, the anti-apartheid fighter with whom I shared honorary degrees at Oxford. He is a little older than I, but a diabetic and physically frail. Mentally full of vigour though. Very much British upper class. His father was a naval officer who finished his career as commander-in-chief of the British Indian Navy and a knight bachelor. I wrote to you before that his religious order sent him to South Africa. He also told us about his work in Mauritius, where he was bishop, and his advocacy of an ecumenism embracing

Trevor Huddleston

not just the different Christian sects but all the world's great religions.

A few days ago we saw him again at a lecture he gave here to the Society of Friends. He talked like an angry young man, making one forget his age, except for his recalling his presence at crucial events long past. He carried everybody away by being transparently motivated only by compassion and a sense of justice, without seeking any power or glory for himself. He is a wonderful new friend to have acquired. I only wish he were younger.

To Lotte Perutz, March 27, 1994

I have very sad news. Werner Weissel died a few days ago. He was my closest and dearest friend.

After this tragedy my doings sound trivial. I have just been through 10 days of lecturing, and all the lectures were different. The first was the introductory talk to a Royal Society Discussion on Drugs by Design, which meant drugs designed to fit the structure of pharmacologically important proteins which had been solved by X-ray analysis. I told them how our unsuccessful search for a drug to relieve sickle cell anaemia has now led to the discovery of a drug that promotes the delivery of oxygen to tumours which helps to reduce the dose of radiation needed to destroy the tumours. On the following Monday I travelled to London for the fourth time, to lecture to a large boy's school on "Life with Living Molecules." It was a day school, fee-paying, in the East End where you would least expect it. I tried to tell them that great dis-

Werner Weissel with his granddaughter Daria

coveries were often made by people only a few years older than they are now, and that they are still being made here and now, not only by old men with long beards, like the traditional portraits of Darwin, in the distant past.

Finally, two nights ago, I was asked to open the final evening's celebration of a Science Festival at a local school, Parkside Community College.

I am obviously pleased to be still so much in demand, and the effort has done me no harm.

In my report to the Pope on the Pontifical Academy meeting on Resources and Population, I recommended that the Church should help to stem the population explosion by promoting breast feeding and girls' education. As a result, the Academy decided to hold a scientific meeting on breast feeding jointly with the Royal Society. They asked me to convene a planning meeting here in Cambridge which took place on 11 March. I feared that it would be useless, seeing that I know nothing about the subject, but luckily the Foreign Secretary of the Royal Society found a very knowledgeable professor of obstetrics in Edinburgh who helped us to draw up a promising programme. He seemed a splendid man, full of fun, and I hope another new friend.

But the new friends do not replace Werner. You never become as intimate as with one who shared a similar background, whose family you knew and who knew yours, with whom you went skiing and climbing, whose children you watched grow up. I have never got over Heini Granichstaedten's death and I shan't get over Werner's.

To Robin Perutz and Family. Geneva to London, April 19, 1994

John Thomas and I were driven up [to Engelberg] together with three other participants in the Forum Engelberg for a symposium on Chemistry and the Quality of Life which was to bring together politicians, business people, journalists and scientists from all parts on Europe. In theory at least.

In fact only the Ministers of Science of Hungary and Slovenia turned up; there was a Hungarian TV crew, a good Austrian and a poor Slovenian journalist, representatives of quite a few chemical and pharmaceutical firms, quite a few Swiss VIPs.

There was some good science, overshadowed by a surfeit of boring speeches; the worst was an evening of speeches about science and spirituality interlaced with dissonant religious songs by a mixed male and female choir in the ornate, icy cold baroque church of the local Benedictine abbey at which I found myself a captive audience.

I tried to teach them the elements of molecular biology and make them understand what biotechnology was about. No sooner had I begun than the entire brass of the conference walked out. After all the blah-blah of what an honour it was for them that I had condescended to edify the meeting with my august presence, I found this strange. I learned later that the organiser-in-chief, a man constantly running hither and thither with an air of great importance, had wisely arranged a press conference to coincide with my lecture.

The positive side was acquaintance with a few interesting people: Nüsch, the Rektor of the ETH [Eidgenössische Technische Hochschule Zürich, Swiss Federal Institute of Technology]; Paul Janssen, head of a large Belgian pharmaceutical firm which he founded when he was a graduate student; the Abbot of the Benedictine monastery; the former President of Kyoto University, an endearing elderly man; [Richard] Ernst the NMR man. All people whom I would not otherwise meet.

To Steffen Peiser, May 8, 1994

The meeting at Engelberg was about Chemistry and the Quality of Life. There were some excellent talks on ways of avoiding environmental damage and enjoying the benefits of technology by better chemistry. Even so, the journalists wanted to concentrate on the damage chemistry has done. I told them that the public has two alternatives: they can decide to do without modern transport, refrigerators, washing machines, and modern medicine, essentially return to the 18th century and accept a reduction in life expectancy to 40 years. But if they want to retain the benefits of modern technology and minimise environmental damage they cannot do it without chemistry. They did not like this blunt message.

Another important message which the Science Exhibition [in Washington] should have drummed home and evidently didn't is that the battle between hosts and their parasites—bacteria, viruses, protozoa—can never be finally won, because the parasites mutate and continuous research is needed to keep them under control.

To Rt. Hon. William Waldegrave, Cabinet Minister with Responsibility for Science, July 4, 1994

Innovation and British Industry In 1981 the British Pharmacological Society invited me to give the Jubilee Lecture on the occasion of their fiftieth anniversary. I talked about the promise of protein crystallography for rational drug design. The lecture was attended by the top ranks of the British pharmaceutical industry, but no one approached me afterwards to discuss how they might put this new approach into practice. In 1985 I gave a talk on the same subject in Vienna to the European Federation of Pharmaceutical Industries Associations with the same disappointing result. At lunch afterwards the head of the ICI Pharmaceuticals promised to invite me to their laboratories. I never heard from him again.

Now to the sequel. An American colleague has just sent me a *World Directory of Industrial Macromolecular Crystallography* dated 21 June 1994. According to this directory 35 American firms now employ 132 such crystallographers, 12 Japanese firms employ 20, and *3 British firms employ 12.*

A few years ago my young colleague Kiyoshi Nagai invented a brilliant way of modifying haemoglobin, the protein of the red blood cell, by genetic engineering so that it could be produced in bulk in cultures of *coli* bacteria and used as a substitute for transfused blood. No British firm was interested in taking up his invention. Eventually, he found a small American biotech company, Somatogen in Boulder, Colorado, which raised the venture capital and engaged the staff needed to develop the synthesis of Nagai's haemoglobins on a production scale and to begin clinical trials. Now the first results look so hopeful that the giant pharmaceutical firm Eli Lilly has made an agreement with Somatogen to assume responsibility for the commercial scale manufacture and to finance phase 3 clinical trials. If successful, sales of this haemoglobin could bring in billions of dollars, because it would do away with blood donors and the accompanying dangers of contamination with HIV and other viruses. The MRC holds the patent and will receive royalties, but the bulk of the profits and increased employment will accrue to the U.S.[19]

HM Government always acts on the notion that the universities and the research councils need reform in order to turn the discoveries of academics into wealth. My experience has been that it is the management of British industry rather which needs reform.

To the Editor, The New York Times, *July 4, 1994*

Your issue of 16 June carried a report by your Rome correspondent of an alleged conflict between the Pontifical Academy of Sciences and the Vatican over the Academy's report on Resources and Population, stating that

---

[19]Disappointingly in later clinical trials problems developed. In July 2003, Baxter International, which had taken over this project, decided to abandon it in view of the substantial investment that might be needed to overcome them.

the Pope John Paul II was infuriated by the report, because it draws attention to the catastrophe which the population explosion threatens to bring upon the world.

The main body of the report was written, not by scientist-members of the Academy, as its opponents allege, but by three internationally reputed Italian demographers and economists, a scientific consultant of ENEA,[20] the formerly state-owned Italian oil company, and a theologian at the Vatican. I added an appendix on medical aspects in which I drew attention to some of the tragic consequences of the population explosion. More than a billion people live in abject poverty and are malnourished. Medical researchers have found that malnourished infants of malnourished mothers grow into physically and mentally handicapped adults. Such adults will be incapable of emancipating from the poverty into which they have been born and will be destined in their turn to produce large numbers of malnourished children, unable to learn the skills necessary to support themselves as adults in modern society. I hoped these and other stark facts would modify the Church's unbending opposition to family planning.

As co-author of the report, I received this letter from the Academy's secretariat:

"We are very pleased to inform you that on 13 December 1993 the Holy Father received representatives of our Academy in private audience. During the meeting the text of the report was formally presented to the Pope.

The Holy Father, who had already received a copy informally several days before, has examined it and expressed himself very positively about the document. He recommended that it should be distributed immediately to all members of the Curia."

No sign of the Pope's fury here. Fury seems rather to have been generated by Cardinal [John Joseph] O'Connor [Archbishop of the Archdiocese of New York] and his ultra-conservative colleagues on finding the appalling threat to which they want to close their eyes confirmed by the authority of the Pontifical Academy itself.

[In a letter dated 17 March 1995 to Dr. Maxine Singer, President of the Carnegie Institution of Washington, Max wrote: "Renato Dardozzi told me that after the publication of the summary report on our meeting on Resources and Population, a Cardinal Lopez came to see him making a ter-

---

[20]Ente per le Nuove Tecnologie, l'Energia e l'Ambiente, that is, the Italian Agency for New Technologies, Energy and the Environment.

rible row and demanding that this should be modified or withdrawn, but Dardozzi stuck to his guns and insisted that full publication should go ahead. He also told me that the Pope had been most impressed by my piece on the 'medical aspects of overpopulation,' but I did not have the courage to reply that I wished he had taken more notice of it in his public pronouncements."]

To John T. Edsall, August 2, 1994

I recovered [from a septic tooth] after a week in our favourite village in the Dolomites where we spent a heavenly three weeks. It is the nearest place to paradise, and I am never as happy as when I am there. The place itself, the walks, the views, the mountains, the flowers, everything combines with the sunshine to make it a spot to which I long to return all the rest of the year. Robin and family, Vivien and a cousin from Paris with her husband all joined us there and made very good company.

To Lotte Perutz, August 5, 1994

Dorothy Hodgkin died last week. I had expected it for the last two years or more. I have been friends with her for nearly 60 years and had a great affection for her, but was unhappy to find my affection fading when I could no longer get any response from her. It was as if she had died already. Dorothy remained ambitious and enterprising to the last. Last summer she insisted on travelling to the International Congress of Crystallography in Beijing despite the fact that she would fall asleep as soon as she settled down to a lecture.

Hotel Rondinella in the hamlet of Feder where we always stayed

Max with Dorothy Hodgkin

To Lotte Perutz, September 1, 1994

My talks to Dorothy became monologues, my letters remained unanswered, my papers uncommented.

Since then Pauling has also died. He was a much greater scientist than Dorothy and also a more colourful personality. Many feel that he was the greatest chemist of this century. He was also instrumental in the protests that led to [President John F.] Kennedy and [Prime Minister Harold] Macmillan's conclusion of the Atmospheric Test ban, and he was one of the original eleven signatories of the Russell-Einstein Declaration Against Nuclear Arms.

Here I have become a student again. A graduate student is teaching me genetic engineering while helping with an experiment designed to put my new ideas about the molecular mechanism of Huntington disease to a rigorous test. After a good holiday the physical effort involved is no problem, but I have difficulty remembering the details of the delicate, intricate operations of the many chemical steps needed to engineer a genetically modified protein. I am not sure if I will.

I have been reading a 600 page-long biography of Charles Darwin recently which is so vivid that you never tire of reading it. It conveys the tragedy of his life after his return from the voyage of the Beagle when he was ill almost continuously, and also the furore aroused by his revolutionary ideas on the evolution of species, especially the notion that man is not a unique creature specially created by God. It seems strange to me that people were so upset, yet it should not seem so to me, because this was what I was taught and firmly believed until I was almost grown up.

To Professor Nicola Cabibbo, President of the Pontifical Academy of Science, and Father Renato Dardozzi, September 28, 1994

After thinking about your kind encouragement to come to the meeting of the Academy, I have come to the conclusion that, basically, the Pope has not moved from the dogma laid down by Pius XI in his Casti Connubis and by Paul VI in Humanae Vitae. I am advised that there is nothing in the Gospels to condemn sexual intercourse as sinful except for the procreation of children, but I learnt that the Catholic Church's attitude to women, marriage and sex is based on the teachings of St. Paul and later on those of St. Augustine.

In your letter to me you quote the Pope's permission to use the rhythm method of birth control, but no other. It is unrealistic and inhuman to expect a young husband and wife to share a bed and abstain from intercourse more than three weeks out of four in every month. It is particularly unrealistic to demand this of many for whom making love is one of the few pleasures in life. I agree with the protest of the over 2000 Catholics who put the enclosed full page advertisement into *The New York Times* on 6 September.

When I wrote my summary on the medical aspects of overpopulation, I hoped that my picture of the effects of malnutrition on children who grow up to be mentally and physically handicapped adults would arouse the Pope's compassion and change his attitude to contraception. I am deeply disappointed that there is no sign of this.

It is true that higher standards of living and education of women reduce fertility but experience has shown that they do not do so sufficiently to reduce birth rates to a level which our world can sustain.

Finally, may I say that it is also unrealistic of the Pope to expect populations of the developing world to abstain from artificial methods of birth control when Catholic Italy has the world's highest fraction of women using them.

For all these reasons I have decided to adhere to my protest and stay away from your meeting next month.

To Lotte Perutz, October 13, 1994

Dorothy: she showed all the signs of brain damage before the final stroke. I was very pleased to receive an interview recorded with her by the BBC years ago, to hear her firm voice and charmingly simple ways of answering the questions put to her.

The symposium in my honour [80th birthday celebration] was a great success scientifically, because all the talks were first class, and touching for me on account of the affection shown to me by everyone. About 350 people attended and more would have come if the railways had not been on strike that day. John Edsall was there aged 93, and another ~90 year old colleague from Scotland. Neither fell asleep. Friends and colleagues came from as far as Oregon, from Indiana, Rome, Paris and Amsterdam. It was all very cheerful and relaxed, no tedious speeches.

Two days earlier there was another dinner at Peterhouse arranged by the new Master, my old chemist friend John Thomas. Thomas first made a speech praising me to the skies which was a bit overdone, but very sincere and heart-warming.

I have given several lectures about my recent work on Huntington disease, the last at St. Mary's Hospital Medical School in London yesterday, where I was shown their newly set up Alexander Fleming museum, a mini

Max lecturing on polar zippers at the symposium in honour of his 80th birthday.

laboratory, with a narrow bench by the window and a diminutive sink, where he discovered penicillin, all cluttered untidily with test tubes, culture dishes and reagents as they were in his time.

Father Huddleston came to visit us again, delighted and optimistic about S. Africa where he stood on Mandela's platform during his inauguration speech as President. He wants to go back to live there, which grieves me, as I shall then not see him again. A wonderful man.

To Lotte Perutz, March 6, 1995

Two days ago Gisela and I went to Oxford for the memorial service for Dorothy in the University Church, where I was asked to give the address. I had prepared it with great care and was quite confident about it, but as the moment came to climb up to the pulpit and address the packed audience of perhaps 500 people, with Isaiah Berlin sitting in the first row as the Queen's representative and Margaret Thatcher in the second, I was seized by the most awful stage fright and had a pulse of almost 120. Once I had started speaking, I calmed down and was quite fluent. Before me Lizzie [her daughter] had read part of a speech that Dorothy had delivered at a Pugwash meeting about the evils of modern arms, and Luke [her son] read a beautiful Shakespeare sonnet about the nature of love. Fortunately there was none of the nonsense about the resurrection and eternal life which always irritates me on these occasions.

After the service we went to a reception at Dorothy's college where the overwhelming tributes to my speech brought lumps to my throat that made it hard for me to reply. The tributes came from Dorothy's family, colleagues and friends and were deeply touching, and I was enormously pleased that everyone thought I had done justice to her memory.[21]

---

[21]Max concluded his funeral oration: "Dorothy radiated love: for chemistry, her family, her friends, her students, her crystals and her college to which she generously gave part of her Nobel Prize.... Her love was combined with a brilliant mind and an iron will to succeed, regardless of her frail and later severely crippled body. There was magic about her person. She had no enemies, not even among those whose scientific theories she demolished or whose political views she opposed.... It was marvellous to have her drop in on you in your lab, like the spring. She brought interest and enthusiasm for your work, making you feel that it was really important, and more often than not she would point out something relevant that you had overlooked, because she knew more about your problem and the ways of solving it than you did yourself....

Her outlook is best illuminated by one of my favourite quotations: Orlando says in *As You Like It*:
Thou are not of the fashion of these times,
Where none will sweat but for promotion.
Dorothy will be remembered as a great chemist, a saintly, tolerant and gentle lover of people and a devoted protagonist of peace."

To Robin and Sue Perutz, April 14, 1995

When I arrived at Edinburgh Airport last Sunday, [Tam] Dalyell was there to meet me and take me to supper at his home. I was prepared for a modest semi-detached, but instead a long drive through the rainy countryside took us to an imposing castle in huge grounds near Linlithgow which turned out to be his ancestral home. It was built by a successful businessman, Dalyell's forebear with the same name and his rich wife in 1612, and the Dalyells have lived there ever since. Most of Tam's ancestors have been generals whose impressive portraits adorn the walls. Tam's parents gave the property to the National Trust in 1943 and Tam lives in part of the castle as the Trust's tenant.

Tam went to Eton, followed by King's College, Cambridge, where he read history. He then became a schoolmaster. When I asked him how he became a Labour MP, he told me, by coaching his school soccer team to country-wide fame, a success that made him acceptable to the mineworkers' union.

Next lunch with the officers of the RSC [Royal Society of Chemistry]. I ended my own talk by telling them that I got into the work on Huntington Disease, because I had wondered why *Ascaris* haemoglobin has such a high oxygen affinity, which makes me sceptical of the value of technology forecasts and the like. This drew lively applause from the audience, with John Cadogan looking rather sour in the front row.

To Robin Perutz and Family. New York—London, May 1, 1995

I had a session [at Princeton] with Tom Spiro who showed me time-resolved picosecond resonance Raman spectra of CO haemoglobin after flash photolysis. The technical advances were impressive, but unfortunately the results have led him to propose yet another wrong mechanism of the Bohr effect. Sadly, there is no end to the papers purporting to prove new features of the allosteric mechanism which confuse what has been thoroughly proved to be the correct one. To comfort me, Bill Eaton also showed me new results that corroborate and add yet further proof to the right one.

At Washington I attended a one day-long haemoglobin meeting which I found cheering. Don Abraham, my long-time collaborator, has finally found a compound that lowers the oxygen affinity of haemoglobin even in the presence of serum albumin. True to present fashion, he has founded a company designed to exploit this compound commercially. It improves delivery of oxygen to tumours which in turn increases their sensitivity to radiation, so that smaller doses can be used. Unexpectedly it also strength-

ens contraction of the heart muscle through increased oxygen
delivery and promises to be useful
in cardiac surgery. I am delighted
that the work which Abraham
and I began in 1980 is finally giving medically useful results.

Between these two meetings
in Washington proper, I attended
a 3-day meeting on signalling proteins at the NIH. I heard that
hydroxy urea is proving a successful treatment of sickle cell
anaemia because it increases production of foetal haemoglobin
which has a strong anti-sickling

Robin Perutz

effect. I heard of a brilliant treatment for septic or wound shock which
promises to save many lives. I was disheartened by the ever-increasing complexity of the signalling systems of the living cell, whose intricate workings
the conference was supposed to clarify and impressed by the progress in 3-
and 4-dimensional NMR. [Marius] Clore and [Angela] Gronenborn expect
soon to have a 750 megahertz machine which will allow them to work with
much lower protein concentrations than those needed for the only just
delivered 600 megahertz machine. These machines and many others
become obsolete as soon as one has got them to work.

I did not find myself shedding many tears for my U.S. colleagues' shortage of funds. As usual on my visits, most of them have just *"happened"* to
move into new buildings or collected superb new X-ray data at Grenoble, or
replaced their almost new image plates by a new superior charge something
device. Crowds of them are tearing the guts out of structural biology, and
most protein structures now emerging resemble one or another seen before.

To Hiradó Udvarhelyi, August 17, 1995

I read [Karl] Popper's *Open Society [and Its Enemies]* when I was invited to
give a lecture on the impact of science on society. I was very impressed by
his analysis of the philosophical foundation of totalitarianism from Plato to
Marx via Hegel. The collapse of Marxism has removed some of the book's
topicality, but you would still find it interesting. At the anniversary meeting

[Ernst] Gombrich told us that he had known Popper before the War, but after Popper's move to New Zealand he had heard nothing from him, until one day in 1943 a letter arrived telling Gombrich that Popper had written a book and asking him to find a publisher for it. This was the first of 92 letters G received from P, some of which G read out to us, to our great amusement, because P sent G long lists of corrections: "Transfer the first half of the 2nd sentence in the 3rd paragraph on p. 339 to the end of the 5th sentence of the 1st paragraph on 340," only to be followed by another letter requesting different changes and a 3rd letter saying that he had rewritten the entire chapter and would G change it, always entirely unconcerned about the hours of work imposed upon G who had the greatest difficulties finding a publisher. The one who finally accepted it paid Popper an advance of £25 and printed only 300 copies due to wartime paper restrictions. We had a representative of the publisher at our meeting, but he had no idea how many copies of the book had been sold since.

To Rita Levi-Montalcini, February 16, 1996

Please excuse this delayed reply to your circular letter of December and the Trieste Declaration.

Of course, I support your document which sets out all the things needed to create a better world, but I would have liked to include a scientist's duties in his own laboratory, because people who preach to the world often use this as a cover for their moral lapses at home. If you are not sure what I mean, read the Goertzels'[22] biography of Linus Pauling, just published.

Here are some of my commandments: Thou shalt not steal books from your departmental library, nor the ideas from papers and grant applications you are asked to review, nor delay publication of other people's papers in order to publish your results first, nor put your name on publications to which you have made no significant contribution nor in other ways exploit the work of your students, and so on. Such rules need to be laid down, because otherwise people do not realise that they are committing crimes.[23]

---

[22]Goertzel, T.G. and Goertzel, B. 1995. *Linus Pauling: A Life in Science and Politics.* Basic Books, N.Y.

[23]In an interview with Harry Kroto [Vega Science Trust] Max remarked: "My teachers were Bernal, Keilin and Bragg and there was a very high moral standard there; neither Bragg nor Bernal would ever put their name on a paper to which they had not themselves made a major contribution. So this German habit, which is now rampant in America, that the head of the laboratory puts his name on any paper even if he's hardly read it, that didn't exist in the Cavendish."

Finally, I have long been in favour of the Hippocratic Oath for Scientists. Was this possibly discussed at your meeting?

To Lotte Perutz, March 31, 1996

You will remember my pleasure at having found what seemed like a clue to the molecular basis of Huntington disease. There was *one* small anomaly about the results which Kelvin Stott, the graduate student whom you may have met in Washington briefly last year, and I decided to investigate further. This work has been going on since last August. Kelvin finally suspected that our favourable results might have been artefactual, and a few days ago confirmed that this is true. There is still a small hope that there was at least partial truth in our results, and Kelvin hopes to find out before I go off to the U.S. This was a shock and sad disappointment for me and makes me fear that it spells the end of my active research career. I still have some minor haemoglobin work in mind, but nothing that people will be very interested in; haemoglobin is largely passé.

To Robin Perutz and Family. New York–London, May 8, 1996

At the Human Rights meeting my opening talk was followed by prisoners of conscience. All the ex-prisoners said how much the letters by colleagues abroad demanding their release helped. The mere fact that their imprisonment is known and condemned abroad was a great help and improved their treatment.

I spent the last 2 days at a Huntington's Disease meeting at Cold Spring Harbor with only 30 people sitting around a few tables. Many of the people there had tried to produce a mouse model of the disease, i.e. a mouse that carries and expresses the gene for the disease and exhibits its symptoms. My patriotic heart leapt when the only one to have succeeded turned out to be a young English woman from Guy's Hospital in London [Gillian Bates]. She "infected" mice with the gene for just the glutamine repeat of the big Huntington's Disease protein, and that is sufficient to induce the symptoms which strikingly resemble the human disease. This mouse can now serve as a model for attempts at possible treatments.

I learnt that 7 different inherited neurodegenerative diseases have now been found to be due to expansion of glutamine repeats. In all of them the disease begins when there are more than 35–40 glutamines in a row. This gave me an idea for a common molecular mechanism which appeals to me very much. I put it to the meeting, but my argument hinged on entropy and the chelate effect which are concepts few of the geneticists, medical people and biochemists there would have understood. So it will take time for the idea to be accepted.

To Vivien and Robin Perutz and Family. Haifa, May 19, 1996

Israel is one huge building site. 3/4 million Russians and other immigrants from Yemen, Ethiopia, Morocco, etc. have arrived recently and most of them have already been decently housed. Much of the housing is attractive and fits the local style. Israel has better architects than most countries. Architecture of the many new labs at the Weizmann Institute is marvellous. No nonsense about post modernism. In fact there are no "issues," no idiotic copying of some fad or other, but each building is an original *and attractive* work of art in its own right. The same is true of some of the public buildings in Jerusalem. I often think our architects are beauty-blind. Israeli architects are not.

The second positive experience is the quality of the science at the Weizmann Institute. The highlight at the meeting was the development of a vaccine which arrests the progress of multiple sclerosis. It has passed all three stages of clinical trials and is being manufactured in quantity by a local firm and should presumably gain FDA approval. Michael Sela, the immunologist in charge of the work, told me that it was the outcome of 27 years' work.

Mummy and I enjoyed long talks with Ephraim Katzir,[24] and also his humorous, compassionate and moving speeches. He speaks of science as the most wonderful thing in the world, the one thing that has kept him from despair in the face of the tragedies that have marred his life.

A negative side is that Israel has lost much of its character and has become like the U.S. Multiple lane highways, dense traffic, supermarkets. Here you feel even more cut off from the rest of the world than in the U.S. Today is the first day when we managed to see the *Jerusalem Post*, the only paper not in Hebrew. Foreign papers are not to be had, but our hotel TV can tune into the BBC World Service.

One of the chemists and his wife took us to Acre. We drove . . . then trudged through narrow slummy streets in the old city, past one or two mosques, walked into the Karn, a wide Arab court where camel caravans unloaded their goods,

---

[24]The biophysicist whom Max first met when he gave the Weizmann lectures in 1961 and who later represented Israel on the EMBO committee which Max chaired. From 1973 to 1978, Katzir was President of Israel. He changed his name from Katchalski to Katzir.

past the coastal fortifications which the Crusaders built, squeezing against the walls of the narrow streets to let cars past, and went to the fisherman's harbour. It was not clear whether the inhabitants of the slums were also the owners of the many cars. No one looked under nourished. I heard that 25,000 Arabs live in Haifa, Arab students attend Haifa University, there was an Arab "village" a few miles south which looked all new and immaculate white from a distance and must have housed several thousand people. It seems that tens of thousands of Arabs live in Israel as Israeli citizens about whom one never hears, because there is no conflict between them and the Jews.

To Vivien and Robin Perutz and Family, May 21, 1996

This morning we took a taxi to the Dome of the Rock. Built around 700 AD, its original structure is still intact as a wonderful monument to Islamic art. Its glistening golden dome has recently been restored at King Hussein's expense ($8m). The decorations are sumptuous but without conveying the ungodly wealth that repelled me in St. Peter's. The Dome is built above the rock from which the Prophet ascended to heaven, and this rock is still exposed under its centre. Through a hole in the fencing around it, the faithful can put in their hands and feel the Prophet's footprint as he took off.

Jerusalem is immense. When you are not in sight of old monuments, Israel looks much like California. Yesterday Gisela's cousin took us to the old city where we walked along the narrow souks or bazaars with its milling crowd of tourists to the Church of the Holy Sepulchre. Its walls were no longer propped up by the steel girders placed against them by the British Army to save them from collapse, but its temporary wooden roof was supported by scaffolding, and several other structures were also concealed by scaffolding. By contrast with the Dome of the Rock, the Church is a mess, apparently because the different Christian sects which claim it as their property cannot agree on who is to pay for its repair.

Boaz Shaanan's wife[25] told us that the old spirit of warmth, friendship and helpfulness is no longer there, that parents come to school and shout abuse at the teachers in front of the children, that the Jewish respect for learning has died and with it the respect for teachers as professionals. In other words, Israel has become just another society chasing wealth.

When we returned to our hotel last night we learnt that a Jewish holiday had started at midday and that the kitchen would therefore be closed

---

[25]Boaz had been Max's postdoc in the early 1980s; his wife Nurit, is a school teacher.

for the next two and a half days. We would have been stranded without food until our departure had not an old colleague, a well-known haematologist, invited us to dinner.

Rabbis in long black kaftans with sidelocks, beards and long hair are all over Jerusalem. Boaz told me that the street with the ultra orthodox that our friends took us to in 1961 has now expanded to a large district. The rabbis lead idle parasitic lives; they are a small minority, but they have a stranglehold over the country. Hotels have rabbinical inspection to see if all rules are strictly observed, otherwise their kosher licenses are withdrawn. Cooking is prohibited on the Sabbath and all food is served cold. Not knowing this, I brought some cooked potatoes done for me by a friend to the country hotel near Caesarea, but they refused to heat them in their microwave, because pressing the buttons of the microwave would break the Sabbath. At supper in Haifa's top hotel I asked for milk in my tea. This was refused because milk must not be served with meat. This morning's El Al flight to London via Copenhagen, which would have allowed us a good night's sleep, was cancelled, I take it for religious reasons. Instead we had to get up at 4.00 am to be at Ben Gurion Airport at 6.00. There we found longer passenger queues than I have seen anywhere. Departure of our aircraft was delayed by over an hour to the British Airways pilot's fury, because passengers could not reach it. The reason: it's a Jewish holiday and religion seems to have kept most of the airport's security staff at home. In hotels and hospitals lifts are programmed to work automatically on the Sabbath stopping at every floor each way, because pressing the buttons would break the Sabbath. Never mind the inconvenience and the delay. I got very angry at this kind of chicanery at times, but the sunshine was a great compensation.

We talked to several friends about the Lebanon war. The papers failed to report that the Hezbollah sent rockets into Northern Israel at the rate of 50 a day for several weeks so that villages and towns had to be evacuated. This situation became intolerable and forced [Shimon] Peres [Prime Minister of Israel in 1996] to order the attack. The bombardment of the refugee camp really seems to have been a mistake.

To Robin Perutz and Family, June 11, 1996

I must tell you an extraordinary story John Kendrew related to me when we celebrated Aaron Klug's OM at Peterhouse.

In the late 60s, at the height of the Cultural Revolution, John went to China and gave a lecture which was interpreted sentence by sentence by a colourless fellow in Maoish drab outfit. John noticed that he knew English rather well and asked him if he had ever been to England, which he denied. "Where had he learned English?" "At school in China."

Last May John went to China again and visited an old friend of ours with whom we had shared a room at the Molteno Institute here until he returned to China after the Communist revolution in 1948/9. He is now retired professor of biochemistry and called Wang.

Wang asked John if he remembered the interpreter at his lecture in the 60s. When John replied that he did, Wang revealed that it was he. The Party had disguised him and forbidden him to mention that he knew John or ever left China, but used him as the only one who could understand both John's English and his subject.

To Lotte Perutz. Dijon, September 8, 1996

You wonder what my scientist friends thought of the Likud victory. We had a very disheartened letter from my host in Jerusalem who fears that violent conflicts between Jews and Arabs will start again, calling [Benjamin] Netanyahu [the new Prime Minister of Israel] an American television actor rather than a statesman and detesting the rule of the rabbis. Did you read that they elevated [Yitzhak] Rabin's murderer to a national hero?

To the Family. Washington, May 12, 1997

One morning was filled by a meeting of the Human Rights Network of the National Academy. The President of the Academy reported on his discussion of the Chinese Government's disregard for human rights with his Chinese counterpart and other officers of the Chinese Academy of Sciences. To his astonishment there was no difference between the American and the Chinese scientists' condemnation of these abuses. On the contrary, at the end of their meeting, the Chinese President put his hand on the shoulder of Torsten Wiesel who heads the committee which intervenes on behalf of imprisoned Chinese dissident scientists, and said to him: "Keep going!"

Things have improved in China in so far as you can abuse the government in private without being denounced and arrested and you are left in peace so long as you don't do it at a public meeting.

A traveller to China said that 90% of Beijing residents support civil and human rights, but most Chinese know the history of the past 150 years and are determined that there should be no repeat of past humiliation of China by foreign powers; therefore they support their government's nationalistic policies.

Educated people know that life expectancy in 1920 was 35 in the cities and 29 in the country. Concern for civil rights is muted by their awareness of economic progress; they are anxious above all for its continuation. He also stressed the importance of traditional Chinese values, such as loyalty to the family. Baruch Blumberg, virologist, thought that Americans could profit from copying Chinese social and economic rights, while the Chinese could profit from American civil rights. He told us that the best Chinese science students go to the U.S. for postdoctoral work. He thought that China will have to improve civil rights if it wanted them to return.

A Chinese dissident who now lives in the U.S. doubted this. He began by telling us that Chinese people, like all others, want a better life, more dignity and more freedom, but he did not believe that freedom will be granted to them. Human rights violation in China had nothing to do with its having a different culture as the authorities maintain, but they were imposed by the Communist Party whose power was based on repression. After Mao's death China had been bankrupt. Deng [Xiaoping] started economic reform because he believed that economic progress was the only way for the Party to retain power. Corruption pervaded Government and Party like a cancer and could not be controlled without a free press. Environmental degradation was disastrous. "Stability" today was being bought at the expense of instability tomorrow.

Lotte and I went to the *most marvellous concert* last Sunday afternoon, part of a Brahms festival. I've rarely heard music played with such verve and produce such wonderful sounds. I was thrilled.

To Jean Floud. Feder, July 26, 1997

I was pleased to read about your happy experience with the Jewish girls at your school and your many Jewish friends. My own experience at school was different. The Jewish boys in my class were not very likeable, and those boys who became lifelong friends were Gentiles. In Vienna of the twenties and thirties, there was no rigid division of society into Jews and Gentiles. My sister's and my friends were all people who shared our love for the mountains and our boundless devotion to skiing in winter and rock climbing in summer. [Ernst] Gombrich's article does not mention the frequent intermarriage between Jews and Gentiles. Our circle contained Gentiles, Jews, half and quarter Jews. We never thought about them as such, none of them cared, they were just people. The categorisation was an invention of the Gestapo.

As I walked up the mountain this morning, your letter went through my mind and it conjured up the images of many dear friends. There was Werner [Weissel] who sat next to me during our last two school years, and who shared my interests in history and literature, and whose political views were as liberal as my own. He became a successful physician and head of a clinic for internal medicine in Vienna. He had to serve in Russia, and was severely wounded at the very end of the war by shrapnel from an American bomb. I met him again in Switzerland in 1947 and was immensely pleased that the war and the Nazis had not divided us; on the contrary, we understood each other better than ever. During the war he had married a Russian émigré, a Princess Troubetskoy, who looked like a queen and was full of fun. Throughout her life, her radiant beauty

René Jaeger on a mountain above Tiers in the Dolomites

and her wit made you feel cheerful the moment she entered the room. She died tragically of a heart attack in her fifties, in the arms of her cardiologist husband who died himself of a heart attack two years ago.

The other school friend was René [Jaeger], a wonderful skier and mountaineer. In 1963 he built himself a house in a lovely spot of the Engadine to which he invited us winter and summer to share his passion for the mountains. Tragically he fell to his death off one of his favourite mountains in 1981.

Then there was my sister's boyfriend, Arne, a Norwegian philosophy student who had come to Vienna for the Vienna Circle and also to learn psychoanalysis, because he said there was no living in philosophy. He need not have worried because he was appointed to the chair of philosophy in Oslo before he was 30. He was a brilliant rock climber and pianist, and lover of debate. He made me read Schopenhauer, Kant, Nietzsche and Freud and opened my horizons in many ways. We visited him once in the 1960s when he thought great thoughts in a cabin two hours' climb from Norway's highest railway station. On a clear day his panorama stretched over most of southern Norway. His only company up there was a very affectionate tame rat. Arne is still alive but a bit cranky, bossed by his Chinese wife.

There was Hermann Mark, the professor of physical chemistry whose brilliant lectures covered the entire subject, a great sportsman and extrovert. Once, when he went skiing with us students, we marvelled how well the old boy could still ski. I later worked out that he was 38 years old then. He emigrated to the U.S., became a professor in Brooklyn, where he did much to bring the American plastics industry into being. When I went there to celebrate his 90th birthday, I found him as bright and active as ever. He was a half or quarter Jew with a Gentile wife, presiding over a Brooklyn laboratory that was 100% Jewish, except for his one-time Viennese assistant Fritz Eirich who joined him at Brooklyn, a brilliant teacher and great nature lover whom I still visit whenever I go to the U.S. Mark and I even once made a film together. Mark was a great show off, but he had a lot to show off with.

Soon after I arrived in Cambridge, one Gerald Seligman, a

Max with Fritz Eirich, 9 years Max's senior. They had been friends since 1928.

member of the former Jewish Frankfurt banking family, more English than the English, engaged me for a glacier research expedition in the Swiss Alps. I spent 4 months on a research station at 13,000 ft with him and a chemistry student, Tom Hughes, son of a Welsh clergyman. To be thrown together, with little other company, can make people lifelong enemies, but Tom and I became good friends. He was one of those people who is never ruffled, full of resource and always cheerful. When I was interned and deported to Canada, leaving my parents behind in Cambridge, he was like a son to them. Seligman, by contrast, did nothing to help them.

When I started as a research student in the Crystallographic Laboratory in Cambridge, Bernal's research assistant was Isidor Fankuchen, the atheist son of a rabbi in Brooklyn, a podgy, childish, naive, good-natured, jealous, aggressively tactless devoted Communist. He and Seligman were the only Jews I got to know here. Later Kendrew, Crick, Sanger, Huxley, my close colleagues were all Gentiles.

I hope I have not tired you with this long letter. By the way, do call me Max.

To Patience Thomson, March 5, 1998

On 16 March I am supposed to distribute the prizes for a Max Perutz Essay Competition instituted by the Medical Research Council for its graduate students. The best two were written by girls. I also find at our lab seminars that the girls are often better at organising their material, expressing themselves and putting themselves in the place of others not familiar with their speciality. Needless to say, I have to make a speech and am just debating what to amuse my audience with.

To André Roch, March 21, 1998

Your cri de coeur made me very sad, but it also reminded me of all your wonderful companionship in the past. Next summer it will be 50 years since you came to the Jungfraujoch to help me drill my borehole into the Jungfrau firn. Both the English students who came out to work with me had broken their legs while learning to ski, and my expedition was on the point of collapse when you came from Davos and revived it.

It was marvellous to work with you. Your enthusiasm, cheerfulness, ingenuity, sheer physical energy and all the laughter you brought with you suddenly made the project go. You showed us how to sledge our steel tubes straight down to the glacier, through a snow-filled gully from the Research

Station, you helped us to set up our drilling rig, and in between work took me up the Mönch along its west ridge.

The next year you and I met on the Jungfraujoch to remeasure the inclination of the tube. We found our borehole snowed up, but you found it and showed me how to build an igloo over it so that we had a shelter for our instruments. I still have the photograph of your igloo.

In 1951 or 2 you invited me to your house for a week to ski with you. One day we walked up a mountain with your small son. To keep him going, you told him Red Indian stories all the way up which you invented. I later followed that recipe with my own children and grandchildren and found that it worked wonders.

I treasure all the books you gave me with your wonderful photographs and I still regret that I was never able to attempt the Haute Route myself.

There are certain people who make you feel cheerful the moment they enter your room and you were one of them. Your very presence breathed laughter, courage and enterprise, competence, always knowing what's the right thing to do and not caring about trivia.

When I stayed with you in Davos your wife complained of your wasting time watering your ice rink instead of answering your letters, but it was your playfulness that made everything you touched work.

I hope that these few memories will give you some pleasure. Let me tell you how much I treasured our friendship and how pleased I was that my students breaking their legs made me get to know you.

Let me wish you, despite all the evil symptoms that Gute Besserung[26] may yet come your way.

To Patience Thomson, June 28, 1998

Your heart-warming response to my book [*I Wish I'd Made You Angry Earlier*] cheered me enormously. I am never confident about my writing: Is it really clear? Will this interest other people? I am easily captivated, but that does not mean that anyone else will be by what I have uncovered. Recently the editor of *The New York Review* sent me a book on engineering principles in nature's designs. It seems very well written but I am not sure that I know enough biology or engineering to do it justice. One useful principle is always to try and make the review more interesting than the book, but I may not succeed there.

[26]The German phrase for "get better," literally "good betterment."

2000s

*"I have had 65 years of productive
work in Cambridge, the most wonderful
centre of learning in the world."*

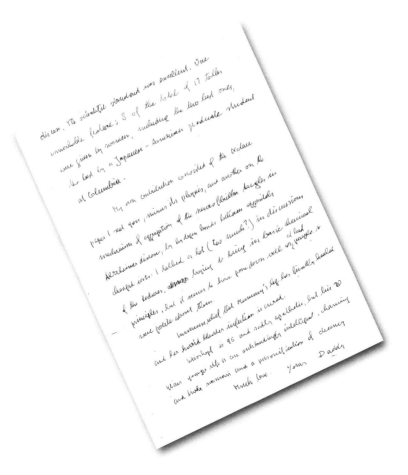

A T THE START OF THE DECADE MAX WAS AS VIGOROUS as before, travelling, lecturing and fighting his scientific corner; but in January 2001 a dermatologist diagnosed Merkel cell cancer, which is so virulent in a third of patients that treatment does not prolong their lives. Luckily, the doctor had told Max that his cancer was harmless, which gave him and us 10 happy months. He died just short of his 88th birthday and 60th wedding anniversary on 6 February 2002, content with a marvellous life, less than two months after the virulence of his cancer became apparent. During this period, family and friends from Britain, mainland Europe, and the United States visited him, and on sleepless nights he composed the remarkable letters reproduced below, letters which he dictated to Mary-Anne Starkey, his former secretary.

To Ron Gray, November 19, 2000

I wrote to you once before about the French poem you sent me "S'il est vrai. . ."[1] This touched a chord, but my letter got lost.

I grew up as a devout, believing Catholic, and also deeply impressed by the horror of the First World War described by [Erich Maria] Remarque's *Im Westen nichts Neues* [All Quiet on the Western Front]. When Mussolini threatened to invade Abyssinia and the League of Nations failed to take action, it seemed to me that the attack on Abyssinia would open the gates to fresh wars. I fervently prayed in church asking God to prevent this happening. When Italian planes then dropped poison gas on defenceless, innocent Abyssinian villages unpunished, I concluded that there can be no omniscient compassionate, just God. "Il ne répondra plus que par un froid silence." [He will only answer with a stony silence]. Shortly afterwards I read of Roman bishops blessing the troops going out to Abyssinia. That killed my respect for the Church.

---

[1] By Alfred de Vigny: The gist of the poem is that if God forsook Jesus as he hung on the cross, then he is deaf to our suffering.

To Marion Perutz, November 19, 2000

This letter is mainly to tell you how pleased I was that Edinburgh is such a success for you. It's marvellous that the lectures are interesting, your company is congenial and that Scotland gives you scope for your spirit of enterprise. Robin told me of your adventurous ascent of Ben Nevis one week and finding conger eels in Loch Long the next. It's marvellous to be young and have infinite stamina. You must feel very cheerful indeed.

I came back from America on Thursday night, also very cheerful and not a bit tired. I attended an excellent meeting on structural and developmental biology in a suburb of Washington for the last two and a half days, delighted to hear how my subject, protein crystallography, is still going from strength to strength 40 years after Kendrew and I launched it with the structures of haemoglobin and myoglobin.

Sue and Marion Perutz

On one weekend I visited my oldest Austrian friends (90+) near Princeton, and they took me to a spectacular concert of Mozart and Schubert chamber music. The players got such wonderful sounds out of their instruments that they lifted me into the clouds from the first bar.

I gave two lectures in Philadelphia and one at the meeting near Washington. One was on Huntington disease and the other had the title: "What is it trying to tell you?" This is what my teacher and patron W.L. Bragg used to ask when looking at a new structure, telling you to look at it with a loving eye to find out its secrets. It is a good way of looking at nature, not just at atomic structures. They often tell you so much, and the same is true, no matter whether it is a fish or the stars that you are looking at.

To An Associate Editor of Nature, January 19, 2001

Your first reviewer understands neither physical chemistry nor structural biology. The intra-nuclear aggregates which are the cause of neural death in Huntington disease were discovered by Stephen Davies at University College here in London in 1997 and had been missed by many of the biomedical scientists working on the disease in America. Perhaps for this reason many of the American workers have been trying to prove that they are not the cause, even though no-one has yet proposed an alternative.

As [Aaron] Klug pointed out, the referee's report never entered into Windle's and my scientific evidence or arguments, but it merely asserted unspecified accumulated evidence against the aggregates being the cause of neural death. [David] Rubinsztein and [Alan] Fersht have shown that evidence to be flawed. As Klug also pointed out, the referee accompanied this by offensive personal remarks about me. I had better not tell you what I think of this.

To a Number of Colleagues, undated

On 3 November I sent the enclosed Brief Communication to *Nature*. On 8 January *Nature* rejected it on the strength of a single referee's report.

The referee ignores our arguments and recommends rejection on the grounds of accumulating evidence against the huntingtin aggregates being the cause of neural death. I am not aware of such evidence.

The exponential dependence of age of onset on length of glutamine repeats now discovered by [James] Gusella and [M.E.] MacDonald is even stronger evidence in support of the nucleation theory than the invariance of the probability of neural death with time. There is no other mechanism that could possibly give this result.

Our paper makes a vitally important point, and as it is a comment on Clarke et al.'s earlier paper *Nature* is the proper place for it. Only support by other workers in the field will persuade the editor that a mistake has been made.

To Ron Gray, February 6, 2001

Thank you so much for the lovely passage from Darwin. In my youth I found that mountaineering as practised at that time taught you the same moral lessons: good-humoured patience, freedom from selfishness and the habit of acting for yourself, but in addition it also taught you to take responsibility for others and courage in the face of difficulties. As to the last sentence, about the many kind-hearted people you encounter on a journey, I experienced this again on my last journey to the U.S., when men for whom I'd never done anything in my life put themselves out for me.

To An Associate Editor of Nature, June 8, 2001

When Galileo found that Copernicus was right that the earth goes round the sun and not, as is written in the Book of Joshua, the sun round the earth, the Church forced him to publish this merely as a *hypothesis*.

Now *Nature* assumes the mantle of the Catholic Church forcing Windle and me to publish our firm evidence as a "hypothesis." I cannot see why our paper cannot go in as a letter. What is the reason?

Your e-mail arrived 30 minutes before I was going to send the paper to Washington by DHL. I have already made the alteration requested by the third referee. There will be a Gordon Conference on Triplet Repeat Diseases in the U.S. starting on 15 July. If you were able to get the paper out before then, this would be some compensation for the inappropriate heading, but as I say, I would rather it came out as a letter.[2]

To the Family. Cambridge, Mass., July 20, 2001

Great news! I climbed a mountain. Altitude 1080 feet but along a steep rocky path, the kind I believed I would never be able to do again. I never intended to. They invited participants to come on a 4 mile walk. Since the country was flat all around I decided this would give me no trouble. We drove off in a cavalcade of cars and stopped at what we used to call "einen Einstieg" [start of the climb], and scrambled up over steep rocks. Nobody said how high it was and the woman who "led" us, it turned out, didn't know the path either. I was doubtful, but there was no turning back. It continued like that for over an hour, and *I was fine*. My only trouble was poor balance. On tricky bits I needed support, just an arm to help me balance.

The meeting on trinucleotide repeat diseases was mainly on Huntington Disease. The scientific standard was excellent.

To Bruce Alberts, President of the National Academy of Sciences, January 10, 2002

It seems that my days are numbered. I am writing to tell you how much I appreciated being a foreign member and also publishing papers which every other journal would have rejected. When I was elected in 1971 the accepted dogma was that the half molecule of haemoglobin was the cooperative unit. This idea was first put forward by the Harvard biophysicist Jef-

---

[2]Max needed a theory to explain how the development and progression of the disease could be explained on the basis of his proposed structural model. Prof. Alan Windle (a materials scientist) suggested that nucleation theory would account for such a random process and the paper models this in three dimensions. It was controversial particularly with the reviewers who may not have been sympathetic to Max's thinking. It was finally published as a hypothesis. Perutz, M.F. and Windle A.H. 2001. Cause of neural death in neurodegenerative disease attributable to expansion of glutamine repeats. *Nature* **412**: 143–144.—AW

fries Wyman in the 1940s, and in 1970 this was the firm view of everyone in the field including John Edsall's postdoc, Guidotti, and of course of his boss Edsall, who was a close friend of Wyman. The first paper I submitted shortly after my election demolished that idea and showed that the tetramer was the cooperative unit. Edsall was then editor of *PNAS*. It is a great tribute to his fairness that he did not reject this paper but accepted it.

In 1994 I conceived the idea that the glutamine repeats whose elongation is the cause of Huntington disease are polar zippers, that they make the huntingtin protein aggregate and that is the cause of the disease. I sent the paper to *Nature* whose editor rejected it as of no interest without even sending it to referees. So I submitted it to *PNAS* where it was published despite the absence of any evidence for these aggregates. Three years later Gillian Bates of Guys Hospital succeeded in producing the disease in transgenic mice. She handed her mice to Stephen Davies at University College Anatomy School, and he found the aggregates; thereupon the people at Harvard looked again at the post-mortem sections of the patients who had died from the disease. They found that the aggregates were there, but had been overlooked. Nowhere else would I have been able to publish this.

I enormously enjoyed the annual meeting, attended by all the interesting people and old friends I used to meet there, and had looked forward to the one next April.

To Monsignor Marcelo Sánchez Sorondo, Chancellor of the Pontifical Academy, January 14, 2002

It seems that my days are numbered and I feel like expressing to you and the President my deep appreciation of having been a member. I received the Pope's telegram appointing me to the Academy at the same moment as the news of the attempt to assassinate him. It roused a terrible conflict of emotion in me, on the one hand my great pleasure about this honour, and on the other hand my deep sorrow at that tragic crime.

I first attended a study week in 1961, in fact organised it myself, which you could almost call "the birth of molecular biology." People presented an extraordinary series of exciting new discoveries and I first met some of the protagonists from other countries. Since then I have attended and organised other study weeks and much enjoyed that privilege, but the greatest privilege was being a member of that unique body, a truly international academy, covering all the natural sciences. I came across many more people there whom I would never otherwise have met, such as the Indian physicist

Menon, and then there was the wonderful setting, that Renaissance court, looking over the back of St. Peter's like the view of the Matterhorn from Zermatt. I think that the Pontifical Academy is a unique institution and I very much hope that the Holy Father and his successors will continue to give it their support.

I should be delighted if you were able to communicate any of this letter to the Holy Father and assure him again how much I appreciated my membership.

To Jim Watson, January 14, 2002

My days are numbered, and I just wanted to let you know how much fun dealing with you gave me in the early days. In 1950 or so, you poked your head through the door and asked shyly: "Can I come and work here?" I had a quick think and recalled that [Salvatore] Luria had written to John about a young postdoc of his, so I said yes without a moment's hesitation. I then asked you what made you decide to join us and expected to hear how much interest reports of our work had aroused in you. Instead you said: "Because Kalckar is getting divorced." When it was all settled, we agreed that you should try to get into a college, but it was already the beginning of term. With great difficulty I persuaded Denis Wilkinson, a physicist friend of mine who was a fellow, to take you into Jesus. After a while I asked you if it was alright there. You replied that they were only interested in rowing and you wanted to get out. Another diplomatic effort of mine got you out of Jesus and into Clare, hoping that you would be happy there. When I tried to sound you out about it, you replied: "The food is awful!" You were awkward and not a model of tact but your arrival had an electrifying effect on our small group, because all our thoughts had been focussed on proteins, that we thought contained the riddle of life, but you convinced us that it was in DNA. Then one Monday morning in March 1953, Francis asked me to come to your room, and there stood your atomic model of the double helix! I realised at once that it must be right. It was the most dramatic moment in my scientific life.

I was sorry not to appear at your launching party at Clare the other day, but I had a very good excuse. I had been working on Huntington disease for some years which also got me interested in the amyloid structure, because the fibres of poly-L-glutamine have the same cross beta X-ray pattern as amyloid. Last September I had an idea what the structure responsible for it might be. The more I thought about it, the more apparent did it become,

Jim Watson and Francis Crick with the double helix in 1953

that it was the only possible solution, so I dropped everything else, replied
to no letters, went to no meetings and concentrated on that one problem. I
finished two papers about the structure of amyloid at 12.50 on 20 December, and Alan Fersht, now an editor, sent them straight to *PNAS*.[3] At 13.00 I
had to be admitted to hospital for an operation on my bile duct which was

---

[3]The final papers were controversial because the evidence was too ambiguous for direct demonstration of Max's hypothesis. Aaron Klug has suggested that these ambiguities might be resolved
if the tubes had collapsed, when the samples were dried for X-ray analysis, to form the stacked
sheets which other scientists have proposed as amyloid's structure (A. Klug, pers. comm., 2008).
A recent paper by S.J. Singer and N.N. Dewji supports Max's water-filled nanotubes by demonstrating that proteins of the length found by Max to form these structures, enter membranes and
act as ion channels, causing cells to burst. As the authors note, "We provisionally regard the Perutz
et al. model as a plausible and attractive but not proven structure" (Singer, S.J. and Dewji, N.N.
2006. Evidence that Perutz's double-β-stranded subunit structure for β-amyloids also applies to
their channel-forming structures in membranes. *Proc. Natl. Acad. Sci.* **103**: 1546–1550.)—AW

blocked by a tumour of a cancer that started with a pimple under my nose last January and is now out of control. I have enjoyed 65 years of productive research here at Cambridge and what more can anyone expect of life? Please give my regards to Liz and tell her that I am sorry I never got to know her better.

To Margaret, the Rt. Hon. Baroness Thatcher, January 14, 2002

It seems that my days are numbered, and I thought that I would let you know how much I enjoyed our meetings. The first time I came across you was at a dinner at Queens' College in honour of some German scientific delegation. You were Minister of Education. Now, I have often heard ministers speak—they pull a speech composed by their secretary out of their pocket and read out a series of platitudes. To my surprise, you got up and made a first-class speech off the cuff.

We next met when you decided in 1980 to pay a visit to our laboratory. It was then headed by my successor Sydney Brenner, who had been severely injured in a motor bike accident, and he asked me as the recently retired head of the laboratory to show you around. During your visit, we had arranged for you a series of 10-minute talks by young people to tell you what was going on in the laboratory. There had been some political crisis which had preoccupied you. Nevertheless you sat down listening with complete concentration to every one of these talks and asked relevant questions about each of them. Then I showed you round and showed you my haemoglobin model. I had arranged for one of our young people to explain computer graphics to you which was something quite new then. So you sat down with him in front of the screen and the moment he tried to show it to you, the computer collapsed. I thought you might say thank-you and go away. Instead you remained very patiently until he had revived the programme and showed you the new magic. I chatted to your secretary during your visit, and he told me what a voracious reader you are and that you dominated every international meeting because you were always better briefed than anyone else.

Next time I called at Number 10, believe it or not, as the messenger of the Pope (I am a member of the Pontifical Academy of Sciences). A physicist friend of mine had persuaded the President to induce the Pope to appeal to the heads of three nuclear states for nuclear disarmament. Members of the Academy took this appeal to Reagan and Brezhnev, and a delegation was to take it to the Queen. The Foreign Office protested that it was

Anne Bloomer showing Margaret and Denis Thatcher her model of tobacco mosaic virus in 1980 with Max in attendance.

a political matter and must go to you. The President of the Academy, a Brazilian neurophysiologist, a Catholic Astronomer Royal in Edinburgh and I appeared at Number 10 with the document. You received us most courteously and the President made a little speech in favour of the Pope's appeal. You produced without a moment's hesitation a cogent, convincing reply that there can be no such thing without verifiable inspection. The President then handed you the Pope's letter to the Queen which you read. "I shall advise the Queen what to reply," you replied icily. I, an ex-Austrian with Jewish parents, felt a real Charlie Chaplin, acting as messenger from the Pope to the Queen. When I thought of it as a great joke, you courteously showed no sign that you did.

I enormously enjoyed the lunch party you gave for the Nobel laureates and the privilege of sitting next to you at lunch. You had just come back from a trip to Africa and I asked you about it. I remember you telling me that the one African leader who impressed you was [Robert] Mugabe [President of Zimbabwe], because he was honest! That must have been the worst misjudgement of your life! I can match that. You asked me for my views about cold fusion, which was all over the news just then, the nuclear energy in the test-tube. I replied that I believed that there must be something in it because the work had been done by very competent people.

Soon afterwards I learnt that it was all nonsense and felt very ashamed of my reply.

I disagreed with many of your political views, but very much appreciated getting to know you as the very remarkable person you are.

To Her Majesty, The Queen, January 14, 2002

My days may be numbered and I have a great urge to tell you how much I appreciated your many kindnesses to me over the years.

In May 1962 you came to open my new laboratory; we were all cheered by the interest you showed in what we were doing, but what particularly impressed me was the way you talked to the instrument mechanics and technicians without a trace of condescension. After that heart-warming visit I learnt that you were never allowed to go to school with other children, but had to be educated by tutors alone. You must have been a lonely girl.

Next time I met you, you would confer the CH [Companion of Honour] on me, so I waited in your anteroom while you first received the ambassador from X, then said good-bye to the British ambassador to Y and received a minister of this or that, then the Privy Council, and when I remarked on this to your private secretary, he said we call it the "treadmill." Since then I have learned that a timetable for several hours of the day is laid down for you often two years in advance. You fulfil all your duties with a smile and never get any thanks but only abuse and ridicule from the press to which your position does not allow you to reply. At a millennium lunch at the Guildhall, Robin Day paid a tribute to you which ended by saying, "She never has a day off." Your devotion to duty is a unique and old-fashioned virtue.

To come back to the CH, after receiving all these various people, you talked to me knowing what I got the CH for, and took an interest in all I told you about my work. It gave me the feeling that you really enjoyed giving me that order. That was wonderful.

Later I was astonished to receive a telephone call inviting my wife and me to a party at Windsor Castle. It was a wonderful occasion. I was treated there like a prince and you were most kind and hospitable. Then came the news of the OM [Order of Merit] which reached me while lecturing in California. It was a tremendous thrill. Later, while I waited in your anteroom I met Ernst Gombrich for the first time, to whom you were giving the OM on the same day. That same afternoon we discovered that we came from the same family background in Vienna with a similar education, that we both emigrated to England before Hitler overran Austria and that we were both anti-Zionists and had the same outlook on many things. Then I discovered that he knew everything that I didn't know. He had an encyclopaedic knowledge of classical literature so that he could match Ovid to Raphael and Claude. He believed that Zeitgeist was a lot of rubbish and that art's history is made by individuals. He didn't believe in abstract art, so a bond of friendship formed, which lasted until his recent death. He was a delightful man who never opened his mouth without saying something either original or witty.

I enormously enjoyed the lunch parties that you gave for the OMs, because I met people there I would never otherwise have encountered, such as Yehudi Menuhin who talked to me with glistening eyes about the school he founded for young violinists. At a later lunch I sat next to Mrs. Menuhin who spent the entire time complaining about her husband. On another occasion, the Librarian at Windsor showed me a letter from your great grandfather, Prince Albert, to the then Prime Minister Lord Russell, telling him to induce Cambridge University to include science in their curriculum. That was fascinating.

I enclose an article, "Long Live the Queen's Subjects" which I was able to write thanks to the help I received from your Private Secretary and the ladies who helped him.[4]

This brought to light some remarkable facts about rising longevity, and without help from the Palace I would never have discovered them. So once again please accept my deepest thanks for the kindness you have shown me over the years. When I was 21 years old I decided to leave my native town, Vienna, and come to Cambridge for my Ph.D. It was the best decision I have ever made in my life. I have had 65 years of productive research in Cambridge, the most wonderful centre of learning in the world, and I could never have accomplished what I did anywhere else.

I looked forward to celebrating your Golden Jubilee to accession and well remember your coronation with thousands of people camping in the streets of London to see the procession. It was in June and it snowed in the night! You must have been freezing in your coronation coach. I think you have often had what we in Austria call *Wetter-Pech* [bad luck with the weather]. Everyone thinks it is a dream to be born as a princess and become queen so young, but I now realise that it has been hard work.

---

[4]Because it is the custom for the Queen to congratulate her subjects on their 100th birthdays and their diamond wedding anniversaries, the Palace was able to give Max statistics from 1952 to 1996.

To Horst Fuhrmann, Vice President, Pour le Mérite, January 21, 2002

Sadly I have contracted a cancer for which, so far, no effective control has been found. So my days are numbered and to my great regret I shall not be able to attend any more meetings of the Pour le Mérite, but I should like to convey to you my enormous pleasure at having been a member. I think it is fantastic that Humboldt should have conceived that constitution of 30 German and 30 foreign members, 10 in the natural sciences, 10 in the humanities and 10 in the arts. I remember the list of original members that included Faraday, Gauss and Chopin.

In 1958 I sold my second-hand car in order to raise the money for a family holiday in Austria. We went to that lovely little resort, Alt-Aussee in the Salzkammergut. In those days tickets to the Salzburger Festspiele were still affordable and we saw *The Marriage of Figaro* and *Fidelio*. In *The Marriage of Figaro* [Dietrich] Fischer-Dieskau sang the count and Schwarzkopf the countess. It never occurred to me that many years later I would actually make friends with Elizabeth Schwarzkopf and have long chats to Fischer-Dieskau. And then there were also many marvellous individuals, Frau Wimmer, that wonderful actress.

So please convey the contents of this letter to Professor Zachau [the President] and, if you feel like it, convey its contents to the members. I enormously enjoyed our friendship and your interesting and perceptive books.

To Lord May, President of the Royal Society, January 21, 2002

It seems that my days are numbered, and I just wanted you to know how enormously I appreciated my fellowship of the Royal Society. People used to ask me occasionally where I really belonged, whether to Austria or Britain, or to the Jews. I would give an evasive reply because I really wanted to say that I belonged to the Royal Society and that was all I needed. It is the best academy in the world and the most active.

Max and Gisela, to whom Max dedicated Science is Not a Quiet Life, *the volume of his most significant papers "for giving me a happy home; it was the ground on which my work grew and prospered."*

Index